Issues for Debate in
American Public Policy

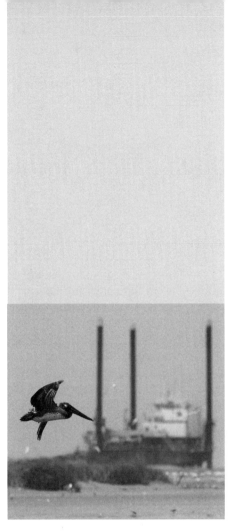

Issues for
Debate in American
Public Policy

**TWELFTH
EDITION**

Los Angeles | London | New Delhi
Singapore | Washington DC

SELECTIONS FROM **CQ RESEARCHER**

CQ Press
2300 N Street, NW, Suite 800
Washington, DC 20037

Phone: 202–729–1900; toll-free, 1–866–4CQ-PRESS (1–866–427–7737)

Web: www.cqpress.com

Cover design: www.RichdesignStudio.com
Cover photos: Getty Images
Composition: C&M Digitals (P) Ltd.

♾ The paper used in this publication exceeds the requirements of the American National Standard for Information Sciences—Permanence of Paper for Printed Library Materials, ANSI Z39.48–1992.

Printed and bound in the United States of America

15   14   13   12   11   1   2   3   4   5

A CQ Press College Division Publication

Director	Brenda Carter
Acquisitions editor	Charisse Kiino
Marketing manager	Christopher O'Brien
Managing editor	Catherine Forrest Getzie
Production editor	Mirna Araklian
Electronic production manager	Paul Pressau

ISSN: 1543–3889
ISBN: 978-1-60871-829-0

Contents

Annotated Contents

The sixteen *CQ Researcher* reports reprinted in this book have been reproduced essentially as they appeared when first published. In the few cases in which important developments have since occurred, updates are provided in the overviews highlighting the principal issues examined.

BUSINESS AND THE ECONOMY

Public-Employee Unions

Public-employee unions, which represent somewhat over one-third of the nation's 21 million government workers, have come under pointed attacks in several states. Republican governors in Wisconsin and Ohio won passage of laws to limit the scope of collective bargaining between unions and government agencies. They say the moves are needed to bring workers' pay under control to help ease state and local budget deficits. Union leaders and their Democratic allies say the measures take away workers' rights for the purpose of reducing unions' political influence. The legislative battles have touched off broad debates about whether government workers are overpaid. Most economists say government workers' wages and salaries are generally not out of line, but benefits and pensions are often more generous than those in the private sector. Unfunded pension liabilities are a looming problem for many states, and governors of both parties are calling for changes to trim the costs.

National Debt

Washington was wracked by intense budget politics in 2011. Spurred by the conservative Tea Party movement, Republican lawmakers point to the federal government's $14 trillion debt as an emergency that demands big cuts in domestic programs, including Social Security, plus tax cuts they say will spur economic growth. But Democrats say government spending is needed to sustain the economy while the private sector struggles back to health. They call for government investment in infrastructure and education, plus tax increases to strengthen programs such as Social Security for future generations. A decade ago the nonpartisan Congressional Budget Office predicted that the federal government would run a $796 billion surplus in 2010, but that rosy future never materialized. Over the past 10 years, a severe recession, tax cuts and spending on two wars put the federal government, and also the states, deeply in the red.

Financial Industry Overhaul

In July 2010, three Republican senators crossed the aisle to help pass the most sweeping financial-regulation overhaul since the Great Depression. Supporters of the 2,300-page legislation say the new rules will rein in investment risk-taking by big financial firms that otherwise might endanger the economic system again. Trading in complex investments known as derivatives will also get closer scrutiny. But some critics say that the law's effectiveness depends on the same federal regulators who missed the signs of the last impending crisis. Other critics say the new law is nowhere nearly as tough as it needed to be. They point out, for example, that the law doesn't prevent banks from growing to enormous size, which many analysts say makes financial institutions unmanageable and leads to conflicts of interest.

Jobs Outlook

The economy has finally started to grow again, but more than 8 million jobs that disappeared after the economic crisis began in late 2007 haven't returned, and the unemployment rate is nearly 10 percent. People who do have jobs are working harder, increasing productivity. In another major change on the job front, advances in technology are intensifying the allure — to employers — of offshore jobs. What's the best strategy for getting a job in today's tough job market? Experts may argue over how many jobs are at risk, but no one disputes that a college degree gives by far the best salaries and the best odds for finding a job — and the ability to switch careers if necessary. Demand is also rising at the low end of the market, but mid-level jobs that fall in between the two extremes may be most at risk.

SOCIAL ISSUES

Income Inequality

A recent Census Bureau report brought a flurry of press attention to the widening gap between rich and poor. The gap in New York City is widening — and is now bigger than in India, noted the *New York Daily News.* Indeed, most analysts agree incomes of the very rich have been pulling away from all others in recent decades. The average pretax income for the bottom 90 percent of households is almost $900 below what it was in 1979, while the average pretax income for the top 1 percent is $700,000 higher. Having a wealthy class with very large amounts of disposable money is valuable — not harmful — to society, some argue. But others say the recent winner-take-all economy helped trigger the massive recession, leaving most people with stagnant incomes. Meanwhile, Republicans argue that Bush-era tax cuts on top earnings should be extended to stimulate the economy, while many Democrats back extensions only for lower earners.

The Graying Planet

The world's populations are aging rapidly, triggering demographic changes that will have a profound impact on economies, government expenditures and international migration patterns. In the past century, life expectancy has doubled, while the average family size has shrunk. By 2050, the number of children under 5 is expected to drop by 49 million, while the number of adults over 60 will skyrocket — by 1.2 billion. An unprecedented number of senior citizens will be depending on diminishing numbers of younger workers to contribute to pension and health care programs for the elderly. And it's not just a problem for wealthy countries: Developing countries' elderly populations are growing faster than in the developed world. For example, in 20 years, China will have 167 million senior citizens — more than half the current U.S. population. On the positive side, some demographers believe aging societies will be more peaceful, since seniors suffer fewer crime and drug-abuse problems. And with fewer children, there could be more money per capita for their education.

EDUCATION
School Reform

With international tests showing that the United States no longer leads in school achievement, a bipartisan coalition of reformers is advocating the creation of more charter schools and a system of basing pay and firing decisions for teachers on students' standardized test scores. Conservatives have long recommended such businesslike approaches for schools, and Republican lawmakers and politicians are pushing for laws to weaken unions' ability to defend teachers against charges of incompetency. Teachers' unions remain opposed to market-oriented reforms, but the philosophy has new adherents among education-reform groups and centrist Democrats such as President Obama, whose administration is providing funding to states to develop data-driven teacher assessments. Meanwhile, some education scholars point out that poorly performing students are concentrated in low-income districts, where funding shortfalls, bad teaching conditions and poverty make educating students more difficult.

POLITICS AND GOVERNMENT
Redistricting Debates

The once-every-decade process of redrawing legislative and congressional districts is getting under way in state capitals around the country. To start, Sun Belt states will gain and Rust Belt states will lose seats in the U.S. House of Representatives. But win or lose, states have to redraw lines to make sure that legislative and congressional districts have equal populations and give fair opportunities to minority groups. The process is intensely political, with parties maneuvering for advantage and incumbents seeking to hold on to friendly territory. Republicans are in a good position after gaining control of legislatures in

a majority of states in November 2010. But demographic trends, especially the growth of Latino populations in some states, may limit the GOP's opportunities. In addition, California and Florida will be operating under new rules pushed by good-government groups that seek to limit "gerrymandering," line-drawing for purely partisan reasons. After redistricting plans are completed, many will be challenged in court, where outcomes are difficult to predict.

States and Federalism

Arizona enacted Medicaid cuts in 2010 only to have the action countermanded by the Obama administration's health care law passed later that year. Arizona is now one of 20 states challenging the new law as unconstitutional. Meanwhile, the state is also tangling with the federal government over national immigration policy. The cases highlight the recurrence of high-profile clashes over federal power and state prerogatives playing out against the backdrop of sharp political attacks on the administration and declining confidence in government at all levels. One federal judge has upheld the new health care law, but the states' suits challenging the law are advancing. Meanwhile, the Supreme Court is set to hear a challenge by business and civil rights groups to Arizona's tough law on hiring illegal aliens even as the state is appealing a lower court ruling that blocks its new measure requiring local law enforcement officers to check the immigration status of anyone arrested, detained or stopped for possible law violations.

Tea Party Movement

The Tea Party movement seemed to come out of nowhere. Suddenly, citizens angry over the multi-billion-dollar economic stimulus and the Obama administration's health-care plan were leading rallies, confronting lawmakers and holding forth on radio and TV. Closely tied to the Republican Party — though also critical of the GOP — the movement proved essential to the surprise victory of Republican Sen. Scott Brown in Massachusetts. Tea partiers say Brown's election proves the movement runs strong outside of "red states." But some political experts voice skepticism, arguing that the Tea Party's fiscal hawkishness won't appeal to most Democrats and many independents. Meanwhile, some dissension has appeared among tea partiers, with many preferring to sidestep social issues, such as immigration, and others emphasizing them. Still, the movement exerts strong appeal for citizens fearful of growing government debt and distrustful of the administration.

ENVIRONMENT
Managing Nuclear Waste

Thousands of tons of lethal nuclear waste from civilian power plants and military sites are stored at more than 100 sites around the country. But the federal government doesn't have a long-term plan today for managing nuclear waste. In the 1980s, Congress decided to build a single underground repository for spent fuel and highly radioactive defense waste in the southern Nevada desert. But work on the Yucca Mountain complex has faced political and technical problems and was canceled by President Obama, who advocates a new storage solution. Cancellation has created uncertainty for the nuclear power industry and for states where military waste is stored. It also is forcing utilities to pay to store used nuclear fuel at reactors — costs they pass on to customers. Some utilities have won multimillion-dollar lawsuits against the federal government, and more cases are pending. Obama supports expanding nuclear power as a clean energy strategy, but if the waste problem isn't solved, new reactors may be a hard sell in many states.

Energy Policy

Gasoline prices are rising above $4 per gallon in many parts of the United States, causing stress for consumers and political finger-pointing. Conservatives say that government overregulates energy companies and limits domestic production, while liberals want to repeal tax breaks for oil companies. But the larger problem is that the United States has an energy-intensive economy and depends heavily on imported oil. The Obama administration, with support from environmentalists, argues that the U.S. needs to use more clean-energy sources, and that investing in these industries will generate high-tech jobs and export revenues. Republicans in Congress want to cut federal energy spending and rely on market forces to determine which fuels and technologies

succeed. Complicating the issue, many forms of energy receive various kinds of government support, although budget debates could provide an opportunity to rethink whether longstanding energy subsidies are still needed.

Climate Change

Delegates from around the globe arrived in Copenhagen, Denmark, for the U.N. Climate Change Conference in December 2009 hoping to forge a significant agreement to reduce greenhouse gas emissions and temper climate change. But despite years of diplomatic preparation, two weeks of intense negotiations and the clamor for action from thousands of protesters outside the meeting, the conferees adopted no official treaty. Instead, a three-page accord — cobbled together on the final night by President Barack Obama and the leaders of China, India, Brazil and South Africa — established only broad, nonbinding goals and postponed tough decisions. Yet defenders of the accord praised it for requiring greater accountability from emerging economies such as China, protecting forests and committing billions in aid to help poorer nations. But the key question remains: Will the accord help U.N. efforts to forge a legally binding climate change treaty for the world's nations?

FOREIGN AND NATIONAL SECURITY POLICY
Afghanistan Dilemma

Nearly ten years ago, U.S. forces first entered Afghanistan to pursue the al Qaeda terrorists who plotted the Sept. 11 terror attacks. American troops are still there today, along with thousands of NATO forces. Under a strategy crafted by the Obama administration, military leaders are trying to deny terrorists a permanent foothold in the impoverished Central Asian country and in neighboring, nuclear-armed Pakistan, whose western border region has become a sanctuary for Taliban and al Qaeda forces. The Afghanistan-Pakistan conflict — "Af-Pak" in diplomatic parlance — poses huge challenges ranging from rampant corruption within Afghanistan's police forces to a multibillion-dollar opium economy that funds the insurgency. But those problems pale in comparison with the ultimate nightmare scenario: Pakistan's nuclear weapons falling into the hands of terrorists, which for-eign-policy experts say has become a real possibility.

Government Secrecy

The online disclosure of thousands of classified diplo-matic, military and intelligence documents by the shad-owy Internet site WikiLeaks has dramatically intensified the debate over government secrecy. Open-government advocates argue that federal agencies, including the CIA, keep too much information from the public, undermin-ing the ability of citizens to keep a check on official wrongdoing. Secrecy supporters argue that modern tech-nology gives far too many people access to sensitive infor-mation that could threaten the nation's welfare if released. The Obama administration is taking steps to open more of the government's business to public scrutiny, but disclo-sure advocates say President Obama needs to do even more. Meanwhile, lawmakers, intelligence officials and secrecy experts are debating whether the Espionage Act of 1917, which prohibits the "willful" disclosure of "informa-tion relating to the national defense," needs to be updated.

HEALTHCARE
Health-Care Reform

The health-care reform legislation signed into law by President Obama in March 2010 marked the biggest attempt to expand access to health care since Medicare and Medicaid were launched in the 1960s. The massive legislation will help 32 million Americans get health insurance coverage and bans insurers from denying cov-erage to those with preexisting illnesses. It also expands Medicaid to all poor people — except illegal immigrants — and gives subsidies to low- and low-middle-income people to buy insurance. But opponents, including every Republican member of Congress, say the coverage expansion is simply too expensive, at a price tag of about $1 trillion over 10 years. They also say new fees and taxes to help pay for the coverage place too big a burden on currently insured people. Meanwhile, a group of state attorneys general is challenging the constitutional-ity of the law's requirement that everyone buy health insurance.

Preface

Is the federal government usurping states' powers? Is the gap between rich and poor getting wider? Should public employees have the right to collective bargaining over pay, benefits and pensions? These questions — and many more — are at the heart of American public policy. How can instructors best engage students with these crucial issues? We feel that students need objective, yet provocative examinations of these issues to understand how they affect citizens today and will for years to come. This annual collection aims to promote in-depth discussion, facilitate further research and help readers formulate their own positions on crucial issues. Get your students talking both inside and outside the classroom about *Issues for Debate in American Public Policy.*

This twelfth edition includes sixteen up-to-date reports by *CQ Researcher*, an award-winning weekly policy brief that brings complicated issues down to earth. Each report chronicles and analyzes executive, legislative, and judicial activities at all levels of government. This collection is divided into seven diverse policy areas: business and the economy; social issues; education; politics and government; the environment; foreign and national security policy; and healthcare — to cover a range of issues found in most American government and public policy courses.

CQ RESEARCHER

CQ Researcher was founded in 1923 as *Editorial Research Reports* and was sold primarily to newspapers as a research tool. The magazine was renamed and redesigned in 1991 as *CQ Researcher.* Today, students are its primary audience. While still used by hundreds of journalists and newspapers, many of which reprint portions of the reports, the *Researcher's* main subscribers are now high school, college and public libraries. In 2002, *Researcher* won the American Bar Association's coveted Silver Gavel award for magazine excellence for a series of nine reports on civil liberties and other legal issues.

Researcher staff writers — all highly experienced journalists — sometimes compare the experience of writing a Researcher report to drafting a college term paper. Indeed, there are many similarities. Each report is as long as many term papers — about 11,000 words — and is written by one person without any significant outside help. One of the key differences is that writers interview leading experts, scholars and government officials for each issue.

Like students, staff writers begin the creative process by choosing a topic. Working with the *Researcher's* editors, the writer identifies a controversial subject that has important public policy implications. After a topic is selected, the writer embarks on one to two weeks of intense research. Newspaper and magazine articles are clipped or downloaded, books are ordered and information is gathered from a wide variety of sources, including interest groups, universities and the government. Once the writers are well informed, they develop a detailed outline, and begin the interview process. Each report requires a minimum of ten to fifteen interviews with academics, officials, lobbyists and people working in the field. Only after all interviews are completed does the writing begin.

CHAPTER FORMAT

Each issue of *CQ Researcher*, and therefore each selection in this book, is structured in the same way. Each begins with an overview, which briefly summarizes the areas that will be explored in greater detail in the rest of the chapter. The next section chronicles important and current debates on the topic under discussion and is structured around a number of key questions, such as "Is the new health-care reform law a good idea?" and "Is transporting radioactive waste dangerous?" These questions are usually the subject of much debate among practitioners and scholars in the field. Hence, the answers presented are never conclusive but detail the range of opinion on the topic.

Next, the "Background" section provides a history of the issue being examined. This retrospective covers important legislative measures, executive actions and court decisions that illustrate how current policy has evolved. Then the "Current Situation" section examines contemporary policy issues, legislation under consideration and legal action being taken. Each selection concludes with an "Outlook" section, which addresses possible regulation, court rulings, and initiatives from Capitol Hill and the White House over the next five to ten years.

Each report contains features that augment the main text: two to three sidebars that examine issues related to the topic at hand, a pro versus con debate between two experts, a chronology of key dates and events and an annotated bibliography detailing major sources used by the writer.

CUSTOM OPTIONS

Interested in building your ideal CQ Press Issues book, customized to your personal teaching needs and interests? Browse by course or date, or search for specific topics or issues from our online catalog of over 150 *CQ Researcher* issues at http://custom.cqpress.com.

ACKNOWLEDGMENTS

We wish to thank many people for helping to make this collection a reality. Thomas J. Billitteri, managing editor of *CQ Researcher*, gave us his enthusiastic support and cooperation as we developed this ninth edition. He and his talented staff of editors and writers have amassed a first-class library of *Researcher* reports, and we are fortunate to have access to that rich cache. We also thankfully acknowledge the advice and feedback from current readers and are gratified by their satisfaction with the book.

Some readers may be learning about *CQ Researcher* for the first time. We expect that many readers will want regular access to this excellent weekly research tool. For subscription information or a no-obligation free trial of *Researcher*, please contact CQ Press at www.cqpress.com or toll-free at 1-866-4CQ-PRESS (1-866-427-7737).

We hope that you will be pleased by the twelfth edition of *Issues for Debate in American Public Policy.* We welcome your feedback and suggestions for future editions. Please direct comments to Charisse Kiino, Editorial Director, College Publishing Group, CQ Press, 2300 N Street, NW, Suite 800, Washington, D.C. 20037, or *ckiino@cqpress.com.*

—The Editors of CQ Press

Contributors

Thomas J. Billitteri is managing editor of the *CQ Researcher*. He has more than 30 years' experience covering business, nonprofit institutions and public policy for newspapers and other publications. He holds a BA in English and an MA in journalism from Indiana University.

Staff writer **Marcia Clemmitt** is a veteran social-policy reporter who previously served as editor in chief of *Medicine & Health* and staff writer for *The Scientist*. She has also been a high school math and physics teacher. She holds a liberal arts and sciences degree from St. John's College, Annapolis, and a master's degree in English from Georgetown University. Her recent reports include "Gridlock in Washington" and "Health-Care Reform."

Alan Greenblatt covers foreign affairs for National Public Radio. He was previously a staff writer at *Governing* magazine and *CQ Weekly*, where he won the National Press Club's Sandy Hume Award for political journalism. He graduated from San Francisco State University in 1986 and received a master's degree in English literature from the University of Virginia in 1988. For the *CQ Researcher*, his reports include "Confronting Warming," "Future of the GOP" and "Immigration Debate." His most recent *CQ Global Researcher* reports were "Attacking Piracy" and "Rewriting History."

Associate Editor **Kenneth Jost** graduated from Harvard College and Georgetown University Law Center. He is the author of the *Supreme Court Yearbook* and editor of *The Supreme Court from A to Z* (both *CQ Press*). He was a member of the *CQ Researcher* team that won the American Bar Association's 2002 Silver Gavel Award. His previous reports include "States and Federalism" and "Campaign Finance Debates." He is also author of the blog *Jost on Justice* (http://jostonjustice.blogspot.com).

Reed Karaim, a freelance writer living in Tucson, Arizona, has written for *The Washington Post, U.S. News & World Report, Smithsonian, American Scholar, USA Weekend* and other publications. He is the author of the novel, *If Men Were Angels*, which was selected for the Barnes & Noble Discover Great New Writers series. He is also the winner of the Robin Goldstein Award for Outstanding Regional Reporting and other journalism awards. Karaim is a graduate of North Dakota State University in Fargo.

Peter Katel is a *CQ Researcher* staff writer who previously reported on Haiti and Latin America for *Time* and *Newsweek* and covered the Southwest for newspapers in New Mexico. He has received several journalism awards, including the Bartolomé Mitre Award for coverage of drug trafficking, from the Inter-American Press Association. He holds an A.B. in university studies from the University of New Mexico. His recent reports include "Prisoner Reentry," "Rise in Counterinsurgency" and "Caring for Veterans."

Alex Kingsbury has written about national security and the intelligence community for U.S. News & World Report. He made several trips to Iraq in 2007 and 2008 to cover the Iraq War. He holds a B.A. in history from George Washington University and an M.S. in journalism from Columbia University.

Jennifer Weeks is a Massachusetts freelance writer who specializes in energy, the environment, science and technology. She has written for *The Washington Post, Audubon, Popular Mechanics* and more than 50 other magazines and websites and worked for 15 years as a public policy analyst, congressional staffer and lobbyist. She has an A.B. degree from Williams College and master's degrees from the University of North Carolina and Harvard.

Issues for Debate in
American Public Policy

1

Public-Employee Unions

Kenneth Jost

Wisconsin Gov. Scott Walker speaks at the state capitol in Madison on March 11 after signing his controversial bill limiting collective bargaining rights of public-employee unions. The bill is one of several proposals being pushed by Republican governors or legislators aimed at curbing public-sector unions.

From *CQ Researcher*,
May 24, 2011.

Steven Reid worked as a consumer-complaint investigator for the state of Wisconsin for 27 years before retiring with a $2,000-a-month pension in 2007. He might have earned more in the private sector, but he felt drawn to public service — and to the promise of a good pension at age 55.

As the son and grandson of longtime union members, Reid joined Local 33 of the American Federation of State, County and Municipal Employees (AFSCME) on his first day on the job.

Though he is retired, Reid is proud to be standing by the union that stood by him. In mid-February he began driving on weekends from his home in the village of Eden to the state capital in Madison to join with his union brothers and sisters and others in protesting a crackdown on public-employee unions by Republican Gov. Scott Walker.

Elected in November 2010 in a wave of state-level GOP victories in legislative and gubernatorial balloting, Walker proposed and won hard-fought legislative approval of a bill that virtually eliminates collective bargaining by public-employee unions except police and firefighters. The measure, delayed from taking effect pending a court challenge, also bars payroll deductions for union dues and requires unions to win approval from workers in a certification election every year.

In introducing the measure Feb. 11, Walker called it a "budget repair bill," aimed at reducing the state's $137 million budget deficit. Nationally, other Republican officials and GOP supporters link states' fiscal woes to what they call overly generous compensation packages for government workers. "Unaffordable and unsustainable

Most States Allow Collective Bargaining

Thirty-one states and the District of Columbia allow unions representing state employees to bargain with the state over their members' wages, hours and conditions of employment. An additional 10 states allow bargaining for some state and/or local employees. Nine states do not allow public workers to bargain collectively.

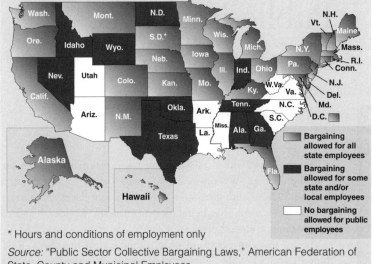

Collective Bargaining by Public-Sector Unions, 2010

Bargaining allowed for all state employees

Bargaining allowed for some state and/or local employees

No bargaining allowed for public employees

* Hours and conditions of employment only

Source: "Public Sector Collective Bargaining Laws," American Federation of State, County and Municipal Employees, www.afscme.org/members/11075.cfm.

salaries, pensions and other benefits for unionized government workers are a substantial part of the problem," U.S. Chamber of Commerce President Thomas J. Donohue wrote recently.[1]

The liberal Center for American Progress counters that state budget deficits are due primarily to lost revenue from the recession. Personnel costs are actually a smaller percentage of state budgets than they were 20 years ago, according to David Madland, director of the American Worker Project with the Center for American Progress Action Fund. "The evidence strongly suggests that conservative attempts to restrict public-sector union rights and slash government employee compensation are driven by motives other than budget necessity," Madland writes.[2]

The Wisconsin act does sharply increase state employees' contributions for health insurance and retirement benefits, amounting to about an 8 percent pay cut. But Reid says the budget issues were a "smokescreen" for Walker's real purpose — undermining the state's Democratic Party by weakening its political ally, public-sector unions.

Public workers are "willing to help with this deficit," Reid says. But cutting back on union rights, he says, "looks like an opportunity for the Republicans to do real damage to the other party."

Walker's bill is only one of several proposals being pushed by Republican governors or legislators aimed at curbing public-employee unions. In Ohio, newly elected Gov. John Kasich on March 30 won legislative approval of a measure to eliminate collective bargaining over health benefits and some working conditions and to make strikes by public workers illegal, with a stiff penalty. As of late March, a database compiled by the National Conference of State Legislatures showed some 300 bills on public-sector labor issues introduced in 37 states.[3]

The surge in activity reflects conservatives' strategy to turn the anti-government feeling and economic angst shared by many Americans into tangible legislative victories against public-employee unions. "There's a general feeling that's been whipped up by conservatives, and particularly Republican governors, that public employees are privileged," says Richard Kearney, a professor at North Carolina State University's School of International and Public Affairs in Raleigh and author of a leading text on public-sector unions.[4]

The stakes for the nation's 7.6 million unionized public workers, ranging from sanitation workers and teachers to state university professors and federal-government scientists — are high. The stakes for the labor movement as a whole are also high. With the percentage of unionized workers in the private sector in sharp decline, public workers now comprise roughly half of union members in the country. But the percentage of unionized public workers — roughly 40 percent today — has remained relatively flat for decades.[5]

Opponents say Walker's bill, with its curbs on collective bargaining and other restrictions, is effectively aimed at busting the public unions. "Sure," says Steve Kreisberg, national collective bargaining director for AFSCME (commonly pronounced as "AF-SMEE). "I think they've stated as much."

With the stakes so high, Walker's proposal provoked a fierce, nationally televised battle waged by labor unions proud of Wisconsin's role in pioneering public-employee rights and by Democratic lawmakers resentful of their relegation to minority status following last November's elections. The weekend after Walker unveiled the proposal, Reid was one of an estimated 150 people who converged on Madison to protest the bill. Police estimated the crowd at 85,000 on March 13 following the bill's enactment. Pro-Walker supporters appear to have numbered in the hundreds, at most.[6]

The legislature's approval of the bill came only after outnumbered Democratic senators staged a three-week boycott. The so-called "Gang of 14" decamped across the Illinois border to deny the Republican-controlled Senate the 20-member quorum needed to pass a budget-related bill. With a 19-vote majority in the 33-seat chamber, Republicans needed at least one Democrat in attendance to approve the bill as introduced with a number of budget-related provisions.

But with Walker's approval, Republicans circumvented the Democrats' boycott by stripping out the budget provisions on March 9, with only minimal public notice. Senate Majority Leader Scott Fitzgerald sent the bill without Senate passage to a joint Assembly-Senate conference committee, which removed the budget provisions and then returned the measure to the Senate for approval minutes later. The lone Democrat present, Assembly Minority Leader Peter Barca, complained that the conference committee met with less than the 24-hour notice required under the state's open-meetings law.[7]

The Senate's approval of the bill on an 18-1 vote — with one Republican voting against it — set the stage for the Assembly to follow suit the next day and Walker to sign it on March 11. But Democratic officials in Dane County (Madison) filed suit the same day to block the

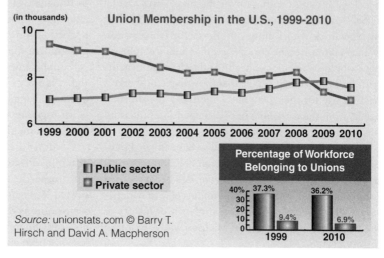

Public-Sector Unions Hold Steady

Membership in public-employee unions grew slightly over the past decade while private-sector unions declined by about a fourth (top). The proportion of public employees belonging to a union changed little during that period, while the percentage of unionized private-sector employees fell sharply (bottom).

(in thousands) Union Membership in the U.S., 1999-2010

1999 2000 2001 2002 2003 2004 2005 2006 2007 2008 2009 2010

☐ Public sector
☐ Private sector

Source: unionstats.com © Barry T. Hirsch and David A. Macpherson

Percentage of Workforce Belonging to Unions

37.3% (1999), 9.4% (1999)
36.2% (2010), 6.9% (2010)

law. County Executive Kathleen Falk and county board Chairman Scott McDonell argued the law should be voided because the conference-committee session failed to comply with the open-meetings law. Judge Maryann Sumi issued a temporary restraining order on March 18 blocking the law from going into effect pending further proceedings, now due to resume in May.

With the Wisconsin law still in court, labor unions and their supporters continued to argue with critics and opponents about the issues. To unions, the limits on collective bargaining eliminate rights won slowly over the last 60 years, the same rights enjoyed by private-sector workers and protected by international worker-rights guarantees. The unions' adversaries insist that the analogy to private-sector workers is inapt and that in practice public-employee unions have exploited collective bargaining rights — and their political clout — to win overly generous compensation packages.

The opposing sides differ as well on whether public employees are generally overpaid or underpaid. In general, economists appear to agree that most state and local government workers lag behind private-sector counterparts with comparable education in terms of wages or salaries, but enjoy somewhat better health and retirement benefits. Using different methodologies, experts from different ideological positions come to differing conclusions on how to compare the overall compensation.

The opposing sides differ as well on responsibility for the shortfalls in public-employee pension funds that loom for many states — red and blue alike. "There is a pension tsunami coming down the pike," says Daniel DiSalvo, a professor of political science at City College of New York who follows public-sector labor issues. Walker epitomizes the critics' view that public employees have won overly generous health and retirement benefits with far lower contributions than private-sector workers have to pay for their benefits. Unions say the shortfall results from the recession's impact on pension funds and inadequate funding by some states in recent years.

In Wisconsin, Walker appeared to have enjoyed public support at the start of the fight, but polls indicate gains by the unions in the weeks since. The debate "has raised people's attention to the role that unions play in society," says William Jones, an associate professor of history at the University of Wisconsin in Madison who is writing a history of AFSCME.

Retired complaint investigator Reid is fully aware of the sharp divisions over the issues. In the cluster of six houses where he lives, three families are Democrats and three are Republicans — and they are not talking to each other these days.

Here are some of the arguments being heard on the major issues in the debate:

Should public employees have the right to collective bargaining over pay, benefits and pensions?

Indiana Gov. Mitch Daniels marked his first full day in office on Jan. 11, 2005, by rescinding collective bargaining rights for the state's 25,000 employees. The Republican governor's move reversed a policy that three Democratic predecessors had followed under executive orders for the previous 15 years.

Daniels depicted the action then as needed to restructure the state's child-welfare bureau. Six years later, the potential GOP presidential contender sees a broader purpose in curbing public-sector unions. "Public jobs grew while private jobs were lost, public salaries went up while private sector salaries are shrinking," Daniels told a Republican fundraiser in Cincinnati Feb. 23, referring to the era since widespread recognition of collective

bargaining for public-employee unions. "It's time to interrupt that loop in the public interest," Daniels said.[8]

Daniels' comments came as his fellow Republican governors in Wisconsin and Ohio were urging GOP-controlled legislatures to approve new restrictions on public-employee unions in their states. In those states, as in Indiana earlier, unions and their allies say the moves eliminate important worker rights, while supporters say restrictions on unions are needed to cut costs and make government more efficient.

"Public employees should have the same bargaining rights as every other employee in society," says AFSCME collective bargaining director Kreisberg. "If they want to work together in the bargaining process, they should have the same right as any other worker in America."

"I don't believe they're rights," counters Matt Seaholm, director of the Wisconsin chapter of Americans for Prosperity, a low-tax advocacy group that has supported Walker's legislation. "It's a privilege for public-sector unions to have collective bargaining ability with government and, frankly, with the taxpayers. That privilege has been abused."

In the past, union rights for public employees were seen by opponents as an infringement of government sovereignty. That argument is rarely heard today. Instead, critics of public-employee unions argue that the unions' combined economic and political clout results in overly favorable deals for public workers when bargaining with government officials and managers.

"The trouble with collective bargaining for public employees is there's no one with skin in the game on the other side of the table," says Chris Chocola, a former two-term Republican congressman from Indiana and now president of the Club for Growth, another low-tax advocacy group. "The people agreeing on one side bear no consequence."

Collective bargaining for public employees "results in pay that you could not get in an arms-length negotiation," says Stephen Bainbridge, a professor at UCLA Law School and a former senior fellow at the Heritage Foundation, a conservative think tank in Washington. "It gets you the kind of gross pension benefits that you see around the country."

Pro-labor experts scoff at the picture of unions overpowering complacent government officials and managers. "Tired arguments," says North Carolina State's Kearney. "There are constraints on public employees," he continues. "When the public perception is that the unions have been too successful and have generated wages, benefits and working conditions that are out of step with those in the private sector, then there can be a reaction."

"The problem is not that the unions exist," says Henry Farber, a professor of economics in the industrial relations section at Princeton University in Princeton, N.J. "The problem is inadequate discipline on the government's side. The solution is not to kill the union."

Kreisberg similarly rejects the argument that government managers are more willing to grant union demands than private companies. "It's easier to make a profit than to raise a tax," he says. He also notes that in many states pensions are set by legislatures, not through collective bargaining. "That's the biggest myth out there right now," he says. "That unions have somehow negotiated fat pensions."

Defending the Wisconsin legislation, Seaholm initially says that it leaves bargaining over wages "intact" and only eliminates negotiations over pensions and benefits. Under questioning, however, he acknowledges that the bill allows bargaining over wages only for raises up to the cost-of-living increase. With that provision, the bill "basically abolishes collective bargaining," Kreisberg retorts. "Let's not mince words."

Walker and other critics are tapping into a sentiment widely shared by the public at large — that public-employee unions have gotten the upper hand. "In some states, the relationship [between state government and public-employee unions] is slightly out of whack," says DiSalvo of the City College of New York. To correct the imbalance, DiSalvo favors either restricting collective bargaining rights or limiting unions' political influence.

Key Provisions of Wisconsin's New Bill

Wisconsin Gov. Scott Walker requested and won legislative approval of a broad overhaul of state and municipal employees' collective bargaining rights and provisions governing public-employee unions. Walker signed the bill March 11, but a state court judge has blocked it from going into effect pending a ruling on a lawsuit alleging that the state Senate failed to comply with the state's open-meeting law two days earlier before voting on the measure.

Here are the major provisions:
- Restricts collective bargaining for state and municipal employees except police and firefighters to "base wages." No collective bargaining for health benefits or pensions.
- Limits increase in base wages to the percentage change in Consumer Price Index.
- Increases employee contribution for health benefits. Family coverage under lowest tier would increase to $208 per month from $78.
- Requires employees to contribute 5.8 percent of pay to retirement system. Currently, most employees pay 0.2 percent.
- Mandates study due by June 30, 2012, on offering employees option of a "defined-contribution" 401(k)-type retirement plan.
- Requires annual certification election for union to represent designated workers. Union would be decertified unless it receives at least 51 percent of all workers in collective bargaining unit, not just those voting. Initial certification elections were to have been held April 1; the date is now uncertain because of the legal challenge to the act.
- Limits collective bargaining agreements to one year, not two years as under current law. Collective bargaining agreements cannot be extended.
- Prohibits payroll deductions for union dues except for public-safety employees.
- Provides for employee to be discharged for participating in a strike or other "concerted" work actions, including sit-downs, slowdowns or mass sick calls.

Source: Wisconsin State Legislature, http://legis.wisconsin.gov/2011/data/acts/11Act 10.pdf.

"If one could restrict one or the other, it could bring things back into equilibrium," he says.

But Thomas Kochan, a professor of management and director of the Institute for Work and Employment Research at the Massachusetts Institute of Technology's Sloan School of Management in Cambridge, says restricting collective bargaining is not the solution. "The beauty of collective bargaining is standards," he says. "That doesn't eliminate politics, but there are standards. To go

State Employees Get Smaller Slice of Pie

The portion of state expenditures devoted to pay and benefits for state employees was lower in 2008 than in 1992, but on the rise.

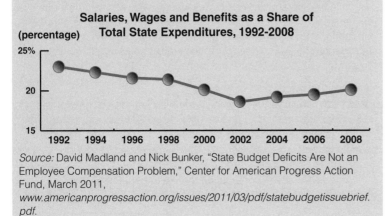

Salaries, Wages and Benefits as a Share of Total State Expenditures, 1992-2008

(percentage)

Source: David Madland and Nick Bunker, "State Budget Deficits Are Not an Employee Compensation Problem," Center for American Progress Action Fund, March 2011, *www.americanprogressaction.org/issues/2011/03/pdf/statebudgetissuebrief.pdf.*

back to the law of the jungle and pure politics is very, very shortsighted."

Are public employees, in general, overpaid, underpaid or fairly paid?

With the Wisconsin collective bargaining bill stalled, *USA Today* stepped into the debate on March 1 with a front-page story listing the state as one of 41 where public workers "earn more" than private-sector employees. Quoting figures from the Commerce Department's Bureau of Economic Analysis (BEA), the newspaper said that state and local government workers in Wisconsin earn $50,774 per year on average, about $1,800 more than the average for private-sector workers.

The Commerce Department data were also said to show that public employees' compensation has grown faster than the earnings of private workers since 2000, primarily because of the rising value of benefits. Only in the seventh paragraph, however, did the story note that the earnings comparisons "did not adjust for specific jobs, age, education or experience."

Unions sharply criticized the story, but so did many economists and media watchers. Within the story, Jeffrey Keefe, an associate professor of economics at Rutgers University in New Brunswick, N.J., called the analysis misleading because it did not reflect factors such as education "that result in higher pay for public employees." In a critique later that day, the progressive media-monitoring

group Fairness and Accuracy in Reporting (FAIR) made the same point, calling the comparison "entirely meaningless."[9]

As the episode illustrates, comparisons between public- and private-sector compensation are both statistically complex and emotionally charged. When *The New York Times* tried to answer the question of which side earns more, it presented a package of charts that began with the BEA comparison but continued with other data showing government workers more likely to be white-collar and better-educated than private-sector workers as a whole.[10]

A wide range of economists agree that the widespread public perception of government workers as overpaid is inaccurate. "I don't think public employees are overpaid," says Princeton's Farber. Pay levels are "fairly comparable," he says, "a bit higher for low-skilled workers, lower for high-skilled workers." Along with others, however, Farber also points out that public employees generally have better health and pension benefits than private-sector workers.

Economists trying to take account of all factors still come to differing conclusions. Keefe has written a series of papers, published by the liberal Economic Policy Institute in Washington, that conclude state employees are generally undercompensated in relation to private-sector workers nationally and in Wisconsin and several other states. In Wisconsin, for example, Keefe found that state workers have a 5 percent gap in total compensation compared to private-sector workers. Conservative economists Andrew Biggs of the American Enterprise Institute (AEI) and Jason Richwine of the Heritage Foundation find instead that Wisconsin government workers have a 10 percent pay premium over private-sector employees.[11]

The dueling studies agree generally in finding private-sector workers better paid except for less-skilled blue-collar workers and public-sector workers with better pension benefits. But Biggs argues that Keefe underestimates pensions' value by calculating their worth not on the basis of the ultimate benefit but the state's current contribution. Because state pension funds generally perform well, the current contribution understates the eventual value of the retirement benefit to the employee, he says.

In their study, Biggs and Richwine also credit state workers with additional compensation — a 15 percent pay premium — in the form of greater job security than private-sector workers. "Job security pulls them ahead," Biggs says. But Keefe says Biggs and Richwine offer no justification for any job-security premium, "much less 15 percent."

Similar arguments over federal workers' compensation were aired in a March 9 hearing by the House Oversight Subcommittee on Federal Workforce, U.S. Postal Service, and Labor Policy. Subcommittee chairman Dennis Ross, a Florida Republican, opened by calling federal workers' pay "not in line" with the private sector. But John Berry, director of the Office of Personnel Management (OPM), rejected what he called "the myth" that federal workers as a whole are overcompensated.

At the hearing, Biggs and Heritage Foundation senior policy analyst James Sherk presented studies showing a substantial 30 percent to 40 percent premium for federal workers over private-sector counterparts even after adjusting for factors such as education and experience. But Colleen Kelly, president of the National Treasury Employees Union, noted that under both Republican and Democratic administrations, the President's Pay Agent has concluded that federal workers have a pay gap of about 20 percent compared to private employees.*[12]

In Wisconsin, Walker and his supporters focused on the benefits issue. A television ad paid for by the Wisconsin Club for Growth, an economically conservative advocacy group unaffiliated with the national organization of the same name, commended Walker for fighting to make public workers "pay their fair share."[13]

Walker's legislation requires government workers to pay half of the contribution toward retirement benefits

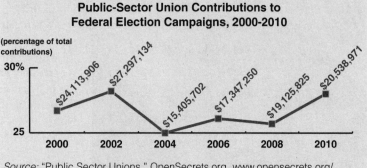

Public-Employee Unions Are Major Donors

Unions representing police, firefighters and other government employees contribute about one-fourth of the donations to federal election campaigns. Yearly amounts have ranged from $15 million to $27 million over the past decade.

Public-Sector Union Contributions to Federal Election Campaigns, 2000-2010

Source: "Public Sector Unions," OpenSecrets.org, www.opensecrets.org/industries/indus.php?cycle=2010&ind=P04#contribtrends.

— 5.8 percent of their paychecks, up from 0.2 percent — and 12.6 percent of the cost of health insurance. AFSCME leaders in Wisconsin and Washington have said throughout the controversy that they were willing to negotiate increased contributions. "While we're certainly going to share in the sacrifices," Martin Beil, executive director of Wisconsin's AFSCME Council 24, said in a video message Feb. 26, "we will not under any circumstances surrender our right to collectively bargain or organize as a union."[14]

Do public-employee unions wield undue political influence?

Public-sector unions are big players in federal and state campaigns, and they play overwhelmingly for Democrats. So Wisconsin party leaders on both sides of the aisle see high political stakes in the debate over Gov. Walker's union legislation.

"I consider organized labor to be the backbone of the Democratic Party," Mike Tate, state party chairman, told the *Wisconsin State Journal* as the union bill was pending in early March. "Part of Scott Walker's strategy is to weaken the infrastructure of the Democratic Party."

Senate Majority Leader Fitzgerald appeared to confirm Tate's accusation a few days later as he finally maneuvered the bill through the chamber. "If we win this battle, and the money is not there under the auspices of the unions," Fitzgerald told Fox News on March 9, "certainly

---

* The President's Pay Agent is composed of the secretary of Labor and the directors of OPM and the Office of Management and Budget.

Firefighter and union supporter Tom Ullom registers his
opposition to SB 5, a bill limiting collective bargaining rights for
government workers in Ohio, during Gov. John Kasich's State of
the State address in Columbus on March 8. Kasich signed the bill
three weeks later, but it is on hold pending a possible referendum
on the measure. The bill is one of several proposals being pushed
by Republican governors or legislators aimed at curbing public-
employee unions.

what you're going to find is President Obama is going to
have a . . . much more difficult time getting elected and
winning the state of Wisconsin."[15]

Over the past 10 years, AFSCME's political action
committee ranks 13th among PACs in giving to federal
candidates, with $9.4 million in total contributions,
according to the Center for Responsive Politics, a
Washington group that monitors campaign finance. All
but a tiny fraction of the donations — 97 percent —
went to Democrats. In Wisconsin, too, public-employee
unions give predominantly to Democratic office-seekers
— about 73 cents of every dollar given, according to an
analysis by the Wisconsin Democracy Campaign prepared for the *State Journal*.[16]

Critics of public-employee unions see the campaign giving as part of a system that uses money and
votes to get government officials to do their bidding,
both at the bargaining table and in the policy arena.
They blame teachers' unions, for example, nationally
for bottling up school reforms that threaten educators'
job security.

"When you combine the realities of campaign finance
with collective bargaining in the public sector, you end
up with a situation in which you have very powerful,
very wealthy unions, such as the teachers' union, financing political campaigns of the people who are running
for political office," says UCLA's Bainbridge. In states
with a Democratic majority, he says, "you've got the
unions and their lackeys on either side of the bargaining
table."

Union officials and their supporters insist the picture of
influence-peddling is overdrawn. "Where's the evidence
that that occurs?" asks AFSCME's Kreisberg. "Where's
the evidence that [unions' influence] is corrosive?"

Labor unions are "a bulwark in favor of democracy,"
Kreisberg continues. "They're part of the democratic
institutions of our government. We extol trade unions
everywhere else in the world except when they are in the
United States."

By reducing public-employee unions' collective bargaining role, Walker's legislation threatens to reduce
their membership. In the six years since Daniels' move in
Indiana to rescind collective bargaining with state
employees, dues-paying union members dropped from
16,408 in 2005 — about two-thirds of the state's public-
employee workforce — to 1,409, according to the
Wisconsin State Journal.[17]

Two distinctive provisions in Walker's bill go further
toward undermining unions by eliminating payroll
deductions for union dues and requiring unions to face
certification elections every year. Walker argued that getting rid of the dues check-off would help offset workers'
increased costs for health and retirement benefits. He said
annual certification elections will force unions to prove
their value to workers.

Labor-oriented experts are sharply critical of the elections provision. "It's totally outside of the mainstream of
collective bargaining statutes in the United States or
Canada," says Martin Malin, a professor of law and director of the Institute for Law and the Workplace at Chicago-
Kent College of Law, Illinois Institute of Technology.

"It's simply nutty," says MIT's Kochan. "You're going to have a perpetual election process."

Even critics of public-sector unions view the provision as punitive. "Clearly, an election costs money and takes up time," says DiSalvo of City College of New York. "That is money and time that from the union's point of view could be dedicated to expressing its interest." Together, he says, the election and dues check-off provisions amount to "a huge one-two punch" against unions.

While supportive of unions, Princeton's Farber says he would like to limit their political clout. "They really shouldn't be contributing to the people they're negotiating with," Farber says. "The management should not be beholden to the union." He concedes, however, that U.S. Supreme Court rulings on campaign finance, including a January 2010 decision guaranteeing unions and corporations the right to spend freely in election campaigns, make it impossible to keep public-sector unions out of political contests.[18]

In Wisconsin, Walker's push for the union bill provoked a fight vigorously waged on the streets, in print and on radio and TV. Bainbridge says the outcome bodes well for other anti-union proposals. "If you have the stomach to wage this fight, it is a fight that Republicans can win," he says. But Kreisberg thinks unions can regain footing if they shift the terms of the debate. "It's really easy to beat up on teacher unions or employee unions," he says. "But when you ask people how they feel about teachers or firefighters, [approval ratings are] much higher."

BACKGROUND

Forging Solidarity

Public employees in the United States have organized to promote their interests since the 1800s, often in the face of resistance from local supervisors and government officials. Civil service reforms in the late 19th century gave some workers protections from politically motivated hiring and firing. Only in the 20th century, however, did public-employee unions win the right to advocate on the full range of workplace issues. The mid-20th century saw cities and then states recognize collective bargaining rights for public employees; the federal government partially followed suit in 1962 by recognizing federal-employee unions. But the advance of public-employee unions halted in the mid-1970s with the

AFL-CIO President Richard Trumka rallies union members and community activists at New Jersey's capitol in Trenton on Feb. 25 to support opponents of Wisconsin legislation restricting collective bargaining. Trumka also blasted cuts in benefits for New Jersey government workers proposed by Republican Gov. Chris Christie.

failure of a federal bill to guarantee collective bargaining rights for government workers at all levels.[19]

Federal shipyard workers organized as early as the early 1800s and achieved their first notable success with a strike at the naval shipyard in Washington, D.C., in 1836 that prompted President Andrew Jackson to grant their demand for a 10-hour day. The New York Letter Carriers formed in 1863 and, with help from the Knights of Labor, became a national organization by 1890. At the local level, teachers organized into the National Education Association in 1870, initially as a mutual-aid society and later as a quasi-union seeking to ease various regulations and restrictions on educators. Police and firefighters similarly organized mutual-aid societies in the late 1800s that later evolved into modern unions.

Civil-service laws passed by Congress and many states in the late 19th century reduced some abuses of political patronage in the hiring and firing of public employees. But the National Association of Letter Carriers' increasing activism prompted Postmaster General William Wilson in 1895 to forbid postal employees from lobbying in Washington. President Theodore Roosevelt in 1902 expanded the "gag rule" to all federal employees. The postal workers responded with a public campaign supported by the American Federation of Labor that won congressional approval in 1912 of the Lloyd-LaFollette Act, guaranteeing federal employees' right to lobby the government. The act laid the groundwork

Pension Woes Blamed on Wall Street Crash, Not Unions

"It's a little perverse to be looking to unions as the main scapegoat."

Public-employee unions are being blamed for underfunded pension plans for state and local government workers. But two Washington research centers lay most of the blame on losses in the stock market and cuts in contributions by state and local governments.

The nonpartisan Pew Center on the States warned in February 2010 that states faced a cumulative $1 trillion gap in covering pensions and health benefits for state and local workers: $452 billion in unfunded liabilities for pensions and $587 billion for health benefits, as of December 2008. The Washington-based center warned that the gap would grow unless states brought down costs or "set aside enough money" to pay for benefits.[1]

In a more recent report, the liberal-leaning Center for Economic Policy and Research (CEPR) concluded that most of what it calculated as $647 billion in unfunded pension liabilities stemmed from the two-year stock market plunge from 2007 to 2009. The Washington-based center listed a second major cause as reduced contributions by states during the downturn.[2]

Unions play only a minor role in both reports. The Pew Center report notes that unions have resisted moves to increase contributions or reduce future benefits in some states, but it found "a greater willingness" to accept changes than in the past. The CEPR report, written by co-director Dean Baker, does not mention unions. In an interview, he says unions "haven't played much of a role."

"The economy went off the cliff," Baker says. "That wasn't the unions. That was bad management of the financial system, bad regulatory management. That wasn't school teachers and firefighters. It's a little perverse to be looking to unions as the main scapegoat."

Jack Dean, a conservative pension-reform advocate who publishes the website pensiontsunami.com, does cite the unions' stance as a factor in causing pension funding problems, but he says state and local governments share the blame.

"The unions have gotten us into this situation, but that's what they're designed to do," says Dean, a former journalist who began monitoring public pensions in 2004 and is now affiliated with the conservative California Public Policy Center in Santa Monica. "We can't fault them for doing what they were set up to do. We need to watch them more closely and prevent them from driving us into bankruptcy."[3]

Both the Pew and CEPR reports show wide variations among the states' pension funds. California, the nation's most populous state, has the biggest pension shortfall or "overhang" — $75 billion, according to the CEPR report. Illinois, with $65 billion, and New Jersey, with $43 billion, rank second and third.

Surprisingly, perhaps, the state where public unions are under severest attack — Wisconsin — gets high marks in both reports. Pew cites Wisconsin as one of four states — along with Florida, New York and Washington — with fully funded pension plans. The CEPR report shows Wisconsin with a minimal $193 million in unfunded pension liabilities. "Wisconsin looks pretty good in the scheme of things," says Baker.

Public workers — federal, state and local — generally enjoy better pension benefits than private-sector workers as a whole, experts agree. Union leaders say the benefits often amount to deferred compensation in exchange for forgoing current wage or salary increases. Critics say government officials agree to boost pension benefits because they satisfy

for formation of other federal-employee unions, including the National Federation of Federal Employees in 1917 and the American Federation of Government Employees in 1932.

Public-sector unionism suffered a decades-long setback, however, with the public backlash against the Boston police strike of 1919. After calling out the Massachusetts National Guard, Gov. Calvin Coolidge, later U.S. president, famously declared, "There is no right to strike against the public

safety" — a view reflected in the widespread bans on public-employee strikes today. By the 1930s, public-employee organizing picked up, as exemplified by the founding of the Wisconsin State Employees Association in 1932, predecessor of present-day AFSCME. But the University of Wisconsin's Jones notes that AFSCME did not initially list collective bargaining as one of its goals. At the federal level, President Franklin D. Roosevelt supported public workers' right to organize, but, in a letter widely quoted by

unions while pushing the fiscal impact of the increases into the future.

Contrary to the picture drawn by critics, however, a pension expert has found limited correlation between union strength and pension levels. In research to be published in the *Journal of Pension Economics and Finance*, economist Sylvester Schieber found, for example, that Colorado has the most generous pension benefits even though it has a relatively low 25 percent unionization rate among public workers.

Several states with high unionization rates do have relatively high pension benefits, including, in descending order, New York, Ohio, New Jersey, California and Wisconsin. But Georgia, with a low unionization rate of 15 percent, ranked third-highest in pension benefits. "I was surprised by the result," Schieber told *The New York Times.*[4]

Both Baker and Pew Center research director Kil Huh say states should be moving toward fully funded pensions through some combination of steps, beginning with keeping up their own contributions. Baker says that state and local payments to pension funds have averaged $6.9 billion less than withdrawals for the past three years.

Huh says states were already considering or adopting such reforms as reducing benefits, changing the retirement age and requiring employee contributions. Nineteen states adopted such changes in 2010, he says, in some instances with union support.

As one example, Ken Brynien, president of New York's Public Employees Federation, notes that public-sector unions worked with Democratic Gov. David Paterson on a package of changes in 2009. New employees are now required to contribute 3 percent of their paychecks to their pension throughout their period of service. In addition, the retirement age was increased from 55 to 62, the minimum years of service for pension vesting from five years to 10 and the use of overtime capped in calculating benefits.

Pension-reformer Dean gives the unions only grudging credit. "They've gone along with some of the changes, and that's because they've seen the handwriting on the

Conservative pension-reform advocate Jack Dean blames both unions and state and local governments for pension problems.

www.fullertonsfuture.org

wall. The problem is that the changes being made are in most cases tweaks."

But Baker says the pension shortfalls are generally "manageable," especially if the stock market avoids another reversal. "You do have states that have serious situations," he says, "but those are the exceptions."

— Kenneth Jost

[1] Pew Center on the States, "The Trillion-Dollar Gap," February 2010, http://downloads.pewcenteronthestates.org/The_Trillion_Dollar_Gap_final.pdf.

[2] Dean Baker, "The Origins and Severity of the Public Pension Crisis," Center for Economic and Policy Research, February 2011, www.cepr.net/documents/publications/pensions-2011-02.pdf.

[3] "PensionTsunami: A Project of the California Public Policy Center," www.pensiontsunami.com/. The site focuses on California but includes extensive reports and commentary on pension issues in other states as well.

[4] Mary Williams Walsh, "The Burden of Pensions on States," *The New York Times*, March 11, 2011, p. B1. Schieber ranked pension benefits by the "replacement rate" — that is, the percentage of a worker's income replaced by the benefit. Colorado's pensions replaced 90 percent of a retiree's income; Wisconsin's, 57 percent.

public-employee union critics today, said that collective bargaining — "as usually understood" — "cannot be transplanted into the public service." He also opposed "militant tactics," including strikes.[20]

Public unions gained solid footing after World War II with the growth of state and local public employment and the gradual recognition of collective bargaining rights by local and state governments. In 1958, New York City's Democratic mayor, Robert F. Wagner Jr. — whose

father, as a U.S. senator, sponsored the private-sector National Labor Relations Act — granted collective bargaining rights to city workers. A year later, Wisconsin's Democratic governor, Gaylord Nelson, later a U.S. senator, won enactment of the first statewide collective bargaining law.

President John F. Kennedy continued the favorable trend for public workers in 1962 by signing an executive order that explicitly guaranteed federal workers' right to organize

Before 1950 *Government workers organize, but have limited rights.*

1912 Lloyd-LaFollette Act guarantees federal workers' right to lobby government.

1919 Boston police strike incites anti-union sentiment in public.

1935, **1937** President Franklin D. Roosevelt signs National Labor Relations Act, guaranteeing union rights to private sector (1935); in later letter, says collective bargaining — "as usually understood" — "cannot be transplanted" into public service (1937).

Late 1940s Government employment begins to grow after World War II.

1950s-1976 *Government workers gain collective bargaining rights.*

Early 1950s About 10 percent of public employees belong to unions.

1958 New York City's "Little Wagner Act" grants collective bargaining rights to public-employee unions.

1959 Wisconsin is first state to pass collective bargaining law for government workers.

1962 President John F. Kennedy signs executive order guaranteeing federal workers' right to unionize and collectively bargain, but not over pay.

1971 Postal workers are granted right to bargain over pay.

1976 Federal bill to grant collective bargaining rights to all state and local government workers fails in Congress.

1977-2000 *Public-sector unions make some gains, suffer some setbacks.*

1977 Unionization rate for government employees is around 40 percent.

1978 Civil Service Reform Act codifies federal workers' right to unionize.

1980 Most states allow collective bargaining for government workers.

1981 Air traffic controllers strike; President Ronald Reagan fires controllers, decertifies union.

1993 President Bill Clinton expands bargaining rights for federal workers.

2000 Unionization rate for government workers holds at around 37 percent.

2001-Present *Public-employee unions take hits from Republican administrations in Washington, several states.*

2001 President George W. Bush rescinds Clinton order on bargaining.

2002 At Bush's insistence, Department of Homeland Security (DHS) is created with president given authority to waive collective bargaining rights.

2003, 2005 Governors in three states rescind collective bargaining: Kentucky (2003); Indiana, Missouri (2005).

2006 Federal appeals court in Washington says Bush administration went too far in curbing collective bargaining with DHS employees.

2007 Missouri Supreme Court rules state constitution guarantees bargaining rights for state workers.

2009 Democrat Barack Obama elected president; federal employee unions expect favorable climate.

2010 Republican New Jersey Gov. Chris Christie wins passage of laws to require teachers to contribute to health insurance (March), limit police, firefighter raises (December). . . . Republicans gain majority in House of Representatives; win majority of governorships, state legislatures (Nov. 2). . . . In new economic and political climate, Obama announces two-year pay freeze for civilian federal workers as budget-cutting step (Nov. 29).

2011 Republican Govs. Scott Walker in Wisconsin and John Kasich in Ohio win passage of omnibus bills to curb collective bargaining for state and local workers (March 11, 30); Wisconsin law blocked by legal challenge; opponents eye referendum on Ohio law.

Federal Pay Freeze Sparks Partisan Bickering

Obama cites budget savings, but GOP says plan includes costly pay raises.

Facing tough budget negotiations with the new Republican-controlled Congress, President Obama found a quick way in November to cut federal spending: a two-year pay freeze for civilian federal workers. Federal-employee unions complained, while Republicans begrudgingly gave the move tepid support.

Three months later, however, Republican lawmakers are complaining the "freeze" still allows federal workers to get "step increases" — graduated pay hikes within each of the 15 defined civil service grades — that they estimate will cost $1 billion for the current fiscal year. [1]

In announcing the move on Nov. 29, Obama tried to cushion the blow by praising federal workers, but said the times required "all of us . . . to make some sacrifices." He said it would save $2 billion a year.

Federal union leaders sharply criticized the move. "Very disappointed," Colleen Kelly, president of the National Treasury Employees Union, told *The Washington Post.* John Gage, president of the American Federation of Government Employees, called the move a "public relations gesture" that would amount to "peanuts" in savings. "The American people didn't vote to stick it to a VA nursing assistant making $28,000 a year or a border patrol agent earning $34,000 per year," Gage added.

Rep. Jason Chaffetz, a Utah Republican who was then expected to head the House Oversight Subcommittee on Federal Workforce, U.S. Postal Service, and Labor Policy, called the move "a good start." (The post eventually went to Florida's Dennis Ross.) But in a subcommittee hearing three months later, House Oversight and Reform Committee Chairman Darrell Issa, a California Republican, sharply challenged Office of Personnel Management Director John Berry on Obama's move.

"There is no freeze because of the step increases," Issa said. "The truth is there will be pay raises."

Berry said he would oppose barring step increases for federal workers because that would cause some workers to leave the government for private-sector jobs. Under friendly questioning later from Democrat Danny Davis of Illinois, Berry said federal workers deserved credit for forgoing pay raises. "They were the first ones who were asked to step up to the plate and make a sacrifice," he said.

— Kenneth Jost

---

[1] Coverage drawn in part from Seth McLaughlin, "GOP pushes total pay freeze," *The Washington Times,* March 10, 2011, p. A4; Lisa Rein and Perry Bacon Jr., "Obama proposes 2-year pay freeze," *The Washington Post,* Nov. 30, 2010, p. A1; Joe Davidson, "President's salary freeze for federal workers gets cold reception," *ibid.,* p. B3. For Obama's remarks, see "Remarks by the President on the Federal Employee Pay Freeze," Nov. 29, 2010, www.whitehouse.gov/the-press-office/2010/11/29/remarks-president-federal-employee-pay-freeze.

---

and bargain collectively, though not over pay. Dissatisfied with some of its restrictions, unions won favorable changes later in revised executive orders issued by two Republican presidents: Richard M. Nixon (1969, 1971) and Gerald R. Ford (1975). Meanwhile, the National Association of Letter Carriers had won the right to bargain collectively over pay as an implicit payback for settling the 1970 postal strike and supporting the reorganization of the Postal Service as an independent government corporation.

Public employees were making gains in pay and benefits, and public unions were growing. By the mid-1970s, nearly one-third of public-sector workers were unionized, compared to about 10 percent in the 1950s.[21] But unions' militancy — notably, the increasing number of strikes in the 1960s and early '70s — was also engendering a backlash. Then in 1976, unions suffered a crushing disappointment at the federal level with the failure of legislation to guarantee union and collective bargaining rights to state and local workers nationwide. Oddly, the bill failed not because of lack of support in Congress, according to Georgetown University historian Joseph McCartin, but because of a Supreme Court decision casting doubt on its constitutionality. McCartin says the bill's death "marked the turning point of the once expansive public-sector labor movement."[22]

Holding Ground

Public-sector unionism held its own during the final decades of the 20th century even as private-sector unions shrank in size and political clout. Federal workers won statutory protection of union rights, while state and local governments continued to enact or enlarge collective bargaining rights for their workers. Public-sector unions grew to surpass 7 million members by century's end, but the percentage of government workers enrolled in unions was essentially flat. And public-employee unions' vulnerability to political attack was vividly demonstrated by President Ronald Reagan's decision to break a nationwide air controllers' strike in 1981 in his first year in the White House.

Congress solidified federal workers' rights somewhat as part of the Civil Service Reform Act of 1978. The act's Title VII — separately entitled the Federal Service Labor Management Statute — codified federal workers' right to organize and slightly expanded the scope of collective bargaining previously established by executive order. The act also created the Federal Labor Relations Authority (FLRA) to interpret and administer the act, with a general counsel to prosecute unfair labor practices under the law. While protecting workers' organizing rights, the act also reinforced federal managers' control over personnel policy, including hiring, promotions and work assignments. Wages and hours remained outside the scope of bargaining, but the law allowed — without requiring — bargaining over procedures for managers to use in exercising their powers.[23]

State and local government workers continued to make incremental gains as well, but with difficulty. The number of states with collective bargaining rights for at least some government workers increased from 16 as of the mid-1960s to 29 by 1980. Victories were hard-fought. In Florida, for example, the legislature passed a statewide collective bargaining law in 1974 only under duress, six years after the state's supreme court found bargaining rights guaranteed under the state constitution. California was one of several states to pass a statewide law, in 1977, after first having extended bargaining rights to specific categories of employees. In some states — for example, Indiana in 1989 — bargaining rights were established by executive order after legislative efforts failed. By the end of the century unions had strengthened some of the laws, but the total number of states with collective bargaining rights remained around 30.

Public unions waged their organizing and lobbying efforts under the cloud cast by the 1981 strike by the Professional Air Traffic Controllers Organization (PATCO) and Reagan's forceful reaction to the work stoppage. The union, formed in 1968, had had a stormy relationship with the Federal Aviation Administration (FAA) for years. In 1981, members voted 20-1 against accepting a proposed contract with a 32-hour workweek and maximum $59,000 salary; on Aug. 3, some 12,000 controllers staged a nationwide walkout.

Reagan, former president of the Screen Actors Guild, declared the job action illegal, fired the striking controllers, hired new ones and decertified the union. The union got little public support, and supervisors along with military and non-striking civilian controllers kept planes in the air without crippling reductions in flights. Years later, in 1987, a new union, the National Air Traffic Controllers Organization, was formed — with an explicit no-strike pledge in its charter.[24]

The PATCO strike was actually exceptional. The number and length of strikes have fallen since the days of public-union militancy in the 1960s and '70s. In fact, 13 states have laws today permitting public-employee strikes, typically with exceptions for police and firefighters; Kearney, the North Carolina State professor, says that the bans are ineffective in preventing strikes and that strikes are actually more frequent in states that ban work stoppages than in those with permissive laws.[25] Whatever the law, however, striking public employees typically draw little public support since the inconvenience to transit riders or parents of school children is easier to understand than the details of labor negotiations.

Throughout the period, and to date, public-sector labor relations have remained a partisan issue in Washington and in many state capitals. President Bill Clinton, a Democrat, gave federal unions a small victory in 1993 with an executive order that required agencies to bargain on the issues left optional in the 1978 law. The act also called for the establishment of labor-management partnerships throughout the executive branch, collaborations that the administration later credited with promoting innovation and productivity. President George W. Bush, a Republican, rescinded the order on Feb. 17, 2001 — less than a month after taking office.[26]

Later, Bush adopted an aggressive, anti-union stance on a more protracted issue: union rights for workers in the newly created Department of Homeland Security.

Bush proposed the creation of the new department — a consolidation of agencies in several departments — in the aftermath of the Sept. 11, 2001, attacks on the World Trade Center and Pentagon. As enacted, the law gave the president the authority to waive collective bargaining rights for designated employees on national security grounds. Bush and GOP lawmakers said the president needed flexibility in structuring the new department. In a key vote, the House of Representatives approved the provision on a party-line vote, 229-201, before final passage on July 26, 2002. The Democratic-controlled Senate passed a bill without the provision, but Bush prevailed by vowing to veto the measure without it.[27]

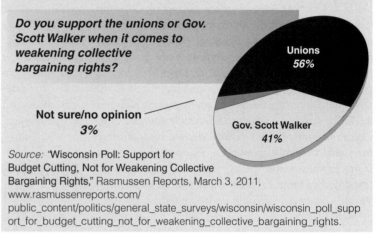

Support Wanes for Wisconsin Governor

A majority of Wisconsin voters initially supported Republican Gov. Scott Walker's effort to curtail bargaining rights for government workers, but public support for the plan has declined. Most voters now back the state's public-employee unions.

Do you support the unions or Gov. Scott Walker when it comes to weakening collective bargaining rights?

Unions
56%

Not sure/no opinion
3%

Gov. Scott Walker
41%

Source: "Wisconsin Poll: Support for Budget Cutting, Not for Weakening Collective Bargaining Rights," Rasmussen Reports, March 3, 2011, www.rasmussenreports.com/ public_content/politics/general_state_surveys/wisconsin/wisconsin_poll_supp ort_for_budget_cutting_not_for_weakening_collective_bargaining_rights.

Taking Flak

The Bush administration's attack on worker rights at the federal level presaged a period of similar pressure on public-employee unions in the states. Republican governors in three states — Kentucky, Indiana and Missouri — rescinded collective bargaining rights previously granted by executive order. Other states moved to limit bargaining with teachers' unions over such issues as class size or teacher evaluations. Public-employee unions limited the damage somewhat by winning favorable court rulings, including a victory over the Bush administration's restrictions on bargaining for Homeland Security employees. But GOP victories in state elections in November 2010 touched off a new round of anti-union moves in several states, including the contentious battle fought most dramatically in Wisconsin.

In contrast to the open-ended scope of bargaining in the private sector, state laws for public employees had long taken some issues off the table. In the 1990s, school-reform issues prompted legislatively enacted limits on bargaining with teachers in such states as Illinois, Michigan, Oregon and Wisconsin. Oregon's law, for example, barred bargaining not only on class size and

teacher evaluations but also on dress and grooming standards and personal conduct such as smoking and chewing gum. The Michigan Supreme Court in 1995 upheld the constitutionality of the bargaining restrictions enacted there. The Ohio Supreme Court struck down a law challenged by state university faculty that barred bargaining over instructional workload, but the U.S. Supreme Court in 1999 reinstated the measure. By 2008, an education group reported that most states limited teacher bargaining to economic issues, such as wages, hours, health benefits and the like.[28]

GOP governors in Kentucky, Indiana and Missouri went further in the 2000s by revoking collective bargaining rights granted by executive orders issued by Democratic predecessors. In Kentucky, Republican Ernie Fletcher rescinded collective bargaining rights on his first day in office in December 2003 following a campaign pledge to reduce state personnel costs. Indiana's Daniels and Missouri Gov. Matt Blunt followed suit shortly after taking office in January 2005. Blunt had vowed in his campaign to rescind the executive order issued by his Democratic predecessor in 2001. Blunt's action was later undone, however, by the Missouri Supreme Court. In a 2007 ruling, the court held that a provision in the state constitution guaranteeing collective bargaining rights for "employees" extended to public as well as private-sector workers.[29]

In Washington, the National Treasury Employees Union had won a more significant victory a year earlier when the U.S. Court of Appeals for the District of Columbia Circuit struck down the Bush administration's effort to all but abolish bargaining rights for Homeland Security employees. The administration argued the new department needed flexible personnel rules to deal with the range of post-9/11 security issues. But in a unanimous ruling, the three-judge appeals panel said the administration had gone too far by claiming a power to unilaterally abrogate existing labor contracts and limit collective bargaining to individual employee grievances. The provisions, Judge Harry Edwards wrote, "plainly violate the statutory command in the Homeland Security Act that the department 'ensure' collective bargaining for its employees."[30]

With Democrat Obama in the White House, public-sector unions breathed a sigh of relief in regard to federal labor-management relations in 2009. A year later, however, New Jersey became the first of the battleground states when public-employee unions clashed with a sacrifice-demanding Republican chief executive: Gov. Chris Christie. Christie, a federal prosecutor who ousted a scandal-tainted Democrat, made attacks on public-employee unions his signature issue throughout 2010. Working with a Democratic-controlled legislature, Christie won passage of a law in March that, among other provisions, required teachers to pay 1.5 percent of their pay for health insurance, as state employees already did. In December, he also signed an act limiting local police and firefighters to 2 percent pay increases if union-management talks hit an impasse.[31]

With the GOP gubernatorial and legislative victories in the November 2010 balloting, Walker in Wisconsin and Kasich in Ohio became the highest-profile of the new combatants with public-employee unions. In Ohio, GOP state Sen. Shannon Jones introduced an omnibus measure, Senate Bill 5 (SB 5), on Feb. 9 that, among other changes, would eliminate collective bargaining for state workers, take health insurance out of collective bargaining for municipal employees and remove binding arbitration for police and firefighters in event of a breakdown in negotiations. The next day, Kasich said he was working on

his own bill, which would include a provision to fire striking workers.[32]

Walker unveiled his proposal in a news conference in Madison the next day, Feb. 11, calling it necessary to trim the state's budget deficit and avoid layoffs. "I get why unions make sense in the private sector," Walker said in explaining the bill. "But at the public level, it's the government, it's the people, who are the ones who are the employers." Republican legislators applauded the proposal, but it drew fierce criticism from union leaders and some municipal leaders. Dane County executive Falk called it a "draconian" plan. "There's a fair and responsible way to do this," Falk said. Walker, she said, "chose a sledgehammer."[33]

CURRENT SITUATION
Continuing Fights

The bitter fights over public-employee union bills in Ohio and Wisconsin are moving into new arenas with political battles possible for the rest of the year.

Wisconsin's bill is on hold at least until late May pending the legal challenge under the state's open-meetings law. In the meantime, opponents are circulating petitions to try to recall eight Republican senators who voted for the measure. Supporters countered by starting drives to recall eight of the 14 Democrats whose boycott stalled passage of the bill for three weeks.

Ohio's new law, SB 5, is also on hold pending a possible referendum on the measure in November.

Opponents have 90 days from Gov. Kasich's signature of the bill on March 30 to gather at least 231,149 signatures of registered voters to put the measure on the Nov. 8 ballot for approval or disapproval.

In Wisconsin, the fight over the labor bill may cost a Republican-appointed state supreme court justice his bid for re-election in April 5 balloting that ended with the outcome in doubt. JoAnne Kloppenburg, an assistant state attorney general, held a 204-vote lead over Justice David Prosser in complete but unofficial returns reported by The Associated Press in mid-afternoon on April 6. Labor, liberal and Democratic groups backing Kloppenburg had portrayed the race as a referendum on Gov. Walker. A recount was expected, possibly several weeks in the future.[34]

Should states limit collective bargaining by public-sector unions?

YES

James Sherk
*Senior Policy Analyst in Labor
Economics, Heritage Foundation*

Written for *CQ Researcher,* April 2011

Federal law does not allow the FBI, CIA or Secret Service to collectively bargain. Is this is a mistake? Collective bargaining gives public unions a monopoly on the government's workforce. It means government can only employ workers on union terms. This often conflicts with serving the public.

Last year, Milwaukee Public Schools laid off Megan Sampson, the district's "Outstanding First Year Teacher." Why? The school district was short of money, and Milwaukee's education union refused concessions.

The union preferred having a few teachers lose their jobs to having all teachers contribute toward their health insurance. That forced the district to close its deficit with layoffs. Under union rules, those layoffs occur strictly on the basis of seniority. So goodbye, first-year teacher Megan Sampson. Her excellence in teaching children did not matter.

The union sacrificed education quality to protect the pay and job security of its senior members. That is its job. Unions exist to get more for their members, not serve the public good.

This is acceptable in the private sector. Unions there negotiate over business profits, so competition holds them in check. If they get too greedy, they know they will drive their customers away.

The government is different. Government employees do not need unions. Civil service laws already ensure they get treated fairly. Further, competition does not restrain government unions. The government has no competitors and earns no profits. Government unions bargain over tax dollars. As long as the government does not go bankrupt they can keep demanding more.

They do.

Unions make firing government employees exceedingly difficult. That keeps ineffective teachers and abusive social workers on the job. In many states government union members retire in their mid-50s at taxpayer expense. Unions push the government to put their interests above the public's.

Historically, even champions of the labor movement thought this a bad idea. George Meany, the first president of the AFL-CIO, believed that "collective bargaining is impossible in government." President Franklin D. Roosevelt agreed. He considered a government-employee strike "unthinkable and intolerable."

Government should serve the public interest, but unions want their interests to come first. They should not get a monopoly on the government workforce to insist that happens. Union organizing is far less important than effectively educating children or stopping terrorists.

NO

David Madland
*Director, American Worker Project, Center for
American Progress Action Fund*

Written for *CQ Researcher,* April 2011

Public-sector workers deserve the right to unionize and collectively bargain with their employers. And governments, like corporations, sometimes need to be reminded by organized workers to treat their employees fairly.

Indeed, the Rev. Martin Luther King Jr. traveled to Memphis in 1968 to help city sanitation workers gain recognition for their union as they faced low pay, terrible working conditions and racist supervisors. Even the conservative icon Ronald Reagan recognized that public-sector workers should be able to collectively bargain. Reagan signed a bill to grant municipal and county employees the right to do so when he was governor of California.

The only reason our country is debating whether public-sector unions should exist is because of an orchestrated political campaign that is trying to use budget deficits as a cover to weaken a political opponent. This smear campaign is deceptive and dangerous.

Opponents claim that public-sector employees are overpaid and are the main drivers of state budget deficits. Both accusations are false. Studies that compare the compensation of public-sector workers to similar private-sector workers — controlling for things like education levels — find that public employees are actually underpaid. Total compensation — including wages and benefits — is less for government workers. Only the erosion of private-sector job quality makes the comparison even somewhat close.

Further, employee compensation is not busting state budget deficits. My research shows that state budget deficits are the result of the Great Recession and that employee compensation as a share of government spending has actually declined over the past decades.

Nor are public-sector unions newly powerful, as opponents argue. Public unionization rates remain at the same level as in the late 1970s. The absence of collective bargaining does not ensure a balanced budget, either. States with very low levels of public-sector unionization — such as Texas, Louisiana and South Carolina — have some of the largest budget shortfalls as a share of their economy.

Finally, collective bargaining is used to negotiate the sharing of pain as well as gain. And government workers are in fact sharing the pain. Significant government jobs have been cut since the recession began. Those still employed in nearly every state have seen cuts in pay and benefits or furloughs.

The bottom line: All workers deserve the right to collectively bargain and negotiate for fair wages and decent working conditions on relatively equal footing with their employer.

Opponents of the Wisconsin labor bill are marking at least one success: After gathering more than 21,000 signatures — 5,000 more than needed — they forced a recall vote against state Sen. Dan Kapanke, a LaCrosse Republican in his second four-year term. Other recall efforts have until the end of April to gather the needed number of signatures.[35]

The recall petitions have to be verified by the state's Government Accountability Board, with an election held within six weeks after verification. In Wisconsin's history, five legislators have faced recalls, and two have been defeated. One expert doubts any of the current recalls will succeed.

"The big uncertainty is how long people will remain angry," says Michael Kraft, a professor of political science at the University of Wisconsin-Green Bay. "It's a different world today from when people were demonstrating in front of the Capitol."

In Ohio, opponents of SB 5 may be planning to ask rank-and-file union members to help fund a referendum campaign with projected costs of up to $20 million. *The Columbus Dispatch* reported that an email from Larry Wicks, the executive director of the Ohio Education Association, said members may be charged a one-time assessment of $50 to finance the campaign. A similar message from the president of the Columbus firefighters union said a $100 assessment was to be considered on April 7. In his email, Wicks said at least $20 million would be needed for "an effective campaign."[36]

The 90-day waiting period for a law to take effect in Ohio is standard except for budget measures, according to Mike McClellan, a spokesman for the Ohio secretary of state's office. Opponents have until July 1 to submit the needed number of signatures, equal to 6 percent of the total vote cast in the most recent gubernatorial election. The secretary of state's office has 20 days to verify the signatures.

Kasich won election in November with 49 percent of the vote and a narrow, 77,000-vote margin over the Democratic incumbent, Ted Strickland. A poll in late March showed Kasich's approval at 30 percent — "shockingly low," according to Alexander Lamis, an associate professor of political science at Case Western Reserve University in Cleveland and co-editor of a book on Ohio politics.[37]

Still, Lamis says labor unions will be challenged to defeat the collective bargaining law in a referendum. "We certainly have strong labor unions," he explains. "But labor has lost a lot of strength. The jobs aren't there anymore."

Wavering Views

Public opinion about government workers appears to be highly malleable even as lawmakers in several states continue to push proposals to limit collective bargaining or other rights of public-employee unions.

Various polls published as the Wisconsin and Ohio legislatures considered bills to limit public-employee unions registered support for requiring government workers to pay more toward health and retirement benefits. But the surveys also found opposition to restricting collective bargaining rights for the unions representing those workers.

The most recent nationwide poll finds that the unions have what the Gallup organization called "a slight edge" over governors in what the survey characterized as "disputes over collective bargaining policies and state budgets." In a telephone survey of slightly more than 1,000 respondents March 25-27, 48 percent said they agreed more with state-employee unions while 39 percent agreed with more with governors. Thirteen percent favored neither side or had no opinion.[38]

The *USA Today*/Gallup survey showed a sharp partisan split on the issue, with 70 percent of Democrats favoring unions and 65 percent of Republicans siding with governors. Independents were close to evenly split: 45 percent favored unions, 40 percent governors. Young people (18-34) sided with unions by a better than 2-to-1 margin; unions had a narrow edge among the 35-55 age group, while those over 55 split evenly.

In its analysis, Gallup noted previous polls that found opposition to restricting collective bargaining rights but mixed opinions on whether public-employee unions are helpful or harmful on balance to states. "Today," the analysis continued, "neither the governors nor the unions appear to have a strong advantage in the court of public opinion nationally, but the unions do have the slight edge."

Two earlier nationwide surveys registered mixed views about public employee unions. Polls by *The New York Times*/CBS News and NBC News/*Wall Street Journal* both found about 60 percent of respondents opposed to "taking away" or "eliminating" what both surveys called "collective bargaining rights." The *Times*/CBS poll also found a 56 percent majority opposed to cutting the pay or benefits of public employees to reduce budget deficits.

On the other hand, the NBC/*Journal* poll found solid support for requiring public employees to contribute more toward retirement benefits (68 percent) and health insurance (63 percent). A majority — 58 percent — also said it would be acceptable to freeze public employees' salaries for one year. And a 37 percent plurality in *The Times*/CBS survey said that public-employee unions have "too much" influence on American life and politics.[39]

One poll in Ohio indicates the importance of the phrasing of questions in surveys on the issues. The Quinnipiac University poll found a 48 percent to 41 percent plurality opposed to bills limiting "collective bargaining," but opposition increased to 54 percent among a different sample asked about a bill to limit "collective bargaining rights."[40]

The Gallup survey noted a significant difference in the split of opinion depending on how closely respondents were following the issues. Those following them "very closely" were almost evenly divided (49 percent to 48 percent in favor of unions); groups paying less attention registered strong support for unions: 52 percent to 41 percent among those following "somewhat closely" and 45 percent to 31 percent among those following "not closely or not at all."

OUTLOOK

Troubled Times

Arising tide lifts all boats, President John F. Kennedy liked to remark in talking about the shared benefits of a growing economy. In a sinking ship, however, the often used idiom is, "Every man for himself."

For the past four years, the U.S. economy has been foundering instead of being lifted up with a rising tide. The housing bubble burst, big banks failed, the economy stalled and unemployment reached nearly 10 percent. With so much economic insecurity, many Americans were open to arguments that government employees were being spared most of the pain thanks to their unions' unfairly exploiting their political and economic power.

The Wisconsin and Ohio laws give effect to the widespread view that public-sector workers should be paying more for health and retirement benefits. But the detailed provisions go much further to limit the power of public-employee unions at the collective bargaining table and in the political arena.

Experts sympathetic to the labor movement see the laws, and the political attacks behind them, as a prelude to a long fight. "We're headed for a prolonged period of conflict and labor war if the Wisconsin model drives this in the future," says MIT professor Kochan. "You just can't attack workers' rights in as bald a fashion as they did in Wisconsin and not get the kind of backlash we've seen."

"This is not an issue the unions are going to give up on," says Kearney at North Carolina State. "These states could be the death knell of collective bargaining."

Critics of public-employee unions likewise expect continued conflict. "As long as the states are in serious financial difficulty, this will remain a political issue," says UCLA's Bainbridge. "I suspect this is not going to go away at the end of the 2012 election cycle."

Union leaders, however, are professing optimism about the likely course of the issues. "I think this anti-union wave has crested," says AFSCME's Kreisberg. He expects some Wisconsin senators to be recalled and the Ohio bill to be repealed by referendum. "We'll be seeing repercussions," he warns.

AFSCME president Gerald McEntee goes further. With the Wisconsin bill pending, he predicted that labor leaders would harness the energy from the anti-Walker protests and turn it into "a real resurgence for labor." But DiSalvo, the union critic at City College of New York, is dubious. "Maybe there's energy, but I don't quite see the avenue that that energy is going to take," he says.[41]

In Wisconsin, Walker's supporters are celebrating their victory, even while the bill is in limbo pending a court challenge of uncertain outcome. "The first round goes to the taxpayer," says Seaholm with Americans for Prosperity, "and we're going to keep fighting until the taxpayers ultimately win."

For state employees, the Wisconsin law is conversely a defeat. Many are apparently considering voting with their feet before current collective bargaining contracts expire and the law's provisions start to bite. The state's Department of Employee Trust Funds reports that it is "experiencing an extremely high volume of calls, emails, and in-person contacts from Wisconsin Retirement System members who are considering retiring on a relatively short timeline."[42]

Already retired, former consumer-complaint invesitgator Reid regrets what he sees as the implication of the controversy. "We seem to have lost the willingness to help each other out," Reid says. "Instead of dragging people down, we should be lifting people up."

NOTES

1. Tom Donohue, "Governors Show Leadership on Budgets," *ChamberPost*, Feb. 24, 2011, www.chamber post.com/2011/02/governors-show-leadership-on-budgets/. For background, see Alan Greenblatt, "State Budget Crisis," *CQ Researcher*, Sept. 11, 2009, pp. 741-764.

2. David Madland and Nick Bunker, "State Budget Deficits Are Not an Employee Compensation Problem: The Great Recession Is to Blame," Center for American Progress Action Fund, March 10, 2011, p. 2, www.americanprogressaction.org/issues/2011/03/pdf/statebudgetissuebrief.pdf. Bunker is a special assistant with the center's economic policy team.

3. National Conference of State Legislatures, "Collective Bargaining and Labor Union Legislation" data base, www.ncsl.org/default.aspx?TabId=22275.

4. See Richard Kearney, *Labor Relations in the Public Sector* (4th ed.), 2009.

5. For background on the labor movement, see these *CQ Researcher* reports: Pamela M. Prah, "Labor Unions' Future," Sept. 2, 2005, pp. 709-732; Kenneth Jost, "Labor Movement's Future," June 28, 1996, pp. 553-576.

6. See Sandy Cullen and Patricia Simms, "Passage Prompts Massive Turnout," *Wisconsin State Journal*, March 13, 2011, p A1; Samara Kalk Derby, "Protests Draw Opponents of Bargaining Proposal," *ibid.*, Feb. 14, 2011. Some other details throughout report drawn from or verified by *Wisconsin State Journal* coverage in February and March.

7. Mary Spicuzza and Clay Barbour, "GOP's Quick Maneuvers Push Bill Through Senate," *ibid.*, March 10, 2011, p. A1.

8. Quoted in Sharon Coolidge, "Daniels: Ohio can follow Indiana's lead," *The Cincinnati Enquirer*, Feb. 24, 2011. For the 2005 action, see Kevin Corcoran and Mary Beth Schneider, "Daniels ends union pacts for 25,000," *The Indianapolis Star*, Jan. 12, 2005, p. A1.

9. Dennis Cauchon, "Wisconsin one of 41 states where public workers earn more," *USA Today*, March 1, 2011, p. 1A. Fairness & Accuracy in Reporting, "Why Does USA Today Hate Public Workers?," March 1, 2011, www.commondreams.org/newswire/2011/03/01-7.

10. "Are State and Local Government Employees Paid Too Much?," *The New York Times*, March 7, 2011, p. A13.

11. Jeffrey H. Keefe, "Are Wisconsin Public Employees Over-compensated?," Economic Policy Institute, Feb. 10, 2011, www.epi.org/publications/entry/6759/; Andrew Biggs and Jason Richwine, "Government vs. unions: Are state's public employees overpaid?," *Milwaukee Journal-Sentinel*, March 10, 2011, www.jsonline.com/news/opinion/117753788.html.

12. David Madland and Nick Bunker, "State Budget Deficits Are Not an Employee Compensation Problem: The Great Recession Is to Blame," Center for American Progress Action Fund, March 10, 2011, p. 2, www.americanprogressaction.org/issues/2011/03/pdf/statebudgetissuebrief.pdf. Bunker is a special assistant with the center's economic policy team.

13. Club for Growth Wisconsin, http://wicfg.com/index.cfm/m/3/s/3.cfm.

14. AFSCME Council 24 SEPAC, Feb. 26, 2011, http://wseusepac.blogspot.com/2011/02/video-message-marty-beil-executive.html.

15. Tate quoted in Mark Pitsch, "Walker Going After 'Backbone' of Democratic Party," *Wisconsin State Journal*, March 6, 2011, p. A1; Fitzgerald's broadcast appearance is posted here: www.newsvideoclip.tv/msnbc-breaking-news-nbc-news-breaking-news/quoted.

16. Pitsch, *op. cit.*

17. Doug Erickson, "Union Membership Plunged in Indiana Following Change," *Wisconsin State Journal*, March 11, 2011, p. A1.

18. The decision is *Citizens United v. Federal Election Commission*, 558 U.S. — (2010). For background, see Kenneth Jost, "Campaign Finance Debates," *CQ Researcher*, May 28, 2010, pp. 457-480.

19. For a compact historical overview, see Richard Kearney, *op. cit.*, pp. 13-21.

20. For the complete letter, written to the president of the National Federation of Federal Employees as Congress was considering a never-enacted ban on federal collective bargaining, see American Presidency Project, University of California-Santa Barbara, www.presidency.ucsb.edu/ws/index.php?pid=15445#axzz1GhcV0NpV.

21. See Karen DeYoung, "Public Employee Militancy," *Editorial Research Reports*, Sept. 19, 1975, p. 688; William A. Korns, "Unionization of Public Employees," *Editorial Research Reports*, July 10, 1957, p. 506.

22. See Joseph A. McCartin, " 'A Wagner Act for Public Employees': Labor's Deferred Dream and the Rise of Conservatism, 1970-1976," *The Journal of American History*, June 2008, pp. 123-148.

23. See Kearney, *op. cit.*, pp. 193-195; "Congress Approves Civil Services Reform," *CQ Almanac 1978*, pp. 813-815, http://library.cqpress.com/cqalmanac/document.php?id=cqal78-1237364&type=hitlist&num=0.

24. See Kearney, *op. cit.*, pp. 250-252.

25. *Ibid.*, pp. 231-236.

26. Executive Order 12871 (Clinton); Executive Order 13203 (Bush). See *ibid.*, p. 55.

27. "Homeland Department Created," *CQ Almanac 2002*, pp. 7-3 — 7-8. See also David Firestone, "Divided House Approves Homeland Security Bill, With Limited Enthusiasm," *The New York Times*, July 27, 2002, p. A1.

28. See Education Commission of the States, "State Collective Bargaining Policies for Teachers," January 2008, www.ecs.org/html/Document.asp?chouseid=3748. The Michigan decision is *Michigan State AFL-CIO v. Michigan Employment Relations Commission*, 212 Mich.App. 472 (1995); the U.S. Supreme Court decision is *Central State University v. American Association of University Professors*, 526 U.S. 124 (1999).

29. The decision is *Independence-National Education Association v. Independence School District*, 223 S.W.3d 131 (Mo. 2007). The ruling overturned a 1947 decision that interpreted the provision to apply only to private-sector workers. For coverage, see Paul Hampel, "Government workers win right to bargain," *St. Louis Post-Dispatch*, May 30, 2007, p. A1.

30. The ruling is *National Treasury Employees Union v. Chertoff*, 452 F.3d 839 (D.C. Cir. 2006). For coverage, see Eric Weiss, "Appeals court vetoes Bush plan to alter U.S. personnel rules," *The Washington Post*, June 28, 2006, p. 23.

31. See Ginger Gibson, "Christie puts pen to pay limits," *The Times* (of Trenton), Dec. 22, 2010, p. A1; Angela Delli Santi, "Christie signs pension bill," *ibid.*, March 23, 2010, p. A9. For contrasting views of Christie's actions and statements on public-employee unions, see Matt Bai, " 'When I Run Out of Fights to Have, I'll Stop Fighting,' " *The New York Times Magazine*, Feb. 27, 2011, p. 32; Richard Pérez-Peña, "Christie's Talk Is Blunt, but Not Always Straight," *The New York Times*, March 11, 2011, p. A1.

32. See Joe Hallett and Jim Siegel, "Kasich: You strike, you get punished," *The Columbus Dispatch*, Feb. 11, 2011, p. A1; Jim Siegel, "Unions in a Fight," *ibid.*, Feb. 10, 2011, p. A1.

33. Walker quoted in Jason Stein and Patrick Marley, "Walker calls for cuts or big layoffs," *Milwaukee Journal Sentinel*, Feb. 12, 2011, p. A1; Falk quoted in Dean Mosiman, "Civic Leaders Slam 'Draconian' Plan," *Wisconsin State Journal*, Feb. 12, 2011, p. A1.

34. Larry Sandler and Patrick Marley, "Supreme Court race too close to call; Kloppenburg has narrow lead over Prosser," *Milwaukee Journal Sentinel*, April 6, 2011, www.jsonline.com/news/statepolitics/119308059.html. This report went to press in late afternoon April 6.

35. Coverage and background drawn from Chris Hubbuch, "Petitions Delivered in Kapanke Recall

Effort," *Wisconsin State Journal*, March 29, 2011, p. A7. Hubbuch is a reporter for the *LaCrosse Tribune*.

36. Joe Vardon, "Unions want members to pay for SB 5 referendum," *The Columbus Dispatch*, April 5, 2011.

37. "Ohio Women Lead in Disapproval of New Governor, Quinnipiac University Poll Finds; Voters Oppose Efforts to Curb Unions," March 23, 2011, www.quinnipiac.edu/x1284.xml?ReleaseID=1570& What=&strArea=;&strTime=0.

38. Gallup Poll, "More Americans Back Unions Than Governors in State Disputes," April 1, 2011, www .gallup.com/poll/146921/americans-back-unions-governors-state-disputes.aspx. *USA Today* published a summary of the survey on April 1 in its online feature "OnPolitics," http://content.usatoday.com/communities/onpolitics/post/2011/04/gallup-poll-governors-unions-wisconsin-ohio-/1.

39. See Michael Cooper and Megan Thee-Brenan, "Majority in Poll Back Employees in Public Unions," *The New York Times*, March 1, 2011, p. A1; "NBC/WSJ poll: 62% against stripping public employees' bargaining rights," First Read, MSNBC, March 2, 2011, http://firstread.msnbc.msn.com/_news/2011/03/02/6171265-nbcwsj-poll-62-against-stripping-public-employees-bargaining-rights. *The Wall Street Journal*'s account of the poll made only a brief reference to the public-employee union issue but suggested the survey showed public opinion "tipping against" Wisconsin Gov. Scott Walker. See Neil King Jr. and Scott Greenberg, "Poll Shows Budget-Cuts Dilemma," *The Wall Street Journal*, March 3, 2011, p. A5.

40. Quinnipiac University poll, *op. cit.*

41. McEntee quoted in Steven Greenhouse, "Organized Labor Hopes Attacks by Some States Help Nurture Comeback," *The New York Times*, March 6, 2011, sec. 1, p. 17.

42. Advisory, State of Wisconsin, Department of Employee Trust Funds, updated April 5, 2011, http://etf.wi.gov/news/Retiring%20on%20Short%20Notice%202%20_2_.pdf.

BIBLIOGRAPHY
Books

Freeman, Richard, and Casey Ichniowsky (eds.), *When Public Sector Workers Unionize*, University of Chicago Press, 1988.
Editors Freeman and Ichniowsky open the collection of articles with an overview that concludes public-sector unions increase government employment, raise wages of unionized and non-union workers alike and increase expenditures in unionized departments. Freeman is a professor of economics at Harvard University, Ichniowski a professor at Columbia University's Graduate School of Business; both also are associated with the National Bureau of Economic Research.

Kearney, Richard, *Labor Relations in the Public Sector* (4th ed.), *CRC Press*, 2009.
The book covers labor relations in the public sector from historical, economic and political perspectives. Includes 24-page list of references. Kearney is a professor of government at North Carolina State University.

Malin, Martin H., Ann C. Hodges and Joseph E. Slater, *Public Sector Employment: Cases and Materials* (2d ed.), *West*, 2011.
The law school casebook comprehensively covers the law of public-sector employment, including the right to organize, collective bargaining, administration of agreements and strikes. Malin is a professor at Chicago-Kent College of Law, Hodges at University of Richmond School of Law and Slater at University of Toledo College of Law. The first edition of the casebook, published in 2004, was co-authored by Joseph R. Grodin, June M. Weisberger and Malin.

Nesbitt, Murray B., *Labor Relations in the Federal Government Service*, Bureau of National Affairs, 1976.
Although dated, the book provides a thorough history of labor relations policy for the federal workforce up to the mid-1970s.

Articles

DiSalvo, Daniel, "The Trouble With Public Sector Unions," *National Affairs*, **fall 2010, www.national-affairs.com/publications/detail/the-trouble-with-public-sector-unions.**

An assistant professor of political science at City College of New York argues that the cost of public-sector pay and benefits, combined with hundreds of billions of dollars in unfunded pension liabilities for retired workers, requires limiting public-employee unions or even reopening the question of whether government workers should enjoy "the privilege" of collective bargaining.

Edwards, Chris, "Public-Sector Unions," *Cato Institute*, **March 2010.**

The director of tax-policy studies at the Washington-based libertarian think tank argues that collective bargaining should be banned in the public sector to give policymakers greater flexibility and improve government efficiency.

Lewis, Finlay, "Should Unionizing Be a Private Right?," *CQ Weekly*, **March 14, 2011, p. 565.**

The story ties proposals to curb public-employee unions as a means to reduce state and local budget deficits to the larger debate over the right of government workers to unionize and bargain collectively over pay, benefits and working conditions.

Orr, Andrea, "Scapegoating public sector workers," *Economic Policy Institute*, **March 8, 2011, www.epi.org/analysis_and_opinion/entry/scapegoating_public_sector_workers/.**

The web editor for the liberal Washington-based think tank says the debate over public-employee unions stems from "a single false argument" that government workers are to blame for state budget crises.

Reports and Studies

Lewin, David, *et al.*, **"Getting It Right: Empirical Evidence and Policy Implications from Research on Public-Sector Unionism and Collective Bargaining,"** *Employment Policy Research Network*, **March 16, 2011, www.employmentpolicy.org/.**

The 32-page report, a collaboration of 10 scholars, reviews evidence on issues of public-employee compensation and benefits, public-employee strikes and public-sector collective bargaining. Much of the current debate is based on "incomplete" or "inaccurate" understanding, the authors say, and "far too much" is "ideologically driven." Lead author Lewin is a professor at UCLA's Anderson School of Management.

Wisconsin Resources

Gov. Scott Walker and his major union adversary in the battle over Senate bill 10, American Federation of State, County and Municipal Employees Council 24, both have extensive material about the bill on websites. The media center page on the governor's website has various releases about the so-called budget repair bill beginning Feb. 11: **http://walker.wi.gov/mediaroom.asp?locid=177** .SEPAC, the union's political arm, has information about what it calls the anti-collective bargaining bill on its website: **www.wseu-sepac.org/**.

Several newspapers have had thorough ongoing coverage, including the *Wisconsin State Journal* (Madison), http://host.madison.com/wsj/, and the *Milwaukee Journal Sentinel*, www.jsonline.com/. In addition, the *Wheeler Report* is a blog aggregator of state news: **www.thewheelerreport.com/**

For More Information

Here are some of the major unions representing public-sector workers, with membership figures as provided by websites or other sources:

American Federation of Government Employees, 80 F St., N.W., Washington, DC 20001; (202) 737-8700; www.afge.org (250,000).

American Federation of State, County and Municipal Employees (AFSCME), 1625 L St., N.W., Washington, DC 20036-5687; (202) 429-1000; www.afscme.org (1.6 million).

American Federation of Teachers, 555 New Jersey Ave., N.W., Washington, DC 20001; (202) 879-4400; www.aft.org (1.5 million).

Fraternal Order of Police, 701 Marriott Drive, Nashville, TN 37214; (615) 399-0900; www.grandlodgefop.org/ (325,000).

International Association of Fire Fighters, 1750 New York Ave., N.W., Suite 300, Washington, DC 20006; (202) 737-8484; www.iaff.org (298,000).

National Education Association, 1201 16th St., N.W., Washington, DC 20036; (202) 833-4000; www.nea.org (3.2 million).

National Treasury Employees Union, 1750 H St., N.W., Washington, DC 20006; (202) 572-5500; www.nteu.org (90,000).

Service Employees International Union, 1800 Massachusetts Ave., N.W., Washington, DC 20036; (202) 350-6600; www.seiu.org (2.2 million).

Other organizations that follow public-employee union issues:

AFL-CIO, 815 16th St., N.W., Washington, DC 20006; (202) 974-8222; www.aflcio.org. Major labor federation formed in 1955 and representing 12.2 million workers.

Americans for Prosperity, 2111 Wilson Blvd., Suite 350, Arlington, VA 22201; (866) 730-0150; www.americansforprosperity.org. Advocacy organization to promote principles of entrepreneurship and fiscal and regulatory restraint.

Center for American Progress, 1333 H St., N.W., #1, Washington, DC 20005; (202) 682-1611; www.americanprogress.org. Advocacy group founded in 2003 to promote progressive ideas and policies.

Center for Economic and Policy Research, 1611 Connecticut Ave., N.W., Suite 400, Washington, DC 20009; (202) 293-5380; www.cepr.net. Research and public-education organization to promote debate on important social and economic issues.

Club for Growth, 2001 L St., N.W., Suite 600, Washington, DC 20036; (202) 955-5500; www.clubforgrowth.org. National network to promote pro-growth economic policies; unaffiliated with state organizations bearing same name.

Crossroads GPS, P.O. Box 34413, Washington, DC 20043; (202) 706-7051; www.crossroadsgps.org. Policy and grassroots advocacy organization focusing on key economic and legislative issues.

Employment Policy Research Network, c/o Labor and Employment Relations Association, University of Illinois, Urbana-Champaign, School of Labor and Employment Relations, 504 E. Armory Ave., Champaign, IL 61820; (217) 244-0725; www.employmentpolicy.org. A network of 120 researchers at 40 research institutions, launched in early 2011, that publishes evidence-based research on the state of work and employment in the United States.

Heritage Foundation, 214 Massachusetts Ave., N.E., Washington, DC 20002; (202) 546-4400; www.heritage.org. Research and educational think tank founded in 1973 to promote conservative policies.

U.S. Chamber of Commerce, 1615 H St., N.W., Washington, DC 20062; (202) 659-6000; www.uschamber.com. Nonprofit organization representing business interests before Congress, federal agencies and the courts.

2

National Debt

Marcia Clemmitt

Activists backing full Social Security and Medicare funding take a breather during the One Nation Working Together rally on the National Mall on Oct. 2, 2010. The protest brought together hundreds of predominantly liberal groups in support of improved social programs following a rally on the mall in August sponsored by conservative commentator Glenn Beck.

From *CQ Researcher*, March 18, 2011

Congress is locked in a titanic struggle over how to reduce the nation's $14.2 trillion federal debt without stalling the fragile economic recovery.*

Led by a newly elected GOP majority in the House of Representatives, Republicans say low taxes and an ultra-lean federal bureaucracy will stimulate growth and cut the debt. Democrats say the answer is more government spending to spur the economy and higher taxes. The debate reflects a deeply partisan philosophical difference over what role the government should play in economic policy and, more broadly, American society.

"There is fundamental disagreement about the size and role of government," says John L. Palmer, a professor of public policy at Syracuse University's Maxwell School. "It's about value choices. How much are you willing to pay for which services? What services should government provide, and how should they be paid for?"

For many congressional Republicans — especially those influenced by the powerful Tea Party movement — chopping federal spending has both economic and symbolic significance. It "sends the signals to the markets, to the small businessmen and women of America, that my taxes aren't going to have to pay for all this borrowing, that interest rates are going to be low," House Budget Committee Chairman Paul Ryan, R-Wis., explained on Fox News. "Getting spending under control today gives confidence for tomorrow, and that leads to more hiring and job creation."[1]

But congressional Democrats see the issue far differently. Sen. Charles Schumer, D-N.Y., argued that spending cuts alone won't get the debt under control. He called for "revenue raisers," including closing loopholes in the tax code and halting across-the-board

National Debt Approaches $14 Trillion

The Treasury now owes $14.2 trillion, including money owed to the government's own trust funds, such as Social Security, and to external investors. Over the past 35 years, the U.S. debt has exploded, surpassing $10 trillion for the first time in 2008.

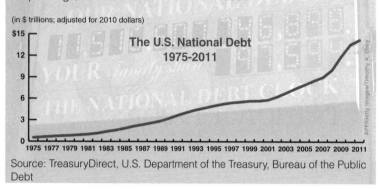

(in $ trillions; adjusted for 2010 dollars)

The U.S. National Debt
1975-2011

Source: TreasuryDirect, U.S. Department of the Treasury, Bureau of the Public Debt

tax cuts passed during the George W. Bush administration that especially favored the wealthy. Raising taxes on the rich "is not a substitute for cutting," Schumer said, "but at some point in the near future, it needs to be a part of the solution."[2]

Finding solutions is urgent business in Washington. This spring, Congress and the White House do battle over appropriations measures to fund the government for the remainder of fiscal 2011, which ends Sept. 30, and through fiscal 2012. Failure to come to terms could result in a government shutdown, a move already narrowly averted once this year when Congress passed a stopgap funding measure. (A second stopgap spending action was expected to pass this week.)

Underlying part of the deficit squabble are competing ideas on how to spur hiring and reduce the nation's worrisome 8.9 percent unemployment rate.

President Obama's fiscal 2012 budget proposal, which combines tax increases with spending cuts, would impose "massive job-killing tax hikes on small businesses," and is thus "hardly the answer" in a time "of record-high deficits and continued high levels of unemployment," said House Ways and Means Chairman Dave Camp, R-Mich. His words reflect the majority view of corporate America, including the U.S. Chamber of Commerce.[3]

But Democratic lawmakers, along with some small-business owners, disagree.

The charge that raising taxes on wealthy Americans "will hamper small businesses' ability to reinvest is a red herring," argues Rick Poore, a business owner in Lincoln, Neb., and member of Business for Shared Prosperity, a left-leaning advocacy group. "The sales dollars I reinvest by hiring more employees or buying equipment" have nothing to do with "my [personal] tax return," he said. "As a fellow businessman once told me: 'Give me more customers and I'll be forced to buy equipment and hire people to meet demand. Give me a tax break without more customers and I'll just go to Aruba.' "[4]

Animating the fiscal fight is a steep and relentless rise in the federal debt. Two years ago, the debt owed to investors outside the government stood at less than $6 trillion, or about 40 percent of the annual value of all the nation's goods and services, or gross domestic product (GDP). By 2010, it was $9 trillion, 62 percent of GDP.[5]

The Treasury owes federal trust funds, including Social Security, about another $4 trillion.

Republicans blame the debt increase on profligate government spending. Sen. Tom Coburn, R-Okla., says overspending has pushed the debt so high that the United States risks foreign investors pulling the plug on further borrowing, a potential catastrophe. To lower the debt, he argued, Washington must drastically — and permanently — reduce the federal workforce and cut spending on job training, education, law enforcement, energy research, environmental protection and other programs.

The bottom line, said Coburn, is that while government employees are "fabulous" workers, they divert scarce funds from the private sector and "produce no net economic benefit in our country."

"If you take the drag off the economy" by trimming government, "you're going to see . . . that capital is then going to be put to use in something . . . productive," he said.[6]

But Democrats argue that spending is only half the problem. Also fueling the debt, they argue, are tax cuts enacted by Republicans over the past decade, plus a severe recession that shrank tax revenues and increased the need for government cash and services to help stave off business bankruptcies and protect Americans from financial ruin.

Businesses' reluctance to hire, say Democrats, is a significant hindrance to economic recovery — and to deficit reduction, since unemployment curtails the flow of income-tax revenue into the Treasury. "Controlling the nation's long-term deficit will benefit the economy in the long haul," wrote Robert Creamer, a longtime political organizer and strategist for Democratic causes. But right now, "companies are sitting on $2 trillion of cash," yet not doing much hiring or expanding, he wrote. With high unemployment making it hard for consumers to spend, only the government can inject demand into the economy by such means as offering financial help to states and paying for new infrastructure projects, Creamer argued.[7]

Center stage in the debate over taxing and spending is Social Security. Conservatives are adamant that, as baby boomers retire, Social Security income they have been promised will be unaffordable and should be slashed immediately to keep the system from going broke. "Social Security is bankrupt and is a Ponzi scheme, and if you've got a young 20-something-year-old, they know for a fact that they're not ever going to see it," said Republican Gov. Rick Perry of Texas.[8]

But liberals vehemently disagree that Social Security is broken. Over the past quarter-century, Social Security has racked up a total surplus of $2.6 trillion, which is invested in interest-bearing U.S. Treasury bonds, says Paul Van de Water, a senior fellow at the Center on Budget and Policy Priorities, a left-leaning Washington think tank. Social Security is expected to continue running surpluses for the next several years and will be able to pay full benefits until 2037 by redeeming, first, the interest income and, later, the principal due on those bonds, Van de Water says.

Some conservative critics suggest the government could fail to pay back what it owes the Social Security Administration on the bonds, but Van de Water sees no

Recession, Tax Cuts Drive Deficits

Recessions, which lower tax revenues while increasing public need, are the biggest single contributor to annual federal budget deficits. According to the nonpartisan Congressional Budget Office, the recent recession accounted for $455 billion of the $1.368 trillion deficit in fiscal 2010.

Projected Budget Deficits
(in $ billions)

Budget year	Total deficit	Biggest Contributors to Annual Deficits				
		Extend tax cuts	Interest payments	Effects of recession	Stimulus spending	War costs
FY2009	1,413	0	0	418	200	178
FY2010	1,368	11	<0.5	455	412	191
FY2011	996	139	3	400	176	193
FY2012	642	247	12	349	58	192
FY2013	525	279	26	244	51	180
FY2014	463	300	44	197	20	163
FY2015	472	318	65	183	60	145
FY2016	513	331	91	200	47	140
FY2017	521	344	120	229	37	143
FY2018	534	356	153	259	42	152
FY2019	641	369	185	N/A	46	162

Source: Kathy A. Ruffing and James R. Horney, "Critics Still Wrong on What's Driving Deficits in Coming Years," Center on Budget and Policy Priorities, June 2010, based on Congressional Budget Office data.

reason to think that would happen — any more than the federal government would refuse to redeem bonds bought by other investors, including other countries such as China and Japan.*

Politicians from both parties hope their budget plans appeal to voters. Yet surveys suggest that the public has only the haziest notion of what government does and how its operations are funded.

In a national poll in February, more Americans than two years ago said they were worried about budget deficits. Nevertheless, a strong majority still said they favored increased government spending on areas such as education and the environment.[9]

This and other recent polls make clear that "people want [federal] spending cut, but are opposed to cuts in anything except foreign aid," and "want state governments to balance their budgets without cutting spending or raising taxes," observed *New York Times* columnist Paul Krugman, a liberal economist and Nobel laureate who teaches at Princeton University. That leaves lawmakers with a tough assignment, Krugman said: To please voters, they must "repeal the laws of arithmetic."[10]

As lawmakers battle over the nation's budget, here are some questions being asked:

Should debt reduction be Washington's top priority?

Rising government debt is damaging the U.S. economy, say conservatives. "We're broke. Broke, going on bankrupt," and "just as a bankrupt business has trouble creating jobs, so does a bankrupt country," said House Speaker John Boehner, R-Ohio.[11]

But many economists say the economic recovery is still too fragile to withstand severe cuts in government spending. For the next year or two, government should keep spending to create demand for goods and services — demand that private buyers can't yet supply, says Syracuse University's Palmer.

Yet, conservatives argue that the debt is the nation's biggest threat and must be cut now. "Our debt is a threat to not just our way of life, but our national survival," said Sens. Mike Crapo, R-Idaho, and Okahoma's Coburn. "We are already near a precipice. In the near future, we could experience . . . hyperinflation" — a rapid decline in the dollar's value that could occur if investors lost confidence in America's ability to pay its debts, they said in a statement.[12]

"The government's too damn big," and large cuts must begin now, said former Minnesota Gov. Tim Pawlenty, a potential 2012 GOP presidential hopeful.[13]

Helping focus Republican lawmakers on debt is the surging influence of the Tea Party movement, which opposes public debt. "I've chopped my credit cards. I'm watching my spending. This country needs to do the same," Texas retiree Carter Brough declared at a Tea Party conference in Phoenix in February.[14]

Economists widely agree that allowing the national debt to balloon compared to GDP involves risk. Interest on ever-increasing debt soaks up money that could go to better purposes, and a huge debt may make investors worry that the U.S. economy is weak.

"There are increasing questions about the rest of the world's appetite for U.S. debt, as the United States has changed from a net creditor country in 1980 to a vast net borrower," wrote Alan J. Auerbach, an economics professor at the University of California, Berkeley, and William G. Gale, chief federal economic policy analyst at the Brookings Institution, a centrist think tank in Washington.[15]

While investors would probably lose their appetite for U.S. Treasury bonds only gradually, "the history of financial markets suggests . . . that shifts in investor confidence can be sudden," wrote economics professors Laurence Ball of The Johns Hopkins University and N. Gregory Mankiw of Harvard. Such a shift could lead investors suddenly to demand much higher interest rates in exchange for lending money to Washington, they said.[16]

"Right now, the U.S. is the best-looking horse in the glue factory," with investors viewing U.S. Treasury bonds as the safest government vehicle in a world replete with troubled economies, says Joseph Minarik, senior vice president and research director at the Committee for Economic Development, a nonpartisan, business-led think tank in Washington. At present, "you may well say, 'If the U.S. isn't a good place to park your money, there is none.' " Nevertheless, Minarik says, "if Europe gets its act together, if China becomes more mature," they could easily become more attractive places for investors. "At the rate we're going, we're deteriorating a lot faster than some other places."

Liberal lawmakers and many economists argue that spending to push the economy back on track is still job one, however.

The danger from today's federal debt "is zero," as evidenced by the fact that Treasury bond investors aren't demanding high interest rates, declared James K. Galbraith, a professor of government at the University of Texas, Austin. "If the markets thought that [the deficit] was a serious risk, the rate on 20-year Treasury bonds wouldn't be [a low] 4 percent and change," he said.[17]

What would be a serious risk, some argue, is a sharp cut in federal spending amid a weak economic recovery. "From President Hoover in the Great Depression to global responses to the East Asia crisis in the late 1990s [when nations beginning with Thailand suffered financial meltdowns], it's clear that government cuts weaken economies rather than alleviating malaise," wrote Joseph E. Stiglitz, a liberal Columbia University economist and 2001 Nobel Prize winner.[18]

Syracuse's Palmer and Rudolph G. Penner, a senior fellow at the Urban Institute, a centrist think tank in Washington, argued that economic stimulus and debt reduction could occur simultaneously — if the debt-reduction moves are implemented gradually. "We could easily continue some short-run stimulus while immediately announcing reforms in Social Security or in health programs," for example, to phase in "slowly beginning in, say 2012 or 2013," they wrote.[19]

Should Congress raise taxes to help cut the national debt?

In December, Obama and congressional Democrats initially fought to end the Bush-era tax cuts for individuals earning more than $200,000 a year and couples earning a combined $250,000 or more. But eventually they bowed to Republican pressure and allowed a two-year extension of the cuts for all income levels.

Yet, while that may look like a victory for Republicans, they want more than just a temporary extension of the cuts. "Congress merely extended the uncertainty that has stifled our economic growth," said Rep. Mike Pence, R-Ind., chairman of the Republican Conference, the GOP party caucus.[20]

Indeed, Republicans are increasingly adamant in their views that anything beyond the most limited taxation infringes on Americans' freedom and that taxes on businesses and the wealthy drag down the economy.

"Keeping pace with its liberal tax-and-spend agenda, the Obama administration hits almost every sector of our economy with a tax hike" in its fiscal 2012 budget proposal, said Sen. Orrin Hatch, R-Utah, the top-ranking Republican on the Senate Finance Committee. "That's not how we get our economy moving forward."[21]

But many economists say the debt cannot be tamed without raising taxes. And that would be a politically charged move that neither Republicans nor Democrats seem willing to make, says Harvard political economist Benjamin M. Friedman. The nonpartisan Congressional Budget Office projects that the federal debt could level off at about 75 percent of annual GDP a decade from now, a level that potentially would quell investors' concerns, Friedman says. But that level could be sustained only "if the Bush tax cuts aren't continued for anybody," Friedman says. "I don't see that happening. I haven't heard anybody talk about discontinuing those cuts for everybody."

By world standards, Americans don't bear a heavy tax burden, noted two University of Maryland School of Public Policy analysts, professor Douglas J. Besharov, a

New parents attend a class on care for newborns funded by the Metro Community Provider Network in Aurora, Colo. Money for the nation's community-health-care system, which has been strained by the high number of uninsured Americans, is slated for large cuts in the House GOP budget.

former fellow at the conservative American Enterprise Institute, and research associate Douglas M. Call. In 2007, for example, total local, state and federal U.S. tax revenues amounted to 28.3 percent of GDP compared to an average 39.7 percent in the European Union, Call and Besharov said. "Despite vociferous opposition from many quarters (not just the Tea Partiers), any realistic solution" to the country's long-term budget dilemmas "will require that *all* Americans pay considerably higher taxes," they wrote.[22]

Liberal analysts argue that because tax rates for wealthy Americans are at historic lows, it is especially inappropriate to declare them off-limits for debt reduction. One "shameless tax loophole . . . allows hedge-fund managers to pay only a 15 percent 'capital gains' tax on their enormous incomes instead of the top income tax rate of 35 percent," according to economics writer Les Leopold. "Closing that tax loophole on just the 25 top hedge-fund managers — just 25 individuals!" — would have the same effect as a two-year salary freeze for 2 million federal workers that President Obama has proposed, Leopold argued.[23]

Newly released 1940s Internal Revenue Service data provide "evidence of just how much America used to expect out of individual wealthy Americans — and just how little, by comparison, we expect out of our wealthy today," wrote Sam Pizzigati, an editor at the Institute on Policy Studies, a liberal think tank in Washington. In

A National Park Service crew packs supplies into the Grand Canyon for a trail-repair project funded by federal stimulus money on June 9, 2009. Stimulus funding for projects across the nation is running out.

1941, top IBM executive Thomas Watson, one of the country's richest executives, paid 69 percent of his earnings in federal income tax. In 2008, the 13,374 Americans who reported incomes of more than $10 million paid an average 24.1 percent, Pizzigati said.[24]

Largely thanks to tax loopholes, "many large U.S. companies use offshore subsidiaries and creative tax planning to lower their tax rates at the expense of the rest of us," wrote Phineas Baxandall, a senior analyst at U.S. PIRG, a grassroots consumer group based in Boston. Since 2007, Google has paid an effective tax rate of 2.4 percent on its profits, and Goldman Sachs — recipient of a $10 billion government bank bailout in 2008 — paid only 1 percent on its 2007 earnings, he said.[25]

Is Social Security a cause of rising national debt?

America's biggest budget problem is its public retirement programs, mainly Social Security and Medicare, which conservatives say will plunge the country into bankruptcy as baby boomers retire. But liberal analysts argue that, while rising health-care costs — in both the public and private sectors — do pose a daunting financial challenge down the road, Social Security faces no current budget crunch and a relatively minor future one that simple tweaks could solve.

As the population ages, fewer working-age people will be available to pay into Social Security compared with the rising numbers who draw benefits. Because Social Security is a "pay-as-you-go" system in which today's worker contributions pay today's retirement benefits, the program rests on shaky ground, wrote Besharov and Call. By 2050, for example, there will be 2.7 workers for each retiree, down from 4.7 in 2008, they noted.[26]

The decline in the number of workers contributing to Social Security makes government retirement programs "little more than Ponzi schemes that are running short of new 'investors,'" Besharov and Call argue.

Social Security has run surpluses for a quarter-century and invested the cash in U.S. Treasury bonds, as do many individual, institutional and government investors. Nevertheless, like many conservatives, Besharov and Call suggest that, if the government faces tough budget demands in the future, it may not consider the bonds held by Social Security a top priority for repayment. "Last year," they wrote, "the government 'owed' the [Social Security] trust fund about $4.3 trillion. (These IOUs are dutifully printed at the Bureau of the Public Debt in Parkersburg, West Virginia, and placed in a filing cabinet.)[27]

Other conservatives state bluntly that the Social Security Administration is unlikely to be allowed to redeem its Treasury bonds. "No administration will admit that Social Security is nothing more than an accounting ledger with no money," said Rep. Ron Paul, R-Tex., a staunch advocate of limited government. "The money you paid into the system is long gone."[28]

Social Security must begin phasing in a new revenue and benefit formula in the next few years to ensure future solvency, says Berkeley's Auerbach. To argue otherwise "is like saying of a diving plane at 30,000 feet that it's not in trouble because it hasn't hit the ground yet," he says.

Nevertheless, if politicians have the will, a range of options is available to balance income and outgo, Harvard's Friedman says. Furthermore, Social Security represents only a small fraction of the retirement-funding burden the country faces, he says. By far the larger problem is steeply increasing health-care costs, such as for Medicare and the state-run Medicaid program for the poor. And while there are "lots of proposals that would work to deal with Social Security, we don't know what would work" to slow spiraling health-care costs, Friedman says.

Social Security took in less in payroll taxes than it paid out last year, but it "is not 'in the red' or 'going bankrupt,' " wrote business journalist Mark Miller. The shortfall "was due mainly to the deep recession, which has cut into payroll tax collections" as the workforce shrank "and pushed more unemployed workers to file for early benefits" when they couldn't find jobs, Miller said. "That's a short-term problem that will reverse itself when the economy improves."[29]

Harry C. Ballantyne, appointed chief actuary for the Social Security Administration during the Reagan administration, and economists Lawrence Mishel and Monique Morrissey of the liberal Economic Policy Institute argued that Social Security should not be viewed as a contributor to the national debt.

By law, "Social Security can only spend what it receives in tax revenues and has accumulated in its trust fund from past surpluses and interest earnings," so it can't ever drive up the debt, they wrote. If in any year current revenues and trust-fund savings aren't enough to pay promised benefits, the benefits must be cut, they explain. "Though modest changes will be needed to put Social Security in balance" a couple of decades from now, "the projected shortfall is less than 1 percent" of GDP, they wrote.[30]

Voters in Both Parties Often Agree on Budget

Republican and Democratic voters are much more in agreement about how to manage the federal budget than are the White House and members of Congress, a recent poll suggests. Voters in both parties agreed that government spending should be cut overall. But unlike most Republican lawmakers, Republican voters agreed with Democrats that Congress should also increase spending in areas such as job training and education. Moreover, Republicans and Democrats both advocate steep cuts in defense spending.

Voter Preferences for Spending Cuts, Increases

Democrats, Republicans and Independents favor increased spending for . . .	Job training Energy conservation/renewable resources Elementary and secondary education Higher education Agricultural subsidies to small farmers
All parties support cuts for . . .	Highway system Air travel and railroads Medical research Subsidies to agricultural corporations with large farms Defense
Only Republicans support increases in . . .	Homeland security
Only Republicans support cuts in . . .	Mass transit Global health International organizations
Only Democrats support increases in . . .	Housing programs
Only Democrats support cuts in . . .	Nuclear weapons Federal law enforcement

Source: Steven Kull, et al., "How the American Public Would Deal With the Budget Deficit," Program for Public Consultation, February 2011

Furthermore, Social Security benefits don't drain money from the economy, as some critics suggest, says Syracuse University's Palmer. Rising health-care costs may divert money from arguably more important purposes, he says. But "Social Security is just a cash-transfer program" that recipients use to pay for goods and services throughout the economy.

Kevin Drum, a political journalist and blogger, pointed out that Social Security currently costs about 4.5 percent of GDP, a share he said will "increase as the baby boomer generation retires" to a bit over 6 percent. But "in 2030 it steadies out forever at around 6 percent of GDP," a far from overwhelming fiscal burden, he argued.[31]

"One way or another, at some level between 75 percent and 100 percent of what we've promised, Social Security benefits will always be there. This is not a Ponzi scheme."[32]

In 1977, Congress capped the level of individual earnings liable for the Social Security payroll tax with the intent of having the tax apply to 90 percent of all wages, says Virginia Reno, vice president of the National Academy of Social Insurance, a nonpartisan research and public-education group. But the share of income going to the highest earners has increased drastically, and the ceiling now captures only 83 percent, she says. Raising it to reflect Congress' original 90-percent goal and making other modest changes "could solve the funding problem without putting an undue burden on anyone," Reno argues.

Nevertheless, many economists argue that while Social Security's future funding problems are solvable, waiting to tackle them would be a mistake. Says Palmer, "We can address all this in a sane and timely manner. Or we can dither and delay until much more painful things need to be done" because a shortfall will be so imminent that fixes can't be phased in or retirees warned in advance, he says.

BACKGROUND

Good, Bad Times

Dubbed "Keynesian economics" for its chief architect, British economist John Maynard Keynes (1883-1946), the idea that government deficits may go up in hard economic times but should be brought down in good times served as a guiding principle in both Democratic and Republican administrations through the 1970s.[33]

"In hard times it is not irreligious to borrow money," says the Committee on Economic Development's Minarik. "If demand is down in the private sector, the public has to do something.

"The presumption has always been that when you get out of bad times you should balance the budget or ideally try to run a surplus," says Minarik. "That's the sophisticated Keynesianism" embraced by economists and politicians alike for much of the 20th century, he says.

Over the past three decades, however, Republicans, in particular, have abandoned Keynes, focusing instead on cutting taxes and government spending as the primary goals of public-sector budgeting. Because of that, Washington's fiscal debates today are even more heated and difficult to resolve than in the past.

Perhaps the most striking illustration of Washington's changed view of budgeting appears in the way lawmakers

approach military expenditures, economists say. Historically, while annual deficits and the national debt have swollen in wartime, Congress has repeatedly raised tax revenues to keep military spending from jacking up the debt permanently.

In 1861, Congress levied the nation's first federal income tax to help defray the expense of the Civil War. Lawmakers repealed the tax in 1872, after the war ended.[34]

In World War II, "we ran very large budget deficits" relative to the GDP but then raised taxes high to pay them off, says Minarik. U.S. income-tax rates are "marginal" rates: Earners pay a different rate on each successive tier of income, with the highest earnings taxed most. During World War II, the top earners paid a 90 percent tax on the highest portion of their income, and the top tax rate remained high during the Korean War (1950-1953).

Even in the Cold War era of the early 1960s, both political parties supported tax increases, says Paul L. Posner, a professor of public administration at George Mason University and longtime chief of federal budget analysis at the Government Accountability Office. "In the Kennedy-Nixon debates [during the 1960 presidential campaign], each was trying to be first out of the blocks to say we need a tax increase for defense," he says.

In 1967 President Lyndon B. Johnson signed a temporary 6 percent surcharge tax on corporate and individual incomes (except for the lowest earners) to pay for the Vietnam War.[35]

The New Deal

Many economists say the Great Depression of the 1930s — the biggest economic crisis the United States has ever faced — illustrates the riskiness of trying to keep government debt low in a struggling economy.

"The Great Depression actually consisted of two sharp downturns," in 1929 and 1938, "with recoveries after each," beginning in 1933 and 1939, wrote Berkeley's Auerbach and Brookings' Gale. These "remarkable economic gyrations" that saw the economy slump after it appeared to be regaining strength were due at least partly to untimely budget-balancing efforts by states and the federal government, they wrote.[36]

"After the sharp downturn in 1929 and 1930, President Hoover continued to try (albeit unsuccessfully) to balance the budget," with the result that the economy continued in the doldrums, they wrote. Franklin D. Roosevelt was elected president in 1932 on a balanced-budget platform but abandoned it when he took office, fueling the first recovery, they wrote. In 1937, however, Roosevelt cut spending and raised taxes to balance the budget, and the move "likely drove the economy back into recession."[37]

Roosevelt's New Deal program, aimed at relieving poverty, reviving the economy and reforming the financial system, also added a new bone of contention to Washington debates over the budget. The New Deal included Social Security, which was intended to enable the elderly — most of whom lacked pensions or other retirement income — to pay for food, shelter and other basics.

Social Security had its roots in Europe. In the late 1880s, a conservative German government was the first to enact government-run social-insurance programs, in hopes of fending off a more radical socialism with government ownership of industries. Supported by mandatory contributions, the programs paid out when people lost their incomes through unemployment, disability or retirement. Soon similar programs became the European norm.

In the United States, lawmakers resisted calls for a government safety net for decades. Conservatives successfully argued that social-insurance programs unfairly required younger, healthier, wealthier people to subsidize support for others and that private enterprise, not government, should provide most services.

In 1935, however, as the Depression deepened, businesses folded and millions sank into poverty, Roosevelt signed into law Social Security as an income-support system for retirees, severely disabled people, widows and under-age bereaved children. Mandatory workplace contributions supported the system.

Social Security greatly increased the government's domestic social spending. Nevertheless, say supporters, it was constructed with budget issues in mind.

For one thing, "Social Security is permitted to pay benefits only to the extent that it has resources to do so," wrote Merton Bernstein, an emeritus professor of law at Washington University, in St. Louis, and his wife, Joan B. Bernstein, former president of OWL (Older Women's League.), a grassroots membership group that advocates for improvement in the economic condition of older women. "Further, it cannot borrow. Those real

Residents in flood-ravaged Pakistan's Swat Valley unload relief materials from a U.S. helicopter on Sept. 2, 2010. American voters say they would cut foreign aid sharply.

life facts shredded the charge that Social Security contributes to the federal deficit," they wrote. "It does not and cannot."[38]

While Social Security can't borrow, however, it does lend to the rest of the government — by purchasing Treasury bonds in any year that the money it collects from workers exceeds benefits paid to retirees and other recipients. This fact has become increasingly germane to budget debates in the past few decades.

'Reagan Revolution'

During Ronald Reagan's presidency (1981-1989), a change in Social Security's funding formula plus Reagan's successful championing of new principles for federal budgeting —"Reaganomics" — helped set the stage for today's contentious budget battles, economists say.

Reaganomics "was the most serious attempt to change the course of U.S. economic policy of any administration since the New Deal," wrote William A. Niskanen, a senior economist at the libertarian Cato Institute, who chaired Reagan's Council of Economic Advisors. Among Reagan's top objectives were chopping tax rates on personal, corporate and investment income, cutting government spending and reducing all forms of government regulation of business. These policies "were expected to increase saving and investment, increase economic growth" and "balance the budget," among other achievements, Niskanen said.[39]

CHRONOLOGY

1930s-1940s *Great Depression and World War II see high tax rates, new anti-poverty programs and high deficits.*

1932 President Herbert Hoover raises top income tax rate to 63 percent.

1937 Social Security begins offering benefits.

1946 National debt totals $271 billion, 122 percent of gross domestic product (GDP).

1950s-1970s *Economic growth shrinks debt-to-GDP ratio.*

1952 Tax rate on highest earnings peaks at 92 percent during Korean War.

1960 In Nixon-Kennedy presidential debates, both candidates recommend tax hike for Cold War military buildup.

1965 Medicare and Medicaid created.

1979 Debt reaches $829 billion, 33 percent of GDP.

1980s *Annual Social Security surpluses allow tax cuts as military budget soars.*

1981 Severe recession persisting into 1982 runs up debt. . . . President Ronald Reagan proposes, and Congress passes, largest tax cuts in U.S. history.

1982 Annual interest payments on debt reach $85 billion.

1990s *Partisan rancor over deficits early in the decade fade as economy booms.*

1995 Government shuts down twice as newly elected congressional Republican majority and President Bill Clinton fail to agree on funding bills.

1997 Bipartisan congressional majorities pass Balanced Budget Act, which includes cuts to Medicare and Medicaid.

1999 Federal government runs first surplus since 1969.

2000s-2030s *War spending, tax cuts and recession swell deficits. Skyrocketing health costs loom.*

2003 In third round of tax cuts initiated by President George W. Bush, rate on the highest earnings is cut to 35 percent. . . . Taxes on dividends and capital gains are cut. . . . Iraq War begins.

2005 Sign-up begins for expensive Medicare Part D drug benefit enacted on bipartisan basis in 2003.

2008 First baby boomers collect Social Security benefits. . . . Recession begins, sinking state and federal tax revenues as unemployment rises. . . . Americans earning over $10 million pay an average 24.1 percent in income tax.

2010 Republicans win control of House, pledging drastic cuts to domestic spending to balance the budget.

2011 First baby boomers eligible for Medicare. . . . States face record-high recession-related revenue shortfalls. . . . Newly elected House Republican majority revises budgeting rules to make it easier to cut taxes and harder to increase spending. . . . Labor protests break out as Republican governors in several states argue that they must limit unionized public workers' bargaining rights to make room for corporate tax cuts to improve the states' economies. . . . Congress must approve raising the statutory debt limit as total outstanding government debt approaches the current limit of $14.29 trillion.

2018 Health-care spending projected to consume 20 percent of GDP.

2020 Medicare projected to account for 17.4 percent of all federal spending.

2030 Social Security costs projected to stabilize at about 6 percent of GDP.

2037 Social Security Trust Fund projected to fall about 25 percent short of paying full benefits in this year.

Not everything worked out as Reaganomics enthusiasts predicted, however. Reagan persuaded a Democrat-controlled Congress to cut domestic spending and slash the top individual income-tax rate from 70 percent to 28 percent and the corporate rate from 48 percent to 34 percent; he also got Congress to significantly loosen government regulation.

However, instead of balancing the budget, Reaganomics led to historically high federal deficits, mainly because military spending soared amid Cold War tensions. Deficits during the eight-year Reagan era totaled more than $1.7 trillion, the largest eight-year total up to that time. The deficit averaged more than $200 billion annually during that period, according to Treasury Department data analyzed by Stephen Bloch, an associate professor of mathematics at Adelphi University, on Long Island.[40]

Harvard's Friedman says the Reagan era and subsequent George H. W. Bush administration (1989-1993) provided an important lesson: that running big federal deficits when unnecessary "did depress investment" by requiring businesses to compete with the government for scarce domestic savings. That boosted inflation and allowed investors in Treasury bonds to demand high interest. The deficits also "caused us to borrow more from abroad," he says.

Meanwhile, some of Reaganomics' apparent achievements, such as low tax rates, owed more than many realize to a hidden part of the budget — borrowing of Social Security surpluses to finance other government functions.

In the early 1980s, a severe recession with high unemployment threatened Social Security with a looming — but temporary — revenue shortfall. In response, Reagan proposed substantial benefit cuts but backed off when Republican and Democratic congressional leaders balked. Reagan subsequently charged the Greenspan Commission, named for its chairman, longtime Federal Reserve Chairman Alan Greenspan, with devising a formula to boost revenue and trim benefits to meet two challenges: Social Security's immediate problem and demands from baby boomers due to start retiring in 2008. Among the commission's moves: It raised the eligibility age for Social Security benefits to save the system money.

Unlike workplace 401(k) retirement programs — in which the benefits fluctuate according to investment

Opponents of a Wisconsin bill that largely eliminates collective-bargaining rights for unionized public workers protest outside the office of Republican Gov. Scott Walker after he signed the measure March 11, 2011. Walker said he hopes the crackdown on public-sector unions will entice business to the state by reducing unions' power to bargain for higher wages and benefits.

performance — Social Security entitles workers to receive a set level of wage replacement. Therefore, "unless you're going to let the payroll tax rise and fall as necessary," which most reject as too uncertain, a multi-year formula to fund a demographic bulge will inevitably bring in surplus taxes in earlier years, explains Syracuse's Palmer.

As a result, Social Security has run surpluses for a quarter-century and lent the money to the Treasury, where it has financed general government programs, such as military spending, and allowed corporate and individual income tax rates to remain low. This practice has "desensitized" the nation to the cost of government and increased lawmakers' fiscal irresponsibility, charges Minarik of the Committee on Economic Development.

For many decades, federal taxes have remained at about the same proportion of GDP — about 19 percent. But since 1983 Social Security taxes have represented a growing share of that amount, while corporate taxes, for example, have represented a shrinking share, Minarik says. "We've more or less been saying that we don't care about the nature of the taxes" with which we pay government bills. As a result, "we've essentially been underfunding the government outside of Social Security" for years, while Social Security picked up the slack, he says.

That practice has helped to create "a substantial shift in the tax burden [for general-government functions] to

Recession Intensifies State Budget Battles

As federal stimulus funds run out, next year may be even tougher.

The recession that began in 2008 caused the biggest drop in state tax revenues on record, with collections now down 11 percent from pre-recession levels.[1] And fiscal 2012, which begins later this year, may be even more difficult, as federal stimulus funds designed to help states get through the recession run out.

Because of revenue shortfalls, states — which are required by law to balance their annual budgets — are having a tougher time than ever providing services such as mental-health care, education, highway maintenance and policing. Meanwhile, a group of newly elected Republican governors and state legislators has vowed to make their states more business friendly to boost their economies. But the effort is leading to some highly contentious budget politics.

The Wisconsin capitol in Madison, for instance, has seen weeks of turmoil after Republican Gov. Scott Walker vowed to offset new business tax cuts by cracking down on public-sector unions. The unions, he says, have too much power to drain money from the state because they can bargain for high wages and benefits.[2]

But he's not the only governor pursuing this course. Ohio's budget is "$8 billion in the hole," and the state has lost 600,000 jobs in the last decade, according to newly elected Republican Gov. John Kasich. To get the recession-strapped state back on its feet, Kasich said he hopes to make the state more welcoming for businesses by cutting taxes and retooling how the state does business.

"I'm going to cut taxes" and "preserve" earlier tax cuts and — as "just one piece of an overall reform program designed to make us competitive again" — end the collective-bargaining rights of public-sector unions, he said.[3]

When public-sector unions have too much power they drive up both taxes and costs for businesses, Kasich said. For example, unions demand that workers on publicly funded projects be paid prevailing wages, said the governor. "I've never been for 'prevailing wage' because it drives up the cost," he explained.[4]

Liberal groups dispute the governors' efforts to link public-sector union power with state budget difficulties. The power and reach of public-sector unions varies widely from state to state, says David Madland, director of the American Worker Project at the Washington, D.C.-based Center for American Progress, a liberal think tank. If strong, intransigent public-sector unions drive state costs

those on lower incomes," wrote Robert Auerbach, a professor of public affairs at the University of Texas, Austin.[41]

Partisan Divide

Despite economists' qualms, a belief among lawmakers that tax cuts are always good — even if the cost is rising debt — has gradually taken over Washington, many commentators say. Further, this belief, rooted in Reaganomics, has taken much stronger hold among Republicans, deepening the partisan divide.

In 1995, President Bill Clinton and Republican congressional leaders reached an impasse in budget negotiations when Clinton refused to cut domestic spending on programs including K-12 education, environmental regulation and the Earned Income Tax Credit for poor families. After Clinton and Congress failed to agree on temporary appropriations measures, federal agencies twice shut down a number of operations.

The first shutdown, which began Nov. 14, 1995, lasted five days, and the second, beginning Dec. 16, 1995, lasted 21, the longest government closure in U.S. history. Essential functions such as military operations, air traffic control and care of prisoners continued, but most other activities ceased. Government agencies did not process passport applications, track infectious-disease outbreaks or keep national parks open. With public distaste for the partisan battling growing, Clinton and Congress agreed on budget compromises in the spring of 1996.[42]

By 1999, the budget and debt had moved to Washington's back burner. An economic boom, plus a tax increase on

too high, he says, then heavily unionized states should have some of the nation's largest budget shortfalls.

But that is not the case, he points out. In fact, "some of the states with the biggest shortfalls, like Texas and Louisiana, don't have strong unions at all." In Texas, which has the third-highest state budget shortfall, only 16.9 percent of public-sector workers are unionized. And in Louisiana, only 9.3 percent of the public-sector workers are unionized while the state has the seventh-highest budget shortfall in the country.[5]

In Wisconsin — ground zero of 2011 state budget battles — 47 percent of public-sector workers are unionized, yet Wisconsin is not among the 10 states with the highest budget shortfalls, says Madland.

— *Marcia Clemmitt*

---

[1] Elizabeth McNichol, Phil Oliff and Nicholas Johnson, "States Continue to Feel Recession's Impact," Center on Budget and Policy Priorities, March 9, 2011, www.cbpp.org/files/9-8-08sfp.pdf.

[2] For background, see Jason Stein, Patrick Marley and Lee Bergquist, "Walker's Budget Cuts Would Touch Most Wisconsinites," [Milwaukee] *Journal-Sentinel*, March 1, 2011, www.jsonline.com/news/statepolitics/117154428.html.

[3] Greta Van Susteren, "Union Battleground Goes to '$8 Billion in the Hole' Ohio," "On the Record," FoxNews, Feb. 21, 2011, www.foxnews.com.

[4] Darrel Rowland, "Points of Division: Jobs Dominate, But 'Hot Button' Issues Remain Important in Governor's Race," *Columbus Dispatch*, Sept. 26, 2010, www.dispatchpolitics.com.

[5] McNichol, *et al.*, *op. cit.*

State Recession Woes to Continue

As tax revenues continue to lag and federal recession-related assistance ends, state budget shortfalls will persist into next year. The states facing the largest budget shortfalls are Nevada, New Jersey and Texas.

States Facing the Largest Shortfalls	Shortfall as Percent of FY2011 Budget
Nevada	45.2%
New Jersey	37.4
Texas	31.5
California	29.3
Oregon	25.0
Minnesota	23.6
Louisiana	20.7
New York	18.7
Connecticut	18.0
South Carolina	17.4

Source: Elizabeth McNichol, et al., "States Continue to Feel Recession's Impact," Center on Budget and Policy Priorities, March 9, 2011

---

high earnings that Clinton pushed through in 1994, raised so much federal revenue that the government ran surpluses for two years. At the same time, military spending shrank in the years after the Soviet Union collapsed in 1991.

But the low debt didn't last. During President George W. Bush's administration [2001-2009], substantial tax cuts in 2001 and 2003 went hand in hand with increased spending for wars in Afghanistan, beginning in 2001, and Iraq, beginning in 2003, and for an expensive Medicare prescription-drug benefit enacted with bipartisan support in 2003 that took full effect in 2006. By the end of Bush's second term, the debt stood at more than $10 trillion, about $4 trillion higher than when he took office in 2001.[43]

Minarik of the Committee for Economic Development cites Bush's anti-tax philosophy in the runup of debt. "In

2000 . . . , the public elected a president who said, 'We've paid too much in taxes and I want a refund,' " he says.

The lesson many took from the Reagan era — that deficits don't matter but tax cuts do — dominated policy in the 2000s, Minarik says. For example, contrary to all U.S. history, "in the current [military] conflicts, [former Republican House Majority Leader] Tom DeLay said that nothing is as important in a time of war as cutting taxes," he says.

Richard Cheney, vice president under Bush, famously told Treasury Secretary Paul O'Neill in 2002 that "Reagan proved deficits don't matter." The comment came during an intra-administration skirmish when O'Neill argued against cutting taxes while increasing spending.[44]

The financial crisis and deep recession that began in 2007 focused Americans' attention anew on fiscal troubles.

The Hidden Cost of Tax Breaks

What look like cuts are really "bigger government in disguise," critics say.

As Congress seeks ways to cut spending programs to reduce budget deficits, a growing category of expenses gets little scrutiny — tax breaks.

Tax breaks on such things as mortgage interest and employer-provided health insurance are "quite simply, spending programs implemented through the tax code," according to the Center for American Progress, a liberal think tank. Dubbed "tax expenditures" by economists, they drive up federal deficits and debt by reducing the taxes individuals and businesses pay, the group argued. [1]

Harvard economist Martin Feldstein, who chaired President Ronald Reagan's Council of Economic Advisors, agrees.

"Tax expenditures increase the deficit by hundreds of billions of dollars a year, more than the total cost of all non-defense programs other than Social Security and Medicare," wrote Feldstein, now a member of the Council of Academic Advisors at the conservative American Enterprise Institute think tank. Rather than wading into the political swamp of deciding just which tax expenditures to eliminate — something both political parties find extremely difficult —"Congress should cap the total benefit taxpayers can receive from . . . tax expenditures," Feldstein argued.[2]

The chief beneficiaries of tax expenditures are not only corporations and the wealthy but also the middle class, says Paul L. Posner, a professor of public administration at George Mason University, in Fairfax, Va., and longtime chief of federal-budget analysis at the Government Accountability Office. "The spending side of the budget goes to the poor and the old," he says. "The tax code is where we subsidize the middle class, the soccer moms and the NASCAR dads," he says.

"Partly due to the large number of spending items in the tax code . . ., I no longer divide the budget balance sheet into spending and taxes but, instead, as 'giveaway' and 'takeaway,' " said C. Eugene Steuerle, a fellow at the Urban Institute, a centrist think tank, and a deputy assistant Treasury secretary in the Reagan administration. When viewed from that perspective, Steuerle told the Senate Budget Committee in February, it becomes clear that "most members in today's Congress," from either party, "have never voted for any significant deficit reduction." [3]

Even Republicans like spending if it comes dressed as a tax cut, wrote Howard Gleckman, a tax expert at the institute. In 2009, for example, House Republicans proposed a "package of massive, new housing subsidies, including a $5,000 credit for those who refinance their homes and a $15,000 credit for buyers. I hate to break the news, but these tax credits are spending," Gleckman pointed out. In 2007, the government "passed out $760 billion in these sorts of tax expenditures," he said. "That is a stunning sum when you consider the government collected only about $1 trillion in individual tax revenues that year." [4]

Every tax expenditure requires a tax increase — or borrowing — elsewhere to fund it, just as surely as any other spending item does, said Steuerle. "Put $1 billion of tax subsidies for farmers in the tax code, and taxpayers must fork over an additional $1 billion in taxes on their earnings and profits to pay for them," he said. "The complication is that the tax subsidies show up in the budget as a reduction in taxes, whereas the corresponding spending items show up as an increase in spending. The former looks like smaller government when it really is bigger government in disguise."[5]

Furthermore, while many spending programs get re-examined by Congress and the White House come budget time, "most tax expenditures are not subject to the same annual appropriations process as other forms of spending" and thus "are less likely to be scrutinized" and "scrapped" if found to do harm than an inefficient or misguided spending program, noted the Center for American Progress.

Of course, some tax expenditures are enacted not just to give individuals and businesses a gift but to encourage behavior that many lawmakers believe is good for the country The mortgage-interest deduction, for example, is widely viewed as encouraging home ownership. Critics argue, however, that many tax expenditures are targeted at special interests and do little to better the nation and the economy.

For example, wrote Seth Hanlon, director for fiscal reform at the Center for American Progress, the government "spends $4-$5 billion per year subsidizing the extremely profitable oil and gas industry through special tax breaks," a completely unnecessary tax expenditure that President Barack Obama and many Democrats are pressing to end. [6]

But conservatives, such as Rep. Joe Barton, R-Texas, argue that the oil and gas subsidies are crucial if "you . . . believe in the free-market capitalist system" and that the companies "should be headquartered in the United States." [7]

Opponents suggest that many tax expenditures are an inefficient use of funds. For example, because many take the form of income-tax deductions, they end up giving more money to richer people, the exact opposite of what should happen, Hanlon wrote. For example, "for a wealthy taxpayer in the highest 35 percent tax bracket, a $100 itemized deduction" such as for a charitable contribution "is worth $35, but for a taxpayer in the lowest 10 percent bracket that same deduction is worth at most $10," he explained. [8]

A few tax breaks that serve especially important social purposes could be retained as is, such as the tax break for savings in an Individual Retirement Account, Feldstein said. Otherwise, the total amount of tax breaks any individual may receive in one year could be capped. "Because the cap would reduce the revenue cost of all tax expenditures without eliminating or reducing specific ones, it would not unfairly burden taxpayers who benefit from one particular type of tax measure. The budget gain would be substantial." [9]

A specific dollar cap would have the added benefit of dinging wealthier people more than those who earn less — and also "produce a larger deficit reduction," Feldstein said. [10]

— *Marcia Clemmitt*

Getty Images/Justin Sullivan

Tax breaks such as deductions that homeowners take for mortgage-interest payments typically get little scrutiny. Opponents of tax breaks say the wealthy benefit most.

[1] "Tax Expenditures 101," Center for American Progress, www.americanprogress.org/issues/2010/04/tax_expenditures101.html.

[2] Martin Feldstein, "How to Cut the Deficit Without Raising Taxes," *The Washington Post*, Nov. 29, 2010, www.washingtonpost.com/wp-dyn/content/article/2010/11/28/AR2010112802912.html.

[3] Testimony before Senate Committee on the Budget, Feb. 2, 2011, www.urban.org/uploadedpdf/1001494-Steuerle-Reforming-Taxes.pdf.

[4] Howard Gleckman, "Why Does the GOP Hate Spending but Love Tax Expenditures?" *TaxVox Blog*, Urban Institute/Brookings Institution Tax Policy Center, March 27, 2009, http://taxvox.taxpolicycenter.org.

[5] Testimony before Budget Committee, *op. cit.*

[6] Seth Hanlon, "Cutting Tax Expenditures," Center for American Progress, Feb. 15, 2011, www.americanprogress.org.

[7] Quoted in Brian Beutler, "Barton: Government Subsidies Necessary to Keep Exxon From Going Out of Business," *Talking Points Memo*, March 10, 2011, http://tpmdc.talkingpointsmemo.com/2011/03/barton-free-market-oil-subsidies-necessary-to-keep-exxon-from-going-out-of-business.php?ref=fpi.

[8] Hanlon, *op. cit.*

[9] *Ibid.*

[10] Feldstein, *op. cit.*

The downturn reduced both personal and business income — and thus tax revenues — while increasing demand for public services. That helped drive deficits sky-high and renewed concern about the national debt.

CURRENT SITUATION

Cutting Spending

With the rise to prominence of the conservative Tea Party movement in 2010, Republicans have rallied around a firm anti-tax, anti-spending agenda, consolidating an ideological view that took hold in the 1990s. Moderate Republicans willing to compromise with Democrats to support higher taxes or oppose large spending cuts have been replaced by lawmakers who argue that, even in hard economic times, shrinking domestic spending is the only way to build the economy.

Shrinking government debt remains a major Republican talking point. "Powerful nations all the way from Rome to Russia have killed their economies by spending more than they had," said Sen. Jim DeMint, R-S.C., who supports a constitutional amendment to require balancing the federal budget annually and allow tax increases only if two-thirds of each chamber votes in favor.[45]

In December, Republicans pushed through a two-year extension of the Bush-era tax cuts for all income levels and pledged to make them permanent in 2012. Congress' Joint Committee on Taxation estimated that extending the cuts for the highest-income Americans — a move Obama and most congressional Democrats oppose — would cost the government $81.5 billion in lost revenues and thus contribute to deficits over 10 years.[46]

But Tea Party-influenced lawmakers reject the committee's formulation. Tax cuts should never be considered a cause of deficits; spending alone should be viewed in that light, said Rep. Michele Bachmann, R-Minn. "When people get to keep their own money [because of a tax cut] that's considered a deficit to government, but it's not a deficit to your pocket or mine," she told NBC News.[47]

Extending the tax cuts does show disregard for debt, however, insisted Stan Collender, managing director of Qorvis Communications, a public relations company in

Washington, and a former congressional budget analyst. Republicans clearly "are willing to increase the deficit if it comes as a result of things they want to do, specifically tax cuts," he said. "It's a little disingenuous at best."[48]

Spending bills begin in the House, newly controlled by Republicans after the November 2010 election, while Democrats control the White House and Senate, which must approve the measures. House Republicans have wasted no time in establishing new budgeting principles.

In the last Congress, which Democrats controlled, a so-called PAYGO rule required new tax cuts or spending increases in some programs to be offset by tax increases or spending cuts elsewhere. In January, the new Republican majority replaced PAYGO with CUTGO — a requirement that new spending must be balanced by spending cuts elsewhere but that tax cuts require no budget-balancing offsets.[49]

The change reflects "the priority of the new Republican majority to reduce spending and, in general, shift the focus of budget rules from controlling the deficit to controlling spending," observes the Committee for a Responsible Federal Budget, a bipartisan policy-analysis and advocacy group.[50]

Democrats, meanwhile, say they support deficit trimming using both tax increases and judicious spending cuts, but that the weak economy demands caution.

"We are willing to cut spending further if we can find common ground on cuts that we can all agree would help reduce the deficit without harming the economy in the short term or harming our long-term competitiveness," said Gene Sperling, chief White House economic adviser.[51]

Debt Action

With Democrats and Republicans able to agree on almost nothing, a complicated game of budget chicken is playing out this spring in Washington.

Because congressional Democrats failed last year to pass a full budget for fiscal 2011, the first order of business on this year's agenda is for the parties to agree on temporary measures to fund government through Sept. 30. Then, lawmakers must try to approve spending and revenue plans for fiscal 2012.

Are Bush-era tax cuts a key driver of federal deficits?

YES
Chuck Marr
Director, Federal Tax Policy, Center on Budget and Policy Priorities

Written for *CQ Researcher*, March 2011

Anyone following today's budget debate could be forgiven for finding it confusing. The entire focus is on the 12 percent of the budget known as "non-security discretionary spending," as if this small part of the budget fueled our deficits and cutting it significantly will address our fiscal challenges.

In fact, even a cursory review of our recent fiscal history would reveal the urgent need to put President George W. Bush's tax cuts of 2001 and 2003 back on the budget negotiating table — particularly for those at the top of the income scale.

A decade ago, with the transition from President Bill Clinton to Bush, federal policymakers reversed course and transformed record surpluses into large deficits. Over the Bush years, the tax cuts account for about half of the policy changes contributing to our fiscal reversal, with the rest driven largely by such other contributing factors as spending for the wars in Afghanistan and Iraq and the creation of prescription drug coverage for Medicare (none of which was paid for).

Just last December, President Barack Obama and Congress extended for two years the Bush tax cuts, which were due to expire on December 31. For this year alone, the tax cuts just for those making over $250,000 will cost the federal government roughly $65 billion. That, by the way, is about the same amount that House Republicans want to cut this year from "non-security discretionary spending" — everything from K-12 education to cancer research, environmental protection to law enforcement.

Think about how all of this might affect two illustrative Americans:

One is a working class high school kid who plans to be the first in his family to go to college. The House GOP's proposal to cut Pell Grant funding by 24 percent would make it harder for him to afford it. It would cut the maximum grant by 15 percent this year and about 30 percent in 2014.

The second is an equity trader who places informed bets on whether particular mergers and acquisitions will happen and at what price. With Bush's high-end tax cuts, he'll continue to enjoy a $130,000 yearly tax break, which is the average for people making over $1 million.

Today's budget debate does not give policymakers the choice between denying college opportunity to a working class kid and denying a tax cut for an equity trader who doesn't need it. It's time to put these tax cuts back on the table

NO
Brian Riedl
Grover M. Hermann Fellow in Federal Budgetary Affairs, Heritage Foundation

Written for *CQ Researcher*, March 2011

The 2001/2003 tax cuts are blamed for past, present and future budget deficits. The numbers tell a different story. When the cuts were enacted in 2001, the Congressional Budget Office (CBO) forecast a $5.6 trillion surplus between 2002 and 2011. Instead, Washington is set to run a cumulative $6.1 trillion deficit. What caused this dizzying $11.7 trillion swing? CBO data reveal that the much-maligned tax cuts, at $1.7 trillion, caused just 14 percent of the swing from projected surpluses to actual deficits (and even that excludes any positive economic impact of the cuts).

The bulk of the swing resulted from two recessions, two stock market crashes and other economic/technical factors (33 percent), other new spending (32 percent), net interest on the debt (12 percent), the 2009 stimulus (6 percent) and other tax cuts (3 percent).

Specifically, the tax cuts for those earning more than $250,000 are responsible for just 4 percent of the swing. Even without any tax cuts, runaway spending and economic factors would have guaranteed more than $4 trillion in deficits over the decade and kept the budget in deficit every year except 2007.

In 2011, low tax revenues are a temporary result of the sluggish economy. The $200 billion annual cost of the tax cuts (three-quarters of which go to those earning under $250,000) is not a major player in the $1.5 trillion deficit.

The tax cuts are not driving future deficits, either. Over the past half-century, tax revenues have deviated little from their 18 percent of the gross domestic product (GDP) average. By the end of the decade (once the economy recovers), tax revenues are projected to reach 18.4 percent of GDP — even with all tax cuts extended — and continue surging thereafter. This is because rising real incomes automatically push taxpayers into higher income-tax brackets, increasing tax revenues' share of the economy.

Runaway federal spending is the real driver of long-term budget deficits. While tax revenues will return to their historical average by decade's end, spending is projected to soar by 6 percent of GDP above its historical average — resulting in deficits approaching $2 trillion annually.

Put differently, the tax cuts are projected to reduce revenues by (at most) $3 trillion over the next decade. By contrast, Washington is projected to spend $48 trillion, including $17 trillion on Social Security and Medicare, and $8 trillion on antipoverty programs.

It's the spending, stupid.

First lady Michelle Obama visits with Head Start students in Silver Spring, Md., on May 19, 2010. Many Republicans say overspending has pushed the nation's debt so high that drastic cuts are needed in education, job training, law enforcement, energy research and other programs.

All plans remain in flux, but Republicans, while trimming their original ambitions for spending cuts, continue to push for major rollbacks in domestic spending. Proposals potentially constitute "the largest reduction in discretionary spending in the history of our nation," said Rep. Hal Rogers, R-Ky., chairman of the Appropriations Committee. Proposed cuts include $899 million from energy-efficiency and renewable-energy programs; $593 million from Internal Revenue Service enforcement; $856 million from state and local law-enforcement programs; $950 million from clean-water funds; $1.3 billion from community health centers; $755 million from public-health and disease surveillance; and $1 billion from high-speed rail projects.[52]

The new class of Republican legislators also was expected to push hard for cuts in military spending because some Tea Party-affiliated voters have supported such a move. But that isn't happening, wrote Benjamin H. Friedman, a research fellow at the Cato Institute. Scrutinizing records of GOP lawmakers, he lamented, "I found little" support for cutting defense spending.[53]

Meanwhile, Democrats call for modest spending cuts, some spending increases on what they call economy boosters, such as infrastructure and education, and modest tax increases.

Obama's 2012 budget, for example, would let Bush-era tax cuts on high earnings expire at the end of 2012; increase taxes on oil, gas, and coal producers, investment hedge-fund managers and U.S.-based multinational corporations; and limit the size of tax breaks the highest earners could get by itemizing deductions for mortgage interest, charitable contributions and state and local taxes. Obama would cut spending for programs including environmental protection, heating assistance for the poor and block grants that localities use to provide services to the poor. The administration also would make minor cuts in the Pentagon's $600 billion-plus annual budget — $78 billion over five years — and increase spending on education, infrastructure and clean energy.[54]

But with Republicans focused entirely on cutting discretionary domestic spending, "a bipartisan compromise simply will not be found," said Sen. Schumer. Nondefense discretionary spending — spending for such programs as energy efficiency and high-speed rail — constitutes such a small fraction of the budget (under 15 percent) that even the deepest imaginable cuts could have little effect on debt, he said.[55]

The parties will also battle over raising the statutory debt limit this spring.

Beginning in 1917, Congress has set a legal limit on how much money the government may owe. If Treasury can't meet the government's expenses with a combination of revenues and debt up to the legal limit, it's "left in a bind," potentially unable to pay bills or repay lenders, explains the nonpartisan Congressional Research Service.[56]

The debt ceiling stands at $14.29 trillion, and some Republicans vow not to vote to raise it unless Democrats accede to Republican budget priorities.

But Federal Reserve Chairman Ben Bernanke warned Republicans that causing investors to believe the government might renege on bond payments would send interest rates into the stratosphere — a likely "recovery-ending" event that would plunge the country back into recession.[57]

Economists argue that policymakers must begin soon to phase in the adjustment to Social Security that will be needed in 2037 to pay for baby boomers' benefits. In addition, economists say, policy makers must seek more ways to stem health-care costs, which are projected to rise exponentially in coming decades.

The Democratic health-care law enacted in 2011 contains numerous pilot projects and research initiatives to control health spending, which is driven mainly by new technology and high prices for medicine and services.[58] Republicans vehemently oppose the law, however, and seek its repeal, saying that its expansion of coverage to most Americans will cost too much and bring unwelcome government interference in what they call the world's premiere high-tech medical system.

Meanwhile, the bipartisan National Commission on Fiscal Responsibility and Reform, appointed by Obama, spent most of 2010 debating budget issues, with an emphasis on Social Security. Like many other recent efforts, however, the panel split over deeply held beliefs on the role of government and taxation and failed to produce a consensus.

Nevertheless, many economists say it is urgent that lawmakers closely examine the analysis by the commission's chairs, Erskine Bowles, White House chief of staff in the Clinton administration, and former Sen. Alan Simpson, R-Wyo. The same is true, economists say, of other long-range budget proposals, such as one from the nonprofit Bipartisan Policy Center's Debt Reduction Task Force.

Few see much hope for progress in today's partisan environment, however.

Says the University of California's Auerbach, "You have to get into a crisis before something can happen."

OUTLOOK

Unhealthy Costs

That the United States prints the world's premiere currency shields it — unfortunately, many say — from the consequences of its indebtedness.

"We're like no other country," explains Posner of George Mason University. Foreign investors are reluctant to demand high interest rates from Washington for fear that if the government defaulted on its loans, the dollar would fall, he says. And if that happened, creditor nations, which hold not only Treasury bonds but also large quantities of dollars, would see their wealth plummet, Posner notes.

Even so, the United States faces fearsome budget challenges in the years ahead, many policy experts say. By far the country's most intractable is health-care spending, which has grown faster than the rest of the economy for decades, says Michael Chernew, a professor of health policy at Harvard Medical School. Such

> "By far the country's most intractable budget challenge is health-care spending, which has grown faster than the rest of the economy for decades."
>
> —*Michael Chernew*
> *Professor of Health Policy,*
> *Harvard Medical School*

a trend is not sustainable for any economic sector and is set in coming decades to devastate both the federal budget — as Medicare and Medicaid spending soars — and budgets of individuals and businesses.

A few decades from now, even with a GDP that continued rising briskly, "spending on everything but health care would actually have to begin dropping" year to year as ballooning medical expenses outstripped the nation's productivity, Chernew says.

By 2018, the federal government projects that health-care spending by the public and private sectors combined will equal 20.3 percent of the national income, if current trends persist.[59] Meanwhile, Medicare alone accounted for slightly more than 15 percent of federal spending in 2010 and is on course to account for 17.4 percent by 2020.[60]

These trends are clearly budget busters, says Syracuse University's Palmer. But the key methods that have helped other countries keep their health-care costs substantially lower than in the United States are "politically unimaginable here," he says. Every developed nation except the United States has a single-payer government-backed health-care system and thus caps its health-care budget to guarantee a base level of coverage for all, he explains. That approach requires holding down the prices doctors and pharmaceutical companies may charge, plus some rationing of care, both of which Americans find worrisome, he notes.

Americans' apparently insatiable appetite for new medical technology is the key driver of medical costs, and "we know some things to try" as cost-control measures, such as beefing up preventive care and giving doctors and hospitals incentives to hold down costs, Palmer says. "But we don't know if they'll work."

In every other area of budgeting, however, "we know the levers" that can bring budgets into balance, he says. Some strategic combination of tax increases and spending cuts will do it, "and choosing which is just a matter of figuring out what we value."

Economists take comfort in that fact but fear lawmakers may not muster the resolve — or the philosophical agreement on the role of government — to address the budget honestly and in a spirit of compromise.

"Four mornings a week I'm optimistic," quips Posner. "Three mornings a week I'm in despair."

NOTES

1. Quoted in Chris Wallace, "Fox News Sunday," Feb. 13, 2011, www.foxnews.com/on-air/fox-news-sunday/transcript/rep-paul-ryan-deficit-reduction-gov-haley-barbour-2012-presidential-politics. For background, see Peter Katel, "Tea Party Movement," *CQ Researcher*, March 19, 2010, pp. 241-264, and Marcia Clemmitt, "Gridlock in Washington," *CQ Researcher*, April 30, 2010, pp. 385-408.

2. Shira Toeplitz, "Chuck Schumer: 'revenue-raisers' necessary," *Politico*, March 9, 2011, www.politico.com/news/stories/0311/50940.html.

3. Quoted in *ibid*.

4. "The Business Case for Letting High-End Tax Cuts Expire," *Business for Shared Prosperity*, Nov. 16, 2010, www.businessforsharedprosperity.org/resources/The+Business+Case+for+Letting+High-End+Tax+Cuts+Expire.

5. "The Budget and Economic Outlook: Fiscal years 2011 to 2021," Congressional Budget Office, January 2011, www.cbo.gov/ftpdocs/120xx/doc12039/SummaryforWeb.pdf.

6. Quoted in Nin-Hai Tseng, "Tom Coburn: Government Employees Are a Drag on the Economy," *Fortune online*, http://finance.fortune.cnn.com/2011/03/07/tom-coburn/government-employees-are-a-drag-on-the-economy.

7. Robert Creamer, "Three Fatal Republican Mistakes That Could Spell Their Defeat Next November," *Huffington Post*, March 7, 2011, www.huffingtonpost.com.

8. Quoted in Josh Baugh, "Perry Calls Social Security Bankrupt 'Ponzi Scheme,'" *My San Antonio website*, Nov. 9, 2010, www.mysanantonio.com/entertainment/books/article/Perry-calls-Social-Security-bankrupt-Ponzi-805696.php.

9. "Fewer Want Spending to Grow, But Most Cuts Remain Unpopular," Pew Research, Feb. 10, 2011, http://pewresearch.org/pubs/1889/poll-federal-spending-programs-budget-cuts-raise-taxes-state-budgets.

10. Paul Krugman, "Don't Cut You, Don't Cut Me," *The New York Times blogs*, Feb. 11, 2011, http://krugman.blogs.nytimes.com.

11. Quoted in Bob Smietana, *Tennessean.com*, Feb. 28, 2011, www.tennessean.com/article/20110228/NEWS02/102280350/-1/RSS03/House-Speaker-John-Boehner-says-debt-sign-moral-failure.

12. "Senators Coburn, Crapo Announce Support for Debt Commission Plan," press release, website of Sen. Tom Coburn, Dec. 2, 2010, http://coburn.senate.gov.

13. Quoted in Marc Lacey, "Tea Party Group Issues Warning to the GOP," *The New York Times*, Feb. 26, 2011, www.nytimes.com/2011/02/27/us/politics/27teaparty.html.

14. Quoted in *ibid*.

15. Alan J. Auerbach and William G. Gale, "The Federal Budget Outlook", Brookings Institution website, Sept. 17, 2010, www.brookings.edu/papers/2010/0917_federal_budget_outlook_auerbach_gale.aspx.

16. Laurence Ball and N. Gregory Mankiw, "What Do Budget Deficits Do?" paper prepared for Federal Reserve Bank of Kansas City, 1995, www.kansascity-fed.org/publicat/sympos/1995/pdf/s95manki.pdf.

17. Quoted in Ezra Klein, "Galbraith: The Danger Posed by the Deficit 'Is Zero,'" *The Washington Post Blogs*, May 12, 2010, http://voices.washingtonpost.com/ezra-klein/2010/05/galbraith_the_danger_posed_by.html.

18. Joseph E. Stiglitz, "Turbulence Ahead," *Truthout blog*, Jan. 24, 2011, www.truth-out.org.

19. John L. Palmer and Rudolph G. Penner, "Have Recent Budget Policies Contributed to Long-Run Fiscal Stability?" Urban Institute, October 2010, www.urban.org/uploadedpdf/412268-recent-budget-policies.pdf.

20. Quoted in Steven Sloan, "Higher Taxes, Few Changes," *CQ Weekly*, Feb. 21, 2011, p. 392.

21. Quoted in Stephen Ohlemacher, "Obama Budget Resurrects Rejected Tax Increases," The Associated Press, Feb. 14, 2011, http://hosted2.ap.org/AP Default/*/Article_2011-02-14-Obama%20Taxes/id-65e41cc1a30c44cb838ef42e93bbb9e0.

22. Douglas J. Besharov and Douglas M. Call, "The Global Budget Race," *The Wilson Quarterly*, August 2010, www.wilsonquarterly.com.

23. Les Leopold, "Wall Street Wins Big in Deficit Battle," *Huffington Post*, Feb. 18, 2011, www.huffingtonpost.com.

24. Sam Pizzigati, "A Tax-the-rich Lesson Finally Goes Public," *Too Much Blog*, Institute for Policy Studies, Dec. 4, 2010, http://toomuchonline.org/a-tax-the-rich-lesson-finally-goes-public.

25. Phineas Baxandall, "In the Public Interest: A (Non) Taxing Issue," *Huffington Post*, Feb. 15, 2011, www.huffingtonpost.com.

26. Besharov and Call, *op. cit.*

27. *Ibid.*

28. Ron Paul, "Social Security Is Not 'Insurance,' " website of Rep. Ron Paul, http://paul.house.gov/index.php?option=com_content&view=article&id=1811:social-security-is-not-qinsuranceq&catid=31:texas-straight-talk.

29. Mark Miller, "How Deficit Reduction Plans Would Affect Social Security," *Retirement Revised website*, Nov. 18, 2010, http://retirementrevised.com/money/how-deficit-reduction-plans-would-affect-social-security.

30. Harry C. Ballantyne, Lawrence Mishel and Monique Morrissey, "Social Security and the Federal Deficit: Not Cause and Effect," Economic Policy Institute, Aug. 6, 2010, www.wowonline.org/documents/EPI SocialSecurityBrief.pdf.

31. Kevin Drum, "Understanding Social Security in One Easy Lesson," *Mother Jones online*, Feb. 15, 2011, http://motherjones.com.

32. *Ibid.*

33. For background, see the following *CQ Researcher* reports by Marcia Clemmitt: "The National Debt,"

Nov. 14, 2008, pp. 937-960, and "Budget Deficit," Dec. 9, 2005, pp. 1029-1052; and Mary H. Cooper, "Budget Surplus," *CQ Researcher*, April 13, 2001, pp. 297-320.

34. For background, see 16th Amendment to the Constitution: Federal Income Tax (1913), National Archives and Records Administration website, www.ourdocuments.gov/doc.php?flash=old&doc=57.

35. Joseph J. Thorndyke, "Historical Perspective: Sacrifice and Surcharge," Tax History Project, Tax Analysts website, Dec. 5, 2005, www.taxhistory.org/thp/readings.nsf/cf7c9c870b600b9585256df80075b9dd/6b24abb33fe1996c852570d200756a5d?OpenDocument.

36. Alan J. Auerbach and William G. Gale, "Activist Fiscal Policy to Stabilize Economic Activity," Aug. 6, 2009, www.kansascityfed.org/publicat/sympos/2009/papers/auerbach-gale.08.08.09.pdf.

37. *Ibid.*

38. Merton and Joan Bernstein, "Deficit Commission Chairs Change Tune: No Longer Assert Social Security Causes Deficit," *Huffington Post*, Jan. 21, 2011, www.huffingtonpost.com.

39. William A. Niskanen, "Reaganomics," Library of Economics and Liberty, www.econlib.org.

40. Stephen Bloch, "U.S. Federal Deficits and Presidents," Sept. 30, 2010, http://home.adelphi.edu/sbloch/deficits.html; "Historical Debt Outstanding — Annual," Treasury Department website, www.treasurydirect.gov/govt/reports/pd/histdebt/histdebt.htm.

41. Robert Auerbach, "The Social Security Lock Box Hoax and the National Debt," *Huffington Post*, March 3, 2011, www.huffingtonpost.com.

42. Sharon S. Gressle, "Shutdown of the Federal Government: Causes, Effects and Process," Congressional Research Service, Nov. 8, 1999, http://ncseonline.org/nle/crsreports/government/gov-26.cfm.

43. "Historical Debt Outstanding — Annual 2000-2010," TreasuryDirect website, U.S. Department of the Treasury Bureau of the Public Debt, www.treasurydirect.gov/govt/reports/pd/histdebt/histdebt_histo5.htm.

44. "Debt and the Bush Years, Ten Trillion and Counting," "Frontline," PBS website, www.pbs.org/wgbh/pages/frontline/tentrillion/themes/bush.html.

45. Jim DeMint, "Balance or Crumble," *Human Events*, June 22, 2010, www.humanevents.com/article.php?id=37615.

46. Catherine Dodge and Peter Cohn, "Republicans Promising Cuts Deliver Deficit-raising Policies," Bloomberg/*BusinessWeek*, Jan. 7, 2011, www.businessweek.com.

47. Quoted in Eric Kleefeld, "Bachmann: I Don't Think Tax Cuts Should Be Defined as part of a Deficit," *Talking Points Memo*, Dec. 10, 2010, http://tpmdc.talkingpointsmemo.com.

48. Quoted in Dodge and Cohn, *op. cit.*

49. For background, see "Understanding the New House Rules," Committee for a Responsible Federal Budget, Jan. 5, 2011, http://crfb.org/document/understanding-new-house-rules.

50. *Ibid.*

51. Quoted in Carl Hulse and Jackie Calmes, "Democrats Open Talks by Offering $6.5 Billion More in Cuts," *The New York Times*, March 3, 2011, www.nytimes.com, p. A18.

52. "CR Spending Cuts to Go Deep," press release, House Committee on Appropriations web site, Feb. 9, 2011, http://appropriations.house.gov.

53. Benjamin H. Friedman, "Tea Party Isn't Mellowing GOP Militarism," Cato @ Liberty website, Jan. 25, 2011, www.cato-at-liberty.org.

54. "The President's Budget for Fiscal Year 2012," Office of Management and Budget, White House website, www.whitehouse.gov/omb/budget.

55. Quoted in Brian Beutler, "Schumer Calls GOP Bluff on Spending and Deficits," *Talking Points Memo*, March 9, 2011, http://tpmdc.talkingpointsmemo.com.

56. D. Andrew Austin, "The Debt Limit: History and Recent Increases," Congressional Research Service, April 29, 2008, http://fpc.state.gov/documents/organization/105193.pdf.

57. Quoted in Ian Talley and Michael R. Crittenden, "Bernanke: Not Raising Debt Limit Would Cause 'Real Chaos,' " *Wall Street Journal online*, March 1, 2011, http://online.wsj.com/article/BT-CO-20110301-712207.html.

58. For background, see Marcia Clemmitt, "Health-Care Reform," *CQ Researcher*, June 11, 2010, pp. 505-528.

59. "Trends in Health Care Costs and Spending," Kaiser Family Foundation, www.kff.org/insurance/upload/7692_02.pdf.

60. "Medicare Spending and Financing: A Primer," Kaiser Family Foundation, 2011, www.kff.org/medicare/upload/7731-03.pdf.

BIBLIOGRAPHY

Books

Choosing the Nation's Fiscal Future, Committee on the Fiscal Future of the United States, *National Academies Press*, 2010.
Economics and public-administration experts lay out the range of revenue and spending options — about which there is little disagreement — for a sustainable federal budget.

Rubin, Irene S., *The Politics of Public Budgeting: Getting and Spending, Borrowing and Balancing*, 6th Edition, *CQ Press*, 2009.
A professor emeritus of political science at Northern Illinois University explains how local, state and national budgets are influenced by a complicated interplay of political considerations and public needs.

Articles

Besharov, Douglas J., and Douglas M. Call, "The Global Budget Race," *The Wilson Quarterly*, Autumn 2010, www.wilsonquarterly.com/article.cfm?AID=1709.
University of Maryland experts, formerly of the conservative American Enterprise Institute, lay out what they see as an unsustainable budget future, with Social Security, Medicare and Medicaid causing the federal budget to balloon.

Collender, Stan, "Don't Believe the Scary Words You Hear About the Debt Ceiling," *Capital Gains and Games* (website), Jan. 11, 2011, http://capitalgainsandgames

.com/blog/stan-collender/2104/dont-believe-scary-words-you-hear-about-debt-ceiling.

A former congressional budget analyst explains strategies the government can use to keep funding itself through a short shutdown, which could happen this year if Congress and the White House fail to agree on funding bills.

Miller, Mark, "Phony Social Security Reform Arguments: When Will the Media Get It?" *Reuters Prism Money*, Feb. 14, 2011, http://blogs.reuters .com/prism-money/2011/02/14/phony-social-security-reform-arguments-when-will-media-get-it.

A Reuters economics blogger says the media fail to differentiate between budget issues involving the general government and Social Security.

Veghte, Benjamin, "Contributions or Taxes? Two Social Security Funding Paradigms," *National Academy of Social Insurance website*, April 15, 2010, www.nasi .org/discuss/2010/04/contributions-taxes-two-social-security-funding-paradigms.

A social-insurance expert explains the pros and cons of treating Social Security taxes as dedicated revenue for the retirement program only or as funds that may be borrowed by the Treasury to fund general-government functions.

Reports and Studies

"The Budget and Economic Outlook: Fiscal years 2011 to 2021," *Congressional Budget Office*, January 2011, www.cbo.gov/doc.cfm?index=12039.

Congress' nonpartisan budgeting arm projects future deficits and debts if current laws continue in effect.

"The Moment of Truth," The National Commission on Fiscal Responsibility and Reform, December 2010, www .fiscalcommission.gov/sites/fiscalcommission.gov/ files/documents/TheMomentofTruth12_1_2010.pdf.

The chairmen of a commission appointed by President Barack Obama to make budget-balancing proposals for the federal government recommend raising the retirement age to 69.

"Restoring America's Future," Debt Reduction Task Force, Bipartisan Policy Center, November 2010, www .bipartisanpolicy.org/library/report/restoring-americas-future.

A bipartisan policy-analysis group recommends improving the long-term federal budget picture. Proposals include a five-year freeze on non-war defense spending, phasing out the tax exclusion for employer-sponsored health insurance, gradually raising the cap on incomes subject to Social Security taxes and instituting a national sales tax on goods and services.

Mitchell, Daniel, "The Impact of Government Spending on Economic Growth," Heritage Foundation, 2005, www.heritage.org/Research/Reports/ 2005/03/The-Impact-of-Government-Spending-on-Economic-Growth.

A conservative analyst concludes that increased government spending harms the economy by transferring too many resources from the private sector.

Palmer, John L., and Rudolph G. Penner, "Committees Tackle the Deficit," Urban Institute Program on Retirement Policy, February 2011, www.urban.org/ uploadedpdf/412298-Committees-tackle-the-Deficit .pdf.

Palmer, a former trustee of the Medicare and Social Security Trust Funds (2000-2004), and Penner, a former Congressional Budget Office chief (1983-1987), examine recent proposals to improve the federal budget's long-term balance.

Stiglitz, Joseph E., "Principles and Guidelines for Deficit Reduction," The Roosevelt Institute, Dec. 2, 2010, www.rooseveltinstitute.org/sites/all/files/ Stiglitz%20White%20Paper%20final.pdf.

A Nobel Prize-winning economist and fellow at a think tank dedicated to furthering the legacy of Franklin Roosevelt's New Deal lays out a framework for deficit-reduction based on the twin goals of improving the economy's efficiency and fairness.

For More Information

Cato Institute, 1000 Massachusetts Ave., N.W., Washington, DC 20001; (202) 842-0200; www.cato.org. Think tank that analyzes budget and tax issues from a Libertarian point of view.

Center on Budget and Policy Priorities, 820 1st St., N.W., Suite 510, Washington, DC 20001; (202) 408-1080; www.cbpp.org. Liberal-leaning think tank that analyzes state and federal budget issues.

Committee for Economic Development, 2000 L St., N.W., Suite 700, Washington, DC 20036; (800) 676-7353; www.ced.org. Nonpartisan advocacy organization of business and academic leaders that analyzes effects of the federal budget on economic development.

Committee for a Responsible Federal Budget, 1899 L St., N.W., Suite 400, Washington, DC 20036; (202) 986-6599; http://crfb.org. Bipartisan nonprofit group of budget experts that provides public information on budget issues.

Concord Coalition, 1011 Arlington Blvd., Suite 300, Arlington, VA 22209; (703) 894-6222; www.concordcoalition.org. Nonpartisan membership organization that advocates for fiscal responsibility in federal budgeting.

Heritage Foundation, 214 Massachusetts Ave., N.W., Washington, DC 20002; (202) 546-4400; www.heritage.org. Conservative think tank that provides budget and tax analysis.

National Academy of Social Insurance, 1776 Massachusetts Avenue, N.W., Suite 400, Washington, DC 20036; (202) 452-8097; www.nasi.org. Nonpartisan expert group that analyzes social-insurance programs such as Social Security and Medicare.

Peter G. Peterson Foundation, 1383 Avenue of the Americas, New York, NY 10019; www.pgpf.org. Research group headed by a former financial executive and Nixon cabinet member; supports research on potential solutions to fiscal challenges and advocates for an urgent national response to budget challenges such as Social Security.

Tax Policy Center, Urban Institute/Brookings Institution, 2100 M St., N.W., Washington, DC 20037; (202) 833-7200; www.urban.org. Provides in-depth nonpartisan analysis of budget issues.

3

Financial Industry Overhaul

Marcia Clemmitt

An independent consumer protection bureau created by the financial system overhaul has the power to regulate consumer loans, credit cards and mortgage-lending practices. However, lawmakers bowed to pressure from the auto industry and exempted automobile dealers from oversight by the agency.

From *CQ Researcher*,
July 30, 2010

W hen 30-year-old Chris Fargis applied for a job on Wall Street a couple of years ago, he didn't have a business degree or experience in finance. His ace in the hole was poker. Fargis had played online since about 2001 — playing up to eight hands at a time — and Toro Trading sought his gambling skills when it hired him as a trader.

"If someone's been successful at poker, then there's a good chance they could be successful in this business," said company founder Danon Robinson.

Robinson isn't the only financial executive who thinks so. "There's a certain maturity and ability to deal with risk that is hard to get any other way — unless you put the money on the table at some point in your life," said hedge fund executive Aaron Brown.[1]

Nevertheless, ever since several big Wall Street firms tumbled to the verge of collapse in 2008, helping precipitate a worldwide recession, economists, lawmakers and the public have grown skeptical of Wall Street's "casino culture" and obsession with risky bets.[2]

Huge "financial supermarkets" like Citigroup and JP Morgan Chase engage in investing that resembles "gambling more closely than banking," even as they ask depositors to trust them with their personal savings, complained Nouriel Roubini, a professor of economics at New York University's Stern School of Business, and Stephen Mihm, a professor of history at the University of Georgia.[3]

Banks' increasingly single-minded pursuit of fast profits rather than longer-term value investments — and the growing use of large amounts of "leverage," or debt, to make trades — has harmed the whole economy, says Dean Baker, chief economist at the Center for Economic and Policy Research, a liberal Washington think tank.

'Too Big to Fail' Banks Hold Most Assets

Banks in the U.S. banking system with assets worth more than $10 billion each are collectively worth $10.4 trillion — or 78 percent of the entire sector — making them "too big to fail" in the eyes of many experts. Smaller banks worth less than $100 million each only make up 1 percent of the system.

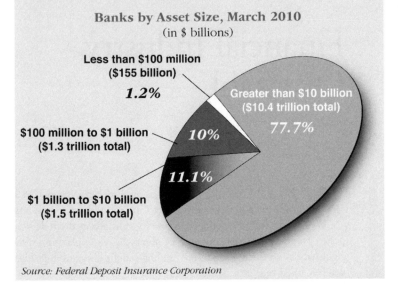

Banks by Asset Size, March 2010
(in $ billions)

Less than $100 million
($155 billion)
1.2%

Greater than $10 billion
($10.4 trillion total)
77.7%

$100 million to $1 billion
($1.3 trillion total)
10%

11.1%

$1 billion to $10 billion
($1.5 trillion total)

Source: Federal Deposit Insurance Corporation

"The reason why we're sitting here with 10 percent unemployment is that we had a housing bubble that was driving the economy down the wrong path," focusing homeowners on the illusory "housing wealth" they believed they were gaining as house prices rose and encouraging investors to buy packages of mortgage loans rather than stock in companies that could have been long-term job creators, he says.

Based on such concerns, when Democrats took control of the White House and both houses of Congress in 2009, debate began on legislation to tighten banking rules to limit the possibility that risky investing with borrowed funds would again sink the financial system. The year-and-a-half struggle to enact the legislation is a testament to both the issue's complexity and banks' political power and intense struggle to fight off new rules. Three Republican senators, Scott Brown of Massachusetts and Maine's Susan Collins and Olympia Snowe finally crossed the aisle to give supporters of the overhaul the 60 Senate

votes they needed to overcome a final Republican filibuster of the plan on July 15, and President Obama signed the measure into law on July 21.

In the wake of the debate, questions persist about whether increased bank regulation is a good idea and whether current proposals would be effective.

Most conservative analysts assert a strong "No" to both.

Government regulation actually encourages carelessness, said Peter J. Wallison, a fellow at the free-market think tank American Enterprise Institute. "Market participants believe that if the government is looking over the shoulder of the regulated industry, it is able to control risk-taking," so customers stop trying to determine for themselves whether a financial firm is behaving responsibly. Regulation also "impairs innovation" and raises prices, Wallison said.[4]

But while the new legislation won't forestall the next economic crash, rules are valuable, and current proposals are a "definite improvement" over the status quo, says Baker.

For example, there will be closer scrutiny of complex investments known as derivatives, whose value is derived by a formula based on the shifting values of some asset or assets, such as the value of the Japanese yen compared to the U.S. dollar. Under the legislation, most derivatives now will "be traded in some regulated way" rather than in unsupervised trader-to-trader deals, says Baker. Supervised trading will pose fewer risks to investors, Baker says.

"Also a clear plus is the Consumer Products Financial Services Agency," says Baker. "People get burned on financial products all the time" so having a government office to look out for consumers' interests will be a help, he says.

In the 2008 crash, the federal government stepped in with taxpayer funds — the Troubled Asset Relief Program (TARP) — to prevent some of the biggest financial firms from collapsing. Policymakers figured the biggest firms were so deeply entwined with the rest of the economy that their demise would take other firms down with them. In short, the mega-firms were "too big to fail," or TBTF.

As a result, many expected legislative efforts to limit banks' size or the scope of activities a single firm could pursue. The Obama administration and many in Congress steadfastly opposed this approach, however.

"The trickiest banks" — the ones good at figuring out ways to circumvent rules to maximize profits — "tend to be large," said Richard W. Fisher, president of the Federal Reserve Bank of Dallas. That being the case, there is "only one way to get serious about [TBTF] — . . . 'shrink 'em,'" he said. "Banks that are TBTF are simply TB — 'too big.' We must cap their size or break them up."[5]

Today's biggest banks have attained a scale "that's impossible to run prudently," says James K. Galbraith, a professor of economics at the Lyndon B. Johnson School of Public Affairs at the University of Texas, Austin.

But while the desire to break up super-big institutions is "understandable," it's "ultimately futile," said Mark Zandi, chief economist for Moody's Economy.com, a West Chester, Pa.-based financial research company. Breaking up banks "would be too wrenching and would put U.S. institutions at a distinct competitive disadvantage vis-à-vis their large global competitors," he said.[6]

Also hotly debated is how big a role unethical conduct played in the crisis. In April, the Securities and Exchange Commission (SEC) filed a civil lawsuit charging the big New York investment bank Goldman Sachs with fraud for selling investors mortgage-backed securities the bank knew were intended to fail. Some analysts say the system's future soundness depends on whether the government will continue to crack down.

Many of today's financial-industry practices amount to "fraud" or "outright criminal negligence," charges Galbraith. When it comes to selling investments made up of packaged mortgage loans — so-called mortgage-backed securities — for example, fraudulent behavior was evident throughout the system, he says.

First, "you had a massive issuance of mortgages to people who couldn't pay them. The guy who made those loans" committed fraud "because he knew they couldn't pay" but made the loans anyway "to generate a fee" for

himself, Galbraith says. Then the ratings agencies — companies such as Fitch, Moody's and Standard & Poor's that assess investments according to relative risk — extended the fraud by "labeling these things triple A," or very low-risk securities. "That's the same thing as money laundering. It takes something dirty and makes it clean," Galbraith argues.

Finally, investment firms that marketed mortgage-backed securities to pension funds and other traditionally low-risk investors misled buyers — by passing off bad goods to suckers, he says. Charging companies who commit such frauds "is the only hope we have" of cleaning up the industry, he says.

But most bankers deny unethical conduct.

"I am saddened and hurt by what happened in the market," said Fabrice Tourre, the 31-year-old Goldman Sachs vice president whom the SEC has charged with helping the bank engineer a fraudulent deal in which two European banks lost $1 billion. "I believe my actions were proper."[7]

As lawmakers, economists and the public wonder whether financial reforms will prevent the next financial-market meltdown, here are some of the questions that are being asked:

Are tougher rules for financial firms needed?

Over the past three decades, many rules governing financial firms have been rescinded as policymakers embraced the philosophy that markets function best when left alone. Following the 2008 crash, however, some economists have called for reinstating stricter curbs on banking.

"I hope it's no longer controversial" to say that a hard-line free-market philosophy has been "thoroughly discredited," says Texas' Galbraith. "When people say this today, they're just covering for the fact that they're backing what special interests want."

"Taxpayers are providing a substantial benefit to the shareholders and creditors of institutions considered too big to fail" by putting up bailout funds, said Zandi of Moody's Economy.com. In return, big financial firms should "be subject to greater disclosure requirements, required to hold more capital, satisfy stiffer liquidity requirements, and pay deposit and other insurance premiums commensurate with . . . the risks they pose to the system."[8]

"The financial reform bill goes in the right direction . . . but it doesn't go far enough," however, said New York University's Roubini. An effective law would have to restructure the industry by limiting bank size and the number of different financial businesses one institution could pursue, he said.[9]

Baker of the Center for Economic and Policy Research would like to see a provision "with teeth" requiring commercial banks, which take deposits and lend to individuals and businesses, to be separate entities from investment banks, which issue, price and trade stocks and bonds.

The legislation is "probably better than nothing," says Galbraith. Nevertheless, "I'm disappointed in it, and if I were a member of Congress, I'm not sure whether I'd vote yes or no."

Behind-the-scenes deals between lawmakers and financial firms turned the legislative process "into a victory lap for Wall Street," charged Simon Johnson, a professor of entrepreneurship at the Massachusetts Institute of Technology's Sloan School of Management. After the 2008 bailout, "administration officials promised they would be back later to fix the underlying problems. This they — and Congress — manifestly have failed to do. Our banking structure remains unchanged . . . and the incentives and belief system that lie behind reckless risk-taking has only become more dangerous."[10]

"Regulatory changes in most cases represent a too-late attempt to catch up with the tricks of the regulated," who will quickly find ways to circumvent new rules, said Dallas Fed chief Fisher.[11]

In addition, many financial regulators come from the banking industry, and that fact will always compromise enforcement, says Baker. "Imagine if we had a Labor Department where most people were from the United

Derivatives Market Dwarfs Global GDP

The value of the worldwide trade in derivatives — financial instruments that represent bets on shifting prices, not real assets — exceeds $1 quadrillion, or more than 20 times the value of the world's gross domestic product.

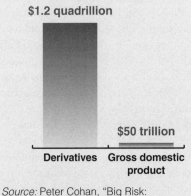

Value of Worldwide Derivatives Market and GDP

$1.2 quadrillion

$50 trillion

Derivatives   **Gross domestic product**

Source: Peter Cohan, "Big Risk: $1.2 Quadrillion Derivatives Market Dwarfs World GDP," Daily Finance, June 2010

Auto Workers. It would be very hard for them to take an independent view" of labor issues and crack down on former colleagues, he says.

But many conservative commentators challenge the notion that the financial industry needs more rules.

As it stands, the legislation is "worse than nothing," says Mark A. Calabria, director of financial regulation studies at the libertarian Cato Institute. There's no need to re-regulate banks because they were never actually deregulated, and any claim that deregulation helped trigger the 2008 crisis ignores history, he says.

As evidence, Calabria points to studies showing that government "outlays for banking and financial regulation increased from only $190 million in 1960 to $1.9 billion in 2000 and to more than $2.3 billion in 2008 (in constant 2000 dollars.)" The annual average of new financial-industry rules proposed by the Treasury Department grew "from around 400 in the 1990s to more than 500 in the 2000s."[12]

Misguided regulation has actually been the key driver of the financial meltdown, not actions financial firms took on their own, Calabria argues.

For example, federal rules "micromanage the relationship between capital and assets," specifying, for example, that banks must hold more capital in reserve to back their lending to corporations than for their lending to national governments, he says. But the recent financial meltdown of Greece demonstrates that government's so-called "sovereign" debt can be far riskier than corporate debt, Calabria argues.

Furthermore, when the Federal Reserve lowered interest rates after the Sept. 11, 2001, terrorist attacks, to jump-start business expansion and consumer spending, Fed Chair Alan Greenspan left the low rates in place too long, fueling the over-borrowing spree that led to the current troubles, Calabria says. The lowered rate "was needed for six months, not three years," he says. "Did the Fed just not get that they were setting up bad incentives" that encouraged too many people to take out mortgages?

The call for more regulation is a "new culture war" launched by pro-government liberals, said American Enterprise Institute president Arthur C. Brooks. The panic the economic downturn engendered among Americans is allowing liberals to "attack free enterprise openly and remake America in [their] own image" by "expand[ing] the powers of government" to rigorously control an industry that was not at fault, Brooks said. "In truth . . . government housing policy," which encouraged too many Americans to take out mortgages to buy homes, "was at the root of the crisis."[13]

Was unethical behavior by bankers a major factor in the economic crash?

Some observers are convinced that financial markets are hotbeds of unethical conduct, but others point out that seeking profit is not only legal but is what the public demands that financial firms do.

Goldman Sachs is "a great vampire squid wrapped around the face of humanity . . . little better than a criminal enterprise that earns its billions by bilking the market, the government, and even its own clients in a bewildering variety of complex financial scams," fumed financial reporter Matt Taibbi.[14]

In 2006, Goldman sold $76.5 billion in mortgage-backed investments, of which about $59.1 billion — more than three-quarters — consisted of hundreds of home loans that either were made to people with very bad credit or had other serious problems, such as risky terms like a no down-payment requirement, Taibbi said. Then, "some Dutch teachers' union that a year before was buying ultra-safe U.S. Treasury bonds . . . runs into a Goldman salesman who offers them a different, 'just as safe' AAA-rated investment that, at the moment anyway, just happens to be earning a much higher return than Treasuries. Next thing you know, a bunch of teachers in Holland are betting their retirement nest eggs on a bunch of meth-addicted 'homeowners' in Texas and Arizona. . . . This isn't really commerce, but much more like organized crime . . . a gigantic fraud perpetrated on

the economy that wouldn't have been possible without accomplices in the ratings agencies and regulators willing to turn a blind eye," said Taibbi.[15]

"It is unacceptable to continue allowing Wall Street to put their short-term gambles ahead of the long-term prosperity of Main Street America," said Sen. Jeff Merkley, D-Ore., who sought to ban so-called "proprietary trading" — banks trading securities for their own profits rather than on behalf of customers — but secured only minor limitations on such trades. "We've seen how proprietary trading can cause conflicts of interest when firms bet against securities they help put together for their clients," Merkeley said.[16]

Sen. Carl Levin, D-Mich., who cosponsored Merkeley's proposal, labeled many bankers' primary motivation "extreme greed."[17]

In many cases, both sellers and buyers of the complex investments called "derivatives" are "cheaters," charged Frank Partnoy, a professor of law and finance at the University of California, San Diego, and a former associate at the New York City-based financial services firm Morgan Stanley. Some derivatives allow people to avoid taxes by making their investment portfolios appear to have a different mix of risks and assets than they actually do, he said. In a so-called "equity swap," a "bank that sells the swap makes money, and the purchaser . . . makes money because they effectively get to liquidate a portion of their stock position without paying tax. They both win," but the public loses a legitimate part of the tax base, Partnoy said.[18]

"Ethical rot" and "perverse incentives . . . caused the ongoing financial crisis," said William K. Black, an associate professor of economics and law at the University of Missouri who was a federal bank regulator during the savings and loan meltdown of the late 1980s. For example, "executive compensation and the compensation systems used for appraisers, accountants and rating agencies were designed" to create a business climate in which "fraudulent and abusive lending and accounting practices drove good practices out of the marketplace."[19]

"I don't think those who went into finance are greedier or more deficient in moral scruples than others," but the incentives in the way financial markets currently operate "led them to behave" as if they were, said Joseph E. Stiglitz, co-winner of the 2001 Nobel Prize for economics and a professor of economics at Columbia University. The idea that "you have to pay me more if I succeed

Lawmakers Reject 'Rainy Day' Fund for Banks

Global finance ministers rejected creation of a similar fund.

While deliberating new banking rules that might mitigate future financial crises, U.S. lawmakers and banking officials considered and rejected a plan to have banks put funds upfront into a fund that would pay creditors and depositors should a large bank fail. Some financial-industry analysts say that such advance preparation for the likely inevitable failure of more big financial firms down the line is a plan well worth pursuing.

"An advance-payment bailout fund was a House proposal that didn't get nearly enough attention," says Dean Baker, chief economist at the Center for Economic and Policy Research, a liberal think tank. The final congressional bill instead included what Baker calls a misguided proposal to have banks ante up such funding only after financial firms actually crash.

Having such a fund available before a crisis "would allow the regulators to shut down" ailing institutions in a quick, orderly fashion before problems worsened and spread, Baker says, Without it, "regulators won't have the tools to shut down" ailing big banks. Furthermore, the plan is a proven idea "that we already have in place" in the Federal Deposit Insurance Corporation (FDIC) and use routinely for smaller banks, Baker says.

Without an advance fund, if a big bank fails, "government regulators can go to Congress and ask for money" to address that specific emergency, "but Congress might say they don't want to provide the money" or ask the financial industry for it, or the request might get tangled up in a legislative logjam of some kind, he says.

The provision might not be needed if the only problems in the system came from a handful of "rogue institutions," says Baker. "But what we got in 2008 was not rogue. You didn't so much have rogue players as a system that was totally out of whack," he says. "A fund that's ready and waiting would be a backstop" for the day when a large firm was "suddenly insolvent."

When failing banks are closed, the money to pay creditors "shouldn't take the form of a post-crisis tax," says Amy Sepinwall, an assistant professor of legal studies and business ethics at the University of Pennsylvania's Wharton School. "I think there should be a perpetual tax on the players" in recognition of the fact that, no matter what laws and regulations are in place, there will always be the possibility of some financial institution taking too many risks and failing.

"People on Wall Street are incredibly intelligent" and may "develop strategies to circumvent whatever rules Congress" puts in place to rein them in, says Sepinwall. "Maybe that's the way it's supposed to be," since the circumvention often leads to innovation, some of which is very valuable. At the same time, however, it's obvious that

in increasing profits" became "conventional wisdom," leading bankers to neglect the fact that banks "are a means to an end" in the economy, "not an end in themselves."[20]

"A good financial system" manages risk, allocates capital and runs the economy's payment system "at low transaction costs," said Stiglitz. "Our financial system created risk and mismanaged capital, all the while generating huge transaction costs" — financial firms' outsized profits compared to other industries. While bankers claim that products like derivatives created real value in the economy, "it is hard to find evidence of any real growth associated" with these "so-called innovations," Stiglitz said.[21]

"So deceptive were the systems of creative accounting" employed in pursuit of large returns that bankers "didn't even know their own balance sheets, and so they knew that they couldn't know that of any other bank," Stiglitz said. No wonder then that lending between banks — which allows bankers quick access to cash they can then loan to businesses — froze up in a crisis of trust that helped topple the world's economy, he said.[22]

Financial-industry executives mostly reject such charges.

Far from ignoring obligations to society, most bankers embrace their social purpose, said Goldman Sachs Chairman Lloyd Blankfein. "I know I could slit my wrists and people would cheer," but accusers don't realize that the bank does "God's work," Blankfein said. "We help companies to grow by helping them to raise

some financial-market innovations will be extremely risky, she says.

For that reason, requiring regular payments from the whole industry into a fund that could serve as a backstop for firms whose innovative financing arrangements go south is probably a good idea, she says. "One could key the tax to the size of the bank," she says. Such an upfront fund would constitute a "recognition of the principle of 'moral luck' " — the idea that, while many people may drink and drive, for example, only some will have an accident, but that everyone who engages in the risky behavior, not just those who crash, actually bears some degree of responsibility, Sepinwall explains.

Like Congress, finance ministers and central-bank chiefs of the G20 — 19 nations and the European Union — considered but rejected an international version of the bank shutdown fund in deliberations this summer. Given the increasingly international nature of the financial system, the European Union and some others want each country to tax its banks to create a pool to be used to resolve failed banks, to avoid delaying the process or sticking taxpayers with the bill.

Some countries that impose limits on how much risk banking institutions may take on, such as Canada, object to the idea. [1] They argue that "since their regulatory systems are strong," their local institutions "shouldn't have to pay for what happens in riskier countries" without the foresight to ban risky practices up front, says Sepinwall.

In the U.S. debate over financial reform, key congressional Republicans persistently demanded that the fund be removed from the bill on the grounds that it might actually be used to keep faltering institutions alive. "The bill reported out of committee sets up a $50 billion fund that, while intended for resolving failing firms, is available for virtually any purpose that the Treasury secretary sees fit," wrote Alabama's Sen. Richard Shelby, the top-ranking Republican member of the Senate Banking Committee. "The mere existence of this fund will make it all too easy to choose bailout over bankruptcy. This can only reinforce the expectation that the government stands ready to intervene on behalf of large and politically connected financial institutions." [2]

The fact-checking website *PolitiFact* notes, however, that Shelby's statement — which was widely echoed by other Republican and conservative commentators — ignores specific bill language that bans use of the funds for any purpose except those connected with closing large firms that falter. "The legislative language is pretty clear that the money must be used to dissolve — meaning completely shut down — failing firms," said *PolitiFact*. "The fund cannot be used to keep faltering institutions alive." [3]

— *Marcia Clemmitt*

[1] For background, see "Canada Urges G20 to Stop Bank Tax Talk," CTV television online, June 1, 2010, www.ctv.ca.

[2] Quoted in "Sen. Richard Shelby Overlooks Safeguards in Financial Regulation Bill," *PolitiFact.com*, http://politifact.com/truth-o-meter/statements/2010/apr/16/richard-shelby/sen-richard-shelby-overlooks-safeguards-financial-/.

[3] *Ibid.*

capital. . . . This, in turn, allows people to have jobs that create more growth and more wealth. It's a virtuous cycle."[23]

Some bankers have exhibited a "failed moral compass" by "hiring people and promoting people based simply . . . on commercial productivity" rather than the "many other criteria that could be used," acknowledged Brian Griffiths, vice chairman of Goldman Sachs International. Nevertheless, "my reading of [Scottish philosopher and economist] Adam Smith is that self-interested actions," though "they may sometimes be selfish," produce social good, he said. (Smith's 1776 treatise *An Inquiry into the Nature and Causes of the Wealth of Nations* theorizes that an "invisible hand" guides the free market to produce and price things correctly, despite seeming chaos.) "I think that the injunction of Jesus to love our neighbors as ourselves is a recognition of self-interest" as a positive social force, said Griffiths.[24]

Banks do only what society asks of them, says Amy Sepinwall, an assistant professor of legal studies and business ethics at the University of Pennsylvania's Wharton School. "We live in a get-rich-quick culture, and we ask people [in the financial industry] on our behalf to make as much money as possible in as little time as possible, so in a way we're sort of licensing this."

"Individuals prefer to spend rather than save, and, as a result, demand the kind of financial alchemy that can transform one's house into a virtual ATM or one's

What's in the New Financial Regulation Law

Here are key provisions of the sweeping 2,300-page financial reform law signed by President Obama on July 21, 2010:

Overseeing the system's financial health: A new 10-member council of financial regulators, drawn from several different agencies, will monitor not just individual financial firms but their interactions, to help head off emerging risks for an economic crash. [1]

Breaking up big banks: Regulators get new authority to seize and break up troubled financial firms whose large size means their troubles could damage the economy. The Treasury would fund the initial costs of winding down the bank, but regulators could recoup those funds from the failed bank and from special fees imposed on all big financial firms.

Curbing financial-market speculation: A watered-down version of part of the so-called Volcker Rule limiting but not entirely banning banks from using depositors' money to speculate in financial markets.

Limiting banks' derivative trading: Phased in over several years, banks are required to spin off some derivatives trading into separate, affiliated companies. For the first time, many derivatives must be traded through clearinghouses or public exchanges, rather than over the counter.

Overseeing insurers, hedge funds, and private equity funds: A new Federal Insurance Office in the Treasury Department will monitor, but not regulate, the insurance industry, which previously has been overseen only by states. Hedge funds and private equity funds must register with the SEC as investment advisers and provide information on trades to help regulators monitor financial-system risk.

Improving how securities are rated: The SEC will conduct a two-year study on whether to create a federal board to assign ratings agencies to each security deal. Some lawmakers had pushed for immediate random assignment of rating agencies as a way to end banks "shopping" for securities they trade.

Overseeing the Federal Reserve: The Fed faces a one-time audit of the emergency loans and other actions it took to help financial firms weather the 2008 crisis, but the central bank's decision-making about monetary policy — how it sets interest rates — will not be audited.

Protecting consumers: An independent consumer financial protection bureau will regulate and police consumer-loan, credit-card and mortgage-lending practices. This provision was enacted despite strong objections from the financial industry and from congressional Republicans. Automobile dealers won an exemption from oversight by the agency.

Cleaning up mortgage lending: Lenders must verify borrowers' income and determine in advance whether they can meet the loan payments before originating a mortgage, thus ending the risky "liar loans" implicated in some home foreclosures.

Curbing executive pay: Shareholders of all publicly traded companies, not just financial firms, get a nonbinding advisory vote on how executives are compensated.

---

[1] See Open Congress website, www.opencongress.org/bill/111-h4173/text; Alison Vekshin and Phil Mattingly, "Overhaul of Financial Regulation on Path to Obama's Desk," Bloomberg/*Business Week*, June 26, 2010, www.businessweek.com.

exceedingly modest savings into a fiscal cushion that can sustain a long, comfortable retirement," Sepinwall said. Thus, the risk that crashed the system "is the inevitable price of our preferences for leisure over toil and consumption over savings."[25]

Should big banks be broken up?

Proponents of limiting the size and scope of each individual bank argue that today's biggest firms are too large to be effectively managed. But other analysts say that

the real problem is not overlarge banks but misguided government policies, such as bailing out institutions the government deems "too big to fail." No matter how large the company, if it fails financially, it should go bankrupt, rather than being rescued, these commentators say.

"The best way to prevent a bank from becoming too big to fail is preventing it from becoming too big in the first place," said Robert Reich, secretary of Labor in the Clinton administration and a professor of public policy at the University of California, Berkeley. Lawmakers should cap the deposits any one bank can hold, reinstate the so-called Glass-Steagall ban on combining an investment bank and a commercial deposit-holding bank in one company and force banks to spin off their derivatives-trading operations into separate companies, Reich said. (Only a limited form of the last of these provisions survives in the current legislation.)[26]

"If they're too big to fail, they're also becoming too big to be saved, too big to be bailed out and too big to be managed," said New York University's Roubini. "No CEO can monitor the activities of thousands of separate profit and loss statements"[27]

"Where within one institution you have commercial banking, investment banking, underwriting of securities, market-making and dealing, proprietary trading, hedge fund activity, private equity activity, asset management, insurance," it "creates massive conflicts of interest," said Roubini. "These institutions are always on every side of every deal. That's an inherent conflict of interest that cannot be addressed" by simply setting up internal barriers within the company.[28]

Bank "swaps desks" that trade in certain risky derivatives should be spun off into separate enterprises that do not have "access to government backstops," said Dallas Fed chief Fisher and Federal Reserve Bank of Kansas City President Thomas M. Hoenig.[29]

Some commentators argue that the biggest banks generally became big through sweetheart deals with the government, and since that makes them both tools and symbols of dangerously consolidated government power, they should be broken up.

"Big banks are bad for free markets" because "they are conducive to what might be called 'crony capitalism,'" said Arnold Kling, an adjunct scholar at the Cato Institute. Thus, "there is a free-market case for breaking up large financial institutions: that our big banks are the product, not of economics, but of politics."

The key example cited by Kling and many other conservative and libertarian commentators is Fannie Mae and Freddie Mac — two huge stockholder-owned but government-sponsored institutions that buy and securitize mortgages. "Created by the government," these two institutions "always benefited from the perception that Washington would not permit them to fail," a fact

that "gave them important advantages in credit markets and allowed them to grow bigger than they otherwise would have," he said.[30]

Some of the biggest private banks also have pursued "public purposes imposed on them by Congress" — such as increasing mortgage lending to expand home ownership — in an attempt to woo lawmakers into regulating them more lightly over the years, said Kling. At the government's instigation, big banks, along with Fannie Mae and Freddie Mac, created a market in which high-risk mortgages were "securitized" — packaged to be sold as investments — driving house prices sky high, and the bursting of this price bubble caused the financial crash, he said. The root cause, however, was "banks' being big enough to achieve real political power. To expand free enterprise, shrink the banks."[31]

But shrinking banks "wouldn't really solve our problems, because it's perfectly possible to have a financial crisis that mainly takes the form of a run on smaller institutions," said Paul Krugman, a professor of economics and international affairs at Princeton University and winner of the 2008 Nobel Prize for economics. In the Great Depression of the 1930s, the "Federal Reserve believed that it was OK to let [the small banks] fail," but "as it turned out, the Fed was dead wrong: the wave of small-bank failures was a catastrophe for the wider economy," he said. Regulators should limit risky lending and the use of borrowed funds to buy investments, rather than trying to cap banks' size, Krugman said.[32]

Unilaterally limiting the size of U.S.-based banks would put the country at a competitive disadvantage because big U.S. companies with international operations would end up using the bigger banks that were based elsewhere, said Rob Nichols, president of the Financial Services Forum, a banking industry trade group.[33]

Rebuilding the Glass-Steagall wall between depository banks and investment banks is completely beside the point because, in fact, "very few financial holding companies decided to combine investment and commercial banking activities," even after Congress allowed them to do so in 1999, says Cato's Calabria. Bear Stearns and Lehman Brothers, "the two investment banks whose failures have come to symbolize the financial crisis,

. . . were not affiliated with any depository institutions," and, in fact, if they had had "a large source of insured deposits, they would likely have survived their short-term liquidity problems" rather than going under and precipitating a wider crisis, he said.[34]

BACKGROUND

Early Bank Battles

Money is power, and even in the earliest days of the republic, lawmakers debated the benefits and dangers of having a large central bank. They worried that big financiers might join with politicians or the wealthy to turn the democratic republic into an oligarchy — a state run for the benefit of a powerful few.[35]

The first such debate centered on whether to establish a single bank with close ties to the federal government.

Backers of the idea, like Treasury Secretary Alexander Hamilton, pointed out the value of having a bank large enough to offer credit to government, issue paper money — currency — that could be used nationwide, and facilitate payments among businesses in multiple states.[36]

Skeptics, like Thomas Jefferson, worried about centralizing economic power. A large bank might easily become a king-maker and make unilateral decisions about how much currency to issue, for example, Jefferson and others said. "I sincerely believe . . . that banking establishments are more dangerous than standing armies," the future third president wrote.[37]

Hamilton won the day, and in 1791 President George Washington signed a law chartering the First Bank of the United States, with 80 percent private and 20 percent government ownership.

During its 20-year charter as the sole federally affiliated bank, the firm collected tax revenues on behalf of the government and issued the only currency accepted as payment of federal tax bills.

State-chartered banks issued the lion's share of paper money in circulation. But the First Bank's role in clearing state-to-state payments meant that it held large amounts of state currency and could demand that states fork over gold or silver reserves to redeem those notes. This gave the bank enormous power to determine the country's money and credit supplies — decisions that affect prices and whether businesses can get loans.

By and large, the bank was a boon rather than a bane to the young republic, helping businesses to thrive. By 1825, when the young United States and the old United Kingdom "had roughly the same population . . . the United States had nearly 2.5 times the amount of bank capital as the UK," as well as a stock market "able to attract capital from around the world," wrote MIT's Johnson and business consultant James Kwak in their 2010 book *13 Bankers: The Wall Street Takeover and the Next Financial Meltdown.*[38]

The Federal Reserve

In the 1830s, President Andrew Jackson — who believed that only gold and silver rather than paper currency should be used as money — railed against what he called a dangerous monopoly held by the Second Bank, chartered in 1816. The battle marked the seventh president as somewhat old-fashioned in an age when industrialization and urbanization created a need for centralized banking, but the behavior of Second Bank president Nicholas Biddle also provided evidence that there was reason to fear big banks' power.

An ally of Jackson rival Kentucky Sen. Henry Clay, Biddle expanded the bank's lending to win support for Clay and the bank. Jackson nevertheless defeated Clay in the 1832 presidential election, but afterwards Biddle drastically cut lending and demanded that states pay gold and silver to redeem their currencies, contracting the money supply and causing loan interest rates to double. "The bank is trying to kill me," Jackson fumed.[39]

Jackson vetoed renewal of the Second Bank's charter. But, at least partly as a result of having no big bank to manage the money and credit supply, "the U.S. economy . . . suffered through severe business cycles" — booms and depression-level busts — "through the rest of the 19th century," Johnson and Kwak write.[40]

Nevertheless, American industry thrived, as railroad, oil and chemical companies launched new products. Then, near the end of the 19th century, many companies in industries like steel merged into huge corporate entities, dubbed "trusts" — monopoly or near-monopoly enterprises that executives argued cut costs. But Presidents William McKinley, Theodore Roosevelt and William Howard Taft tried to break up the trusts, saying they had power to raise prices and lower wages without restraint.

CHRONOLOGY

1900s-1920s *Federal Reserve system is launched to curb the cycle of steep economic booms and busts, but stock market crashes, triggering economic collapse.*

1930s-1970s *Banking rules are tightened. Following the Great Depression, the economic boom-and-bust cycle stabilizes.*

1933 Glass-Steagall Banking Act separates investment banks from commercial — deposit-holding — banks and establishes federal deposit insurance.

1934 Securities and Exchange Commission established to regulate stock trading.

1935 Fed's regulatory powers expanded.

1936 Commodity Exchange Act requires commodity futures to be traded on public exchanges.

1938 Federal National Mortgage Association (Fannie Mae) established.

1974 Congress creates Commodity Futures Trading Commission (CFTC).

1980s-1990s *Banking regulations ease, and new products like adjustable-rate mortgages and mortgage-backed securities are introduced.*

1980 Congress allows banks to compete for deposits by offering higher interest, expands loans savings & loans (S&Ls) may make, and bans state caps on first-mortgage interest rates.

1984 Congress eases rules to allow investment banks to package and sell mortgages as securities with varying risk levels.

1989 Resolution Trust Corp. created to take over insolvent S&Ls.

1994 Congress lifts restrictions on interstate banking.

1995 Nearly a third of S&Ls have failed and been shut down.

1998 Losses on derivatives bought with borrowed funds sink big hedge fund Long-Term Capital Management.

1999 Gramm-Leach-Bliley Act repeals 1933 ban on combining investment and commercial banking in one company.

2000s-2010s *Housing price bubble swells then pops, triggering worldwide recession.*

2000 Commodity Futures Modernization Act deregulates derivatives trading.

2006 High-risk loans, such as interest-only and no-documentation loans, account for 13 percent of new mortgages, up from 2 percent in 2003.

2007 Two hedge funds run by investment firm Bear Stearns go bankrupt. . . . German bank IDK suffers heavy losses on subprime investments. . . . May foreclosure filings up 90 percent from May 2006. . . . Government takes over Fannie Mae and Freddie Mac, the two big government-sponsored institutions that buy and securitize mortgages.

2008 Federal Reserve lends JP Morgan Chase $29 billion to buy Bear Stearns. . . . Lehman Brothers investment firm goes bankrupt. . . . Fed creates $85 billion loan fund to rescue insurer AIG. . . . Congress passes $700 billion bailout plan — the Troubled Asset Relief Program (TARP) — devised by Bush Treasury Secretary Henry Paulson to buy up risky investments held by "too big to fail" financial firms.

2009 Congress restricts compensation for highly paid workers at firms bailed out with TARP funds. . . . Congressional Oversight Panel for TARP says the Treasury paid more than market value for bank assets. . . . Bank of America and Citigroup return their TARP funds to the government.

2010 SEC charges Goldman Sachs bank with fraud in derivative-trading case; in July Goldman settles the case for $550 million. . . . On July 15, Congress passes sweeping legislation tightening rules for the financial industry. . . . A White House report says that many banks overpaid their executives during the financial crisis. . . . Federal Financial Crisis Inquiry Commission threatens to audit Goldman's derivatives-trading business.

Did Weakened Regulations Fuel the Economic Crisis?

Critics of regulation say "constant vigilance" by bank customers is the only answer.

The weakening or elimination of many banking and investing regulations over the past three decades contributed to the financial crisis, many analysts say. Conservative commentators, on the other hand, argue that most regulation fails to address the real problems behind troubled financial markets and only hinders financial firms in finding creative solutions.

Even small rules can make a big difference, some analysts say.

In June 2007, for example, the Securities and Exchange Commission eliminated a Depression-era rule intended to keep traders from driving down a company's stock to the point of ruin when market prices were falling. The so-called "uptick rule" imposed limits on "short selling" — borrowing, rather than buying, stocks whose price was dropping; selling them; and then buying them back at a lower price and pocketing the difference between the two prices before giving the stocks back to their real owner.

The uptick rule had banned short selling unless a stock's price had recently "ticked up," thus eliminating some of the profit motive in quick sales rather than longer-term investments. In the 1930s, the SEC determined that short selling by people who were not really investing in a company but merely trading borrowed stock in search of quick profits had worsened the stock-market crash and ruined some companies.[1]

The rule's repeal is partly responsible for recent financial-market plunges, said Muriel Siebert, former state banking superintendent of New York state and the first woman member of the New York Stock Exchange.[2] "The SEC took away the short-sale rule and when the markets were falling . . . investors just pounded" some companies' stocks.

Reinstating the rule "might have had some benefit" in mitigating the 2008 crash, said Federal Reserve Chairman Ben S. Bernanke.[3]

To have their full effect, the new rules Congress created should cover all kinds of financial traders, but mostly won't, many industry critics say.

"Current reforms won't deter the reckless financial engineering, investing, and inflation of values" that create speculative financial "bubbles" whose collapse can bring down the system, said Nomi Prins, a senior fellow at Demos, a New York City-based liberal research and advocacy group.[4]

For example, drafters of current legislation largely have ignored the "shadow-banking system," a group of financial players who take big risks but because most regulation doesn't apply to them never will have to pay for problems they exacerbate, said Prins. Investment groups called "private-equity funds," for example, "are financial-pyramid bottom-feeders. . . . They buy distressed companies or assets, load them up with debt, extract near-term profit, and are gone before any collapse occurs," she said. Such actions increase the risk of a system collapse because they usually buy complex, poorly understood assets that may be very risky and use borrowed money to do so, just as happened in the mortgage meltdown, said Prins.

Instead of ignoring some financial enterprises, lawmakers should require "leveraged funds" of all kinds — that is, any organizations that borrow money to invest — to register with the SEC, report their borrowing and trading activities to regulators in detail, and have limits on how much they can borrow, she said.[5]

The Federal Reserve system — the public-private banking network that not only regulates banks but also makes key decisions about the country's credit and money supply — also got too little attention from lawmakers this year, some analysts say. Although Congress approved some additional auditing for the Fed, lawmakers left too many of its

---

The rise of the trusts ushered in a new era of big banking, this time allied with big industry, rather than government. The banking empire of Connecticut-born J.P. Morgan had become financier of choice for fast-consolidating industries, lending money to buy stock and helping arrange mergers. By 1900, Morgan's banks were raising 40 percent of all industrial capital in the United States.

activities in darkness, says Robert D. Auerbach, a professor of public affairs at the University of Texas, Austin.

The Fed has "done a lot of devilish things" over many decades, such as secretly lending money to foreign governments at the behest of the White House, and "there should be checks and balances. They should tell Congress" of their activities because in many ways, "they run the country, as unelected officials with no accountability," Auerbach says. What's required is not full public disclosure but merely disclosure to the members of Congress with oversight authority. "If the CIA can make disclosures" to congressional oversight panels, then the Fed can do so without damage also, he says.

But many conservative commentators argue that regulation simply can't be the answer to creating a sounder banking system.

"Regulation as protection is a false promise, and to the extent that any new regulation is presented to the public as a protection" against future harms, "people are being misled," says Marvin Goodfriend, a professor of economics at the Carnegie-Mellon Tepper School of Business in Pittsburgh.

History has plenty of examples showing that financial regulation often does not work, Goodfriend says. "There were plenty of regulations in the mortgage markets, for example, but they didn't protect people. There is a role for regulation, but it should not be oversold." For example, "a too big to fail" rule — should one be enacted — "could be gotten around by the industry, and they would get around it," he says.

Instead, to create a well-functioning market in which frauds and risk are at a minimum, "there is no solution except constant vigilance" by "informed customers," — borrowers, depositors, stockholders, and investors, among others — who "discipline firms" by their vigilant search for value, Goodfriend says.

On that basis, rather than rules per se, he would like to see more standardization of financial products. "Standardization is a public good" because it leads to more informed customers who keep banks honest. "I want to be able to compare" investments.

Goodfriend says that he'd start an effort to standardize financial-product descriptions by examining how more transparent labeling was achieved for other products, such

Federal Reserve Chairman Ben S. Bernanke said a rule regulating "short selling" might have softened the 2008 economic crash.

as nutritional labeling on food. Because of that history, "we're not flying blind" in trying to accomplish standardized labeling for investments, he says. Transparency might extend to all types of investments, including initial public offerings — IPOs — of company stock, he says.

— *Marcia Clemmitt*

[1] For background, see Robert Holmes, "Uptick Rule: Meaningful or Meaningless," *The Street.com*, Feb. 27, 2009, www.thestreet.com.

[2] Quoted in Gretchen Morgenson, "Why the Roller Coaster Seems Wilder," *The New York Times*, Aug. 26, 2007.

[3] Quoted in Jesse Westbrook, "Bernanke Says There May Be Benefit to Uptick Rule," Bloomberg.com, Feb. 25, 2009, www.bloomberg.com.

[4] Nomi Prins, "Shadow Banking," *The American Prospect*, May 4, 2010, www.prospect.org

[5] *Ibid.*

In 1907, however, a failed scheme by some investors to manipulate the price of copper stocks panicked Wall Street, triggering a run on New York banks and a market crash that saw stocks lose nearly 50 percent of their value. The so-called Banker's Panic demonstrated that while a large corporation-allied bank like J.P. Morgan's may help industries grow, it does not promote economic stability the way a federal bank could, by managing money and credit supplies.

Although Morgan used his own cash to help keep the banks afloat, the federal government ultimately had to deposit $25 million into banks in New York to bail out the banks and prevent economic meltdown.

After the panic, bankers pushed for a government-affiliated bank to act as lender of last resort to head off crashes. Rep. Charles A. Lindbergh, Sr., R-Minn., father of famed aviator Charles A. Lindbergh, Jr., grumbled that it was "a wonderfully devised plan specifically fitted for Wall Street securing control of the world," using taxpayer cash.[41]

Democratic President Woodrow Wilson engineered a compromise proposal to create a central banking system that would be privately owned but receive some government input. The Federal Reserve Act of 1913 established a network of private regional banks empowered to use public funds to shore up troubled banks, loosely overseen by the presidentially appointed Federal Reserve Board.

The system exists today in much the same form in which it was created. To get some idea of its power, one need only observe that "every dollar bill in the country says 'Federal Reserve Note' on it," says Robert D. Auerbach, a professor of public affairs at the University of Texas, Austin.

Regulation, Deregulation

It soon became clear, however, that the system was no panacea for financial busts.

In the 1920s, good times rolled, industry grew and stock prices soared, tempting more stock investors into the game, with a growing number buying securities with "leverage," or using borrowed cash.

The young Federal Reserve had considerable power to affect the money and credit supply and thus slow an economy where debt was growing excessive. But slowing a boom is "never popular with politicians concerned about the next election, banks making large profits . . . or ordinary people benefiting from a burgeoning economy," so the Fed kept interest rates low, said Johnson and Kwak.

In October 1929, an increasingly unstable stock market began experiencing unnerving one-day price drops. At the same time, housing prices were dropping around the country. Panic about financial firms' stability led to bank runs that helped trigger the Great Depression of the 1930s.

President Franklin D. Roosevelt, inaugurated in March 1933, sought a law to stop banks from making risky Wall Street investment bets with Main Street depositors' money. The Banking Act of 1933 — dubbed the Glass-Steagall Act after cosponsors Sen. Carter Glass, D-Va., and Rep. Henry B. Steagall, D-Ala. — required traditional "commercial" banks — which take deposits and make loans — to be separate entities from "investment" banks, which help raise corporate capital and issue and trade securities. It also created the Federal Deposit Insurance Corporation to insure bank deposits and facilitate an orderly shutdown of commercial banks that got into trouble.

Decades of moderate business cycles, without steep booms and busts, followed, although historians disagree about whether stricter banking laws were largely responsible. By the late 1970s, however, a new school of free-market economists joined with banks to press for loosening the restraints.

Beginning with the Reagan administration, in 1981, banking rules were relaxed, and financial firms got larger and took on a more varied and riskier mix of investments, loans and deposits.

At the same time, Americans became more comfortable with borrowing; and workers whose companies once offered pensions now had to invest retirement money in stocks and bonds. Wages stagnated, leading to increased borrowing as Americans sought the higher standard of living that by now was considered an American birthright.

A new era of steeper booms and busts was about to begin.

In the 1980s, savings and loan associations (S&Ls) — local institutions that took deposits and made mortgage loans — were among the first financial firms to be deregulated. Initially, profits soared. Between 1986 and 1995, however, regulators closed 1,043 failing S&Ls — about a third of the total — mainly because they'd lent to risky borrowers who defaulted. By 1999, around $124 billion in taxpayer money had shielded S&L depositors from losing their savings.[42]

The advent of fast computers allowed financiers to design new investment instruments — "derivatives" — whose values, often based on complex formulas, could make them effective "hedges" against failing bets on traditional investments, like a company stock. Mostly traded over-the-counter rather than in managed exchanges as stocks are, derivatives are essentially bets on how some shifting quantity or quantities will change. A derivative's value can derive from literally any changing quantity, such as stock prices, the value of one nation's currency in terms of another, or even how many sunny days a region will experience. Derivatives can theoretically be designed to hedge against any risk.

Derivatives markets boomed in the 1990s, with many individual and institutional investors borrowing millions or even billions of dollars to buy them. Nevertheless, as the investments grew more complex, their risks became harder to discern, triggering huge losses for some.

In the late 1990s, Brooksley Born — then chair of the Commodities Futures Trading Commission (CFTC), which oversees the "futures contracts" that help farmers lock in favorable prices for wheat and other crops — sought to have her agency designated to oversee derivatives trading. Born made her pitch after the spectacular demise of Long-Term Capital Management (LTCM), a huge "hedge" investment fund that collapsed "because it had $1.25 trillion worth of derivative contracts at the same time as it had less than $4 billion in capital to support them" and thus was utterly unable to make good on its losing bets.[43]

But financial firms and policymakers, including Federal Reserve Board chairman Alan Greenspan, shot down Born's proposal, arguing that the LTCM crash was an aberration.

In 2000, President Bill Clinton signed the Commodity Futures Modernization Act, eliminating a longstanding legal rule that over-the-counter derivatives "contracts" were valid only if one of the trading parties actually owned the security that they were betting against, explained Lynn A. Stout, a professor of corporate and securities law at the University of California, Los Angeles.[44]

Under the new law, even a person who does not own a particular security may invest in an over-the-counter derivative that will pay off if that security fails. Supporters argued the change would keep American investment firms competitive with those in countries that do not restrict derivatives trades. But Stout compares it to permitting "the unscrupulous to buy fire insurance on other people's houses." In that case, "the incidence of arson would rise dramatically," she notes dryly. Similarly, under the 2000 law, some derivatives dealers certainly design some securities

to fail, just so they can make surefire bets against those failures, she said.[45]

Nevertheless, as regulations loosened, the financial industry increased its profitability and thus its importance to the country's overall financial picture. Between 1980 and 2005, financial-sector profits grew by 800 percent, compared to 250 percent in other industries.[46]

Crash of 2008

The economy enjoyed a wealth boom as the 21st century began. Home ownership soared as borrowers took advantage of low interest rates set by the Federal Reserve to keep the economy moving after the 9/11 terrorist attacks.

New kinds of mortgages — with ultra-low introductory interest or requiring no downpayment — enticed many to take out second mortgages to get cash to spend. Speculators buying houses today so they could "flip" them at higher prices to other buyers tomorrow helped drive real-estate prices skyward and, along with them, Americans' perception that their personal wealth was soaring. Another computer-based banking innovation, "securitization," increased mortgage availability by allowing banks to package hundreds of mortgages and sell them to investors, thus getting the loans off banks' own books and freeing them to make new loans.[47]

In 2007 the wheels came off the wealth machine.

Some of the riskiest mortgage holders were defaulting. And since not local banks but investors owned the "securitized" debt — as well as derivatives based on the mortgage-backed securities, which many had taken on large amounts of additional debt to buy — financial losses from the unpaid mortgages quickly spread around the globe.

The amount of apparent wealth that a highly leveraged system with multiple complex paper assets can produce is enormous. Currently, the worldwide derivatives market alone is said to have a value of about $1.2 quadrillion, or about 24 times the value of the entire world's annual gross domestic product (GDP). Such a wealth bubble may quickly deflate, however, if the value of underlying assets wanes or grows suspect, as happened with high-risk mortgage loans in the 2000s and with sketchy start-up companies in the 1990s' Internet stock bubble.[48]

Most banks knew they had risky securities on their books and, suspecting that other banks did too, refused

Mystery of the May Mini-crash

Did big banks use ultra-high-speed trading to spook Congress?

By April 2010, the Dow Jones Industrial Average had climbed to 11,205 — nearly 70 percent over its March 2009 level — and Wall Street seemed to have put the 2008 financial-market crash behind it. Then, on May 6, a so-called "flash crash" sent the Dow plummeting 998 points — nearly a tenth of its value — in just a few minutes, before regaining about 600 of those points by day's end.[1]

High-frequency trades (HFT) — instantaneous stock trades generated by computers — were widely blamed for the dizzying drop.

Only a handful of big firms, such as the investment bank Goldman Sachs, use HFTs, but the trades represent about 75 percent of overall trading volume and have enormous power to push the market sharply up or down, "usually without fundamental or technical reason," charged financial blogger Tyler Durden. High-frequency traders can make lightning-quick trades and thus turn a profit based on market shifts that are actually created by HFT itself, he said.[2]

As a result, "based on a few lines of code" in a big bank's HFT computers, "retail investors," who don't understand that the market is being driven by computerized buying rather than real-world events, "get suckered into a rising market that has nothing to do with" factors that might legitimately raise stock prices, such as "some Chinese firms buying a few hundred extra Intel servers," Durden said.[3]

Some in Washington are sounding alarms. "I'm afraid that we're sowing the seeds of the next financial crash," said Sen. Ted Kaufman, D-Del., who holds an MBA from the University of Pennsylvania's Wharton School and was a longtime aide to Vice President Joseph Biden. "We're dealing with something highly complex and completely unregulated. The last time we had that mix, with the practitioners telling us, 'Don't worry about it,' things didn't end well."[4]

Moreover, some high-frequency traders use their speed advantage to profit in ways that are, if not illegal, at least highly unfair, said David Weild, a former vice chairman of the NASDAQ stock exchange. Some HFT firms use their high speed and the slower trading algorithms used by investors like pension funds to buy the next stock those investors will want, and then sell it back at a higher price. "It is increasingly clear that there are quite a number of [such] high-frequency bandits in the high-frequency-trading community," said Weild.[5]

Some commentators even suspect that big-bank, high-frequency traders deliberately created the May 6 market tumble to warn Congress of what havoc bankers could cause if lawmakers passed a tough banking law. On the day

to offer them the short-term credit they needed to make business loans. The supply of home buyers dried up, and house prices dropped, wiping out the paper wealth against which many consumers had borrowed their spending money. The economy ground to a halt, and some financial institutions that were believed — rightly or wrongly — to have the riskiest investment portfolios stumbled.

Beginning in 2008, the Treasury Department and the Federal Reserve worked together to save some "too big to fail" financial institutions, — while allowing others, like the financial-services firm Lehman Brothers, to go under.

In March, the Federal Reserve lent $29 billion to help the JP Morgan Chase bank acquire the failing investment firm Bear Stearns. In September, the Federal Reserve put up $85 billion — later increased to over $180 billion — to save AIG, Inc., an insurance firm that had helped investors "hedge" bets with a risky derivative called a "credit default swap." When investments tumbled in value in the general slump, AIG was unable to pay off its many CDS obligations. Also in September, the government seized the government-sponsored mortgage giants Fannie Mae and Freddie Mac, as mortgage defaults swelled.

of the 998-point drop, Congress was deliberating two provisions that were anathema to the financial industry — a forced breakup of the nation's six largest banks and a requirement for an independent audit of the Federal Reserve's 2008 bailout of the banks. That the "flash crash" occurred during discussion of these proposals suggests it "could have been an act of financial terrorism," wrote liberal blogger David DeGraw.[6]

"The amalgamation of events is eerily similar to what took place on Sept. 29, 2008," when the House of Representatives voted to reject the federal bailout plan for banks, the Troubled Asset Relief Program (TARP), said DeGraw. "Immediately after the vote, big banks made the market plunge a record 778 points, sparking widespread . . . panic that helped convince Congress to eventually pass" the measure.[7]

Many in the HFT community dismiss such claims as nonsense, however, and argue that HFT did not cause the May 6 crash. "This crisis was precipitated by panic selling by humans," not HFT, because "we just had had a huge run-up in the equities markets, we were in the midst of a 10 percent correction before the mayhem unfolded, and on top of that you had very vexing news" about the financial collapse of the Greek government, said Manoj Narang, founder of the New York City-based HFT information firm Tradeworx.[8]

Meanwhile, the Securities and Exchange Commission is proposing additional "circuit-breaker" mechanisms that would halt securities trading briefly if any stock price declined by a large amount within a five-minute period, to forestall panic sell-offs that turn into market crashes.[9]

But some analysts say that ever-rising trading speeds simply make the market too difficult to control by such mechanisms. "There's a speed that's too fast, and right now we're at it," said Michael Goldstein, a professor of finance at Babson College, a business school in Wellesley, Mass. "Like our highways have a minimum speed and a maximum speed, maybe it's time for our highways in trading to have a minimum speed and a maximum speed as well."[10]

— Marcia Clemmitt

[1] For background, see Matthew Philips, "Fast, Loose, and Out of Control," *Newsweek*, June 1, 2010, p. 42.

[2] Tyler Durden, "Goldman's $4 Billion High Frequency Trading Wildcard," Zero Hedge blog, July 2009, http://zerohedge.blogspot.com.

[3] *Ibid.*

[4] Quoted in Philips, *op. cit.*

[5] Quoted in Timothy Lavin, "Monsters in the Market," *The Atlantic*, July/August 2010.

[6] David DeGraw, "Was Last Week's Market Crash a Direct Attack by Financial Terrorists?" AlterNet web site, May 10, 2010, www.alternet.org.

[7] *Ibid.*

[8] Quoted in "'Flash Crash,' the Untold Story by Tradeworx's Manoj Narang, at High-Frequency Trading Leaders Forum," press release, Golden Networking web site, June 2, 2010, www.prlog.org.

[9] Jim Puzzanghera, "New Circuit Breakers Will Likely Prevent 'Flash Crash,' Experts Say," *Los Angeles Times*, June 3, 2010, p. B3.

[10] Quoted in *ibid.*

Despite the taxpayer-funded "bailout" of big financial companies, however, a deep economic recession spread worldwide and persists.

CURRENT SITUATION

Reform Legislation

After a long and intense battle on Capitol Hill, financial reform legislation is now in place.

The fierce 2010 congressional battle to enact the legislation was Washington's response to widespread anger over the Wall Street bailout and public distaste for companies many believe handed out huge bonuses to the very executives who put profits ahead of customers' interest and helped precipitate the economic crash.

Passing the legislation has not been easy, however. The year-and-a-half struggle to get a majority of House members, 60 senators and the White House to agree on just what new rules are needed reveals both the issue's complexity and banks' enormous political clout. In the early morning hours of Friday, June 25, a House-Senate conference committee agreed on final details to merge separate versions of financial-reform legislation passed earlier

Do Fannie Mae and Freddie Mac bear primary responsibility for the financial crisis?

 Mark A. Calabria
Director of Financial-Regulation Studies, Cato Institute

From Cato Institute website, June 25, 2010, www.cato.org.

 Julia Gordon
Senior Policy Counsel, Center for Responsible Lending

From testimony before Financial Crisis Inquiry Commission, Jan. 13, 2010

Perhaps it should come as no surprise that Sen. Christopher Dodd, D-Conn., and Rep. Barney Frank, D-Mass, the 2010 financial-reform bill's primary authors, would fail to end the numerous government distortions of our financial and mortgage markets that led to the crisis. Both have been either architects or supporters of those distortions.

Nowhere in the bill will you see even a pretense of rolling back the endless federal incentives and mandates to extend credit, particularly mortgages, to those who cannot afford to pay their loans back. After all, the popular narrative insists that Wall Street fat cats must be to blame for the credit crisis. Despite the recognition that mortgages were offered to unqualified individuals and families, banks will still be required under the Dodd-Frank bill to meet government-imposed lending quotas.

Apologists for government-mandated lending are correct in pointing out that much of the worst lending was originated by state-chartered lenders, such as Countrywide, and not federally chartered banks. However, they either miss or purposely ignore the truth that these non-bank lenders were selling the bulk of their loans to Fannie Mae, Freddie Mac or the government corporation Ginnie Mae. About 90 percent of loans originated by Countrywide, the largest subprime lender, were either sold to Fannie Mae or backed by Ginnie Mae. Subprime lenders were so intertwined with Fannie and Freddie that Countrywide alone constituted over 25 percent of Fannie's purchases.

While one can debate the motivations behind Fannie and Freddie's support for the subprime market, one thing should be clear: Had Fannie and Freddie not been there to buy these loans, most of them would never have been made.

And had the taxpayer not been standing behind Fannie and Freddie, they would have been unable to fund such large purchases of subprime mortgages. Yet Congress believes it is more important to expand federal regulation and litigation to lenders that had nothing to do with the crisis rather than fix the endless bailout that Fannie and Freddie have become.

Nor has there been any discussion in Congress about removing the tax preferences for debt. Washington subsidizes debt, taxes equity and then acts surprised when everyone becomes extremely leveraged.

Until Washington takes a long, deep look at its own role in causing the financial crisis, we will have little hope for avoiding another one.

Since the problems in the subprime market became evident in early 2007, many in the mortgage industry evaded responsibility by blaming the borrowers.

However, the stereotypes of the risky borrower or the borrower overreaching to purchase a McMansion turn out to be false. Research shows that an elevated risk of foreclosure was an inherent feature of the defective, exotic loan products that produced this crisis. Loan originators frequently specialized in steering customers to higher-rate loans than those for which they qualified, which are loaded with risky features.

In addition, given the long-standing political dispute over the very existence of the Federal National Mortgage Association (Fannie Mae) and the Federal Home Loan Mortgage Corporation (Freddie Mac), it is not surprising that these government-sponsored enterprises (GSEs) are often blamed for the crisis. Those blaming the GSEs point to their decision to purchase subprime securities from Wall Street.

The fact is, while we agree that Fannie Mae and Freddie Mac should not have purchased subprime mortgage-backed securities (MBS), their role in purchasing and securitizing problem loans was small in comparison with that of private industry. All subprime mortgage-backed securities were created by Wall Street. Fannie Mae and Freddie Mac did not securitize any of these loans because the loans did not meet their standards. When they finally began to purchase the MBS, they were relative late-comers to a market that had been created by private-sector firms and they purchased the least risky and most easily sellable of the securities.

In fact, the GSEs' role in the overall mortgage market diminished substantially as subprime lending rose. As of 2001, Fannie Mae and Freddie Mac funded almost two-thirds of home mortgage loans across the United States. These were loans that Fannie Mae and Freddie Mac purchased directly from originators who met the GSE guidelines and either held on their balance sheets or securitized and sold to investors. Subprime loans accounted for just 7 percent of the market.

Around 2003, private issuers began to introduce new, riskier loan products into the market and began to displace the GSEs. In early 2004, private-issue MBS surpassed the GSE issuances of all loans and by early 2006, Fannie and Freddie's market share of new issuances had dropped to one-third of the total. As the role of the GSEs was declining, the percentage of subprime loans in the mortgage market almost tripled.

this year by the two chambers. No conference-committee Republican voted to approve the bill, arguing that it would cripple the financial industry and the economy, although it contains far less stringent curbs on banks than many economists, and even some bankers, recommend.

In the full Senate, however, three Republicans, Scott Brown, (Mass.) and Maine's Susan Collins and Olympia Snowe, crossed the aisle on July 15 to give supporters the 60 votes they needed to overcome a final Republican filibuster of the plan, and President Obama signed the measure into law on July 21.

Republican opposition to the measure remains strong, however. "I think it ought to be repealed," said House Minority Leader John Boehner, R-Ohio. "I think it is going to make credit harder for the American people to get."[49] The new law:

- Gives regulators authority to assess whether a bank poses a risk to the economy and to break apart or close such banks;
- Limits some derivatives trading;
- Tightens capital standards;
- Sets up a consumer-credit watchdog agency in the Federal Reserve; and
- Allows Congress to seek audits of the Federal Reserve.

"We shouldn't put in place a regulatory regime that overly reacts and, as a result, significantly dampens our capacity to have the most vibrant capital and credit markets in the world," said Sen. Judd Gregg, R-N.H.[50]

Some Republicans did seek tough rules, however. In May, for example, the Senate approved an amendment from Collins requiring banks with more than $250 billion in assets to meet slightly stricter capital requirements than in the past, and the plan made it into the final package. Collins' amendment would prevent the biggest banks, which make many high-risk trades, from trading with too much borrowed money.[51]

Democrats including the Obama administration are all over the map in their views, hotly debating nearly every proposed provision. The Obama administration actually opposed Collins' amendment, for example.[52]

In both the current and recent administrations, Treasury Department leaders mainly come from the financial industry and the Federal Reserve, a fact that likely drives White House wariness of some rule tightening, many observers say. "Isn't it interesting that the White House is opposing" an amendment to require the Federal Reserve to undergo stringent independent auditing, given that Treasury Secretary Timothy Geithner "is a former head of the New York Fed," says Texas' Auerbach.

Some Democrats have fought for very strict regulation. Sens. Sherrod Brown (Ohio) and Ted Kaufman (Delaware) proposed forbidding any single bank from holding more than 10 percent of the country's deposits, and Sen. Al Franken (Minnesota) wanted an independent board to assign financial firms a credit ratings agency for each project, rather than letting banks "shop" for agencies as they do now. Neither measure made it into the law.[53]

But many Democrats also have fought to soften bill provisions. For example, Sen. Tom Harkin (Iowa) and Rep. Greg Meeks (New York) successfully pushed to keep the SEC from regulating so-called equity-indexed annuities — products often fraudulently sold to seniors as ultra-safe, fixed-income investments, even though their value depends on stock prices, and both the SEC and the courts have ruled that the SEC should regulate them.[54]

Its architects praise the law. "This is going to be a very strong bill, and stronger than almost everybody predicted it could be," said House Financial Services Committee Chairman Barney Frank, D-Mass.[55]

But many analysts say the legislation will do little to limit banking risk.

"Lobbying in the gazillions predictably stopped the needed major structural reforms . . . revealed by the scope and scale of the financial crisis," said Robert Johnson, director for global finance at the Roosevelt Institute, a liberal think tank in New York City. "We still have many practices that are not transparent and many off-balance-sheet problems that disguise the conditions of our financial firms."[56]

Fraud Enforcement

In the end, laws make no difference unless they're enforced, and financial-sector enforcement has been chancy at best over the years, partly because of the industry's vast influence, many observers say.

Nevertheless, no matter how lightly an industry is regulated, the ability to crack down on at least the most abusive behavior always exists, says Texas' Galbraith. "You can't decriminalize fraud. Good accounting, good auditing and appropriate criminal referrals are what we need" from regulators, he says. "My sense is that once the wheels [of civil and criminal investigations] start turning, the effects are pretty powerful," including making other industry players "think twice" about their behavior. At present "it's hard to judge" how much enforcement activity is bubbling, but there are encouraging signs, Galbraith says.

On April 16, for example, the SEC filed a civil lawsuit charging Goldman Sachs with fraud for selling mortgage-backed securities the bank knew were intended to fail. The so-called Abacus securities were designed by a hedge-fund manager, John Paulson, who did not buy any of the securities but designed them to fail so that he could profit by betting against them using derivatives, under the legal permission granted by the 2000 Commodity Futures Exchange Act.[57] In mid-July, Goldman agreed to pay $550 million to settle the case, an amount the SEC notes is "the largest-ever penalty paid by a Wall Street firm." In the settlement, the bank neither admitted nor denied the SEC's allegation that it had committed fraud, however.[58]

Some analysts say that the fine is far too small to deter bad behavior by the high-rolling financial industry.

For one thing, the fine amounts to only about two weeks' worth of profits for Goldman Sachs, according to the independent, foundation-funded investigative journalism organization ProPublica.[59]

"It's the largest fine in SEC history, and that's the bad news . . . because it shows how ineffective the SEC has been for decades now," said the University of Missouri's Black. While "losses caused by securities fraud have grown into the multibillion dollars" over the past few decades, "the SEC not only didn't bite, but it forgot that it had teeth." The Goldman Sachs fine "is very, very weak; it's not going to have any significant deterrent effect," said Black. Furthermore, civil lawsuits against the bank will be extremely difficult to pursue, since the SEC did not exact an admission of intentional deception from the bank, he said.[60] Goldman, in fact, reportedly expected to have to pay a $1 billion fine.[61]

Meanwhile, states, especially in the West, are said to be pursuing numerous fraud cases involving the mortgage industry, and some in Congress also have shown interest, Galbraith notes. Last November, for example, Rep. Marcy Kaptur, D-Ohio, introduced legislation to hire up to 1,000 new FBI agents to pursue cases of suspected corporate, securities, and mortgage fraud.[62]

White-collar enforcement, especially in finance, has always faced severe challenges, at least partly because regulators mostly come from the regulated industries, says Baker of the Center for Economic and Policy Research. "It's as if [big pharmaceutical manufacturers] Pfizer and Merck appointed members to the Food and Drug Administration," Baker says. "This remains an enormous problem not addressed by" legislation.

In the Federal Reserve system, for example, which is charged with overseeing banks, "you've got the New York banks electing" the very officials who will oversee them, says Texas' Auerbach, author of the 2008 book *Deception and Abuse at the Fed: Henry B. Gonzalez Battles Alan Greenspan's Bank.*

"There was massively too much leverage" — the use of large amounts of debt, rather than actual assets or capital, to purchase investments —"in the financial system" before the last crash, noted Richard Breeden, who chaired the Securities and Exchange Commission from 1989 to 1993. "Regulators had the authority to control that and eliminate it" but didn't. "We can keep passing laws, but if the regulators don't have the backbone to enforce the rules and to be realistic, then that's a different problem."[63]

Currently, for example, pro-regulation, liberal advocates are pressing the administration to appoint Elizabeth Warren, a Harvard Law professor and head of Congress' oversight committee for the financial-industry bailout, as chief of the new consumer-protection agency created by the reform law. "Professor Warren has a proven track record as a smart and tough consumer advocate" and in fact was the first person to propose that there be such an office, said Sen. Bernie Sanders, I-Vt., in a letter to President Obama urging Warren's appointment.[64]

However, with the banking industry believed to strongly oppose Warren's nomination, Senate Republicans would likely filibuster it, and even with all Democrats and Independents voting "yes," Senate Democratic leaders would still have to win over at least one Republican vote to get the 60 votes needed to end a filibuster and approve her nomination.[65] If Obama "nominates a zealot or an activist, I think it will bring to life our greatest fears about this consumer protection agency," said Sen. Bob Corker,

R-Tenn.[66] Meanwhile, Wall Street activities continue much as they did pre-crash, observers say.

For example, "many big banks have not modified their [employee compensation] practices from what they were before the crisis," paying executives in ways that incentivize "excessive risk-taking," said Federal Reserve Chairman Ben S. Bernanke in June.[67]

"Despite all those dramatic congressional hearings, average compensation of Wall Street bankers rose by 27 percent in 2009," said Nomi Prins, a senior fellow at the liberal New York City-based think tank Demos. Meanwhile, "banks posted their lowest lending rates since 1942, despite all the subsidies and cheap money they received from, well, us" as a supposed incentive to help the economy by making business loans, she said.[68]

OUTLOOK

New Crash Ahead?

Most analysts don't see an end to extreme boom-and-bust cycles in financial markets.

The new financial industry overhaul legislation "will have relatively little impact" on slowing growth of speculative "bubbles," like the vastly inflated stock prices for fledgling Internet companies in the so-called dot.com bubble of the 1990s and the soaring house prices of the early 2000s, says Baker of the Center for Economic and Policy Research.

"I believe that nothing in the [new legislation] will prevent another crisis," said Richard Marston, a professor of finance at the University of Pennsylvania's Wharton School. The basic problem is that "securitization" — conversion of pools of loans, like mortgages and credit-card debt, into packages to be sold as investments —"has changed banking in a fundamental way," he says. "It ties all financial institutions and investors together," so that risky investment activities can't easily be walled off from the rest of the system, and risk spreads easily throughout the economy.[69]

Congress didn't even pretend to address the real causes of the crash, some analysts say.

No legislation to reform the financial industry could "address the underlying problems" that really triggered the economic meltdown, said Wharton finance professor Franklin Allen. Low interest rates and "global imbalances" of wealth, such as large reserves of currency in Asia, led to over-borrowing, visible in the proliferation of high-risk mortgages, and the law's provisions "do nothing" to address these.[70]

"A number of . . . provisions in the bill . . . run far afield from Wall Street reform and will ultimately harm Main Street," said American Bankers Association President Edward L. Yingling. "This bill will, in the end, add well over a thousand pages of new regulations for even the smallest bank," with the result that "the capability of traditional banks to provide the credit needed to move the economy forward has been undermined."[71]

Some analysts say it's unlikely lawmakers can ever effectively address the problem of "wealth bubbles," whose rapid deflation triggers financial and economic meltdowns.

"I don't think the problem of bubbles is an economic problem. It's a political problem," says Cato's Calabria. "The public loves a bubble" because people rejoice when their house values or stock portfolios make them feel wealthy, he says. That being the case, neither lawmakers nor regulators nor banks will ever get much support for deliberately trying to pop wealth bubbles or slow their development, he suggests.

"Based on what's in the bills, in 10 to 15 years there will be another crash," Calabria predicts.

NOTES

1. For background, see Nathaniel Popper, "Trading Firms Put Their Money on Poker Experts," *Los Angeles Times*, May 1, 2010.

2. For background, see Kenneth Jost, "Financial Crisis," *CQ Researcher*, May 9, 2008, pp. 409-432, and Thomas J. Billitteri, "Financial Bailout," *CQ Researcher*, Oct. 24, 2008, pp. 865-888.

3. Nouriel Roubini and Stephen Mihm, "Bust Up the Banks," *Newsweek*, May 17, 2010, p. 42.

4. *Ibid.*

5. Remarks at the SW Graduate School of Banking 53rd Annual Keynote Banquet, Federal Reserve Bank of Texas website, June 3, 2010, http://dallasfed.org.

6. Testimony before House Financial Services Committee, Sept. 24, 2009, www.house.gov/apps/list/hearing/financialsvcs_dem/zandi_testimony.pdf.

7. Quoted in Chris Adams and Greg Gordon, "Goldman Executives: 'No Regrets' for Deals that Accelerated Crisis," McClatchy Newspapers, April 27, 2010, www.mcclatchydc.com.

8. Testimony before House Financial Services Committee, Sept. 24, 2009, www.house.gov/apps/list/hearing/financialsvcs_dem/zandi_testimony.pdf.

9. Zach Carter and Nouriel Roubini, "How to Break Up the Banks, Stop Massive Bonuses, and Rein in Wall Street Greed," Alternet blog, May 18, 2010, www.alternet.org.

10. Simon Johnson, "Wall Street's Victory Lap," *Huffington Post blog*, May 26, 2010, www.huffington post.com.

11. Remarks at the SW Graduate School of Banking, *op. cit.*

12. Mark A. Calabria, "Did Deregulation Cause the Financial Crisis," *Cato Policy Report*, July/August 2009, www.cato.org.

13. Arthur C. Brooks, "The New Culture War," *The Washington Post*, May 23, 2010, p. B1.

14. Matt Taibbi, "Will Goldman Sachs Prove Greed is God?" *The Guardian* [UK], April 24, 2010, www.guardian.co.uk/business/2010/apr/24/will-goldman-prove-greed-is-god.

15. Matt Taibbi, "The Greatest Non-Apology of All Time," *The Smirking Chimp blog*, June 19, 2009, www.smirkingchimp.com.

16. "Merkley-Levin Amendment to Crack Down on High-Risk Proprietary Trading," press release, Office of Sen. Jeff Merkley, May 10, 2010, http://merkley.senate.gov.

17. *Ibid.*

18. Joe Kolman, "The World According to Frank Partnoy," DerivativesStrategy.com, October 1997, www.derivativesstrategy.com.

19. William K. Black, "The Audacity of Dopes," *Huffington Post blog*, May 28, 2010, www.huffington post.com.

20. Testimony before House Committee on Financial Services, Jan. 22, 2010.

21. *Ibid.*

22. *Ibid.*

23. Quoted in John Arlidge, "I'm Doing 'God's Work.' Meet Mr. Goldman Sachs," *London Times online*, Nov. 8, 2009, www.timesonline.co.uk.

24. Regulation, Freedom and Human Welfare, St. Paul's Institute panel discussion, transcript, Oct. 20, 2009, www.stpauls.co.uk/documents/st%20paul%27s%20institute/regulation%20freedom%20and%20human%20welfare%20transcript.pdf.

25. Quoted in " 'A Race to the Bottom': Assigning Responsibility for the Financial Crisis," *Knowledge at Wharton newsletter*, Dec. 9, 2009, http://knowledge.wharton.upenn.edu.

26. Robert Reich, "Why the Finance Bill Won't Save Us," *Huffington Post blog*, May 24, 2010, www.huffington post.com.

27. Carter and Roubini, *op. cit.*

28. *Ibid.*

29. Shahien Nasiripour, "Regional Fed Chiefs Lining Up to Support Tough Derivatives Provision, Obama Administration Still Opposed," *Huffington Post blog*, June 11, 2010, www.huffingtonpost.com.

30. Arnold Kling, "Break Up the Banks," Cato Institute, March 26, 2010, www.cato.org.

31. *Ibid.*

32. Paul Krugman, "Financial Reform 101," *The New York Times*, April 2, 2010, p. A23.

33. Quoted in Martha C. White, "Should We Break Up Big Banks?" Walletpop.com, Dec. 5, 2009, www.walletpop.com.

34. Calabria, *op. cit.*

35. For background, see Simon Johnson and James Kwak, *13 Bankers: The Wall Street Takeover and the Next Financial Meltdown* (2010).

36. For background, see "The First Bank of the United States: A Chapter in the History of Central Banking," Philadelphia Federal Reserve, www.philadelphiafed.org/publications/economic-education/first-bank.pdf.

37. "Private Banks," *Thomas Jefferson Encyclopedia online*, wiki.monticello.org/mediawiki/index.php/Private_Banks_%28Quotation%29.

38. Johnson and Kwak, *op. cit.*, p. 17.

39. Quoted in *ibid.*, p. 20.

40. *Ibid.*

41. Quoted in *ibid.*, p. 28.

42. Timothy Curry and Lynn Shibut, "The Cost of the Savings and Loan Crisis: Truth and Consequences," *FDIC Banking Review*, December 2000, p. 26, www.fdic.gov/bank/analytical/banking/2000dec/brv13n2_2.pdf.

43. Quoted in Les Leopold, *The Looting of America: How Wall Street's Game of Fantasy Finance Destroyed Our Jobs, Pensions, and Prosperity* (2009), p. 68.

44. Lynn A. Stout, "The Natural Result of Deregulation," *The New York Times online blogs*, April 16, 2010.

45. *Ibid.*

46. Johnson and Kwak, *op. cit.*, p. 60.

47. For background, see Marcia Clemmitt, "Mortgage Crisis," *CQ Researcher*, Nov. 2, 2007, pp. 913-936.

48. Peter Cohan, "Big Risk: $1.2 Quadrillion Derivatives Market Dwarfs World GDP," *Daily Finance*, AOL, June 9, 2010, www.dailyfinance.com.

49. "Boehner Wants Reg Reform Repealed," *Politico*, July 15, 2010, www.politico.com/blogs/glenn-thrush/0710/Boehner_sees_Democratic_civil_war.html?showall.

50. Quoted in Herszenhorn and Wyatt, *op. cit.*

51. Pat Garofalo, "Fed and Treasury Work to Nix Collins' Amendment Mandating More Capital for Risky Banks," Think Progress blog, May 20, 2010, http://wonkroom.thinkprogress.org.

52. *Ibid.*

53. Ryan Grim, "Wall Street Reform: Progressive Dems Glimpse Victory," *Huffington Post*, May 6, 2010, www.huffingtonpost.com.

54. Shahien Nasiripour, "Dem-sponsored Loophole in Financial Reform Bill Could Hurt Seniors," *Huffington Post*, June 24, 2010, www.huffingtonpost.com.

55. Quoted in "Lawmakers Agree on Wall Street's Biggest Overhaul Since 1930s," Bloomberg/*Business Week*, June 25, 2010, www.businessweek.com.

56. Quoted in Lynn Parramore, " 'Disappointing and Inspiring': Roosevelt Fellows and Colleagues React to FinReg," *Huffington Post*, June 25, 2010, www.huffingtonpost.com.

57. For background, see "What Goldman's Conduct Reveals," *The New York Times online blogs*, April 16, 2010, http://roomfordebate.blogs.nytimes.com.

58. Marian Wang, "Goldman's SEC Settlement by the Numbers: We Do the Math," ProPublica blog, July 15, 2010, www.propublica.org.

59. *Ibid.*

60. Quoted in "Goldman 'Too Big to Prosecute,'" The Real News website, July 17, 2010, http://therealnews.com.

61. Susan Pulliam and Susanne Craig, "Goldman Talks Settlement with SEC," *The Wall Street Journal*, May 7, 2010, http://online.wsj.com/article/SB10001424052748704370704575228232487804548.html?mod=WSJ_business_LeadStoryRotator.

62. For background, see "Kaptur Introduces Legislation to Beef Up FBI Anti-fraud Efforts," press release, office of Rep. Marcy Kaptur, Nov. 3, 2009, www.kaptur.house.gov/index.php?option=com_content&task=view&id=502&Itemid=86.

63. Jesse Westbrook and Otis Bilodeau, "Regulatory Overhaul Won't Stop Next Crisis, Say Levitt, Breeden," Bloomberg, June 16, 2010, www.bloomberg.com.

64. Quoted in "Will President Obama Appoint Elizabeth Warren to Head the Consumer Financial Protection Bureau," ABC News Political Punch blog, July 20, 2010, http://blogs.abcnews.com.

65. For background, see Marcia Clemmitt, "Gridlock in Washington," *CQ Researcher*, April 30, 2010, pp. 385-408.

66. Quoted in Brian Beutler, "Signs Point to Tough Haul for a Potential Elizabeth Warren Nomination," *Talking Points Memo blog*, July 21, 2010, http://tpmdc.talkingpointsmemo.com.

67. Quoted in Eric Dash, "Fed Finding Status Quo in Bank Pay," *The New York Times*, June 8, 2010, p. B1.

68. Nomi Prins, "Speculating Banks Still Rule — Ten Ways Dems and Dodd Are Failing on Financial Reform," AlterNet website, April 14, 2010, www.alternet.org.

69. Quoted in "Regulating the Unknown: Can Financial Reform Prevent Another Crisis," *Knowledge at Wharton newsletter*, June 9, 2010, http://knowledge.wharton.upenn.edu.

70. Quoted in "Banking Reform Proposals: Why They Miss the Mark," *Knowledge at Wharton newsletter*, Feb. 17, 2010, http://knowledge.wharton.upenn.edu.

71. Edward L. Yingling, press statement, American Bankers Association, June 25, 2010, www.aba.com.

BIBLIOGRAPHY

Books

Black, William K., *The Best Way to Rob a Bank Is to Own One: How Corporate Executives and Politicians Looted the S&L Industry, University of Texas Press,* **2005.**
An associate professor of economics and law at the University of Missouri-Kansas City and former bank regulator describes how savings and loan executives, abetted by many government regulators and lawmakers, committed accounting fraud and looted their banks.

Johnson, Simon, and James Kwak, *13 Bankers: The Wall Street Takeover and the Next Financial Meltdown, Random House,* **2010.**
Johnson, a professor of entrepreneurship at the Massachusetts Institute of Technology and former International Monetary Fund chief economist, and business journalist Kwak argue that banks have repeatedly fought the U.S. government for political power and generally won the battle.

Ritholtz, Barry, Bill Fleckenstein and Aaron Task, *Bailout Nation: How Greed and Easy Money Corrupted Wall Street and Shook the World Economy,* **Wiley, 2009.**
Money manager Ritholtz, hedge fund manager Fleckenstein and business reporter Task trace the history of U.S. business bailouts, arguing that financial firms' political power has gradually allowed corporations to police themselves in economic booms and rely on docile government bailouts when times are bad.

Woods, Thomas E., Jr., *Meltdown: A Free-Market Look at Why the Stock Market Collapsed, the Economy Tanked, and Government Bailouts Will Make Things Worse, Regnery Press,* **2009.**
A senior fellow at the libertarian Mises Institute argues that Federal Reserve attempts to manage the money supply are a root cause of financial collapses.

Articles

Dorgan, Byron L., "Very Risky Business: Derivatives," *Washington Monthly,* **October 1994, http://findarticles.com/p/articles/mi_m1316/is_n10_v26/ai_15818783/?tag=content;col1, p. 7.**
In the early years of the now gigantic derivatives-trading market, a U.S. senator discusses his qualms about the complex investments in light of the recent S&L collapse.

Lavin, Timothy, "Monsters in the Market," The Atlantic, July/August *2010,* **www.theatlantic.com/magazine/archive/2010/07/monsters-in-the-market/8122.**
The Securities and Exchange Commission is trying to monitor how computer-driven high-frequency trading at ever faster speeds affects financial markets.

Ornstein, Charles, and Tracy Weber, "Texas Mortgage Firm Survives and Thrives Despite Repeat Sanctions," Pro Publica web site, *July 2, 2010,* **www.propublica.org.**
Despite piles of customer complaints, a mortgage company escapes regulatory consequences.

Philips, Matthew, "Fast, Loose, and Out of Control," *Newsweek, June 1, 2010,* **www.newsweek.com/2010/06/01/fast-loose-and-out-of-control.html, p. 42.**
Is new ultra-fast stock-trading technology a boon or a bane to financial markets?

Roubini, Nouriel, and Stephen Mihm, "Bust Up the Banks," *Newsweek,* **May 17, 2010, p. 42.**
Roubini, a New York University professor of business, and Mihm, a University of Georgia history professor, argue that the biggest banks are too big to be properly managed and should be broken up.

Taibbi, Matt, "The Great American Bubble Machine," *Rolling Stone online*, April 5, 2010, www.rollingstone.com/politics/news/12697/64796.
A business reporter argues that the growing number of Goldman Sachs' veterans serving as government officials in both parties has given the bank unfair opportunities to manipulate financial markets and public policy.

"What Goldman's Conduct Reveals," *The New York Times blogs*, April 16, 2010, http://roomfordebate.blogs.nytimes.com/2010/04/16/what-goldmans-conduct-reveals.
Experts representing numerous points of view on financial-industry practices comment on the meaning and probable outcome of the Securities and Exchange Commission's April civil lawsuit filed against investment bank Goldman Sachs.

Reports and Studies

Gokhale, Jagadeesh, "Financial Crisis and Public Policy," *Cato Institute*, March 23, 2009, www.cato.org/pubs/pas/pa634.pdf.
A senior fellow at a libertarian think tank argues that government policies encouraging home ownership — including loose regulation of risky mortgage lending — were the real root of the financial crash.

Miller, Rena S., "Key Issues in Derivatives Reform," *Congressional Research Service*, Dec. 1, 2009, www.fas.org/sgp/crs/misc/R40965.pdf.
An analyst at Congress' nonpartisan research office describes how derivatives work and what regulatory safeguards have been proposed to guard against their risks.

For More Information

Cato Institute, 1000 Massachusetts Ave., N.W., Washington DC 20001-5403; (202) 842-0200; www.cato.org. Libertarian think tank analyzes financial-reform and other public policies.

Center for American Progress, 1333 H St., N.W., 10th Floor, Washington DC 20005; (202) 682-1611; www.americanprogress.org. Progressive policy analysis and advocacy group on issues including banking reform and the economy.

Center for Capital Markets Competitiveness, U.S. Chamber of Commerce, 1615 H St., N.W., Washington, DC 20062; (202) 463-3162; www.uschamber.com. Business group opposed to tightening regulation of financial industry offers information and commentary.

Congressional Oversight Panel, 732 North Capitol St., N.W., Rooms C-320 and C-617, Washington, DC 20401; (202) 224-9925; http://cop.senate.gov/index.cfm. Web site of the congressionally appointed panel overseeing the TARP bailout program includes testimony and reports on how the TARP bailout of firms like insurer AIG is affecting financial markets and the economy.

Financial Crisis Inquiry Commission, 1717 Pennsylvania Ave., N.W., Suite 800, Washington, DC 20006-4614; (202) 292-2799; www.fcic.gov. Web site of the government-appointed panel researching causes of the 2008 financial-market crash includes reports on how financial markets operate.

Pew Financial Reform Project, 901 E St., N.W., Washington, DC 20004-2008; (202) 552-2000; www.pewfr.org. Foundation-funded group provides nonpartisan analysis of financial reform and the 2008 financial crisis.

Roosevelt Institute, 570 Lexington Ave., 18th Floor, New York, NY 10022; (212) 444-9130; www.rooseveltinstitute.org. Nonprofit group studies and promotes policies related to the progressive legacy of President Franklin D. Roosevelt and first lady Eleanor Roosevelt.

Zero Hedge blog, www.zerohedge.com. Financial analysts blog on market and economic news.

4

Jobs Outlook

Peter Katel

Solar electric panels are installed on a home in Santa Monica, Calif., last year. The Obama administration is emphasizing "green" jobs as a major field of new employment, but Republicans, and some Democrats, remain skeptical. "In areas like advanced manufacturing of wind turbines and solar turbines, for instance, we can help turn good ideas into private-sector jobs," the president said in December. The economic recovery package passed last year includes $500 million for green job training.

From *CQ Researcher*,
June 4, 2010

S tatistically — and in the eyes of many of her friends — 22-year-old Alyssa Jung is to be envied: She landed a job right out of college. But Jung doesn't consider herself particularly blessed, even in today's desolate job market.

"Honestly, I can't say that I have my life on track right now, despite having a job," says Jung, who graduated last year from the State University of New York at New Paltz. "I never thought that when I graduated high school I would end up working in the same place where I grew up. I can come home and my mom has dinner ready."

Yet many would call Jung lucky, despite the fact that she can't afford her own apartment and must live at home. After all, she got a job in journalism, a field that's reeling from its own economic shock even as the entire country tries to fight its way out of a recession that has cost more than 8 million jobs in the past two years. Among the unemployed, 46 percent have been jobless for six months or more — a post-World War II record.[1]

Jung had big aspirations when she began job hunting, contacting big-city media in Atlanta, New York and Washington. "When I heard back, they said there were already many experienced journalists in the market who were more attractive even for entry-level positions." So she set her sights lower. At the end of her five-month search, Jung got a job reporting for *Spotlight*, a suburban weekly in her hometown of Albany, N.Y. She won't say what she's making.

The American workforce — 154 million strong — is going through hard times.[2] At the end of May an average of 5.5 unemployed workers were competing for each job opening of any kind.[3]

Even with 290,000 jobs added to the economy in April — the biggest increase in four years — the monthly unemployment rate

Female Workers Benefit More From Education

At every educational level women's earnings have risen significantly more than men's since 1979. Female college graduates are earning nearly 30 percent more than in 1979, while earnings for men at the same educational level rose only 10 percent.

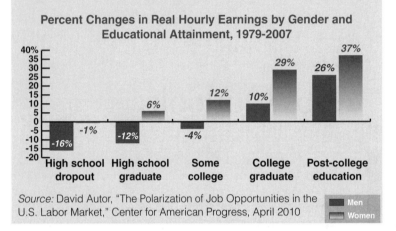

Percent Changes in Real Hourly Earnings by Gender and Educational Attainment, 1979-2007

Source: David Autor, "The Polarization of Job Opportunities in the U.S. Labor Market," Center for American Progress, April 2010

Men
Women

Republicans also tend toward skepticism about the administration's emphasis on "green" jobs as a major field of new employment. Some Democrats are also dubious. But expectations that the health care sector will keep expanding as the population ages run across political lines. "I have been involved in discussions about how do we train enough health care workers for what is an expanding sector and will continue to be an expanding sector, given demographics," Assistant Treasury Secretary Alan B. Krueger told Congress' Joint Economic Committee in early May.[7]

Views divide over how the future prospects of another existing — and troubling — trend: the exportation of jobs that can be performed remotely from abroad. Even highly skilled tasks — university teaching, for instance — could be "offshored," some argue.

ticked up from 9.7 percent to 9.9 percent. The reason, experts said, was that people who had abandoned job hunting were back in the market. A return to economic growth since the third quarter of 2009 encouraged hopes of finally finding work.[4]

The Obama administration has been doing its part to build optimism. "Despite all the naysayers in Washington, who are always looking for the cloud in every silver lining, the fact is our economy is growing again," President Obama told workers in May at a pipe-making plant in Youngstown, Ohio. Its workforce is growing thanks to infrastructure projects financed by the 2009 Recovery Act — the $787 billion "stimulus" — which will benefit the factory.[5]

Republicans insist the White House is hiding failure behind a scattering of good-news anecdotes. "The fact that the president has come to cheerlead the 'stimulus' in a city where unemployment is 15.1 percent demonstrates just how out of touch Washington Democrats are with the harsh realities many communities are facing today," House Republican Leader John A. Boehner of Ohio said. "During this time of hardship, the last thing the people of the Mahoning Valley need is more of the president's job-killing agenda that is only making matters worse."[6]

Whatever the accuracy of that prediction, debates over uncertain future developments may not grab the attention of people caught up in the jobs crisis. The pool of even traditionally recession-proof jobs, such as teaching, is drying up as state and local governments deal with revenue shortfalls by slashing budgets. Nationwide, as many as 300,000 teachers may be laid off next year. The Port Washington school district on Long Island's affluent North Shore has received 3,620 applications for eight slots.[8]

At colleges and universities, job-placement counselors are warning students to keep their grades up and start their job hunts early. "Hiring still remains competitive, and companies selectively look for top-tier talent," says Jim Henderson, an associate director of career services at Virginia Tech. "This tends to include a high GPA cutoff, and a big segment of the student body finds this challenging."

For all of the job-market hardships that college graduates face, as a group they are among the most fortunate members of the labor force, whether they're employed or still hunting.

The college-attendance rate is declining, so higher-education credentials command a premium. And college graduates' earnings have been increasing steadily for the past 25 years, while the pay of those with lesser educational credentials has been declining. Money aside, "College-educated workers have more stable employment," MIT economist David Autor told a jobs conference organized in April by the Brookings Institution's Hamilton Project and the Center for American Progress. "They spend less time unemployed. They have more fringe benefits. They have safer working conditions."[9]

Women in the United States have gotten the message and are becoming "the educated sex," Autor said, while men aren't keeping up.[10]

Demand for well-educated workers makes up part of what Autor calls a "polarized" job market in the United States: the simultaneous growth of jobs at the two ends of the wage spectrum: high-wage, high-skill jobs and low-wage, low-education jobs. But middle-education, middle-skill, middle-wage jobs are suffering.[11]

Some conference panelists argued that today's joblessness crisis overlays several worrisome trends that have been developing for decades as economies worldwide cope with economic and technological transformation.

"Forty years ago, one in 20 men [ages] 25 to 54 was not working at a given point in time," Lawrence H. Summers, director of the White House National Economic Council, said. "Today the number is one in five. And a good guess, based on extrapolating the trends in this area, is that when the economy recovers five years from now . . . one in six men, 25 to 54, will not be working at any point in time."[12]

Automation has eliminated several categories of jobs, and others have been exported to countries with lower labor costs, Summers said. "For the long run, long after this recession, finding ways of developing the skills and potential of all Americans — not just the majority who are working — becomes a critical priority," he argued.[13]

Those conservative economists who are speaking openly about job-market trends largely agree that technology and globalization explain the changes under way. But they disagree with Summers and others who argue for government investment in activities that stimulate employment.

Government, these conservatives argue, should lessen — rather than step up — its presence in the market. "Congress should say, 'This is an emergency, we're going to freeze tax rates,' " Diana Furchtgott-Roth, director of the Center for Employment Policy at the Hudson Institute, a conservative think tank, told Congress' Joint Economic Committee in late April. "And we're going to let the minimum wage go down to $5.15 an hour so that low-skilled workers can get their foot on the first rung of the career ladder . . . we are going to focus on basically measures that help employers to create jobs."[14]

Still, Furchtgott-Roth, the chief Labor Department economist in the George W. Bush administration, and other conservatives favor expanding community colleges and improving public schools — also types of public investment — with a view to bettering employment options for those not college-bound.

Meanwhile, the Great Recession could cut into the advantage that college and university graduates enjoy. "Graduating from college in a bad economy has a long-run, negative impact on wages" of as much as 7 percent for each percentage point increase in the unemployment rate immediately following graduation, economist Lisa B. Kahn of Yale University concluded after studying data from the 1981-82 recession.[15]

Laura Vanderkam, a New York-based writer who specializes in career issues, takes a rosier view, based on her confidence in the dynamism of the U.S. economy, including the freedom employers have to lay off and rehire. "The U.S. unemployment rate hit 10.8 percent in 1982," Vanderkam wrote in *City Journal*, published by the conservative Manhattan Institute. "At the time, one might have thought that people born in 1960 would become a lost generation. But today's 50-year-olds don't appear lost in their careers."[16]

Some labor economists do worry that workers in that age bracket who find themselves jobless and with skills not in demand might give up the work world entirely, while newcomers are more open to the possibility of jumping into new careers.

Back in Albany, Jung is determined to stay in journalism, even after a long job hunt that ultimately didn't take her where she wanted to go. But her ambitions remain undimmed. "I do plan on moving to a larger city than Albany," she says. "I feel like I'm at the point of my life where I need to explore what's out there and what I'm capable of."

College Graduations Increased Sharply

The percentage of young adults with college degrees rose significantly among all races and both genders — more than tripling in the case of black females and nearly tripling for white females. White males, who posted one of the highest graduation percentages in 1970, had the lowest growth rate and in 2008 one of the lowest graduation percentages. The increases have saturated the job market with far more educated candidates than before.

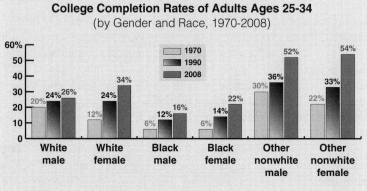

College Completion Rates of Adults Ages 25-34
(by Gender and Race, 1970-2008)

Source: David Autor, "The Polarization of Job Opportunities in the U.S. Labor Market," Center for American Progress, April 2010

As Americans of all ages hunt for jobs, here are some of the questions they are asking:

Is the job market most dynamic only at the high and low ends of the scale?

Highly trained and well-educated workers fare extraordinarily well in the U.S. economy — far better than those who didn't go to college.

In March, N. Gregory Mankiw, a politically conservative economist at Harvard, discussed the gap in a paper on wealth distribution. "In 1980, each year of college raised a person's wage by 7.6 percent. In 2005, each year of college yielded an additional 12.9 percent," Mankiw wrote. "Over this time period, the rate of return from each year of graduate school has risen even more — from 7.3 to 14.2 percent."[17]

Mankiw points to evidence that supply and demand play a role. The share of the working population with college and postgraduate degrees has dropped in recent decades. Members of that group benefit from their relative scarcity in the form of higher pay.[18]

Liberal economist Autor of MIT found similar results after tracking the wage-education divide over a longer period of time. In 1963, he reported, a college graduate earned about 1.5 times more per hour than a high school graduate. By last year, a college graduate's earnings had increased by 45 percentage points.[19]

Postgraduate studies are even more richly rewarded, Autor found. Real wages for men with bachelor's degrees rose by 10 percent from 1979 to 2007 — but by 26 percent for those with master's and doctoral degrees.[20]

The consensus over the practical value of higher education breaks down over another conclusion that Autor has been exploring. "The shape of employment opportunities is shifting toward the extremes — toward high-wage, high-skill, and low-wage, low-skill — at the expense of the middle," he said.

Many low-skill jobs can't be shifted abroad, Autor noted, citing house cleaners and medical assistants. But — throughout the industrialized world — vast improvements in information technology have eliminated whole categories of jobs in the middle that Autor calls "repetitive information-processing and manual tasks: sorting, copying, filing, typing" as well as equivalent jobs on factory production lines. "It's estimated that the price of information technology has fallen 2 trillion-fold in the last 50 years," Autor told the jobs conference. "If you're a worker who's doing something that computers potentially do and the price of that computing power falls 2 trillion-fold, that's not necessarily good for your earnings power."

Furchtgott-Roth at the Center for Employment Policy accepts the evidence of higher rewards for higher education. But she argues that the new health care law will ratchet up unemployment, especially in the fast-food and retail sectors because requirements that businesses provide health coverage or pay fines will force payroll cuts. "I don't see polarization, I see a decline in the number of jobs at the low-skill end," she says.

"There are a number of very large enterprises with a large number of minimum-wage workers that don't provide health insurance," says Furchtgott-Roth. "It will be difficult for them to raise their prices" to cover the costs of coverage or of fines, she argues.

But Chad Stone, chief economist at the liberal Center on Budget and Policy Priorities, says that new health care requirements aren't weighty enough to alter the polarized job-market landscape. Businesses can pay the higher costs by combining slightly higher prices with reductions in profitability while holding down wage increases, he says. "The shareholders absorb part of it, the customers absorb part of it, the workers absorb part of it," he says. "It's not going to drastically shrink the low-wage workforce."

But, Stone argues, the magnitude of the low-end sector poses a deep challenge that may well persist even after the economy recovers. "Are we going to have shared benefits of economic expansion," he asks, "or are we going to have real winners and real losers?"

Russell Roberts, a conservative economist of libertarian bent at George Mason University in Fairfax, Va., agrees that times of economic transformation create hardships for workers in some industries. But he argues that the vision of a polarized labor market leads too easily to an argument for protecting medium-skilled industries from change. "People say we've got to bring back manufacturing," he says. "That's like saying that if you knew how to shoe a horse 100 years ago you had a good job. We don't want to preserve the jobs of 100 years ago."

Top Jobs for Men and Women Differ Markedly

Lists of top jobs for men and women tend to confirm gender stereotypes about who does what. The most common occupations for women are secretaries and administrative assistants, nurses and teachers. Men most commonly work as drivers, managers and retail supervisors. The lists also confirms that men and women continue to work in gender segregated workplaces: Only four occupations (shown in boldface) appear on the lists for both women and men.

Top 20 Occupations for Women and Men, 2008

WOMEN		MEN	
Occupation	Share of female workers (in millions)	Occupation	Share of male workers (in millions)
Secretaries and administrative assistants	4.7	Driver/sales workers and truck drivers	4.1
Registered nurses	3.8	**All other managers**	**2.9**
Elementary and middle-school teachers	3.7	**First-line supervisors/ managers of retail stores**	**2.6**
Cashiers	3.0	Construction laborers	2.1
Retail salespersons	**2.5**	Carpenters	2.1
Nursing, psychiatric, and home health aides	2.5	**Retail salespersons**	**2.0**
First-line supervisors/ managers of retail stores	**2.3**	Laborers and freight, stock, and material movers	2.0
Waiters and waitresses	2.1	Janitors and building cleaners	1.8
Bookkeeping, accounting, and auditing clerks	1.9	Chief executives	1.6
Receptionists and information clerks	1.9	**Cooks**	**1.5**
All other managers	**1.9**	Grounds maintenance workers	1.5
Customer service representatives	1.9	Construction managers	1.5
Maids and housekeeping cleaners	1.9	Sales representatives, wholesale and manufacturing	1.3
Child care workers	1.8	First-line supervisors/ managers of non-retail sales workers	1.2
First-line supervisors/ managers of office and administrative support workers	1.8	Stock clerks and order fillers	1.2
Accountants and auditors	1.6	Electricians	1.1
Office clerks, general	1.5	Automotive service technicians and mechanics	1.1
Teacher assistants	1.4	First-line supervisors/ managers of construction trades and extraction workers	1.1
Cooks	**1.1**	Computer software engineers	1.1
Personal and home care aides	1.1	First-line supervisors/ managers of production and operating workers	1.0
Share employed in top 20 occupations	**44.4 million**	**Share employed in top 20 occupations**	**34.8 million**

Source: Maria Shriver, "A Woman's Nation Changes Everything," Center for American Progress, October 2009

Nevertheless, Roberts and other conservatives do agree with liberal economists that the limited prospects for high school graduates amount to a case for deep educational reform.[21] "I'd like to see us make better high schools," Roberts says. "They're part of the reason that people with only high school educations don't do well."

Does offshoring present a major threat to U.S. jobs?

The Great Recession forced policymakers and experts to confront a series of urgent problems in the labor market — mainly, how to stem the tide of job loss. Issues of less immediate concern were pushed to the back burner.

But this year, with indications that an economic recovery has slowly begun, arguments have restarted over some longer-term trends, including foreign competition for American jobs. That problem isn't new, but some economists argue that foreign competition will reach far more widely into the job market than most people had imagined.[22]

Factories have been closing in the United States and opening in Mexico and Asia for decades. But continuing advances in communications technology may enable jobs once thought of as securely tied to the United States to be moved abroad — "offshored." In other words, the advances that have marked the U.S. and global economies for the past two decades come with risks as well as benefits for skilled, white-collar workers who never imagined that their work could be performed at long distance.

Alan S. Blinder, a Princeton University economist who launched the thesis in 2006, argues that only high-level managerial jobs and those that depend entirely on direct physical contact — carpentry, for instance — are entirely safe from the possibility that they could be replaced by offshoring. Even an American university professor could be displaced by an Asian academic who lectures to students via hologram, Blinder speculates.

Given the pace of ongoing technological developments, he has written, offshoring has barely gotten off the ground. In fact, it could launch another industrial revolution, he argues, exposing as many as 40 million U.S. jobs to direct foreign competition.[23] "I've had any number of people write or e-mail or talk to me to say that I'm understating the potential for offshoring," Blinder says. "I've had hardly any fan mail in the opposite direction." One of those commentators was a civil engineer who wrote

that he and his colleagues never visit construction sites any more but work from digital photos — which could be examined by a civil engineer on another continent.

Offshoring of jobs that extend far beyond the factory floor has been taking place quietly for some time. Blinder himself says that for the 11th edition of a textbook he authored, he's working with layout people in India.

Nevertheless, other labor experts argue that Blinder may be overstating the trend's potential. "I suspect he's undervaluing the importance of proximity," says Autor of MIT. "You could have told the story 20 years ago that with the rise of the Internet we wouldn't have cities any more, but just the opposite has occurred. Why do people pay very high amounts to live in very crowded cities? Clearly, there must be something that causes people to need to be together even with abundant communications technology that seems to make that unnecessary."

So far, Autor argues, jobs that have been offshored are those that don't require any direct personal contact, such as routine computer programming, and technical support delivered by phone. "Not everything can be deconstructed and done in a million places and nobody loses anything," he says "Certain jobs seem to demand close physical proximity."

But Ron Blackwell, chief economist of the AFL-CIO, says the expansion of offshoring over the past several decades supports Blinder's argument that job exporting is likely to expand, especially given the present state of the global economy. "The crisis has motivated firms to rethink their competitive strategies because of the pressure on profits," he says. "You can build state-of-the-art plants in many industries in any country."

Blackwell also suggests that the "jobless recovery" trend that first appeared following the 1990-91 recession resulted from exporting manufacturing jobs and what he calls its boost to profitability at the price of U.S. jobs. "Technological change interacts with global competition," at U.S. workers' expense, he says.

Roberts of George Mason University argues that global trade creates as many jobs as it destroys. And even if U.S. companies didn't open factories in countries with lower labor costs, production-line jobs would still be drying up in the United States. "We've gotten better at manufacturing stuff," he says. "You don't need a lot of folks any more to make a car."

The U.S. economy has weathered transformations at least as massive as offshoring, Roberts argues. He takes a view that's common among economists of varying political inclinations, who note that farm work now occupies fewer than 2 percent of the labor force. "In 1900, 40 percent of the American people worked on farms," he says. " 'What are they going to do?' you would have asked. You'd say that there would be rioting in the streets."

Do "green" jobs represent an important potential source of new employment?

President Obama's campaign vow to stimulate the creation of green jobs fired the hopes of employment-seekers and the imaginations of politicians, environmental-protection activists and entrepreneurs. One year into his term, Obama is maintaining the strategy. "In areas like advanced manufacturing of wind turbines and solar turbines, for instance, we can help turn good ideas into private-sector jobs," the president said last December at the Brookings Institution, a think tank filled with former and future government officials of both parties.[24]

"Green jobs" is a term that's elastic enough to include many kinds of work. Still, the description is more than a catch-phrase, some experts say. A detailed study last year by the Pew Charitable Trusts concluded that the "green energy economy" includes clean energy production and transmission, energy efficiency, environmentally friendly production in any field, conservation and pollution mitigation, and training and support.[25]

Seen in that light, green jobs aren't a new phenomenon. A follow-up Pew study this year calculated that from 1998 to 2007, the last year for which data are available, a total of 770,000 jobs had been created in what Pew researchers define as the clean energy economy.

To be sure, that number is a drop in the very large bucket of the U.S. economy, even in its present state. The

Fastest-Growing Jobs Call for Limited Education

On-the-job training rather than a four-year college degree is needed in all but two of the 15 occupations expected to have the most new jobs by 2016. Women have at least a two-thirds share of 11 of the occupations.

Occupations with Largest Projected New Jobs, 2006-2016

Occupation	Number employed (in thousands)	Salary level	Main post-secondary education or training	Percentage that is female, 2008
Registered nurses	587	VH	Associate's degree	91.7%
Retail salespersons	557	VL	Short-term on-the-job training	51.8
Customer service representatives	545	L	Moderate-term on-the-job training	68.2
Combined food preparation and serving workers, including fast food	452	VL	Short-term on-the-job training	69.8
Office clerks, general	404	L	Short-term on-the-job training	85.7
Personal and home care aides	389	VL	Short-term on-the-job training	84.1
Home health aides	384	VL	Short-term on-the-job training	88.2
Postsecondary teachers	382	VH	Doctoral degree	48.0
Janitors and cleaners, except maids and housekeeping cleaners	345	VL	Short-term on-the-job training	31.9
Nursing aides, orderlies, and attendants	264	L	Postsecondary vocational award	88.2
Bookkeeping, accounting, and auditing clerks	264	L	Moderate-term on-the-job training	92.1
Waiters and waitresses	255	VL	Short-term on-the-job training	73.0
Child care workers	248	VL	Short-term on-the-job training	95.5
Executive secretaries and administrative assistants	239	H	Work experience in a related occupation	96.3
Computer software engineers, applications	226	VH	Bachelor's degree	21.2

Source: Maria Shriver, "A Woman's Nation Changes Everything," Center for American Progress, October 2009

Salary Levels:	
Very high	$46,360 or more
High	$30,630-$46,300
Low	$21,260-$30,560
Very low	Up to $21,220

manufacturing sector, for instance, still employs 11.6 million people even after decades marked by a massive shift of factory production to Asian countries.[26]

"Clean tech is where [information technology] was 30 years ago and biotech was 20 years ago; we're way early in the innovation cycle," David Prend, managing partner of RockPort Capital and director of the National Venture Capital Association, told Pew.[27]

But even some economists with Obama administration ties express skepticism about green jobs as a major employment source, at least in the foreseeable future.

"Ultimately, having lots and lots of green jobs would rest on a fundamental change in our energy system," says Michael Greenstone, director of the Brookings Institution's Hamilton Project on the economy, and a former chief economist for the White House Council of Economic Advisers. "And I think that is unlikely to occur without legislation that makes emitting carbon and other greenhouse gases expensive."

Greenstone acknowledges that skepticism can sound discordant in the present economic climate. "We all want to be able to point to an industry that is going to be able to employ everyone at high wages," he says. "The truth is that it's very difficult to make those predictions."

Nevertheless, Maria Flynn, a vice president at Jobs for the Future (JFF), a Boston-based nonprofit that develops and promotes job-training and education programs nationwide, argues that a number of "green jobs" have immediate practical application in many big cities. "Neighborhoods of these cities have very high poverty rates, and are developing career pathways for people who may start out in jobs like weatherization," Flynn says. Weatherization fits in the green-job category because it is a form of energy conservation.

Flynn acknowledges that all training programs present the constant problem of ensuring that jobs are available for the newly trained. JFF isn't "training folks for training's sake," she says.

Weatherization jobs in poor neighborhoods largely exist thanks to U.S. Energy Department government grants, which have financed insulation repair and installation in 6.4 million homes over the past 33 years, the department says.[28] Conservative economists point to dependence on government funds throughout the clean-energy field as a basic flaw. Here, in a nutshell, is George Mason University economist Roberts' description of a green-jobs strategy: "We should make windmills because windmills are clean, so there needs to be windmill manufacturing in the United States."

In fact, Roberts argues, "If they are a good idea, we should make them where it's cheaper to make them," even if that means a lower-cost manufacturing country such as China. "To create green jobs because green is good is a bizarre concept to an economist."

But Blackwell of the AFL-CIO argues that a major set of green jobs can also be defined as public-works projects. He and others have been advocating major new government investment in public works not only as sources of employment but as vital upgrades or replacement of roads, bridges and other infrastructure that is widely reported to be strained or outmoded, with consequences for the private sector as well as individuals. "If we're going to spend in building infrastructure and increasing the productivity of the infrastructure that we have," Blackwell says, "let's do that so that they use clean energy."[29]

Meanwhile, the infrastructure-building and rebuilding jobs would provide the basis for training and retraining programs that serve as a pipeline to real jobs. "We can't afford to have workers work at jobs that demand less than they're able to do," he says. "In the U.S. if you lose your job, the object is to get you the next job ASAP whether as a greeter at Wal-Mart or whatever. That is not worthy of a real human resources policy."

BACKGROUND
Economic Transformation

The U.S. economy began a transformation in the 1970s that is still under way.

In the country that had been the world's leading maker of cars, airplanes and machinery, the role of manufacturing had diminished. Services — or all activities that don't involve producing things — expanded.

In 1959, 40 percent of all jobs were in the "goods producing" sector, which includes manufacturing along with mining and construction. By 1980, that sector accounted for 30 percent of employment. Today, 14.2 percent of workers produce goods. Meanwhile, the service sector, which accounted for 60 percent of jobs in 1959, accounted for 70 percent by 1980 (farming provided the remainder). Presently, service employees make up 77 percent of the work force.[30]

The scale and pace of change gave rise to an intense debate — one still echoing today — over the future of the U.S. economy and, ultimately, American society.

Then as now, that debate began to unfold in the early 1980s against the backdrop of a severe recession that cost millions of workers their jobs and prompted widespread doubts and fears about the country's economic future. By September 1982, the unemployment rate had hit 10 percent for the first time since 1941. Approximately 12 million people were jobless — an increase of 4.2 million since mid-1981. The black community was especially hard-hit, because about one-third of black men in their 20s were employed in manufacturing. By 1987, their share of the manufacturing workforce had fallen to 20 percent. Overall, joblessness hit hardest in manufacturing, which accounted for 90 percent of job losses in 1982.[31]

In that year, two left-wing economists, Barry Bluestone, now the director of Northeastern University's Kitty and Michael Dukakis Center for Urban & Regional Policy, and Bennett Harrison of the Massachusetts Institute of Technology, helped frame the argument. "Capital . . . has been diverted from productive investment in our basic national industries into unproductive speculation, mergers and acquisitions and foreign investment," they wrote in a widely discussed book. "Left behind are shuttered factories, displaced workers and a newly emerging group of ghost towns."[32]

Bluestone and Harrison proposed an "industrial policy." Companies would be required to prove a legitimate need to close factories; the government would hold minority or majority stakes in manufacturing companies, and thereby have a say — or the final word — on when and how companies could relocate, how much they would charge and what forms of automation they would use.[33]

Robert Reich, then a Harvard professor of public policy who later became President Clinton's labor secretary, advocated a softer version of "industrial policy" that would enable the government to shape the country's economic future in cooperation with big business and unions. "The American business community is beginning to understand that it desperately needs the government's aid in helping it adjust to the new demands of the world market," Reich wrote in 1982.[34]

Despite the demoralizing effects of the recession, the industrial policy advocates were making their argument at the wrong political moment. President Ronald Reagan, who

had taken office in 1981, was determined to lessen — not strengthen — government regulation. "Industries that innovate and utilize the latest technology to respond to market competition . . . grow rapidly without political assistance," wrote economist Dwight R. Lee of George Mason University in 1983 for the Heritage Foundation, which had been founded 10 years earlier to advocate the doctrines that Reagan's administration represented.[35]

Meanwhile, by the end of the 1980s the economy had registered what was then a record peacetime expansion. The unemployment rate plunged from 8.3 percent in 1983 to 5.4 percent in 1989.[36]

Economic growth accelerated economic transformation. By the end of the decade, the service sector accounted for 75 percent of all jobs. Business services were the most dynamic of all, adding 2.9 million jobs, as companies started contracting for work that they previously had done in-house, including advertising, public relations and building management. Health services grew as well, adding 2.6 million workers.[37]

Bust and Boom

But the good times didn't last for everyone. The 1990s opened with a new recession. This time, white-collar workers as well as their blue-collar counterparts felt the pain — a marked contrast from the 1980s, and from earlier economic slowdowns. White-collar employees accounted for 34 percent of the increase in unemployment in 1990-91, and blue-collar workers for 43 percent. But in past recessions more than half of increases in joblessness came from the blue-collar sector, and 20 percent from the white-collar workforce.[38]

"Unlike the early '80s, we're seeing accountants, engineers, lawyers, financial types, people from all across the spectrum," Charles Albrecht, executive vice president at Drake Beam Morin, a job-search firm, told *The New York Times* in 1992.[39]

Technology played a major role in the trend. Growing use of computers throughout the business world made many clerical jobs redundant, while thinning the ranks of mid-level workers. In addition, manufacturing was increasingly moving to China and other low-wage countries.

Even the return of economic growth in March 1991, didn't spark major increases in employment, which had been typical of post-recession periods in the past. "Jobless recovery" entered the national vocabulary. By April 1993 the unemployment rate remained at a high 7 percent for the third straight month.[40]

Tellingly, businesses that did gain workers included temporary-help agencies. Companies in growing numbers were turning to "temps," who were registered in federal unemployment statistics as hired by these agencies, not by the companies that used their services for short periods of time. The trend stayed in place well past the early '90s. "Firms are demanding more temporary help in part due to increased competition; rising costs of hiring, firing, and providing benefits to relatively permanent workers, and a sufficiently low fee charged by temporary-help firms," two staff members of the Federal Reserve Bank of Kansas City wrote in 2003. By then, more than 3 million jobs were filled by temporary workers.[41]

Politically, the jobless early phase of the 1991 recovery played a major role in the defeat of incumbent President George H. W. Bush by then-Arkansas Gov. Bill Clinton in 1992. The last unemployment report before the election showed joblessness at 7.5 percent, with 25,000 fewer jobs in the private sector than when Bush had taken office in 1989.[42]

With Clinton in office, the country suffered the last period of the jobless recovery before enjoying an economic boom that took off in 1995. Enormous strides in technology, marked by the migration of retail and business functions to the Web, helped propel the economic expansion, whose ripple effects reached throughout the economy. Employment shot upward.

Aerospace companies, for instance, which had been decimated by the end of the Cold War, were recruiting engineers to work on rockets and communications satellites. As global telecommunications surged, the number of satellites bouncing voice and data signals between distant locations rose from 27 in 1994 to 200 in 1998.[43]

Software companies and Web-based startups — "dot-coms" — that sprang up to exploit the seemingly limitless possibilities of the Web launched intensive searches for anyone who could write computer code. Demand was so intense that the Clinton administration authorized $28 million for programs to stimulate training in computer programming, including one aimed at laid-off workers looking to switch careers.[44]

And middle managers who'd been laid off in the 1990s found employers eager for their services. "Even the *Fortune* 1000 firms are looking for these people,"

John Challenger of Challenger, Gray & Christmas, a Chicago-based recruiting firm, told *USA Today* in 1998. "A lot of the big companies want them back."[45]

By early 1999, the joblessness rate was at 4.4 percent. That rate in practical terms means full employment, economists say, because that relatively low percentage reflects "frictional" joblessness resulting from people changing jobs or careers for reasons not related to economic slumps. However, the job scene was still marked by the transformation of the '90s. Employers felt relatively little pressure to raise workers' pay because of the availability of a large pool of "temps." And the manufacturing sector continued weakening, with 50,000 jobs lost in early 1999.[46]

Bursting Bubbles

The technology-fueled boom of the 1990s was reflected — and fueled even further — on Wall Street. There, enthusiasm for technology startups fueled a bubble of rising stock prices. It burst in 2000, and the Sept. 11 terrorist attacks the following year triggered a recession that intensified the job-market effects of the dot-com bust.

Even before the attacks, tech firms responded to the crash by slashing their payrolls. On one day alone in July 2001, a total of 31,000 tech firm workers were laid off (not all in the United States). Some were firms that had been supplying communications hardware to dot-com startups whose value collapsed when tech stock prices plunged.[47]

But even before that, some analysts had been warning that the dot-com bubble was diverting attention from long-term problems in the job market. "Job growth in the 1990s was the slowest since the 1950s," wrote lawyer and political scientist David Friedman, then a fellow at the New America Foundation, a liberal think tank. "For the first time, retail and service occupations, the lowest paid of all major industry groups, now comprise nearly half of U.S. employment, up from just 37 percent in 1980."[48]

Even after the recession ended, Americans both employed and unemployed clearly had changed their expectations about the job world. For many, the ups-and-downs of the recent past pointed to the value of stability and security, even if it required lower pay and less exciting work. "People are going to the safer jobs that were so unsexy in the dot-com era," Samantha Ettus, a career consultant, told *USA Today* in 2003. "The trend is to go [with] what's safe."[49]

CHRONOLOGY

1980s *Recession and high unemployment, coupled with a decline in heavy manufacturing, prompt worries over the future of the U.S. job market.*

1982 Unemployment rate hits 10 percent for first time since 1941, with 90 percent of job losses occurring in manufacturing; African-American community is especially hard-hit because one-third of black men in their 20s worked in that sector. . . . Two left-wing economists advocate federal "industrial policy" to preserve manufacturing; conservative Heritage Foundation opposes industrial policy strategy on grounds it would interfere with market forces.

1983 Unemployment drops to 8.3 percent.

1989 With economy in record peacetime expansion, joblessness falls to 5.4 percent. . . . Manufacturing's decline is compensated for by expansion of service sector, now accounting for 75 percent of all jobs.

1990s *Recession is followed by prosperity and optimism accompanied by rapid spread of digital technology.*

1990-1991 Unemployment sparked by recession strikes with unprecedented force at white-collar workers, who account for a record 34 percent of the increase in joblessness.

1992 Recession is a major cause of incumbent President George H. W. Bush's defeat by Gov. Bill Clinton.

1993 Unemployment rate remains at 7 percent despite recession's end, prompting new term: "jobless recovery."

1998 A tech boom under way for the past three years sparks an overall business expansion prompting high demand for programmers and middle managers.

1999 Unemployment rate falls to 4.4 percent, the functional equivalent of full employment. . . . Nevertheless, pay doesn't rise across the board because employers are making extensive use of large pools of temporary workers, and relatively low-paid retail and other service jobs employ half the workforce.

2000s *The bursting of the "dot-com bubble" is followed by yet another recession, but recovery brings no*

major increases in full-time employment before the Great Recession hits.

2000-2001 Dot-com crash brings major cutbacks in tech firms. . . . Sept. 11 attacks push the country into recession.

2003 Spooked by long-running economic instability, employment agencies report that job-seekers opt for security over pay and excitement. . . . Employed workers include 4.9 million freelancers and part-timers who would prefer steady, fulltime jobs. . . . Acceleration of real-estate boom leads to sudden, high demand for mortgage officers.

2007 Wave of about 2 million foreclosures signals the bursting of the real-estate bubble. . . . Recession begins at year-end in a sign of property market's key role in the economy.

2008 Unemployment rate grows steadily from 5 percent in January to 7.4 percent in December. . . . Congress enacts $700 billion package to rescue financial system.

2009 Congress passes Obama administration's $787 billion "stimulus" bill in hopes of creating and saving jobs. . . . State governments begin wrestling with budget shortfalls totaling $145 billion. . . . Economy shows growth in third quarter, but unemployment rate climbs to 10 percent by year's end.

2010 Number of "discouraged" unemployed no longer looking for work reaches 1.2 million. . . . National League of Cities projects 1.5 million layoffs of municipal employees through 2011. . . . Obama touts "stimulus"-financed job creation, but Republicans dispute law's effectiveness. . . . Enactment of health-care coverage law prompts partisan debate about its effects on labor market, if any. . . . Unemployment rate hits 9.9 percent for April despite continuing signs of economic growth. . . . Economists at April jobs conference warn that men are falling behind women in higher education, a key to quality employment. . . . President Obama tells Ohio factory workers that economy is on the mend. . . . House Republican Leader John Boehner of Ohio cites persistently high joblessness to dispute president. . . . House passes legislation to extend unemployment insurance, but Senate doesn't act in time to prevent expiration of benefits to some recipients.

Women Are Better Educated, But Still Earning Less

Jobs have yet to catch up to their educational achievements.

Women are famously more adept than men at interpreting social cues. Indeed, their decoding abilities may extend further, says Michael Greenstone, director of the Brookings Institution's Hamilton Project, which is researching economic growth and equality.

"The labor market is sending a really, really clear signal: You've got to get more education," he says. "To a large degree, women have responded, and men have not."

Data from recent decades all point in one direction: Women are entering and graduating from college at greater rates than men. "Across industrialized economies, women are now — among younger cohorts — the more educated sex," MIT economist David Autor told a recent conference on the job market. "And maybe that's the way it should always have been and will always be."[1]

Women's educational advances coincide with another major trend. After decades of increasing female participation in the workforce, the nation's working population is now half female. But women are still earning less — 77 cents for every dollar earned by a male, on average — in part because their educational advancement has yet to be widely felt. "The most common occupations for women are secretaries and administrative assistances, nurses and schoolteachers," concluded a massive report by the liberal Center for American Progress last year. "Of the top 20 jobs for women, only nurses and schoolteachers required advanced degrees."[2]

Meanwhile, the higher-education gap between men and women remains sizable. In 2008, 34 percent of white females ages 25-34 had graduated college, versus 26 percent of men. Among African-Americans, 22 percent of women graduated, versus 16 percent of the men.[3]

Among all young adults, 57 percent of the college graduates in 2008 were women and 43 percent were men.[4]

Gender-based statistics, however, don't take social class and race into account.

"Overall, the differences between blacks and whites, rich and poor, dwarf the differences between men and women within any particular group," Jacqueline King, director of the American Council on Education's Center for Policy Analysis, told *The New York Times*.[5]

In a recent study, King found that Hispanic males have the lowest bachelor's degree attainment rate of all — 10 percent. Among Hispanic women, the rate is about 18 percent, roughly the same as for African-American women.[6]

Other researchers studying barriers to higher education for young people from poor families argue that a gender gap coexists with economic and social obstacles.

"Young women are more likely than young men to enroll in and complete college in every major racial and ethnic group, with the largest gaps found among African-Americans," three social policy experts wrote in a report for the Pew Charitable Trusts. "We should continue to explore the causes and consequences of the new gender gap in higher education and consider efforts that target the specific barriers and disincentives experienced by low-income boys."[7]

One effect of the gender gap is clear. In more than 51 percent of black households, working women earn as much

Others, by choice or necessity, opted for freelance work in various forms — as individual contractors, temp service workers and independent professionals. Some, by choice, were unattached to single employers. But by 2003, when the unemployment rate was a moderate 5.9 percent, those who did have jobs included 4.9 million part-time and freelance workers who would have preferred full-time employment.[50]

Some of the un- and under-employed learned the new skills necessary to enter fields in which demand was strong and seen as secure — especially teaching and health care. Others leapt into a newly expanding industry.

One former tech staffer for a major accounting firm told *USA Today* in 2003 that he had found a lucrative and reliable new career: mortgage loan officer. "Mortgage

as or more than their husbands. By comparison, about 36 percent of both Hispanic and white women earn more than their husbands.[8]

The gender gap in higher education narrows toward the top of the socioeconomic ladder. Overall, 79 percent of children from the top-earning families go to college, and 53 percent graduate. At the lower end of the ladder, 34 percent enter college and only 11 percent graduate. "Family background is still a formidable barrier to earning a college degree as a way to increase economic mobility," the Pew report concluded.[9]

But even at top universities, whose students tend disproportionately to come from high-earning families, gender differences have emerged. At Harvard, 55 percent of women graduated with honors in 2006 compared with 50 percent of the men. In 2009, 13 percent of Harvard's female BA recipients graduated with high honors versus 10 percent of the men. Among nine BS degree recipients, the only graduate with highest honors (summa cum laude) was a woman.[10]

In some professions, the female surge is extraordinary. In 1961, less than 6 percent of medical school graduates were women; by 2009, they represented fully half. Likewise, women make up about half of both U.S. law school enrollments and recipients of postgraduate degrees of all kinds.[11]

But women's pay doesn't yet reflect the female educational surge. Women doctors earn 59 cents for every dollar paid to their male colleagues, and women lawyers make 77 cents to the male dollar. The wage differential largely reflects an oft-cited male-oriented bias in medicine and law, in which the main ages for demonstrating talent and dedication — one's 20s and 30s — coincide with women's peak child-bearing years.[12]

Pay inequality may not last. And women's march into the workplace may be only beginning, said Heather Boushey, senior economist at the Center for American Progress. "If you look at those top 30 occupations that are estimated to create the most net new number of jobs," she said, "nearly two-thirds of the workers that are currently in those jobs are women."[13]

— *Peter Katel*

[1] "The Future of American Jobs," The Hamilton Project, Center for American Progress, April 30, 2010, www.americanprogress.org/events/2010/04/inf/jobs.pdf.

[2] Heather Boushey and Ann O'Leary, eds., "The Shriver Report: A Woman's Nation Changes Everything," Center for American Progress, October 2009, pp. 39, 57, www.americanprogress.org/issues/2009/10/pdf/awn/a_womans_nation.pdf; Quoted in Tamar Lewin, "At Colleges, Women Are Leaving Men in the Dust," *The New York Times*, July 9, 2006, p. A1.

[3] David Autor, "The Polarization of Job Opportunities in the U.S. Labor Market: Implications for Employment and Earnings," The Hamilton Project, Center for American Progress, April 2010, pp. 24-26, www.brookings.edu/~/media/Files/rc/papers/2010/04_jobs_autor/04_jobs_autor.pdf. For background, see Thomas J. Billitteri, "Women's Pay Gap," *CQ Researcher*, March 14, 2008, pp. 241-264.

[4] "College Gender Gap Appears to be Stabilizing With One Notable Exception," American Council on Education, Jan. 26, 2010, www.acenet.edu/AM/Template.cfm?Section=Press_Releases2&TEMPLATE=/CM/ContentDisplay.cfm&CONTENTID=35338.

[5] Quoted in Lewin, *op. cit.*

[6] "College Gender Gap," *op. cit.*

[7] Ron Haskins, Harry Holzer and Robert Lerman, "Promoting Economic Mobility by Increasing Postsecondary Education," Economic Mobility Project, Pew Charitable Trusts, May 2009, p. 12, www.urban.org/uploadedpdf/1001280_promotingeconomic.pdf.

[8] Boushey and O'Leary, *op. cit.*, p. 38.

[9] *Ibid.*, p. 52, n. 13.

[10] "358th Commencement," *Harvard Gazette*, June 4, 2009, http://news.harvard.edu/gazette/story/2009/06/358th-commencement-harvard-confers-6777-degrees-and-81-certificates/; Lewin, *op. cit.*

[11] Mark J. Perry, "Chart of the Day," *Carpe Diem* (blog), Nov. 24, 2009, http://mjperry.blogspot.com/2009/11/chart-of-day-medical-school-graduates.html; Boushey and O'Leary, *op. cit.*, p. 186.

[12] *Ibid.*

[13] "The Future of American Jobs," transcript, Center for American Progress, Hamilton Project, April 30, 2010, www.americanprogress.org/events/2010/04/inf/jobs.pdf.

companies are hiring as fast as they can," said the San Diego-based newcomer to the field. "It's very secure."[51]

Over the next several years, mortgage companies made loans to virtually anyone who applied. An entire sector of the mortgage business grew up around loans to people who wouldn't have been able to qualify for mortgages only a few years earlier. The new sector was known as the "subprime" market.

Fueling the lending, investing and building was the steady rise of real-estate prices. Because the increase seemed to have no ceiling, some business analysts theorized that even people with few resources could stay in the market by refinancing their mortgages, or by selling quickly and making a profit.

But in 2007, reality began setting in as the real-estate market started tanking. By year's end, 2 million foreclosures were projected on properties whose owners had fallen behind on payments.[52]

Initial hopes that the crisis would be limited to the real-estate sector proved illusory. Wall Street and its equivalents in Europe had sunk billions into the mortgage market, buying and selling securities made up of shaky mortgages that had been "bundled "into packages.

By late 2008, after President Bush and Congress had authorized $700 billion in loans to Wall Street firms in order, they said, to stave off the collapse of the entire financial system, former Federal Reserve Chairman Alan Greenspan accepted some of the blame for the crisis, conceding that the huge wave of lending to borrowers with few assets contradicted his view that markets are largely self-regulating. He also pointed the finger at investment banks. They were strongly encouraging mortgage lenders to keep up the stream of loans, he told the House Committee on Government Oversight and Reform.[53]

The intricacies of the mortgage securities market may have seemed far removed from the workplace realities of most Americans. But as the construction business virtually stopped and banks quit lending to millions of business borrowers, employers of all kinds began massive layoffs. The layoffs further weakened consumer demand, and the collapse of the real-estate bubble led inexorably into the Great Recession.

CURRENT SITUATION

Unemployment Insurance

President Obama and his Democratic allies may be trumpeting the early signs of an end to the Great Recession, but they're aware that with unemployment still close to 10 percent, millions of jobless workers are still counting on unemployment insurance checks. Those checks are now set to stop after June unless Congress extends — again — the unemployment insurance time period. The House passed the legislation on a 215-204 vote before the Memorial Day break. But the Senate won't return from the recess until June 7, which would mark the earliest point at which that chamber could consider the bill. The legislation would also boost taxes on oil companies to benefit the proposed Oil Spill Liability Trust Fund, a response to the BP oil disaster in the Gulf of Mexico.

According to House Speaker Nancy Pelosi, D-Calif., the bill aims at "meeting the needs of those who have lost their jobs through no fault of their own."[54]

In its unextended form, unemployment insurance in most states stops at 26 weeks. During recessions, Congress typically stretches out the eligibility period. Since the present crisis began, lawmakers have granted three extensions. If the new bill passes, the insurance program would have run for a total of 99 weeks before the cutoff.[55]

By last month, the Bloomberg news service reported that even some senior Democrats had decided that 99 weeks should be the upper limit. "You can't go on forever," Senate Finance Chairman Max Baucus of Montana told Bloomberg. "I think 99 weeks is sufficient."[56]

If lawmakers are loathe to cut off the income lifeline for jobless constituents, they are also increasingly nervous about the price tag. Total costs of unemployment insurance this year could reach nearly $200 billion — a significant amount at a time when the federal deficit has become a headline issue.[57]

Republicans maintain their long-held position that extending unemployment insurance amounts to providing an incentive not to find work. "We have study after study that shows people are more anxious to get a job after they run out of benefits," said Rep. John Linder of Georgia, the ranking Republican on the House Ways and Means subcommittee that oversees the benefits program. "Continuing to extend this isn't helping them or us."[58]

Those studies are irrelevant to today's massive joblessness crisis, some labor experts say. "Most of the estimates of the adverse effects of unemployment insurance on raising unemployment durations come out of the '70s and '80s in a just very different world where most unemployment insurance recipients were on temporary layoff," Harvard economist Lawrence F. Katz told the jobs conference in late April.[59]

Katz also argued that because unemployment insurance recipients are required to look for work, the benefits keep them from giving up entirely on seeking employment and joining the "discouraged worker" category. That group has more than doubled in size from 457,000 in April 2009, to 1.2 million last month.[60]

"The huge worry about the long-term unemployed is they psychologically give up," Katz said. "That they stop looking. . . . Many who are 40-65 often apply for disability benefits. Once they leave the workforce and move on

How to Face a Tough Job Market

Career centers and job-seekers fine-tune their strategies.

This year's college graduates are entering a labor market decimated by the worst economic downturn since the Great Depression.

To help new graduates find jobs in an already saturated labor force, job-seekers and university career centers are refocusing their strategies and emphasizing the details that employers look for.

In some industries, high grade-point averages are no longer enough to set exceptional students apart in the recruitment process. "In this recession what tends to make or break a candidate is how well they articulate their stories to the work that they will be doing and how it translates to different industries," says Lynne Sebille-White, senior assistant director of employer relations at the University of Michigan. "Once interviews are secured, employers look for the best fit. This is determined most by connecting with candidates much more than any kind of pedigree relating to GPA or even previous experience."

Many universities, moreover, are encouraging their students to start their job searches much earlier, sometimes as early as their sophomore years. Perhaps, though, the greatest tools available to students remain networking and summer internships prior to graduation.

"I don't think a lot has changed in our strategy during the recession. We have just stressed things more emphatically," says Alan P. Goodman, director of career services at The Catholic University of America. "For example, the notion of how important it is to network. Some students don't want to do that and want to do things on their own, or because they don't feel like asking for help from others. But that is the nature of how many people get jobs."

Internships, meanwhile, can serve as de facto interviews for students regardless of whether or not they are paid. "The good thing about an internship is that it's like a really long interview process for the employer," says New York University's director of employer services, Diana Gruverman. "They can see if a candidate would be a good fit for a full-time position after graduation. But in addition to having a good experience, a student can also see if a specific position is right for them . . . whether they like what the position entails and whether they feel that a company's culture is right for them."

Here are some tips offered by university career centers during tough job markets:

Start early. Many recruiters target students as early as their sophomore years to fill internships that may eventually lead to full-time positions upon graduation.

Network. Increasing numbers of students find jobs and internships through networking. Employers tend to favor familiar faces. Students should start establishing contacts early in their college careers.

Tailor cover letters and résumés. Generic cover letters and résumés are too broad and don't focus on skills and qualifications that companies are looking for. Every job or internship application should be hand-tailored.

Research a company thoroughly. Once interviews are secured, companies will look for the best fit over educational pedigree. Doing your homework on a company can help you articulate how your skills match up with its needs.

Summer internships. Internships completed during the summer before a student's senior year may lead to an immediate offer to begin working permanently after graduation.

Be flexible. Positions for which you may be overqualified, such as an administrative assistant, can help you get a foot in the door and lead to a different position within a company later on. The same holds true for postgraduate internships.

Focus on "soft" skills. Leadership potential and good communication skills help sell a candidate. Pedigree and educational accomplishments sometimes matter less later on in a person's career.

Informational interviews. Try to schedule information sessions with companies whether or not they are hiring. They can give good advice on the path you should take. They also serve as a valuable networking tool.

Visit the career center early. Career centers allow students to make connections, learn of events and openings, and learn the "game" earlier than others. Students should begin visiting once they arrive on campus.

Practice interviewing. Students should take advantage of practice interview sessions offered by career centers to identify and correct their mistakes. Better to flub an answer in practice instead of during the interview for your dream job.

Social networking. Sites such as LinkedIn and Facebook help expand networks and can provide leads as to who's hiring.

Be persistent. Don't give up; if the door isn't slammed in your face, keep coming back. The tougher the job market, the tougher and more persistent you must be.

— Darrell Dela Rosa

to disability benefits, they're pretty much a long-term loss to the labor market. So even on fiscal grounds, keeping up unemployment insurance is both a humanitarian and a fiscally sensible policy."[61]

Politics of Unemployment

Weak but persistent signs of economic growth are giving Democrats hope that they can overcome the political ravages of high unemployment in the fall congressional elections.

"Unemployment changes very slowly . . . but if the economy is growing quickly or declining, voters can perceive that very directly and can vote on that," University of Denver political scientist Seth Masket said in April.[62]

Before indicators maintained their upward trend this year, conventional wisdom about the elections was that voters would punish many Democratic candidates for persistently high unemployment and the lingering effects of the recession. And given the strong opposition to Obama, who ranks at just below 50 percent in voter-approval surveys, Republicans have declared the goal of retaking control of the House, which would require them to win 40 seats. Indeed, Rep. Pete Sessions of Texas, chairman of the National Republican Congressional Committee, told reporters that if the GOP doesn't win the House, his stint at the committee would have been worth no more than "a warm bucket of spit."[63]

And for months, Republicans have pointed to the economy in general and unemployment in particular as major handicaps for the Democrats.

"The biggest threat to the president's party is not health care, a climate-change bill or Afghanistan. It's jobs," John Feehery, a Republican strategist, told *The Wall Street Journal* last October.[64]

Women's Share of High-Skilled Jobs Rose Most

The number of females working in high-skilled occupations rose about 15 percent from 1979 to 2007, versus 3 percent for men. The share of jobs fell, however, among both men and women in medium-skilled occupations.

Changes in Occupational Employment Shares by Gender, 1979-2007

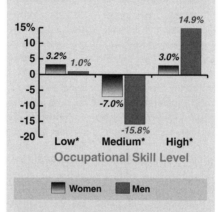

* High: managerial, professional and technical occupations

Medium: Sales, office/admin, production and operators

Low: Protective service, food prep, janitorial/cleaning, personal care/services

Source: David Autor, "The Polarization of Job Opportunities in the U.S. Labor Market," Center for American Progress, April 2010

But jobs can be a political weapon for Democrats as well as Republicans. In a special election in May to choose a successor to the late Democratic Rep. John Murtha of Pennsylvania, Democrat Mark Critz trounced his Republican opponent 53 percent to 45 percent. "Mark Critz focused on creating jobs for middle-class families," Democratic Congressional Committee Chairman Rep. Chris Van Hollen, D-Md., said in a statement hailing the outcome.

Critz had been Murtha's economic-development director, overseeing the disbursement of hundreds of millions of dollars in federally funded projects that the congressman channeled into his district.[65]

That district is dominated by conservative, white, working-class voters on whom Republicans have pinned their hopes for the Northeast and Midwest — "exactly the kind of seat that we have to win," Republican National Committee Political Director Gentry Collins said after the vote. The Republican candidate for the seat, Tim Burns, who had founded and sold a software company that developed prescription-management programs for pharmacies, tried to use Critz' past against him, calling the Democrat a Washington insider. Burns welcomed support from the Tea Party, the loosely knit movement of Republicans critical of government and federal spending.[66]

But Critz' service as a congressional aide may have served as an advantage, not handicap, in an economically hard-hit area with a long tradition of federally financed employment.

Republicans argued that Critz triumphed largely because he took Republican positions on some major issues, including opposition to the new health-care law.

Because the election only decided who would fill out the remainder of Murtha's term, Critz and Burns and their respective parties will have another chance at each other in November.

By then, economic indicators may have moved more decisively in a direction that favors Republicans or Democrats. "This political moment . . . is about performance," John Sides, a George Washington University political scientist who specializes in the connections between economic conditions and voter sentiments, wrote in a recent blog post. "People want conditions in the country to improve. They want a growing economy. Once that happens, peoples' assessments of the government's performance will also improve."[67]

Government Jobs

Long seen as the gold standard in secure employment, government jobs turn out to be as subject to economic conditions as other employment. From coast to coast, state and city governments are laying off, furloughing and not filling empty positions. The National League of Cities projects that state and local governments will have laid off up to 1.5 million workers by the end of 2011.[68]

No definitive national unemployment figures for government workers are available yet, with governors, legislators, local officials and unions still negotiating and maneuvering. The possibility of a federal rescue for teachers is fading. Sen. Tom Harkin, D-Iowa, has introduced legislation to spend $23 billion to prevent layoffs of educators, but the bill is languishing in the Senate for lack of support.[69]

Still, the magnitude of the shortfalls limits the extent to which officials can lessen the effects of spending cuts. State deficits so far this year add up to $196 billion, the National Conference of State Legislatures reports (2009 deficits amounted to $145 billion). "A budget gap of 5 percent or 10 percent in any given year is a tough problem," said Corina Eckl, fiscal director at the conference. "But we're talking about gaps in excess of 20 percent over multiple years. The size of these gaps is staggering."[70]

And cities face 2010-2012 deficits that total at least $56 billion, Ronald O. Loveridge, mayor of Riverside, Calif., and president of the National League of Cities, told a congressional subcommittee in April.[71]

Laying off employees can be problematic for elected officials. Government employee unions are a major electoral force. Nationwide, 37 percent of public-sector workers (including federal employees) are represented by unions — in sharp contrast to a 7 percent union-representation rate in the private sector. Teachers, police officers and firefighters are among the most heavily unionized employee groups.[72]

Nevertheless, public officials do enjoy an asset in the battle for public opinion: Government workers may command less support from ordinary voters than in the past, because the public employees enjoy benefits that private-sector employees can only dream of. "In New York City, in our uniformed services, the benefits are equal to 100 percent of their salaries," New York Mayor Michael Bloomberg told the Hamilton-CAP jobs conference.

"Very generous" benefits are the rule in all big cities, he said. "Every mayor is trying to address the problem."[73]

Major deficits are likely to hobble municipalities for some time, Loveridge added. Recessions hit city governments late, because the effects on property tax payments are delayed by as long as two years. Economic recoveries are late in making themselves felt as well. "Cities will be dealing with the downturn even after federal and state economies improve," he testified. The vast majority of city fiscal officers report spending cuts in 2009 and expect further reductions in 2010 that will result in layoffs, delayed or canceled infrastructure projects or cuts to public safety, libraries, parks and other municipal services."[74]

Meanwhile, job actions already ordered include the laying off and non-replacement of about 2,500 faculty members at California State University's 23 campuses; proposed elimination of 761 jobs in Los Angeles city government, following the elimination of 2,400 jobs through early retirements and other moves; layoffs of more than 1,000 New York transportation workers and layoffs of 500 city workers in Boston.[75]

Another growing trend is to cut pay by sending workers home for short furloughs. In New York, Gov. David A. Paterson ordered a one-day furlough in May, only to see a federal judge block the move pending a hearing. The furloughs would have kept about half of the state's 200,000 employees away from their work sites, as part of an effort to save $250,000 million in payroll costs. Overall, the state is facing a budget deficit of more than $9 billion.[76]

Are "green" jobs an important potential source of new jobs?

YES

Hilda Solis
Secretary of Labor

From testimony before House Appropriations Subcommittee on Labor, Health and Human Services, and Education, and Related Agencies, March 10 and 25, 2010

We view green jobs as a key driver of America's economic revitalization and sustained economic stability. The demand for green job training has been enormous, and it has come from the private sector. We have simply not been able to keep pace with the record number of applications. We believe this interest represents the need for assisting people who are already working, but who may be underemployed.

We're committed to linking this training with job-certain efforts in green industries, and expect our grantees to work with employers and other participants to gain those valuable skills and industry-recognized credentials that will help them move into better and higher-paying jobs in emerging industries, where we know there are jobs, such as clean energy, an area where we see a lot of potential for additional training efforts. Potentially, these jobs will provide 10 to 20 percent more in wages.

This means looking at new opportunities, retraining those workers who lost their jobs in the automobile industry; electrical workers, plumbers and pipefitters that may now need to take a different approach in terms of what other job careers are available. For example, a community in Tennessee was doing televisions before; now they're doing solar panels.

The Green Jobs Innovation Fund would build on the lessons learned from the Recovery Act's $500 million investment in green jobs, and the $40 million Congress provided to support this initiative in fiscal 2010. Complementary to our efforts, the U.S. Bureau of Labor Statistics has also been working to develop and implement the collection of new data on green jobs, critical to assisting policymakers in planning policy initiatives and understanding their impact on the labor market. In addition, other federal agencies will be investing in complementary green industry activities, and the leveraging of these resources will be critical to developing the green workforce as jobs are emerging in state and regional economies. We have created new partnerships with other departments, such as the U.S. Department of Housing and Urban Development, so that we connect residents in public housing with green jobs.

We've really lost hold in the manufacturing arena. That's been happening for the last decade. Making investments in new technologies, in green energy, biofuels and transportation is going to help us in the long run. But we have to be competitive and make sure that we have an appropriate workforce.

NO

Diana Furchtgott-Roth

Director, Center for Employment Policy, Hudson Institute; former Chief Economist, Department of Labor

From testimony before Joint Economic Committee, April 29, 2010

No one has properly defined a "green" job, the kind that Mr. Obama wants to encourage, but many believe such jobs include installers of insulation and energy-efficient windows and producers of renewable energy, as from sunshine and wind. Tax revenues used to subsidize the manufacture of these products create jobs in those sectors, but leave less to be spent on other activities.

In Spain, economics professor Gabriel Calzada Alvarez . . . has calculated that his country has spent $763,383 (at today's exchange rates) per green job. Higher energy costs have driven away jobs in metallurgy, mining and food processing, so over two jobs have been destroyed for every job created.

Mr. Obama believes that increases in greenhouse gases contribute to global warming, which purportedly hurts plants and animals by damaging their environments and harms humans by flooding. Even if true, unilateral emissions reduction by America, without similar action by China and India, would have a negligible effect on global warming.

At a time of fragile employment growth, President Obama's "Clean Energy Economy" proposals would worsen unemployment. American greenhouse gas emissions, chiefly carbon dioxide, would decline on a per person basis to late-19th-century levels. Businesses would be required to invest in energy efficiency and low-carbon or zero-carbon fuels to offset emissions through investments in agriculture and trees, and to pour money into emission-offset activities abroad.

At the same time, as the administration moves to lower greenhouse gas emissions it also proposes getting rid of incentives for American workers to produce oil, natural gas and coal in the United States. Over the next decade, oil, gas and coal companies would lose almost $39 billion in exploration and production incentives if Congress adopts the Obama budget policy.

The American Clean Energy and Security Act, sometimes known as the cap-and-trade bill, would raise energy prices, impose strict new efficiency standards on automobiles and appliances, require firms to use nonexistent technology and mandate greenhouse gas emissions per person back to 19th-century levels by 2050. Its [House] cosponsor, Democrat Ed Markey of Massachusetts, said the bill would "create jobs by the millions," and Speaker Nancy Pelosi said it was about "jobs, jobs, jobs and jobs."

[But] many solar panels and wind turbines are being manufactured in China, hence creating jobs for the Chinese.

Furloughs amount to involuntary pay cuts, which allow government entities to cut costs without layoffs. However, in California, at least, many employees have been making up for smaller paychecks by working more overtime — $1 billion worth last year, compared to $808 million in 2005.[77]

Overall, service cutbacks at city and state levels can reverberate far beyond state employee ranks, even when the cuts don't directly affect payrolls.

In many states, massive reductions in child care that's funded by federal and state governments are effectively preventing low-income women from finding or keeping jobs. "We're going the wrong way," Ron Haskins, a senior fellow at the Brookings Institution think tank, told *The New York Times*. As a Republican congressional aide, Haskins helped author the 1996 welfare reform law that authorized subsidized daycare for working mothers. "The direction public policy should move is to provide more of these mothers with subsidies. To tell people that the only way they can day care is to go on welfare defeats the purpose of the whole thing."[78]

OUTLOOK

Fingers Crossed

Whatever their political leanings, economists tend to see a rebound of the economy as likely, with job creation a leading result. When that may happen and what elements of industry or commerce serve as the mainspring of recovery remain uncertain. But, says economist Autor of MIT, "Hopefully we'll have bounced back. The best-case scenario is that in 10 years things will look a lot like 1999."

Government can help create the conditions in which the economy can flourish, creating jobs for nearly everyone who wants to work. "It depends on having sound tax and spending policies," Autor says, "so that we don't have government being a huge drain on the economy — not fighting wars and not paying for them."

For Autor and others, the issues to worry about have less to do with overall economic growth and more to do with how widely the benefits of expansion are spread. And those concerns don't only focus on poor people with little education.

"Unemployment has disproportionately been created in many of those previously high-paying middle-wage jobs, whether middle management, clerical, construction," Harvard economist Katz told the Hamilton-CAP conference in late April. "We're not going to reconstruct the economy as we go into recovery with the same type of job mix we had before."[79]

Those who find that their skills aren't in demand may have to limit their aspirations, Katz said.

Expectations about the effects of the economic reshaping already under way are echoing widely. "The construction and finance industries, bloated by a decade-long housing bubble, are unlikely to regain their former share of the economy," writes Don Peck, deputy managing editor of *The Atlantic*, "and as a result many out-of-work finance professionals and construction workers won't be able to simply pick up where they left off when growth returns — they'll need to retrain and find new careers. (For different reasons, the same might be said of many media professionals and autoworkers.)"[80]

Meanwhile, concerns about the lopsided distribution of wealth are spreading into conservative ranks. "We are in the middle of the largest transfer of wealth from the average American to the richest people in history," says George Mason University economist Roberts, criticizing the multibillion-dollar business and industry rescue packages that began in the final months of the Bush administration. "Wall Street has made a killing. Bush started it, and Obama continued it. And the Democrats, supporters of the president, have embraced it."

If suspicions of big finance are no longer an exclusive province of the left, some Democrats acknowledge that government programs can't fix everything that's wrong with the economy. The Hamilton Project's Greenstone, reflecting on how men are falling behind women in higher education, says, "The government can do things to help make it easier to get more education, but at the end of the day it will be up to people themselves to do that."

Nevertheless, Greenstone says, some issues do demand a government role. One is educational quality, as opposed to educational attendance. "We spend the most of OECD [Organization for Economic Cooperation and Development] countries, and get the worst results," he says. "The productivity of our K-12 system is not up to task." And investment in another longtime U.S. economic strength — research and development — is faltering, he says.

Liberal economists worry about the erosion of both public education, a powerful engine of social mobility, and research, which fuels innovation and productivity. Stone of the Center for Budget and Policy Priorities has no doubt that present conditions will improve. "Surely, the unemployment rate will get down to 5 percent in a certain number of years," he says.

But that is no guarantee that job-hunters will be able to work themselves up to decently paying jobs. "The expansion of the 2000s," he says, "did get the unemployment rate down to 5 percent, but it didn't deliver the goods for most people."

Amid these grim assessments, one note of optimism echoes widely.

"We've had industrial revolutions before that have displaced huge numbers of workers," says Princeton economist Blinder, "and new jobs in new industries have always sprouted up."

NOTES

1. "Of Total Unemployed, Percent Unemployed 27 Weeks & Over," U.S. Bureau of Labor Statistics, http://data.bls.gov/PDQ/servlet/SurveyOutput Servlet.

2. "Civilian Labor Force and Participation Rates With Projections: 1980 to 2016," U.S. Census, updated 2010, www.census.gov/compendia/statab/2010/tables/10s0575.pdf.

3. Testimony by Alan B. Krueger, assistant secretary for economic policy and chief economist, U.S. Treasury Department, before Joint Economic Committee, May 5, 2010, www.ustreas.gov/press/releases/tg688.htm.

4. Motoko Rich, "Economy Gains Impetus as U.S. Adds 290,000 Jobs," *The New York Times*, May 7, 2010, www.nytimes.com/2010/05/08/business/economy/08jobs.html?pagewanted=all.

5. Quoted in Jackie Calmes, "Obama Tells Ohio, 'Our Economy Is Growing Again,' " *The New York Times*, May 18, 2010, www.nytimes.com/2010/05/19/us/politics/19obama.html; "Gross Domestic Product: First Quarter 2010 (Advance Estimate)," U.S. Bureau of Economic Analysis, April 30, 2010, www.bea.gov/newsreleases/national/gdp/gdpnewsrelease.htm.

6. "Mind the (Credibility) Gap: White House Rhetoric vs. Main Street Reality," Rep. John Boehner Web site, May 18, 2010, www.republicanleader.house.gov/News/DocumentSingle.aspx?DocumentID=186169.

7. "Joint Economic Committee Holds Hearing on Job Creation," CQ Congressional Transcripts May 5, 2010.

8. Greg Toppo, "Pink slips on the way to teachers," *USA Today*, May 4, 2010, p. D4; Winnie Hu, "Teachers Facing Weakest Market for Jobs in Years," *The New York Times*, May 20, 2010, p. A1.

9. "The Future of American Jobs [transcript]," Center for American Progress, Hamilton Project, April 30, 2010, www.americanprogress.org/events/2010/04/inf/jobs.pdf. Wage statistics in David Leonhardt, "The Value of College," *The New York Times*, Economix blog, May 17, 2010, http://economix.blogs.nytimes.com/2010/05/17/the-value-of-college-2/?ref=business.

10. *Ibid.*

11. "Future of American Jobs," *ibid.*

12. *Ibid.*

13. *Ibid.*

14. "Joint Economic Committee Holds Hearing on Long-Term Unemployment," CQ Congressional Transcripts, April 29, 2010.

15. Lisa B. Kahn, "The Long-Term Labor Market Consequences of Graduating from College in a Bad Economy," Yale School of Management, updated Aug. 13, 2009, pp. 5, 27, http://mba.yale.edu/faculty/pdf/kahn_longtermlabor.pdf.

16. Laura Vanderkam, "A Not-Lost Generation," *City Journal*, winter 2010, www.city-journal.org/2010/20_1_youth-unemployment.html.

17. N. Gregory Mankiw, "Spreading the Wealth Around: Reflections Inspired by Joe the Plumber," March 12, 2010, p. 5, www.economics.harvard.edu/faculty/mankiw/files/Spreading%20the%20Wealth%20Around.pdf.

18. *Ibid.*

19. David Autor, "The Polarization of Job Opportunities in the U.S. Labor Market: Implications for Employment and Earnings," The Hamilton Project, Center for American Progress, April 2010, p. 5,

www.brookings.edu/~/media/Files/rc/papers/2010/04_jobs_autor/04_jobs_autor.pdf.

20. *Ibid.*, pp. 26-27.

21. For background, see the following *CQ Researcher* reports: Kenneth Jost, "Revising No Child Left Behind," April 16, 2010, pp. 337-360; Marcia Clemmitt, "AP and IB Programs," March 3, 2006, pp. 193-216, and Thomas J. Billitteri, "Discipline in Schools," Feb. 15, 2008, pp. 145-168.

22. For background, see Mary H. Cooper, "Exporting Jobs," *CQ Researcher*, Feb. 20, 2004, pp. 149-172.

23. Alan S. Blinder, "Free Trade's Great, But Offshoring Rattles Me," *The Washington Post*, May 6, 2007, www.washingtonpost.com/wp-dyn/content/article/2007/05/04/AR2007050402555.html; Alan S. Blinder, "Offshoring: The Next Industrial Revolution?" *Foreign Affairs*, March-April, 2006, p. 113.

24. "An Address on Jobs and the Economy by President Barack Obama," Brookings Institution, Dec. 8, 2009, www.brookings.edu/events/2009/1208_jobs_obama.aspx.

25. "The Clean Energy Economy: Repowering Jobs, Businesses and Investments Across America," Pew Charitable Trusts, July 10, 2009, p. 5, www.pewcenteronthestates.org/uploadedFiles/Clean_Economy_Report_Web.pdf.

26. "Employees on nonfarm payrolls by industry sector and selected industry detail," U.S. Bureau of Labor Statistics, updated May 7, 2010, www.bls.gov/news.release/empsit.t17.htm.

27. Quoted in "Who's Winning the Clean Energy Race?" Pew Charitable Trusts, March 24, 2010, p. 13, www.pewtrusts.org/uploadedFiles/wwwpewtrustsorg/Reports/Global_warming/G-20%20Report.pdf.

28. "Weatherization Assistance Program," U.S. Department of Energy, undated, www1.eere.energy.gov/wip/wap.html.

29. For background, see Marcia Clemmitt, "Public-Works Projects," *CQ Researcher*, Feb. 20, 2009, pp. 153-176; and Marcia Clemmitt, "Aging Infrastructure," *CQ Researcher*, Sept. 28, 2007, pp. 793-816.

30. Ronald E. Kitscher and Valeri A. Personick, "Deindustrialization and the shift to services," *Monthly Labor Review*, U.S. Bureau of Labor Statistics, June 1986, pp. 4-5, www.bls.gov/opub/mlr/1986/06/art1full.pdf; "Employment by major industry sector," U.S. Bureau of Labor Statistics, updated November 2009, www.bls.gov/emp/ep_table_201.htm.

31. Michael A. Urquhart and Marilyn A. Hewson, "Unemployment continued to rise in 1982 as recession deepened," *Monthly Labor Review*, U.S. Bureau of Labor Statistics, February 1983, pp. 3-4, www.bls.gov/opub/mlr/1983/02/art1full.pdf; Don Peck, "How a New Jobless Era Will Transform America," *The Atlantic*, March 2010, www.theatlantic.com/magazine/archive/2010/03/how-a-new-jobless-era-will-transform-america/7919.

32. Barry Bluestone and Bennett Harrison, *The Deindustrialization of America: Plant Closings, Community Abandonment, and the Dismantling of Basic Industry* (1982), p. 6.

33. *Ibid.*, pp. 233-255.

34. Robert Reich, "Making Industrial Policy," *Foreign Affairs*, spring 1982. The article was expanded into a book, Robert Reich, *The Next American Frontier* (1983).

35. Dwight R. Lee, "The Faulty Logic of Industrial Policy," Heritage Foundation, Oct. 26, 1983, p. 6, www.policyarchive.org/handle/10207/bitstreams/9174.pdf.

36. "Labor Force Statistics From the Current Population Survey," U.S. Bureau of Labor Statistics, http://data.bls.gov/PDQ/servlet/SurveyOutputServlet.

37. Lois M. Plunkert, "The 1980s: A decade of Job Growth and Industry Shifts," September 1990, in Harold G. Vatter and John F. Walker, eds., *History of the U.S. Economy Since World War II* (1996), pp. 168-171.

38. Jennifer M. Gardner, "The 1990-91 recession: how bad was the labor market?" *Monthly Labor Review*, U.S. Bureau of Labor Statistics, June 1994, pp. 9-10, www.bls.gov/mlr/1994/06/art1full.pdf.

39. Quoted in Silvia Nasar, "Overhauling Services: The Long, Painful Process," *The New York Times*, Jan. 2, 1992, p. A1.

40. Robert Burns, "Sluggish Job Growth Held Unemployment at 7 Percent in April," The Associated Press, May 7, 1993.

41. Stacey L. Schreft and Aarti Singh, "A Closer Look at Jobless Recoveries," *Economic Review*, Second Quarter 2003, pp. 51-53, www.kc.frb.org/Publicat/econrev/Pdf/2q03schr.pdf.

42. Robert D. Hershey Jr., "Few Bright Spots in last Job Report Prior to Election," *The New York Times*, Oct. 3, 1992, p. A1.

43. Barry Stavro, "At Rocketdyne, Hiring Has Been Taking Off," *Los Angeles Times*, Nov. 9, 1997, p. A1.

44. Amy Harmon, "Vacant Cubicles; Software Jobs go Begging," *The New York Times*, Jan. 13, 1998.

45. Quoted in Stephanie Armour, "Middle management boom," *USA Today*, May 14, 1998, p. B1.

46. Jonathan Peterson, "Favorable Job Report Lifts Dow to Record High," *Los Angeles Times*, March 6, 1999, p. A1; Louis Uchitelle, "Strong Summer Apt to Propel Economic Boom to a Record," *The New York Times*, Oct. 29, 1999, p. A1; Louis Uchitelle, "Big Increases in Productivity by Workers," *The New York Times*, Nov. 13, 1999, p. C1; Arleen J. Hoag and John H. Hoag, *Introductory Economics* (2002), pp. 221-222.

47. Karen Kaplan, "A Bad Day for Tech: 31,000 Jobs Slashed," *Los Angeles Times*, July 27, 2001, p. A1.

48. David Friedman, "The New Economy," *Los Angeles Times*, Feb. 6, 2000, p. M1.

49. Quoted in Stephanie Armour, "Wanted: A job with security," *USA Today*, July 9, 2003, p. B1.

50. David Streitfeld, "Jobless Count Skips Millions," *Los Angeles Times*, Dec. 29, 2003, p. A1.

51. Quoted in Armour, *op. cit.*, July 9, 2003.

52. For background, see Marcia Clemmitt, "Mortgage Crisis," *CQ Researcher*, Nov. 2, 2007, pp. 913-936.

53. Edmund L. Andrews, "Greenberg Concedes Error on Regulation," *The New York Times*, Oct. 23, 2008, www.nytimes.com/2008/10/24/business/economy/24panel.html?_r=1.

54. Quoted in Stephen Ohlemacher, "Bill aims to expand benefits for the unemployed," The Associated Press, May 21, 2010.

55. Brian Faler, "More Than a Million in U.S. May Lose Jobless Benefits (Update2)," Bloomberg.com, April 29, 2010, www.bloomberg.com/apps/news?pid=20601074&sid=aXwP.wJosrtY.

56. Quoted in *ibid.*

57. *Ibid.*

58. Quoted in *ibid.*

59. "The Future of American Jobs," *op. cit.*

60. "Employment Situation Summary," U.S. Bureau of Labor Statistics, May 7, 2010, www.bls.gov/news.release/empsit.nr0.htm.

61. "The Future of American Jobs," *op. cit.*

62. Quoted in Ed Stoddard, "Could growth trump unemployment in election?" Reuters, April 28, 2010, www.reuters.com/article/idUSTRE63R3K020100428.

63. Quoted in Christina Bellantoni, "'94 or Bust: Republicans Drafting New Contract With America in Effort to Retake Congress," TalkingPointsMemo, April 22, 2010, http://tpmdc.talkingpointsmemo.com/2010/04/94-or-bust-republicans-drafting-new-contract-with-america-in-effort-to-retake-house.php#more; Jeff Zeleny and Adam Nagourney, "G.O.P. Threatens Seats Long Held by Democrats," *The New York Times*, April 25, 2010, p. A1.

64. Quoted in Neil King Jr., "Jobless Rate Is Key to Fate of Democrats in 2010," *The Wall Street Journal*, Oct. 7, 2009, http://online.wsj.com/article/SB125487096440369163.html.

65. Amanda H. Allen, "Rep. Mark Critz (D-Pa.) — CQ Politics in America Profile," *CQ Politics in America*, May 20, 2010.

66. Collins quoted in Steve Benen, "Where is the Wave," *Political Animal* (blog), *Washington Monthly*, May 19, 2010, www.washingtonmonthly.com/archives/individual/2010_05/023869.php. Johanna Neuman, "How Republicans lost PA-12," *Los Angeles Times*, May 19, 2010, http://latimesblogs.latimes.com/washington/2010/05/how-republicans-lost-pa12-and-why-democrats-think-the-mark-critz-prototype-could-save-them-in-2010.html.

67. John Sides, "Will the Tea Party Succeed?" *The Monkey Cage* (blog), May 20, 2010, www.themonkeycage.org/2010/05/will_the_tea_party_succeed.html.

68. Richard Simon, "Cities wait for their bailout," *Los Angeles Times*, April 25, 2010, p. A1.

69. Greg Toppo, "Secretary Duncan warns that the situation is dire," *USA Today*, May 4, 2010, p. D4.

70. Quoted in Jennifer Steinhauer, "New Year but No Relief For Strapped States," *The New York Times*, Jan. 6, 2010, p. A15; Stephen Ohlemacher and Andrew Taylor, "Senate OKs war funding," The Associated Press, May 28, 2010.

71. "Actions and Proposals to Balance FY 2011 Budgets: State Employee Actions: Furloughs and Layoffs," National Conference of State Legislatures, updated May 2010, www.ncsl.org/default.aspx?tabid=19647; Ronald O. Loveridge, president, National League of Cities, testimony before House Judiciary Committee, Commercial and Administrative Law Subcommittee, April 15, 2010, www.nlc.org/ASSETS/F338E80A56 3D433CB8206E41B28E7C4B/HouseJudTest4.15 .pdf.

72. "Union Members Summary," U.S. Bureau of Labor Statistics, Jan. 22, 2010, www.bls.gov/news.release/ union2.nr0.htm.

73. "Future of American Jobs," *op. cit.*

74. *Ibid.*

75. Carla Rivera, "Cal State's faculty cut by 10%, says union," *Los Angeles Times*, May 21, 2010, p. AA6; David Sahniser, "L.A. layoff cost could top $32 million," *Los Angeles Times*, May 11, 2010; Michael M. Grynbaum, "M.T.A. Plans More Rounds Of Layoffs By July 4," *The New York Times*, April 29, 2010, p. A27; Loveridge, *ibid.*

76. Nicholas Confessore, "U.S. Judge Blocks State Worker Furloughs," *The New York Times*, May 13, 2010, p. A25.

77. Patrick McGreevy, "Overtime may offset furloughs," *Los Angeles Times*, March 7, 2001, p. A1.

78. Peter S. Goodman, "Cuts to Child Care Subsidy Thwart More Job Seekers," *The New York Times*, May 24, 2010, p. A1.

79. *Ibid.*

80. Don Peck, "How a New Jobless Era Will Transform America," *The Atlantic*, March 2010, www.theatlantic .com/magazine/archive/2010/03/how-a-new-jobless-era-will-transform-america/7919/.

BIBLIOGRAPHY
Books

Cottle, Thomas J., *Hardest Times: The Trauma of Long Term Unemployment*, Praeger, 2001.
A professor of education at Boston College undertook the first major 21st-century examination of a major problem.

Goldin, Claudia, and Lawrence F. Katz, *The Race Between Education and Technology*, Harvard University Press, 2008.
Widely cited by scholars and officials across the political spectrum, an analysis by two Harvard economists provides vast detail on the U.S. education lag.

Vatter, Harold G., and John F. Walker, eds., *History of the U.S. Economy Since World War II*, M.E. Sharpe, 1996.
The collection of readings covers all major economic trends through the final decade of the 20th century.

Articles

Ahrens, Frank, "Payrolls grow, yet jobless rate holds," *The Washington Post*, April 3, 2010, p. A1.
A veteran correspondent reports on one of the most pressing issues of the day.

Brownstein, Ronald, "Repairing the Job Machine," *National Journal*, May 15, 2010, www.nationaljournal .com/njmagazine/nj_20100515_5237.php.
A dispassionate analysis by a longtime Washington journalist concludes that the next major engine of job-creation hasn't yet been discovered.

Calmes, Jackie, "Democrats Shifting Focus Back to Jobs Creation," *The New York Times*, May 17, 2010, www.nytimes.com/2010/05/18/us/politics/ 18stimulus.html.
As elections loom, the party in power focuses on the country's major economic and social issue.

Conda, Cesar, and Diana Furchtgott-Roth, "Job Creation under Obama: Nothing to Crow About," *National Review* (The Corner, blog), May 18, 2010.
Two conservative economic-policy experts argue that the administration is hyping the effects of the 2009 financial "stimulus."

Goodman, Peter S., "Cuts to Child Care Subsidy Thwart More Job Seekers," *The New York Times*, May 23, 2010, www.nytimes.com/2010/05/24/business/economy/24childcare.html.
Goodman takes an in-depth examination of the ripple effects of recession — from state governments' revenue losses to the effect on working mothers of cutbacks in subsidized child care services.

Peck, Don, "How a New Jobless Era Will Transform America," *The Atlantic*, March 2010, www.theatlantic.com/magazine/archive/2010/03/how-a-new-jobless-era-will-transform-america/7919.
The magazine's deputy managing editor, an economics and public-policy specialist, argues at length that long-term unemployment is changing the U.S. social landscape.

Wessel, David, "Meet the Unemployable Man," *The Wall Street Journal*, May 6, 2010, http://finance.yahoo.com/career-work/article/109471/meet-the-unemployable-man?mod=career-work.
An economic-policy specialist reports on job polarization and its effects on a big segment of the workforce — men without much education.

Reports and Studies

Autor, David, "The Polarization of Job Opportunities in the U.S. Labor Market: Implications for Employment and Earnings," Center for American Progress/Hamilton Project, April 30, 2010, www.americanprogress.org/issues/2010/04/pdf/job_polarization.pdf.
This detailed examination of the changing employment market by an MIT economist framed a discussion on jobs at a Washington conference of high-level economists with close administration ties.

Boushey, Heather, and Ann O'Leary, eds., "The Shriver Report: A Woman's Nation Changes Everything," Center for American Progress, October 2009, www.americanprogress.org/issues/2009/10/pdf/awn/a_womans_nation.pdf.
In exhaustive detail, labor experts explore the expanding role of women in the workplace and the ways in which social structures and pay rates have and haven't kept up.

Haskins, Ron; Harry Holzer and Robert Lerman, "Promoting Economic Mobility by Increasing Postsecondary Education, Economic Mobility Project," Pew Charitable Trusts, May 2009, www.urban.org/uploadedpdf/1001280_promoting economic.pdf.
A trio of policy hands explores ways to expand higher-education opportunities for young people with low incomes.

***Independent, Innovative, and Unprotected: How the Old Safety Net is Failing America's New Workforce*, Freelancers Union, November 2009, http://fu-res.org/pdfs/advocacy/surveyreport_overview.pdf.**
Leaders of a new organization to represent freelancers' interests expose what they call critical deficiencies in their growing corner of the job world, including lack of access to unemployment insurance.

For More Information

AFL-CIO, 815 16th St., N.W., Washington, DC 20006; (202) 637-5018; www.aflcio.org. Major labor federation advocating stepped-up government efforts to bolster job market.

Bureau of Labor Statistics, Postal Square Building, 2 Massachusetts Ave., N.E., Washington, DC 20212; (202) 691-5200; www.bls.gov. Federal agency offering an enormous, constantly updated, compilation of data on all aspects of employment and the economy.

Center for Employment Policy, Hudson Institute, 1015 15th St., N.W., Washington, DC 20005; (202) 974-2400; www.hudson-employment.org. A conservative think tank exploring policies, including low taxation and limits on regulation, designed to encourage economic growth and job creation.

CLASP, 1200 18th St., N.W., Washington, DC 20036; (202) 906-8000; www.clasp.org. Nonprofit group, formerly named Center for Law and Social Policy, advocating stronger government programs to expand employment opportunities for the poor.

Hamilton Project, Brookings Institution, 1775 Massachusetts Ave., N.W,, Washington, DC 20036; (202) 797-6000; www. brookings.edu/projects/hamiltonproject.aspx. A project of the moderate think tank studying proposals to strengthen economic growth and widen the benefits of prosperity.

Jobs for the Future, 88 Broad St., Boston, MA 02110; (617) 728-4446; www.jff.org. Nongovernmental organizer of training and education programs geared to changing needs of employment market; publishes research on job-opportunity expansion.

5

Income Inequality

Marcia Clemmitt

A Ferrari complements the conspicuous consumption on display along Rodeo Drive in Beverly Hills, Calif. Experts agree the rich are pulling away from other Americans, but not all think it's a problem. Some say investments by the wealthy stimulate the economy by building businesses and driving demand for labor, but others say the result has been a severe recession and stagnant incomes for most Americans.

From *CQ Researcher*, Dec 3, 2010.

A Census Bureau report released in September brought a brief flurry of press attention to rising income inequality in America.

"The gap between rich and poor in New York is getting worse," noted the *New York Daily News*. In 2009, 18.7 percent of New York City's population lived in poverty, and the median household income fell to $50,033, from $51,116 in 2008, even as the combined worth of the city's 58 richest residents rose by $19 billion. As a result, the earnings gap among New Yorkers "is now larger than the gap in India and the African nation of Burkina Faso," Joel Berg, executive director of the New York City Coalition Against Hunger, told the paper.[1]

The finding that income inequality is increasing is generally accepted by analysts across the political spectrum, with the exception of libertarian commentators, who argue that no existing data set accurately depicts how money is distributed. What provokes debate in all quarters, however, is whether steep income inequality in an industrialized nation is something to worry about and, if it is, what policies would address it effectively.

The main story is that the very rich have been pulling away from all others in income over the past three decades, most analysts agree.

"The average pretax income for the bottom 90 percent of households is almost $900 below what it was in 1979, while the average pretax income for the top 1 percent is over $700,000 above its 1979 level," according to the Center on Budget and Policy Priorities (CBPP) a liberal-leaning think tank.[2]

After-tax incomes also have risen more for the highest earners, says CBPP. From 1979 to 2007, the average after-tax income of the

Richest Americans Have Biggest Share of Income

The top 1 percent of income earners in the United States control nearly 18 percent of Americans' total income, the world's highest such concentration. In 1949, however, the top American earners lagged behind those of several other countries, including Indonesia, Germany and the United Kingdom.

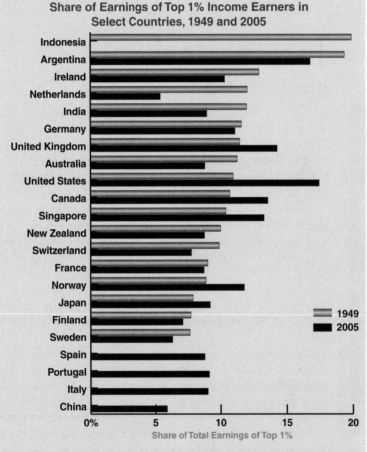

Share of Earnings of Top 1% Income Earners in Select Countries, 1949 and 2005

Share of Total Earnings of Top 1%

Source: Anthony B. Atkinson, et al., "Top Incomes in the Long Run of History," National Bureau of Economic Research, January 2010

fifth saw its average after-tax income grow from $15,300 to $17,600, or 16 percent.[3]

Citigroup, the financial-services conglomerate, concurs. As of 2006, "the richest 10 percent of Americans account for 43 percent of income, and 57 percent of net worth," based on Federal Reserve data, says a Citigroup analysis. The United States, Canada, Australia and the United Kingdom "have seen the rich take an increasing share of income and wealth over the last 20 years, to the extent that the rich now dominate income, wealth and spending." The distribution of wealth — the value of one's assets such as real estate and stocks, minus one's debts —"continues to be even more aggressively skewed" than income, it said.[4]

But having an economic class with very large amounts of disposable money is valuable — not harmful — to society, some argue. That's because only the very richest can make the investments vital to building businesses and driving demand for labor, wrote George Reisman, a professor emeritus of economics at Pepperdine University, in Malibu, Calif. "In a market economy, the wealth of the rich . . . is overwhelmingly invested in means of production, that is, in factories, machinery and equipment, farms, mines, stores, and the like."[5]

Other analysts question that proposition. "We've had a natural experiment recently with what can happen to the economy" when the richest

top 1 percent of earners "nearly quadrupled, from $347,000 to over $1.3 million," a 281-percent increase, based on data from the nonpartisan Congressional Budget Office. Over the same period, the aftertax income of the middle fifth of the population rose from $44,100 to $55,300, or 25 percent, while the bottom

people make extraordinary gains compared to others, says Yale University political scientist Jacob S. Hacker. "We've had a winner-takes-all economy for a while, and it's provided limited benefits," leaving the country with a severe recession and virtually stagnant incomes for most people.

Simmering debates over rising income inequality in America — not to mention the solvency of Social Security and the growing federal deficit — lie behind many of this year's policy and political battles.

At the heart of the debates is the system of taxing income: In the United States each additional increment of an individual's income is taxed at a different rate in a so-called "marginal" tax scheme; marginal income tax rates on higher earnings are generally higher — known as a "progressive" taxation scheme. And while many liberals this year have called for raising the marginal tax rate on the highest earners, that's a bad idea, said Sen. Joseph Lieberman of Connecticut, a former Democrat who became an independent during a tough reelection campaign a few years ago. "To me, these are the people we need to be protecting — their income to spend and invest to spur growth and job creation. The fact is that the top 3 percent of . . . earners account for 25 percent of the consumption in our economy."[6]

But history casts doubt on whether holding down taxes on the highest earnings boosts the economy, said Cenk Uygur, a journalist and political commentator on the Internet and the Sirius Satellite Radio show "The Young Turks." "From 1925 to 1931, the highest marginal tax rate was as low as it has almost ever been — between 24-25 percent. And between 2003-2010, the highest marginal tax rate was also at one of its lowest points — 35 percent," he said. "So what happened . . . ? The Great Depression and the Great Recession."[7]

The current high-profile debate over whether Social Security benefits must be cut to keep future federal budgets in balance is skewed by lack of attention to growing income inequality, argued Robert Kuttner, founder and co-editor of the liberal magazine *The American Prospect*. Social Security is funded by payroll taxes on earnings beneath a certain cap — around $107,000 in 2010. In other words, people who earn above $107,000 only pay Social Security tax on that

Tax Rates Drop for Highest Earners

The average income of the top 400 American households increased from $71 million in 1992 to $357 million in 2007 — a 403 percent rise — while the effective tax rate dropped from 26 percent to 17 percent. By comparison, the bottom 90 percent of earners saw their income rise from about $29,000 to about $33,000 — a modest 14 percent increase.

Income and Tax Rates of 400 Highest-Income American Households, 1992-2007

	Average income in 2009 dollars (in millions)	Effective tax rate
1992	$71.5	26.4%
1995	$71.6	29.9
1998	$125.0	22.0
2001	$158.8	22.8
2004	$196.2	18.2
2007	$356.7	16.6

Source: David Cay Johnston, "Tax Rates for Top 400 Earners Fall as Income Soars, IRS Data," Tax.com, February 2010

$107,000. Thus, lower-earning people pay a much higher percentage of their income to sustain the system than high earners, he said. "If you want to get Social Security well into the black for the indefinite future, the easiest way is to restore wage growth" among low earners, which would boost Social Security's take. Instead, recent earnings growth has gone almost entirely to people whose incomes are high above the cap and thus hasn't helped at all to shore up Social Security, he wrote.[8]

As economists, lawmakers and the public debate whether economic inequality should be an important public-policy agenda item, here are some questions being asked:

Is income inequality growing in the United States?

In recent years, many analysts have come to agree that income inequality is rising, mostly because incomes of the top earners have skyrocketed. However, some say that studies that find very high inequality are based on incomplete or misleading data.

In comparisons that include people's spending, for example, the effective income gap between the rich and poor is narrower, say some economists. Contrary to what some other studies find, "poor households systematically pay less than richer households for identical goods . . . in part because they shop in cheaper stores and in part because they pay less for the same goods even in the same store," most likely by buying things on sale, wrote University of Chicago professor of economics and business Christian Broda, U.S. Department of Agriculture economist Ephraim Leibtag and Columbia University professor of Japanese economy David E. Weinstein. As a result, poorer people effectively have higher-value incomes, something that most research fails to acknowledge, they argue. When the differential spending is taken into account, poverty rates turn out to be "less than half of the official numbers."[9]

Income studies generally examine "households," not individuals, and changes in household size over the years mean that supposed inequality problems are much lower than many estimate, wrote Stephen J. Rose, a research professor at the Georgetown University Center on Education and the Workforce. "Americans today are more likely to live in single-adult households than they were 30 years ago," so actual per-person earnings growth for middle-class people is considerably higher than other studies suggest, he said.[10]

The most recent statistics that indicate poverty is rising don't depict long-term poverty but recession-related job loss, argued Atlanta-based, nationally syndicated libertarian radio host and commentator Neal Boortz. "If you're out of work, you have no income. Snap! You're living in poverty. It doesn't matter what your net worth actually is" or if you "own $3 million homes free and clear."[11]

"The evidence is incontrovertible that American income inequality has increased . . . since the 1970s," said Robert J. Gordon, a professor of economics at Northwestern University. Nevertheless, its rise "has been exaggerated" since the most recent increase consists entirely of a tiny group of very high earners pulling far ahead of everyone else. Analysis of census and tax data reveals that "there was no increase in inequality after 1993 in the bottom 99 percent of the population, and the remaining increase . . . can be entirely explained by the behavior of incomes in the top 1 percent."[12]

Many other commentators, however, including some conservatives, stress that the income gap that opened between 1980 and 2000 is indeed very wide.

"Income inequality is real; it's been rising for more than 25 years," said President George W. Bush in 2007. Furthermore, the gap is serious enough to warrant careful watching, said Bush.[13]

This "growth in wage inequality is one of the most spectacular and consequential developments of our time," partly because most people have expected that economic development and modernization would create more economically equitable societies, said David B. Grusky, director of Stanford University's Center for the Study of Poverty and Inequality, and Kim A. Weeden, an associate professor of sociology at Cornell University.[14]

"Data from both . . . income tax returns and . . . W-2 records tell a simple and similar story" to the tale of inequality told by analysis of census figures, which is often criticized — to some extent correctly — for including data on too few people, said Gary Burtless, a senior fellow at the center-left Brookings Institution think tank. "The relative incomes and the relative wages of top income recipients have been increasing much faster than the incomes and wages of people further down in the distribution." W-2 records show that an earner in the top .01 percent of the income distribution made 46 times as much as the country's median wage earner in 1990, but 81 times as much in 2005, for example.[15]

Does increasing economic inequality harm society?

Most analysts agree that a certain amount of income inequality is valuable because it gives people incentives to work hard and try out new business ideas, in hopes of reaping big rewards. However, many are skeptical that current U.S. inequality levels are risk free or contribute much to building the economy.

Some international data suggest that countries with more extreme income inequality experience faster economic growth overall, said Brookings' Burtless. From 1990 to 2000, economic growth in the G-7 countries — Canada, France, Germany, Italy, Japan, the United Kingdom and the United States, whose top finance officials have met regularly since 1976 — was fastest in the United States and the United Kingdom, the countries that also "experienced the fastest growth in inequality," he said. While not constituting conclusive evidence, this fact is at least "consistent with the view that the rapid rise in U.S. inequality has contributed to the relatively good performance of American output and employment since the late 1970s."[16]

While "it's true that the share of national income going to the richest 20 percent of households" has risen, and "families in the lowest fifth saw their piece of the pie fall," income statistics don't tell the whole story of Americans' living standards, which provide evidence that rising income inequality is highly compatible with a system that produces a better life for all, wrote W. Michael Cox, director of the O'Neil Center for Global Markets and Freedom at Southern Methodist University and senior fellow at the Federal Reserve Bank of Dallas, and Richard Alm, an economics writer. Today, large majorities of Americans enjoy the convenience of once-unheard-of consumer goods like cars and clothes dryers while most are employed in "clean, well-lit, and air-conditioned environment[s]," unlike in the past, they said.[17]

Furthermore, "a far more direct measure of American families' economic status [rather than tax or census data] — household consumption — indicates that the gap between rich and poor is far less than most assume, and that the abstract, income-based way in which we measure the so-called poverty rate no longer applies to our society," they said. In 2006, while the income ratio between the highest- and lowest-earning quintiles was 15 to one, the spending ratio was only four to one, demonstrating the similarity in living standards. Lower-income families can spend more than many believe because they "have access to various sources of spending money that doesn't fall under taxable income," including "sales of property like homes and cars and securities that are not subject to capital gains taxes, insurance policies redeemed," and "the drawing down of bank accounts," they pointed out.[18]

But markets that produce income inequalities at the present scale are in fact failed markets, inefficient because they provide unreasonably high levels of return — what economists dub "rents" — to some people who don't deserve so much, argues Grusky, at Stanford's Center for the Study of Poverty and Inequality. For example, some top executives win extremely high paydays not because they lead their companies to prosper beyond expectations but due to various "sweetheart deals" and the machinations of corporate governing boards who approve outsize CEO payments because they're personally beholden to the executives, he argues.

International studies conducted over the past decade by the Organization for Economic Co-operation and Development have "found no evidence that inequality may be conducive to growth in OECD countries, as some had suggested," said OECD Secretary-General Angel Gurria. "On the contrary, our work shows that greater inequality stifles upward mobility between generations, making it harder for talented and hard-working people to get the rewards they deserve. And the resulting inequality of opportunities . . . inevitably impacts economic performance as a whole."[19]

Some fear that having too much income concentrated at the top compromises the ability of a democracy to give equal political voice to all citizens.

In international studies, nations with wider income inequality often have political structures in which fewer people have an equal voice and there is less government accountability, said Nancy Bermeo, a professor of comparative politics at Oxford University, in England.[20]

"The ability of citizens to influence public policy is the 'bottom line' of democratic government," but in recent decades in the United States the ability to influence policy has skewed toward the most affluent people, whose priorities often don't coincide with those of people who earn less, said Martin Gilens, an associate professor of politics at Princeton University.[21]

Based on survey data from 1981 to 2002, on issues where "Americans with different income levels differ in their policy preferences, actual policy outcomes strongly reflect the preferences of the most affluent but bear virtually no relationship to the preferences of poor or middle-income Americans." So stark is this finding that it may "call into question the very democratic character of our society," according to Gilens.[22]

With money concentrated at the top, "there may be a demand for private jets and yachts, but you need a healthy middle-income group" to drive the massive consumption that promotes real economic growth, said Kemal Dervis, director of the global economy and development division at the Brookings Institution.[23]

Furthermore, "when we see income inequality rising, we ought to start looking for bubbles" — fast-rising prices in some investment sector like the Internet stock bubble of the 1990s and the housing bubble of the 2000s, said Mark Thoma, a professor of economics at the University of Oregon. Such investment bubbles aren't sustainable because they ultimately price things beyond their value and out of reach of too many buyers, and their collapse leads to heavy losses and, often, economic recessions.[24]

Rising inequality also played another role in sparking the financial-market crash and recession, according to University of Chicago professor of finance Raghuram Rajan. Because policy makers have few tools available for directly raising incomes, Washington took the dangerous step of subsidizing large numbers of high-risk mortgage loans — such as no-down-payment loans — to people who may have had limited ability to pay, out of concern that the "American dream" might be slipping away from many people as inequality increased, he said. Those actions helped create the swelling bubble of mortgage debt that exploded when some people began defaulting on their risky loans, said Rajan.[25]

Should the government act to limit inequality?

Not surprisingly, those who argue that income inequality boosts the economy strongly oppose government actions intended to limit its growth or redistribute incomes. Meanwhile, analysts who argue that inequality is risky don't necessarily agree about policies to address it.

"Democrats are right about one thing: I can afford to pay more in taxes," said Harvard economics professor N. Gregory Mankiw. "My income is not in the same league as superstar actors and hedge fund managers, but I have been very lucky. . . . I don't have trouble making ends meet," and "indeed, I could go so far as to say I am almost completely sated. . . . Nonetheless," neither high earnings nor large inherited estates should be subject to higher taxes because such taxes would sap the incentive of top professionals to work hard, Mankiw said.[26]

Mankiw noted that he is "regularly offered opportunities to earn extra money," but if Bush-era tax rates were raised, the resulting gains for him and for his children — who will inherit the money down the line — would be too small to provide an incentive for him to take those extra jobs, he wrote. The same would hold true for other "high-income taxpayers whose services you enjoy," like movie actors, pop singers, blockbuster novelists, top surgeons, and orthodontists, Mankiw argued. "As they face higher tax rates, their services will be in shorter supply. . . . Don't let anyone fool you into thinking that when the government taxes the rich, only the rich bear the burden."[27]

Attempts to put a floor under the lowest income, such as a minimum wage, also harm society, said Art Carden, an assistant professor of economics and business at Rhodes College in Memphis. A higher minimum wage is "likely to exacerbate rather than mitigate social inequalities" because when potential hires aren't permitted to compete intensely for jobs by offering to work for very low wages, then "firms can discriminate on the basis of something other than productivity," he argued.[28]

With no minimum wage set, a "historically disadvantaged" jobseeker, such as "Crackhead Carl, a middle-aged African-American male who was just released from jail," could win a job over "Tad Vanderbilt Rockefeller, a flaxen-haired white teenager from an affluent suburb" — even from a racially biased employer — simply by accepting a rock-bottom wage, said Carden But with a minimum wage in place, Carl could offer a racially biased employer no incentive to hire him rather than Tad, he explained.[29]

Many scholars say that if greater economic equity is the goal, it's hard to imagine it coming about without government action.

"What are the pathways to create a more equal society? Taxation, education and health care," says Dan Ariely, a professor of behavioral economics at Duke University.

"There's nothing anti-capitalist about saying that the sharp edges of capitalism should be softened by government," says Yale's Hacker. A quick look around the globe "shows that capitalism is consistent with a lot of different ways of organizing the economy," including some with high taxes and strict regulations. The wide variation in income-inequality ratios in countries with market economies show that high U.S. ratios aren't simply the inevitable product of a market economy, he says.

In 2008, the ratio between the pay of the average CEO and the average worker was 319 to one in the United States but only 11 to one in Japan, 12 to one in Germany, and 47 to one in Mexico, suggesting that the U.S. distribution is out of line with those in other market economies, including some that are doing fairly well economically, such as Germany, according to the progressive Institute for Policy Studies.[30]

In the past, strong economic growth has proven to be compatible with high tax rates on top earnings, argued Clinton administration Secretary of Labor Robert Reich, a professor of economics at the University of California, Berkeley. "Under President Dwight Eisenhower (whom no one would have accused of being a radical) it was 91 percent. Now it's 36 percent," the "lowest it's been in more than 80 years."[31]

The highest earners have benefited disproportionately from recent workplace productivity gains, so taxing top earnings higher would seem only fair, suggested Northwestern's Gordon and Ian Dew-Becker, a doctoral candidate at Harvard University. Between 2001 and 2004, for example, the U.S. labor force produced an "explosion" in productivity — over 3 percent a year — higher productivity gains than at any other period since World War II, they wrote. Nevertheless, median family income actually fell by 3.18 percent from 1999 and 2004, and — for the whole period of rising productivity between 1995 and 2004, — increased annually by only 0.9 percent, compared to an annual rate of productivity gains in non-farm businesses of 2.9 percent, they said.[32]

During this period of skyrocketing productivity, "only the top 10 percent of the income distribution enjoyed a growth rate of total real income . . . equal to or above the average rate of economywide productivity growth." Thus, the "no-brainer solution to central social objectives" including the budget deficit, Social Security and health care is to "raise taxes on the top 1 percent by a major amount, say from 33 to 50 percent," Gordon and Dew-Becker recommended.[33]

"I know many well-educated professionals convinced that nobody works as hard as they do," wrote Jonathan Cohn, senior editor of *The New Republic*. . . . But I've met many people at the bottom of the income ladder who work just as hard, for far less reward. Between 1980 and 2005, the richest 1 percent of Americans got more than four-fifths of the country's income gains. Does

Rich Got Richer While Poor Lagged

The top 1 percent of American earners took in an average of $1.3 million after taxes in 2007, nearly a 300 percent increase over 1979. By contrast, income for the bottom 20 percent of earners rose only 16 percent over the same period.

Average After-tax Income, 1979 and 2007
(in 2007 dollars)

Income category	1979	2007	% change	$ change
Lowest fifth	$15,300	$17,700	16%	$2,400
Second fifth	$31,000	$38,000	23%	$7,000
Middle fifth	$44,100	$55,300	25%	$11,200
Fourth fifth	$57,700	$77,700	35%	$20,000
Top fifth	$101,700	$198,300	95%	$96,600
Top 1 percent	$346,600	$1,319,700	281%	$973,100

Source: Arloc Sherman and Chad Stone, "Income Gaps Between Very Rich and Everyone Else More Than Tripled in Last Three Decades, New Data Show," Center on Budget and Policy Priorities, June 2010

anybody seriously believe that the other 99 percent didn't deserve to take home a much larger share?"[34]

An investment in postsecondary skills training and education for people who can't find jobs in an increasingly technology-based job market would ease income inequality by holding wages for high-skill jobs down a bit as the supply of skilled workers came closer to meeting the full demand, says Anthony P. Carnevale, a research professor at the Georgetown University Center on Education and the Workforce. The 11 million or so "low-income, dislocated or imprisoned adults with an immediate ability to benefit" from new training programs "are the low-hanging fruit," he wrote.[35]

Government policy should focus on education rather than any direct means of redistributing income such as through tax policy, wrote University of Chicago economists Kevin M. Murphy and Gary S. Becker, winner of the 1992 Nobel Prize for economics. Taxing higher incomes is tantamount to taxing college tuition while giving subsidies "for dropping out of high school," a strategy no one would recommend, Murphy and Becker write. Instead, "the public should focus attention on how to raise the fraction of American youth who complete high school."[36]

Not everyone is sure that education funding will help ease inequalities.

Bleak Futures Await Those with Limited Education

"You need to target kids who are coming out of prison for the first time."

"People up to age 30 who only have a high school diploma or less are in trouble," potentially facing a lifetime of incomes sagging farther and farther behind those of people with a college education or technical training, says Timothy M. Smeeding, a professor of public affairs and economics at the University of Wisconsin, Madison.

They face a bleak future because most of the "traditional roads" to a middle-class income for people with that level of education, such as manufacturing, have dried up. The resulting large oversupply of workers must fight for jobs with low skill requirements, driving down the wages for those positions even further and increasing the nation's income inequality, Smeeding says.

When the recession ends, "it will become clear that there is no work for these people," except jobs like waiting table or mowing lawns. "We have to get more people employed or we'll lose a whole generation. We need to get the less-skilled people to work before they all turn to crime," Smeeding says. Worse, among young men with a high school education or less, 73 percent are fathers by age 30. Furthermore, a high school dropout is likely to have 2.7 children, compared to the 1.9-child average for college graduates, creating a huge additional economic disadvantage for children of low-skilled parents.

If after 1983 the country had continued to produce bachelor's and associate's degree holders at the same rate of increase as it did in earlier years, there would be 10 million more such degree holders competing for high-skill jobs, and "the income distribution would look like it did in 1979," according to Anthony P. Carnevale, director of the Georgetown University Center on Education and the Workforce. Instead, high school graduation rates stalled beginning in the mid-1970s and even dropped in some years, curtailing the number of people eligible for post-secondary training, even as the rates of high school graduates who went to college rose.

The workplace income gap between high-skilled and low-skilled employees relates more to specific occupations, such as engineering, than to education itself, says Carnevale. For example, "you can get a 13-month certificate in engineering and earn more" than a significant chunk of people with B.A.s, he says. "It's access to an occupation that makes the difference, and education gets you that access."

The country needs to produce more people with post-secondary education, especially in technical fields, Carnevale says. "Are we going to be able to do that? It's doubtful." Unlike with K-12 education, "we tend to see higher education as something families do, not as a public

"The last 15 years" have actually "seen significantly slower job growth in high-earnings growth sectors than in the economy at large," wrote James K. Galbraith, a professor of government, and J. Travis Hale, a graduate student, at the University of Texas, Austin. "So even if large numbers of young people 'acquire the skills needed to advance,' there is no evidence that the economy will provide them with suitable employment. Moreover, investments in education presuppose that we know, in advance, what education should be for." For example, "students who studied information technology in the

mid-1990s were lucky; those completing similar degrees in 2000 faced unemployment."[37]

BACKGROUND

All That Glitters

At the end of the 18th century, the young United States was known as the "best poor man's country" in the world, with fertile farmland plentiful enough for most people to earn a decent living and little of either extreme poverty or extreme wealth to be found.[38]

good," and the result is that it's tough to expand higher-education opportunities and especially tough to bridge a spending gap between institutions — "we have huge differentials in spending," he says.

The Obama administration is taking a different and somewhat more promising tack than previous administrations, understanding that "community colleges and public universities are where the students and the voters are,' says Carnevale.

Meanwhile, the "premium" salaries that go to college-educated people increase income inequality, representing a "market failure" in the education system, says David B. Grusky, director of Stanford University's Center for the Study of Poverty and Inequality.

In a rational market, schools "would see rising demand" for post-secondary education and open up more spots, says Grusky. "Any rational market will do that." If a car manufacturer sees more demand, the company increases production of cars. But universities, especially high-status schools like Stanford, are likely to continue to limit their spots, despite increasing demand, because by doing so the degrees and certificates their graduates obtain will be worth higher salaries in a marketplace where demand for the degrees outstrips supply, he explains.

As a result, the salary "return for a college degree is too high today," and "the college-educated people are getting a free ride," Grusky says. "We haven't had substantial investments" in public higher education for a long time, but making them could help, he says.

Young people coming out of jail and prison, who are overwhelmingly urban teenagers, face the worst lifetime income gap, says Smeeding. "I told our governor that you need to target kids who are coming out of prison for the first time, help them get jobs. Because if they don't get a job quickly, within a few weeks they'll be career criminals," and since three of four are fathers, helping them is a twofer.

The widespread incarceration of young men — mostly African-American but also Latino and white men — who have a high school education or less is driving increased social and economic inequality in our society that is "sizable . . . enduring" and "intergenerational," said sociologists Bruce Western at Harvard and Becky Pettit at the University of Washington, Seattle. "The social and economic penalties that flow from incarceration are accrued by those who already have the weakest economic opportunities," and their prison records impose additional "significant declines in earnings and employment" that affect them and their children. [1]

Ironically public-spending trends over the past several decades have reinforced these inequality-creating trends, especially at the state level. For example, 30 years ago, 10 percent of California's general fund went to higher education and 3 percent to prisons. Today, higher education's share has dropped to 8 percent, and nearly 11 percent goes to prisons, so that the state spends more on inequality-increasing incarcerations than on inequality-reducing education. [2]

— *Marcia Clemmitt*

[1] Bruce Western and Becky Pettit, "Incarceration and Social Inequality," *Daedalus*, summer 2010, p. 8.

[2] "Rising Above the Gathering Storm, Revisited: Rapidly Approaching Category 5," Members of 2005 Rising Above the Gathering Storm Committee, National Academies of Sciences and Engineering and Institute of Medicine, 2010, www.nap.edu/catalog/12999.html.

A century later, however, with the industrial age booming, the United States experienced the first of three eras of very high income inequality.

The first stretched from around 1870 through the early 1900s and was characterized by ostentatious spending by industrial titans, even as poverty deepened. Humorist and social critic Mark Twain and essayist and novelist Charles Dudley Warner dubbed the period "the Gilded Age" in their 1873 novel satirizing the corruption in Washington that accompanied what the authors depicted as a mad national scramble after wealth, at the expense of other values.[39]

Gradually, unease grew about economic inequality that might threaten the country's cherished reputation as a land where all residents had the chance to rise.

In hopes of demonstrating that Americans at all income levels were enjoying the fruits of booming industry, University of Wisconsin statistician Willford I. King launched the first major study of U.S. wealth and income distribution, publishing two books on the subject. King unhappily reported, however, that economic inequality was steeper than he had expected, with the richest 1 percent of the population taking home about 15 percent of the national income in 1910, giving the wealthiest Americans an income hundreds or even thousands of times greater than that of a working-class citizen.[40]

"It is easy to find a man in almost any line of employment who is twice as efficient as another employee, but it is very rare to find one who is ten times as efficient," mused King. "It is common, however, to see one man possessing not ten times but a thousand times the wealth of his neighbor," largely due to some people's "greater facility of taking advantage of . . . laws and circumstances to acquire property rights" and the fact that "wealth tends to breed wealth," he wrote. "Is the middle class doomed to extinction, and shall we soon find the handful of plutocrats, the modern barons of wealth, lined up squarely in opposition to the property-less masses?"[41]

The vast sums of heritable wealth amassed by industrialists also posed a danger to society if they were simply passed on to the next generation, opined steel magnate Andrew Carnegie in his 1889 essay "The Gospel of Wealth." "In many cases the bequests are so used to become only monuments of . . . folly." Far better to establish a charitable institution that pursues a public good that's in accordance with the wealth earners' own ideas, said Carnegie, whose own fortune established universities, libraries, museums, research institutions, a pension fund for his former employees and the think tank Carnegie Endowment for International Peace.[42]

Leeriness about the rising concentration of income and the political corruption it might spawn built support among the middle and upper classes for a so-called Progressive Era in politics, which brought new regulations for business and the modern-day progressive federal income tax, which taxes higher earners at a higher percentage, among other changes.

Congress had levied an income tax in 1861, to help pay for the Civil War. The tax withstood a court challenge but was eventually repealed when military needs lessened. In 1894, Congress enacted a second income tax, in the form of a 2 percent levy on all incomes over $4,000 (the equivalent of around $100,000 today), aimed at harnessing some of the income of the richest Americans for public purposes.[43]

But this time a Supreme Court divided 5-4 struck down the tax a year later. The Constitution barred Congress from enacting any so-called "direct" federal tax — a tax based on ownership, such as the ownership of property — unless it would be paid proportionately by the states according to their population, said the court. Unlike the earlier court, the 1895 Supreme Court deemed the income tax such an "ownership" tax.[44]

Proponents were not long deterred, however. In 1909, President William Howard Taft proposed the 16th Amendment to the Constitution to allow Congress to enact a tax on income — from any source, such as property or wages — without apportioning the tax among states based on population. By February 1913 the amendment had been ratified by the required 36 out of the 48 states.

The fortunes of the Gilded Age had largely deflated by 1920, mainly because of capital losses related to catastrophic events like World War I rather than Progressive Era reforms, according to Thomas Piketty, a professor at the Paris School of Economics, in France, and Emmanuel Saez, a professor of economics at the University of California, Berkeley.[45]

In the 1920s, however, both the stock market and the nation's top incomes began soaring again, and income inequality reached another peak in 1929. The crash of financial markets late in that year, and the Great Depression that followed, cut this second period of inequality very short, however. A number of factors kept economic inequalities from rising steeply again until around 1980, including the loss of capital by the wealthy during the Depression, World War II, and government actions to bolster lower earners and tax the wealthy more.

"The stability in income equality, where wages rose with national productivity for a generation after the Second World War, was the result of policies that began in the Great Depression with the New Deal and were amplified by both public and private actions after the war," wrote Massachusetts Institute of Technology professor of urban economics Frank Levy and professor of economics Peter Temin.[46]

For example, in the early days of the Depression President Herbert Hoover raised marginal tax rates for the highest earnings from 25 to 63 percent. Then, in 1936, President Franklin D. Roosevelt, architect of the New Deal, raised the top rate to 79 percent, with the goal of narrowing the income distribution.[47]

The first federal minimum wage was enacted in 1933, but the Supreme Court struck it down in the 1935 case *Schechter Poultry Corp. v. United States.*[48] In 1938, Congress passed another minimum-wage law, which has survived

C H R O N O L O G Y

1860s-1910s *Income and wealth inequality increase to unprecedented levels in the Gilded Age.*

1868 Massachusetts-born writer Horatio Alger publishes *Ragged Dick*, the first of dozens of popular Alger novels depicting the American dream of poor boys rising to wealth through talent and hard work.

1889 In "The Gospel of Wealth," industrialist Andrew Carnegie urges rich people to endow charities rather than passing their money on to their children.

1894 Congress passes a 2 percent tax on incomes over $4,000 (about $100,000 today); the Supreme Court deems it unconstitutional a year later.

1913 The Constitution's 16th Amendment, permitting Congress to enact a federal income tax, is ratified by the required 36 out of 48 states.

1915 In the largest such study to date, University of Wisconsin statistician Willford I. King reports that the richest 1 percent of Americans get at least 15 percent of the income.

1920s *Income inequality rises again. The top marginal income tax rate is at an all-time low 25 percent.*

1929 Driven by a growing economic bubble at the top, the stock market booms, and then crashes.

1930s-1960s *During the Depression, government safety-net programs support low earners; in World War II the top income tax rate rises to over 90 percent.*

1932 President Herbert Hoover raises top income tax rate to 63 percent.

1935 Supreme Court strikes down a minimum-wage law.

1938 Fair Labor Standards Act sets federal minimum wage at 25 cents an hour and survives a court challenge.

1959 Since 1950, the percentage of Americans in poverty has dropped from 32 to 22 percent, and median family income has risen 43 percent.

1970s-1980s *Inequality rises as top incomes soar, high school graduation rates stagnate and computers and automation squeeze out middle-earning manufacturing and other jobs.*

1973 High school graduation rates peak.

1979 U.S. manufacturing employment peaks at 21.4 million workers.

1981 President Ronald Reagan fires 11,000 striking members of the air traffic controllers union, helping to weaken the power of organized labor. . . . Reagan persuades Congress to pass the largest tax cuts in U.S. history.

2000s *U.S. productivity continues to increase, but gains go mostly to highest earners. During the economy's expansion from 2002-2007, the top 1 percent of earners capture two-thirds of income gains.*

2003 Top marginal tax rate is cut to 35 percent.

2006 Richest 10 percent of Americans account for 57 percent of the nation's net worth.

2007 Since 1979, the average after-tax income for the top 1 percent of earners nearly quadruples, rising from $347,000 to more than $1.3 million; after-tax income for the bottom fifth averages $17,600, up 16 percent from 1979.

2008 Ratio between the pay of the average CEO and the average worker is 319 to one in the United States, 11 to one in Japan, 12 to one in Germany and 47 to one in Mexico.

2010 Since 1979, the average pretax income has dropped $900 for the bottom 90 percent of households but risen $700,000 for the top 1 percent. . . . The nation's growing income gap since 1993 is entirely accounted for by soaring incomes for the top 1 percent of earners. . . . Large majorities of Americans support raising the minimum wage and taxing the wealthy more and creating a more equal income structure, such as that in Sweden; Republicans, who oppose these actions, nevertheless regain control of the House of Representatives in the midterm elections.

Is Upward Mobility Still Possible?

Research suggests it's becoming more difficult.

The gap between rich and poor may be wider than ever in the United States, but the U.S. remains, in the dreams of many, a land of equal opportunity — where talent and hard work are the tickets to a better future for anyone. Current data suggest, however, that the dream may have faded a bit.

"The U.S. today has a lower rate of intergenerational mobility than Europe, and that would be a surprise to most Americans," says Richard J. Murnane, a professor of education and society at the Harvard Graduate School of Education. "The key reason for this is the difficulty the poor face trying to get the education they need" to get into occupations that would allow them to move ahead, according to Murnane.

"Americans have an optimistic faith in the ability of individuals to get ahead within a lifetime or from one generation to the next," believing this much more strongly than people in other countries, wrote Julia B. Isaacs, a policy fellow at the Brookings Institution, a center-left think tank. In a survey of people from 27 countries, for example, only 19 percent of Americans thought that coming from a rich family was essential or very important to getting ahead, compared to a median of 28 percent in all the other countries.[1]

In reality, however, Americans are much less likely to move from one economic level to another than people in many other countries, said Isaacs. In a study of eight of the most highly industrialized countries, the link between parents' earnings and children's economic attainment was strongest in the United States and the United Kingdom, where it takes an average of six generations for wealthy families' economic advantage to stop influencing the economic status of their children, she reported. In Canada, Norway, Finland and Denmark, by contrast, it takes only three generations "to cancel out the effects of being born into a wealthy family."[2]

Being born at the top or the bottom of the income distribution affects people much more in the United States than in Canada, said Miles Corak, a professor of economics at Canada's University of Ottawa. For example, in the United States, 22 percent of sons born to fathers in the bottom tenth of the income distribution remain in the bottom tenth as adults, while 18 percent move up only into the next decile; in Canada only 16 percent of those born into the bottom decile stay there and 14 percent move up to the next decile. A similar "stickiness" holds for the top-earning decile, Corak said.[3]

Race plays a major role in trapping people at the bottom of the ladder, according to a 2009 report from the Pew Charitable Trusts Economic Mobility Project. About 47 percent of black children born to families in the middle fifth of the income distribution fall into the bottom fifth as adults, "compared to only 16 percent of middle-income white children."[4]

Some analysts further argue that society has built-in mechanisms to keep people from high-earning families

legal challenge. Meanwhile, the National Labor Relations Act of 1935 — often called the "Wagner Act," for its sponsor Sen. Robert F. Wagner, D-N.Y. — endorsed the right of workers to unionize, strike and engage in collective bargaining with management while limiting the means employers could use to fight unions.[49]

Inequality Rises

When the most recent new era of rising inequality began, around 1980, many were surprised.

As Galbraith at the University of Texas explained, "the very essence" of being a "developed" nation lies in industrialization, long believed to foster both democracy and "the emergence of a stable, middle-class working population, paid at rates which vary only by the range of skills in the workforce." By contrast, "the very essence of underdevelopment is not poverty per se" but a skewed income and wealth distribution with a few very wealthy people at the top and the vast majority of people struggling below.[50]

Nevertheless, in the past three decades the United States and to a lesser extent other industrialized countries, especially Canada and the United Kingdom, have seen a rise of economic inequality whose cause analysts struggle to understand.

Initially, suspicion focused on supply-and-demand trends in the workforce stemming from increased immigration

from falling out of their spots. For example, in a recent analysis of so-called "legacy" college admissions, Richard D. Kahlenberg, a senior fellow at the Century Foundation, a liberal think tank, reports that at selective colleges alumni children generally make up 10 to 25 percent of the student body. Since the proportion of alumni children each college accepts varies little from year to year, that suggests "an informal quota system," he says. Statistical analysis suggests, he says, that being a legacy boosts a student's chance of admission to a selective school by about 20 percentage points — say, from a 40-percent to a 60-percent chance — over a non-legacy student with a similar transcript and scores. [5]

The existence of such a strong tradition of legacy admissions by the most selective colleges — whose graduates also may have a leg up in many job markets — is especially damaging to African-American and Hispanic students, for example, who have been underrepresented at America's most prestigious colleges in the past and thus will continue to get no legacy boost for several generations to come, Kahlenberg said. [6]

Many conservative and libertarian analysts, however, argue that, as with many purported measures of economic inequality, researchers who find low economic mobility in the United States look at the wrong studies and interpret them too narrowly.

Some studies show high mobility, said Jagadeesh Gokhale, a senior fellow at the libertarian Cato Institute, and Pamela Villarreal, a graduate student fellow at the conservative National Center for Policy Analysis. For example, a study has shown that between 1984 and 1994 almost two-thirds of families in the lowest tenth of the income ladder in 1984 had reached a higher rung 10 years later, they pointed out. Meanwhile, 47 percent of the families in the top tenth of earners in 1984 had fallen to a lower decile 10 years later. [7]

Furthermore, "wealth is highly mobile in the United States," where "most fortunes are earned, rather than inherited," write Gokhale and Villarreal. On *Forbes* magazine's annual list of the 400 richest Americans, for example, the vast majority of the 2,218 people listed from 1995 to 2003 — 87 percent — made the cut for only one or two years during the period, they note, indicating that most of the very top earners don't hold onto their top incomes long, as others climb to take their place. [8]

— Marcia Clemmitt

[1] Julia B. Isaacs, "International Comparisons of Economic Mobility," Economic Mobility Project, Pew Charitable Trusts, February 2008, www .economicmobility.org/assets/pdfs/EMP_InternationalComparisons_ ChapterIII.pdf.

[2] *Ibid.*

[3] Miles Corak, "Chasing the Same Dreams, Climbing Different Ladders," Economic Mobility Project, Pew Charitable Trusts, January 2009, www.pewtrusts.org/uploadedFiles/wwwpewtrustsorg/Reports/ Economic_Mobility/EMP_Chasing%20the%20Same%20Dream_ Full%20Report_2010-1-07.pdf.

[4] "Renewing the American Dream: A Road Map to Enhancing Economic Mobility in America," Economic Mobility Project, Pew Charitable Trusts, November 2009, www.economicmobility.org.

[5] Richard D. Kahlenberg, "10 Myths About Legacy Preferences in College Admissions," *The Chronicle of Higher Education*, Sept. 22, 2010, http:// chronicle.com.

[6] *Ibid.*

[7] Jagadeesh Gokhale and Pamela Villarreal, "Wealth, Inheritance and the Estate Tax," NCPA Policy Report No. 289, September 2006, www. ncpa.org/pub/st/st289.

[8] *Ibid.*

and more women workers. Recent analyses find that these suspect trends don't tell the whole story, however.

For example, since women first began entering the workplace in large numbers, beginning in the 1970s, studies show that they've actually outperformed men on average when it comes to "moving out of moderately skilled jobs" and into higher-level, better-paid occupations, said journalist Timothy Noah in a recent series of articles in the online magazine *Slate*. That statistic means that women's employment isn't holding workers' wages down substantially. [51]

Immigration, meanwhile, has had some effect in holding down wages for low-skilled workers, but its overall contribution to inequality is less than expected.

In 2000, the average income of a native-born high school dropout was about 7.4 percent lower than it would have been that year had the immigration that occurred between 1980 and 2000 never occurred, concluded George J. Borjas, a professor of economics and social policy at Harvard. Immigration depressed the incomes of high school graduates by only 2.1 percent over the two-decade period, however, Borjas said. [52] It appears that only about 5 percent of the overall increase in income inequality observed over the past three decades is due to immigration, according to Noah. [53]

A bigger culprit may be what scholars call skill-based technological change (SBTC) — technology-driven

Courts Open Door to Big-Money Political Donors

Do the rich wield more political power than the poor?

In the 2010 campaign season, a single political action committee (PAC) poured $600,000 into the Nevada Senate race on behalf of the Republican challenger, Sharron Angle, who came close to unseating Senate Democratic Majority Leader Harry Reid on Nov. 2. Big spending by PACs is nothing new in political campaigns, but the Ending Spending Fund that operated in Nevada represents a new wrinkle — a PAC funded by a single big donor. [1]

Two 2010 court rulings — the Supreme Court's controversial January decision in the so-called *Citizens United* case and a March ruling by the U.S. Court of Appeals for the District of Columbia Circuit in *Speechnow.org vs. the Federal Election Commission* — cleared the way for outside donors to pour unlimited funds into elections, as long as they don't coordinate with political candidates or party committees. [2] Outside donors can now sponsor election advertising, for example, without abiding by older campaign rules, such as individual-donor spending limits. That opens the door for a PAC like the Ending Spending Fund, bankrolled by J. Joseph Ricketts, the Omaha-based founder of the discount online stock brokerage Ameritrade. [3]

This new avenue for wielding political clout is part of a historical trend over the past several decades that is consolidating disproportionate political power in the hands of the richest citizens, some scholars argue.

"The Founding Fathers believed in political equality, meaning that whether one is rich or poor would determine a person's market power but not their power in the democracy," says Jacob S. Hacker, a professor of political science at Yale University. "I believe we're falling quite dramatically short of this," as wealthier people have gradually developed institutional means like PACs and lobbies to see their favored policies enacted into law and regulation, and the government has become more friendly to these efforts, he says.

"There may exist mechanisms or pathways of influence by which a very small set of oligarchs" — rich people who wield political power —"could, to a far greater extent than their numbers alone would suggest, have a major impact on policy outcomes," wrote Northwestern University political scientists Benjamin I. Page and Jeffrey A. Winters. They

point to the many "highly professionalized and extremely expensive" lobbying organizations that have sprung up in Washington since the mid-20th century, mostly representing business and professional groups. Meanwhile, once-powerful labor unions now represent only about 15 percent of the U.S. workforce, mostly government workers. "The pluralist dream of balance among competing interest groups" is thus "largely discredited," while "those who are able and willing to invest large sums of money" in increasingly professional and expensive lobbying efforts have "a big advantage," they argue. [4]

Politicians' increasing need for fundraising has helped lobbies to increase the power of big-money business interests, wrote Hacker and Paul Pierson, a professor of political science at the University of California, Berkeley. For example, beginning in the 1970s, television advertising and modern public-opinion polling allowed candidates to reach unheard of numbers of people with messages shrewdly crafted to tap into voters' prime desires. The ads and the "pricey political consultants" whom candidates hired to poll and develop campaign strategies greatly increased politicians' reliance on big-money donors, Hacker and Pierson argue. [5]

Based on decades of detailed polling data on different income groups, it's clear that "when the opinions of the poor diverged from those of the well-off, the opinions of the poor ceased to have any apparent influence: If 90 percent of poor Americans supported a policy change, it was no more likely to happen than if 10 percent did," according to political scientist Martin Gilens at Princeton University. [6]

By contrast, when well-off people supported a policy change, it was three times more likely to occur than if they opposed it. Furthermore, the middle class did not fare much better than the poor when their opinions departed from those of the well-off. When median-income people strongly supported a policy change, it had hardly any more chance of occurring than a change that they strongly opposed, Gilens said. [7]

The policy preferences of wealthy people tend to diverge from those of other citizens on various issues, according to

Page, who has begun an extensive study of this question. His preliminary work finds that 58.8 percent of the richest Americans — in the top 4 percent of income — identify as Republicans, for example, compared to 36.1 percent of others. Very high-income Americans are more likely than others to be liberal or libertarian on social issues — favoring abortion rights and the right of atheists to teach, for example. But they are more likely than others to be conservative on economic issues, not favoring government efforts to reduce economic inequalities. [8]

In the 2010 midterm elections, high earners showed a strong preference for Republican candidates and, presumably, policies, while 58 percent of those earning $30,000 or less and 52 percent of those earning between $30,000 and $50,000 voted for Democratic candidates, according to a *Wall Street Journal* analysis. The Republican preference strengthened all the way up the income ladder, with 52 percent of those earning between $50,000 and $75,000 voting GOP; 56 percent of the $75,000 to $200,000 earners; and a whopping 62 percent of those earning over $200,000. [9]

Conservative and libertarian analysts remain skeptical that economic clout helps some gain undue political influence.

While highly educated people wield greater influence, "it is very difficult to see how income in excess of the threshold necessary to receive a high-quality education adds much to most people's pool of political resources," said Will Wilkinson, a research fellow at the libertarian Cato Institute. "Ideologically motivated wealthy Americans are limited by the menu of preexisting organizations, prevailing ideas and the supply of ideologically congenial labor," he argued. "No amount of money can buy you a think tank with your politics if there is no one with your politics to work in it." [10]

"Capitalism might indeed preclude democracy if capitalism meant that rich people really were a permanent class," wrote Council on Foreign Relations Senior Fellow Amity Shlaes. But "one capitalist idea (the railroad, say) brutally supplants another (the shipping canal)," and "within a few generations . . . this supplanting knocks some parties out of the top tier and elevates others to it." [11]

A focus on the dangers of wealth concentration simply "provides a political justification for encouraging envy," a state that leads to neglect of "family and friends, community involvement" and "charitable work" and "bolsters an empty materialism," wrote Jeffrey M. Jones, assistant director of Stanford University's Hoover Institution, a conservative

public-policy research organization, and Daniel Heil, a graduate student at Pepperdine University. [12]

Ironically, when Americans become aware that income inequality is on the rise, that knowledge actually sways the voting public away from liberal policies aimed at decreasing inequality, according to Nathan J. Kelly, an assistant professor of political science at the University of Tennessee, Knoxville, and Peter K. Enns, an assistant professor of government at Cornell University, in Ithaca, N.Y. In the United States, "public opinion moves in a conservative direction in response to income inequality," among both rich and poor Americans, potentially making income inequality a "self-reinforcing" phenomenon, they wrote. [13]

— *Marcia Clemmitt*

[1] Amanda Terkel, "The One-Person Funded Super PAC," *Huffington Post blog*, Oct. 22, 2010, www.huffingtonpost.com.

[2] The cases are *Citizens United v. Federal Election Commission*, 130 S.Ct. 876 (2010), www.law.cornell.edu/supct/html/08-205.ZS.html and *Speechnow.org, et al. v. Federal Election Commission*, No. 08-5223, http://pacer.cadc.uscourts.gov/common/opinions/201003/08-5223-1236837.pdf. For background, see Kenneth Jost, "Campaign Finance Debates," *CQ Researcher*, May 28, 2010, pp. 457-480.

[3] Terkel, *op. cit.*

[4] Jeffrey A. Winters and Benjamin I. Page, "Oligarchy in the United States?" *Perspectives on Politics*, December 2009, p. 731.

[5] Jacob S. Hacker and Paul Pierson, *Winner-Take-All Politics: How Washington Made the Rich Richer — and Turned Its Back on the Middle Class* (2010), p. 171.

[6] Quoted in *ibid.*, p. 111.

[7] *Ibid.*

[8] Benjamin I. Page and Cari Lynn Hennessy, "What Affluent Americans Want From Politics," paper delivered to the American Political Science Association, annual meeting, Washington, D.C., Sept. 2-5, 2010, www.russellsage.org/sites/all/files/u4/Page%20%26%20Hennessy%2C%20What%20Affluent%20Americans%20Want%20from%20Politics.pdf.

[9] "Democratic Coalition Crumbles, Exit Polls Say," *The Wall Street Journal online*, Nov. 3, 2010, http://online.wsj.com/article/SB10001424052748703778304575590860891293580.html?KEYWORDS=voters+election+2010#project%3DEXITPOLL101102%26articleTabs%3Dinteractive.

[10] Will Wilkinson, "Thinking Clearly About Economic Inequality," *Policy Analysis No. 640*, Cato Institute July 14, 2009, www.cato.org.

[11] Amity Shlaes, "An Age of Creative Destruction," *The Wall Street Journal online*, Oct. 29, 2010, http://online.wsj.com.

[12] Jeffrey M. Jones and Daniel Heil, "The Politics of Envy," tech-archives.net website, Aug. 21, 2009, http://sci.tech-archive.net.

[13] Nathan J. Kelly and Peter K. Enns, "Inequality and the Dynamics of Public Opinion: The Self-Reinforcing Link Between Economic Inequality and Mass Preferences," *American Journal of Political Science*, October 2010, p. 855.

changes in the skills workers need to get good jobs, especially as many medium-skill jobs, such as manufacturing, move overseas in a globalized economy where companies can pay people less to do the same work in less-developed economies.

"The American economy grew rapidly and its people 'grew together'" from World War II to about 1973, wrote Harvard economists Claudia Goldin and Lawrence F. Katz. "Each generation of Americans achieved a level of education that greatly exceeded that of the previous one," and this situation allowed businesses based on new technologies to find enough high-skilled workers. At the same time, the emergence of new, larger cohorts of skilled Americans generally created a demand and supply balance in the workforce that kept skilled workers' salaries from rising too high — and thus driving income inequality compared to low-skilled workers — because many people could compete for high-skilled occupations, Katz and Goldin wrote.[54]

"Historically, education has been the primary pathway of upward mobility in the United States," says Richard J. Murnane, a professor of education and society at the Harvard Graduate School of Education. In 1973, the United States had the highest high school graduation rate among OECD [Organization for Economic Co-operation and Development] countries, but the education engine "stopped in the mid-1970s" as high school graduation rates stalled, he says.

Levels of income inequality "depend very strongly on the supply and demand for skills," at least among people between the 10th and the 90th percentile of the income distribution, says David Autor, an economist at the Massachusetts Institute of Technology. For example, in the early 1970s, when the huge Baby Boom generation saw a rising proportion of its members go to college, wages for higher-skilled workers temporarily fell somewhat.

In the mid-1970s, as high school graduation rates stalled and smaller generational cohorts attained adulthood behind the Baby Boomers, the supply of high-skill workers began to shrink compared to the growing demand for them in technology-based industries, Autor says. At that point, "we began to get a [wage] premium for college grads," and their rising incomes helped increase income inequality.

At the same time, the advent of the computer age allowed automation of virtually any repetitive task so that middle-skill jobs — like bookkeeping, many manufacturing jobs and even many computer programming and sales positions — gradually evaporated from the workplace or shifted overseas, explains Carnevale, at Georgetown's Center on Education and the Workforce. With high school graduation rates stagnant, a growing pool of U.S. workers are left to compete for low-skilled jobs like security guards and home-health workers, where the large supply of available workers drives down wages further, Carnevale says.

In 1973 the majority of people with a high school education or less were in the middle 40 percent of the income distribution — solidly middle class, says Carnevale. "Now that number is below 30 percent." People with B.A.s, by contrast, have remained in the middle class, and about a third have moved into the top 30 percent of incomes, he says.

This workforce "polarization" that drives income inequality is evident in European Union and OECD countries, too, says Autor.

Winners Take All

Other scholars point to a different trend as the key driver of income inequality — a "winner-take-all" economy in which a few high earners rack up income gains that far outstrip those of everyone else.

"There was no increase in inequality after 1993 in the bottom 99 percent of the population, and the remaining increase . . . can be entirely explained by the behavior of incomes in the top 1 percent," said Northwestern's Gordon.[55]

Unlike in the Gilded Age, it wasn't investment income but high-rising salaries for people like top executives and Hollywood stars that fueled the outsized gains at the top, according to Piketty and Saez.[56]

Some argue that superstar salaries simply represent a new, globalized market rationally presenting very high rewards to people whose wares sell to tens of millions of people worldwide. "I think there are people, including myself at certain times in my career, who because of their uniqueness warrant whatever the market will bear," said Leo J. Hindery, a managing partner of the New York City-based private equity fund InterMedia Partners.[57]

But others say that government structures and policies — not just market forces — have played a large role in the U.S. shift of income toward the very top earners.

For one thing, financial-industry executives make up nearly 20 percent of the people with salaries in the top

1 percent of the U.S. income distribution, and "it strains credulity to say they are . . . the talented tamers of technological change" who've benefited from skill-based technological workplace change, write Yale's Hacker and University of California, Berkeley, political scientist Paul Pierson. The financial crisis demonstrated that "plenty of the so-called financial innovations that their complex computer models helped spawn proved to be just fancier (and riskier) ways of . . . benefiting from short-term market swings," not the true innovation that markets presumably reward.[58]

Over the past several decades, wealthy business interests have organized into lobbies, political action committees (PACs) and think tanks, at the same time as the main organizations that once represented the working class — labor unions — have shrunk, leaving some business sectors like finance with enormous power to influence government policies, Hacker and Pierson argue. Furthermore, beginning in the 1970s, TV ads and pricey opinion-poll surveying became a necessity for political campaigns, greatly increasing politicians' need for high-dollar contributors and increasing those contributors' influence in Washington, they contend. As a result, "government policy has grown much more generous toward the fortunate."

"Financial deregulation didn't just happen, nor did tax policy" that saw corporate and inheritance taxes as well as marginal taxes on high incomes drop significantly, says Hacker. "The government has made and remade markets" by law and regulation, and the much smaller income differentials that prevail in every other market-based industrialized economy make clear that U.S. income inequalities result from policy choices, he says.

For example, not market forces alone but deliberate government policies drove the "precipitous" decline in U.S. union membership that began just after World War II — when more than one in three workers was a union member — and continues today, when about one in nine is, and most union members are government, not private-sector, workers, Hacker says. While unions aren't blameless in their own demise, and globalization has realigned markets, over the past few decades Congress, state legislatures and successive White Houses dragged their feet on measure after measure that would have strengthened unions' bargaining power, he says.

The result is the loss of a key political force that was "broadly representative of the middle class" in a way that

no other large, politically influential organization has been —"a key source of voter turnout" and "a counterweight in boardrooms" to represent the interests of middle- and low-wage workers, Hacker says.

Economic troubles fueled lawmakers' increasingly business- and wealth-friendly policies beginning in the late 1970s, said University of Arizona professor of sociology and political science Lane Kenworthy. "Stagflation" — slow economic growth combined with rising prices and high unemployment —"and a surge in imports had turned [Americans' long-held] optimism [about the economy] to worry," and the "underlying pessimism" persisted through the late 1990s, making policy makers "more willing to entertain the pleas of business interests," whatever they might be.[59]

CURRENT SITUATION
Policies Debated

Although few members of Congress or candidates in the hotly contested 2010 elections have specifically addressed the question of whether growing economic inequality is bad or good, the issue simmers beneath many of the hottest election-year debates, including taxes, the minimum wage and the power of unions.

In light of the country's fiscal problems, many Democrats in Congress, along with President Obama, have called for the wealthiest to take on a greater share of the public burden. In a heated debate that remained unresolved when Congress adjourned its main session in the fall to campaign, the White House and most Democrats backed the idea of extending Bush-era tax cuts for family earnings under $250,000 and letting the cuts expire for dollars earned above that level.[60]

"In order to save our children from a future of debt, we will . . . end the tax breaks for the wealthiest 2 percent of Americans," said Obama.[61]

But Republicans and some conservative Democrats argue that high-earners' money is the key driver of the whole economy. "History shows and good economic theory shows, if you reduce taxes, you're going to have more economic activity," said Republican Minnesota Gov. Tim Pawlenty, on CBS News' "Face the Nation" on Oct. 31. "If you don't extend those Bush tax cuts — all of them — it's going to send a very negative signal," said

Should tax cuts on high earnings be extended?

YES
Alan Reynolds
Senior Fellow, Cato Institute

Written for *CQ Researcher*, November 2010

In 2001, Congress assembled a time bomb with a 10-year fuse. Unless the lame duck Congress acts with atypical urgency, all tax cuts enacted in 2001-2003 will vanish on Dec. 31.

If lawmakers fail to defuse the tax time bomb by the end of the year, withholding taxes will increase dramatically. Moreover, if lawmakers and the president can't agree on a solution by year's end, the top tax on dividends would jump from 15 percent to 39.6 percent, ensuring a stock market crash. The estate tax would jump to 55 percent with only a $1 million exemption. Marginal tax rates would rise by 3-5 percentage points across the board.

President Obama has appeared eager to hurl himself on top of this bomb. He threatened economic homicide and political suicide by threatening to veto any solution that did not impose much higher taxes on two-earner couples and small businesses earning more than $250,000. Yet the president has had eight months to enact the tax hikes in his 2011 budget. If he couldn't do it then, he certainly can't now. Everyone knows this is playing with fire. The targets of Obama's planned tax increases account for a fourth of all consumer spending, and a greater fraction of entrepreneurship and investment.

Christina Romer, formerly Obama's top economic adviser, found that a U.S. tax increase amounting to 1 percent of gross domestic product (GDP) reduces real GDP by nearly 3 percent within three years, with employment falling 1.1 percent. Harvard economists Alberto Alesina and Silvia Ardagna found that "fiscal adjustments, those based upon spending cuts and no tax increases, are more likely to reduce deficits . . . [and] less likely to create recessions."

Under the fanciful assumption that Obama's tax hikes on "the rich" did no damage to the economy, his plan is estimated to raise $35 billion next year. That would cover the budget deficit for just nine days. This is all risk and no reward.

The White House is now rumored to be willing to compromise on legislation that postpones the president's planned tax hikes on upper-income families while supposedly making "permanent" all other Bush tax cuts. That may not be the ideal solution, but it buys time for the new Congress to tackle the budget in an economy that is rising slowly rather than falling fast.

NO
Chuck Marr
Director of Federal Tax Policy, Center on Budget and Policy Priorities

Written for *CQ Researcher*, November 2010

Letting President Bush's tax cuts for incomes over $250,000 expire on schedule at the end of December is the right move from the standpoint of both equity and economic efficiency.

Recent decades have witnessed a stunning shift in incomes from the middle class to those few at the top. Between 1980 and 2005, about 80 percent of the country's total income gains went to the top 1 percent of the population, according to a report by MIT researchers Frank Levy and Peter Temin. Moreover, while incomes stagnated for middle-class Americans in recent decades, they surged for the wealthy — in stark contrast to the decades between the mid-1940s and mid-1970s, when income growth was widely shared. The average middle-income American family had $13,000 less after-tax income in 2007 than it would have had if incomes of all groups had grown at the same average rate since 1979.

Tax policy is one of the best tools we have to help offset the troubling trend of growing inequality. Unfortunately, President Bush's tax cuts have had the opposite effect, providing much larger benefits — both in dollar terms and as a percentage of income — to people at the very top than to middle- and lower-income people.

In fact, people making more than $1 million a year get an average of about $129,000 each year from the Bush tax cuts, according to the Urban Institute-Brookings Institution Tax Policy Center. The main reason, of course, is the large tax cuts targeted specifically at high-income households. Extending the tax cuts for high-income people would only make inequality worse. (High-income people would still benefit from an extension of the so-called "middle-class" Bush tax cuts, since the first $250,000 of their income would be taxed at the lower marginal tax rates.)

Extending the high-end tax cuts doesn't make sense from an economic perspective, either. The Congressional Budget Office (CBO) rated it the least cost-effective of 11 options for boosting economic growth and job creation. A far better alternative would be to extend President Obama's Making Work Pay tax credit, which is targeted to people who live paycheck-to-paycheck but is also scheduled to expire at the end of December. This would generate two to three times the economic growth and job creation as extending the high-end Bush tax cuts, according to CBO.

The right course, then, would be to let the high-end Bush tax cuts expire, locking in significant long-term budgetary savings, while temporarily extending the Making Work Pay credit while the economy remains weak.

Pawlenty, who is reportedly mulling a run for the White House in 2012.[62]

Most recently, the White House reportedly favors a plan to temporarily extend the cuts for earnings over $250,000 while extending the cuts permanently for earnings under that amount. With Congress in upheaval following the elections, it's not clear whether lawmakers will tackle the issue in the final days of the 2010 "lame duck" session, when most newly elected members won't yet be seated.

Conservative candidates campaigning around the country this fall spoke out against government mechanisms intended to push the income distribution more in favor of lower earners.

John Raese, West Virginia's Republican nominee for the Senate, and Joe Miller, the Republican nominee for Senate in Alaska, for example, argued that the Constitution does not give Congress the power to set a minimum wage for the nation but reserves that power for states.[63] (Similar arguments were made on the two occasions when Congress enacted federal minimum-wage laws, in 1933 and 1938. The Supreme Court struck down the first law as unconstitutional in 1935,[64] but upheld the 1938 Fair Labor Standards Act in a unanimous 1941 decision, *U.S. v. Darby*.[65])

Linda McMahon, the Republican nominee for Senate in Connecticut, opposed increasing the minimum wage, and Rand Paul, Republican nominee for the Senate in Kentucky, suggested a very cautious approach to minimum-wage increases.[66]

How big a role candidates' views on income redistribution played in election results isn't clear, but for these Senate hopefuls the results were mixed: Paul won his race; Raese, McMahon and Miller lost, but Miller is contesting his narrow defeat to write-in candidate Republican Sen. Lisa Murkowski, the incumbent.

Meanwhile, four states voted on ballot measures in November that would slow the growth of unions, and all the measures were approved. Voters in Arizona, South Carolina, South Dakota and Utah approved making a secret vote by workers the sole allowable means of determining whether an authorized workplace union has been formed, outlawing an alternative practice that requires an employer to recognize that a union has been formed any time a majority of workers have signed cards authorizing union formation.[67]

Ambivalent Public?

The public, meanwhile, remains both confused and ambivalent about the underlying question of whether economic inequalities are worrisome.

"It is usually only left-leaning rich people that care about inequality in the U.S.," said Carol Graham, a senior fellow at the Brookings Institution think tank.[68]

Nevertheless, some polling suggests that the public may be fairly supportive of government policies to prop up lower incomes, in particular. For example, an October poll found 67 percent of respondents favoring an increase in the minimum wage from its current $7.50 an hour to $10 an hour, even including a majority — 51 percent — of Republicans. Among people who identified themselves as belonging to the Tea Party, however, 50 percent opposed the increase and 47 percent supported it.[69]

Underlying the ambivalence is the fact that few Americans accurately gauge the level of income inequality, some researchers say.

The public tends to guess right about lower- and middle-income wages, but few seem aware of how high the highest salaries actually are, reports Benjamin I. Page, a professor of decision making in Northwestern University's political science department, and Lawrence R. Jacobs, a professor of political studies at the University of Minnesota. The average person surveyed estimated $250,000 to be the annual income for a heart surgeon and $500,000 for the CEO of a large corporation. The guesses were well off the mark, especially for CEOs. The average heart surgeon earns over $400,000, while the CEOs of Standard & Poor's 500 companies average over $14 million in annual income.[70]

"Even professional economists" generally underestimate current levels of inequality, says Duke's Ariely.

This finding isn't surprising, says Michael I. Norton, an associate professor of business administration at Harvard Business School. "As an average person, we don't really see the very rich or their wealth. It's in trusts" and other financial forms "that make it mostly invisible. People don't see very poor people in their lives, either."

At the same time, the public generally believes that society would be more just if incomes varied a bit less widely, says Norton, who, along with Ariely, conducted a recent study asking people how they would like to see income distributed in a hypothetical society, if they knew that they would be placed into that society at some random spot.

"When you ask people a specific question about a tax cut or some other proposal, you tend to have a very hostile debate. So we stepped back and looked at a very broad level" of what kind of society people actually desire, "and when we did that, people agreed a lot," Norton says.

When shown unlabeled diagrams that actually depicted the income distributions of the United States and Sweden — where inequality is much lower than in the United States — fully 92 percent of Americans surveyed preferred to live in the unlabeled country with the Swedish distribution, says Ariely. Furthermore, "when you look at the apparently differing ideology of Republicans and Democrats, the differences" in how members of the two parties answered the question "are very, very small," with 90 percent of Republicans opting for the Swedish distribution, compared to 93 percent of Democrats.

A desire for overall fairness seems to be the key motivation for most, says Norton. "When people are asked about how they'd redistribute" society's wealth, "they don't just give it to poor, they give it to everybody," and the main sentiment people express is "the rich just have somewhat too much."

When it comes to "taking that broad vision and boiling it down to policy, though, that's very hard to do," Norton acknowledges. "At both the macro and the micro level, people have certain ideas about what they want their lives to be, but very often our decisions go the other way."

OUTLOOK

Progressive Era Redux?

Whether the American economy will continue the trend toward greater inequality or adopt policies to rein in the widening gap is unclear, and lawmakers and the public vary widely in their views of which course is preferable and what policies might change things for the better.

"If you look back at the 1890s — ultimately there was a reaction to it, there was a cycle" that saw an era of progressive taxation and other measures to limit the income inequalities that marked the Gilded Age, says Northwestern's Page. "A lot of these reforms were undertaken by the upper middle class" and even some wealthier people, he says. "And there does now seem to be something in the air" that could portend a similar shift to progressive policies, as billionaires like Microsoft founder Bill Gates and investor Warren Buffett suggest that the wealthy should devote large portions of their estates to charitable and public purposes, he says.[71]

Indeed, in the Progressive Era, "the economic problems dwarfed those we have today," but the nation still came together to shape national policies to overcome them and to rein in rampant inequality, says Yale's Hacker. The same thing could happen today, Hacker says. "Whatever pessimism I have is not over the scope of the problem but over the lack of a widespread recognition" that a problem of inequality exists, he says. "We have really only begun to have this debate. We are where we were on climate change a few decades ago."

Hacker focuses on government policies related to unions, taxation and business regulation as keys to keeping economic inequalities at a reasonable level, but MIT's Autor worries that such a focus might leave Americans "thinking that the whole thing is out of our hands."

The best cure for extreme inequality is education because it creates economic opportunity, he says. "We haven't been keeping pace with the demand for skilled labor," and bolstering technical education and skills training for more young people could go a long way toward rebuilding the American workforce and the businesses that support it, he says. This issue "may not matter much to businesses," most of which can locate anywhere in the world that a skilled workforce exists, "but it matters greatly to our prosperity."

The stagnant buying power of middle- and lower-earning Americans is a severe, growing problem for the wealthiest Americans, whether they realize it or not, says Max Fraad Wolff, an economics writer and commentator who teaches at the New School University Graduate Program in International Affairs. Business leaders may bank on the emergence of global markets to replace U.S. buying power, but that's not a winning strategy, he says.

"What we know is that Americans can sell to Americans," Wolff says. "In this early phase of modernization [in emerging economies like China and India] what it means to be modern is to be Americanized," but "in the early history of the United States being modern meant being Europeanized, too," he says. "Eventually

American pride overtook that, and that will happen" to currently modernizing countries like China, too. That makes bolstering the average American's earning power a critical issue for U.S. businesses, he says.

NOTES

1. Christina Boyle, "Rich-Poor Gap Grows in the City," *Daily News* [New York], Sept. 29, 2010, p. 5.

2. *Ibid.*

3. Arloc Sherman and Chad Stone, "Income Gaps Between Very Rich and Everyone Else More Than Tripled in Last Three Decades, New Data Show," Center on Budget and Policy Priorities, June 25, 2010, www.cbpp.org.

4. Ajay Kapur, Niall Macleod and Narendra Singh, "Revisiting Plutonomy: The Rich Getting Richer," *Industry Note*, Citigroup, March 5, 2006.

5. George Reisman, "For Society to Thrive, the Rich Must Be Left Alone," *Mises Daily blog*, Ludwig von Mises Institute, March 2, 2006, http://mises.org.

6. Sen. Joseph Lieberman, press statement, Sept. 13, 2010, http://lieberman.senate.gov.

7. *Ibid.*

8. Robert Kuttner, "What Planet Are Deficit Hawks Living On?" *Huffington Post blog*, Nov. 14, 2010, www.huffingtonpost.com.

9. Christian Broda, Ephraim Leibtag and David E. Weinstein, "The Role of Prices in Measuring the Poor's Living Standards," *Journal of Economic Perspectives*, spring 2009, http://faculty.chicagobooth .edu/christian.broda/website/research/unrestricted/ z30002092155p%20%282%29.pdf.

10. Stephen Rose, "Five Myths About the Poor Middle Class," *The Washington Post*, Dec. 23, 2007, www. washingtonpost.com.

11. Neal Boortz, "Nine in 10 Politicians Will Rip This Column," *Atlanta Journal-Constitution online*, Sept. 17, 2010, www.ajc.com.

12. Robert J. Gordon, 'Misperceptions About the Magnitude and Timing of Changes in American Income Inequality," National Bureau of Economic Research, *Working Paper 15351*, September 2009.

13. "Growing Unequal? Income Distribution and Poverty in OECD Countries," Organization for Economic Co-operation and Development, October 2008, www. oecd.org/els/social/inequality.

14. David B. Grusky and Kim A. Weeden, "Is Market Failure Behind the Takeoff in Inequality?" forthcoming in David B. Grusky and Szonja Szelenyi, eds., *The Inequality Reader: Contemporary and Foundational Readings in Race, Class, and Gender*, 2nd ed.

15. Gary Burtless, "Comments on 'Has U.S. Income Inequality Really Increased?' " Jan. 11, 2007, www .brookings.edu/views/papers/burtless/20070111.pdf.

16. Gary Burtless, "Has Widening Inequality Promoted or Retarded U.S. Growth?" *Canadian Public Policy*, January 2003, p. S185, www.irpp.org/events/archive/ jan01/burtless.pdf.

17. *Ibid.*

18. W. Michael Cox and Richard Alm, "You Are What You Spend," *The New York Times*, Feb. 10, 2008, www .nytimes.com.

19. Angel Girria, remarks delivered at OECD conference in Paris, France, Oct. 21, 2008, www.oecd.org.

20. "Conference Report: Poverty, Inequality, and Democracy," Network of Democracy Research Institutes, Bratislava, Slovakia, April 26-28, 2009, p. 2, www .wmd.org/ndri/ndri.html.

21. Martin Gilens, "Inequality and Democratic Responsiveness," *Public Opinion Quarterly*, 2005 (Special Issue), pp. 778-796, http://poq.oxfordjournals.org/ content/69/5/778.full.

22. *Ibid.*

23. Quoted in Emily Kaiser, "Special Report: The Haves, the Have-nots, and the Dreamless Dead," Reuters, Oct. 22, 2010, www.reuters.com/article/idUSTRE69 L0KI20101022.

24. Quoted in *ibid.*

25. Quoted in David Wessel, "Professor Finds Many Fault Lines in Crisis," *The Wall Street Journal*, April 22, 2010, http://online.wsg.com.

26. N. Gregory Mankiw, "I Can Afford Higher Taxes. But They'll Make Me Work Less," *New York Times*, Oct. 9, 2010, www.nytimes.com.

27. *Ibid.*

28. Art Carden, "The Minimum Wage, Discrimination, and Inequality," *Mises Daily blog*, Ludwig von Mises Institute, Jan. 19, 2009, http://mises.org.

29. *Ibid.*

30. Sidney Weintraub, "U.S. Tolerance of Income Inequality," *Issues in International Political Economy*, Center for Strategic and International Studies, January 2010, www.csis.org.

31. Robert Reich, "The Perfect Storm that Threatens American Democracy," *Huffington Post blog*, Oct. 18, 2010, www.huffingtonpost.com.

32. Ian Dew-Becker and Robert J. Gordon, "Where Did the Productivity Growth Go? Inflation Dynamics and the Distribution of Income," paper presented at the Brookings Institution panel on economic activity, Sept. 8-9, 2005, www.brookings.edu/es/commentary/journals/bpea_macro/forum/200509bpea_gordon.pdf.

33. *Ibid.*

34. Jonathan Cohn, "Moral Arguments for Soaking the Rich," *The New Republic online*, Oct. 17, 2010, www.tnr.com.

35. Anthony P. Carnevale, "Postsecondary Education and Training As We Know it Is Not Enough," paper prepared for a Georgetown University/Urban Institute conference on poverty, Jan. 15, 2010, www.urban.org/uploadedpdf/412071_postsecondary_education.pdf.

36. Gary S. Becker and Kevin M. Murphy, "The Upside of Income Inequality," *The American: A Magazine of Ideas online*, The American Enterprise Institute, May/June 2007, www.american.com.

37. James K. Galbraith and J. Travis Hale, "The Evolution of Economic Inequality in the United States, 1969-2007," University of Texas Inequality Project, *Working Paper 57*, Feb. 2, 2009, http://utip.gov.utexas.edu/papers.html.

38. Claudia Goldin and Lawrence F. Katz, "The Race Between Education and Technology: The Evolution of U.S. Educational Wage Differentials, 1890 to 2005," May 2009, www.economics.harvard.edu/faculty/katz/files/Chapter8_NBER_1.pdf.

39. Mark Twain and Charles Dudley Warner, *The Gilded Age: A Tale of Today* (1873).

40. Timothy Noah, "The Great Divergence, Part One," *Slate*, Sept. 3, 2010, www.slate.com/id/2266025/entry/2266026.

41. Willford I. King, *The Wealth and Income of the People of the United States* (1915), p. 60, http://books.google.com/books?id=dmFsmjE-TqIC&pg=PA287&lpg=PA287&dq=%22willford+i+king%22+%22the+wealth+and+income+of+the+people+of+the+united+states%22&source=bl&ots=0hVvJxnasb&sig=ilCydUCzxxTa1YW85i40XnS7ZAA&hl=en&ei=Y8HFTK36CMH7lwfBhokG&sa=X&oi=book_result&ct=result&resnum=5&ved=0CCAQ6AEwBA#v=onepage&q=efficient&f=false.

42. Andrew Carnegie, *The Gospel of Wealth and Other Timely Essays* (1901), p. 10, http://books.google.com/books?id=gAGvb5vIh-AC&printsec=frontcover&dq=%22the+gospel+of+wealth%22&source=bl&ots=DMxn1bs71e&sig=7CUUj34D-ignVkYztYo05sC0Rf4&hl=en&ei=JMTFTPjVMoSBlAeV_cED&sa=X&oi=book_result&ct=result&resnum=4&ved=0CCkQ6AEwAw#v=onepage&q&f=false.

43. For background, see *16th Amendment to the Constitution: Federal Income Tax* (1913), National Archives and Records Administration website, www.ourdocuments.gov/doc.php?flash=old&doc=57.

44. *Pollack v. Farmers' Loan and Trust Company*, 157 U.S. 429, www.law.cornell.edu/supct/html/historics/USSC_CR_0157_0429_ZS.html.

45. Thomas Piketty and Emmanuel Saez, "The Evolution of Top Incomes: A Historical and International Perspective," *Working Paper 11955*, National Bureau of Economic Research, January 2006, http://elsa.berkeley.edu/~saez/piketty-saezAEAPP06.pdf.

46. Frank Levy and Peter Temin, "Inequality and Institutions in 20th Century America," MIT Industrial Performance Center, *Working Paper*, June 27, 2007, www.economics.harvard.edu/faculty/katz/files/Chapter8_NBER_1.pdf.

47. *Ibid.*

48. *Schechter Poultry Corp. v. United States*, 295 U.S. 495, www.law.cornell.edu/supct/html/historics/USSC_CR_0295_0495_ZS.html.

49. Levy and Temin, *op. cit.*

50. James K. Galbraith, "Inequality and Economic and Political Change," University of Texas Inequality Project, *Working Paper 51*, Sept. 21, 2008, http://utip .gov.utexas.edu/papers.html.

51. Noah, *op. cit.*

52. *Ibid.*

53. *Ibid.*

54. Goldin and Katz, *op. cit.*

55. Gordon, *op. cit.*

56. Piketty and Saez, "The Evolution of Top Incomes," *op. cit.*

57. Quoted in Louis Uchitelle, "The Richest of the Rich, Proud of a New Gilded Age," *The New York Times*, July 15, 2007, www.nytimes.com.

58. Jacob S. Hacker and Paul Pierson, *Winner-Take-All Politics: How Washington Made the Rich Richer — and Turned Its Back on the Middle Class* (2010), p. 46.

59. Lane Kenworthy, "Business Political Capacity and the Top-heavy Rise in Income Inequality: How Large an Impact?" *Politics & Society*, June 2010, p. 255.

60. For background, see Richard Wolf, "How the Tax Cut Debate Affects You," *USA Today*, Sept. 21, 2010, www.usatoday.com.

61. Quoted in *ibid.*

62. Transcript, "Face the Nation," CBS News, Oct. 31, 2010, www.cbsnews.com/htdocs/pdf/FTN_103110 .pdf.

63. Adam Cohen, "Could the Courts Outlaw the Minimum Wage?" *Time online*/CNN, Oct. 20, 2010, www.time.com.

64. *A.L.A. Schechter Poultry Corp. v. United States*, 295 U.S. 495 (1935). www.law.cornell.edu/supct/html/ historics/USSC_CR_0295_0495_ZS.html.

65. *U.S. v. Darby*, 312 U.S. 100 (1941), http://caselaw. lp.findlaw.com/cgi-bin/getcase.pl?court=us&vol= 312&invol=100.

66. Cohen, *op. cit.*

67. For background, see "Anti-Union Ballot Measures Target Workers' Rights," *AFL-CIO NOW blog*, Oct. 27, 2010, and James Parks, "Corporate-Backed, Anti-Union 'Secret Ballot' Measures Pass in Four States,"

AFL-CIO NOW blog, Nov. 4, 2010, http://blog.aflcio .org.

68. Quoted in Kaiser, *op. cit.*

69. Arthur Delaney, "Two-Thirds of Americans Support Raising Minimum Wage: Poll," *Huffington Post blog*, Oct. 6, 2010, www.huffingtonpost.com.

70. Benjamin I. Page and Lawrence R. Jacobs, "Economic Inequality and the American Public," paper delivered at a conference at the Federal Reserve Bank of Chicago, April 2-3, 2008, http://ctcp.edn .depaul.edu/HGEwebsite/Abstracts/BenjaminPage_ Paper.pdf.

71. For background see Peter Katel, "Philanthropy in America," *CQ Researcher*, Dec. 8, 2006, pp. 1009-1032.

BIBLIOGRAPHY

Books

Cox, W. Michael, and Richard Alm, *Myths of Rich and Poor: Why We're Better Off Than We Think*, Basic Books, 2000.
Cox, a senior fellow at the Dallas Federal Reserve Bank, and Alm, a business reporter, argue that higher living standards for all Americans offset any increases in income inequality that have occurred over the past few decades.

Hacker, Jacob S., and Paul Pierson, *Winner-Take-All Politics: How Washington Made the Rich Richer — and Turned Its Back on the Middle Class*, Simon & Schuster, 2010.
Professors of political science at Yale (Hacker) and the University of California, Berkeley (Pierson), argue that the widening income gap has not occurred mainly because lower-educated workers don't have the skills to compete for jobs in a technological workplace but because the U.S. government has gradually adopted many policies that support the growth of income and wealth at the top.

Articles

Kaiser, Emily, "Special Report: The Haves, the Have-nots, and the Dreamless Dead," Reuters, Oct. 22, 2010, www.reuters.com/article/idUSTRE69L0KI20 101022.

By examining parallels between two eras when economic inequality ran high in the United States — the 1920s and the 2000s — economists struggle to understand why both periods preceded huge crashes of the financial markets and lengthy economic depressions.

Noah, Timothy, "The Great Divergence," *Slate,* **September 2010, www.slate.com/id/2267157/.**
In a 10-part series, a reporter for the online magazine discusses recent research examining the possible causes and effects of rising economic inequality.

Reports and Studies

"Income, Poverty, and Health Insurance Coverage in the United States: 2009," *Current Population Reports,* **U.S. Census Bureau, September 2010, www .census.gov/prod/2009pubs/p60-236.pdf.**
This government report finds that the median household income did not change from 2008 to 2009 but that the poverty rate increased.

Isaacs, Julia B., Isabel V. Sawhill and Ron Haskins, "Getting Ahead or Losing Ground: Economic Mobility in America," Economic Mobility Project/Brookings Institution/Pew Charitable Trusts, October 2008, www.brookings.edu/~/media/Files/rc/reports/2008/02 _economic_mobility_sawhill/02_economic_mobility_ sawhill.pdf.
Scholars from across the ideological spectrum examine research showing that social and economic mobility have been diminishing in the United States compared to other nations, despite the widespread belief that Americans have greater equality of opportunity than elsewhere.

Lindsey, Brink, "Paul Krugman's Nostalgianomics: Economic Policies, Social Norms, and Income Inequality," Cato Institute, 2009, www.cato.org/pub_ display.php?pub_id=9941.
The libertarian think tank's vice president for research argues that U.S. income dispersion resulted from technological change that keeps low-skilled workers out of many jobs, not from economic or social policies and practices like tax rates or unionization of labor.

Norton, Michael I., and Dan Ariely, "Building a Better America — One Wealth Quintile at a Time," forthcoming, *Perspectives in Psychological Science,* **www.people.hbs.edu/mnorton/norton%20ariely%20 in%20press.pdf.**
When surveyed about their preferred society, large majorities of Americans across demographic groups and the political spectrum opt for an income distribution less skewed toward the top than the current U.S. distribution.

Sherman, Arloc, and Chad Stone, "Income Gaps Between the Very Rich and Everyone Else More Than Tripled in Last Three Decades, New Data Show," Center on Budget and Policy Priorities, June 25, 2010, www.cbpp.org.
In an examination of tax and wage data from the nonpartisan Congressional Budget Office, analysts from a liberal-leaning think tank report that U.S. income is more concentrated at the very top of the economic ladder than at any time since 1928, with the income gap between the richest 1 percent of Americans and the lowest three-fifths more than tripling between 1979 and 2007.

Weintraub, Sidney, "U.S. Tolerance of Income Inequality," *Issues in International Political Economy,* **Center for Strategic & International Studies, January 2010, http://csis.org/files/publication/issues201001 .pdf.**
A political economist from a bipartisan foreign-policy think tank argues that U.S. citizens and policy makers tolerate and even promote greater economic inequality than people in many other developed nations consider fair or economically efficient.

Wilkinson, Will, "Thinking Clearly About Economic Inequality," *Cato Institute Policy Analysis 640,* **July 14, 2009, www.cato.org/pub_display.php?pub_id= 10351.**
A research fellow at the libertarian think tank argues that income statistics are a misleading measure of economic inequality and that dispersion of incomes has little relation to either human welfare or social justice.

For More Information

Cato Institute, 1000 Massachusetts Ave., N.W., Washington, DC 20001-5403; (202) 842-0200; www.cato.org. Analyzes economic issues from a libertarian point of view.

Center on Budget and Policy Priorities, 820 First St., N.E., Suite 510, Washington, DC 20002; (202) 408-1080; www.cbpp.org. Liberal-leaning think tank that analyzes economic policy implications for low- and moderate-income families.

Economic Mobility Project, The Pew Charitable Trusts, 901 E St., N.W., 10th Floor, Washington, DC 20004; www.economicmobility.org. Nonpartisan group studying trends in economic and social mobility.

Emmanuel Saez's website, http://elsa.berkeley.edu/~saez. Analysis by University of California, Berkeley, economist supports many arguments about fast-rising income inequality.

Ludwig von Mises Institute, 518 West Magnolia Ave., Auburn, AL 36832-4528; (334) 321-2100; http://mises.org.

Organization of libertarian economists who argue that economic inequalities are both smaller and less troubling than many believe.

My Budget 360 website, www.mybudget360.com/home. Advertising-supported online investment magazine posts data and analysis on economic inequalities.

Too Much website, Program on Inequality and the Common Good, Institute for Policy Studies, 1112 16th St., N.W., Suite 600, Washington, DC 20036; (202) 234-9382; http://toomuchonline.org. A liberal think tank's website posting news and commentary about economic inequality.

U.S. Census Bureau, 4600 Silver Hill Road, Washington, DC 20233; (301) 763-4636; www.census.gov. Federal agency publishes periodic reports and analysis on the economy, including income distribution.

University of Texas Inequality Project, http://utip.gov.utexas.edu. Austin-based group studying economic inequality around the world.

6

The Graying Planet

Alan Greenblatt

Health check-ups are included at a job fair for senior citizens in Seoul, South Korea. The nation's rapidly aging population threatens economic progress. Experts worldwide say that as workforces shrink and governments raise the retirement age, employers must be more willing to hire and retain older workers.

From *CQ Researcher*, March 15, 2011.

The Fahua Home for the Aged in Shanghai is full to overflowing. Tiny rooms are filled with three to four residents lying in beds crammed so tightly together that they touch. There's hardly room for anyone to walk in.

The tight squeeze is a source of continual surprise to Qing Zhuren, the manager. Traditionally, Chinese elders could depend on their children or grandchildren to take care of them in old age. But decades of strict population controls have brought down China's fertility rate at an unprecedented speed, leaving fewer children to care for their aging parents.[1]

And the size of China's elderly population is set to explode. The number of Chinese over the age of 65 is expected to triple by 2050 — faster than the worldwide aging rate. Over the next 20 years, the number of Chinese 65 and over is projected to reach 167 million — more than half the current U.S. population.

China is experiencing in fast motion what has been happening over decades in Western Europe. Far more people are living longer than ever before, which will eventually turn the traditional familiar population age "pyramid" — with lots of younger people on the bottom helping to support fewer seniors on top — on its head.

The eastern part of Germany, for instance, has seen a precipitous decline in its birth rate, leading to a rapidly aging population. In 1988 — the year before the Berlin Wall fell — 216,000 babies were born in East Germany. In 1994, only 88,000 births were reported.

Populations Worldwide Are Growing Older

European countries and Japan already have older populations than the rest of the world, but developing countries will catch up quickly. By 2050 China and Russia, along with Canada and Europe, will have the highest percentages of elderly populations, followed by India, the Middle East and parts of Africa.

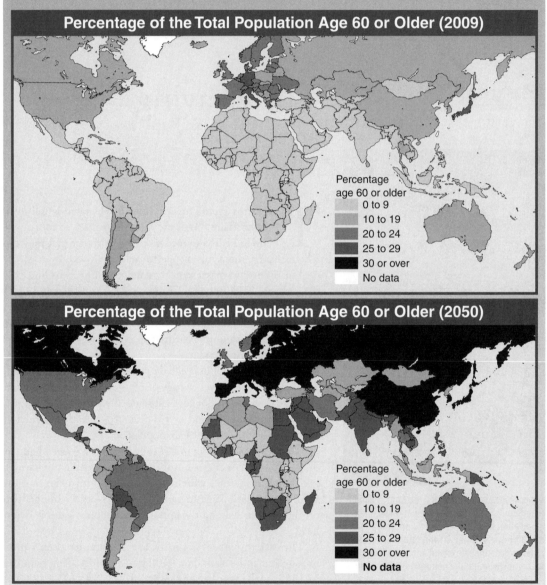

Percentage of the Total Population Age 60 or Older (2009)

Percentage age 60 or older
- 0 to 9
- 10 to 19
- 20 to 24
- 25 to 29
- 30 or over
- No data

Percentage of the Total Population Age 60 or Older (2050)

Percentage age 60 or older
- 0 to 9
- 10 to 19
- 20 to 24
- 25 to 29
- 30 or over
- **No data**

Source: "Population Ageing and Development, 2009," U.N. Department of Economic and Social Affairs, 2009

"There has been nothing comparable in world peacetime history," said Jean-Claude Chesnais, a French demographer.[2]

At one point Eastern Germany's fertility rate — the average number of children born to a given population's women over the course of their lifetimes — plunged below 1. That's well under the "replacement rate" of 2.1, or the average number of births per woman needed to replace the current population. Birthrates have picked up a bit in Eastern Germany, but not by much. In Hoyerswerda, a German city experiencing rapid population decline, schools are closing, and the town's former birth clinic is now a nursing home.

If current demographic trends persist, Germany will lose 83 percent of its native population by 2100. "Germany would have fewer natives than today's Berlin," writes British author and environmental consultant Fred Pearce in his 2010 book *The Coming Population Crash.*[3]

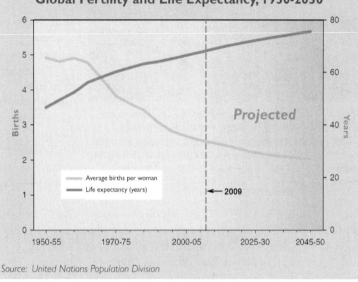

Life Expectancy Rises While Births Decline

Two trends are hastening the "graying" of the world's population: Fewer babies are being born and people are living longer. By 2050, the world's fertility rate (births per woman) is expected to have dropped to about two — less than half the rate in the 1950s. Life expectancy is expected to have increased by 29 years, to an average of 75.5, compared with a century earlier.

Global Fertility and Life Expectancy, 1950-2050

Source: United Nations Population Division

This year, the oldest members of the post-World War II "baby boom" generation (those born between 1946 and 1964) are turning 65, the vanguard of an aging population that will have immense effects on the workforces and economies in most of today's rich nations.

As people live longer, families are growing smaller. The result is a graying — and eventually shrinking — population. World population is likely to reach 7 billion in the coming months and will continue to grow beyond 8 and perhaps past 9 billion. But by mid-century it's likely to stabilize or start shrinking.

By 2050, the number of children under age 5 is expected to fall by 49 million, while the number of people over 60 will grow by 1.2 billion. In fact, by 2150 the global population could be half what it is now, according to a U.N. projection.[4]

"If you are over 45, you have lived through a period when the world population has doubled," which is both unprecedented and unrepeatable, Pearce argues. If you are under 45, he points out, "you will likely see world population decline for the first time since the plague known as the Black Death, nearly 700 years ago.

"This is the first time in history that we have been able to foresee with some certainty a decline in our numbers," Pearce writes.[5]

Rapid aging is happening first in rich countries. Italy stands to lose even more of its native population than Germany by century's end. Japan was the developed world's youngest nation in 1980 but is now the oldest country on the planet. In fact, Japan's birth rate is so low that its government has forecast that the last Japanese baby will be born in 2959 if existing trends continue.[6]

In Russia, low fertility is combined with a high death rate — caused by various health problems, including HIV/AIDS and alcoholism rates that are among the

AFP/Getty Images/Frederic J. Brown

A Chinese woman exercises at an outdoor fitness station, one of many in Beijing's residential neighborhoods. Rapidly aging nations like China face enormous challenges, especially as health care costs rise. To keep costs down, officials urge senior citizens to remain fit — both physically and cognitively — for as long as possible.

world's highest.[7] Since 1992, Russian deaths have outnumbered births by about 50 percent.[8] As a result, Russia stands to lose about one-third of its population by 2050, "a rate of population decline that has no historical precedent in the absence of pandemic," according to demographers Richard Jackson and Neil Howe of the Global Aging Initiative at the Center for Strategic and International Studies (CSIS).[9]

In most countries, rapidly aging populations are a byproduct of prosperity. Infant mortality rates have been slashed over the past century, while medical advances and improved sanitation and nutrition continue to increase life expectancy.

Throughout most of the 19th century, life expectancy was just 40 years, even in advanced economies. Today, it's 77 in developed countries and 69 worldwide, according to the Population Reference Bureau.[10]

"It's clear that life expectancy is increasing two to three years per decade," says Wolfgang Lutz, director of the Vienna Institute of Demography in Austria. "We're talking about four months per year. People are aging only from January to September."

People are not only living longer but also postponing getting married and having children. "There is a delay in all life-cycle stages: end of education, entry into the labor market, exit from the parental home, entry into union and managing an independent household," said Alessandra De Rose, a demographer at Sapienza University in Rome.[11]

Many women are staying single through their 20s and later. Fewer than 25 percent of American women are now married in their early 20s. Fifty years ago, two-thirds married by then. In Hungary, 30 percent of the women in their 30s are single, compared to 6 percent in their mothers' generation. In Japan, half of all 30-year-old women are unmarried; in South Korea, it's 40 percent.[12]

Women are not only marrying later but having children later — if at all. Over the past century, the average family in developed countries has plunged to half the size of its parents' families, although birthrates are still high in many developing countries.

But while affluent countries are aging faster, developing countries also are starting to age. Half of the world's women are now having two children or fewer — even in some developing countries, such as Iran, Burma, Brazil and Vietnam. "To make people have children they don't want to have, that's beyond the power of any despot," says Phillip Longman, a senior research fellow at the New America Foundation and author of the 2004 book about falling birthrates, *The Empty Cradle.*

Perhaps the most challenging aspect of the aging global population is the fact that longer life expectancies and declining birthrates are shrinking the working-age (15 to 64) population. Some parts of Europe already have fewer than two taxpaying workers per pensioner, making the outlook dismal for the solvency of worker-supported social security systems.

Such a fiscal course is not sustainable, says Jackson, the director of the CSIS Global Aging Initiative. In 1980, there were 62 people between the ages of 50 and 64 for every 100 people between 15 and 29 in developed countries, Jackson says. By 2005, that number had climbed to 94. Over the next 20 years, it will reach 112 and even higher in rapidly aging countries such as Germany and Japan.

And older populations are growing even faster. In developed countries, the 65-79 age group is projected to grow by 57 percent by 2050, while the number of people age 80 and older will rise by 173 percent. The populations of centenarians will rise even faster.[13]

The explosive growth of the oldest population means current expectations about pension levels and access to health care must be painfully adjusted. "The whole premise that has to underlie any social or generational contract is that it be sustainable," Jackson says. "In today's rapidly aging developed countries, the current deal is not sustainable."

As demographers, economists and policymakers prepare for an aging world, here are some of the questions they are debating:

Should official retirement ages be increased?

With the recent near-collapses of the Greek and Irish economies, fiscal policy has become a primary concern across Europe. Faced with rising pension costs and rapidly expanding senior populations, several countries have raised official retirement ages and changed other labor rules affecting older workers.

The list includes not just larger economies such as the United Kingdom, France and Spain but smaller countries such as Bulgaria and Slovenia. "Life expectancy increases by three months every year, and the current pension system does not follow such demographic changes," said Slovenian Labor Minister Ivan Svetlik, who introduced legislation passed late last year to increase the nation's retirement age for all to 65, up from 60 for men and 58 for women.[14]

The idea has been hugely unpopular. A French proposal last fall to increase the age for receiving minimal pension benefits from 60 to 62 (and from 65 to 67 for full benefits) triggered weeks of street protests. On at least two occasions, more than a million people took to the streets, while a blockade of France's main refinery led to fuel shortages at half the nation's gas stations and hundreds of canceled flights.

But the plan, touted by French President Nicolas Sarkozy, prevailed. Now, Sarkozy and German Chancellor Angela Merkel are pushing for a uniform retirement age of 67 across all countries that use the euro.

"As a response to aging populations and sustaining fiscal policies and budgets, raising the retirement age is probably one of the most important policy responses," says Vegard Skirbekk, director of the Age and Cohort Change Project at the International Institute for Applied Systems Analysis in Laxenburg, Austria.

Nearly all the longevity gains have been added to retirement years, says Lutz, of the Vienna Institute of Demography. "How should those additional years of life be allocated?" he asks. "It seems fair that not all of these years should be allocated to retirement."

But raising the retirement age remains politically unpopular, especially with aging electorates, many of which aren't convinced it's necessary. And even when countries have changed their pension plans, they haven't always stuck. Nearly 30 years ago, the United Kingdom changed its formulas for pension adjustments, pegging them to prices rather than to wages. Over time, the elderly fell behind financially. So in 2007, Britain changed its formula back.

"There's been dramatic progress in Europe and in Japan — unlike the United States — in terms of reducing the long-term burden," says Jackson, at CSIS' Global Aging Initiative. "But it's not clear whether those reforms are politically and socially sustainable."

Even demographers and economists who support later retirement ages say that won't ensure that older people will be able to find continued employment. "You can't have a blank demand that everybody works more," says Ted C. Fishman, author of the 2010 book about global aging, *Shock of Gray*. "But you can have incentives for people who want to work longer."

British author Pearce says seniors must keep their skills up to date and perhaps work in new roles, such as consulting with younger people still working in their field.

Pearce also alludes to a delicate balancing act. If older workers stay in their jobs longer, younger people may feel that they will have less opportunity for advancement. But older workers won't be able to hold onto important positions unless they can maintain their skills.

"Lifelong education can't just be a program that people pay lip service to," says Nicholas Eberstadt, a demographer at the American Enterprise Institute (AEI), a conservative think tank in Washington. "If people want to have a high standard of living, there will have to be some sort of arrangement for continuing learning, because skills that are absorbed in your 20s are out of date by your 40s, let alone your 60s."

Moreover, he says, older people will have to be paid based not on seniority but on their levels of productivity. "If an older person's productivity declines, it will have to be reflected in pay," he says. "The idea of a lifelong [salary] escalator is going to be a nonstarter."

Skirbekk agrees that "in order for individuals to remain competitive" training and education will become increasingly important for aging workers trying to keep up with technological change. And productivity declines will have to be reflected in wage decreases, he says. But employers will have to adjust as well. Companies often are reluctant to hire older workers for fear they will not bring as much energy and stamina to the job and will cost more in health insurance.

Some countries are experimenting with new policies designed to encourage hiring of older workers. As of this April, U.K. employers will no longer be allowed to force qualified workers over age 65 to retire. In January, Singapore passed a law requiring companies to re-hire qualified workers even after they reach the official retirement age of 62, becoming the second country, after Japan, to legislate "re-employment." The following month, the government announced a plan to heavily subsidize the cost of employing lower-wage older workers over the next three years.[15]

"We not only have to change the attitudes of the employees, we might have to change the social benefits they get," says Norbert Walter, former chief economist at Deutsche Bank. "At the same time, we have to educate and help the employers.

"Higher employment of older people will only make good sense if the jobs that the elderly get are appropriate for their age," he says.

China Is Aging Faster Than Rest of World

The proportion of China's population age 65 and older is expected to triple to 24 percent by 2050, while the percentage of the worldwide population age 60 and older is only expected to double during a similar period.

Proportion of Chinese Population age 65 and Older, 2007-2050

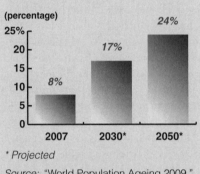

Projected

Source: "World Population Ageing 2009," U.N. Department of Economic and Social Affairs

Do younger generations bear most of the cost of aging populations?

Christopher Buckley's 2007 novel *Boomsday* opens with a scene in front of a gated retiree community in Florida, where a mob of young people are rioting, angry about having to pay for seniors' Medicare and Social Security benefits. One 29-year-old character suggests a solution to the problem of funding entitlements for older Americans: Pay them to commit suicide.

While the book was darkly satirical, some economists say intergenerational warfare could become a reality. In Germany in 2003, Philipp Mißfelder, the leader of the youth wing of the Christian Democratic Party, sparked a major controversy when he suggested that 85-year-olds should start paying for their own false teeth and hip replacements.

Mißfelder later sought to walk back his remark, saying, "Reform is needed, but there must not be a war between generations."[16] But as societies age, it's difficult to pay for skyrocketing pension and health care costs without putting a growing burden on younger workers.

Such costs will be enormous. Pension costs are likely to double in many developed countries as a share of gross domestic product (GDP), and health care will jump even faster, according to a study, "The Graying of the Great Powers," by CSIS' Jackson and Howe.

If current benefit levels are maintained for the burgeoning number of Japanese seniors, for instance, pension costs in Japan would rise from 8.7 percent of GDP in 2005 to more than 20 percent in 2050. Health care costs would rise even faster — tripling across much of the developed world by 2050.[17]

If wealthy countries weren't already running deficits, they might be able to offer generous solutions that would be less painful for people of all generations, says Walter, the former Deutsche Bank economist.

But that is not the case. "We have not prepared society for the change, and the transition process will be painful and not short," says Walter. "We will have not only younger people protesting but older people as well."

In the United States, cutting popular senior entitlement programs such as Social Security and Medicare remains difficult for politicians to contemplate, so they are proposing serious cuts in programs aimed primarily at younger people, including education and infrastructure. "In a democracy, where every vote counts the same, the elderly have a tendency to vote more frequently than young people," says Lutz, the Austrian demographer.

"It's against their personal interest to reallocate money from pensions to helping the younger people," Lutz says. "The good news is that many surveys show that elderly people who have their own children and grandchildren feel a great intergenerational solidarity and want to help them."

But author Fishman notes that there's a difference between wanting to help the young within one's own family and helping young people in general. "It changes the whole underpinning of projects like public education," Fishman says. "In families, money flows down between generations. In the public realm, money flows up to the older generation."

While the scramble for ever-scarcer resources may have a generational element, it also has a racial and ethnic tinge. In the United States, Hispanics comprise a much larger share of the under-20 population than they do among seniors. The same is true among Muslims in Europe.

Minorities now make up more than two-fifths of all Americans under 18 and will represent a majority of them by 2023, according to William Frey, a demographer at the Brookings Institution, a think tank in

Washington. Non-Hispanic whites, by contrast, make up more than four-fifths of American seniors — a share that will only slip slowly in the future.

"Over time, the major focus in this struggle is likely to be between an aging white population that appears increasingly resistant to taxes and dubious of public spending and a minority population that overwhelmingly views government education, health and social-welfare programs as the best ladder of opportunity for its children," American political reporter Ronald Brownstein wrote in the *National Journal* last year.[18]

And the competition for resources between generations will not always favor the elderly. Younger people may rebel at footing the bill for seniors' entitlements and for the interest on deficits that such programs help cause, CSIS demographer Jackson says.

"Will young, brown people, already sending money home to their country of origin to support their aging parents, cough up an ever-rising share of payrolls to support a population of old Anglos here?" Jackson asks.

Older Nations Concentrated in Europe

Africa is home to nine of the 10 countries with the largest percentages of young people, while nine of the 10 countries with the oldest populations are in Europe.

Countries With the Youngest and Oldest Populations, 2010

YOUNGEST	% under age 15	OLDEST	% over age 65
Niger	50.1	Japan	22.6
Uganda	48.7	Germany	20.5
Burkina Faso	46.4	Italy	20.4
Congo, Dem. Rep.	46.4	Greece	18.3
Zambia	46.2	Sweden	18.3
Afghanistan	45.9	Portugal	17.9
Malawi	45.9	Austria	17.6
Chad	45.6	Bulgaria	17.6
Somalia	44.9	Belgium	17.4
Tanzania	44.7	Latvia	17.4

Source: "2010 World Population Data Sheet," Population Reference Bureau, 2010

'Youth Bulges' Can Spur Violence

"Most of the world's violence and mayhem are committed by young men."

At the same time that European and other developed societies are growing older, "it's the reverse in Arab countries," says Brian Katulis, a senior fellow at the Center for American Progress, a liberal-leaning think tank in Washington.

In fact, the Muslim world has been getting younger in recent years. In Pakistan, Iran and Saudi Arabia — for example — the share of the population made up of young males grew by more than 25 percent since the mid-1990s. [1] That helps to explain, in part, the current political upheaval that has spread from Tunisia and Egypt to Libya, Bahrain and beyond, experts say.

"The problems certainly transcend the 'youth bulge' [a disproportionate share of a nation's population falling between age 15 and 29], but in all these places it starts out with youth discontent," says Ray Takeyh, senior fellow in Middle Eastern studies at the Council on Foreign Relations, a New York-based think tank.

"Well-educated groups of young people who can't find the right jobs and are suppressed by the government . . . are a very strong force for change," says Wolfgang Lutz, an Austrian demographer. Educated youths are also most likely to access social media, the Internet and satellite television, which allows them to see how their countries' economies are faltering compared with the rest of the world.

"The youth component is crucial," says Shadi Hamid, director of research at the Brookings Institution's Doha Center in Qatar. "They're the ones most affected by structural underemployment." And that can lead more readily to discontent than unemployment, he adds, because rising expectations are not being met.

The presence of a large percentage of young people in a country — particularly if they are repressed or economically frustrated — has played out in a variety of eras and locales, from the French Revolution to the Parisian *banlieues* — the suburbs where riots among youths have broken out in recent years. "Certainly the presence of a large youth bulge can be destabilizing," says Richard Jackson, a senior fellow at the Center for Strategic and International Studies.

In addition, demographic studies statistically establish "what we've intuitively known all along," he says, "which is that most of the world's violence and mayhem are committed by young men."

Countries where people 15 to 29 made up more than 40 percent of the adult population were more than twice as likely to see civil conflict during the 1990s, according to a study by Population Action International, a Washington-based organization that advocates family planning. [2]

Young people are more prone to engage in civil disobedience for several reasons. For one thing, their risks are

Many observers are growing concerned that programs benefiting the elderly are coming under attack. Most attempts at changing pension rules target current workers to avoid hurting those who are already retired and wouldn't have time to adjust to the new rules. But policymakers increasingly are contemplating changes that would affect current retirees, since they are the source of existing deficit pressures.

Longman, at the New America Foundation, warns that poverty rates among the elderly may soon rise rapidly due to cuts in government programs, reversing trends dating back to the 1960s. And, he points out, in countries where pension and health costs have driven taxes to exorbitant levels, more and more economic activity takes place off the books.

"That's a large part of what's happening in Greece and Italy," he says. "Pension costs are too high, and younger people trade with younger people in an underground [tax-free] economy. In that sense, the young win, or hurt less than the elderly."

Can aging nations increase their birthrates?

Some nations are aging so rapidly — with birthrates too low to replace the current child-bearing generation — that they fall into what Austrian demographer Lutz calls "the fertility trap."

After fertility rates are low for a generation or so, small families become the norm, and it's difficult to raise them back up. More and more women choose to have fewer children — or none at all. In countries such as

often smaller. Many don't yet have families they would have to worry about supporting from a jail cell. They also suffer more in an economic downturn. During the recent recession, youth unemployment has spiked much higher than the workforce as a whole — a particularly acute problem in Arab countries, where jobless rates are among the world's highest.

In Saudi Arabia, unemployment among men is 10 percent, but among college-educated men the number leaps to 44 percent.[3] "If you're a young person coming of age in a country with a large youthful population, your prospects often are not very good," says Elizabeth Leahy Madsen, a senior research associate with Population Action International.

Some countries have enjoyed a "youth advantage," Madsen says, by investing in education and putting their young people to work. In the 1980s and '90s, for instance, the East Asian "tiger" economies — such as Thailand, Indonesia and South Korea — were able to shift from agriculture to more knowledge-based economies by investing in their suddenly abundant youthful human capital.

But the job market must keep up with the rise in educated youth. Most countries now experiencing a youth bulge — such as sub-Saharan Africa, Pakistan and Afghanistan — are not creating jobs fast enough to keep up with population growth, leading to mass frustration. Many societies now under siege have invested heavily in educating their young people but have not provided them with enough to do after graduation.

"We're talking about people who are college-educated and ambitious and want to accomplish something with

Getty Images/Carsten Koall

Young Egyptians participate in an anti-government rally in Cairo on Feb. 25, part of the revolution that ousted President Hosni Mubarak. Egypt's "youth bulge" has been instrumental in organizing the recent protests. With young people making up 29 percent of the country's population, many young Egyptians can't find jobs.

their lives," says Hamid. "But the jobs aren't out there, so they have to be taxi drivers."

— Alan Greenblatt

[1] Fred Pearce, *The Coming Population Crash* (2010), p. 198.

[2] Richard P. Cincotta, Robert Engelman and Daniele Anastasion, "The Security Demographic: Population and Civil Conflict After the Cold War," Population Action International, 2003, p. 13, www.populationaction .org/Publications/Reports/The_Security_Demographic/The_Security_ Demographic_Population_and_Civil_Conflict_After_the_Cold_War.pdf.

[3] Deborah Amos, "Rise of Education Lifts Arab Youths' Expectations," National Public Radio, Feb. 18, 2011; www.npr.org/2011/02/18/133 779699/rise-of-education-lifts-arab-youths-expectations.

Germany and Japan, according to AEI's Eberstadt, the number of women who end up having no children at all is approaching 30 percent.[19]

In response, numerous countries — including Australia, Poland, South Korea and Spain — have introduced programs recently to raise the birth rate by encouraging women to have more children.

Germany has built more state-financed day care centers and created a parental leave policy in 2007. Spain offers parents "baby bonuses," while Japan has allowed shorter work days for women with children. In Singapore, the official family-planning slogan has shifted from "Stop at Two" to "Three Children or More If You Can Afford It."[20]

But while programs to discourage child-bearing have worked in some countries, such as China's "one child"

policy, it's been harder to encourage women to have more children. "You can keep people from having babies through coercive state measures," says AEI's Eberstadt. "It's harder to make them have babies."

And heavy-handed government efforts to control child-bearing can have horrific, unintended consequences. China's one-child policy, for instance, has been blamed for a rise in female infanticide because of a cultural preference for boys. And in the 1960s, Romanian President Nicolae Ceausescu banned contraception and abortion in an effort to boost population growth. Thousands of women who had more babies than they could support abandoned them in Romania's 600 state orphanages. The notoriously overcrowded institutions housed an estimated 100,000 children — often

Crowds march in Toulouse, France, during nationwide strikes on June 24, 2010, to protest President Nicolas Sarkozy's plan to raise the retirement age from 60 to 62. France's state-run pension system has been under increasing pressure because people are living longer, according to Sarkozy. The plan was approved in October.

malnourished, neglected and physically or sexually abused.[21]

Still, offering incentives to boost birthrates is not a new idea. The ancient Romans offered money to families with many children, penalized bachelors and encouraged immigration by offering citizenship to immigrants. Fifteen centuries later, Jean-Baptiste Colbert, Louis XIV's finance minister, offered up the same basic menu. "Leaders have been perpetually disappointed by their population policies," CSIS analysts Jackson and Howe conclude.[22]

Falling birthrates are driven by deeply rooted social and economic developments, so a few financial incentives — what Eberstadt calls "baby bribes" — aren't going to convince people to have multiple children. At most, policies such as tax incentives merely change people's timing, economists say.

Jackson says pro-natal policies can be effective, but they must be permanent. And they can be expensive. Countries such as France and Sweden that offer extensive government support to families with children spend 3 to 4 percent of GDP on such programs — double the rate of less-generous countries such as Germany and Japan.

Immigration also can help counter population aging. If not for its immigrant population, Canada's demographic profile would look like Germany's. Instead, it looks more like the United States, an immigration magnet with a relatively high fertility rate by today's rich-nation standards.

But immigrants also grow old. Typically, within a generation or two their fertility rates come to mirror those of their new nation's population. "Foreign-born women have a higher fertility rate than Spanish women," says Margarita Delgado, a sociologist at the Spanish National Research Council. "However, it doesn't take long for this to decrease and get closer to Spanish women's behavior."[23]

Also, there aren't that many young immigrants to go around. With few exceptions, most of the world's populations are aging, even relatively young countries, such as those in Africa, the Muslim world and Latin America. So, while immigrants can help lower the median age of a tiny country like Singapore, there aren't enough available to curb aging in, say, China.

Some scholars suggest that policies making it easier for women to balance work with child-rearing are the most helpful.

Traditionally, women were more concerned with child-bearing and other family concerns than working outside the home. Now that they have opportunities for jobs and careers, Jackson says, it's important that governments and employers make it easier for workers to balance their family and working lives. "You would assume that having a female workforce . . . means fewer babies, but the opposite is actually true," Jackson says. When it's easier for women to balance work and family — and get some help at home from their spouses — women are more likely to have a second or third child. But, if women are forced to choose between family and work, many today choose to work — or to delay procreation long enough to make having multiple children unlikely.

"It's important that employers understand that the employee is a human being integrated into a family, with prior family obligations," says former Deutsche Bank chief economist Walter.

According to Eberstadt, "the best single predictor of fertility in different societies" is not external factors — such as availability of contraceptives or women's workforce participation — but cultural preferences. "It's desired family size as reported by women of childbearing age."

Perhaps that's why high fertility rates are more commonly found in religious communities. Religious fundamentalists tend to produce more babies. Heavily Mormon

Utah has a birth rate 50 percent larger than more secular-minded Vermont. "In Israel, in 1948, 4 percent of the population was ultra-Orthodox," Longman says. "Now, they're already up to 16 percent of the children of Israel."

Most monotheistic religions promote or even mandate large families. Many were founded at a time when nations or tribes were often surrounded by hostile neighbors, so large populations were viewed as defense against attack.

"Injunctions similar to Jehovah's command, 'Increase and multiply,' are found in the religions of practically every nation," Charles E. Strangeland wrote in his history of population doctrines more than a century ago.[24]

Experts predict heightened competition for resources among groups with widely differing fertility rates within the same country. Alexandra Parrs, a French scholar of the Middle East who lectures at The Johns Hopkins School of Advanced International Studies in Washington, D.C., notes that in Bahrain the Shiites have roughly double the fertility rate of Sunnis. The split between the ruling Sunni and the majority — and faster-growing — Shiite population is a major factor underlying the recent unrest in Bahrain.

"The Shia don't have power, and they outnumber the people who are trying to rule over them," Parrs says. "Hence, their anger."

Even religious orthodoxy, however, may not be enough to slow the trend toward smaller families. "Iran is usually not seen as a poster child for secularization, but its birth rate is way below replacement levels," Eberstadt says. "Tehran's birth rate is lower than New York's."

Summing up, Jackson says, "Nobody thinks you can dramatically raise the fertility rate through government policies. If children are not part of your life plan, you're not going to do anything with incentives to change that."

But, he warns, "If you don't raise birth-rates, there's no long-term solution."

BACKGROUND

Demographic Transitions

For most of human history, Fishman points out in *Shock of Gray*, people who lived past 45 had beaten the odds. Life expectancy barely budged from 25 years in Roman times to 30 years at the dawn of the 20th century.[25]

Up until the Industrial Revolution, people who were 65 or older never comprised more than 3 or 4 percent of the population. Today, they average 16 percent in the developed world — and their share is expected to rise to nearly 25 percent by 2030.[26] Demographers call such shifts from historic norms "demographic transitions."

A confluence of factors has led to the current transition. Aging was once largely synonymous with death. Older people were both rarer and more vulnerable to sudden death due to such things as infectious diseases and poor sanitation. But even as modern medicine has conquered diseases that afflict the old, it has done even more to address infant mortality. Pearce points out in *The Coming Population Crash* that when he was born, 150 out of every 1,000 babies worldwide died before celebrating their first birthdays. That number today is down to 50.[27]

With fewer people dying young, life expectancy has increased. And healthier babies have coincided with other societal and economic factors to bring birthrates down. As prosperity grows, death rates fall and people feel less pressure to have large numbers of children to help support them in their old age.

Meanwhile, women's roles have changed in most countries. Many now balance reproduction with concerns and responsibilities outside the home. Contraceptives are more widely available, while abortion has become legal and available in many countries.

Finally, as societies urbanize, fewer families need to have multiple children to help work in the fields. And the advent of pensions and other social-insurance programs means parents no longer need large families to support them as they age.

Population Boosterism

Concern that women aren't having enough children is not new. From around 1450 to 1750, write Jackson and Howe in "The Graying of the Great Powers," monarchs "showcased an unparalleled obsession" with the connection between demographics and geopolitics. Population growth was seen as a predominant source of strength, both for nations and for leaders. Kings Henry IV of France and Frederick the Great of Prussia, for instance, believed that crowded nurseries translated into large armies and navies.[28]

By the late 18th century, however, opinion among the intelligentsia began to shift away from population booster-ism. By then, much of Europe had begun its demographic transition, with mortality rates dropping as living standards improved.

In England, the population doubled between 1750 and 1800 and then again between 1800 and 1830, reach-ing 24 million.[29] Population growth emerged as a pressing concern, particularly after the 1798 publication of British economist Thomas Malthus' hugely influential *An Essay on the Principle of Population*. Malthus argued that grow-ing populations drain resources and ultimately impoverish societies. Among other things, Malthusian theory led to fear that social-welfare policies would encourage the poor to have more children.

"Dependent poverty ought to be held disgraceful," Malthus wrote. "A man who is born into a world already possessed, if he cannot get subsistence from his parents, or if the society do [sic] not want his labor, has no claim of right to the smallest portion of food and, in fact, has no business to be where he is. At nature's mighty feast there is no cover for him. She tells him to be gone."[30]

Malthus turned out to be wrong. Resources were no more finite than population levels. The Industrial Revolution helped increase the world's "carrying capacity" for feeding growing numbers of people — and increased demand for labor.

Still, concerns about population growth outstripping the supply of food and other essentials persisted well into the 20th century. Eugenics, or the attempt to control the qualities of the population by discouraging reproduction among those with so-called undesirable traits, became official policy in many countries early in the century. Japan, for instance, forcibly sterilized tens of thousands of criminals, lepers and those with mental illness. Sweden also sterilized the mentally ill. Between World War I and World War II, 60,000 "feebleminded" people were steril-ized in the United States, and some laws prevented the mentally ill from marrying.[31]

After the defeat of Nazi Germany in World War II revealed the horrific extent of the regime's eugenics experimentation — designed to create an Aryan master race partly through genocide against "undesirable" popu-lations — eugenics became a disgraced notion. In its 1948 Universal Declaration of Human Rights, the United Nations banned forced sterilization, among other practices.

Population Control

After World War II, fast-rising populations led to renewed concerns that the planet was filling up too fast. Countries such as Indonesia, El Salvador, Nigeria, Brazil, Turkey and Kenya were on course to double their populations within a generation.

From the 1940s to the '60s, both the U.S. govern-ment and private groups such as the Rockefeller Foundation sponsored family-planning efforts around the world. Mortality rates came down quickly in India after World War II and independence from the U.K., thanks largely to an effort to eradicate malaria. Fertility rates, meanwhile, were climbing fast. With births out-numbering deaths by a 2-to-1 ratio, government officials worried that population growth would prove economically devastating.

"We produce more and more food, but also more and more children," complained Jawaharlal Nehru, India's first prime minister. "I wish we produced fewer children."[32]

In 1952, Nehru released a population-control plan that encouraged vasectomies. In the coming decades, states such as Kerala and Gujarat organized mass vasectomy camps, carrying out tens of thousands of vasectomies. Some states sought to impose sterilization, requiring, for instance, that couples show proof of sterilization when seeking new housing.

Neighboring China also grew concerned about popula-tion growth. The postwar communist regime of Mao Zedong had had enormous success with health initiatives, including mass distribution of vaccines and antibodies and improved sewers. China immunized almost a half-billion people against smallpox and trained 750,000 midwives in sterile techniques.

"The results were dramatic," Pearce writes. "In Mao's first eight years in charge, Chinese life expectancy rose from 35 to 50 years."[33]

With deaths down and births up, China had a growth spurt, its population spiking from 583 million in 1953 to 700 million a decade later. In 1979, Mao's successor Deng Xiaoping introduced the "one-child policy," which limited families to one child each.

Every unit of population — every farm, workplace and street — faced limits on the number of babies they

C H R O N O L O G Y

1940s-1970s *Fast-growing populations lead to worries about overcrowding and government programs to limit fertility.*

1946 First of the 78 million American baby boomers are born; other English-speaking countries also see higher fertility rates after World War II.

1952 Indian Prime Minister Jawaharlal Nehru creates the world's first comprehensive population-control plan, promoting vasectomies.

1970 Developing countries' average fertility rate reaches 5.1 percent; it will drop to 2.9 percent by 2005.

1979 China launches its one-child policy. . . . After Iran's Islamic Revolution, government initiates programs to encourage high fertility and rapid population growth.

1980s-1990s *As the baby boom winds down, birth-rates slow. . . . The specter of aging populations emerges as a growing concern.*

1980 With only 9 percent of its population over 65, Japan is the youngest among developed countries; within 25 years it will become the world's oldest country.

1992 Abortions in Russia outnumber live births by more than 2-to-1; total births will decline by 40 percent over the next 15 years.

1994 World Bank publishes *Averting the Old Age Crisis*, promoting pension privatization in more than 30 countries.

2000s *The effects of aging are beginning to be felt as growth declines among working-age populations.*

2004 The percentage of women with no children rises from 10 percent to 16 percent in the United States, and to 18 percent among Germans.

2005 In developed countries, the share of the working-age population peaks at 61 percent. . . . Life expectancy reaches 77 in the United States and 82 in Japan.

2006 Russian government says it will raise fertility rates and reduce mortality by 2025.

2007 To encourage more women to have babies, Germany introduces a new parental-leave benefit. . . . United Kingdom reverses course on a program to index pension benefits to prices rather than wages.

2009 Japan's fertility rate drops to 1.21, among the world's lowest.

2010s *Governments begin to formulate policies to deal with their aging societies.*

2010 France raises the retirement age from 60 to 62. . . . Average life expectancy in developing regions reaches 67 except in sub-Saharan Africa, where it has tumbled due to AIDS. . . . Russia's population, expected to decline rapidly due to low birthrates and high mortality, is already 7 million below 1991 levels. . . . A study finds that 40 percent of Americans age 50 to 64 have difficulty performing basic physical tasks.

2011 United Kingdom changes compulsory retirement rules so that employers will no longer be able to force qualified workers to retire at 65. . . . In January, Spain strikes a deal with the country's two largest unions to raise the retirement age to 67. . . . Singapore announces subsidies for employers who hire low-wage older workers. . . . China is considering allowing elderly parents to demand that courts order their children to visit and look after them. . . . "Youth bulge" in Arab world contributes to unrest throughout the Middle East and North Africa.

2015 Working-age populations are projected to begin declining in the developed world, with the United States the sole major exception.

2025 Population growth will stall or decline in every major developed country except the United States, which will also be the only developed country with more children under 20 than elderly over 65.

2030 Developed countries will have 42 seniors for every 100 working-age adults.

2050 The median age is expected to reach 56 in Japan, 49 in Western Europe and 40 in the United States.

Aging Trends Affect Economic Migration

Laborers seek work in countries with older populations.

It's a bit like the weather. Just as high- and low-pressure zones move air around, differences in aging rates among countries also affect the rate of human migration.

"Instead of air pressure, you can talk about median age," says Richard Jackson, director of the Global Aging Initiative at the Center for Strategic and International Studies in Washington, D.C. "You'll tend to see population flow from countries with lower median ages to countries with higher median ages."

That's especially true in today's world, where some countries are aging rapidly and the economies in countries with higher shares of young people — such as Uganda and Afghanistan — cannot employ them all. Most immigrants leave their countries for economic reasons, although a small percentage leaves to escape political persecution.

Prior to 1990, most migrants were in developing countries, but that is no longer the case. In the past 20 years, the number of immigrants entering developed countries has more than doubled — from 48 million to 100 million — while immigrants in developing countries only rose from 52 million to 65 million, according to Stefano Zamagni, an economist at the University of Bologna, Italy. [1]

The list of countries with mismatches between labor and jobs changes over time. Fifty years ago, Spain saw a large share of its population leaving in search of work abroad. In those days, foreign-born residents were rarities in Spain — just one out of every 500 persons in 1953. Today, 12 percent of Spain's population — nearly one in eight — is foreign born.

With its elderly population on the rise, Spain now needs to import workers. A dozen years ago, Ecuadorians were

scarce in Spain. Today, some 700,000 Ecuadorians live there — a major chunk of Ecuador's expatriate population. [2]

For aging countries, attracting and keeping foreign workers at the height of their earning powers is hugely attractive economically, says Ted C. Fishman, author of the 2010 book *Shock of Gray*. The workers' home countries also benefit: Remittances — money sent home by so-called guest workers abroad — make up an important or even leading share of GDP in countries that export labor.

But countries don't like to see huge percentages of their populations go abroad — particularly the working-age cohort that is both the most productive and the most likely to leave. But incentive programs — instituted in countries ranging from the Czech Republic to the Philippines — have failed to keep workers at home.

In the receiving countries, meanwhile, there is always the risk of a backlash developing against immigrants, who often are seen as a threat to native workers' jobs or a country's values. Several European countries have been experiencing such a backlash since the economic recession began in 2008. [3]

Echoing remarks made by his French and German counterparts, British Prime Minister David Cameron complained in February that "multiculturalism" had led to segregation and encouraged radicalization of Muslim youths. "We have failed to provide a vision of society to which they feel they want to belong," Cameron said. "We have even tolerated these segregated communities behaving in ways that run counter to our values." [4]

"The prime minister was speaking to the pressure to limit the number of migrants coming in," says Fred Pearce, an author and consultant in Great Britain. That sentiment runs

were allowed. Women who were illegally pregnant were often forced to have abortions, sometimes after being abducted and taken to clinics in the dead of night. [34]

Falling Fertility

China's crackdown caused a dramatic decline in birthrates. In 1963, 43 children were born per 1,000 people. By 2003, it had dropped to just 12. Over that same 40-year period, China's fertility rate has dropped from about 6 to below 2. The government estimates that during the first

30 years of the one-child policy, China added 400 million fewer people to its population than it otherwise would have. [35] Partly as a result, China's population today is aging faster than the rest of the globe. Worldwide, the percentage of the over-60 population will double — from 11 percent in 2009 to 22 percent in 2050. But in China the percentage of the over-65 population will triple between 2007 and 2050 — to 24 percent. [36]

Meanwhile, fertility rates have been dropping in many countries for decades, interrupted only by a postwar baby

counter to the coming economic reality of aging populations. "Others, including the mayor of London, are saying that we need more migrants, they're needed in the economy."

Aside from the political push-pull regarding immigration, there also are large economic forces at play. Partly due to the high pension and health care costs associated with supporting older populations, multinational corporations may prefer to move more of their operations to countries with young workers, rather than have workers migrate in search of jobs.

"It's true that people move around in an aging world," Fishman says. "But capital also moves in an aging world, seeking young people unencumbered by age-related expenses."

And developing countries whose young people have long gone abroad for work are starting to catch up with the developed world — both in terms of aging and, to some extent, in terms of standards of living. People don't like to emigrate, so the differences in standards of living must be great enough to convince them it's worth it to pack up and move.

In Mexico, the number of children under 4 has been falling rapidly for 15 years. As the country starts to age, it won't be subject to the same level of population pressures that have contributed greatly to mass emigration over the past half-century.

"Unidirectional migration [within] Europe has stopped," says Wolfgang Lutz, leader of the World Population Program at the International Institute for Applied Systems Analysis in Austria. "In the 1970s, thousands moved from Italy to Germany and from Portugal to France or Luxembourg.

"Today, movement between those countries is free, and people in Portugal are still earning a quarter less than in Germany, but hardly anyone is coming for a higher wage."

Still, given the prospect of labor shortages in the aging rich world and continuing poverty in most of the countries

Would-be immigrants — probably from North Africa — approach the Italian island of Lampedusa on March 7, 2011. In the past 20 years, the number of job-seeking immigrants entering developed countries like Italy has more than doubled, from 48 million to 100 million. Job prospects are better in nations with aging workforces.

with the lion's share of births, economic migration appears bound to continue and even accelerate in coming years.

"As long as there are big economic differences between countries, there's going to be an incentive for migration," says Nicholas Eberstadt, a demographer at the conservative American Enterprise Institute think tank in Washington.

— *Alan Greenblatt*

[1] Stefano Zamagni, "On the Move," *SAISPHERE*, 2010-2011, School for Advanced International Studies, The Johns Hopkins University, p. 66.

[2] Ted C. Fishman, *Shock of Gray* (2010), p. 95.

[3] For background, see Sarah Glazer, "Europe's Immigration Turmoil," *CQ Global Researcher*, Dec. 1, 2010, pp. 289-320.

[4] John F. Burns, "Prime Minister Criticizes British 'Multiculturalism' as Allowing Extremism," *The New York Times*, Feb. 6, 2011, p. A6; www.nytimes.com/2011/02/06/world/europe/06britain.html.

boom that was especially pronounced in the United States and other English-speaking countries.

From 1950 to 1973, the world's population grew by an unprecedented average of 2 percent a year.[37] But demographers increasingly believe the subsequent "baby bust" will prove more the norm than the preceding boom. Fertility rates, in fact, have fallen almost continuously since the 19th century. Where it was once common to find fertility rates of 4 to 6 or even 7 in the United States and Western Europe, by the 1930s most had dropped

closer to 2. And since 1930, the average number of children born to each succeeding cohort of women ending their child-bearing years declined in nearly every developed country.[38]

Today, much of the world is not just getting old, but dramatically older. The United Nation projects that by 2025 life expectancy will rise to 84 in the developed world — up from today's 79.

Some demographers believe that the U.N. estimate is too low, because it assumes life expectancy will increase by only 1.2 years per decade, or about half the rate over the past 50 years.

CURRENT SITUATION

Aging States

Although every developed country is aging — along with most less-developed countries — they are not all aging at the same rate or in the same way. The United States is aging more slowly than Western Europe, for instance. The U.S. birth rate is the highest in the developed world, remaining close to replacement levels, and the country remains a powerful draw for immigrants, who tend to be younger than the native-born population.

While the rest of the developed world is set to lose 18 million people by midcentury, the United States is on course to gain 119 million. By 2025, it will be the only major developed country with more people under 20 than over 65 — and, thus, the only one with a working-age population that will continue to grow.[39]

By some measurements, the United States is in comparatively good shape on pensions. Social Security eats up only about half as much of GDP as more generous pension programs in France, Germany and Italy. And American men over 65 are at least three times as likely to continue working as older men in those countries.

The bad news, however, is that U.S. pension funds — both public and private — are underfunded by trillions of dollars.

Older Population to Double by 2050

The proportion of the world population age 60 and older is expected to double to 22 percent by 2050. The number of individuals age 80 and older is expected to nearly quadruple to almost 400 million during the same period.

Proportion of World Population Age 60 and Older, 1950-2050

(percentage)

- 1950: 8%
- 2009: 11%
- 2050*: 22%

World Population Age 80 and Older, 1950-2050

(in millions)

- 1950: 14.5
- 2009: 101.9
- 2050*: 394.7

* Projected

Source: "World Population Ageing 2009," U.N. Department of Economic and Social Affairs

"This has made American companies relatively uncompetitive when compared to their international counterparts, which have much more flexibility in the labor space and have not had the burden of pension costs anywhere to the degree that Western industrial companies have," said Dambisa Moyo, a Zambian international economist who has worked for Goldman Sachs and the World Bank.[40]

And the United States faces other looming age-related fiscal challenges, because health costs through Medicare and other programs far outweigh those in other countries. "The U.S., demographically, looks pretty good on paper compared to anyone else," says Longman, of the New America Foundation, "until you remember our health care encumbrance. We can't afford to get old, even a little."

Exporting Jobs

Japan, by contrast, is aging at warp speed. In 1980, Japan was the youngest of the developed countries. Now, it is the oldest country on Earth. Japan has the world's highest life expectancy — 83 — with birthrates below any other developed nation except Italy and Spain.

In 1963, there were 100 centenarians in all of Japan. By 2050, their ranks are projected to reach 1 million. Already, more than a fifth of Japan's population is over 65 — a percentage that will double by midcentury.[41] Meanwhile, Japan recorded only about 40 percent as many births in 2008 as it did 60 years earlier.[42]

AT ISSUE

Should official retirement ages be raised?

 YES

Ursula von der Leyen
Minister, Labor and Social Affairs Germany

 NO

Florian Blank, PhD
*Senior Researcher, Institute of Economic and
Social Research Hans-Böckler-Foundation
Düsseldorf, Germany*

Written for *CQ Global Researcher*, March 2011

Tomorrow's working world will be different from the one we know today. The German population is getting smaller and older. By 2030, the number of 20- to-64-year-olds will have declined by more than 6 million, while the number of those 65 and older will have risen by over 5 million.

Persistent low birthrates and longer life expectancy are to blame. By 2030, men age 65 can expect to live 19 additional years on average and women almost another 23 years — up more than two years from present rates.

Raising the standard retirement age is not just a pension-policy measure. It is also intended to convey a clear message to society and business and industry: Change your attitudes toward the potential of older employees and take appropriate action.

Demographic change will cause a substantial contraction of the labor pool, which will also be considerably older. The future task for businesses, social partners and policymakers will be to create suitable conditions for an aging labor force to maximize productivity and innovation. This can be done if company labor organization and workplace design are tailored to the specific abilities and competencies of older employees.

Longer life expectancy also means more years in good health. The aim must be to share the burden resulting from demographic change equitably among all generations. Strengthening the generational contract will avoid distribution conflicts between young and old, provided the necessary change of course is made early on. If this is not done in good time, larger adjustments will be needed later.

To safeguard social welfare and international competitiveness, we must harness more future labor potential through greater labor-force participation by older people. Switzerland and the Scandinavian countries have proven that it is not only necessary but also feasible to adjust the supply of and demand for jobs to the abilities and needs of different age groups.

Longer lifetimes also mean an increase in the time people remain healthy and capable in older age. Developments on the labor market in recent years confirm the federal government's view that labor-force participation and labor-market opportunities have much improved for the older generation. With their adherence to the new standard retirement age, policymakers have laid a firm foundation for the realignment now under way.

Written for *CQ Global Researcher*, March 2011

In 2007, the German government decided to raise the standard retirement age in the public pension insurance system from 65 to 67 by 2029. The main reason — as stated by the government — is that demographic change threatens the pension insurance fund's finances. The decision provoked fierce criticism, especially from trade unions, and probably contributed to the electoral loss of the Social Democrats in 2009.

German society, like others, is aging, and it seems to be widely accepted that this process will affect the social security system, too. However, raising the retirement age does not seem to be an adequate reaction. Not only is it seen as an affront by many future retirees, but it obscures other possible responses.

Demographic change and pension finances are not directly linked. In a contribution-based system, pension finances are heavily influenced by employment and wages. Enabling more people to keep a well-paying job until reaching the retirement age of 65 would directly affect pension finances. But today, only 38.4 percent of those between the ages of 60 and 65 are employed, and only 23.4 percent have a job subject to social insurance.

Raising the retirement age before substantially increasing labor market participation of elderly workers is putting the cart before the horse — and certain groups of employees will still need public support and ways to leave the labor market before age 65, even if employment rates of older workers rise.

Furthermore, according to government's calculations, raising the retirement age will lower future contribution rates by 0.5 percentage points while increasing future pension benefits by 0.6 percentage points.

These seem to be pretty small advantages, compared with the anxiety associated with worrying about potentially being forced to leave the workforce early due to illness, and thus receive smaller benefits.

So raising the retirement age does not tackle the real problem of how to keep people on the job and stabilize contributions through good jobs and decent wages. And since the impact on retirement incomes of raising the retirement age is ambiguous, it does not answer the question of how to guarantee retirement without financial worries.

The number of Chinese senior citizens is projected to triple by 2050 — faster than the worldwide aging rate. Within 20 years, the number of Chinese over age 65 is expected to reach 167 million — more than half the current population of the United States.

Traditionally, Japanese sons take in their aging parents, but this has created a vicious circle when it comes to the nation's aging population. Women put off getting married longer because they fear getting sandwiched between the responsibilities of caring for aging in-laws and their own children, which has translated into more women having fewer children.

Indeed, some Japanese demographers say nearly a third of the current generation of young women will have no children at all. "Some people believe the Japanese economy's lack of growth in the last couple of decades may be traceable to its aging population," says Pearce, the British author.

Japan has sought to attract some immigrants, particularly descendants of Japanese who emigrated to Latin America 100 years ago when Japan had a surplus working-age population. But the country's xenophobic immigration policies and cultural mores remain highly restrictive toward foreigners.

Instead, Japanese companies are exporting manufacturing jobs to countries with younger workers. Already, 20,000 Japanese companies have operations in China, employing 1 million people. "The model for Japan in the future is to make money from Japanese factories in foreign places where other people will do the work," said Masanao Takahashi, whose company, Taisei Industries, supplies steel parts.[43]

'Six Elders Per Child'

But China will not be able to indefinitely take up the slack left by other countries' aging workforces. China is aging so fast that some observers wonder whether it will grow old before it can grow rich enough to support an older population.

"Each country, as it develops, seems to age faster than its neighbors," *Shock of Gray* author Fishman says. "China is aging faster than South Korea, which aged faster than Japan."

China has what some demographers call a 4-2-1 problem. That is, each young adult today may be responsible for supporting not just two parents, but four grandparents, as well. "The one-child policy could just as accurately be called the 'Six Elders Per Child' policy," Fishman writes.[44]

From 1980 to 2010 — when China was growing incredibly fast — the country's working-age population grew by about 1.8 percent per year, until it reached 72 percent of the overall population. But that percentage will peak in 2016, and by 2030 it will be shrinking by nearly 1 percent a year.[45]

Already, Beijing's 60,000 nursing home beds are filled, unable to meet the needs of 2.3 million senior citizens. Nationwide, China has fewer than half as many elder-care beds per 1,000 people over 65 than is the average in developed countries.[46]

The suicide rate among Chinese elderly has been growing rapidly, and the government is considering allowing elderly parents to sue their children if they don't visit regularly.[47] "Their old-age poverty will be a big issue in the '20s and '30s of this century," predicts Walter, the former chief economist at Deutsche Bank.

Other economists note that China's aging is happening much more rapidly than occurred in the West. "China will be growing old before it becomes affluent and before it's had time to put in place the protections of a modern welfare state," the CSIS' Jackson says.

Aging Workforces

China now has three young workers — age 20 to 29 — for every two older workers age 55 to 64. Twenty years from now, that ratio will be reversed.[48]

By that time, China will be facing some of the same issues already bedeviling older societies. Economic growth has been tied strongly to employment growth — something few countries can count on in the coming decades.

CSIS analysts Jackson and Howe estimate that the lack of growth in working-age populations will markedly slow economic growth. While the U.S. GDP doubled during the 22 years leading up to the 2008 worldwide recession, experts say it will take 33 years for that to happen again, due, in part, to the aging workforce. Western Europe's economy will be hit even harder, taking an estimated 64 years to double, while Japan's will take "an incredible 168 years," according to Jackson and Howe.[49]

Severe economic consequences will become evident as the age pyramid continues to invert, with those ages 50-to-80-plus making up an increasingly large share of populations. Not only will pension and health care costs continue to escalate, but there will be less innovation and entrepreneurship, since younger workers are disproportionately responsible for such activities.

And many of today's comparatively young countries, such as Egypt and China, are facing "marriage squeezes" in coming years, with the share of men who will remain single rising rapidly to well above 20 percent. In China, this may be in part because of the gender selection that favored boy babies during the one-child policy period.[50] Worldwide, say researchers, as many as 100 million females are "missing" in cultures that traditionally prefer boy babies, due to selective abortions and female infanticide — usually by poisoning or starvation.[51]

Global aging also affects international and internal migration. "Virtually all the additional population, as we go from 7 to 9 billion people, will be urban," says author Fishman, "and urban families rarely have more than two children."

And while Western countries such as the U.K. and Germany had a century-and-a-half to adjust to their demographic transitions, newly emerging countries will see that sort of change telescoped into one or, at most, two generations, says Jackson, potentially triggering social upheaval. "These are societies experiencing a kind of future shock," he says.

Societies are just beginning to grapple with the effects of an aging world — and doing what they can to prevent it. "Have babies — Allah wants it," Turkey's prime minister, Recep Tayyip Erdogan, told a 2002 gathering in Istanbul, reacting to proposals to expand the use of contraception. "To recommend to people to not procreate is straight-out treason to the state."[52]

OUTLOOK

Age Adjustment

Aging populations — barely on the radar screens of most policymakers a decade ago — will become central to

> **"We have not prepared society for the change, and the transition process will be painful and not short. We will have not only younger people protesting but older people as well."**
>
> **— Norbert Walter, former chief economist, Deutsche Bank**

fiscal, economic and security discussions over the next decade, especially in the developed world. "It will be a decade of economic crisis and economic stagnation in most of the developed world," says Jackson, director of the CSIS Global Aging Initiative. "We will be coming to terms in a real way with the diminished economic and geopolitical stature of current [rich] countries."

Jackson believes aging societies will have to renegotiate social contracts that are no longer sustainable, triggering epochal arguments about who will bear the burden of paying for pensions and health care. Many observers worry that most societies may have already waited too long to start such debates.

"This issue is no longer neglected, but we have not yet reached a comprehensive willingness to respond in a profound way," says Walter, the former Deutsche Bank chief economist. "I'm 66, and when I say that we, the older, have to work longer hours, I get very nasty e-mails from my age cohort, even sometimes from organized groups. If I were a politician, they would be nastier."

Adjusting to aging populations won't be easy, but neither will it necessarily be all bad, suggests Pearce, the British author. It will be a problem "if we just blunder into an aging population without changing our attitudes toward the old," he says. "But if societies help . . . make it easier for older people to keep working — whether full time or in second careers as consultants — they will benefit. We will want to use the skills of old people more wisely. It may happen almost without us noticing, in the way the dominance of the youth culture crept up on us."

The elderly must stay fit longer, both physically and cognitively, says Lutz, the Austrian demographer. That presents some challenges. According to the U.S. Centers for Disease Control and Prevention, even in the United States — where older people are more inclined to keep working after age 60 than in most Western European countries — only one American in five stays physically active on a regular basis.[53] According to a recent study by the RAND Corporation think tank and the University of Michigan, more than 40 percent of Americans aged 50 to 64 have difficulty performing simple physical tasks such as walking a quarter-mile or climbing 10 steps — a big increase from a decade ago.[54]

But, Lutz says, older societies could end up being more peaceful, since seniors suffer fewer problems such as crime and drug abuse. And having fewer children may actually be a good thing, because more per capita can be spent on their education. "This can even overcompensate for their smaller numbers," Lutz says.

"Aging is part of the prosperity equation," notes *Shock of Gray* author Fishman. "I'm not sure we want to reverse this entirely."

Rapidly aging populations will present especially enormous challenges as the cost of their health care goes up. A recent Johns Hopkins University study, for instance, projected that the number of cases of Alzheimer's Disease — the debilitating form of dementia among the elderly that eventually requires the equivalent of full-time nursing home care for the patient — will quadruple by 2050, with one in 85 persons worldwide suffering from the disease.[55]

It will also require some attitude adjustment as societies learn to take full advantage of older workers' knowledge, rather than putting them out to pasture. According to a recent Wellesley College study, more over-55 workers who need to work longer than expected due to losses in their retirement savings accounts may be forced to retire than will be able to hang onto their jobs.[56]

For aging societies to prosper, many habits — including ageism and the desire of the old to seek retirement and leisure — must change. "The big thing is how to get through these first times when we're older," Fishman says, "and figure out how to reap the benefits of being older."

NOTES

1. Phenola Lawrence, "Double-Whammy: Aging China Has Fewer Children to Care for It," *Chicago Tribune*, June 30, 2010, p. 30; www.mcclatchydc.com/2010/06/24/96489/double-whammy-aging-china-has.html.

2. Quoted in Fred Pearce, *The Coming Population Crash* (2010), p. 89.

3. *Ibid.*, p. 247.

4. Phillip Longman, "Think Again: Global Aging," *Foreign Policy*, November 2010, www.foreignpolicy.com/articles/2010/10/11/think_again_global_aging.

5. Pearce, *op. cit.*, p. xviii.

6. Longman, *op. cit.*

7. Bulat Akhmetkarimov, "In Russia, Ambitions vs. Demography," *SAISPHERE*, 2010-2011, p. 14.

8. Nicholas Eberstadt, "The Demographic Future," *Foreign Affairs*, November-December 2010, p. 54.

9. Richard Jackson and Neil Howe, "The Graying of the Great Powers," 2008, p. 3.

10. "2010 World Population Data Sheet," Population Reference Bureau, 2010, www.prb.org/Publications/Datasheets/2010/2010wpds.aspx.

11. Pearce, *op. cit.*, p. 98.

12. *Ibid.*, p. 122.

13. Fishman, *op. cit.*, p. 69.

14. "Slovenia Adopts Pension System Reform, Raises Retirement Age," Agence France-Presse, Dec. 14, 2010.

15. Jeremy Au Yong, "One-off Subsidy for Hiring Low-Wage Older Workers," *The Straits Times*, Feb. 19, 2011, http://justice4workerssingapore.blogspot.com/2011/02/budget-2011-cpf-contributionswage.html.

16. Jack Ewing, "Germany: Revolt of the Young," *Business Week*, Sept. 22, 2003, www.businessweek.com/magazine/content/03_38/b3850051_mz014.htm.

17. Jackson and Howe, *op. cit.*, p. 64.

18. Ronald Brownstein, "The Gray and the Brown: The Generational Mismatch," *National Journal*, July 24, 2010; www.nationaljournal.com/magazine/the-gray-and-the-brown-the-generational-mismatch-2010 0724.

19. Stefan Theil, "Beyond Babies," *Newsweek International*, Sept. 4, 2006, www.newsweek.com/2006/09/03/beyond-babies.html.

20. Michael Cardiosk, "Singapore's Aging Population," Yahoo.com, April 19, 2009, www.associatedcontent.com/article/1621347/singapores_aging_population_the_stop.html?cat=9.

21. Kate McGeown, "What happened to Romania's orphans?" BBC News, http://news.bbc.co.uk/2/hi/europe/4629589.stm.

22. Jackson and Howe, *op. cit.*, p. 26.

23. Delgado was interviewed via email with translation assistance by Cecilia Cortes-Earle.

24. Charles E. Strangeland, *Pre-Malthusian Doctrines of Population* (1904), p. 40.

25. Fishman, *op. cit.*, p. 13.

26. Jackson and Howe, *op. cit.*, p. 7.

27. Pearce, *op. cit.*, p. xvi.

28. Jackson and Howe, *op. cit.*, p. 22.

29. Pearce, *op. cit.*, p. 6.

30. *Ibid.*, p. 5.

31. *Ibid.*, p. 24.

32. *Ibid.*, p. 59.

33. *Ibid.*, p. 77.

34. Louisa Lim, "Cases of Forced Abortions Surface in China," National Public Radio, April 23, 2007, www.npr.org/templates/story/story.php?storyId=9766870.

35. Fishman, *op. cit.*, p. 306.

36. "World Population Ageing, 2009" Population Division, United Nations Department of Economic and Social Affairs, 2010, www.un.org/esa/population/publications/WPA2009/WPA2009-report.pdf; "Asian Demographic and Human Capital Data Sheet, 2008," Asian MetaCentre, www.populationasia.org.

37. Jackson and Howe, *op. cit.*, p. 25.

38. *Ibid.*, p. 46.

39. *Ibid.*, p. 40

40. "Pensions Dull America's Global Edge, Economist Says," National Public Radio, Feb. 18, 2011, www.npr.org/2011/02/18/133860435/Pensions-May-No-Longer-Be-Sustainable.

41. Fishman, *op. cit.*, p. 144.

42. Eberstadt, *op. cit.*

43. Fishman, *op. cit.*, p. 185.

44. *Ibid.*, p. 308.

45. Nicholas Eberstadt, "The Demographic Risks to China's Long-Term Economic Outlook," Swiss Re: Centre for Global Dialogue, Jan. 24, 2011, http://cgd.swissre.com/global_dialogue/topics/ageing_longevity/Demographic_risks_to_China.html.

46. Lan Fang, "Future Starts to Age: China's Elderly," *Caixin Online*, Sept. 6, 2010, www.marketwatch.com/story/china-begins-to-suffer-aging-population-pressures-2010-09-06.

47. Sharon LaFraniere, "China Might Force Visits to Mom and Dad," *The New York Times*, Jan. 29, 2011, www.nytimes.com/2011/01/30/world/asia/30beijing.html?_r=1&ref=asia.

48. Eberstadt, "The Demographic Risks to China's Long-Term Economic Outlook," *op. cit.*

49. Jackson and Howe, *op. cit.*, p. 75.

50. Ching-Ching Ni, "The World; China Confronts Its Daunting Gender Gap; Officials seek corrective measures as a one-child policy and a preference for male offspring mean men now significantly outnumber women," *Los Angeles Times*, Jan. 21, 2005, p. A6.

51. Nicolas Kristoff, "Stark Data On Women: 100 Million Are Missing," *The New York Times*, Nov. 5, 1991, www.nytimes.com/1991/11/05/science/stark-data-on-women-100-million-are-missing.html.

52. "Contraception Is Treason, Turkish Islamist Leader Says," Agence France-Presse, Feb. 16, 2002.

53. Fishman, *op. cit.*, p. 29.

54. Linda G. Martin, Robert F. Schoeni and Patricia M. Andreski, "Trends in Disability and Related Chronic Conditions Among People Ages Fifty to Sixty-Four," *Health Affairs*, April 2010, p. 725. For background, see Beth Baker, "Treating Alzheimer's," *CQ Researcher*, March 4, 2011, pp. 193-216.

55. Ron Brookmeyer, *et al.*, "Forecasting the Global Burden of Alzheimer's Disease," Johns Hopkins University Department of Biostatistics, 2007, http://works.bepress.com/cgi/viewcontent.cgi?article=1022&context=rbrookmeyer.

56. Kelly Evans and Sarah Needleman, "For Older Workers, a Reluctant Retirement," *The Wall Street Journal*, Dec. 8, 2009, http://online.wsj.com/article/SB126022997361080981.html.

BIBLIOGRAPHY

Books

Fishman, Ted C., *Shock of Gray*, Scribner, 2010.
A former financial trader describes how aging is presenting fiscal, health and economic challenges to countries like Japan, China and the United States.

Longman, Phillip, *The Empty Cradle: How Falling Birthrates Threaten World Prosperity (and What to Do About It)*, Basic Books, 2004.
A senior fellow at the New America Foundation examines why birthrates are falling and suggests that societies find economical ways to reward child-bearing to bring rates back up.

Pearce, Fred, *The Coming Population Crash and Our Planet's Surprising Future*, Beacon Press, 2010.
A development and environmental consultant for *New Scientist* magazine traces the history of population shifts and examines past state-sponsored efforts at population control.

Willetts, David, *The Pinch*, Atlantic Books, 2010.
A member of the British parliament examines the implications of the fact that the postwar baby boomers are running up retirement bills that younger generations will have to pay.

Articles

Anderson, Gerald F., and Peter Sotir Hussey, "Population Aging: A Comparison Among Industrialized Countries," *Health Affairs*, May/June 2000, p. 191, http://content.healthaffairs.org/content/19/3/191.
Johns Hopkins University researchers compare countries' health spending, long-term care and retirement policies.

Brownstein, Ronald, "The Gray and the Brown: The Generational Mismatch," *National Journal*, July 24, 2010, www.nationaljournal.com/magazine/the-gray-and-the-brown-the-generational-mismatch-20100724.
The United States is seeing a divergence in attitudes and priorities between a heavily nonwhite population of younger people and an overwhelmingly white cohort of older people.

Eberstadt, Nicholas, "The Demographic Future: What Population Growth — and Decline — Means for the Global Economy," *Foreign Affairs*, November-December 2010, p. 54.
A demographer at the American Enterprise Institute says the "coming demographic challenge of stagnant and aging populations" threatens to put constraints on economies worldwide.

Longman, Phillip, "Think Again: Global Aging," *Foreign Policy*, November 2010, www.foreignpolicy.com/articles/2010/10/11/think_again_global_aging.
A senior fellow at the New America Foundation tries to sort out facts and myths about aging populations, pointing out that aging is not just a rich-world phenomenon. Moreover, he says, seniors can work longer only if their health improves.

Studies and Reports

"Foreshadowing the Future? The Impact of Demography," *SAISPHERE*, The Johns Hopkins University School of Advanced International Studies, 2010-2011.
SAIS scholars focus on demographic topics, many related to aging and showing its effects on health, migration and military strategy (both in general and in individual countries and regions such as Russia, Japan and Latin America).

"World Population Aging 2009," United Nations Population Division, 2010, www.un.org/esa/population/publications/WPA2009/WPA2009-report.pdf.
The latest in a series of U.N. studies finds that aging of societies is pervasive, profound and irreversible because fertility rates will not return to higher past levels.

Cincotta, Richard P., Robert Engelman and Daniele Anastasion, "The Security Demographic: Population and Civil Conflict After the Cold War," Population Action International, 2003, www.populationaction.org/Publications/Reports/The_Security_Demographic/The_Security_Demographic_Population_and_Civil_Conflict_After_the_Cold_War.pdf.
Civil conflicts between 1970 and 2000 were often sparked by demographic factors, such as youth bulges.

Haub, Carl, "2010 World Population Data Sheet," Population Reference Bureau, July 2010, www.prb.org/pdf10/10wpds_eng.pdf.
The cost of entitlements and other supports for aging populations will burden working-age people in the coming decades.

Jackson, Richard, *et al.*, "The Graying of the Great Powers: Demography and Geopolitics in the 21st Century," Center for Strategic and International Studies, 2008.
This comprehensive survey of aging trends in the developed and developing world projects how global aging will affect economic growth, national security and "social mood."

Lutz, Wolfgang, Vegard Skirbekk and Maria Rita Testa, "Forces that May Lead to Further Postponement and Fewer Births in Europe," International Institute for Applied Systems Analysis, March 2007, www.iiasa.ac.at/Admin/PUB/Documents/RP-07-001.pdf.
Three Austrian demographers say governments must revise assumptions about ideal family size and income expectations in order to avoid the "trap" of low fertility rates.

For More Information

Berlin Institute for Population and Development, Schillerstrasse 59, 10627 Berlin, Germany; 49 302 232 4645; www.berlin-institut.org. An independent institute that researches and publishes studies examining the impact of international demographic changes, including aging, on sustainable development.

Center for Strategic and International Studies, Global Aging Initiative, 1800 K St., N.W., Washington, DC 20006; (202) 887-0200; www.csis.org/gai. Explores the fiscal, economic, social and geopolitical implications of population aging.

China Ageing International Development Foundation, Room 1907, Tower B, Winterlesscenter, No.1 West Dawang Rd., Chaoyang District, 100026 Beijing, China; 10 65388759; www.caidf.org.cn. Manages several funds that aimed at serving aging populations in areas such as health.

International Longevity Center, 60 E. 86th St., New York, NY 10028; (212) 288-1468; www.ilcusa.org/. Conducts research and advocates for maximizing the benefits of the current age boom.

The Johns Hopkins University, School of Advanced International Studies, 1740 Massachusetts Ave., N.W., Washington, DC 20036; (202) 663-5600; www.sais-jhu.edu. Is sponsoring a "year of demography," holding lectures and conferences devoted to global aging and other demographic issues. Devoted entire 2010 issue of SAISPHERE magazine to "the impact of demography."

Oxford Institute of Aging, 66 Banbury Rd., Oxford OX26PR, United Kingdom; 44 (0) 1865 612800; www.ageing.ox.ac.uk. Institution that studies the effects of demographic change on income, health and other issues in the U.K. and in the less-developed world.

Population Action International, 1300 19th St., N.W., Suite 200, Washington, DC 20036; (202) 557-3400; www.populationaction.org. A research and advocacy group that aims to improve access to family planning and reproductive health care around the world.

Stanford University Center on Longevity, Landau Building, 579 Serra Mall, Stanford, CA 94305; (650) 736-8643; http://longevity.stanford.edu/. Focuses on improving quality of life, from early childhood to old age. Its Global Aging Program conducts research on the geopolitical impacts of different aging trends in developed and less-developed regions.

United Nations Population Division, 2 United Nations Plaza, Rm. DC2-1950, New York, NY 10017; (212) 963-3179; www.un.org/esa/population/. Monitors a broad range of areas within the field of population; has produced a series of conferences and publications related to aging.

U.S. Census Bureau, 4600 Silver Hill Rd., Washington, DC 20233; 1 (301) 763-4636; www.census.gov/ipc/www/idb/. Population Division's International Data Base publishes various demographic indicators for countries and areas of the world with populations above 5,000.

World Population Program, International Institute for Applied Systems Analysis, Schlossplatz 1, A-2361 Laxenburg, Austria; 43 2236 807 0; www.iiasa.ac.at. Studies how population trends influence society, the economy and the natural environment.

Voices From Abroad:

YUAN XIN

Professor of Population Studies, Nankai University China

Sacrificing for country

"China implemented its family planning policy and achieved its objective within three decades, which will, in turn, intensify some side effects. In China, the family planning policy rapidly sped up the process, with many having made or having been forced to make, a personal sacrifice to help achieve the national goal."

The Statesman (India) September 2010

HENRY KAJURA

Public Service Minister Uganda

Youth must be guided

"I agree with the members [of parliament], we cannot run a country by the youth, the youth have to be guided by older people. This is the reason why we want to establish a Civil Service College to help the youth get competence before they get jobs."

The Monitor (Uganda), July 2010

ANNE O'REILLY

Chief Executive, Age NI* Northern Ireland

Raise the retirement age

"Ageing is a global phenomenon. We believe it to be a demographic bounty that offers exciting opportunities. Policies like the default retirement age must be scrapped to ensure that there are no barriers to the full and equal participation of older people in Northern Ireland. The default retirement age is acutely ageist,

counter-intuitive and stamps an expiry date on thousands of older workers."

Belfast (Northern Ireland) Telegraph, April 2010

XIE LINGLI

Director, Shanghai Population and Family Planning Commission China

Elder care a serious issue

"Compared to families with multiple children, the offspring in single child [Chinese] families have to bear the burden of elderly parents on their own. The problem of how to provide for the aged is a serious issue."

Chinadaily.com.cn, June 2010

ANATOLIY KINAKH

Director, Ukrainian League of Industrialists and Entrepreneurs

The meaning of pension reform

"The retirement age is a part of the problem, and the government, unfortunately, is going about it the wrong way.

---

* A nonprofit that deals with problems affecting the elderly.

Ask anyone on the street what pension reform in Ukraine is all about, and, unfortunately, the answer will be this: An increase in the retirement age for women. But that's wrong."

Interfax news agency (Russia) December 2010

GIYAS GOKKENT

Chief Economist, National Bank of Abu Dhabi United Arab Emirates

Older population = slower growth
"Conceptually, growth is a function of a growth in inputs such as labour and productivity. An older population profile suggests slower growth and, therefore, slower economic growth."

Gulf News (United Arab Emirates), January 2011

BARRY DESKER, DEAN

S. Rajaratnam School of International Studies, Nanyang Technological University, Singapore

Sources of rebellion
"The youth uprising in Egypt draws attention to the impact of similar youth bulges as a result of rapid population increases over the past 20 years. . . . The authoritarian policies and lack of employment opportunities in many of these states will fuel youth rebellion. . . . The volatile mix in the greater Middle East makes this the region with the highest potential for political violence and conflict."

Straits Times (Singapore) February 2011

KIM ENG TAN

Credit Analyst, Standard & Poor's, South Korea

Pension reforms needed
"The proportion of China's population contributing to the government's revenue is likely to begin to fall soon. Unless China is able to carry through reforms in its health-care and pension financing systems, it may have to increase government funding in these areas."

Yonhap (news agency) (South Korea), October 2010

7

School Reform

Marcia Clemmitt

Thousands of young college graduates teach in urban schools through Teach for America, a nonprofit group that receives support from venture philanthropy groups such as the Bill & Melinda Gates Foundation. Above, Erin Gavin conducts a discussion with her seventh-graders in Brooklyn Center, Minn., on Feb. 4.

AP Photo/Andy King

From *CQ Researcher*,
Apr 29, 2011.

K aren Caruso, a third-grade teacher in Los Angeles, read the embarrassing news last August in the *Los Angeles Times*: She was in the bottom 10 percent of city elementary teachers, according to the paper's analysis of seven years of students' performance on standardized math and English tests.

Yet, that poor showing didn't fit Caruso's profile. A 26-year classroom veteran, she was among the district's first teachers certified by the prestigious National Board for Professional Teaching Standards, and her principal had named her one of the best teachers at Hancock Park Elementary School, which serves a mainly upper-middle-class neighborhood.

Caruso was taken aback by the *Times*' findings but told the newspaper she was determined to do better. "If my student test scores show I'm an ineffective teacher," she said, "I'd like to know what contributes to it. What do I need to do to bring my average up?"[1]

It's a question teachers nationwide may soon be asking. With international tests showing that the United States no longer leads in K-12 learning, an emerging coalition of reformers is aiming to use market-based ideas to improve the nation's 99,000 public schools.[2] The ideas include paying teachers based on student performance and creating more publicly funded, privately run, charter schools to compete with public institutions.

Conservative analysts have long recommended such measures. But now they are joined by Democratic politicians, including President Barack Obama, and "venture philanthropists," led by Microsoft cofounder Bill Gates, who are bringing the ideas they

U.S. Lags Behind Asia in Math Scores

U.S. eighth-graders rank ahead of those in several European countries but behind students in England, Japan, South Korea and Taiwan.

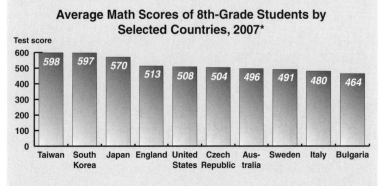

Average Math Scores of 8th-Grade Students by Selected Countries, 2007*

Test score

Taiwan	598
South Korea	597
Japan	570
England	513
United States	508
Czech Republic	504
Australia	496
Sweden	491
Italy	480
Bulgaria	464

* Scores are based on an 800-point scale. Top-scoring countries average about 600.

Source: Patrick Gonzales, et al., "Highlights From Trends in International Mathematics and Science Study 2007: Mathematics and Science Achievement of U.S. Fourth- and Eighth-Grade Students in an International Context," National Center for Education Statistics, September 2009, nces.ed.gov/pubs2009/2009001.pdf.

used to achieve business success to the domain of public education. Gates, Los Angeles insurance magnate Eli Broad and other wealthy donors have poured billions of dollars into market-oriented reform efforts, arguing that failing schools jeopardize the nation's economic competitiveness in the global market.

International data comparing K-12 student achievement across many nations clearly show that U.S. schools are failing, according to Eric Hanushek, a senior fellow at the Hoover Institution, a conservative think tank based at Stanford University in California. "While many people want to be reassured that things are going just fine, ignoring the real message" of these comparisons "actually imperils our economic future," he wrote.[3]

Key to gaining elusive public support for large-scale educational changes is persuading families, who generally support their local schools, that past strategies have been costly failures. Reformers have not been shy about making that case.

"Over the past four decades, the per-student cost of running our K-12 schools has more than doubled, while our student achievement has remained virtually flat," Gates wrote recently. "To build a dynamic 21st-century

economy . . . we need to flip the curve."[4]

But teachers and many education scholars argue that reformers seek a simple fix for a complex problem. Low-performing students are concentrated in the lowest-income districts, where inadequate funding, teacher turnover and the ravages of poverty make it difficult for students to excel, critics of market-based reforms say.

"Achievement differences between students are overwhelmingly attributable to factors outside of schools," wrote Matthew Di Carlo, a senior fellow at the Albert Shanker Institute, a research and advocacy group affiliated with the American Federation of Teachers (AFT), the nation's second-largest teachers' union. Research shows that about 60 percent of variation in students' school achievement is "explained by student and family background characteristics," many related to income, Di Carlo wrote. Only 10 or 15 percent of achievement differences can be laid to teachers, he argued.[5]

Reform critics also argue that the emphasis on rising educational costs is misplaced.

For one thing, said Richard Rothstein, a research associate at the liberal Economic Policy Institute, a large chunk of the cost increase Gates mentions has been used to educate children with disabilities. That segment of K-12 school spending has swelled from 4 percent to 21 percent over the past four decades, he said. Previously, schools largely ignored the special needs of children with disabilities, he said.[6]

Henry Levin, a professor of economics and education at Columbia University in New York, says, too, that "no other country has to include [teachers'] health-care costs and pensions" in school-cost calculations. (Health insurance and retiree benefits add at least 20 percent in costs beyond salary for a public-sector worker, such as a teacher, according to the Bureau of Labor Statistics.)[7]

"Our per-pupil expenditures are the highest in the world," Levin acknowledges. But he argues that it isn't fair to criticize schools for this because of the vast difference in employee costs between countries.

None of these arguments, however, are persuasive to reform proponents, who say ample evidence exists to show that parental choice, school competition and data-based decision-making are needed to drive improvement.

New York Federal Reserve Bank economist Rajashri Chakrabarti found "unambiguous improvement in public school performance" in Florida and Wisconsin as a result of offering parents a choice of schools, according to the Center for Education Reform, in Washington, D.C. The center also cites research by the Manhattan Institute, a conservative think tank in New York, concluding that all students in a Florida program that offered wide school choice to students with disabilities "made greater academic improvements" as their school options expanded — and that included students who stuck with their neighborhood schools.[8]

In recent school-reform battles, such as last winter's hot dispute in Wisconsin over newly elected Republican Gov. Scott Walker's plan to drastically limit teachers' collective-bargaining rights, unions have been heavily criticized for running up costs while allowing poor teaching to flourish.[9]

"The unions have been pushing the case that there is a war against teachers, but I don't think that's true," says the Hoover Institution's Hanushek. "There is a war against teachers' unions" that unions have brought on themselves by opposing reform proposals such as basing firing decisions on student achievement, he says.

Linking teacher evaluations and student performance on standardized tests is indeed among the most contentious topics in public education.

Earlier this month, the Los Angeles Unified School District announced that it will privately inform individual teachers of their ratings on a so-called "value-added" success scale that it uses to link teacher performance and test scores. The approach is a favorite of many reform advocates, and it was the L.A. district's data that the *Los Angeles Times* plumbed to create its rankings of Caruso and other teachers in the city.

The district is negotiating with the local teachers' union, the United Teachers Los Angeles, which is affiliated with both the AFT and the nation's largest teachers' union, the National Education Association, to include the measurements in formal performance reviews, a move the union strongly opposes.[10]

Times reporters argue that opposition is unwarranted because a "value-added" analysis compares teachers by evaluating the progress of each individual student in their classrooms against that student's own progress in earlier school years. By comparing a student's achievement only to his or her own record, the "value-added" approach takes into account such factors as poverty and learning disabilities, over which an individual teacher has

Reading Proficiency Highest in Northeast

Connecticut ranks first in eighth-grade reading ability followed closely by other Northeastern states, including Massachusetts and New Jersey. The District of Columbia ranks below all 50 states.

State Rankings by 8th-Grade Reading Level, 2009		
1. Connecticut	18. Wyoming	35. Tennessee
2. Massachusetts	19. Idaho	36. Alaska
3. New Jersey	20. Illinois	37. Arizona
4. Vermont	21. Kansas	38. Arkansas
5. Pennsylvania	22. Kentucky	39. Georgia
6. New Hampshire	23. New York	40. Texas
7. Minnesota	24. Oregon	41. Oklahoma
8. Montana	25. Utah	42. Alabama
9. Ohio	26. Colorado	43. South Carolina
10. South Dakota	27. Florida	44. California
11. Maryland	28. Indiana	45. Hawaii
12. Washington	29. Iowa	46. Nevada
13. Maine	30. Virginia	47. New Mexico
14. Nebraska	31. Delaware	48. West Virginia
15. Missouri	32. Michigan	49. Louisiana
16. North Dakota	33. North Carolina	50. Mississippi
17. Wisconsin	34. Rhode Island	51. District of Columbia

Source: "8th Grade Reading 2009 National Assessment of Education Progress," Federal Education Budget Project, New America Foundation, febp.newamerica.net/k12/rankings/naep8read09.

Putting Teachers to the Effectiveness Test

"Whether someone is capable or not is way more complex than it may seem."

Earlier this year, the Bill & Melinda Gates Foundation — one of the nation's biggest funders of school-reform projects — announced it would use the Memphis and Pittsburgh school districts, among others, as laboratories for developing "teacher effectiveness" programs using data on student achievement and teachers' classroom behaviors.

The idea is to figure out the connection between student achievement and actions of individual teachers and use the linkage to make "high-stakes" educational decisions — decisions, for example, on which teachers to fire, which to reward with merit pay or other recognition and which teaching practices to replicate.[1]

Microsoft cofounder Bill Gates told *The Wall Street Journal* that he will deem the project a success if "10 years from now . . . we have a very different personnel system that's encouraging effectiveness [in teaching] and our spending has contributed to that."

He went on to say that education-improvement efforts have suffered because data on teacher and school performance haven't been available. Contrast that situation, he

said, to "professions like long-jump or tackling people on a football field or hitting a baseball," where "the average ability is so much higher today because there's this great feedback system, measurement system."[2]

Many education analysts agree that traditional teacher-evaluation practices haven't been of much use. "A principal sitting in the back of the room checking off things on a list" of recommended teacher behaviors "made almost no sense," partly because "it's bound to involve many very subjective judgments," says Aaron Pallas, a professor of sociology and education at Columbia University in New York. "Almost everybody does well" on such evaluations, proving that the approach isn't very accurate or useful, he says.

Nevertheless, Pallas maintains, while old-style evaluations "provide almost no guidance about what to do" to improve one's teaching, new data-oriented evaluation systems don't either — at least so far.

Yet, rejecting the data approach means "sticking our heads in the sand," says Valerie E. Lee, an education professor at the University of Michigan in Ann Arbor. "These things can be good so long as they're done right," she says.

---

no control. Thus, it is a fair way to judge teachers' success, the *Times* argued.[11]

Opponents maintain, however, that inciting teachers to compete with one another for pay is the wrong way to go about improving education.

Diane Ravitch, a research professor of education at New York University who recently disavowed her long-time support for market-based reforms, noted that legendary business-improvement consultant W. Edwards Deming believed that merit pay for workers was even "bad for corporations."

"It gets everyone thinking about what is good for himself," Ravitch wrote, "and leads to forgetting about the goals of the organization."[12]

Columbia's Levin argues that teaching requires collaboration more than competition. For example, he says, teachers who want their students to improve "need to talk to the teachers at lower grades about whether they're teaching" skills on which higher grades' lessons are based

and seek their cooperation to do so, he says. "It's hard to say that the future really is in competition."

As policymakers, schools and families debate how to improve schools, here are some questions they are asking:

Are the public schools failing?

Behind the push to reform K-12 education lies the proposition that wide-scale failure of American schools bears significant responsibility for a lagging economy. But critics of that view argue that reform enthusiasts ignore data showing progress alongside problems. What's more, they argue, it makes no sense to hold schools responsible for the nation's economic woes.

"American education is in a state of crisis," according to the Heritage Foundation, a conservative think tank in Washington. "Millions of children pass through America's schools without receiving a quality education that prepares them . . . to compete in the increasingly competitive global economy."[13]

That means including other measures besides standardized-test scores and being careful not to jump at untested teacher-evaluation approaches, she says. If developed and used judiciously, Lee says, a good system could control for individual differences in students, such as attendance and home life, over which a teacher has no influence. And that, she says, would make for fairer teacher-to-teacher comparisons than those that simply look at student test scores.

Donald B. Gratz, an education professor at Curry College in Milton, Mass., cited a bit of history in arguing that programs linking teacher merit pay and student test scores are ill-conceived. "In the mid-1800s, British schools and teachers were paid on the basis of the results of student examinations, for reasons much like" those cited by today's reformers, Gratz wrote. After about 30 years, however, "the testing bureaucracy had burgeoned, cheating and cramming flourished" and, with public opposition swelling "dramatically," the practice "was abandoned as a failure."[3]

Basing pay on test scores poses another problem, too, Gratz says: Fewer than half of teachers teach subjects whose material is contained in standardized tests.

Furthermore, Gratz notes, at grades six and up, students typically have six or seven different teachers during a given year. "Who gets the credit or the blame" for a student's success or failure?" he asks. "It looks like a field day for labor lawyers."

Offering merit pay for good teaching hasn't been shown to improve instruction either, Gratz argues. Instituting merit-pay programs "assumes that teachers know what to do and just aren't doing it," but that's likely not the case, he says. "We do know a lot about how to teach," but teaching is an extremely complex task, and it's not as easy as it may seem for teachers to change their behavior to incorporate research findings about student learning, for example, he says.

Complicating matters is the fact that educators' and education administrators' ability to succeed relates to the situation in which they're working, says Jeffrey Henig, a professor of education at Columbia. "We have superintendents and principals, for example, who succeed in one school, then go somewhere else and fail," he notes. "So the question of whether someone is capable or not is way more complex than it may seem on the surface."

— *Marcia Clemmitt*

[1] Stephanie Banchero, "Bill Gates Seeks Formula for Better Teachers," *The Wall Street Journal online*, March 22, 2011, http://online.wsj.com/article/SB10001424052748703858404576214593545938506.html.

[2] Quoted in *ibid*.

[3] Donald B. Gratz, "The Problem with Performance Pay," *Educational Leadership*, November 2009, pp. 76-79.

Reform critics cite international PISA (Programme for International Student Assessment) tests, which compare student performance in dozens of countries, in arguing that U.S. teachers are, by and large, doing a good job. But the Hoover Institution's Hanushek dismisses that claim as "largely wrong."

It's true, Hanushek wrote, that recent PISA tests find U.S. 15-year-olds "above the developed-country average in reading, at the average in science, and below average in math," results that make it seem that "perhaps we are not doing so badly." But that's a faulty conclusion, he argued, because "reading is very difficult to assess accurately in the international tests. And reading scores have proven less important than math and science for both individual and national success."[14]

Furthermore, "international performance on these tests is very closely related to . . . economic growth," so that small score differences among countries may add up

to big differences in economic well-being over time, Hanushek wrote.[15]

In an article co-authored with two other scholars, one of them German, Hanushek argued that economic productivity depends on "developing a highly qualified cadre of scientists, engineers, entrepreneurs and other professionals." International tests show, for example, that the United States produces fewer top scorers in math than countries it competes with, the scholars said.[16]

Furthermore, school failure is not confined to low-income neighborhoods, Hanushek says in an interview. "Some suburban schools seem to be great," he says, "but it's because of things parents are providing" for their children, which may mask the fact that the schools themselves do a poor job.

But many education scholars say that while some individual schools are in trouble, claims of widespread failure in American education are false.

The Economic Policy Institute's Rothstein wrote that the National Assessment of Educational Progress (NAEP), which tracks math and reading skills by following groups of students from fourth through 12th grades, shows that "American students have improved substantially, in some cases phenomenally," over the past two decades.[17]

Both black and white fourth- and eighth-graders have improved in math, the Economic Policy Institute's Rothstein wrote. What's more, he said, African-American students have, at the fourth-, eighth- and 12th-grade levels, improved their math and reading skills the most, achieving "a rate of progress that would be considered extraordinary in any area of social policy."[18]

The Organisation for Economic Cooperation and Development (OECD), an international intergovernmental group that manages the PISA tests, also cites U.S. educational improvement. Since 2006, "the United States has seen significant performance gains" on international science assessments, mainly because America's lowest-scoring students have been closing the gap that separates them from the top scorers, the OECD said.[19]

"Overall, the American public school system is pretty decent," says Katrina Bulkley, an associate professor of education at New Jersey's Montclair State University. "It's just that in pockets, it's served badly."

Those pockets are mainly in urban and rural districts with the greatest poverty.[20]

In low-poverty schools — where fewer than 10 percent of students qualify for free or reduced-price lunches — 15-year-old American students score above the international average in reading on the PISA assessment, according to Stephen Krashen, a professor emeritus of education at the University of Southern California. By contrast, in schools where low-income students make up more than 75 percent of enrollment, 15-year-old students scored second to last among the 34 OECD nations.[21]

The U.S. education system doesn't provide enough classroom resources to overcome the disadvantages wrought by poverty, analysts from the OECD argue. "The United States is one of only three OECD countries" in which class sizes in high-poverty schools are routinely much larger than in schools in higher-income districts, said a recent report. As a result, disadvantaged American students are at risk of receiving fewer educational resources, including teacher time, than richer students, the analysts said.[22]

Poverty imposes often-overlooked handicaps. "I can guarantee you right now that at least 20 percent of our kids need glasses," said Ramón González, principal of a public middle school in New York City's South Bronx who struggles to get private funding for vision tests and glasses. "They're in their classrooms right now, staring at blackboards with no idea what they're looking at," said González. "You can have the best teachers, the best curriculum and the greatest after-school programs in the world, but if your kids can't see, what does it matter?"[23]

Educational reformers such as former New York City school Chancellor Joel Klein "have said that to fix poverty you have to fix education," says Aaron Pallas, a professor of sociology and education at Columbia University. "Schools can partner with others to help do this," Pallas says. "But the idea that schools are going to transform poverty on their own is just giving schools too much credit."

Many school reformers argue that Americans are losing jobs to oversees competition because the United States isn't adequately educating its students, says Donald B. Gratz, an education professor at Curry College in Milton, Mass. But the real reason is that "American workers are expensive," he says. American workers' productivity has soared in the past 20 years, demonstrating that graduating good employees is not the problem, he says.

At the same time, universities — not the public schools — are the real culprits in failing to prepare students to compete in the emerging globalized economy, some critics contend.

"The quality of teaching in higher education is worse than at the lower levels, terrible," but "that's going unnoticed," says Richard Ingersoll, a professor of education and sociology at the University of Pennsylvania. "Professors lead the ranks of those who want to impose [standardized-test-based] evaluations on K-12 teachers, but nobody's asking for similar tests to be used on them. The double standard is striking."

But the higher-education scene is changing. In a study of 2,300 students at 24 U.S. universities, Richard Arum, a New York University professor of sociology and education, found that more than a third showed no improvement in critical thinking and writing skills after four years of college.[24] Their professors may soon find themselves on the test-score hot seat, Arum said.

Beginning in 2016, the OECD will use the same test he used to compare college achievement internationally.

Said Arum, "The U.S. higher-education system has been living off its ... reputation," but professors "will increasingly be held accountable."[25]

Are teachers' unions a major barrier to improving schools?

Many reform advocates say teachers' unions are blocking change by being obsessed with job protection. They point to sensational cases, such as the infamous "rubber rooms" in which hundreds of New York City teachers deemed unfit for the classroom by school administrators sat for months, or even years, drawing their salaries, while their cases awaited due-process hearings.[26]

But teacher advocates argue that, despite their flaws, such due-process protections are needed to shield teachers from politically motivated firings or firings based on prejudice.

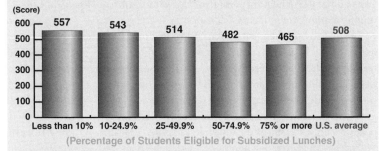

Lower Math Scores Tied to Poverty

Students who qualify for free or reduced-price lunches tend to score lower in mathematics than those whose family income is high enough to make them ineligible for subsidized lunches. The correlation suggests poverty contributes to lower achievement.

Average Mathematics Scores of 8th-Grade Students Eligible for Free or Reduced-price Lunches, 2007*

(Score): Less than 10%: 557; 10-24.9%: 543; 25-49.9%: 514; 50-74.9%: 482; 75% or more: 465; U.S. average: 508

(Percentage of Students Eligible for Subsidized Lunches)

* Scores are based on an 800-point scale. Top-scoring countries average about 600.

Source: Patrick Gonzales, et al., "Highlights From Trends in International Mathematics and Science Study 2007: Mathematics and Science Achievement of U.S. Fourth- and Eighth-Grade Students in an International Context," National Center for Education Statistics, September 2009, nces.ed.gov/pubs2009/2009001.pdf.

They also say that reform proposals are drastic enough to warrant caution. What's more, they point out that unions are not uniformly opposed to reforms.

Because of union contracts, "it takes two years, $200,000 and 15 percent of the principal's total time to get one bad teacher out of the classroom," said Terry M. Moe, a senior fellow at the Hoover Institution. "If we figure that maybe 5 percent of the teachers ... are bad teachers nationwide, that means that 2.5 million kids are stuck ... with teachers who aren't teaching them anything," said Moe. "The unions are largely responsible."[27]

School systems in cities such as Chicago that have tried to pioneer substantial reforms have not been able to produce evidence confirming their value because unions and others "have nipped them in the bud," said Hanushek.[28]

In districts with strong unions, policy change takes longer, according to Katharine O. Strunk, an assistant professor of education and policy at the University of Southern California, and Jason A. Grissom, an assistant

professor of public affairs at the University of Missouri. "Stronger unions are better able ... to negotiate contracts that constrain districts' flexibility in policy setting," they wrote.[29]

Yet, unions aren't the only ones who make it hard to implement change in schools, some analysts argue. They point to resistance by school boards to expanding charter schools, which compete with regular public schools but are exempt from many regulations public schools must follow. "Local school boards have been as great a roadblock, and in some cases even fiercer opponents" of reforms, than unions, wrote PBS education reporter John Merrow. "They go to court to keep charter schools from opening or expanding. Why? It's about money and control."[30]

Blasting unions as driven solely by self-interest ignores facts, union supporters say.

For one thing, "there is no research ... that correlates student achievement to collective bargaining rights," despite many reformers' claims that ending bargaining rights will improve schools, said Kate McLaughlin, executive vice president of the United Teachers of Lowell, the AFT local in Lowell, Mass. Massachusetts students, for example, "perform higher than anybody else in this country academically. Yet we have the strongest collective bargaining rights," she said.[31] Massachusetts teachers bargained for and won the right of every teacher to have "a qualified and trained mentor" during the first three years on the job to help them improve, a clear instance of unions working for students, McLaughlin said.[32]

Even many teachers agree that the most commonly used method of teacher evaluation — classroom evaluation by a school administration — usually doesn't work well, and some unions are trying to lead development of new methods, says Gratz of Curry College.

The Massachusetts Teachers Association (MTA) proposes basing evaluations on multiple measures that can be "validated against one another." Under the plan, the MTA says, "no high-stakes decisions" such as firing or raising pay would be based solely on test scores or any other single factor, such as expert evaluation of teachers' classroom and planning practices. Instead, if apparently good practices aren't matched by good scores or vice versa, evaluators would be "required to find out why" before acting.[33]

Union-management partnerships have "fostered reform" in places such as Toledo, Ohio, and Norfolk, Va., according to researchers led by David Lewin, a management professor at the University of California, Los Angeles. In those cities, administrators and unions emphasize professional development, teacher evaluation and mentoring to improve teacher quality. As an apparent result, school districts experience "very low levels of voluntary teacher turnover," the group wrote. Unions and administrators collaboratively make "difficult decisions to not retain ineffective teachers," they reported.[34]

Countries whose students regularly surpass U.S. students on international tests "without exception have strong unions," observed Dennis Van Roekel, president of the National Education Association (NEA). Teachers must implement administrators' policies, so a collaborative environment matters, he said.[35]

Green Dot, a nonprofit organization founded in 1999, operates 17 charter high schools and one middle school in high-poverty areas of Los Angeles and one high school in New York City, all unionized. "I've seen what happens to working people when they don't have . . . somebody fighting for them," said founder Steve Barr, a Democratic political activist and fundraiser who in 1990 cofounded the nonprofit, nonpartisan Rock the Vote group that aims to increase young people's political participation. When disagreements surface, Barr recommends that administrators and unions ask, "Is there 75 percent of this issue we all agree on?"[36]

The University of Pennsylvania's Ingersoll says that while the current reform movement "has a punitive cast toward teachers" that unions understandably resent, he doesn't absolve unions altogether. "Many unions aren't helping much," he says. "It would be good for them to get out in front on defining what a good, medium and bad teacher" is, but unions have done little of that. "Sometimes I think the unions are their own worst enemies."

Whatever the case, school management plays a huge role — negative or positive — in improving schools, says David Menefee-Libey, a professor of politics at Pomona College, in Claremont, Calif. There is "very strong research support" for five specific factors that underlie school improvement, "and, surprise! Those five factors frequently aren't present in schools where low-income students are," he says.

The five factors — which were validated in research by Anthony S. Bryk, president of the Carnegie Foundation for the Advancement of Teaching — are, according to Menefee-Libey:

- Support systems to guide teachers in what and how to teach;
- Good working conditions;
- Strong ties between the school and community;
- Safe, orderly environments, and
- Principals who prioritize learning.[37]

Is business-style competition a good model for improving schools?

Evidence shows that market-style competition and performance-measurement statistics can improve education, reform advocates say. But skeptics argue that reshaping education to operate like a business is, at best, an unproven strategy that may in fact be contrary to the goals of schooling.

Using data to figure out who is best at vital tasks — such as educating teachers — is crucial, says Gregory McGinity, managing director for education policy at the Los Angeles-based Broad Foundation, one of a small group of philanthropies making grants aimed at spurring education reforms and measuring their results.

Rather than propping up all teacher-training programs, he says, "governors and school superintendents must be more aggressive in using data to determine which schools of education are doing a good job" and then "put the dollars into the schools that provide the best teachers."

Critics focus too much on proposals for firing unsuccessful teachers while ignoring plans to use merit pay and public recognition to reward teachers whose students improve, McGinity says.

Some researchers have found data that links improved education to market-oriented changes, such as providing families with a wider choice of schools.

For example, a school-choice program in Chicago produced modest improvement in on-time high-school graduation rates for students who exercised the option to switch from their assigned neighborhood schools, reported Douglas Lee Lauen, an assistant professor of public policy at the University of North Carolina, Chapel Hill. Students who were high achievers and those from neighborhoods with low poverty rates benefited most, Lauen found.[38]

In a school system overhauled along market lines, schools would be closed and replaced rather than tinkered with in hopes of improvement, wrote Andy Smarick, a visiting fellow at the conservative Thomas B. Fordham

How U.S. Teacher Salaries Compare

Compared with salaries of other college-educated workers, U.S. teacher salaries are further behind than teacher salaries in many other countries.

Ranking of Selected Countries in Teacher Pay Compared with Other College-educated Workers

Spain

Germany

Australia

Finland

Sweden

France

England

South Korea

United States

Italy

Source: "Building a High-Quality Teaching Profession: Lessons From Around the World," Organisation for Economic Co-operation and Development, 2011, www2.ed.gov/about/inits/ed/internationaled/background.pdf.

Institute, an education-policy think tank. In other words, schools would be treated like businesses — those that fail or consistently produce losses are shuttered, and competition fills the gap.

"Once persistently low performing, the majority of schools will remain low performing despite being acted upon in innumerable ways," Smarick said. In what he calls an "alarming" record, only 14 percent of California schools restructured under the 2002 No Child Left Behind Act (NCLB), a major education-reform measure signed into law by President George W. Bush, achieved "adequate yearly progress" in the first year after the changes. The proportions for schools in Maryland (12 percent) and Ohio (9 percent) were even worse, Smarick wrote.[39]

(Under NCLB, "restructuring" means firing and replacing a school's principal and most of its teachers and/or reopening the school as a charter school or under the management of a private school-management company or the state government.)[40]

Frederick M. Hess, director of education policy at the conservative American Enterprise Institute, argues that the public-school system is too stodgy, rule-burdened and old-fashioned to improve. Furthermore, efforts to "scale up" and apply small improvements to many schools routinely fail, he says.

Thus, he argues, "instead of taking this 19th-century box called school and making it better, we ought to" scrap the traditional school system altogether and "think about how to help people get what they need." The way to do that, Hess says, is by harnessing entrepreneurs' energy to provide students and teachers with education products and services geared to their individual needs, such as instructional computer programs based on new brain research, and creating "virtual schools" that students can attend online.

But New York University's Ravitch said she saw "no reason to believe that closing a school and opening a new one would necessarily produce superior results." In fact, she wrote, half of New York City's 10 worst-performing schools on 2009 state math tests "were new schools that had been opened to replace failing schools."[41]

Firing teachers is also a dicey strategy, says Columbia's Pallas. "We know that new teachers, no matter where they come from, often are foundering" for at least a few years, he says. A more realistic approach would be to focus on improving "how we prepare teachers, both in school and once they get on the job," he contends.

Do reformers "think there's a huge army of new teachers to jump in to replace" those who are pushed out? asks Menefee-Libey, of Pomona College. "We haven't seen them."

Kenneth J. Saltman an associate professor of education at DePaul University in Chicago, worries that in the race to require schools to produce measurable outcomes, "the value of intellectual curiosity," among other things, will be lost. "What happens to the country when the curriculum gets narrowed" to exclude skills like deep reading and detailed debate of issues "because these skills aren't easily testable?" he asks.

"All of these reforms have been advanced as accomplishing really big stuff — bringing low-income kids fully into the mainstream," where they'll achieve on a par with higher-income students, says Columbia's Levin. But even studies that show positive effects of market-oriented strategies "show quite small effects," he says.

In Washington, D.C., schools recorded gains in test scores under the direction of Chancellor Michelle Rhee, a hard-nosed reformer best known for firing hundreds of low-performing teachers before resigning — possibly under pressure from a newly elected mayor — a mere three years into her tenure. But as Levin says, reading scores that apparently soared in the second year of Rhee's tenure "disappeared in the third year."

He adds, "If you're only looking for tiny gains, then you've evaded the original argument" for market-based reform.

BACKGROUND

Engine of Opportunity

Today's school-reform debates are the latest in a long line of disputes over public education dating back to the 19th century.

For two centuries, many have hoped that the public schools could help the United States break the historical mold of nations stratified by class. America's excellent universal education promises that "the rail-splitter . . . at 20 years of age may become the chief magistrate of 50 millions of free people before he is 50," declared William A. Mowry (1829-1917), a school administrator in Rhode Island and Massachusetts.[42]

Expectations for what schools should accomplish have continuously risen.

In 1870, only 2 percent of Americans graduated from high school, and 30 years later the rate was only 6.4 percent.[43] By 1940, however, fully half of American students graduated from high school, and in 1969 the graduation rate peaked at 77 percent.[44]

Despite the seemingly much greater progress made by American schools than in the past, however, the 20th century also saw virtually constant calls for improvement and reform, according New York University's Ravitch. Notwithstanding the remarkable gains in American students' educational attainment, "it is impossible to find a period in the 20th century in which education reformers, parents and the citizenry were satisfied with the schools," although few agreed about what should be done to improve them, she wrote.[45]

Beginning in the 1970s, oil shocks, recessions and a globalizing economy shook Americans' confidence in what had seemed an endlessly bright economic future. The schools came under new criticism as the United States found its world-beating school-completion rates surpassed by other nations. By the late 1980s, high-school graduation rates declined to just under 70 percent and leveled off. In 2007, the rate stood at 68.8 percent.[46]

Current reform projects aimed at retooling schools as an engine of economic prosperity trace their history at least as far back as 1957, when the Soviet Union launched *Sputnik*, the first spacecraft to orbit the earth, says Curry College's Gratz. *Sputnik*, he says, sparked worries that the United States might be losing its global technological superiority, and schools came under sharp criticism for not doing enough to prepare students in math and

C H R O N O L O G Y

1990s *Interest in school-reform grows, with limited results. Republicans push for expanded school choice; Democrats support developing compatible curriculum and nationwide learning standards.*

1990 Wisconsin legislature establishes nation's first school-voucher pilot program, to help 1,100 low-income Milwaukee students attend nonreligious private schools. . . . Princeton graduate Wendy Kopp turns her 1989 senior-thesis idea on eliminating education inequities into Teach for America, which recruits elite-college graduates to teach for two years in low-income districts.

1991 Minnesota enacts first charter-school law.

1992 First charter school opens in St. Paul, Minn. . . . California enacts second charter law.

1993 Tennessee adopts "value-added assessment system" to measure how much individual teachers increase or decrease students' test scores.

1994 President Bill Clinton signs Goals 2000: Educate America Act, creating the National Education Standards and Improvement Council with authority to approve states' academic standards; short-lived effort effectively ends when Republicans win control of the House in November. . . . Microsoft cofounder Bill Gates and his wife establish Bill & Melinda Gates Foundation, soon to become a major funder of school-reform projects.

1995 Teach for America alumni Michael Feinberg and David Levin launch Knowledge Is Power Program (KIPP) charter schools. . . . Ohio state legislators pilot a voucher program for low-income Cleveland students to use at either religious or nonreligious schools. . . . Illinois legislature hands control of Chicago public schools to Democratic Mayor Richard Daley.

1999 Florida establishes first statewide school voucher program.

2000s *No Child Left Behind law focuses attention on "failing" schools. Reformers seek to weed out teachers who don't raise students' achievement scores and reward those who do.*

2002 U.S. Supreme Court rules in favor of Ohio's voucher program. . . . Broad Foundation's first annual Broad Prize of $1 million, for an urban district that reduces achievement gaps for low-income students, goes to Houston.

2003 Gates Foundation awards millions to Boston and other cities to break large high schools into smaller units, based on the theory that a more personal environment aids learning.

2007 Newly elected Democratic Mayor Adrian Fenty of Washington is the latest official to wrest control of schools from the local school board; he appoints high-profile reformer Michelle Rhee as school chancellor. . . . New York City school Chancellor Joel Klein says he will fire principals of schools with lagging test scores. . . . Teach for America, which placed 500 teachers its first year, receives 18,000 applications for 2,900 positions.

2009 Citing disappointing results, Gates Foundation ends small-school program after awarding $2 billion in grants. . . . President Barack Obama announces Race to the Top grants for states to develop student-achievement databases, expand charter schools and improve teacher retention and recruitment.

2010 Using previously confidential school data, *Los Angeles Times* names L.A. elementary-school teachers who score high and low on "value-added" teacher assessments. . . . Fenty loses re-election after many residents protest Chancellor Rhee's teacher and principal firings; Rhee resigns. . . . Gates Foundation will fund development of databases to assess teachers' achievement.

2011 Newly elected Republican governors and legislators in states including Wisconsin, Ohio, Indiana, Idaho, New Jersey and Florida propose bills to lower costs and improve education by ending tenure, limiting teachers' union collective bargaining rights, instituting merit pay and firing teachers based on student-achievement assessments. . . . *USA Today* reports possible evidence of cheating on standardized tests at D.C. schools that former Chancellor Rhee praised as successful examples of school reform.

Charter Schools Draw Mixed Reviews

Education experts say only a few have merit.

The nation's 5,000 charter schools — taxpayer-funded institutions freed of some rules that public schools must follow — figure big in school reformers' plans to improve American education. But education experts say that while some individual charter schools have merit, the charter movement as a whole is not a panacea for what ails the nation's public-school system.

That assessment has not discouraged education-reform advocates from embracing charter schools. So-called venture philanthropies such as the Bill & Melinda Gates Foundation generously fund charter school-management organizations, such as San Francisco-based Knowledge Is Power Program (KIPP). Moreover, the Obama administration's school-reform funding program, Race to the Top, encourages states to make their school laws friendlier to charter development.

But information on how well charter schools perform is only gradually emerging. So far, the results are mixed, with some charter schools producing impressive learning results compared with demographically similar public schools, some lagging at the bottom on many measures and most ensconced somewhere in the middle of the pack on student achievement.

Valerie E. Lee, a professor of education at the University of Michigan in Ann Arbor, says that only "a few charter schools are really good" at improving student achievement, while "a few are absolutely awful, and the rest are no different" from traditional public schools. "Is this research solid enough to use as a basis for a large expansion of many of these schools?" she asks. "I'd probably say, 'No.'"

Charter schools are not covered by laws in some states that require a unionized teaching staff. What's more, they do not have to follow state and school-district requirements on curriculum and mode of instruction. While most charter schools operate similarly to traditional public schools, others use longer school days or avant-garde teaching methods, such as curricula built around music education or experiential learning.

While reformers' interest in charter schools has grown sharply in recent years, the charter-school movement isn't new. Minnesota's charter-school law, the first in the nation, is 20 years old this year. And with charter-school laws in effect in 40 states and the District of Columbia, the number of students enrolled in such schools tripled to 1.3 million between 2000 and 2008. [1]

Some of the newest research shows that while few charter schools seem to substantially improve students' test scores, "they do produce much higher graduation rates" — in other words, they instill students with motivation, says John Witte, a professor of public affairs and political science at the University of Wisconsin, Madison. "This parallels the old research on Catholic schools," showing that their students also were more likely than comparable public-school students to persist through graduation, Witte says.

In a 2010 analysis of 22 of the 99 schools managed by the San Francisco-based KIPP charter school-management organization, most of the schools had "positive, statistically significant and educationally substantial" effects on students' scores on state mathematics and reading tests. Furthermore, while KIPP schools serve smaller numbers of students for whom English is a second language and fewer special-education students, they also enroll "a

science. But he says efforts to blame the schools for the nation's large economic and technological challenges have an air of "unreality" because schools can't possibly be held responsible for globalization, growing income inequality and other such factors that shape the economy.

Even as Americans have had high hopes for schools, they've been skeptical about teachers.

Over the 20th century, national magazines regularly "fretted about teacher hygiene, perversion, patriotism and

competence," wrote Hess of the American Enterprise Institute.[47]

The first U.S. teachers' union, the Chicago Teachers Foundation, was established in 1897.[48] At the time, many teachers faced unfair treatment, wrote Ravitch. The New York City Board of Education fired female teachers if they married and, after teachers successfully fought for the right to wed, it fired those who became pregnant. As late as the mid-20th century, in Texas, a "right to

disproportionate share of low-income students" compared to other local schools, analysts wrote. [2]

A 2009 Stanford University study, meanwhile, found that charter-school students outperformed their public-school counterparts in Arkansas, Louisiana, Missouri, Denver and Chicago. But charter students significantly lagged in achievement in Arizona, Florida, Minnesota, New Mexico, Ohio and Texas and performed on a par with public-school students in California, Georgia, North Carolina and the District of Columbia. Nationwide, 17 percent of charter schools improved students' math achievement significantly, compared with public schools, but 37 percent lagged behind public schools on math achievement, according to the analysis. [3]

Furthermore, while reformers push to close low-achieving public schools, researchers have also found that, like public schools, low-achieving charter schools are extremely difficult to shut down. "Are bad schools immortal?" lamented researchers at the conservative Fordham Institute in a 2010 analysis. In follow-up research on both public and charter schools found to be low achievers in 2003-2004, a foundation analyst found that 72 percent of the low-achieving charters were still operating — and still "bad" — five years later. (Eighty percent of low-achieving public schools in the study also remained in operation.) [4]

The bottom line, say many scholars: Don't count on charter schools to drastically improve education.

Originally, many hoped that the freedom granted to charter schools would allow them to develop new modes of instruction that other schools could adopt. But so far, "there's not much evidence of charters serving as incubators for innovation," says Aaron Pallas, a professor of sociology and education at Columbia University in New York. "I can't say there's one reform that's come out that can be widely adopted," he says. Some charter-management organizations such as KIPP have significantly raised student achievement after lengthening the school day and school year, he says. "But when it comes to the curriculum and ways of teaching, they're not looking much, if any, different from the public schools."

The number of charter schools "is always going to be limited because they require entrepreneurial people at the center," says Wisconsin's Witte.

That means that the existence of even the best charter schools in low-income districts does not let the community off the hook for making its public schools as good as they can be, says Lee. She says many families lack the time or knowledge to compete for the limited number of slots typically available in local charter schools. Parents usually must participate in a lottery for available seats.

Concern also exists among civil rights groups about the very large numbers of minority children enrolled in charter schools, which often don't have the same ties to the community or public accountability as do public schools, says Janelle Scott, an assistant professor of education at the University of California, Berkeley. Civil rights organizations and charter-management organizations "haven't been terribly involved with each other," she says. "So there's some concern about who's shaping education for people of color."

— Marcia Clemmitt

[1] "Fast Facts," National Center for Education Statistics, U.S. Department of Education, http://nces.ed.gov/fastfacts/display.asp?id=30.

[2] Christina Clark Tuttle, *et al.*, "Student Characteristics an Achievement in 22 KIPP Middle Schools," Mathematica Policy Research, Inc., June 2010, www.mathematica-mpr.com/publications/pdfs/education/kipp_fnlrpt.pdf.

[3] "Multiple Choice: Charter School Performance in 16 States," CREDO, Stanford University, 2009, http://credo.stanford.edu/reports/MULTIPLE_CHOICE_CREDO.pdf.

[4] David A. Stuit, "Are Bad Schools Immortal?" Fordham Institute, December 2010, www.edexcellence.net/publications-issues/publications/are-bad-schools-immortal.html.

work" state where teachers' unions have had little success in organizing and thus enjoy little clout, "an ultraconservative group called the Minute Women . . . would drop in unannounced to observe classes . . . to find out whether teachers expressed any unacceptable political opinions," such as support for desegregation, Ravitch wrote. [49]

Organized teachers won passage of the first tenure law in 1909, in New Jersey, to protect against firings based on race, gender or unpopular political opinions or to make way for cronies of school management. [50]

Public and Private

As early as the mid-19th century, charities used private money to try to reshape the nation's public schools.

After the Civil War, abolitionist charity groups who feared that Southern states would not provide education to freed slaves took on the job themselves, notes Janelle Scott, an

Teaching Is a Prestige Profession in Some Countries

Education experts say only a few have merit.

Today's U.S. school reformers, alarmed at what they see as widespread failure in the classroom, tend to focus on removing bad teachers, reducing the collective bargaining power of teacher unions and reducing the authority of teachers to stray from standardized curricula.

But in some other countries where students outpace American pupils on international tests, the focus is on giving teachers greater autonomy and elevating them to a professional status often reserved for lawyers and doctors.

"Finland has raised the social status of its teachers to a level where there are few occupations with higher status," states a report prepared for an international education summit organized by U.S. Education Secretary Arne Duncan in March.[1]

Test scores in Finland were below the international average 25 years ago but have recently risen to the top of the global rankings.

Finland focuses on bringing the best students into teaching and ensuring that the job confers respect in society, according to the report, prepared by the Organisation for Economic Cooperation and Development (OECD). In contrast to the United States, where elementary-school teachers, especially, come from the lower half of college classes, top students in Finland battle for primary-school teaching spots. In 2010, for example, "over 6,600 applicants competed for 660 available slots in primary-school preparation programs . . ., making teaching one of the most sought-after professions," the OECD said.[2]

Finnish teachers' unions play a key role in shaping education policy, too. "It's a totally different situation in Finland" than in the United States when it comes to the relationship between unions and school administrators, said Henna Virkunnen, the country's minister of education. "Our teachers' union has been one of the main partners — We are working very much together with the union," she said. "Nearly all of the teachers are members. I think we don't have big differences in our thinking."[3]

Virkunnen acknowledged that comparing education policies is not easy. Schooling is "very much tied to a country's own history and society, so we can't take one system from another country and put it somewhere else," she said. Still, national differences aside, paying close attention to teachers' pre-service and in-service training, developing teachers who "are experts of their own work," respecting their professional autonomy and knowledge and providing good workplace conditions are key, Virkunnen said.[4]

---

assistant professor of education at the University of California, Berkeley. For example, the American Missionary Association, a nondenominational Protestant group, opened more than 500 schools for freed slaves.[51]

Many private fortunes have helped shape U.S. education. The Carnegie Foundation for the Advancement of Teaching, established in 1905 by industrialist Andrew Carnegie, helped found the Educational Testing Service (ETS), for example. The ETS developed and to this day manages standardized tests that include the SAT. In addition, the Carnegie Foundation led the fight for federal Pell grants for low-income college students.[52]

In 1955, Milton Friedman, a University of Chicago libertarian economist and 1976 Nobel Prize winner, introduced a new twist to the idea of linking the public and private sectors on schooling. As part of his overarching theory that all public-sector enterprises overspend and underperform because they are not disciplined by market supply and demand, Friedman proposed that public funds should be directed to private schools.

The government should fund education but should not, in general, run schools, because government, by nature inefficient, should run as few institutions as possible, Friedman theorized. His plan would offer parents vouchers

Singapore also assigns high status to the teaching profession. It "carefully selects young people from the top one-third of the secondary-school graduating class whom the government is especially interested in attracting to teaching and offers them a monthly stipend, while still in school," the OECD said. The stipend, it said, is competitive with salaries for new graduates in other professional fields. In exchange, recipients must make a three-year commitment to teaching. They get a choice of career paths: becoming master instructors who train others, curriculum and research specialists or future administrators.[5]

Some have noted an irony in the fact that Education Secretary Duncan not only organized the international summit but co-authored a newspaper column with the top official of the event's host: Fred van Leeuwen, general secretary of 30-million-member Education International, the largest international teachers' union.

The Obama administration has vocally supported many of the principles of the U.S. school-reform movement, including the championing of charter schools, most of which employ nonunionized teachers and are intended to compete with traditional public schools.

Yet Duncan and his co-authors wrote that "increasing teacher autonomy" is "vital" for improving the schools. Contrary to arguments of many current U.S. school reformers, "many of the world's top-performing nations have strong teacher unions that work in tandem with local and national authorities to boost student achievement," they said. "These high-performing nations illustrate how tough-minded collaboration more often leads to educational progress than tough-minded confrontation."[6]

AFP/Getty Images/Olivier Morin

Finland focuses on bringing the best students into teaching. Above, a second-grade class in Vaasa.

— *Marcia Clemmitt*

[1] "Building a High-Quality Teaching Profession: Lessons from Around the World," Organisation for Economic Co-operation and Development, 2011, p. 11, www.oecd.org/document/53/0,3746 ,en_21571361_44315115_47386549_1_1_1_1,00.html.

[2] *Ibid.*

[3] Quoted in Justin Snider, "An Interview With Henna Virkunnen, Finland's Minister of Education," *The Hechinger Report*, March 16, 2011, http://hechingerreport.org/content/an-interview-with-henna-virkkunen-finlands-minister-of-education_5458.

[4] Quoted in *ibid.*

[5] "Building a High-Quality Teaching Profession," *op. cit.*, p. 9.

[6] Arne Duncan, Angel Gurría and Fred van Leeuwen, "Uncommon Wisdom on Teaching," Dept. of Education website, March 16, 2011, www.ed.gov/blog/2011/03/uncommon-wisdom-on-teaching.

"equal to the estimated cost of . . . a government school" to send children to private schools. Such a scheme would "permit competition to develop" and "not least . . . , make the salaries of school teachers responsive to market forces," Friedman wrote.[53]

Little noticed at first, the idea was promoted in the 1980s by a burgeoning network of conservative think tanks such as the American Enterprise Institute.[54]

The New Reformers

A wealth boom in the 1990s built fortunes for entrepreneurs in such fields as electronics and finance and gave rise to a new breed of school reformers, typified by Gates, the Microsoft cofounder, and Broad, who made his first fortune in Detroit real estate development before turning to insurance. This group has been dubbed "venture philanthropists" for their efforts to fuse business methods with their social activism.

Venture philanthropists' "critique of traditional philanthropy is that it's been far too incremental" in achieving goals, says the University of California's Scott. As a result, while old-style foundations generally announced broad funding areas, then solicited grant applications from experts in those fields, "venture philanthropists often don't ask you to apply." Instead, they "seek you out, if you're doing specific work that they support, because they tend to believe they already know" what works in a given field, Scott says.

But the venture philanthropists' ideas don't always pan out in practice.

For example, one of the Gates Foundation's early initiatives — running from 2001 to 2009 — funded the breakup of large high schools into small ones of a few hundred pupils each, on the theory that better education occurred in a more personal environment, Scott says. At the time, research showed that medium-sized high schools of 500 to 1,200 students got the best results. But Gates poured money into tiny schools anyway. Then, after several years, when the small schools didn't produce improvement, the foundation quietly dropped the program, says Scott. One person involved with the initiative told Scott that "researchers had told us" that medium-sized, rather than very small, high schools showed the best results, "but we didn't listen," she says.

On the positive side, the episode demonstrates that the Gates Foundation, at least, is willing to learn from poor results, says Scott. But it also illustrates the potential danger of privately funding a crucial public resource, she says. What happens to schools created with private dollars when that money is withdrawn? Should taxpayers support them? Scott asks.

Still, venture philanthropists are gaining power as they support mainly market-oriented school reforms in concert with like-minded politicians, such as New York City Mayor Michael Bloomberg and Chicago Mayor Richard Daley. Also working with the philanthropists are "education entrepreneurs" such as Wendy Kopp, the Princeton graduate who founded Teach for America, a nonprofit group that has placed thousands of young graduates of elite colleges into temporary teaching slots in urban schools.

Scott says venture philanthropists have "followed the lead of conservative funders" who in the 1970s began to build a network of professors, academic research centers and think tanks that today buttresses the powerful conservative movement. By funding multiple groups and individuals and providing multiyear funding to cover operating costs, rather than making single-project grants, the venture philanthropists have formed a coherent philosophical network with lasting power, she says.

"There's power because people aren't working at cross-purposes."

In recent years, "joint grant making" by education funders has increased, says Sarah Reckhow, an assistant professor of education at Michigan State University in East Lansing. While many cities and organizations get no venture-philanthropy cash, those that do — including the New York City and Los Angeles school districts and groups such as Teach for America —"get a lot," from multiple sources, which helps them make large-scale, high-profile changes, Reckhow says.

"Historically, education politics has been local," with reformers focusing on change in a single district, says Jeffrey Henig, a professor of political science and education at Columbia University. Today's "coalition is focused on changing the national system," such as by persuading the federal government to add public dollars for programs that echo foundation initiatives. "I don't think this would have been possible without the growing role" that states and the federal government have played in education policy, Henig says.

(Beginning in the 1970s, most states began creating statewide school-funding formulas to replace purely local ones. The 2002 No Child Left Behind law helped increase federal involvement in assessing student achievement.)

Compared to a school system's annual budget, philanthropy dollars are "a drop in the bucket," says Reckhow. However, since most school-district money is tied up in salaries, "the funding actually provides powerful leverage" because it's "nearly the only money available for new initiatives."

Wealthy investment-fund managers who pump money into school-reform efforts such as charter schools "honestly think they're doing good. Plus, it's a very strong goodwill builder" for an industry whose reputation has suffered from the financial crash and recession, says Columbia's Levin. A few million dollars "is a rounding error for a wealthy investor." But it "is huge for a school." Such funding, Levin says, can make a school highly influential by providing extra resources that may help achieve better results and allow adoption of interesting programs that gain public and media attention.

Education Entrepreneurs

Conservative reformers and venture philanthropists tend to stress different aspects of and reasons for school reform, says Montclair State's Bulkley.

Conservatives, who tend to be skeptical of public systems of any kind, often argue that reform's greatest value is to offer families free choice and to create a market where none existed, she says. By contrast, she continues, venture philanthropists "tend to believe in public purposes" for schools and often stress the importance of building a public system better equipped to produce a skilled workforce.

The Broad Foundation, for example, awards an annual prize to districts that improve disadvantaged students' achievement, citing as a key motivation the need to restore "the public's confidence in . . . public schools by highlighting" success.[55]

With their focus on freedom and individual choice, many conservative reformers are as supportive of small one-of-a-kind charter schools as they are of multischool charter-school groups, says Bulkley. But venture philanthropists "have their DNA in entrepreneurship" — having launched small companies that grew into giants — and this background translates into a strong interest among venture philanthropists in so-called "charter-management organizations" that seek to run many individual schools based on a single school-management philosophy, Bulkley says.

Venture philanthropy dollars have spurred development of numerous entrepreneurial groups. New Leaders for New Schools is a New York City-based private training program for aspiring urban-school principals. The Brooklyn-based New Teacher Project — founded in 1997 by Rhee before she became D.C. school chancellor — aims to change school practices to allow more hiring of teachers without traditional certifications.[56]

Venture philanthropists favor working with cities where mayors, not school boards, are in control. Both Chicago and New York, where schools have been under mayor control since 1995 and 2002, respectively, receive substantial private funding.[57]

"Old-style industrial-based foundations tended to work within institutional constraints," taking local politics into account, for example, Henig says. But "Silicon Valley-influenced" philanthropists inhabit a fast-moving world.

"I do understand the frustration" that leads them to prefer the one-stop shop of mayoral control, Henig says. "Why would you want to wait two generations to implement change incrementally, in part because it's hard to get top-heavy bureaucracies to move?" Nevertheless, incremental

change that seeks widespread buy-in is probably the best path to lasting improvement, he suggests.

CURRENT SITUATION
Budget Battles

Several newly elected conservative governors are bringing school reform to the front pages this spring. Recession-triggered budget problems in such states as Wisconsin, Ohio, Idaho, Florida and New Jersey have opened the way for battles over teachers' benefits and unions' cherished right to bargain collectively.

Conservative reformers, especially, have welcomed the reform efforts. "Except for one year during the Great Depression," public-school funding "has gone up every year for 100 years," says the Hoover Institution's Hanushek. Much of the money "went into salaries and retirement" plans for teachers and for "reducing class sizes," neither of which improves education, he argues.

The budget battles provide an entry point for ensuring "accountability for every dollar and every child," wrote former Washington school chancellor Rhee, who continues to enjoy heavy venture-philanthropy backing. To save money, wrote Rhee, "districts must shift new employees from defined-benefit pension programs" — traditional pensions that promise retired workers a specific benefit level for the rest of their lives —"to portable, defined-contribution plans" whose payout depends on investment returns. And because "the budget crisis inevitably requires layoffs," she said, states can take the opportunity to begin basing firing decisions "on teachers' effectiveness, not on their seniority," as most districts do today.[58]

In March, Florida Republican Gov. Rick Scott, who has hired Rhee as a consultant, signed legislation to gradually eliminate tenure and base firings and pay raises on teachers' performance in raising student test scores.[59] In April, Republican Gov. C.L. "Butch" Otter of Idaho signed a measure ending tenure for new teachers, instituting merit pay and banning unions from bargaining over workload and class size.[60]

"There have also been lots of state-law proposals for school choice" this year, says John Witte, a professor of public affairs and political science at the University of Wisconsin, Madison. In the past, Republican lawmakers have pushed bills to bolster charter schools but haven't often

Has spending on public schools risen too high?

YES

Adam B. Schaeffer
Policy Analyst, Cato Institute

Written for CQ Researcher, April 2011

Real, per-pupil spending, adjusted for inflation, has more than doubled over 40 years, while test scores have remained flat at the end of high school. That's around $12,000 or $13,000 per student every year.

We've spent more every decade with no return in student performance. That's not investment — defined as getting a positive return on your money. It's just spending.

This poses a particularly difficult problem for state and local governments who bear most of the burden. State and local education spending consumes 46 percent of all tax revenue, or two-and-a-half times what's spent on Medicaid/CHIP.

It's also taking a bigger *share* of tax revenue. State education spending as a share of tax revenue has increased 90 percent in two decades. It's increased over 70 percent as a share of local revenue.

It's time to replace the "spending" model of education policy with an "investment" model.

We can make public education a lot more efficient. The number of public school staff per student increased 70 percent since 1970; cutting back on unnecessary personnel will bring significant savings.

But school choice, particularly through education tax credits, is the best way to *invest* in education. It's a proven way to improve *public* school performance, save money and increase choice. It's an effective, efficient investment in education.

Choice is the most intensively studied education reform there is, and the verdict is clear: It works. Decades of evidence and dozens of studies provide proof. It works in Chile and Sweden, and it works in Florida and Wisconsin and a dozen other states.

The vast majority of studies analyzing private choice policies demonstrate positive impacts on participants and children who remain in public schools. None have shown negative impacts. And choice programs are far less costly to taxpayers.

According to a 2008 fiscal analysis by the state Office of Program Policy Analysis and Government Accountability in Florida, the state gained $1.49 in savings for every $1 it lost in tax revenue to its education tax credit program. David Figlio, a Northwestern University researcher and official analyst of the program, found it significantly boosted performance in Florida's public schools.

Citizens and businesses want to invest directly in our education system. We should encourage them to do so.

Let's stop just *spending* money on education. Let's really start *investing* in it.

NO

Richard Rothstein
Research Associate, Economic Policy Institute

Written for CQ Researcher, April 2011

States' education spending varies widely, even after adjustment for purchasing-power differences. Real costs also vary, because disadvantaged students need more support than those whose early-childhood, after-school, home-literacy and cultural experiences supplement their schooling.

For decades, spending nationwide increased, largely for children with disabilities. Their individualized attention accounts for much of the staff increases. Nonetheless, achievement for regular students also improved, substantially so for the disadvantaged: On the "gold standard" National Assessment of Educational Progress, black 12th-graders gained nearly two-thirds of a standard deviation in math and reading since 1980.

Some states clearly spend too little. Others may spend more than needed for graduates' workplace success, because wealthier taxpayers choose to provide more fulfilling (and expensive) experiences for their children. Mississippi spends less per pupil — about $8,500 — than almost any state. Its percentage of low-income children is higher, test scores are lower and capacity to fund education (per-capita personal income) is less.

Massachusetts spends more — about $14,500 — with proportionally fewer low-income children than elsewhere. Its test scores are highest of all. Its fiscal capacity is greater than most states'.

Then there is California, spending less — about $10,000 — than most, with many low-income children, low scores and high income. It chooses not to tax itself to educate disadvantaged youth well, spending instead on prisons for those who fail.

More money should not be spent unwisely, but Mississippi cannot spend what's needed without greater federal aid. California should spend more, but with greater state effort. Both should invest in early childhood. Children from less literate homes have worse verbal skills than middle-class children — by age 3. This early gap cannot be overcome by more spending later, but better schools can sustain benefits from early investments. Well-qualified (and better-paid) teachers in smaller primary-grade classes for low-income children would be wise.

Massachusetts should also invest more in early childhood for disadvantaged students, but it need not boost average spending. Wealthy taxpayers should contribute more, choosing whether to do so by reducing suburban expenditures.

Today, federal aid exacerbates inequality. Subsidies for low-income students are proportional to existing state spending, so Massachusetts inexcusably gets more federal dollars per child than Mississippi. The question is not whether we overspend but whether we spend on the right programs for children most in need. The answer is "no".

sought voucher expansions, partly because their mostly suburban constituents like their local schools and wouldn't seek vouchers. "But now something on the right has changed," and voucher-expansion proposals are on the table "all around the country," Witte says.

Wisconsin's Gov. Walker has proposed repealing enrollment caps both for vouchers and for the number of students who can attend so-called "virtual" — or online — schools. He also wants to phase out income limits for voucher eligibility.[61] "That's a huge change" because voucher programs have previously assisted only the poor, says Witte.

Walker also proposes ending a requirement that students who use vouchers at private and online schools take state achievement tests. But that would be contrary to the stated principles of some venture-philanthropy reformers.

"If you're going to have a system of choice," then a common set of learning and achievement standards — preferably nationwide — is crucial for all schools, not just public ones, says Broad Foundation policy director McGinity. Otherwise, "you're not going to have a transparent market in which people can make comparisons." Ultimately, the standards would include both test scores and comparative information to help parents choose a school "with the best arts program," for example, he says.

Such developments cast doubt on just how much reforms backed by conservatives and venture philanthropists actually coincide, says Columbia's Henig. "There's also cleavage on how much money should be spent," he says. Venture philanthropists "have learned from charters and cities with mayoral control that it's expensive to do this," while conservatives stress cutting education spending.

Racing to the Top?

The Obama administration has worked in concert with reformers since taking office in 2009. Obama's Secretary of Education, Arne Duncan, was CEO of Chicago's public schools and gained reformers' favor through his strategy of closing down chronically low-performing schools and reopening them with new staff.[62]

Under Obama's Race to the Top program, states have pledged to:

- Adopt statewide learning standards and assessments;
- Build data systems to measure achievement;
- Recruit, retain and reward effective teachers and principals through measures such as merit pay and retention bonuses;

- Foster education innovation through such means as laws encouraging charter-school development; and
- Focus on turning around the lowest-performing schools.

Last year, 11 states and the District of Columbia won $4.35 billion in Race to the Top grants, including $350 million to support joint work among states on student assessment.[63]

This year, states are pushing forward with these projects. For example, Rhode Island is field-testing a teacher-evaluation program in two districts and a charter school. Delaware will pilot in-school expert coaches to help staff members analyze achievement data and adjust instruction to individual needs. Massachusetts will establish career ladders to encourage teachers to remain in the profession.[64]

Yet, some reformers have hit bumps in the road in recent months, at least partly because of public skepticism.

Last October, Rhee resigned from her post in Washington after then- mayor Adrian Fenty, who appointed her in 2007, lost his reelection bid, in large part because many city residents were fed up with Rhee. Some teachers and parents complained, for example, that teacher firings Rhee claimed she based on merit actually occurred before her new teacher-assessment plan had even gone into operation.[65]

Much of Rhee's "impatience was merited," says Columbia's Levin. "The idea that the school system is an employment agency for my friends" is a bad feature of many districts, including Washington, and needs changing, he says. "But I would try to build community support before doing that," he says. Rhee "has a big ego, and she instead took pride in her tactics."

Levin and others also say that Rhee's so-called "IMPACT" teacher-evaluation plan has merit. The plan is a useful, multifaceted attempt to produce an overall picture of teachers, including not just test scores "but evaluations by master teachers," who would seek "to recognize good teacher practices both in the classroom and in planning" lessons, says Columbia's Pallas.

Ultimately, external funders helped cause the "mischief" in Washington, says Levin. Through their venture-philanthropy ties, Rhee and Fenty "were getting national attention, funding and chances to air their views, so they took their eye off the local population" and viewed funders "as their constituency," Levin says. They failed to "strike the needed balance between getting external funding and then using it to build capacity" for improvement from within, he says.

Earlier this month, New York City Mayor Bloomberg's hand-picked chancellor, Cathleen P. Black, resigned under pressure after less than four months on the job. Black had been a top publishing executive, heading both Hearst Magazines (publisher of *Cosmopolitan* and *Popular Mechanics*, among others) and *USA Today.* But she had no education-management or teaching experience.[66] Black quickly ran afoul of teachers and parents by making what many considered insensitive jokes about school problems. "Could we just have some birth control for a while? It could really help us all out a lot," Black quipped at a parents' meeting to discuss school overcrowding.[67]

"Those kinds of comments show a lack of understanding of what parents are going through," said one parent.[68]

But McGinity, of the Broad Foundation, argues that Black's ouster actually makes "a great case" for one school-management principle reformers consider key — mayoral control. Unlike in districts where school-board politics dominate, Black and Bloomberg "could see that the situation wasn't working and made a change quickly" before problems worsened, he points out.

OUTLOOK
Common Standards

American education will change in the coming decades, but the shape of what's to come is hard to discern.

Some reform critics fear that private interests could dismantle the public schools Americans once prized.

The United States has long had a two-tier system, with schools in higher-income areas having many more resources, observes DePaul's Saltman. "But what you're seeing now is a new kind of two-tier system being created, in which schools in the bottom tier will be privately managed," he predicts.

"In poor city and rural areas," reform advocates are "quickly turning public distrust into short-term profit-making industries" that will seek some quick bucks from taxpayer-supported schools and get out, he warns. "Most Americans don't realize how far along this privatization agenda has gone." But with many Democratic politicians now agreeing "that public schools need to compete with the private sector, privatization has largely won," he says.

There's little doubt that databases tracking student performance will be established everywhere fairly soon. But while unions fear that teachers will lose their job security to overly simplified interpretation of standardized test scores, even some reform critics see possible long-term upsides to data tracking.

Databases now under construction will include school data only, but down the line databases from multiple social-service agencies might link information about health, poverty, homelessness and more to school records, muses Columbia's Henig. Such data could be "revolutionary" in revealing all factors that contribute to students' achievement, or lack thereof, and help propel holistic solutions, he says.

With Republicans and many Democrats now backing school choice, the national learning standards some have recommended for decades will appear at last, some analysts say.[69]

Prior to 2002's No Child Left Behind law, "everybody said they met standards because they could make up their own rules," says Kenneth K. Wong, an education professor at Brown University. But as assessments increasingly become comparable across state lines, this convenient mode of hiding failure is evaporating, he says. In addition, while accountability requirements so far apply only to public schools, with nearly 5,000 charter schools now in operation, "we must think about how we know they are meeting standards, too," Wong says. "If we are going to move toward school choice," the nation must confront the highly contentious question of "whether we're going to have something like a national examination," he says.

"My hope is that there will soon be a strong set of core [learning] standards with a common assessment" for all schools nationwide, says the Broad Foundation's McGinity.

Expansion of school choice to allow out-of-district enrollments and virtual schools will accelerate a "revolutionary" trend — delinking schooling from one's neighborhood, says Wisconsin's Witte. "For a hundred years people went to their neighborhood schools, and 90 percent still do. But until 20 years ago, everybody did," he says. Ultimately, "this change will affect everything" in schools, he says. For example, "We govern public schools through an elected school board, so should open-enrollment people [from out-of-district] also have seats on the board?"

Before the nation simply lets such large changes happen, however, "I think people need to ask themselves, 'What are our goals for our children?'" says Curry College's Gratz.

NOTES

1. Jason Felch, Jason Song and Doug Smith, "Who's Teaching L.A.'s Kids?" *Los Angeles Times*, Aug. 14, 2010, www.latimes.com/news/local/la-me-teachers-value-20100815,0,258862,full.story, p. A1.

2. "Public elementary and secondary schools by type of school," *Digest of Education Statistics*, National Center for Education Statistics, http://nces.ed.gov/programs/digest/d09/tables/dt09_093.asp.

3. Eric A. Hanushek, "Feeling Too Good About Our Schools," Education Next website, Jan. 18, 2011, http://educationnext.org.

4. Bill Gates, "How Teachers Development Could Revolutionize Our Schools," *The Washington Post*, Feb. 28, 2011, www.washingtonpost.com.

5. Matthew Di Carlo, "Teachers Matter, But So Do Words," *Shanker blog*, July 14, 2010, http://shanker-blog.org/?p=74.

6. Richard Rothstein, "Fact-Challenged Policy," *Economic Policy Institute website*, March 8, 2011, www.epi.org/analysis_and_opinion/entry/fact-challenged_policy.

7. "Employer Costs for Employee Compensation," press release, Bureau of Labor Statistics, March 9, 2011, www.bls.gov/news.release/ecec.nr0.htm.

8. "Fact-Checking School Choice Research," The Center for Education Reform, October 2010, www.edreform.com/_upload/No_More_Waiting_School_Choice.pdf.

9. For background, see Kenneth Jost, "Public-Employee Unions," *CQ Researcher*, April 8, 2011, pp. 313-336.

10. Jason Song and Jason Felch, "L.A. Unified Releases School Ratings Using 'Value-Added' Method," *Los Angeles Times*, April 12, 2011, www.latimes.com, p. A1.

11. *Ibid.*

12. Diane Ravitch and Deborah Meier, "Bridging Differences," *Education Week blogs*, March 29, 2011, http://blogs.edweek.org.

13. "Education, Leadership for America," Heritage Foundation website, www.heritage.org/Initiatives/Education.

14. Hanushek, *op. cit.*

15. *Ibid.*

16. Eric A. Hanushek, Paul E. Peterson and Ludger Woessmann, "Teaching Math to the Talented," *Education Next*, Winter 2011, http://educationnext.org. Peterson is a government professor at Harvard University; Woessmann is an economics professor at the University of Munich.

17. Rothstein, *op. cit.*

18. *Ibid.*

19. "Strong Performers and Successful Reformers in Education: Lessons from PISA for the United States," Organisation for Economic Co-operation and Development, 2011, p. 26, www.oecd.org/dataoecd/32/50/46623978.pdf.

20. For background, see Marcia Clemmitt, "Fixing Urban Schools," *CQ Researcher*, April 27, 2007 (update, Aug. 5, 2010), pp. 361-384.

21. Cited in Richard Kahlenberg, "Debating Michelle Rhee," *Taking Note blog*, Century Foundation, Feb. 25, 2011, http://takingnote.tcf.org/2011/02/debating-michelle-rhee.html.

22. "Strong Performers and Successful Reformers in Education," *op. cit.*, p. 28.

23. Quoted in Jonathan Mahler, "The Fragile Success of School Reform in the Bronx," *The New York Times Magazine*, April 6, 2011, p. 34. See also Joe Nocera, "The Limits Of School Reform," *The New York Times*, April 26, 2011, p. A23.

24. "A Lack of Rigor Leaves Students 'Adrift' in College," NPR website, Feb. 9, 2011, www.npr.org.

25. Quoted in Timothy J. Farrell, "Arum Research Calls Out 'Limited Learning' on College Campuses," *New York University blogs*, March 25, 2010, http://blogs.nyu.edu/blogs/dbw1/ataglance/2010/03/arum_research_calls_out_limite.html.

26. For background, see Jennifer Medina, "Teachers Set Deal with City on Discipline Process," *The New*

York Times, April 15, 2010, www.nytimes.com/2010/04/16/nyregion/16rubber.html.

27. "Don't Blame Teachers Unions for our Failing Schools," debate transcript, *Intelligence Squared U.S.*, March 16, 2010, http://intelligencesquaredus.org/wp-content/uploads/Teachers-Unions-031610.pdf.

28. Quoted in Carlo Rotella, "Class Warrior," *The New Yorker*, Feb. 1, 2010, p. 28.

29. Katharine O. Strunk and Jason A. Grissom, "Do Strong Unions Shape District Policies?: Collective Bargaining, Teacher Contract Restrictiveness, and the Political Power of Teachers' Unions," *Educational Evaluation and Policy Analysis*, December 2010, p. 389.

30. John Merrow, "The Road Not Traveled: Tracking Charter Schools Movement," *Taking Note blog*, Dec.1, 2009, http://takingnote.learningmatters.tv.

31. "Don't Blame Teachers Unions for our Failing Schools," *op. cit.*

32. *Ibid.*

33. "A Stronger Evaluation System," Massachusetts Teachers Association, March 22, 2011, http://massteacher.org/news/archive/2011/03-22.aspx; "MTA's Reinventing Educator Evaluation: Answers to Frequently Asked Questions," www.seateachers.com/HTMLobj-1742/MTAReinventing_Educator Eval12011.pdf.

34. David Lewin, *et al.*, "Getting It Right: Empirical Evidence and Policy Implications from Research on Public-Sector Unionism and Collective Bargaining," Employment Policy Research Network, March 16, 2011, www.employmentpolicy.org/sites/www.employmentpolicy.org/files/EPRN%20PS%20draft%203%2016%2011%20PM%20FINAL tk-ml4%20edits.pdf.

35. Quoted in Liana Heitin, "16 Nations Meet to Discuss Improving Teaching," *Education Week blogs*, March 17, 2011, http://blogs.eduweek.org.

36. Quoted in Bill Turque, "Green Dot's Barr: Unions Part of Solution," *The Washington Post*, Sept. 8, 2009, http://voices.washingtonpost.com.

37. For background, see Anthony S. Bryk, "Organizing Schools for Improvement," *Phi Delta Kappan*, April 2010, pp. 23-30.

38. Douglas Lee Lauen, "To Choose or Not to Choose: High School Choice and Graduation in Chicago," *Educational Evaluation and Policy Analysis*, September 2009, p. 179.

39. Andy Smarick, "The Turnaround Fallacy," *Education Next*, Winter 2010, http://educationnext.org/the-turnaround-fallacy; For background, see Kenneth Jost, "Revising No Child Left Behind," *CQ Researcher*, April 16, 2010, pp. 337-360.

40. "School Restructuring Options Under No Child Left Behind," *Education.com*, www.education.com/reference/article/Ref_School_Restructuring.

41. Diane Ravitch, *The Death and Life of the Great American School System* (2010), pp. 86-87.

42. Quoted in Diane Ravitch, *Left Back: A Century of Battles Over School Reform* (2000), p. 19.

43. Christopher B. Swanson, "U.S. Graduation Rate Continues Decline," *Education Week online*, June 2, 2010, www.edweek.org/ew/articles/2010/06/10/34swanson.h29.html?qs=historical+graduation+rates.

44. *Ibid.*

45. Ravitch, *The Death and Life*, *op. cit.*, p. 13.

46. Swanson, *op. cit.*

47. Frederick M. Hess, "A Policy Debate, Not an Attack," *Room for Debate blogs*, *The New York Times online*, March 6, 2011, www.nytimes.com.

48. "Chicago Teachers Federation," *Encyclopedia of Chicago*, www.encyclopedia.chicagohistory.org/pages/271.html.

49. Ravitch, *The Death and Life*, *op. cit.*, p. 174.

50. Trip Gabriel and Sam Dillon, "Teacher Tenure Targeted by GOP Governors," *The New York Times*, Jan. 31, 2011, p. 1, www.nytimes.com/2011/02/01/us/01tenure.html.

51. "American Missionary Association," *Encyclopedia Britannica online*, 2011, www.britannica.com/EBchecked/topic/19996/American-Missionary-Association.

52. "About Carnegie," *Carnegie Foundation for the Advancement of Teaching website*, www.carnegiefoundation.org/about-us/about-carnegie.

53. Milton Friedman, "The Role of Government in Education," *School Choices website*, www.school-choices.org/roo/fried1.htm.

54. For background, see Kenneth Jost, "School Voucher Showdown," *CQ Researcher*, Feb. 15, 2002, pp. 121-144, and Charles S. Clark, "Charter Schools," *CQ Researcher*, Dec. 20, 2002, pp. 1033-1056.

55. For background, see "Frequently Asked Questions," *The Broad Prize for Urban Education website*, www.broadprize.org/about/FAQ.html#2.

56. "Overview," The New Teacher Project website, http://tntp.org/about-us.

57. For background, see Ruth Moscovitch, Alan R. Sadovnik, *et al.*, "Governance and Urban School Improvement: Lessons for New Jersey from Nine Cities," Institute on Education Law and Policy, Rutgers University at Newark, 2010, http://ielp.rutgers.edu/docs/MC%20Final.pdf.

58. Michelle Rhee, "In Budget Crises, an Opening for School Reform," *The Wall Street Journal Online*, Jan. 11, 2011, http://online.wsj.com/article/SB10001424052748704739504576068142896954626.html.

59. Isabel Mascarenas, "Student Teachers Speak Out on SB 736 on Teacher Merit Pay," *WTSP News website*, March 25, 2011, www.wtsp.com/news/article/183421/250/Student-teachers-speak-out-on-teacher-merit-pay; Michael C. Bender, "Rick Scott Names Michelle Rhee, Patricia Levesque to Education Transition Team," *Miami Herald blogs*, Dec. 2, 2010, http://miamiherald.typepad.com/nakedpolitics/2010/12/rick-scott-names-michelle-rhee-patricia-levesque-to-education-transition-team.html.

60. Laura Zuckerman, "Idaho Governor Signs Education Overhaul Into Law," Reuters, April 8, 2011, www.reuters.com/article/2011/04/09/us-idaho-education-idUSTRE7380GA20110409.

61. Amy Hetzner and Erin Richards, "Budget Cuts $834 Million from Schools," [Milwaukee] *Journal Sentinel online*, March 1, 2011, www.jsonline.com/news/statepolitics/117192683.html.

62. Rotella, *op. cit.*

63. "Nine States and the District of Columbia Win Second Round Race to the Top Grants," press release, U.S. Dept. of Education, Aug. 24, 2010, www.ed.gov/news/press-releases/nine-states-and-district-columbia-win-second-round-race-top-grants.

64. For background, see Michele McNeill, "Race to Top Winners Work to Balance Promises, Capacity," *Education Week*, March 30, 2011, www.edweek.org/ew/articles/2011/03/30/26rtt-states_ep-2.h30.html?tkn=RMOFJADRisIf48BKX1kxGbHNaOeVRca26WD1&print=1.

65. Andrew J. Rotheram, "Fenty's Loss in DC: A Blow to Education Reform?" *Time*, Sept. 16, 2010, www.time.com/time/nation/article/0,8599,2019395,00.html.

66. "Cathie Black," *Executive Profiles*, Bloomberg/ *Business Week*, http://investing.businessweek.com/businessweek/research/stocks/private/person.asp?personId=79286149&privcapId=23675200&previousCapId=4160895&previousTitle=Bill%20&%20Melinda%20Gates%20Foundation.

67. Yoav Gonen, "Parents Fume Over Black's 'Birth Control' Quip About Overcrowding," *New York Post online*, Jan. 15, 2011, www.nypost.com/p/news/local/black_wisecrack_on_birth_control_a0EUsHTDjV-vWAMvA5qf6KI.

68. *Ibid.*

69. For background, see Kathy Koch, "National Education Standards," *CQ Researcher*, May 14, 1999, pp. 401-424.

BIBLIOGRAPHY

Books

Hess, Frederick M., *Education Unbound: The Promise and Practice of Greenfield Schooling*, Association for Supervision and Curriculum Development, 2010.
An analyst at the conservative American Enterprise Institute argues that today's schools shouldn't be reformed so much as scrapped so education entrepreneurs can devise specific solutions for different educational needs.

Merrow, John, *The Influence of Teachers: Reflections on Teaching and Leadership*, LM Books, 2011.
Based on his reporting throughout the country, a long-time PBS education reporter explores issues such as teaching quality, payment and evaluation of teachers.

Ravitch, Diane, *The Life and Death of the Great American School System: How Testing and Choice Are Undermining Education*, Basic Books, 2010.
A longtime education policymaker explains why she now rejects the market-oriented education-reform

theories she helped to develop for President George H. W. Bush.

Weber, Karl, ed., *Waiting for "Superman": How We Can Save America's Failing Public Schools*, PublicAffairs, 2010.

The companion book to the acclaimed 2010 school-reform documentary "Waiting for Superman" includes essays on how to improve U.S. education by charter-school leaders, education journalists and a teachers' union leader.

Articles

"Grading the Teachers: Value-Added Analysis," *Los Angeles Times* online, www.latimes.com/news/local/teachers-investigation.

An ongoing series of investigative articles from 2010 and 2011 explores the effectiveness of teacher evaluations based on students' standardized test scores. Includes a database with rankings of individual teachers and schools.

Banchero, Stephanie, "Bill Gates Seeks Formula for Better Teachers," *The Wall Street Journal* online, March 22, 2011, http://online.wsj.com/article/SB1000142405 274870385840457621459345938506.html.

Microsoft cofounder and philanthropist Bill Gates explains how he's trying to develop better teacher evaluations and argues that cutting education budgets is probably unwise.

Barkan, Joanne, "Got Dough? How Billionaires Rule Our Schools," *Dissent*, winter 2011, www.dissent-magazine.org/article/?article=3781.

A writer for a left-leaning magazine argues that venture philanthropists like Bill Gates are gaining too much power.

Bryk, Anthony S., "Organizing Schools for Improvement," *Phi Delta Kappan*, April 2010, www.kappanmagazine.org/content/91/7/23.abstract, p. 23.

The president of the Carnegie Foundation for the Advancement of Teaching describes his research on Chicago's schools, showing that several critical aspects of a school's organization and leadership are major determinants of whether that school can improve.

Pellissier, Hank, "The Finnish Miracle," Great Schools website, www.greatschools.org/students/2453-finland-education.gs.

Finland's schools, which rose from mediocre to outstanding over the past quarter-century, have lessons for schools, teachers and parents. Notably, teaching is among Finland's most respected professions.

Rotella, Carlo, "Class Warrior: Arne Duncan's Bid to Shake Up Schools," *The New Yorker*, Feb. 1, 2010, p. 24.

President Obama's Secretary of Education is the former CEO of Chicago's public schools, with a reputation for closing low-achieving schools and reopening them with new staffs.

Reports and Studies

"Building a High-Quality Teaching Profession: Lessons from Around the World," Organisation for Economic Cooperation and Development, 2011, www.oecd.org/dataoecd/62/8/47506177.pdf.

Analysts for the international organization find that most countries with high-achieving schools recruit the best students as teachers, provide extensive on-the-job training and mentoring and involve teachers closely in efforts to improve schools.

Corcoran, Sean P., "Can Teachers be Evaluated by their Students' Test Scores? Should They Be? The Use of Value-Added Measures of Teacher Effectiveness in Policy and Practice," Annenberg Institute for School Reform, 2010, www.annenberginstitute.org/products/Corcoran.php.

A Columbia University assistant professor of economics explains how value-added evaluations of teacher quality work and examines the evidence on their reliability and implications for schools.

Suffren, Quentin, and Theodore J. Wallace, "Needles in a Haystack: Lessons from Ohio's High-performing, High-need Urban Schools," Thomas B. Fordham Institute, May 2010, www.scribd.com/doc/31987794/Needles-in-a-Haystack-Full-Report.

Analysts for a research organization supportive of school choice examine a group of public, magnet and charter schools in low-income urban areas in search of factors that help the schools improve student achievement.

For More Information

Albert Shanker Institute, 555 New Jersey Ave., N.W., Washington, DC 20001; (202) 879-4401; www.ashankerinst. org. An arm of the American Federation of Teachers that brings together experts to discuss education issues.

Annenberg Institute for School Reform, Brown University, Box 1985, Providence, RI 02912; (401) 863-7990; www. annenberginstitute.org. Analyzes school-system issues, works with community partners to improve school districts and publishes the quarterly journal *Voices in Urban Education.*

Economic Policy Institute, 1333 H St., N.W., Suite 300, East Tower, Washington, DC 20005-4707; (202) 775-8810; www.epi.org/issue/education. Examines school reform from a liberal viewpoint.

Education Next, Program on Education Policy and Governance, Harvard Kennedy School of Government, 79 JFK St., Cambridge, MA 02138; (877) 476-5354; http:// educationnext.org/sub/about. A reform-oriented online publication that examines all aspects of K-12 education.

The Hechinger Report, http://hechingerreport.org. A nonprofit online news organization based at the Teachers College of Columbia University that publishes in-depth reporting and commentary on education issues.

Hoover Institution, 434 Galvez Mall, Stanford University, Stanford, CA 94305-6010; (650) 723-1754; www.hoover. org. Studies and publishes reports on school reform and other topics from a conservative perspective.

National Center for Education Statistics, U.S. Department of Education, 1990 K St., N.W., Washington, DC 20006; (202) 502-7300; http://nces.ed.gov. Provides statistics on every aspect of American education.

Thomas B. Fordham Institute, 1016 16th St., N.W., 8th Floor, Washington, DC 20036; (202) 223-5452; www .edexcellence.net. A think tank dedicated to improving school performance through accountability and expanded options for parents.

8

Redistricting Debates

Kenneth Jost

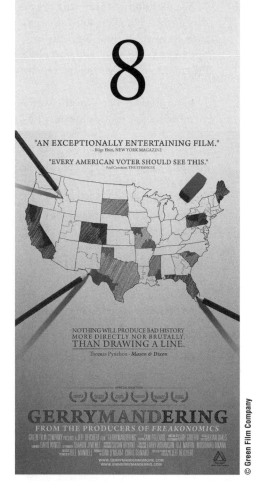

A poster promotes Gerrymandering, a documentary released last fall that sharply criticizes the controversial practice of drawing congressional districts to help political friends and hurt foes. Jeff Reichert, a self-described liberal who made the film, says he wants "more people involved in the redistricting process."

From *CQ Researcher*,
Feb 25, 2011.

Meet Cynthia Dai: high-tech management consultant in San Francisco, Asian-American, outdoor adventurer, out lesbian, registered Democrat.

Meet Michael Ward: chiro-practor in Anaheim, Calif., disabled veteran, former polygraph examiner, Native American, registered Republican.

Dai has been interested in politics since 1984, when she helped register voters before reaching voting age herself. Ward has worked with college Republican groups since his undergraduate days.

Despite their interests, neither Dai nor Ward had ever held or sought public office until last year. For the next year, however, they and 12 other Californians, most with limited if any political experience, will be up to their necks in politics as members of the state's newly established Citizens Redistricting Commission.[1]

Along with the rest of the states, California must redraw its legislative and congressional maps in 2011 to make districts equal in population according to the latest U.S. Census Bureau figures. The every-10-year process is required to comply with the Supreme Court's famous "one person, one vote" rule, which requires districts to be divided according to population so each person is equally represented in government. The intricate line-drawing invites political maneuvering of all sorts, including the practice known as "gerrymandering" — irregularly shaping district maps specifically to help or hurt a political party or individual officeholder or candidate.

With the redistricting cycle just getting under way, California's citizens commission provides a high-profile test of the latest idea for reforming the often-discredited process. By taking the job away

GOP Has Grip on Redistricting Authority

Republicans control 23 of the state legislatures that draw either state or congressional districts or both, including Nebraska's nominally nonpartisan legislature; Democrats control only 12. Legislatures in seven states with redistricting authority are split, with each of the major parties having a majority in one of the chambers. Eight states use commissions to draw both legislative and congressional lines; five others use commissions just for congressional redistricting.

Congressional Redistricting Authority by State

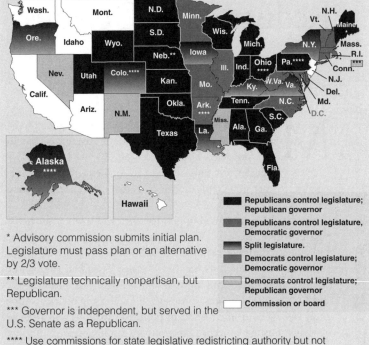

Republicans control legislature; Republican governor

Republicans control legislature, Democratic governor

Split legislature.

Democrats control legislature; Democratic governor

Democrats control legislature; Republican governor

Commission or board

* Advisory commission submits initial plan. Legislature must pass plan or an alternative by 2/3 vote.

** Legislature technically nonpartisan, but Republican.

*** Governor is independent, but served in the U.S. Senate as a Republican.

**** Use commissions for state legislative redistricting authority but not congressional.

Sources: National Conference on State Legislatures; U.S. Department of Justice Civil Right Division; U.S. House of Representatives

of the problem is the politicians have had the right to pick the voters instead of voters picking politicians, which seems like a very big myth in our democracy."

Ward, one of the five registered Republican commissioners, agrees. "The condition of California is evidence that politicians draw districts that serve their own interests and not necessarily first and foremost the communities that they serve," he says.

Completing the commission's membership are four people unaffiliated with either of the two major parties. The maps to be drawn by the commission, due to be completed by Aug. 15, must meet a series of criteria, including "to the extent practicable" compactness. But the commission is specifically prohibited from "favoring or discriminating against" any incumbent, candidate or political party. The final maps must be approved by a bipartisan supermajority of the commission, with votes from at least three Democrats, three Republicans and three independents.

No one knows how the experiment will work. "It's fair to say that the mechanism that we came up with is not simple, but we're hopeful that it will work out," says Derek Cressman, Western regional director for the public interest group Common Cause.

from the state legislature through ballot measures approved in 2008 and 2010, California voters sought to cut out the bizarre maps and unsavory deal-making that good-government groups say prevent the public from ousting incumbents or holding them accountable for their performance in office.

"There's a fair amount of cynicism about how California is being run now," says Dai, one of five Democrats on the partisan-balanced commission. "Part

Along with the state's former Republican governor, Arnold Schwarzenegger, California's Common Cause chapter was the driving force behind Proposition 11, which in 2008 created the new commission to redraw state legislative districts.

With approval of the measure, California became the second state, after Arizona, to establish a citizens redistricting commission. Arizona's commission, created through a ballot initiative approved in 2000, has responsibility for legislative and congressional districts. California voters in 2010 approved a second measure, Proposition 20, that gave the commission power over congressional districts too. *

Redistricting is an arcane process that stirs more interest among political junkies than the general public. But experts say the decennial line-drawing helps shape voters' relationships with their elected officials and can affect the balance of power between rival political parties. "This is one of the most important events in our democracy," says Kristen Clarke, co-director of the political participation group for the NAACP Legal Defense and Educational Fund, a major advocacy group for African-American interests.[2]

The redistricting cycle flows out of the Constitution's requirement that seats in the U.S. House of Representatives be "apportioned" among the states according to an "enumeration" of the population — the census — to be conducted every 10 years (Article I, Section 2). Under the figures released by the U.S. Census Bureau in December, eight states will gain and 10 will lose House seats to be filled in the 2012 election.

The new apportionment has the potential to strengthen the Republican majority that the GOP gained in November 2010. States gaining seats are mostly in the Republican-leaning Sun Belt in the South and West, while states losing seats are mostly in the Democratic-leaning Rust Belt in the Northeast and Midwest.

Thanks to gains in state elections in November, Republicans are positioned to take control of the micro-level line-drawing of congressional and state legislative districts in a near majority of the states. Among states where legislatures draw either congressional or legislative

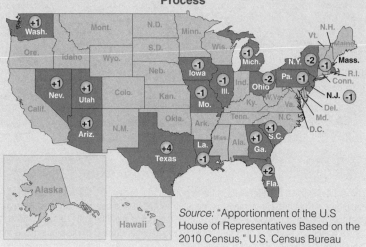

Twelve Seats Shift in Reapportionment Process

Ten states will lose a total of 12 seats in the U.S. House of Representatives during reapportionment. Those seats will be reallocated among eight other states, with Texas and Florida the big winners. They will gain four and two seats, respectively.

States Gaining or Losing House Seats in Reapportionment Process

Source: "Apportionment of the U.S House of Representatives Based on the 2010 Census," U.S. Census Bureau

maps or both, Republicans have undivided control in 19, including Nebraska's nominally nonpartisan unicameral legislature; Democrats in only eight. "Republicans are in the best position ever in the modern era of redistricting," says Tim Storey, a veteran redistricting expert with the National Conference of State Legislatures.

Democrats are disadvantaged not only because they lost ground at the polls in November but also because some states with Democratic-controlled legislatures — most notably, California — assign redistricting to non-legislative boards or commissions. "Democrats are going to have less influence [in California] than they had in the past," says Charles Bullock, a professor of political science at the University of Georgia in Athens.

In fact, California's post-2000 redistricting is Exhibit No. 1 in the reformers' case against the prevailing practice of allowing state lawmakers to draw their own districts as well as those of members of Congress. In the reformers' view, Democrats and Republicans in the state legislature agreed on district lines aimed at protecting incumbents of both parties — a so-called bipartisan gerrymander.

---

* The commission is also charged with drawing the four districts for the state's Board of Equalization, which administers the state's tax laws.

Commissioner Filkins Webber · Commissioner Galambos Malloy · Commissioner Ward · Commissioner Yao

Over the next year, 14 Californians, all with post-graduate degrees but most with limited if any political experience, will redraw the state's legislative and congressional maps as members of the state's newly established Citizens Redistricting Commission. Here they pose for an official photograph midway through a three-day public meeting Feb. 10-12. Michael Ward, a chiropractor, presided as rotating chair; Connie Galambos Malloy, a community organizer, is to his right. Others standing, left to right, are Jodie Filkins Webber (attorney), Gabino Aguirre (city councilman; retired high school principal), Vincent Barabba (online-commerce consultant), Michelle DiGuilo (stay-at-home mom), Maria Blanco (foundation executive), Peter Yao (ex-city council member; retired engineer), Cynthia Dai (management consultant), Libert "Gil" Ontai (architect), Jeanne Raya (insurance agent), Angelo Ancheta (law professor), Stanley Forbes (bookstore owner) and M. Andre Parvenu (urban planner). The panel includes four Asian-Americans, three Hispanic-Americans, one African-American, one Native American and five whites.

Supporters of the new citizens commission say the legislative plan worked as the lawmakers intended. In the five elections from 2002 through 2010, only one of the state's 53 congressional seats changed hands. The districts "represent the legislators' interest, not the voters,'" says Cressman of Common Cause.

Some redistricting experts, however, discount the reformers' complaints about self-interested line-drawing. "The effect of redistricting in the incumbency advantage is unclear," says Nathan Persily, director of the Center for Law and Politics at Columbia University Law School in New York City. "Incumbents win not only because they draw the district lines, but for all kinds of reasons."

Political calculations in redistricting are also limited by legal requirements dating from the Supreme Court's so-called reapportionment revolution in the 1960s. In a series of decisions, the justices first opened federal courts to suits to require periodic redistricting by state legislatures and then mandated congressional and legislative districts to be equal in population within each state.

The Voting Rights Act, passed in 1965, has also played a major role in redistricting. In particular, the act's Section 5 requires that election law changes in nine states and local jurisdictions in seven others be "pre-cleared" with the Justice Department or a federal court in Washington, D.C. Beginning with the post-1990 redistricting cycle, the Justice Department used its leverage to pressure states into drawing "majority-minority" districts to protect African-Americans' and Latinos' voting rights, with some of the districts very irregularly shaped. The Supreme Court limited the practice somewhat, however, with rulings in the 1990s that bar the use of race or ethnicity as the "predominant" factor in a district's boundaries.[3]

African-American and, in particular, Latino groups are looking for more "minority opportunity" districts in the current redistricting cycle. "I hope we will have an increase in the number of districts where Latinos can elect candidates of their choice," says Arturo Vargas, executive director of the National Association of Latino Elected and Appointed Officials (NALEO). Among the states being closely watched is Texas, which will gain four House seats in large part because of the state's growing Hispanic population.

The Supreme Court decisions limiting racial line-drawing came in suits filed by white voters and backed by groups opposed to racial preferences, including the Washington-based Project on Fair Representation. Edward Blum, the group's president, says it will bring similar legal challenges if it sees "evidence of unconstitutional racial gerrymandering" in the current redistricting.

As Blum acknowledges, however, the Voting Rights Act requires some consideration of race, nationwide, to prevent what is termed "retrogression" — new districts that reduce the ability of minority groups to elect their preferred candidate. "Race must be one factor among many that line drawers use," says Clarke with the Legal Defense Fund. It has joined with the Mexican American Legal Defense and Educational Fund (MALDEF) and the Asian American Justice Center in publishing a 78-page booklet aimed at educating and mobilizing minority communities on redistricting issues.

Increased public participation is also the goal of good-government groups, including Common Cause and the League of Women Voters. "There are a lot of opportunities for greater public participation and better maps," says Nancy Tate, the league's executive director.

In addition, two reform-minded academics — George Mason University political scientist Michael McDonald and Harvard University quantitative social scientist Micah Altman — have formed the straightforwardly named Public Mapping Project to put mapping data and software into the hands of interest groups, community organizations and even students to propose redistricting plans. The goal, McDonald says, "is to allow redistricting to be done out of people's homes."

Despite the reformers' hopes, one longtime redistricting expert doubts that public or media pressure will carry much weight as state legislatures go about their work. "I don't see state legislatures buckling much to that," says Peter Galderisi, a lecturer in political science at the University of California-San Diego. "In most situations, they don't have the direct ability to influence this at all."

As state legislatures and redistricting commissions get down to work, here are some of the major questions being debated:

Should partisan gerrymandering be restricted?

Texas Republicans chafed for more than a decade under the post-1990 congressional redistricting, a Democratic-drawn plan that helped Democrats hold a majority of the House seats through the decade. When Republicans gained control of both houses of the state legislature and the governorship in 2002, it was payback time.

Despite an attempted boycott by outnumbered Democrats, the GOP majorities approved an artful plan aimed at giving Republicans an edge wherever possible. In the first election under the new map, the GOP in 2004 gained 21-11 control of the state's congressional delegation. Democrats cried foul and argued all the way to the U.S. Supreme Court that the plan was a partisan gerrymander that violated Democratic voters' constitutional rights. The justices could not agree on a legal rule to govern gerrymandering, however, and left the map intact except to require redrawing a majority Latino district in the Rio Grande Valley.

The ruling in the Texas case marked the third time that the Supreme Court had entertained a constitutional claim against gerrymandering — and the third time that the justices failed to give any guidance on when, if ever, federal courts could strike down a partisan power-grab as going too far.[4]

Legal experts say the judicial impasse is likely to continue. Justice Anthony M. Kennedy straddles the divide between four conservatives uncomfortable with or opposed to gerrymandering challenges altogether and four liberals unable to agree on a standard to police the practice. "Four-and-a-half justices have demonstrated that they don't want to deal with this, and the other four-and-a-half cannot agree on how to deal with it," says Justin Levitt, an associate professor at Loyola Law School in Los Angeles who formerly worked on redistricting issues at the Brennan Center for Justice at New York University School of Law.

For many political scientists, the effort to control gerrymandering through the courts is simply at war with U.S. political traditions dating back to the 19th century. "We've gotten used to the fact that when one party controls, you get partisan gerrymanders," says Galderisi at UC-San Diego.

With courts on the sidelines, the critics of partisan gerrymandering are looking to two approaches in the current redistricting cycle to control the practice. The California citizens commission — and the citizens commission created in Arizona for the post-2000 cycle — take the job away from legislators and establish guidelines, including geographically compact districts. In Florida, reform groups, allied with major Democratic interest groups, won adoption of constitutional amendments in November that prohibit the legislature from drawing districts "with the intent to favor or disfavor a political party or an incumbent."

Bullock, the University of Georgia professor, says the commission approach has the potential to create more competitive districts, one of the main goals of the gerrymandering critics. (Competitiveness is one of the criteria in Arizona, though not in California.) But longtime political expert Thomas Mann, a senior fellow in governance studies at the Brookings Institution in Washington, says geographically compact districting schemes do not necessarily increase competitiveness because like-minded voters often live in the same neighborhood. "In some states, you've got to do real gerrymandering to create more competitive districts," Mann says.

In Florida, even supporters of the anti-gerrymandering amendment acknowledge doubts about how faithfully the Republican-controlled legislature will comply with the provision. "Your guess is as good as mine," says Ellen Freidin, a Miami attorney-activist who headed the Fair Districts Florida campaign for the amendments. Meanwhile, some political scientists see the command not to favor or disfavor an incumbent in drawing district lines as a logical impossibility. "Either it's going to favor them or disfavor them," says Thomas Brunell, a professor of political science at the University of Texas at Dallas. "It's got to be one of those things."

Brunell, in fact, takes the contrarian position of opposing the maximization of competitive districts. In his book *Redistricting and Representation*, Brunell argues that competitive elections are not essential for good

government and in fact increase voter discontent. "The more competitive the district, the more upset voters you have," he says.[5]

For incumbents, partisan gerrymandering may actually have a downside, according to UC-San Diego's Galderisi, if likely party voters in one district are spread around to enhance the party's chances of winning in others. "Incumbents don't feel well off unless they have a comfortable margin of victory," he says.

In fact, cutting political margins too thin in a particular district can result in a party's loss of a once-safe seat — a process that redistricting expert Bernard Grofman at the University of California-Irvine calls "a dummymander." In the current cycle, Galderisi thinks Republicans may take that lesson to heart and concentrate on protecting the gains they made in November. "A lot of efforts are going to be to shore up new incumbents rather than engage in traditional partisan gerrymanders," he says.

McDonald, the George Mason University political scientist in the Public Mapping Project, says that with so much political volatility in the last few elections, Democrats and Republicans alike will be more interested in political security than partisan advantage. "Incumbents are going to want safer districts," he says.

Should district lines be drawn to help minorities get elected to office?

Rep. Luis Gutierrez, a Chicago Democrat, has represented since 1993 a congressional district that only a redistricting junkie could love. Dubbed the "ear muff" district, Illinois-4 includes predominantly Latino neighborhoods from close-in suburbs along the city's southern border and other Latino neighborhoods in Chicago itself that are connected only by a stretch of the Tri-State Tollway.

The district was drawn that way in 1991 not to help or hurt an individual officeholder or candidate but to comply with the federal Voting Rights Act. In a city with a history of racially polarized voting and a state with no previous Hispanic member of Congress, Latinos were entitled to a majority Latino district, a federal court ruled. But the new map had to avoid carving up the majority African-American districts that lay between Latino neighborhoods. "This is not gerrymandering," the Mexican American Legal Defense and Educational

Fund explains, "but rather protecting voting rights."[6]

Latino and African-American groups will be working again in the current redistricting cycle to try to protect minority incumbents and increase opportunities for minority candidates. "We know that Latinos have increased significantly in population," says Nina Perales, MALDEF's litigation director. "We hope to see a redistricting that fairly reflects that growth."

With the African-American population growing less rapidly, Clarke says the NAACP Legal Defense Fund will first be "looking to ensure that existing opportunities are not taken away." In particular, Clarke says LDF wants to guard against the possibility that the Supreme Court's most recent decision on racial redistricting is not "misinterpreted" to call for dismantling so-called crossover or influence districts — districts where a racial or ethnic minority comprises less than a majority of the population but can form coalitions with white voters to elect a candidate.

For their part, critics of racial redistricting would like to see less attention to race and ethnicity in map-drawing. Blum, with the Project on Fair Representation, says district maps should be drawn without access to racial and ethnic data and checked only at the end to see whether redistricters had "inadvertently" reduced minority voting rights.

The Supreme Court has played the lead role in shaping the current law on racial redistricting. In a trio of decisions in the 1990s, the court struck down oddly shaped, majority-minority congressional districts in Georgia, North Carolina and Texas on the grounds that race or ethnicity was the predominant factor in drawing them. But the court in 1998 upheld the Illinois redistricting with the majority-Latino "earmuff" district. And in 2001 the court ruled in effect that redistricters may draw a majority-minority district if done for a partisan purpose — in the specific case, to make the district Democratic.[7]

Rules of the Road for California Redistricting

Ballot measures creating the California Citizens Redistricting Commission to redraw the state's legislative and congressional maps set out mandatory criteria and prohibited districts aimed at helping or hurting an incumbent, candidate or political party.

Districts must:

- Have "reasonably equal population," except where "deviation" is required to comply with the federal Voting Rights Act.
- Comply with the Voting Rights Act. The law prohibits race- or ethnicity-based interference with voting rights
- Be "geographically contiguous."
- Respect the "geographic integrity" of any county, city, neighborhood or "community of interest" to the extent possible. "Communities of interest" do not include "relationships with political parties, incumbents or political candidates."
- Be "drawn to encourage geographical compactness" to the extent practicable.
- Be drawn, to the extent practicable, so that each state Senate district encompasses precisely two Assembly districts.
- The commission is prohibited from considering an incumbent's or candidate's residence in drawing district lines. Districts "shall not be drawn for the purpose of favoring or discriminating against an incumbent, political candidate, or political party."

Source: California Citizens Redistricting Commission, http://wedrawthelines.ca.gov/downloads/voters_first_act.pdf

---

The post-2000 redistricting generated fewer major decisions on racial redistricting, but the court's 2009 ruling on a North Carolina legislative map troubles minority groups. The decision, *Bartlett v. Strickland*, required the redrawing of a once majority-black legislative district that had been reconfigured in a way to prevent the African-American population from falling below the threshold needed to form a "crossover" district. In a splintered 5-4 decision, the Supreme Court said a racial or ethnic minority could not challenge a redistricting map as impermissible "vote dilution" under the Voting Rights Act unless it comprised a majority of the district's population.[8]

The ruling "is not an invitation to dismantle existing influence districts," says Clarke. "Majority-minority districts along with influence and crossover districts continue to represent some of the most diverse constituencies in our country."

Minority groups bristle at the criticism of racial line-drawing as gerrymandering. They argue that oddly shaped districts are often the only way to bring together "communities of interest." "People don't live in squares, circles and triangles," says Vargas, with the Latino office-holders' group. "So it's hard to draw districts that have nice geometric shapes."

Blum counters that the dispersal of ethnic and racial minorities from central cities into suburbs forces redistricters to ignore geographic communities in order to create majority-minority districts. "What you have to do is draw a district that basically harvests African-Americans block by block, neighborhood by neighborhood, all across the county or across multiple counties," Blum says. "That breaks up communities of interest that are far more powerful in America today than cobbling together these racially apartheid homelands."

As in Chicago, some of the line-drawing may come in areas with Latino, African-American or Asian-American neighborhoods in close, sometimes overlapping, proximity. Both Clarke and Perales acknowledge the potential for cross-racial tensions but say their groups aim to work cooperatively.

In any event, redistricting experts say minority groups have a huge stake in the maps to be drawn. "Racial and ethnic minorities have historically been disadvantaged by deliberate efforts to mute their voices in redistricting cycles," says Costas Panagopoulos, an assistant professor of political science at Fordham University in New York City and executive editor of the magazine *Campaigns and Elections.* "Minority groups want to be sure that that does not happen this time."

Should redistricting be done by independent commissions instead of state legislatures?

As head of Arizona's first citizens' redistricting commission, Steve Lynn spent thousands of hours over the past decade redrawing legislative and congressional districts in Arizona and defending the new maps in federal and state courts. Lynn, a utility company executive in Tucson who says he is both a former Democrat and former Republican, counts the commission's work a success: no judicial map-drawing, more opportunities for minorities and — in his view at least — more competitive districts.

Surprisingly, however, Lynn voted against Proposition 106 when it was on the Arizona ballot in 2000. Back then, he had no quarrel with the state legislature doing the job. Today, Lynn endorses independent commissions, but somewhat equivocally. "It's one way to do it," Lynn told a redistricting conference sponsored by the National Conference of State Legislatures in late January. "It's not the only way to do it. Either way can work."[9]

Thirteen states now have redistricting commissions or boards with primary responsibility for drawing legislative districts; seven of those also have responsibility for drawing congressional districts. * Apart from the Arizona and California citizen commissions, the other bodies consist of specifically designated officeholders or members chosen in various ways by political officeholders with an eye to partisan balance. Five other states have backup commissions that take over redistricting in the event of a legislative impasse; two others have advisory commissions.

Two of the non-legislative bodies are long-standing: Ohio's, created in 1850; and the Texas backup commission, established in 1947. McDonald, the George Mason professor with the Public Mapping Project, says those commissions and others created in the 1960s and since were designed to make sure that redistricting was completed on time, not to divorce the process from politics. Indeed, McDonald says, there is "no evidence" that the commissions, despite their description as "bipartisan," have reduced the kind of self-interested or partisan line-drawing that gives redistricting a bad name.

By contrast, the Arizona and California commissions consist of citizens who apply for the positions in screening processes somewhat akin to college admissions. Candidates must specify that they have not served within a specified time period in any party position or federal or state office.

In Arizona, applicants for the five-member commission are screened by the appellate court nominating commission, which approves a pool of 25 candidates: 10 Republicans, 10 Democrats and five independents. From that pool, the majority and minority leaders of the state House of Representatives and Senate each pick one member; those four then pick one of the independents to serve as chair.

---

* The number includes Montana, which currently has one House member, elected at large; Montana lost its second House seat after the 1990 census.

California's process is even more complex. The state auditor's office screens candidates, forming a pool of 60, equally divided among Republicans, Democrats and independents. Those lists are provided to legislative leaders, who can strike a total of 24 applicants. The auditor's office then chooses the first eight commissioners by randomly pulling names from a spinning basket: three from each of the major parties and two independents. Those eight then pick six more: two Democrats, two Republicans and two independents.

Cressman, with Common Cause, acknowledges the complexity of the process. "It is challenging to come up with a system that gives you a combination of expertise and diversity and screens out conflict of interest and self-interest," he says.

Opponents of California's Proposition 11 cited the complexity in campaigning against the ballot measure in 2008. They also argued the commission would be both costly and politically unaccountable. In 2010, opponents qualified an initiative to abolish the commission, which appeared on the same ballot with the measure to expand the commission's role to congressional redistricting. The repealer, Proposition 27, failed by a 40 percent to 60 percent margin.

Political veterans in California continue to complain about the commission — in private. But longtime redistricting expert Bruce Cain, a professor of political science at the University of California-Berkeley and now executive director of the university's Washington, D.C., program, publicly challenged the commission approach in a presentation to the state legislators' group in January.

Cain told the legislators that commissions result in added costs because of the need to train commission members, hire additional staff and consultants and hold extra rounds of public hearings. In any event, Cain said that reformers "oversell" the likely benefits of commissions. Commissions "cannot avoid making political judgments" and are as likely as legislatures to run afoul of legal requirements, he says.

"It doesn't matter whether you have a pure heart," Cain concludes. "If you wind up with a plan that's unfair to one group or another, you're going to have trouble."

Cressman is optimistic about the California commission, which heard from a series of experts in training sessions in January and held its first public hearing in February. "They have a lot of expertise," Cressman says. "They strongly reflect the diversity of California. And they are quite ready to attack their job quite seriously."

Still, experts across the board profess uncertainty about whether the California commission will deliver on the supporters' promise of a fairer redistricting plan. "It's a very open question whether those hopes will be realized," says Douglas Johnson, president of the National Demographics Corporation, which consults on redistricting issues for governments and public interest groups. Johnson himself helped draft the initiative.

BACKGROUND
Political Thickets

The modern era of redistricting began in the 1960s when the Supreme Court intervened to force an end to state legislatures' decades-long neglect of the obligation to redraw legislative and congressional districts to reflect population changes. In a series of decisions, the court first opened the federal courts to redistricting suits and then laid down the famous "one person, one vote" requirement of mathematical equality — strict for congressional districts, slightly relaxed for legislative lines. The rulings redressed the underrepresentation of urban and suburban voters, but they also forced legislatures and the courts into the political thicket of redistricting every 10 years.[10]

The political uses of redistricting date back more than two centuries. Patrick Henry engineered district lines in an unsuccessful effort to prevent the election of his adversary James Madison to the House of Representatives in the nation's first congressional vote in 1788. The salamander-shaped district that Gov. Elbridge Gerry crafted for an 1812 legislative election in Massachusetts gave birth to the pejorative term "gerrymander" for politically motivated line-drawing.*

Through the 19th century, Congress passed laws requiring representatives to be elected in contiguous, single-member districts. A 1901 act — re-enacted in 1911 — specified that districts also be compact and contain "as nearly as practicable an equal number of

---

* Gerry pronounced his name with a hard "g," but "gerrymander" came to be pronounced with a soft "g."

CHRONOLOGY

Before 1960s *Congress, courts take hands-off approach to reapportionment, redistricting lapses.*

1908 House of Representatives refuses to enforce equal-population requirement, allows seating of member chosen from malapportioned district in Virginia.

1932 Supreme Court rejects voters' suit challenging malapportioned Mississippi congressional districts.

1946 Supreme Court rejects voters' suit challenging malapportioned Illinois congressional districts.

1960s-1970s *Supreme Court's "one-person, one-vote" revolution forces states to redraw legislative and congressional districts.*

1962-1964 Supreme Court says federal courts can entertain suits to challenge state legislature's failure to reapportion (1962). . . . Adopts "one-person, one-vote" requirement for state legislative districts (1963). . . . Applies equal-population requirement to House seats, both chambers of state legislatures (1964).

1965 Voting Rights Act prohibits interference with right to vote based on race (Section 2); imposes "preclearance" requirements for election law changes on nine states, local jurisdiction in seven others (Section 5).

1969-1973 Supreme Court strikes down congressional districting plan because of 3 percent population variation (1969), but later allows nearly 10 percent variation for state legislative districts (1973).

1980s-1990s *Supreme Court allows suits to challenge partisan gerrymanders, racial line-drawing.*

1980-1982 Supreme Court says Section 2 of Voting Rights Act prohibits only intentional discrimination; two years later, Congress adds "effects" test to prohibit any election law changes that abridge right to vote because of race.

1983 Supreme Court strikes down congressional map with 1 percent variation between districts.

1986 Supreme Court, in Indiana case, says federal courts can entertain suits to challenge legislative districting as partisan gerrymander; on remand, Republican-drawn plan is upheld against Democratic challenge.

1993-1996 Supreme Court allows white voters' suit to challenge majority African-American congressional district in North Carolina (1993). . . . Later rulings strike down majority-minority districts in Georgia (1995), North Carolina (1996), Texas (1996).

2000s *Redistricting reform proposals advance.*

2000 Arizona voters approve creation of independent citizens' redistricting commission (Prop. 106).

2001 Supreme Court upholds creation of majority African-American district in North Carolina; motivation was partisan, not racial, court finds.

2001-2004 Republican-controlled Pennsylvania legislature redraws congressional districts to GOP's benefit (2001); Republicans gain 12-7 majority in state delegation (2002); Supreme Court rejects Democrats' challenge to plan; in splintered ruling, Justice Kennedy leaves door open to gerrymandering suits (2004).

2003-2006 Republican-controlled Texas legislature reopens congressional districts, draws new map to GOP's benefit (2003); Republicans gain 21-11 majority in state delegation (2004); Democrats' challenge rejected by Supreme Court (2006).

2008-2010 California voters approve citizens' commission to redraw state legislative districts (Prop. 11); two years later, add congressional redistricting to commission's responsibility (Prop. 20).

2009 Supreme Court says states may reduce minority voters' influence if they constitute less than majority of voters in district.

2010 Florida voters approve anti-gerrymandering constitutional amendments (Nov. 2). . . . House seats shift from Northeast, Midwest to South, West (Dec. 21).

2011 States begin work on redistricting. . . . Louisiana, Mississippi, New Jersey, Virginia to hold legislative elections in November.

inhabitants." The provisions went unenforced, however. Most notably, the House failed to act on a committee's recommendation to bar a representative elected in 1908 from a malapportioned Virginia district redrawn earlier in the year to his benefit.[11]

Twice in the first half of the 20th century, the Supreme Court also balked at enforcing reapportionment requirements. In 1932, the court rejected a suit by Mississippi voters challenging the congressional district map drawn by the state legislature on the ground that it violated the 1911 act's requirements. The majority opinion held that the 1911 law had lapsed; four justices went further and said the federal courts should not have entertained the suit. The high court adopted that latter position in 1946 in turning aside a suit by Illinois voters challenging a congressional map as violating a state law requiring equal-population districts. Writing for a three-justice plurality in *Colegrove v. Green*, Justice Felix Frankfurter sternly warned against judicial review. "Courts ought not to enter this political thicket," Frankfurter wrote. A fourth justice joined in a narrower opinion, while three justices said in dissent they would have allowed the suit to go forward.[12]

The Supreme Court reversed direction in its landmark ruling in a Tennessee case, *Baker v. Carr*, in 1962. With Frankfurter in dissent, the court detailed Tennessee's failure to reapportion state legislative districts since 1901 and found urban voters entitled to use the Equal Protection Clause to challenge the malapportionment in federal court. The ruling went only so far as to send the case back to a lower court for a full trial, but in short order the Supreme Court went further. In 1963, it struck down Georgia's county-unit system for apportioning state legislative seats on the grounds that it disadvantaged large urban counties. "The concept of political equality," Justice William O. Douglas wrote in the 8-1 ruling, "can mean only one thing — one person, one vote." A year later, the court applied the equal-population requirement to congressional districts and to both chambers of bicameral state legislatures.[13]

The Supreme Court's rulings opened the door to a flood of reapportionment and redistricting lawsuits in the states. By one count, more than 40 states faced legal challenges by the time of the 1964 decisions. State legislatures across the country became more representative of the growing urban and suburban populations. In Tennessee,

for example, both the House of Representatives and the Senate elected urban members as speakers at the turn of the decade. The rulings also affected membership in the U.S. House of Representatives, if somewhat less dramatically. After the 1970 reapportionment, one study found that the number of members from rural districts had dropped from 59 to 51 while the number from urban and suburban districts rose from 147 to 161.[14]

In further cases, the court confronted how close to equal districts had to be to meet the one-person, one-vote test. For Congress, the court required strict and later stricter equality. In 1969, the justices rejected a Missouri redistricting plan because it resulted in as much as a 3.1 percent variation from perfectly equal population districts. Years later, the court in 1983 rejected, on a 5-4 vote, a New Jersey plan with less than 1 percent variation in population because the state had offered no justification for the discrepancies. States were given somewhat more leeway. In a pair of decisions in 1973, the court upheld Connecticut and Texas plans with variances, respectively, of 7.8 percent and 9.9 percent. And in 1983, on the same day as the ruling in the New Jersey case, the court upheld a Wyoming plan that gave each county at least one member in the state House of Representatives despite the large variation in district population that resulted.[15]

Legal Puzzlers

The Supreme Court in the 1980s and '90s confronted but gave only puzzling answers to two second-generation redistricting issues: whether to open federal courts to challenges to partisan or political gerrymandering or to racially or ethnically based line-drawing. On the first issue, the court ostensibly recognized a constitutional claim against partisan gerrymandering, but gave such little guidance that no suits had succeeded in federal courts by the turn of the 21st century — or, indeed, have since. On the second issue, the court in a series of decisions in the 1990s allowed white voters to challenge racially or ethnically based districting plans and eventually barred using race or ethnicity as the "predominant" motive in redrawing districts.

The political gerrymandering issue reached the Supreme Court in a challenge by Indiana Democrats to a state legislative redistricting plan drawn by Republicans after the 1980 census that helped fortify GOP majorities in the 1982 elections. A federal district court agreed with the Democrats that the plan violated

'Underrepresented' Voters Get No Help in Court

"It's pretty clear that this is not equal and it's not as equal as practicable."

The Constitution created the House of Representatives with 65 members, each representing no more than 30,000 people. Today, the House has 435 members, and their districts average about 710,000 constituents, according to the 2010 census.

That average conceals a wide variation from one state to another. Delaware's only congressman, freshman Democrat John Carney, represents about 900,000 people. In Wyoming, the state's only member of Congress, two-term Republican Cynthia Lummis, represents about 563,000 people. [1]

"One person, one vote" requires congressional districts to be equal in population within each state so that each person is equally represented in government. But the constitutional provision allotting one seat to each state combines with the need to round some fractions up and others down to make mathematical equality impossible from state to state.

Plaintiffs from five of the states disadvantaged in House seats under the 2000 census — Delaware, Mississippi, Montana, South Dakota and Utah — filed suit in federal court in Mississippi to challenge the disparities as a violation of their rights to equal representation in Congress. At the time, Montana had more than 900,000 people, just below the threshold then needed for a second House seat.

"We believe that it's pretty clear that this is not equal and it's not as equal as practicable," says Michael Farris, a constitutional lawyer in Northern Virginia and well-known conservative activist. Farris, a home-schooling advocate, recruited the plaintiffs for the case after being approached by another home-schooling father in the area.

In defending the suit, the government argued that complete elimination of the interstate disparities would require "an astronomical increase" in the size of the House. The number of House seats has been fixed since 1911 except for temporary increases to accommodate new states: Arizona and New Mexico in 1912, Alaska and Hawaii in the late 1950s.

Farris countered that an increase of as few as 10 seats would have reduced state disparities by half. And he noted that the British House of Commons has more than 500 members for a country with 62 million residents — one-fifth of the U.S. population of 308 million.

the Equal Protection Clause because it was intentionally designed to preserve Republicans' dominance. The Supreme Court ruled, 6-3, in *Davis v. Bandemer* (1986) that the suit presented a "justiciable" claim — that is, one that federal courts could hear. Only two of the six justices, however, agreed that the Indiana Democrats had proved their case. As a result, the case was sent back to the lower court, with no guidelines and for an eventual ruling against the Democrats. Challengers in gerrymandering cases over the next two decades were similarly unsuccessful.[16]

The Supreme Court first encountered a racial gerrymander in the late 1950s in a case brought by African-American voters who, in effect, had been carved out of the city of Tuskegee, Ala., by new, irregular municipal boundaries. The court in 1960 ruled unanimously that district lines drawn only to disenfranchise black voters violated the 15th Amendment.[17] The Voting Rights Act, passed and signed into law five years later, went further by specifically prohibiting interference with the right to vote (Section 2) and forcing states and counties with a history of discrimination against minorities to preclear any election or voting changes with the Justice Department or a federal court in Washington (Section 5).

The Supreme Court upheld the act, but in 1980 held that Section 2 barred election law changes only if shown to be intentionally discriminatory. Two years later, Congress amended Section 2 by adding a "results" or "effects" test that prohibits any voting or election law change, nationwide, that denies or abridges anyone's right to vote on account of race or color. In applying the law to a North Carolina legislative redistricting case, the court

The government also contended that the suit raised a "political question" that, in effect, was none of the federal courts' business. Ruling last summer, the three-judge district court hearing the case held that the plaintiffs had no right to equal representation in the House. "We see no reason to believe that the Constitution as originally understood or long applied imposes the requirements of close equality among districts in different States that the Plaintiffs seek here," the court wrote in the July 8 ruling. [2]

On appeal, the Supreme Court rejected the suit even more firmly by setting aside the district court's ruling with instructions to dismiss the case altogether. The court gave no explanation, but Farris says he assumed the justices decided the case on political-question grounds.

Farris is not the only advocate for increasing the size of the House. In an op-ed essay in *The New York Times*, two professors argued that a significantly larger House would allow representatives to be closer to their constituents, reduce the cost of campaigns and limit the influence of lobbyists and special interests. "It's been far too long since the House expanded to keep up with population growth," New York University sociologist Dalton Conley and Northwestern University political scientist Jacqueline Stevens wrote. As a result, Conley and Stevens contended, the House "has lost touch with the public and been overtaken by special interests." [3]

Farris also believes a larger House would be politically more responsive — and, in his view, more conservative. "Bigger districts create more liberal legislators," he says.

"The more it costs to campaign, the more beholden you are to people who want something from government."

Farris also warns that the disparities in the size of districts will increase over time. But he acknowledges that another court challenge may meet the same fate as his and that House members are unlikely to vote, in effect, to reduce their power by increasing the body's size. "The foxes have been given complete control of the henhouse," he says.

In the meantime, however, one of the states with the greatest underrepresentation under the 2000 apportionment — Utah — will be picking up a seat in the 2012 election. Under the new apportionment, Utah's four representatives will have about 692,000 constituents each, slightly below the national average. Delaware, Montana and South Dakota each remains well above the average district size, while Mississippi's four districts have about 744,000 people each, only slightly above the national average.

— *Kenneth Jost*

---

[1] For an interactive map showing average size of House districts state by state, see the Census Bureau's website: http://2010.census.gov/2010 census/data/.

[2] *Clemons v. Department of Commerce*, No. 3:09-cv-00104 (U.S.D.C. — N.D. Miss.), July 8, 2010, www.apportionment.us/DistrictCourtOpinion .pdf. For coverage, see Jack Elliott Jr., "Judges reject lawsuit to increase size of House," The Associated Press, July 9, 2010.

[3] Dalton Conley and Jacqueline Stevens, "Build a Bigger House," *The New York Times*, Jan. 24, 2011, p. A27.

---

crafted a three-part test for a so-called vote dilution claim. Under the so-called *Gingles* test, a plaintiff must show a concentrated minority voting bloc, a history of racially polarized voting and a change that diminishes the minority voters' effective opportunity to elect a candidate of their choice.[18]

Under President George H. W. Bush, the Justice Department interpreted the act in advance of the 1990 redistricting cycle to require states in some circumstances to draw majority-minority districts. Along with other factors, including incumbent protection and partisan balance, the requirement resulted in some very irregularly shaped districts. White voters challenged the district plans in several states, including North Carolina, Georgia and Texas, and won favorable rulings from the Supreme Court in each. The 1993 ruling in *Shaw v. Reno* reinstated a

challenge to a majority-black district created by stitching together African-American neighborhoods in three North Carolina cities. Subsequent rulings threw out majority-black districts in Georgia in 1995 and in Texas in 1996. In the Georgia case, the court declared that a district map could be invalidated if race was shown to be "the predominant factor motivating the legislature's decision to place a significant number of voters within or without a particular district."[19]

With a new decade beginning, however, the court recognized an escape hatch of sorts for states drawing majority-minority districts. In *Hunt v. Cromartie*, the court in 2001 upheld North Carolina's redrawing of the disputed majority-black 12th Congressional District in the center of the state. A lower federal court had found the district lines still to be "facially race driven," but the Supreme

Court instead said the state's motivation was "political rather than racial" — aimed at putting "reliably Democratic," African-American voters in the district. The message of the ruling, as *New York Times* reporter Linda Greenhouse wrote at the time, "was that race is not an illegitimate consideration in redistricting as long as it is not the 'dominant and controlling' one."[20]

The racial line-drawing combined with demographics to increase minority representatives in Congress. The number of African-Americans in the House of Representatives increased from 26 in 1991 to 37 in 2001, and the number of Hispanics from 11 to 19.[21] Minority groups hoped to continue to make gains in the new cycle.

Meanwhile, states braced for more litigation as the new redistricting cycle got under way. In the 1990s, 39 states were forced into court to defend redistricting plans on substantive grounds.[22] Most were upheld, but some legislatures were forced to redraw lines. And courts took over the process altogether in a few states, most notably California. There, a Democratic-controlled legislature and a Republican governor deadlocked at the start of the decade, forcing the California Supreme Court to appoint a team of special masters to draw the legislative and congressional maps.

Crosscurrents

The post-2000 redistricting cycle brought a new round of political fights and legal challenges along with the nation's first experience in Arizona with an independent citizens redistricting commission. As in the previous decade, state or federal courts in many states forced legislatures to redraw redistricting plans or drew redistricting plans themselves after legislative impasses. Arizona's independent commission itself faced protracted litigation over its plans but ended with its maps left largely intact. The Supreme Court, meanwhile, retreated somewhat from its activist posture of the 1990s. The court declined twice to crack down on partisan gerrymandering, while its rulings on racial line-drawing gave legislatures somewhat more discretion to avoid drawing favorable districts for minorities.[23]

Arizona's Proposition 106 grew out of discontent with a Republican-drawn redistricting plan in 1992 that solidified GOP control of the legislature while giving little help to the state's growing Hispanic population. The ballot measure gained approval on Nov. 7, 2000, with 56 percent of the vote after a campaign waged by good-government groups, including Common Cause and the League of Women Voters, and bankrolled by a wealthy Democratic activist. The congressional and legislative plans drawn by the five-member commission were challenged in court by Democrats and minority groups for failing to create enough competitive districts. In state court, the congressional map was upheld, while the legislative map was initially ordered redrawn. In a second ruling, however, the state court in 2008 found the commission had given sufficient consideration to competitiveness along with the other five criteria listed in the measure.

In other states, redistricting was still being played as classic political hardball. In Pennsylvania, a GOP-controlled legislature and Republican governor combined in 2001 to redraw a congressional map after the loss of two House seats that helped the GOP win a 12-7 edge in the state's delegation in the 2002 election. The Democratic challenge to the Pennsylvania plan went to the Supreme Court, where the justices blinked at the evident partisan motivation. Justice Kennedy's refusal to join four other conservatives in barring partisan gerrymandering suits left the issue for another day. But the four liberals' failure to agree on a single standard for judging such cases gave little help to potential challengers in future cases.[24]

Two years later, the Texas redistricting case produced a similarly disappointing decision for critics of partisan gerrymandering. Preliminarily, the court found no bar to Texas's mid-decade redistricting. On the gerrymandering claim, Kennedy wrote for three justices in finding that the new map better corresponded to the state's political alignment than the previous districts; two others — Antonin Scalia and Clarence Thomas — repeated their call for barring gerrymandering challenges altogether. Kennedy also led a conservative majority in upholding the breaking up of African-American voters in Dallas and Houston, but he joined with the liberal bloc to find the dispersal of Latino voters in the Rio Grande Valley a Voting Rights Act violation.[25]

In other Voting Rights Act cases, the Supreme Court and lower federal courts generally moved toward giving state legislators more leeway on how to draw racial and ethnic lines. In 2003, the high court upheld a Democratic-drawn plan in Georgia that moved African-American voters out of majority-black legislative districts to create adjoining "influence" districts where they could form majorities with like-minded voters. In the North Carolina case six years

Bringing Redistricting to the Big Screen

"I would like to see more people involved in the redistricting process."

Jeff Reichert, a self-described left-wing political junkie, remembers being both fascinated and outraged at the political shenanigans that Texas Republicans carried out to redraw congressional districts to their benefit in 2003. Reichert, who was working with a film-distribution company at the time, began to think of going behind the camera himself to bring the somewhat arcane subject of redistricting to the big screen.

"I just couldn't shake it," Reichert says today of his urge to make *Gerrymandering*, an 81-minute documentary released to theaters in fall 2010. "I thought there was a way of making a movie out of this."

True to its origins, the film takes a hard and mostly critical look at legislators' time-dishonored practice of drawing district lines to help one's friends and hurt one's foes. [1] Presidents of both parties — Democrats John F. Kennedy and Barack Obama and Republicans Ronald Reagan and George H. W. Bush — denounce the practice in the film's opening. The Texas story is told at length, with semicomic efforts by outvoted Democrats to decamp to Oklahoma to deny Republicans a quorum needed to complete their legislative coup.

The film gains more structure and immediacy from the successful effort in 2008 to pass California's Proposition 11, a ballot initiative to create an independent citizens redistricting commission charged with drawing state legislative boundaries. Gov. Arnold Schwarzenegger, the face of the initiative, and state Common Cause Executive Director Kathay Feng, the organizational mastermind, are presented as crusaders for the public good. "Pass Proposition 11," placards read, "to hold politicians accountable."

The film cost "mid-six figures" to produce, Reichert says, with much of that money coming from "folks in California who had worked on the reform effort." The reformers made good use of the investment. In 2010, supporters of the 2008 ballot initiative put their weight behind a new effort — Proposition 20 — to give the citizens' commission responsibility for congressional redistricting as well. The supporters bought 660,000 copies of Reichert's DVD to send to California voters before the November midterm elections. Proposition 20 passed, with a better margin than its predecessor two years earlier.

Documentary filmmaker Jeff Reichert defends Gerrymandering's one-sided examination of redistricting practices. "A lot of people feel that redistricting isn't working," he says.

© Green Film Company

The film drew some attention when shown in festivals in spring and summer 2010. The reviews on *Rotten Tomatoes*, a popular movie-fan website, are mixed. "Sincere but slick," one commenter writes. *New York Times* film critic Stephen Holden faulted the Proposition 11 story as "sloppily told" and took Reichert to task for failing to show anyone in defense of redistricting practices. [2]

Reichert makes no apologies for the film's one-sided critique of gerrymandering. "Documentary filmmakers aren't journalists," he says. "I have a perspective. I would like to see more people involved in the redistricting process."

Still, Reichert takes a time-will-tell attitude toward California's experiment with citizen-drawn district lines and reform efforts in other states. Some will succeed, he says, and some won't. For now, however, "a lot of people feel that redistricting isn't working."

— Kenneth Jost

---

[1] For background, see the film's website: www.gerrymanderingmovie.com.
[2] Stephen Holden, "The Dark Art of Drawing Political Lines," *The New York Times*, Oct. 15, 2010, p. C18.

later, however, the court made plain that legislators were also free to decide not to create such "crossover" or "influence" districts. In that case, a lower state court had interpreted the Voting Rights Act to require concentrating minority voters even if they did not constitute a majority in the district.[26]

As the decade neared an end, new attention was focused on reform proposals. In California, Gov. Schwarzenegger had made redistricting reform a major issue since taking office in 2003. In 2005, voters rejected by a 3-2 margin his ballot measure, Proposition 77, to give redistricting authority to a panel of retired judges. Three years later, Schwarzenegger worked closely with Common Cause and the League of Women Voters to push the more complex citizens' commission proposal, Proposition 11. In a crucial decision, supporters sought to neutralize potential opposition from members of Congress by leaving congressional redistricting in the legislature's hands. The plan won approval by fewer than 200,000 votes out of 12 million cast (51 percent to 49 percent). Two years later, with House Democrats focused on midterm elections, the measure to add congressional redistricting to the commission's authority, Proposition 20, passed easily.

In Florida, reformers suffered a setback mid-decade when the state supreme court barred a redistricting proposal in 2005 as violating the state's "single-subject rule" for initiatives. The redrawn proposals, on the ballot in November 2010 as Amendments 5 and 6, set out parallel criteria for the legislature to follow in redrawing legislative and congressional districts: contiguous, compact where possible, "not drawn to favor or disfavor an incumbent or political party" and "not drawn to deny racial or language minorities the equal opportunity to participate in the political process and elect representatives of their choice." Fair Districts Florida received major contributions from teachers' unions; the opposition group, Protect Our Vote, got the bulk of its money from the state's Republican Party. The measure passed with 62.6 percent of the vote.

CURRENT SITUATION

Advantage: Republicans

Republican control of congressional redistricting machinery in major states adding or losing House seats puts the GOP in a favorable position to gain or hold ground in the 2012 elections. But Democrats will try to minimize partisan line-drawing and lay the groundwork for court challenges later.

The November 2010 elections gave Republicans undivided control of 25 state legislatures plus Nebraska's nominally nonpartisan unicameral body. Democrats control 16, while eight other states have divided party control between two chambers. "Republicans control more legislatures," says Columbia law professor Persily. "They are in the driver's seat when it comes to drawing lines."

But Jeffrey Wice, a Democratic redistricting attorney in Washington, says pressure by good-government groups for greater transparency and public participation adds a new element that may reduce partisan gerrymandering. "We're too early in the game to predict winners and losers," Wice says. "There's no simplicity in this process."

Out of eight states picking up House seats in the current reapportionment, Republicans control both houses of the state legislature and the governor's offices in five, including the two biggest gainers: Texas, with four new seats, and Florida, with two. The GOP also has undivided control in Georgia, South Carolina and Utah, each picking up one seat. All five states currently have majority-Republican delegations.

Republicans also have undivided control in three states to lose seats: Ohio, giving up two seats, as well as Michigan and Pennsylvania. In those states, Republican lawmakers are likely to draw maps to try to avoid losing House seats in the currently majority-GOP delegations.

Democrats start the congressional redistricting process with significantly less leverage. They have undivided control of redistricting machinery in none of the three other states to gain seats. Arizona and Washington both use bipartisan commissions to redraw congressional districts. In Nevada, Democrats have majorities in both legislative chambers, but Republican Gov. Brian Sandoval could veto a redistricting plan approved by the legislature.

Among states losing seats, Democrats have undivided control only in Illinois, where Republicans currently have an 11-8 majority in the House delegation, and Massachusetts, where Democrats hold all nine current House seats. In New York, which loses two seats, Democrats control the Assembly and Republicans the Senate — setting the stage for a likely deal in which each party yields one House district.

Louisiana's legislature is also divided, with Republicans in control in the House and the two parties tied with

AT ISSUE

Should redistricting be done by independent commissions?

YES
Derek Cressman
Western regional director, Common Cause

NO
Bruce E. Cain
Heller Professor of Political Science, University of California, Berkeley, and Executive Director, UC Washington Center

Written for CQ Researcher, February 2011

Throughout 2011, states will redraw their political districts in a process usually controlled either directly or indirectly by state legislators, the very people with the most to gain or lose from the outcome. The process will almost always cater to incumbent or partisan self-interests. Too often, it also will divide communities, dilute the political strength of ethnic voters and virtually guarantee re-election for the vast majority of incumbents. Unable to hold politicians accountable, too many voters will be left feeling powerless, and citizen participation in politics will suffer.

Reforming this dysfunctional process is fundamental to restoring both a truly representative government and one that can solve societal problems. When voters are disengaged and stay home on election day, legislators have little incentive to act, whatever the issue.

Gerrymandering — manipulating district lines in a way that essentially predetermines election results — has been with us since the early days of our republic. Today, it's more sophisticated, and more sinister, than ever.

Using powerful computer-mapping software, legislators and their political consultants can draw boundaries that remove a potential opponent from a district, add or subtract voters of a certain ethnicity, bring in big donors or concentrate members of an opposing party in a single district to reduce their overall representation. Elections in the ensuing decade are so predetermined that there is little left for voters to choose.

This is a mess best addressed by turning over redistricting to independent, citizen commissions whose members have no stake in where the lines are drawn. California recently made this move, creating a citizens commission of five Democrats, five Republicans and four independent or minor-party voters. The new law requires the panel to make compliance with the federal Voting Rights Act a priority and avoid splitting communities. The commission is prohibited from drawing districts to aid any incumbent legislator off-the-record. Most important, the commission has to conduct all hearings in public, with no off-record conversations about maps allowed.

Other states have created similar panels, though none go as far as California to wring partisanship and self-interest from the redistricting process. And while no commission can be expected to produce maps that please everyone, any effort that shifts the focus of redistricting toward the voters' interest in accountable, effective government and away from the politicians' interest in self-preservation and partisan advantage is a step in the right direction.

Written for CQ Researcher, February 2011

Replacing legislative redistricting with independent commissions is high on the reform agenda, but is it really so obviously irrational or shameful for a state to resist this trend?

Even the most independent commissions, such as those in Arizona and California, have peculiar issues. Most basically, there is the composition problem. Legislatures are imperfectly reflective of state populations, but they are at least democratically elected and relatively large. Commissions are both appointed (in California's case by an odd, convoluted mix of jury selection and college application-style procedures) and small (making it harder to reflect population diversity). If there is controversy over the lines, as there usually is, these composition disputes can figure prominently in the ensuing litigation.

For good and bad reasons, commissions tend to be more expensive. There are high costs associated with being more open and independent. Greater transparency means more hearings and outreach efforts, which are costly and time consuming to set up, and the yield in terms of broad public participation as opposed to the usual interested groups will likely be low. And given that any association with political parties or elected officials is grounds for exclusion by virtue of excessive political interest, commissions cannot borrow from legislative and political staff. They must hire consultants instead.

Commissions are also no less likely to end up in lawsuits or political controversies. Redistricting is inherently political, involving choices and trade-offs related to race, communities of interest, the integrity of city and county boundaries, the number of competitive seats and so on. However one chooses, someone is going to feel aggrieved. Commissioners cannot be sequestered like jury members or insulated from political influences. Doing without political or incumbency data only means making controversial decisions blindly, not avoiding them. The losers in redistricting disputes will derive little consolation from the commission's efforts at impartiality by empirical blindness, which is why commissions to date have been no more successful in avoiding legal challenges.

On the other side, the sins of legislative redistricting have been grossly exaggerated. Partisan redistricting is rare, and in states with term limits, redistricting is less important than it used to be. Studies show that effects of redistricting on competition and party polarization are marginal at best, casting doubt on the hyperventilated assertions of commission advocates.

So adopt a commission if you must, but expect no miracles. Just be prepared to pay the consultants' bills.

AP Photo/Charlie Neibergall

Ed Cook, legal counsel for the Iowa Legislative Services Agency, displays a map Feb. 9 that is being used to help draw new congressional district lines in the state. Iowa is losing a seat in the U.S. House of Representatives during reapportionment. Unique among the states, Iowa essentially assigns legislative and congressional redistricting to professional staff, subject to legislative enactment and gubernatorial approval.

one vacancy in the Senate. Democrats hold only one of the state's current seven House seats. In Missouri, a Republican-controlled legislature will draw congressional districts, but Democratic Gov. Jay Nixon has to sign or veto any plan approved by lawmakers.

New Jersey, the one other state losing a House seat, uses a bipartisan commission. Democrats have a 7-6 majority in the state's current congressional delegation, but the state is losing population in the predominantly Democratic north and gaining population in Republican areas to the west and south.

California poses the biggest question mark for the 2012 congressional districts. The state's current congressional map favors Democrats, who hold 35 of the 53 House seats. Democrats also hold a nearly 2-to-1 majority in both legislative chambers.

A chart presented to the Citizens Redistricting Commission in an early training session shows that congressional districts in predominantly Democratic Los Angeles and San Francisco are now underpopulated, while districts in some Republican areas — such as the so-called Inland Empire to the east of Los Angeles — are overpopulated.[27] As a result, Los Angeles and San Francisco could lose seats or at least shed voters to adjoining districts.

The commission has pointedly avoided deciding so far whether — or to what extent — to use the existing

legislative and congressional districts as a starting point for the new maps. But commission members Ward and Dai both stressed that the ballot measures creating the commission specifically prohibit any consideration of protecting incumbents. "The idea of creating competitive districts," Ward adds, "seems to be unanimous among the commissioners."

In some Republican-controlled states, demographics may limit the GOP's opportunity to gain ground. In particular, Latino advocacy groups believe that Texas will be required to make two of the four new congressional districts majority Latino. That would benefit Democrats since Latinos in Texas and elsewhere have been voting predominantly Democratic in recent elections.

In Virginia, a different demographic change — the growth of the Northern Virginia suburbs surrounding Washington, D.C. — is seen as a possible benefit for Democrats in redrawing the existing 11 House seats despite the GOP's control of the redistricting machinery. Northern Virginia is seen as more liberal than rural counties in the state's south and west, some of which are losing population, according to the Census Bureau.

Forecast: Cloudy

California's new Citizens Redistricting Commission is just getting organized even as a midsummer deadline looms for the 14 map-drawing neophytes to complete the nation's largest legislative and congressional redistricting.

The commission spent two-and-a-half days in mid-February working on housekeeping matters without touching on any of the politically sensitive issues members will face in redrawing lines for 53 congressional districts, 40 state Senate districts and 80 state Assembly districts in the nation's most populous state

"We do believe we're behind schedule," says Ward, the Anaheim chiropractor who held the rotating position of chair for the commission's Feb. 10-12 sessions. "Given the compressed time line, I don't believe you can ever be on schedule."

As in California, redistricting is still in initial stages in most states, but is moving faster in the four that must redraw legislative lines quickly because of general elections scheduled this fall and primary elections beginning this summer. Besides New Jersey, the others are Louisiana, Mississippi and Virginia — Southern states with divided legislatures and significant African-American populations.

Under the Voting Rights Act, all three must have redistricting maps precleared by either the Justice Department or a federal court in Washington.

The California commission is working on an ambitious series of four public sessions in each of nine regions in the state, with informational or educational workshops to explain the redistricting process hoped to begin in March. Plans then call for more formal public-input meetings to be held before maps are drawn, as they are being drawn and again after the maps are completed.

Proposition 20, the 2010 ballot measure, established an Aug. 15 deadline for the maps to be certified to the state's secretary of state. But commission member Dai explains that to allow time for public notice and for preclearance — five of the state's counties are subject to the Voting Rights Act's Section 5 — the commission's target date for completion is July 25.

The four states with legislative elections this year are all moving to get redistricting maps up for decisions in March or April.

In New Jersey, the 10-member legislative redistricting commission — with five members appointed by each of the Democratic and Republican state chairs — is holding a series of public hearings aimed at submitting a map by an early April deadline. "The two delegations have been working on tentative maps," says Alan Rosenthal, a professor of political science at Rutgers University in Newark, who is a likely candidate to be named by the state's chief justice as a tie-breaker if the commission reaches an impasse. The separate commission to redraw New Jersey's congressional districts — to be reduced from 13 to 12 — has not been appointed yet.

In Louisiana, the legislature's governmental affairs committees were due to complete eight public hearings around the state by March 1; the legislature was then to convene on March 20 in special session to redraw legislative and congressional districts. Mississippi's Standing Joint Committee on Reapportionment also held public hearings in February, with an announced plan to bring redistricting proposals to the floor of each chamber in early March.

In Virginia the General Assembly's Joint Reapportionment Committee set up an Internet site in December for public comment on redistricting proposals and then laid plans for a special session to begin April 6. Meanwhile,

Republican Gov. Bob McDonnell fulfilled a campaign pledge on Jan. 9 by appointing a bipartisan, 11-member advisory commission on redistricting. The commission plans to propose legislative and congressional redistricting plans by April 1, but the legislature will not be bound to follow the recommendations.

Meanwhile, political skirmishes are breaking out in other states. Litigation is already under way in Florida over the newly passed anti-gerrymandering ballot measures. Two minority-group members of Congress filed a federal court suit immediately after the election challenging Amendment 6 on congressional redistricting as a violation of the Constitution and the Voting Rights Act. Reps. Mario Diaz-Balart, a Hispanic Republican, and Corrine Brown, an African-American Democrat, argue standards for congressional district-drawing are up to Congress, not the states; in addition, they say the Voting Rights Act requires protection for already-elected minority legislators. Separately, supporters of the amendment have filed suit against Republican Gov. Rick Scott for failing to submit Amendment 6 to the Justice Department for preclearance.[28]

In other states, Democratic legislators in New York are pressing the GOP-controlled state Senate to stick to pre-election campaign pledges by Republican members and candidates to support an independent commission to redraw lines. In Michigan, a coalition of reform groups is urging the GOP-controlled legislature to allow more public input by posting any redistricting maps on the Internet at least 30 days before taking action. And in Illinois, Democratic Gov. Pat Quinn is weighing whether to sign a bill approved by the Democratic-controlled legislature to require four public hearings on any redistricting proposal and, significantly, to require creation of minority group-protective "crossover" and "influence" districts where feasible.

OUTLOOK

Not a Pretty Picture?

The 20 "most gerrymandered" congressional districts in the United States selected by the online magazine *Slate* present an ugly picture of the redistricting process. The boundaries of the districts — 16 of them represented by

Democrats as of 2009 — zig and zag, twist and turn and jut in and out with no apparent logic.[29]

To redistricting expert Storey, however, many of the districts amount to marvels of political-representation engineering. As one example, Storey points to Arizona-2, which stretches from the Phoenix suburbs to the state's northwestern border and then connects only by means of the Colorado River to a chunk of territory halfway across the state to the east.

As Storey explains, the safely Republican district was drawn in the post-2000 cycle to include a Hopi reservation while placing the surrounding reservation of the rival Navajo nation in an adjoining district. And the districting scheme was crafted not by a politically motivated legislature but by the then brand-new independent citizens redistricting commission.

Among *Slate*'s list of worst districts are others drawn to connect minority communities, such as Illinois-4 (majority Hispanic) and several majority African-American districts in the South (Alabama-7, Florida-23, North Carolina-12). "Lines that look funny may represent real communities without any partisan motivation," says Loyola law professor Levitt.

"There are reasons why districts aren't pretty," adds Cynthia Canary, director of the Illinois Campaign for Political Reform. "But people want pretty."

The people who "want pretty" may well be disappointed again with the post-2010 redistricting cycle despite the concerted efforts of reform-minded groups and experts to improve the process. "This is going to be hardball politics," Sherri Greenberg, a professor at the University of Texas Lyndon B. Johnson School of Public Affairs in Austin and a former Texas legislator, says of the state's redistricting process just now under way. "This is a process that creates enemies, not friends."

In California, however, members of the Citizens Redistricting Commission are professing optimism that they can reach a bipartisan agreement on maps that are both fairer and more competitive than the existing legislative and congressional districts. "There really has been no evidence of partisanship among the commissioners," says Dai, one of the Democratic members. Asked whether a bipartisan agreement is "doable," Republican commissioner Ward replies simply: "Undoubtedly, yes, it is doable."

Reformers are similarly hopeful about the likely outcome of the anti-gerrymandering measures in Florida. "It's going to stop the most egregious gerrymanders," says MacDonald, the professor who co-founded the Public Mapping Group. But John Ryder, the Tennessean who heads the Republican National Committee's redistricting committee, says the Florida measures — with the stated prohibition against helping or hurting a political party or candidate — defy logic. "It's simply an unenforceable standard," he says.

Latino advocacy groups have high hopes — and expectations — for the current round of redistricting. MALDEF president Thomas Saenz predicts nine new majority-Hispanic districts, including two in Texas. Perales, the group's litigation director, makes clear that MALDEF is prepared to go to court to defend plans that increase Latinos' political influence and challenge any that do not.

For her part, the NAACP Legal Defense Fund's Clarke declines to predict whether the redistricting cycle will help elect more African-Americans to the next Congress. "We don't have quotas," Clarke says. But she stresses that the Legal Defense Fund is closely monitoring developments in states to try to prevent dismantling existing influence districts as well as those with majority black population.

Politically, experts are predicting Republican gains in the 2012 congressional elections, thanks to geographic shifts as well as political control of redistricting machinery in close to half the states. Galdaresi, the UC-Irvine professor, expects the GOP to pick up seven to 15 House seats.

Political pros profess uncertainty. "I think it takes a pretty good crystal ball to predict what the net effect of redistricting is," the RNC's Ryder says. Democratic attorney Wice thinks public pressure may reduce Republicans' ability to engineer favorable plans. "It's not over by any means to give the Republicans the final word," he says.

Whatever happens in the first round, many, perhaps most, of the redistricting plans will be headed for a second round in the courts. "It's hard not to predict litigation in redistricting," says Perales. "Somebody's always unhappy after the plan is done."

Increased public participation may influence the process not only in legislatures and commissions but also in the courts, according to Norman Ornstein, a longtime Congress watcher now at the conservative

American Enterprise Institute think tank. "Courts will have more information to use in evaluating or drawing maps," he says.

But the calls for more public participation will be a challenge to citizen groups. "This is an incredibly complex topic," says Canary. "Nobody out in the public knows why it is so complicated."

NOTES

1. Dai's and Ward's background taken in part from their application for the positions, posted on the California Citizens Redistricting Commission's website: http://wedrawthelines.ca.gov//.

2. For previous *CQ Researcher* coverage, see Kenneth Jost, "Redistricting Disputes," March 12, 2004, pp. 221-248; Jennifer Gavin, "Redistricting," Feb. 16, 2001, pp. 113-128; Ronald D. Elving, "Redistricting: Drawing Power With a Map," Feb. 15, 1991, pp. 98-113.

3. For background, see Nadine Cohodas, "Electing Minorities," *CQ Researcher*, Aug. 12, 1994; pp. 697-720.

4. The Texas case is *League of United Latin American Citizens (LULAC) v. Perry*, 548 U.S. 399 (2006). The previous cases are *Vieth v. Jubelirer*, 541 U.S. 267 (2004); and *Davis v. Bandemer*, 478 U.S. 109 (1986).

5. Thomas Brunell, *Redistricting and Representation: Why Competitive Elections Are Bad for America* (2008).

6. The quote is from a power-point presentation, "Redistricting 101," by the Brennan Center for Justice and MALDEF, dated Feb. 23, 2010, www.midwest-redistricting.org/. The court case is *Hastert v. State Board of Elections*, 777 F.Supp. 634 (N.D. Ill. 1991). For coverage, see Thomas Hardy, "GOP in clover as federal judges approve congressional remap," *Chicago Tribune*, Nov. 7, 1991, p. 2.

7. The first three decisions are *Miller v. Johnson*, 515 U.S. 900 (1995) (Georgia); *Shaw v. Hunt*, 517 U.S. 889 (1996) (North Carolina); and *Bush v. Vera*, 517 U.S. 952 (1996) (Texas). The Supreme Court summarily upheld the Illinois plan in *King v. Illinois Board of Elections*, 522 U.S. 1087 (1998). The final ruling is *Hunt v. Cromartie*, 532 U.S. 234 (2001). For a summary compilation, see "Redistricting Disputes," *op. cit.*, p. 228.

8. The citation is 556 U.S. 1 (2009).

9. The Arizona Independent Redistricting Commission's website is at www.azredistricting.org/?page=.

10. For a comprehensive overview, see "Reapportionment and Redistricting" in *Guide to Congress* (6th ed., 2008), pp. 1039-1072. See also "The Right to an Equal Vote" in David G. Savage, *Guide to the U.S. Supreme Court* (5th ed., 2010), Vol. 1, pp. 640-653.

11. Edward W. Saunders was elected from Virginia's 5th congressional district in 1908 after Floyd County was transferred to the adjoining 6th district. The transfer left the 5th district with significantly less population than the 6th. Saunders' opponent, who would have won the election in the district as previously drawn, challenged Saunders' seating on the ground of the 1901 apportionment act; a committee recommended the challenger be seated, but the House did not act on the recommendation. See "Reapportionment and Redistricting," *op. cit.*, p. 1049.

12. The Mississippi case is *Wood v. Broom*, 287 U.S. 1 (1932). The citation for *Colegrove v. Green* is 327 U.S. 549 (1946). The dissenting justices were Hugo L. Black, William O. Douglas and Francis Murphy.

13. See *Baker v. Carr*, 369 U.S. 186 (1962); *Gray v. Sanders*, 372 U.S. 368 (1963); *Wesberry v. Sanders*, 376 U.S. 1 (1964); *Reynolds v. Sims*, 377 U.S. 533 (1964).

14. Jack L. Noragon, "Congressional Redistricting and Population Composition, 1964-1970," *Midwest Journal of Political Science*, Vol. 16, No. 2 (May 1972), pp. 295-302, www.jstor.org/pss/2110063.

15. The cases are detailed in Savage, *op. cit.*, pp. 646-650.

16. The citation is 478 U.S. 109 (1986).

17. The case is *Gomillon v. Lightfoot*, 364 U.S. 339 (1960).

18. The decision is *Thornburg v. Gingles*, 478 U.S. 30 (1986); the earlier ruling is *Mobile v. Bolden*, 446 U.S. 55 (1980).

19. For a summary compilation, with citations, see "Redistricting Disputes," *op. cit.*, p. 228.

20. See Linda Greenhouse, "Justices Permit Race as a Factor in Redistricting," *The New York Times*, April 19, 2001, p. A1.

21. "Redistricting Disputes," *op. cit.*, p. 233.

22. *Outline of Redistricting Litigation: The 1990s*, National Conference of State Legislatures, www.senate.mn/departments/scr/redist/redout.htm.

23. Coverage drawn in part from *Outline of Redistricting Litigation: The 2000s, National Conference of State Legislatures*, www.senate.mn/departments/scr/redist/redsum2000/redsum2000.htm.

24. The case is *Vieth v. Jubelirer, op. cit.* For a comprehensive account, see Kenneth Jost, *Supreme Court Yearbook 2003-2004*.

25. The case is *LULAC v. Perry, op. cit.* For a comprehensive account, see Kenneth Jost, *Supreme Court Yearbook 2005-2006*. See also Steve Bickerstaff, *Lines in the Sand: Congressional Redistricting in Texas and the Downfall of Tom DeLay* (2007).

26. The decisions are *Georgia v. Ashcroft*, 539 U.S. 461 (2003); *Bartlett v. Strickland, op. cit.*

27. Karin MacDonald and Nicole Boyle, "Redistricting California: An Overview of Data, Processes and GIS," Statewide Database_Berkeley Law, p. 53, http://wedrawthelines.ca.gov/downloads/crc_public_meeting_20101130_training_karin_mac_donald_nicole_boyle.pdf.

28. See Marc Caputo and Lee Logan, "Redistricting Amendment Challenged," *St. Petersburg Times*, Nov. 4, 2010, p. 4B; Steve Bousquet, "Scott's Action May Stall Ban on Gerrymandering," *ibid.*, Jan. 26, 2011, p. 1B.

29. See "The 20 Most Gerrymandered Districts," *Slate*, www.slate.com/id/2274411/slideshow/2208554/fs/0//entry/2208555/. The unsigned, undated slide show was apparently posted in 2009.

BIBLIOGRAPHY

Books

Brunell, Thomas, *Redistricting and Representation: Why Competitive Elections Are Bad for America*, Routledge, 2008.
A professor at the University of Texas at Dallas argues that competitive elections are not vital for effective representation, but in fact increase the number of people who "are left unrepresented in Congress." Includes notes, references.

Bullock, Charles S. III, *Redistricting: The Most Political Activity in America*, Rowman & Littlefield, 2010.
A professor at the University of Georgia summarizes background information on congressional and legislative redistricting and examines the strategies and tactics of a process that he says is inevitably political if in control of elected officials. Includes notes.

Cox, Gary W., and Jonathan N. Katz, *Elbridge Gerry's Salamander: The Electoral Consequences of the Reapportionment Revolution*, Cambridge University Press, 2002.
The authors argue that, contrary to conventional wisdom, the reapportionment revolution of the 1960s onward was not without political consequence but had two lasting effects: strengthening the Democratic advantage in the U.S. House of Representatives and the advantage of incumbents over challengers. Cox is a professor emeritus at the University of California-San Diego, Katz a professor at the California Institute of Technology. Includes notes, references

Galderisi, Peter F. (ed.), *Redistricting in the New Millennium*, Lexington Books, 2005.
The 14 essays by 18 contributors include overviews of events through the turn of the 21st century, detailed examination of race and redistricting and case studies of redistricting in several states. Editor Galderisi is a lecturer at the University of California-San Diego. Includes notes, 12-page bibliography.

Winburn, Jonathan, *The Realities of Redistricting: Following the Rules and Limiting Gerrymandering in State Legislative Redistricting*, Lexington Books, 2008.
A professor at the University of Mississippi examines the "realities" of redistricting as seen in four institutional settings: unified partisan control of the state legislature; divided partisan control; partisan commission; and bipartisan commission. Includes selected bibliography.

Yarbrough, Tinsley, *Race and Redistricting: The Shaw-Cromartie Cases*, University Press of Kansas, 2002.
A professor at East Carolina University chronicles the decadelong fight over congressional redistricting in

North Carolina that first recognized constitutional objections to racially drawn district lines but ended with upholding a plan with district lines drawn to take race into account to some degree. Includes chronology, short bibliographical essay.

Articles

"Reapportionment and Redistricting," in *Guide to Congress* (6th ed.), CQ Press, 2007, pp. 1039-1072, http://library.cqpress.com/congressguide/toc.php? mode=guides-toc&level=3&values=Part+VII%3A+Con gress+and+the+Electorate~Ch.+33++Reapportionment +and+Redistricting (purchase required).

The chapter provides a comprehensive overview of developments in regard to congressional reapportionment and redistricting from the Constitutional Convention through the mid-2000's. Includes select bibliography.

Reports and Studies

"The Impact of Redistricting in YOUR Community: A Guide to Redistricting," NAACP Legal Defense and Educational Fund/Asian American Justice Center/Mexican American Legal Defense and Educational Fund, 2010.

The 78-page guide covers redistricting practices and policies as they affect racial and ethnic minorities. Includes state-by-state listing of contact information for redistricting authorities.

Levitt, Justin, "A Citizen's Guide to Redistricting," Brennan Center for Justice at New York University School of Law, 2010, http://brennan.3cdn.net/7182a7 e7624ed5265d_6im622teh.pdf.

The 127-page guide published by the nonpartisan public policy and law institute covers from an often critical perspective the basics of current redistricting practices and outlines current reform proposals. Includes additional resources, notes, other appendix materials. Levitt is now an associate professor at Loyola Law School in Los Angeles.

"Redistricting Law 2010," National Conference of State Legislatures, 2009.

The 228-page guide covers current redistricting practices, step by step and subject by subject. Includes notes, extensive appendix materials.

On the Web

GovTrack, www.govtrack.us/congress/findyourreps. xpd.

This private, unofficial website includes well-organized, state-by-state information and maps on congressional districts and current members of Congress.

Note: For earlier works, see "Bibliography" in Kenneth Jost, "Redistricting Debates," CQ Researcher, March 12, 2004, p. 243.

For More Information

Asian America Justice Center, 1140 Connecticut Ave., N.W., #1200, Washington, DC 20036; (202) 296-2300; www.advancingequality.org. Organization founded in 1991 to advance human and civil rights of Asian Americans.

Brennan Center for Justice, New York University Law School, 161 Sixth Ave., 12th Floor, New York, NY 10013; (646) 292-8310; www.brennancenter.org. Nonpartisan public policy and law institute founded in 1995 that focuses in part on voting rights and campaign and election reform.

Common Cause, 1250 Connecticut Ave., N.W., #600, Washington, DC 20036; (202) 833-1200; www.commoncause .org. Nonpartisan public-interest advocacy organization founded in 1970.

League of United Latin American Citizens, 2000 L St., N.W., Suite 610, Washington, DC 20036; (202) 833-6130; www.lulac.org. Organization founded in 1929 to advance the economic condition, educational attainment, political influence, housing, health and civil rights of the U.S. Hispanic population.

League of Women Voters, 1730 M St., N.W., Suite 1000, Washington, DC 20036-4508; (202) 429-1965; www.lwv. org. Nonpartisan organization founded in 1920 to promote government reform through education and advocacy.

Mexican American Legal Defense and Educational Fund, 634 S. Spring St., Los Angeles, CA; (213) 629-2512; www. maldef.org. Leading Latino civil rights advocacy organization, founded in 1968.

NAACP Legal Defense and Educational Fund, 99 Hudson St., 6th Floor, New York, NY 10013-6289; (212) 965-2200; http://naacpldf.org. Nonprofit civil rights law firm founded in 1940.

National Association of Latino Elected and Appointed Officials, 600 Pennsylvania Ave., S.E., Suite 230, Washington, DC 20003; (202) 546-2536; www.naleo.org. Organization founded in 1976 as a national forum for Latino officials.

National Conference of State Legislatures, 7700 E. First Place, Denver, CO 80230; (303) 364-7700; www.ncsl.org. Bipartisan organization that provides research, technical assistance and other support for legislators and legislative staff in the states, commonwealths and territories.

Project on Fair Representation, 1150 17th St., N.W., #910, Washington, DC 20036; (703) 505-1922; www. projectonfairrepresentation.org. Legal defense fund founded in 2005 to support litigation that challenges racial and ethnic classifications and preferences in state and federal courts.

Public Mapping Project, Prof. Michael MacDonald, George Mason University, Department of Public and International Affairs, 4400 University Drive — 3F4, Fairfax, VA 22030-4444; www.publicmappingproject. A project founded for the post-2010 redistricting cycle to make census data and redistricting software available to general public.

The two major political parties' national committees:

Democratic National Committee, 430 South Capitol St., S.E., Washington, DC 20003; (202) 863-8000; www.dnc .org.

Republican National Committee, 310 1st St., S.E., Washington, DC 20003; (202) 863-8500; www.rnc.org.

9

States and Federalism

Kenneth Jost

President Obama signs new health care reform legislation on March 23, 2010, providing insurance for some 30 million uninsured Americans. Twenty states have sued to invalidate the controversial legislation, claiming the added costs it requires amounts to an unconstitutional intrusion on the states' sovereignty.

From *CQ Researcher*,
Oct 15, 2010.

Arizona Gov. Jan Brewer worked hard with the state's legislature to come up with $1.1 billion in spending cuts early this year to avoid a big budget deficit in 2011. A big chunk of savings came from eliminating health care coverage for 47,000 low-income children and 310,000 childless adults.

"This is the most significant streamlining of state government ever undertaken," the Republican chief executive said as she signed a series of budget bills on March 19.

Only a few days later, however, Arizona's budget-cutting effort ran headlong into President Obama's plan to cover most of the estimated 50 million Americans without health insurance. Under the health care overhaul that Congress passed and Obama signed into law on March 23, states are prohibited from reducing their current health care funding.

"The short version is that states are locked into their existing programs at the moment the president signs the bill," Monica Coury, spokeswoman for the Arizona Health Care Cost Containment System, told the *Arizona Republic* on the eve of Obama's signing. The agency operates the state's Medicaid system, the federal-state health care program for low-income persons.[1]

Barely a month later, Brewer found herself in another power struggle with Washington as she signed a controversial immigration law on April 23 making it a state crime to be in the country illegally and requiring local police to enforce federal immigration law. Brewer said the law — passed by the GOP-controlled legislature — was necessary "to solve a crisis we did not create and the federal government has refused to fix — the crisis caused by illegal immigration and Arizona's porous border."

Confidence in Government Lags

Fifty-nine percent of Americans have limited or no confidence in either the federal or their state government (top graph). In five economically stressed states — Arizona, California, Florida, Illinois and New York — a majority of voters say they can trust their state governments only some of the time (chart).

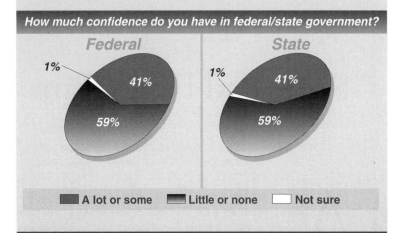

How much confidence do you have in federal/state government?

Federal: 41% A lot or some, 59% Little or none, 1% Not sure

State: 41% A lot or some, 59% Little or none, 1% Not sure

■ A lot or some ■ Little or none □ Not sure

How much of the time do you think you can trust your state government to do what is right?

State	Just about always	Most of the time	Only some of the time	Never	Don't know
Arizona	4%	29%	60%	6%	1%
California	3	15	70	10	2
Florida	4	27	59	8	2
Illinois	2	17	71	9	1
New York	3	16	67	12	2

* Figures may not total 100 due to rounding.

Sources: "Voter Confidence in Big Banks, Corporations & Wall Street Even Lower Than That of Government," Zogby, February 2010, www.zogby.com/news/Read News.cfm?ID=1817; "Facing Facts: Public Attitudes and Fiscal Realities in Five Stressed States," Pew Center on the States, October 2010, www.pewcenteronthe states.org/uploadedFiles/PCS_PPIC.pdf?n=4566

The very same day, Obama in Washington called the law "misguided" and pledged an administration review of its implications. The Justice Department followed through on July 6 by filing a federal court suit in Phoenix to invalidate the law as conflicting with the federal government's plenary power over immigration matters. "The Constitution and the federal immigration laws do not permit the development of a patchwork of state and local immigration policies throughout the country," the suit says.[2]

The two issues are as current as the upcoming 2010 midterm congressional elections. Republican candidates and activists in the diffuse Tea Party movement are depicting the health care overhaul as a massive power grab by the federal government at the expense of state prerogatives and individual rights. Along with immigration-control advocacy groups, they are also blaming Washington for the failure to seal U.S. borders from illegal immigrants and urging the feds to get out of the way of state and local governments wanting to adopt tougher policies.[3]

The conflicts over federal and state powers, however, are also as old as the Republic itself. The Constitution, drafted in the summer of 1787, called for replacing the weak national government created by the Articles of Confederation with a federal system of divided powers between the national and state governments, known as federalism. The new national government was to be stronger, but how much stronger was unclear. The issue was fiercely debated in the state-by-state battles that led up to ratification of the Constitution nine months later.

"From the beginning there was ambiguity in the Constitution," says Timothy Conlan, a professor of political science at George Mason University in Fairfax, Va., and author of two books and numerous articles on federalism, "And the scope of ambiguity has grown over time as we've been forced to adapt an 18th-century document to the realities of 20th-century government."[4]

Federal powers have grown over time, particularly since the 1930s, when President Franklin D. Roosevelt put Washington into the economic-recovery and regulation business. The Supreme Court initially struck down some of FDR's legislative initiatives, but reversed course in 1937.

"The federal government clearly has grown in power since 1938," says Robert A. Schapiro, a professor of constitutional law at Emory University School of Law in Atlanta. "The scope of federal regulation has increased," Schapiro adds, "but the scope of state regulation has also increased."

Roosevelt set the pattern for Democratic presidents, including John F. Kennedy and Lyndon B. Johnson in the 1960s, of being associated with expanding the scope and size of the federal government. Two Republican successors, Richard M. Nixon and Ronald Reagan, countered with federalism reforms that purported to transfer power back to the states. Conlan notes, however, that both of the GOP chief executives also adopted some policies that centralized powers in Washington.

Today, Obama and his fellow Democrats in Congress are under fierce criticism for supposedly expanding federal powers and spending to unprecedented levels. "No government-controlled health care," read one commonly seen placard at a Tea Party rally in Washington on Sept. 12. Another: "The more the government takes, the le$$ we make. Cut taxes + spending now!"

Experts with differing political views say the attacks are overdrawn. "Like most administrations, [Obama's] is somewhat conflicted," says Jonathan Adler, a conservative law professor at Case Western Reserve University in Cleveland. "In some areas, the administration has sought to be responsive to the desire of the states to do their own thing. But in other areas, the administration has certainly been aggressive in maintaining federal supremacy to preempt state actions."

Doug Kendall, president of the consumer-oriented Constitutional Accountability Center in Washington, agrees. "The administration's record could be viewed as pointing in a couple of directions," Kendall says. He notes that the administration issued a policy statement early in 2009 generally pledging to minimize the use of the doctrine of federal preemption to supersede state laws. But he acknowledges that the administration has vigorously claimed preemption to override some of the

Demonstrators block a street in downtown Phoenix on July 30 to protest Arizona's tough new immigration law requiring local police to enforce federal immigration law. Gov. Jan Brewer said the law was necessary "to solve a crisis we did not create and the federal government has refused to fix — the crisis caused by illegal immigration and Arizona's porous border."

flurry of state and local immigration laws passed in the past few years.

Adler, Kendall and others also note that Obama's Republican predecessor, George W. Bush, pursued several power-centralizing policies despite the GOP's general association with favoring states' interests over Washington's. "There was a dramatic growth of federal mandates under Bush," Conlan says.

Whether overdrawn or not, discontent with Obama administration policies is fueling interest in ambitious but long-shot campaigns to rewrite the U.S. Constitution to limit federal power. Some conservatives are pressing a campaign to get the required number of states — 34 — to call on Congress to convene a constitutional convention, a procedure never before used to amend the nation's foundational document. Meanwhile, a libertarian-minded Georgetown University law professor is drawing attention for a proposed constitutional amendment to allow two-thirds of the states to repeal a federal law unless Congress reenacts it in the face of the states' opposition.

Federalism issues routinely end up in the courts, often at the Supreme Court. In the 1990s under Chief Justice William H. Rehnquist, the court breathed new life into federalism principles with several decisions that trimmed

States Look to Article V to Limit Federal Power

Conservative advocates push for a state-led convention to amend Constitution.

Conservative scholars and activists, frustrated with mounting federal debt and expansion of federal powers, are looking to an unused provision in the Constitution for a remedy. They want to convene a convention under Article V, which permits applications from two-thirds of the states (now 34) to force Congress to call a convention where state delegates would debate constitutional amendments. To ratify the proposed amendments, three-fourths of the state legislatures (38) would then have to approve them.

"This current debt is unconscionable," says Bill Fruth, an economist and founder of 10 Amendments for Freedom, a Florida-based advocacy group working to create a convention to propose a balanced budget amendment. "An amendment is necessary to force Congress to stop borrowing. They won't do it themselves, so we have to force them," Fruth says.

Randy Barnett, a law professor at Georgetown Law Center, agrees. "People are looking for levers to pressure Congress," says Barnett. "We can't rely on Congress to police themselves or for the courts to police Congress, so

Article V provides an alternate way of reining in federal power."

Barnett, a prominent advocate of limiting federal power, is also pushing his own proposed constitutional amendment to allow two-thirds of the states to "repeal" a law passed by Congress. The repeal would take effect unless Congress decided to reenact the measure, with only a simple majority required. As Barnett explained in an op-ed in *The Wall Street Journal*, the amendment would effectively force Congress to take a second look at a new law if a solid majority of states opposed it. The op-ed was co-authored by William J. Howell, speaker of the Virginia House of Delegates, who said he would introduce the measure in a coming session. [1]

Paradoxically, efforts to block the proposed convention are being led by conservative groups that also want to limit federal power but worry about the risk of potentially damaging changes to the Constitution. Lobbying by the Eagle Forum and the far-right John Birch Society have prompted at least 13 states to withdraw their applications for conventions in the last decade.

federal powers. The so-called federalism revolution began to peter out, however, at the turn of the century. After five years in office as Rehnquist's successor, Chief Justice John G. Roberts Jr. has shown little interest in the area.

The court does have several federalism-related cases on its calendar for the current term, however, including a closely watched challenge to Arizona's controversial law tightening prohibitions against employers' hiring illegal aliens. The federal appeals court in San Francisco upheld the law. The U.S. Chamber of Commerce, along with immigrant-rights groups and the U.S. government, is asking the justices to strike the law down. The case will be argued on Dec. 8.

Meanwhile, federal judges in two states are considering suits by states challenging the new health care law.

The states say the Patient Protection and Affordable Care Act — sometimes referred to by the acronym PPACA or, pejoratively, as "Obamacare" — will cost states so much money that it infringes on their power to control their own affairs. The administration, along with health reform advocates, contends that any additional costs for states will be minimal and will be offset by other savings.

The administration's challenge to Arizona's newest immigration law is also advancing in the courts. U.S. District Judge Susan Bolton issued an injunction on July 28 blocking the law from going into effect as scheduled at 12:01 a.m. the next day. The federal appeals court in San Francisco is scheduled to hear the state's appeal Nov. 1.

"There is no provision in the Constitution for how a convention would run," says Republican New Hampshire state Rep. Tim Comerford, who sponsored a successful effort in the 2010 legislative session to rescind a pending convention application. Comerford began his efforts after learning about the dangers of a constitutional convention from a John Birch Society video, "Beware of Article V."

"The only constitutional convention we ever had was the original one, and that was a runaway convention because they set out to amend the Articles of Confederation and wound up creating a whole new document," says Comerford. "A new convention could put the First and Second Amendments — any of the Constitution — under fire."

Virginia Sloan, director of The Constitution Project, a non-partisan group that fosters discussion of constitutional issues, is also critical of the convention process. "In the construction of the Constitution, the framers were trying to avoid people using the Constitution as a political tool," says Sloan. "Most people are reluctant to support an amendments convention because we could destroy what we have."

Calling for an amendments convention is nothing new. In the 1960s and again in the '80s, 32 of the 34 states needed sought to establish a convention, proposing, respectively, amendments on legislative reapportionment and balanced budgets. In both cases, the fear of a runaway, free-for-all convention motivated Congress to address the issues.

This time, experts are not convinced that the threat of a convention will compel Congress to act. "My prediction is no," says Robert G. Natelson, a senior fellow in constitutional jurisprudence at the Denver-based Independence Institute, which describes itself as a "free-market, pro-freedom" think tank. "I hear some people say, 'Maybe Congress will just cave,' but I think people who want to apply for a convention should be prepared for a convention."

Organizing a convention comes with many obstacles. "When you call a convention, you have to do a lot of organization beforehand, and you need a way of sharpening the issues," says Jack Balkin, a law professor at Yale University. "It's a very tall order."

Also, Balkin says, if a convention is held and actually sends proposed amendments to the states, they are very difficult to pass, as proven by the struggle and eventual failure to add the Equal Rights Amendment to the Constitution.

As of Sept. 1, 20 state legislatures have voted to force Congress to hold an amendments convention. Fruth's 10 Amendments for Freedom plans to have sponsors in all 50 state legislatures in January 2011 introduce the group's petition for a convention.

The ramifications of calling a convention could be huge. "The mere fact of having a convention would set all eyes on constitutional issues," says Balkin. "Even if the convention failed, those issues would be setting the political agenda. It would suck all the air out of the political room."

— Maggie Clark

---

[1] Randy Barnett and William J. Howell, "The Case for a 'Repeal Amendment,'" *The Wall Street Journal*, Sept. 16, 2010, p. A23.

As the court cases proceed and the congressional elections approach, here are some of the major questions being debated:

Is the federal government taking on too much power from the states?

Four weeks after an upset win in Alaska's Republican primary, U.S. Senate candidate Joe Miller used a nationwide television appearance on Sept. 19 to call for cutting back the size of the federal government. "The first thing that needs to be done," the Tea Party-backed candidate told host Chris Wallace on "Fox News Sunday," "is, again, restricting the growth and actually reversing the growth of government and, in the process, transferring power back to the states."

Anxiety about the size of the federal government had been growing since Obama's early months in office when he proposed a $900 billion stimulus plan to try to lift the country out of the recession that began while Bush was president. Obama agreed to trim the request to gain Republican votes needed to pass the bill in the Senate. As enacted, the American Recovery and Reinvestment Act of 2009 provided $787 billion in stimulus — divided between tax breaks for individuals and businesses; funds for education, health care and entitlement programs, including unemployment benefits; and funds for federal contracts, grants and loans.

Meanwhile, the administration was also continuing the financial industry bailout — the Troubled Asset Relief Program or TARP — that had been enacted in the final months of the Bush administration. And with General Motors, the nation's largest automaker, on the verge of financial collapse, Obama decided in June 2009 effectively to force the company into a federal bankruptcy court for reorganization, with the government acquiring a 60 percent ownership stake.

The government had no shortage of interest from states for funds from the economic stimulus. Officials in the states most directly affected also generally backed the government's financial rescue plans for Wall Street (New York) and GM (Michigan). Emory law professor Schapiro finds the states' support for the expanded federal roles unsurprising. "Often what the federal government is trying to do is the same thing the state governments are trying to do," he says. "It's just that the federal government can do it more effectively."

On regulatory issues, Obama reversed the Bush administration's stance of invoking federal preemption to supersede state laws or state court rulings. "The Bush administration was completely hostile to regulation at the state level," says Kendall of the Constitutional Accountability Center. The administration signaled the shift toward what is sometimes called "progressive federalism" with a decision in January 2009 to allow California and other states to set their own standards on greenhouse gases from cars and trucks. Later, Obama cautioned agency and department heads against issuing regulations that preempted state laws without clear federal statutory authority. Obama's memo, issued in May 2009, favorably quoted Supreme Court Justice Louis Brandeis' observation that states can serve as a "laboratory" for "novel social and economic experiments."[5]

Obama also revised another Bush policy initiative that intruded on state prerogatives: the No Child Left Behind Act, with its combination of curriculum and testing mandates and financial penalties for non-performing schools. The act was challenged in court on states' rights grounds but upheld. Federalism expert Conlan calls the law "unquestionably the most intrusive federal policy on elementary and secondary education since the Great Society, and perhaps ever."

Instead of using mandates and penalties, the Obama administration is promoting education reform in the states through a $4.35 billion competitive grant program known as "Race to the Top." Eleven states and the

District of Columbia have been selected to receive grants — two in March, the others in late August — based on detailed proposals that generally hewed to the administration's support for charter schools and performance-based pay for teachers. In all, 40 states and the District of Columbia submitted applications for the funds.[6]

Despite some states-minded shifts, the administration's reputation on federalism among Republicans and conservatives today appears to be uniformly negative, largely because of the state mandates in the health care law and the immigration policy stance. Writing in *The American Spectator* in July, Andrew Cline, editorial page editor of the conservative New Hampshire *Union Leader*, denounced what he calls the administration's "crazy quilt federalism."[7]

In similar vein, Gene Healy, a vice president at the libertarian Cato Institute and columnist for the *Washington Examiner*, accuses the administration of "fair-weather federalism." The administration "allows states license when they're pursuing policies that the Obama administration and its supporters favor and brings the hammer down when they're doing policies that [the administration opposes]."

Healy says the Obama administration is not unique in adopting an inconsistent attitude toward state-federal relations. "It's quite common for politicians to wave the 10th Amendment flag," he says. The Bush administration, Healy says, was "quite abysmal" on federalism. As examples, he notes the Bush policies of challenging state initiatives in California on medical marijuana and in Oregon on assisted suicide.

Emory law professor Schapiro says the policy shifts from one administration to another indicate that federalism provides no fixed answer on the respective powers of the federal and state governments. "Federalism debates have often been policy debates in constitutional language," he says. "To the extent that some states don't like what the federal government is doing, that's the issue."

Does the federal health care law infringe on the powers of the states?

On the day before President Obama was to sign the federal health care law, Florida Attorney General Bill McCollum promised to file a suit challenging the act as an infringement of states' rights immediately afterward. The legislation would cost the states "billions of dollars" and go "far

Arizona Law Blocked by Federal Judge

U.S. law preempts parts of tough anti-immigration law, judge says.

Major provisions of Arizona's Support Our Law Enforcement and Safe Neighborhoods Act have been blocked from going into effect by a federal judge's ruling on July 28. U.S. District Judge Susan Bolton in Phoenix ruled that federal law preempts provisions in four sections of the controversial act that:

- Require law enforcement officers to make a reasonable attempt to determine the immigration status of a person stopped, detained or arrested if there is a reasonable suspicion that the person is unlawfully present in the United States; and require verification of the immigration status of any arrested person before release. The provision, Bolton said, is "likely to burden legally present aliens" and "to impermissibly burden federal resources and redirect federal agencies away from the priorities they have established."
- Create a crime for the failure to apply for or carry alien registration papers. The provision, Bolton ruled, "alters the penalties established by Congress under the federal registration scheme."
- Create a crime for an unauthorized alien to solicit, apply for or perform work. The provision, the judge said, "conflicts with a comprehensive federal scheme. . . ."
- Authorize the warrantless arrest of a person if there is probable cause to believe the person has committed a

public offense that makes the person removable from the United States. Bolton found "a substantial likelihood that officers will wrongfully arrest legal resident aliens" under the provision.

The judge found two challenged provisions were not preempted and could be enforced. Those provisions:

- Create a separate crime to transport or harbor an unlawfully present alien or encourage or induce an unlawfully present alien to come to or live in Arizona.
- Permit impoundment of vehicles used in the transporting or harboring of unlawfully present aliens.

Many other provisions of the law remain enforceable because the government did not seek to enjoin them. They include a provision creating a new crime of stopping a motor vehicle to pick up day laborers if the action impedes normal traffic.

The state's appeal of the issuance of the preliminary injunction is to be heard by a panel of the Ninth U.S. Circuit Court of Appeals in San Francisco on Nov. 1.

— Kenneth Jost

Source: *United States v. Arizona*, CV10-1413-PHX-SRB, July 28, 2010, http://docs.justia.com/cases/federal/district-courts/arizona/azdce/2:2010 cv01413/535000/87/.

beyond any unfunded mandate we've ever seen," McCollum said on March 22. "Anything that really manipulates the states like this," he continued, "is unconstitutional under the 10th Amendment, under the sovereignty of the states."

The Obama administration is vigorously defending against Florida's federal court suit, now joined by 19 other states, and a similar suit filed separately by Virginia. Supporters of the health care law and many legal experts voice doubts about the states'- rights challenge, though some experts see a stronger basis for attacking the law's individual-insurance mandate. In any event, the two federal judges hearing the cases — one in Pensacola, the other in Alexandria — have both signaled they are unlikely to dismiss the suits at an early stage.[8]

Supporters of the law sharply dispute the opponents' claims, including the claimed fiscal impact on the states. The law expands health insurance coverage by requiring participating states — and all do participate — to extend Medicaid eligibility beginning in 2014 to a new, nationwide standard: all adults with incomes up to 133 percent of the federal poverty level.

The new requirement is projected to add 16 million to 22 million people to Medicaid rolls nationwide. The federal government will pay 100 percent of the cost of new enrollees for the first three years, with the percentage declining gradually to 90 percent in 2020 and future years.

The change amounts to "a massive expansion of the states' Medicaid programs," according to Robert

Alt, a senior legal fellow and deputy director of the Center for Legal Studies at the conservative Heritage Foundation. "Representatives of states are genuinely concerned about how much more this is going to cost," Alt says, "and whether or not it's simply going to bankrupt them."

John Holahan, director of the Health Policy Research Center at the liberal-oriented Urban Institute, calls the argument by the objecting states "grotesquely flawed." The new law, he says, would mean "a small increase" in state Medicaid spending but would also allow states to reduce current spending in several areas — notably, unreimbursed medical care for the uninsured. The savings, Holahan says, "will be more than enough to offset" the new spending under the law.

In their lawsuits, the states contend that the new law fundamentally changes the Medicaid program from "a voluntary federal-state partnership into a compulsory top-down federal program." In its reply, the government says the new law imposes valid conditions on the states' acceptance of federal aid comparable to changes in Medicaid rules enacted periodically since the program was created in 1965.

Health policy experts on both sides agree with the states' argument that participation in Medicaid is, in practical terms, obligatory. "That's been true for a long time," says Holahan. "No state has ever seriously considered walking away from [the program]."

Two legal experts on federalism, however, say they doubt that the states' coercion argument will carry the day. "The legislation is a dramatic assertion and exercise of federal authority," says Adler, the conservative law professor at Case Western Reserve. Even so, Adler says, the states' spending arguments "are difficult to make."

Conlan, a more centrist-minded federalism expert, is also dubious. "There's no question that the law does entail new opportunities and responsibilities for the states," he says. But he calls the states' arguments "overdrawn." In its brief, the government says that the Supreme Court has never struck down a federal state-aid program on the grounds that a condition for receiving the assistance was coercive.

The states are also challenging provisions of the new law for the states to establish health-insurance exchanges to offer moderately priced insurance coverage for small businesses and individuals. The states depict the provisions as mandatory and, on that basis, as an impermissible command to operate a federal regulatory program. The government counters that the states in fact are free to decide whether or not to create the insurance exchanges.

The states are also attacking the most politically contentious aspect of the new law: the individual health insurance mandate. In their suit, the states call the provision "an unprecedented encroachment on the sovereignty of the Plaintiff States and the rights of their citizens." The government calls the claim premature and denies the states' legal standing to bring the claim. But on the law's merits the government says the mandate is a valid exercise of Congress' authority to regulate the market in health care.

The Heritage Foundation's Alt says the argument contradicts federalism principles. "If the Commerce Clause were read this broadly, then the federal government could do anything," he says. Emory law professor Schapiro calls it "surprising" for the states to raise a sovereignty-based argument against a regulation affecting individuals, not the states themselves. But he adds, "It's a little late in the day for states to say that health is a local matter."

Do state and local immigration laws infringe on federal powers?

When two illegal aliens were involved in a fatal shooting in the small town of Hazleton in northeastern Pennsylvania in 2006, Mayor Lou Barletta responded by proposing a local ordinance aimed at making his city "the toughest place in the United States" for illegal immigrants. As approved by the town council, the Illegal Immigration Relief Act provided for lifting the business license of any company that employed or the rental license for any landlord that rented housing to an illegal alien.

The ordinance was promptly challenged by Hispanic residents and immigrant-rights groups, blocked from going into effect and now has been struck down by a federal appeals court as conflicting with federal law. In a massive, 188-page decision on Sept. 9, a three-judge panel of the Third U.S. Circuit Court of Appeals said that it was "required to intervene when states and localities directly undermine the federal objectives embodied in statutes enacted by Congress."⁹

The appeals court ruling conforms to the general view, dating to the 19th century, that federal law is preeminent on immigration matters. But critics of the federal government's inability in recent years to stem the influx of undocumented aliens insist that states and localities are on sound ground in passing laws that they say will strengthen the enforcement of federal laws.

"The primary responsibility for immigration policy and immigration enforcement rests with the federal government," says Ira Mehlman, national media director for the Federation for American Immigration Reform (FAIR). "But Congress has made it clear over the years that they welcome state and local cooperation in enforcing immigration laws."

As one example, Cory Andrews, a senior litigation counsel with the conservative Washington Legal Foundation (WLF), points to an immigration law — passed in 1995 and known as section 287(g) — that authorizes state and local law enforcement officers to perform immigration law enforcement functions. WLF filed a friend-of-the-court brief supporting the Hazleton ordinance as well as the Arizona employer-sanctions law pending before the Supreme Court.

Immigrant-rights advocates say the states have far less power to deal with immigration-related matters. The federal government has "supreme" power over "anything that touches on who can enter the country and the conditions under which they may remain," says Karen Tumlin, managing attorney with the Los Angeles-based National Immigration Law Center. "State attempts to legislate in that area are strictly prohibited."

Tumlin acknowledges section 287(g) but notes that the provision permits agreements between the federal government and local law enforcement only if local officers receive specialized training from federal agents.

As with the health care issue, experts Conlan and Adler both doubt the states' arguments despite the differences in their political perspectives. Both scholars acknowledge the states' concerns about the impact of illegal immigration but question the states' authority to take on enforcement responsibilities themselves.

"The federal government is failing perhaps to adequately perform one of its constitutional responsibilities," says Conlan. "The corollary of that is not that [the states] get to address immigration. That does not follow constitutionally."

States may have "legitimate policy complaints" about federal enforcement, Adler says, but that does not mean that the states can enact their own policies. "If the federal government believes that the immigration laws are to be enforced in a particular way," he says, "the federal government has the ability to make that a national rule."

Despite the legal doubts, state and local governments have enacted well over 1,000 immigration-related laws in the past six years. Many but not all of the laws have been struck down or blocked from going into effect.

The Supreme Court will have its first chance to rule on the recent spate of laws during the current 2010-2011 term when the justices hear a challenge to Arizona's tough 2007 employer-sanctions law on Dec. 8. The case, *Chamber of Commerce v. Whiting*, pits business and civil rights groups challenging the law against Arizona and groups favoring a tougher stance against illegal immigration. The federal appeals court in San Francisco upheld the law.

Schapiro, the Emory law professor, acknowledges the federal government's argument for preempting state and local laws aimed at more stringent enforcement of federal laws may seem paradoxical. "It's a hard argument to make," he says. In briefs in the *Hazleton* case and the two cases challenging Arizona laws, the government argues that overenforcement by state and local governments risks burdening aliens legally in the United States, deterring employers or landlords from hiring or renting to legal aliens and overwhelming federal resources to enforce immigration laws.

The appeals court in the *Hazleton* case credited those arguments. The law's employment provisions created an "obstacle" to federal policy, the court said, by emphasizing enforcement but not the anti-discrimination protections included in the federal employer sanctions law. As for the housing provisions, the court said that regulation of the residency of immigrants was "clearly within the exclusive domain of the federal government."

In *Hazleton*, Mayor Barletta is vowing to appeal the decision. "I have said repeatedly over the years that the main line of defense against illegal immigration is to eliminate the availability of jobs to illegal aliens," Barletta said on the day of the decision. "If illegal aliens have no place to work, they will self-deport."

BACKGROUND

Dual Sovereigns

The Constitution established a national government with some powers defined specifically and others more generally, but it also preserved state governments with most but not all of their residual powers retained. Over the course of two centuries, the federal government has grown in size and scope, but so too state governments. Congress and presidents have naturally gravitated toward federal solutions to perceived national problems but with the ever-present constraint of political and public support for states' prerogatives. The Supreme Court at times limited federal powers somewhat, but since the 1930s has generally upheld the growing federal role exemplified in direct regulation and in conditions attached to federal aid to states.[10]

The Constitution sets forth in Article I Congress' so-called "enumerated powers," including most significantly the power to tax and spend and to regulate interstate and foreign commerce. Article I also includes some limitations on the states, including a prohibition on any "tax or duty" on exports from other states. In urging ratification of the Constitution, James Madison and Alexander Hamilton stressed in *The Federalist Papers* the continued importance of the states. In *Federalist 45*, Madison said the federal government's powers were "few and defined," while the states' were "numerous and indefinite." In *Federalist 51*, Hamilton argued that the federal structure would help preserve liberty. "The different governments will control each other," he wrote.[11]

Under Chief Justice John Marshall (1801-1835), the Supreme Court generally upheld federal powers, including an 1819 decision that gave a broad but not unlimited reading to Congress' authority to enact "all laws . . . necessary and proper for . . . the execution" of its enumerated powers and limited the states' ability to interfere with those powers. Under Chief Justice Roger Taney (1835-1864), the court tilted slightly toward the states. Taney's "dual federalism" is illustrated in a pair of immigration-related cases, a decade apart. One upheld as a proper exercise of a state's police powers a law requiring ship

masters to provide the names and other information about disembarking passengers. The other struck down a state law imposing a tax on those beginning a voyage.[12]

The Civil War and the post-Civil War amendments established a national policy on an issue that the Constitution had left to the states: slavery. The 14th Amendment also laid the basis for expansion of federal powers by prohibiting the states from denying "to any person" equal protection or due process. The late-19th century Industrial Revolution also encouraged Congress to exercise its Commerce Clause powers, sometimes to protect nationwide enterprises such as the railroads and sometimes to safeguard workers or consumers from exploitative practices by business. The Supreme Court, however, often set itself against economic regulation by either the federal or state governments in a laissez-faire period that extended into the 1930s. The court struck down or limited some federal laws by narrowly defining "commerce" as trade, not manufacturing. But it also struck down some state laws — notably, limits on working hours — as infringing on constitutionally protected property rights.

Federal powers were lastingly expanded in the 1930s as President Franklin D. Roosevelt pushed through Congress and later won Supreme Court approval of the now-familiar laws regulating the economy and creating some elements of a social safety net. In three critical decisions in 1937 that overturned prior rulings, the court upheld the National Labor Relations Act, a federal unemployment compensation law and the Social Security Act for old-age benefits. The court also upheld state wage-and-hour laws and, in 1941, similarly upheld the federal Fair Labor Standards Act.[13]

A year later, the court gave its most expansive construction to Congress' commerce power by enforcing a production quota on a farmer's cultivation of wheat solely for his own use with no intention of selling it. Congress' power, the court wrote in *Wickard v. Filburn*, extended to any activity that "exerts a substantial effect on interstate commerce."[14]

The New Deal and post-New Deal laws and programs did not, however, reduce the states to nonentities. Indeed, the unemployment compensation system upheld in 1937 was to be administered by the states. Instead, the federal government worked through the states in what has been called "cooperative federalism."

C H R O N O L O G Y

1970s-1980s *Federalism "reform" is persistent theme in Washington, state capitals.*

1972 Congress passes and President Richard M. Nixon signs general revenue sharing for state, local governments.

1981 Budget Reconciliation Act signed by President Ronald Reagan consolidates federal grant programs, cuts overall state aid.

1987 Supreme Court says Congress can require states to set minimum drinking age at 21 as condition to receive highway construction funds.

1990s *"Federalism revolution" at Supreme Court limits federal power.*

1995 Congress passes and President Bill Clinton signs Unfunded Mandates Act, limiting new federal mandates on states without federal funding (March 22).

1995-2000 Chief Justice William H. Rehnquist leads Supreme Court in limiting Congress' ability to force state governments to administer regulatory programs, protecting state governments from damage suits for violating federal law and limiting Congress' use of Commerce Clause power to regulate non-economic matters.

2000-Present *Presidents George W. Bush and Barack Obama push centralizing policies in Washington despite nods to state prerogatives; federalism revolution stalls at Supreme Court.*

2001 President Bush wins congressional approval of No Child Left Behind Act; measure establishes national standards on curriculum, testing, school performance; Bush signs into law Jan. 8, 2002; act is challenged in court but upheld.

2002 Help America Vote Act establishes nationwide minimum election standards, provides funds to replace punch-card, lever-based voting systems (Oct. 22).

2005 Real ID Act, requiring states to adopt uniform procedures for driver's licenses as individual identification

(May 11). . . . Supreme Court rules federal drug laws preempt state measures to legalize medical marijuana; ruling seen as retreat from Rehnquist's federalism revolution (June 6).

2006 Hazelton, Pa., enacts ordinance to punish employers for hiring or landlords for renting to illegal aliens; measure is one of hundreds enacted by state or local governments over several years to counter illegal immigration.

2007 Arizona's Legal Arizona Worker Act makes it a crime for illegal alien to seek employment in state and puts employer out of business for second offense of hiring illegal alien; act is challenged by business, civil rights groups but upheld by federal appeals court in September 2008.

2008 Democrat Barack Obama elected after presidential campaign with minimal attention to state-federalism issues.

2009 Obama makes health care overhaul a major domestic policy goal; works with Congress to craft bill to expand Medicaid eligibility with federal financing, use states to create health insurance exchanges to provide affordable coverage for individuals, small businesses.

2010 Obama signs Patient Protection and Affordable Care Act into law (March 23); Virginia files suit same day challenging law as violating state law barring individual health insurance mandate; Florida files suit next day, challenging act as unconstitutional because of fiscal impact on state. . . . Arizona's Support Our Law Enforcement and Safe Neighborhoods Act (SB 1070) requires police to determine immigration status of any person arrested or stopped (April 23); federal judge, ruling in suit by U.S. government, enjoins major provisions as preempted by federal immigration law (July 28). . . . *Hazelton* ordinance struck down on preemption grounds by federal appeals court (Sept. 9). . . . Federal judge in Detroit upholds health care law (Oct. 7); suits by states still pending. . . . Federal appeals court to hear appeal in SB 1070 case (Nov. 1). . . . Supreme Court to hear challenge to Arizona's employer sanctions law (Dec. 8).

Will Staggering New Medicaid Costs Hit the States?

Dueling studies examine impact of new health care reform law.

Nebraska spends about $742 million a year in its Medicaid program to provide health care to low-income persons. In August, Gov. Dave Heineman released an actuarial study claiming that the state's costs could increase by somewhere between $526 million and $766 million over the next 10 years under the new federal health care reform law enacted in March.

Heineman, a Republican, called the price tag from the state-commissioned study "staggering and shocking" and urged Congress to repeal or substantially modify the law. Heineman also supports Nebraska's participation with other states in a federal court suit in Florida challenging the constitutionality of the law.

A study by researchers at the liberal-oriented Urban Institute, however, estimates Nebraska's added costs much lower: $106 million to $155 million. And the report notes that Nebraska will receive more than $2 billion in new federal matching funds during the period under the law.[1]

The dueling cost studies are highly dependent on differing assumptions about new Medicaid enrollment and health care cost trends. The price tags figure not only in political debate but also in the federal court case. Florida, the lead plaintiff in the case, is claiming that it faces $4 billion in additional Medicaid costs from 2014 when the law is to take effect through 2019.

Florida's suit says the added cost —"a price the state simply cannot afford to pay" — represents an unconstitutional intrusion on the state's sovereignty. The Urban Institute researchers, however, estimate a substantially lower price tag: $1.2 billion to $2.5 billion. Overall, they estimate the states will pay about $21 billion for Medicaid expansion through 2019 — with the federal government picking up the lion's share: $444 billion.

With different but somewhat comparable projections, the nonpartisan Congressional Budget Office says the federal price tag for expanding Medicaid and the Children's Health Insurance Program (CHIP) — put at $434 billion

---

The federal government's revenue-raising powers allowed it to expand its role from providing technical assistance to state governments to bestowing financial grants aimed at furthering federal goals, typically with significant conditions attached. These programs grew in FDR's so-called "Second New Deal" (mid-1935 to 1939); under his Democratic successor, Harry S. Truman (1945-1953); and, despite his supposed conservatism, under the Republican president, Dwight D. Eisenhower (1953-1961). By 1960, historian David B. Walker counts some 132 grant-in-aid programs with total outlays to the states of $6.8 billion — nearly triple the amount at the start of Eisenhower's presidency.[15]

'New' Federalisms

Federalism reform became a persistent theme in Washington and state capitals in the second half of the 20th century. Officials at both levels endeavored to find the right balance between federal and state responsibilities and to manage federal-state programs more efficiently and more effectively. Two Republican presidents in particular, Nixon (1969-1974) and Reagan (1981-1989), adopted policies aimed at "returning" powers to the states. State governments became more influential with increased revenue and administrative modernization, but they remained subject to mandates from Washington established by Congress or the executive branch and generally upheld by the Supreme Court.[16]

The number and dollar amounts of federal aid programs grew, and their management became more complex, under the two Democratic presidents of the 1960s, Kennedy and. Johnson. The increased complexity of federal aid prompted proposals for intergovernmental reform under Johnson and that Nixon developed and adopted as a signature domestic policy goal. Initially, Nixon pushed to consolidate federal aid in block grants. He broadened the effort with a proposal

— represents just under half of the estimated $938 billion increase in total health-care spending under the law. The other costs include $464 billion in subsidies for individuals and small businesses and $40 billion in small-employer tax credits.[2]

The Medicaid expansion costs represent the price for setting a national household income standard of Medicaid eligibility at 133 percent of the poverty level: $29,300 for a family of four or $14,400 for a single person. Currently, eligibility varies greatly between states. Many Southern states provide Medicaid only for persons well below the poverty level, while a few Northeastern states extend Medicaid to families with incomes as high as 150 percent of the poverty level.

The federal government currently pays about half the costs of Medicaid in the wealthiest states and a larger fraction in less-wealthy states. Under the new law, the federal government will pick up 100 percent of the cost of newly eligible Medicaid participants for the first three years — 2014 to 2016 — with the percentage declining gradually to 90 percent in 2020 and subsequent years.

In a critical report, two health care experts at the conservative Heritage Foundation say the reimbursement provision amounts to an attempt "to appease state lawmakers." They put the total cost of Medicaid expansion for the states at $33 billion, including $12 billion in administrative costs. And while they acknowledge that state lawmakers may view the provision as "a relatively good fiscal deal," they also warn that state taxpayers "will face higher tax bills . . . not just for the state costs but for the federal costs as well."[3]

John Holahan, director of the Urban Institute's Health Policy Research Center, says, however, that states will save money by spending less on uncompensated care for uninsured individuals. State spending on health care for low-income children will also be reduced, he says, because many will gain coverage under the insurance exchanges to be established under the law. "I don't agree that states will be worse off financially," Holahan concludes.

— *Kenneth Jost*

[1] The eight-page report by Milliman, Inc., dated Aug. 16, 2010, is available at www.governor.nebraska.gov/news/2010/08/pdf/Nebraska%20Medicaid%20PPACA%20Fiscal%20Impact.pdf. The report by Urban Institute researchers John Holahan and Irene Headen, "Medicaid Coverage and Spending in Health Reform," Henry J. Kaiser Family Foundation, May 2010, www.kff.org/healthreform/upload/Medicaid-Coverage-and-Spending-in-Health-Reform-National-and-State-By-State-Results-for-Adults-at-or-Below-133-FPL.pdf. For coverage, see these stories by Nancy Hicks in the *Lincoln* (Neb.) *Journal Star*: "Medicaid expert says state's report flawed," Sept. 16, 2010, p. B1; "Nebraska Medicaid costs likely to soar," Aug. 19, 2010, p. A1.

[2] Congressional Budget Office figures cited in *Landmark: The Inside Story of America's New Health-Care Law and What It Means for Us All*, by The Staff of *The Washington Post* (2010), p. 173. Other background drawn from the chapter, "Medicaid's Expansion: The Impact on the States," pp. 163-168.

[3] Edmond F. Haismaier and Brian C. Blaise, "Obamacare: Impact on the States," Heritage Foundation, July 1, 2010, p. 3, http://thf_media.s3.amazonaws.com/2010/pdf/bg2433.pdf.

for general revenue sharing with state and local governments that Congress cleared for his signature in October 1972. The five-year, $30 billion program gave broad discretion to state and local officials.

As George Mason professor Conlan notes, however, the Nixon presidency also saw "a dramatic increase in federal regulations aimed at state and local governments" — notably, in the areas of environmental protection, health planning and highway construction.[17]

Reagan opened his presidency by proposing a major federalism reform: a consolidation of scores of federal grant-in-aid programs into nine block grants. States were to get more discretion but also to suffer a significant cut in overall federal aid. After a contentious congressional debate, Reagan got most of what he asked for in the Omnibus Budget Reconciliation Act of 1981. But he failed in subsequent efforts to consolidate more categorical programs into block grants.

Reagan also failed with a bold plan announced in December 1981 for the federal government to take over Medicaid funding while giving the states responsibility for 43 other programs, including welfare and many other social services. The proposal fell under criticism from social service advocates and from many state officials who viewed it as requiring state tax increases. The administration also promised to ease regulatory restrictions on state governments.

Nevertheless, the administration supported spending mandates that effectively required states to raise limits on trucking weights and to adopt a uniform minimum drinking age of 21. By the end of the 1980s, Conlan says, the number of new intergovernmental regulatory provisions enacted at the federal level surpassed the number for any previous decade.[18]

The regulatory spike underlay the Clinton era's most important federalism reform: the Unfunded Mandates

Supreme Court to Consider Order to Reduce Prison Crowding

Hearing set on inmate-release order in California.

Can a federal court order the state to reduce its prison population? California prisons have been filled to nearly double their capacity over the past decade. Now the state is now facing a federal court order to reduce inmate population by around 40,000 within a two-year period.

California officials, however, are urging the Supreme Court to set aside the order as a misapplication of a law Congress passed specifically to make it difficult for federal judges to issue inmate-release decisions. Seventeen other states are backing California's appeal.

The order, issued by a special three-judge federal district court in August 2009, would require California to reduce its inmate population to 137.5 percent of the prisons' combined designed capacity of 84,000. The court found that the population cap — to be met through a combination of early releases and diversions of low-risk offenders at sentencing — was needed to ensure constitutionally adequate medical and mental health care for state prisoners.[1]

In appealing the decision, California contends that the three-judge court failed to follow the restrictions of the Prison Litigation Reform Act, which Congress passed in 1996 establishing new procedural and substantive restrictions on inmate-release orders by federal courts. Specifically, the law requires any inmate-release order to be issued by a three-judge court, not an individual judge, and only after any remedial order by a single judge has been given "reasonable time" to remedy any constitutional violations. The law also requires that overcrowding be found to be the "primary" cause of a constitutional violation and that "no other relief" will remedy the violation.[2]

Congress passed the law in response to lobbying by state attorneys general and district attorneys in the wake of a controversial federal court order requiring release of thousands of inmates from Philadelphia jails over a period of years. "What we were asking," explains Sarah Vandenbraak Hart, a deputy Philadelphia district attorney who helped draft the law, "was that they make a prison release order an absolute last resort remedy and only if absolutely necessary to remedy an ongoing constitutional violation."

Lawyers for the California inmates contend the three-judge court followed the law's requirements. Congress

Reform Act of 1995. With some exceptions — notably, civil rights statutes — the act requires Congress to specify the cost of any new mandate on state and local governments and permits a point of order against any mandate unless fully funded in the bill. The act began with bipartisan cosponsorship when Democrats controlled the House and Senate in 1993; it won enactment in 1995 after Republicans had gained control of both chambers, but only after the GOP majorities had beaten back a string of weakening, Democratic-backed amendments. In signing the bill, President Bill Clinton called it historic, but Conlan says that — as in the Reagan era — Congress and the White House continued to establish new regulatory mandates despite the professed reform.

In the meantime, the Supreme Court had dealt two major blows to state prerogatives in federalism cases. In 1985, the court ruled that Congress could require state governments to follow minimum-wage and overtime requirements of federal labor law. The decision overturned a ruling favoring state governments on the issue a decade earlier. Then in 1987, the court upheld the federal law to withhold highway construction aid to any state that did not set the minimum drinking age at 21. In a 7-2 decision written by Chief Justice William H. Rehnquist, the court ruled the law a proper exercise of Congress' spending power even though Congress had no authority to regulate the drinking age directly.[19]

In the 1990s, however, Rehnquist led a revival of federalism principles to benefit states. In one line of decisions, the court prohibited Congress from requiring state or local governments to administer federal regulatory systems — notably, the background check for gun purchasers. In another, the court held state governments immune from money-damage suits for violating federal

"succeeded in making it harder . . . but not impossible" for courts to issue release orders, says Donald Specter, director of the Prison Law Office, a Berkeley-based inmate rights organization. "They set the threshold, and our position is that we've met the threshold."

Federal court orders in so-called institutional litigation have long been a bane of the states. State governments can find themselves on the losing end of decisions that not only require wide-ranging and sometimes expensive changes in operation of programs and facilities but also expose them to six- or seven-figure attorney fee awards to lawyers on the other side. In a significant decision in April, the Supreme Court ordered a lower court to reconsider a $10.5 million fee award to public-interest lawyers for a case that forced broad changes in the state's foster care system.[3]

The court order in the California case came after more than a decade of litigation over medical care for state inmates in separate cases filed before single-judge courts in Sacramento and San Francisco. The two district courts decided in 2007 to convene a three-judge court as provided in the 1996 law after finding medical care still constitutionally deficient. The three-judge court presided over a trial from November 2008 to February 2009 before issuing its 185-page decision on Aug. 4, 2009.

The state says the order, which has been stayed pending the Supreme Court appeal, would require release of between 38,000 and 46,000 inmates. In its appeal, the state contends the requirements for a three-judge court were not met and the cases should be sent back to the separate district courts.

In accepting the appeal on June 14, the Supreme Court said it would consider the jurisdictional issue at the same time as the merits of the case. Oral arguments, now set for Nov. 30, will feature two highly regarded Supreme Court advocates: Carter Phillips for the state and Paul Clement, U.S. solicitor general under President George W. Bush, for the inmates.

In his brief for the inmates, Specter discounts the potential impact of the case on other states, describing California's prison crisis as unique. But he also discounts the states' concerns about improper federal court intrusion into prison systems.

"Federalism is not a one-way street," Specter says. "It doesn't mean only that states have rights. It also means that federal courts have obligations to enforce constitutional rights against the states."

— *Kenneth Jost*

---

[1] The decision came in two consolidated cases: *Coleman v. Schwarzenegger* (medical care), *Plata v. Schwarzenegger* (mental health care), CIV S-90-0520 LKK JFM P, U.S. Dist. Ct., N.D./E.D. Calif., Aug. 4, 2009, www.caed.uscourts.gov/caed/Documents/90cv520o10804.pdf. For coverage, see Carol J. Williams, "State gets two years to cut 43,000 from prisons," *Los Angeles Times*, Sept. 5, 2009, p. A1. The appeal at the Supreme Court is *Schwarzenegger v. Plata*, 09-1233; background and briefs on SCOTUSBlog: www.scotusblog.com/case-files/cases/schwarzenegger-v-plata/?wpmp_switcher=desktop.

[2] The act is codified at 18 U.S.C. §3626. Background at http://en.wikipedia.org/wiki/Prison_Litigation_Reform_Act.

[3] The decision is *Perdue v. Kenny A.*, 559 U.S. — — (April 21, 2010), www.supremecourt.gov/opinions/09pdf/08-970.pdf.

---

law, including the federal wage and hours act. And in a pair of decisions written by Rehnquist, the court limited Congress' power to use the Commerce Clause to regulate non-economic activity. One ruling struck down the federal Gun Free School Zones Act, which made it a crime to possess a gun within a minimum distance of a school. Another struck down a provision of the Violence Against Women Act that allowed victims of "gender-motivated" violence to sue their assailants in federal court. In both cases, Rehnquist said Congress had infringed on the states' traditional police powers.[20]

Federal Powers

Federalism concerns have been given a low priority in Washington in the 21st century under two presidents of different parties: Republican George W. Bush and Democrat Barack Obama. Bush pursued centralizing

policies on a range of issues despite his background as a former governor and the GOP's professed support for state prerogatives. The Supreme Court also appeared to step back from its resistance to expanding federal powers even after two appointments by Bush. Obama took office with some nods to the states, but he stirred strong opposition from many states to his health care reform and then set the administration against state and local laws aimed at strengthening immigration enforcement.[21]

Bush trampled on federalism concerns with his signature domestic policy initiative: education reform. The No Child Left Behind Act mandated student testing, imposed curriculum and teacher standards and threatened non-performing schools with penalties up to takeover by independent operators. Some states called the law unconstitutional, but court challenges failed to invalidate it. States also complained about the strictures in two other major laws: the Help America Vote Act, which set federal standards for voting and voter registration, and the Real ID Act, which established new requirements for state driver's licenses. All three laws provided some funds for the mandated changes, but education authorities in particular said federal aid fell short of the promised amounts.

The Bush administration overrode state interests in several other areas. Siding with business interests, the administration repeatedly interpreted federal laws or regulations to preempt state laws or court suits. On social issues, the administration won enactment of a nationwide ban on so-called "partial birth abortions" and pushed unsuccessfully for a constitutional amendment to ban same-sex marriages. The administration also attempted to use federal drug law to nullify Oregon's assisted-suicide initiative, but the Supreme Court in 2006 rejected the attempt.[22]

A year earlier, the high court had stepped back from its federalism stance of the 1990s with a decision upholding federal power to override a California initiative permitting medical use of marijuana. With Rehnquist and Justice Sandra Day O'Connor among three dissenters, the court in June 2005 held that the government can ban private, noncommercial use of marijuana because of its potential impact on the admittedly illegal market in the drug.[23] O'Connor retired and Rehnquist died later that year. As their successors, Bush chose John G. Roberts Jr. as chief justice and Samuel A. Alito Jr. as O'Connor's replacement, two Eastern conservatives less identified with federalism issues than the two Westerners they followed.

Neither Obama nor his Republican opponent, Sen. John McCain of Arizona, made federalism a major issue as such in the 2008 presidential campaign. But both men professed support for states' interests in the area, according to an assessment by federalism experts John Dinan and Shama Gamkhar. McCain self-identified as a federalist to explain, for example, his opposition to a constitutional amendment to ban same-sex marriage. Obama identified himself with some of the states' criticisms of No Child Left Behind. And both men buttressed their health care proposals by citing state initiatives: Obama pointed to Massachusetts Gov. Mitt Romney's universal coverage plan, McCain to Indiana Gov. Mitch Daniels' market-oriented approach.[24]

Early in his presidency, Obama made gestures and took some concrete actions favorable to states' interests. In a meeting in February 2009, he promised the states' governors to try to make their lives "easier, not harder." As part of his economic-stimulus plan, Obama proposed — and eventually won congressional approval of — substantial aid to financially beleaguered states with few strings attached. Obama also reversed some Bush decisions to give states more discretion — significantly, to pursue liberal policies in such areas as children's health and air pollution control. And Attorney General Eric H. Holder Jr. announced in February 2009 that the Justice Department would discontinue raids on medical marijuana dispensaries in the 13 states that had legalized the practice.

The administration worked to accommodate the states' interests during the yearlong struggle that ended in March 2010 with enactment of the health care law. Broadening eligibility for Medicaid was always seen as the principal vehicle for expanding health insurance coverage, but from the outset the federal government was to bear most of the cost. Obama's proposal included a variety of mandates for health insurers, but states continued to have principal responsibility for insurance regulation. Republicans and conservatives opposed to the bill cited the fiscal impact on the states in their arguments, but the issue was overshadowed by the individual insurance mandate — and, at the end, by arguments over the potential for government-subsidized abortions under the law.[25]

Meanwhile, the administration was weighing a request made by the Supreme Court in November 2009 to state the government's view on the challenge to Arizona's employer-sanctions law. The government's brief, filed on May 28, marked the first time the government had weighed in against any of the flurry of state and local immigration laws enacted in the last few years. The brief pointed to the number of similar laws in urging the justices to hear the case. It went on to argue that Arizona's law "disrupt[s] a careful balance" that Congress struck between preventing employment of illegal aliens and preventing discrimination against racial or ethnic minorities. A month later, the court agreed to hear the case, setting the stage for arguments by year's end.[26]

CURRENT SITUATION

Health Suits Advancing

The Obama administration is applauding a federal judge's ruling upholding the new individual health insurance mandate even as it awaits pivotal developments in two similar suits by states that federal judges refused to dismiss at the earliest stage.

In a ruling on Oct. 7, U.S. District Judge George Caram Steeh in Detroit accepted the administration's basic legal argument that Congress could require individuals to purchase health insurance as part of its power to regulate interstate commerce. When "viewed in the aggregate," Steeh said, individual decisions to buy health insurance or go without "have clear and direct impacts on health care providers, taxpayers, and the insured population who ultimately pay for the care provided to those who go without insurance."[27]

Steeh's ruling came in a case filed by the conservative Thomas More Law Center and several Michigan residents, one of 15-20 cases challenging the health care law, according to a compilation by the Justice Department. The ruling came as two higher-profile challenges by state governments were proceeding in federal courts in Virginia and Florida.

U.S. District Judge Henry Hudson is scheduled to hear legal arguments in Richmond, Va., on Oct. 18 in competing motions for summary judgment by the state of Virginia and the federal government. Hudson had rejected the government's motion to dismiss the case in a 32-page opinion on Aug. 2 that called the applicable legal precedents "informative but inconclusive."

Meanwhile, U.S. District Judge Roger Vinson in Pensacola, Fla., was due to rule by his self-announced deadline of Oct. 14 on the government's similar motion to dismiss the suit by Florida and 19 other states challenging the health care law. In a hearing on Sept. 14, Vinson appeared sympathetic to the states' claim about their costs once the law takes full effect in 2014. "Doesn't this really put all 50 states on the short end of the stick?" Vinson asked the government's attorney at one point.

In his opinion, Hudson, who was appointed to the federal bench by President George W. Bush in 2002, preliminarily upheld the state's standing to bring the case in order to give effect to its law, the Virginia Health Care Freedom Act, prohibiting any individual health insurance mandate. On the merits, Hudson said the government had failed at this stage to overcome the state's constitutional arguments against the law. "No reported case from any federal appellate court," the judge wrote, "has extended the Commerce Clause or the Tax Clause to include the regulation of a person's decision not to purchase a product, notwithstanding its effect on interstate commerce."[28]

The case, *Virginia ex rel. Cuccinelli v. Sebelius*, is being brought in the name of Virginia's conservative Republican attorney general, Ken Cuccinelli. He depicted Hudson's ruling as a significant setback for the Obama administration. In her comments, Health and Human Services (HHS) Secretary Kathleen Sebelius emphasized the preliminary nature of the ruling. The two sides recapitulated their arguments in parallel, competing motions for summary judgment filed with the court on Sept. 3 in advance of the Oct. 18 hearing.

The health care mandate issue also figured prominently in the Sept. 14 arguments in the Florida case before Judge Vinson, a Reagan appointee to the federal bench in 1983.[29] For the states, Washington attorney David Rivkin argued that Congress has no authority to regulate citizens' decisions not to buy health insurance. "Congress can regulate commerce," he said. "But Congress cannot create it." For the government, Ian Gershengorn, a deputy assistant United States attorney general, countered that uninsured individuals nevertheless use medical services. "This is not telling people you have to buy a product," he said. "It's saying this is how you have to pay for your health care."

On the fiscal issue, Blaine Winship, representing Florida, said the new law "transformed" Medicaid beyond its original purpose. "It's quite a budget buster for us," he said. Gershengorn countered that any state can opt out of Medicaid. The states' position, he added, would prevent Congress from making any changes in the program. Vinson, however, appeared sympathetic to the states. "The states are in a catch-22 situation," the judge said, "because the government dominates the ability to raise income."

Expectations that Vinson would reject the government's effort to dismiss the case were fed by his decision to schedule further arguments on Dec. 16. Vinson rejected an effort by four states to join the suit on the federal government's side but said he would reconsider the issue later.

The Florida and Virginia suits had been the most closely watched of the various challenges to the new health care law, including two previously dismissed on procedural grounds. In his ruling in the Michigan case, Judge Steeh rejected the administration's procedural arguments that the challengers lacked legal standing to bring the suit and that the suit was premature. He went on in a 20-page ruling, however, to say that Congress had "a rational basis to

Is the Obama administration taking on too much power from the states?

YES
Robert Alt
Senior Legal Fellow and Deputy Director,
Center for Legal & Judicial Studies, The
Heritage Foundation

Written for *CQ Researcher,* October 2010

The Obama administration has used federal authority in a schiz-ophrenic fashion: making illegitimate claims of authority to achieve desired ends, while disavowing legitimate authority where doing so proved beneficial to favored special interests. From a constitutional and policy perspective, this is the worst of both worlds.

The most audacious claim of federal authority comes in the health care mandate, which requires all individuals to purchase health insurance or pay a penalty enforced through the tax code. Despite Speaker Nancy Pelosi's incredulity to a press question asking where Congress found the constitutional authority for the mandate — she responded, "Are you kidding?" — Congress is still subject to the requirements of the Constitution, which grants to Congress limited and enumerated legislative powers.

Where, then, does the Obama administration point to as its constitutional justification for this sweeping new authority? It claims that Congress has the authority to regulate individual "acts" of not purchasing a product (i.e., not entering into com-merce) pursuant to Congress' authority to regulate — wait for it — interstate commerce.

The term "unprecedented" is thrown around lightly, but here I use the literal meaning — this assertion of authority has no prec-edent. There is simply no example in federal law which supports this usurpation. Indeed, the first federal court to hear a challenge noted that "[n]o reported case from any federal appellate court has extended the Commerce Clause or Tax Clause to include the regulation of a person's decision not to purchase a product."

While in health care the Obama administration suffers from delusions of grandeur, in the area of federal regulatory preemption — that is, the authority to set uniform regulations for products that actually are in interstate commerce to avoid a patchwork of 50 dif-ferent regulations — the administration has an inferiority complex.

The administration has asserted a narrow view of preemp-tion in a memorandum to the heads of all executive agencies and has disclaimed federal authority in court filings. This deci-sion might seem difficult to understand in light of the previously bold assertions of federal authority — until one realizes that this position is advantageous to the trial lawyers (major donors to the Obama administration), who find it easier to win cases if courts and juries are not bound by blanket federal product-liability requirements.

As these examples suggest, the administration's assertions of federal authority are not circumscribed by the Constitution, but by political expediency.

NO
Doug Kendall
President, Constitutional Accountability Center

Written for *CQ Researcher,* October 2010

The charge that the Obama administration has concentrated too much power in the federal government is not only unsupporta-ble, it is in important respects counter-factual.

Early in his presidency, President Obama issued a sweeping policy memorandum that reaffirmed the critical role that state and local governments play in protecting the health and safety of their citizens and directed executive branch officials to review every regulation adopted in the past 10 years to scrub them of language that inappropriately displaced states.

Obama's shift in policy has led to reversal of several Bush administration policies and has empowered states to take a lead in a whole series of areas where state-level innovation is most needed, from environmental regulation to drug laws to financial reform. In one prominent example, the Obama administration granted California its long-sought waiver of federal preemption, restoring this state to its historic role as a path-breaker in the regulation of auto emissions.

Even President Obama's health care reform law is an example of balancing the need for a national solution with the benefits that accompany state innovation. Learning from state experiences, such as the Massachusetts plan signed into law by then-Gov. Mitt Romney, the new health care law preserves the states' regu-latory flexibility by (1) allowing states to form their own insur-ance exchange or join with a regional exchange; (2) giving states significant discretion over plan specifics like whether to cover abortion; and (3) permitting states to set up their own programs — with or without an individual mandate — so long as certain requirements are met.

Only when the Constitution explicitly places sole power with the national government — such as the provision that gives the federal government the power to make "uniform" rules for immigration and naturalization — has the Obama administration jealously guarded federal power and challenged the ability of states like Arizona to create their own system of immigration enforcement.

Reviewing these actions collectively, President Obama has appropriately balanced state-level innovation with national inter-ests, viewing federalism as a structure for allocating government power in ways that improve how the government serves its citi-zens rather than as a zero-sum struggle between the national government and the states. Even when confronting issues of clear national concern, such as health care reform, the Obama administration has recognized the critical role states play in our federal system. The result is federalism at its best and a govern-ment that works better for everyone.

conclude that, in the aggregate, decisions to forego [sic] insurance coverage in preference to pay for health care out of pocket drive up the cost of insurance."

A Justice Department spokeswoman voiced satisfaction with the ruling. "We welcome the court's decision upholding the health care reform statute as constitutional," said spokeswoman Tracy Schmaler. Robert J. Muise, senior trial counsel for the Thomas More Law Center, told *The New York Times* the case was "set up nicely for appeal."[30]

Immigration Cases Set

Closely watched challenges to two Arizona statutes aimed at tougher enforcement of federal immigration laws are being readied for oral arguments soon before federal appellate courts.

The Ninth U.S. Circuit Court of Appeals, with jurisdiction over nine Western states, is set to hear arguments during the week of Nov. 1 in Arizona's effort to reinstate its law enacted in April making it a state crime to be in the country in violation of federal immigration laws.

Meanwhile, the Supreme Court is due to hear arguments on Dec. 8 from business and immigrants rights groups seeking to invalidate the 2007 law stiffening the penalties for employers who hire illegal aliens.

Both laws are being challenged under the doctrine known as preemption as intruding on the federal government's primacy over states on immigration-related matters. The justices are also hearing three other preemption cases this fall testing the relationship of state and federal laws in arbitration, auto safety and vaccine safety.

The Ninth Circuit will be reviewing the July 28 ruling by federal judge Bolton in Phoenix that blocked major provisions of the act from going into effect. In her ruling, Bolton, appointed to the bench by President Clinton in 2000, acknowledged the state's interest in "controlling illegal immigration and addressing the concurrent problems with crime." But, she continued, "it is not in the public interest for Arizona to enforce preempted laws."[31]

Bolton's ruling blocked the most controversial parts of the law, including a requirement that state and local law enforcement officers determine the immigration status of anyone arrested, detained or stopped that they reasonably suspect is "unlawfully present" in the country. The ruling also blocked the new state crime of failing to carry alien registration papers. And it enjoined the provision making it a crime for illegal immigrants to apply for a job.

Immigration rights advocates hailed the ruling. "It's a victory for the community," Lydia Guzman, president of Somos America (We Are America), said. Gov. Brewer voiced disappointment but called the ruling "a bump in the road" and vowed a quick appeal. The Ninth Circuit set an expedited briefing schedule in the case with arguments to be heard by a three-judge panel on Nov. 1.

Earlier, a three-judge Ninth Circuit panel upheld Arizona's employer-sanctions law in a unanimous, 23-page opinion in September 2008.[32] The business and immigrant rights groups challenging the law argued that it created the risk of "conflict preemption" because state courts could rule differently on an alien's status than federal immigration authorities would. They also said that an "express preemption" clause precluded the state from revoking an employer's business license because the federal law prohibited any penalties other than those provided there.

Writing for the court, Judge Mary Schroeder, a Clinton appointee, rejected the challengers' arguments. She said the "speculative, hypothetical possibility" of a conflict with federal law was insufficient to invalidate the law in its entirety. As for the license-revocation provision, she said it fell within an exception in the federal law for "licensing" provisions. She also found no conflict with federal law in the state act's requirement that employers use the voluntary federal E-verify system to verify a job applicant's status.

The Supreme Court agreed to hear the case on June 28. The Chamber filed its opening brief on Sept. 1, followed a week later by friend-of-the-court briefs from the U.S. government, business groups, immigrant rights groups and a major labor union: the Service Employees International Union. The state's brief and any supporting briefs were to be filed in October.

In the other preemption cases, the high court will decide these issues being closely watched by business and consumer groups as well as state governments:

• Can the victim of a vaccine-related injury sue the manufacturer in state court for a "design defect" despite the no-fault, administrative system established by the National Vaccine Injury Compensation Act? (*Bruesewitz v. Wyeth*; argument: Oct. 12.)

• Does the Federal Arbitration Act prevent a state from requiring that any consumer arbitration agreement permit the use of classwide arbitration allowing the consolidation of claims by all similarly situated persons? (*AT&T Mobility v. Concepcion*; argument: Nov. 9.)

- Do federal auto safety laws block an accident victim from suing a manufacturer in state court for failing to install a lap/shoulder belt in the middle back seat when not required to do so by federal regulations? (*Williamson v. Mazda Motor of America*; argument: Nov. 3.)

OUTLOOK

Federalism's Meanings

The Framers of the Constitution created a government unlike any other before. "Federalism was our Nation's own discovery," Supreme Court Justice Anthony M. Kennedy has written. The Constitution, Kennedy said, "split the atom of sovereignty" between the national and state governments, with each "protected against incursion by the other."[33]

In their deliberations, the Framers strove to divide powers between a strong and stable federal government and states whose prerogatives were to be protected from incursion by the new national government. Writing in *Federalist No. 37*, James Madison described the process of partitioning the respective powers of the federal and state governments as "arduous."

Now more than two centuries later, federalism issues remain contentious, but the context is much changed. The "dual federalism" concept of the 19th century has been displaced by usages such as "cooperative" or "collaborative" federalism that describe powers and responsibilities intertwined among rather than partitioned between Washington and state capitals. In his book, *Polyphonic Federalism*, Emory law professor Schapiro sees this overlapping of power as promoting "the traditional federalism values of responsiveness, self-governance and liberty."[34]

Legislative debates and court challenges in today's major federalism controversies, however, still tend to be waged under the old zero-sum game concept of dividing rather than sharing power. State officials challenging the new health care law attack the fiscal impact of Medicaid expansion with little acknowledgment in their public comments of the joint federal-state structure of the program since its inception. From the opposite perspective, the business groups that press for federal preemption to supersede state law give no recognition to the states' role in the 20th century in promoting stronger protections for workers, consumers and the general public — ultimately to the benefit, not the detriment, of business itself.

Meanwhile, Americans are evincing middling confidence at best in government at all levels. For several years, polls have been detecting declining public confidence in the federal government generally. But a recent Zogby International poll found public trust in state governments no higher — with only a minority of respondents placing much trust in either Washington or their own state government.

Health care and immigration illustrate reasons for the public's angst. The inability to stem the rising cost of health care or the continuing flow of illegal immigration test the public's belief in the power of government to deal with contemporary problems. Ironically, the loudest voices in the debates are complaining that the federal government is taking on too much power to try to confront them.

"This is a classic example of what seems to be a growing pace of volatility in our system," says George Mason professor Conlan. "This is like a case of whiplash. It was not that long ago when people were talking about this era of devolution," or returning power to the states.

The court cases on the health care law are proceeding against the backdrop of strong political criticism by Republican lawmakers, many of whom are campaigning for Congress by promising to repeal and replace it. Neither the GOP lawmakers nor the states in their lawsuits provide details on how they would replace the law if successful in their goal of knocking it out. If the law stays on the books, a definitive Supreme Court decision is likely to be at least two years away.

Meanwhile, immigrant rights groups that challenge tough-minded state and local laws acknowledge the problem of illegal immigration but look for a solution to the unlikely prospect of Congress and the president agreeing on some form of legalization as part of a broad overhaul of immigration law. For their part, the groups that support the states' initiatives take no note of the Obama administration's sharp increase in deportations — a record 392,000 during the year that ended Sept. 30, an increase of 81,000 over the number in President Bush's final year in office.[35]

In Schapiro's metaphor, however, these conflicts should be seen not as discordant, but euphonious — the arguments and power struggles apt to lead to better policies with broader support in the long run. The state of federalism today, Schapiro says, is good. "It's good when the question of allocation of power in the United States is debated."

NOTES

1. Quoted in Casey Newton, "End of Kids Care could cost state billions from feds," *The Arizona Republic* (Phoenix), March 23, 2010, p. A1; see also Casey Newton, "Budget for 2011 signed by Brewer," *ibid.*, March 19, 2010, p. B1.

2. The case is *United States v. Arizona*, U.S. Dist. Ct., Ariz., 2:2010cv01413, http://dockets.justia.com/docket/arizona/azdce/2:2010cv01413/535000/. See Jerry Markon and Michael D. Shear, "Justice Dept. sues Arizona over law," *The Washington Post*, July 7, 2010, p. A1. For coverage of the law's enactment, see Craig Harris, Alia Beard Rau and Glen Creno, "Center of the storm," *The Arizona Republic* (Phoenix), April 24, 2010, p. A1.

3. For background on the Tea Party, see Peter Katel, "Tea Party Movement," *CQ Researcher*, March 19, 2010, pp. 241-264.

4. Conlan's books are listed in Bibliography. For previous coverage, see Kenneth Jost, "States and Federalism," *CQ Researcher*, Sept. 13, 1996, pp. 793-816.

5. "Memorandum for the Heads of Executive Departments and Agencies, May 20, 2009, www.whitehouse.gov/the_press_office/Presidential-Memorandum-Regarding-Preemption/. For coverage, see Philip Rucker, "Obama curtails Bush's policy of preemption," *The Washington Post*, May 22, 2009, p. A3. See also John Schwartz, "Obama Seems to Be Open to a Broader Role for States," *The New York Times*, Jan. 30, 2009, p. A16.

6. For background, see Kenneth Jost, "Revising No Child Left Behind," *CQ Researcher*, April 16, 2010, pp. 337-360.

7. Andrew Cline, "Obama's Crazy-Quilt Federalism," *The American Spectator*, July 13, 2010, http://spectator.org/archives/2010/07/13/obamas-crazy-quilt-federalism/print.

8. The cases are *Florida v. U.S. Dep't of Health and Human Services*, No. 3:10-cv-91-RV/EMT, *Virginia ex rel. Cuccinelli v. Sebelius*, U.S. Dist. Ct., E.D. Va., 3:2010cv00188. McCollum was interviewed for White House Brief, allpoliticsradio.com, March 22, available on You Tube: www.youtube.com/watch?v=TzRqc8MrGtc.

9. The case is *Lozano v. City of Hazleton*, 07-3531, 3d Circuit, Sept. 9, 2010, www.ca3.uscourts.gov/opinarch/073531p.pdf. Documents and updates can be found on the American Civil Liberties Union's website: www.aclu.org/immigrants-rights/anti-immigrant-ordinances-hazleton-pa. For coverage, see Julia Preston, "Court Rejects a City's Effort to Restrict Immigrants," *The New York Times*, Sept. 10, 2010, p. A12.

10. Background drawn in part from David B. Walker, *The Rebirth of Federalism: Slouching toward Washington* (2d ed., 2000). See also Michael Greve, *Real Federalism: Why It Matters, How It Could Happen* (1999). For a succinct overview, see "Federalism" in Kenneth Jost, *Supreme Court from A to Z* (4th ed., 2007), pp. 189-190.

11. *The Federalist Papers* are online at the Library of Congress' Thomas website: http://thomas.loc.gov/home/histdox/fedpapers.html.

12. The cases are *McCulloch v. Maryland*, 17 U.S. 316 (1819); *New York v. Miln*, 36 U.S. 102 (1837); and *Passenger Cases* (*Smith v. Turner, Norris v. Boston*), 48 U.S. 283 (1849).

13. The cases are *National Labor Relations Board v. Jones & Laughlin Steel Corp*, 301 U.S. 1 (1937); *Steward Machine Co. v. Davis*, 301 U.S. 548 (1937) (unemployment compensation); *Helvering v. Davis*, 301 U.S. 619 (1937) (Social Security); *West Coast Hotel Co. v. Parrish*, 300 U.S. 379 (1937) (state minimum wage); *United States v. Darby Lumber Co.*, 312 U.S. 100 (1941) (Fair Labor Standards Act). See individual entries in Melvin I. Urofsky and Paul Finkelman, *Landmark Decisions of the U.S. Supreme Court* (2d ed.), 2007.

14. The case is *Wickard v. Filburn*, 317 U.S. 111 (1942).

15. See Walker, *op. cit.*, p. 99.

16. Background drawn from Walker, *op. cit.*; Timothy Conlan, *From New Federalism to Devolution: Twenty-Five Years of Intergovernmental Reform* (1998).

17. *Ibid.*, pp. 85-91.

18. *Ibid.*, pp. 259-260.

19. The cases are *Garcia v. San Antonio Metropolitan Transit Authority*, 469 U.S. 528 (1985), overruling *National League of Cities v. Usery*, 426 U.S. 833 (1976); and *South Dakota v. Dole*, 483 U.S. 203 (1987).

20. The decisions include *Printz v. United States*, 527 U.S. 598 (1999) (gun background checks); *Alden v. Maine*, 527 U.S. 706 (1999) (Fair Labor Standards Act); *United States v. Lopez*, 514 U.S. 549 (1995) (Gun-Free School Zones Act); *United States v. Morrison*, 529 U.S. 598 (2000) (Violence Against Women Act).

21. Background drawn in part from Tim Conlan and John Dinan, "Federalism, the Bush Administration, and the Transformation of American Conservatism," *Publius: The Journal of Federalism*, Vol. 37, No. 3 (winter 2007), pp. 279-303, http://publiusoxford-journals.org; and Tim Conlan and Paul Posner, "Inflection Point? Federalism and the Obama Administration," paper presented to American Political Science Association, September 2010, http://papers.ssrn.com/sol3/papers.cfm?abstract_id=1642264.

22. The decision is *Gonzales v. Oregon*, 546 U.S. 243 (2006).

23. The decision is *Gonzales v. Raich*, 545 U.S. 1 (2005).

24. John Dinan and Shama Gamkhar, "The State of American Federalism 2008-2009: the Presidential Election, the Economic Downturn, and the Consequences for Federalism," *Publius: The Journal of Federalism*, Vol. 39, No. 3 (winter 2009), pp. 369-407, http://publius.oxfordjournals.org. Dinan teaches at Wake Forest University, Gamkhar at the University of Texas-Austin.

25. For a full account, see *Landmark: The Inside Story of America's New Health Care Law and What It Means for All of Us*, by the staff of *The Washington Post* (2010).

26. The government's brief can be found on SCOTUSB log: www.scotusblog.com/wp-content/uploads/2010/05/09-115_cvsg-grant-limited.pdf.

27. The case is *Thomas More Law Center v. Obama*, 10-CV-11156, U.S. Dist. Ct. E.D. Mich., Oct. 7, 20910, www.mied.uscourts.gov/News/Docs/09714485866.pdf. For coverage, see Lyle Denniston, "Health insurance mandate upheld," SCOTUSBlog, Oct. 7, 2010, www.scotusblog.com/2010/10/health-insurance-mandate-upheld/.

28. The judge's decision in *Virginia ex rel. Sebelius* is available at http://docs.justia.com/cases/federal/district-courts/virginia/vaedce/3:2010cv00188/252045/84/. All other case documents are also on the site. For coverage, see stories by Rosalind S. Helderman, "U.S. judges allows Va. health care lawsuit to move ahead," *The Washington Post*, Aug. 3, 2010, p. A2; "Va. begins courtroom assault on health care law," *ibid.*, July 2, 2010, p. B1.

29. Quotes from these stories: N.C. Aizenman, "A first step in health care suit," *The Washington Post*, Sept. 15, 2010, p. A4.; Kevin Sack, "Suit on Health Care Bill Appears Likely to Advance," *The New York Times*, Sept. 15, 2010, p. A20; Kris Wernowsky, "Health care suit lives to see another day," *Pensacola News Journal*, Sept. 15, 2010.

30. See Kevin Sack, "Judge rules health law is constitutional," *The New York Times*, Oct. 8, 2010.

31. The decision in *United States v. Arizona* can be found at http://docs.justia.com/cases/federal/district-courts/arizona/azdce/2:2010cv01413/535000/87/. Reaction drawn from news coverage: Nicholas Riccardi and Anna Gorman, "Judge blocks key parts of Arizona immigration law," *Los Angeles Times*, July 29, 2010, p. A1.

32. The decision in what was then known as *Chicanos por la Causa, Inc. v. Napolitano* can be found at www.ca9.uscourts.gov/datastore/opinions/2008/09/17/0717272.pdf. Janet Napolitano, then governor of Arizona, is now U.S. secretary of Homeland Security. For materials on the Supreme Court case, now known as *Chamber of Commerce v. Whiting*, see www.scotusblog.com/case-files/cases/chamber-of-commerce-of-the-united-states-v-candelaria/?wpmp_switcher=desktop.

33. *U.S. Term Limits v. Thornton*, 514 U.S. 779 (1995) (Kennedy, J., concurring).

34. Robert A. Schapiro, *Polyphonic Federalism: Toward the Protection of Fundamental Rights* (2009), p. 177.

35. See Shankar Vedentam, "U.S. deportations reach record high," *The Washington Post*, Oct. 8, 2010, p. A10; Julia Preston, "Deportations From U.S. Reach a Record High," *The New York Times*, Oct. 8, 2010, p. A21.

BIBLIOGRAPHY

Books

Conlan, Timothy J., *From New Federalism to Devolution: Twenty-Five Years of Intergovernmental Reform*, **Brookings Institution Press, 1998.**
A professor at George Mason University traces and analyzes federalism reforms from the 1970s through the mid-1990s. Includes detailed notes. The book is a continuation of Conlan's earlier title, *New Federalism: Intergovernmental Reform from Nixon to Reagan* (Brookings Institution Press, 1988). In acknowledgments, Conlan foreswore writing a third edition, but he has continued to write articles on the topic.

Greve, Michael S., *Real Federalism: Why It Matters, How It Could Happen*, **AEI Press, 1999.**
The conservative activist-scholar, now at the American Enterprise Institute, argues that a revival of federalism — possible but "not inexorable" — is needed to counter centralizing tendencies and protect citizens' liberty and welfare. Includes detailed notes.

Holahan, John, Alan Weil, and Joshua M. Wiener (eds.), *Federalism and Health Policy*, **Urban Institute Press, 2003.**
The book comprehensively details the respective roles of federal and state governments in setting and implementing health policy in the United States. Holahan is director of the institute's Health Policy Research Center; Weil was director of its New Federalism Project; Wiener a principal research associate. Notes and references with each chapter.

Schapiro, Robert A., *Polyphonic Federalism: Toward the Protection of Fundamental Rights*, **University of Chicago Press, 2009.**
The Emory law professor's theory of "polyphonic federalism" views the organizational principle of multiple, overlapping decision-making authorities as the best means to promote responsiveness, self-government and liberty.

Walker, David B., *The Rebirth of Federalism: Slouching toward Washington* **(2d. ed.), Chatham House, 2000 (originally published 1995).**
The book traces the history of American federalism and analyzes its condition at the end of the Clinton presidency. Walker, now retired, was a professor at the University of Connecticut and Bowdoin College after having worked for many years with the Advisory Commission on Intergovernmental Relations. Includes detailed notes.

Articles

Conlan, Tim, and John Dinan, "Federalism, the Bush Administration, and the Transformation of American Conservatism," *Publius: The Journal of Federalism*, **Vol. 37, No. 3 (winter 2007), pp. 279-303, http://publiusoxfordjournals.org (subscription required).**
Conlan and coauthor Dinan, an associate professor of political science at Wake Forest University, write that President George W. Bush "is the latest in a string of presidents" to sacrifice federalism concerns for the pursuit of specific policy goals at the federal level. The issue included nine other articles assessing the Bush presidency's impact on federalism in such specific areas as education, environmental policy, preemption and federal assistance to states.

Conlan, Tim, and Paul Posner, "Inflection Point? Federalism and the Obama Administration," paper presented to American Political Science Association, Washington, D.C., Sept. 2-5, 2010, http://papers.ssrn.com/sol3/papers.cfm?abstract_id=1642264.
Conlan and George Mason University colleague Posner write that President Obama is practicing "nuanced federalism," with some areas of "unprecedented federal reach" alongside "impressive examples of intergovernmental consultation and deference to state regulatory prerogatives."

Greenblatt, Alan, "Federalism in the Age of Obama," *State Legislatures*, **July/August 2010, pp. 26-28, www.ncsl.org/?tabid=20714.**
The article, published in the magazine of the National Conference of State Legislatures, examines the Obama administration's exploitation of states' fiscal woes to press them to implement initiatives in education, health care and other areas. Greenblatt, a former staff writer for *Governing*, is a *CQ Researcher* contributing writer. The online edition includes a Q&A with Paul Posner, a federalism expert at George Mason University.

Reports and Studies

"2010 Immigration-Related Laws and Resolutions: January-June 2010," National Conference of State Legislatures, July 20, 2010, www.ncsl.org/default .aspx?TabId=20881.

The report traces the growth in the number of immigration-related laws passed by the states since 2005 and categorizes the nearly 200 laws passed by state legislatures during the 2010 legislative season.

Thomas, Kenneth R., "Federalism, State Sovereignty, and the Constitution: Basis and Limits of Congressional Power," Congressional Research Service, Feb. 1, 2008, http://assets.opencrs.com/rpts/RL30315_ 20080201.pdf.

The 24-page report by a CRS legislative attorney summarizes Supreme Court decisions governing the extent and the limits of federal power vis-à-vis the states from the early days of the Constitution to the present.

For More Information

10 Amendments for Freedom, 2740 S.W. Martin Downs Blvd., Suite 235, Palm City, FL 34990; (772) 781-6112; 10amendments.org. Nonprofit working to amend the Constitution by proposing initiatives that will restrain the power of Congress.

Constitution Project, 1200 18th St., N.W., Suite 1000, Washington, DC 20036; (202) 580-6920; www.constitutionproject.org. Seeks consensus solutions to difficult legal and constitutional issues through dialogue across ideological and party lines.

Federation for American Immigration Reform, 25 Massachusetts Ave., N.W., Suite 330, Washington, DC 20001; (202) 328-7004; www.fairus.org. Promotes immigration reform through increased border security and limits on the number of immigrants allowed per year.

Heritage Foundation, 215 Massachusetts Ave., N.E., Washington, DC 20002; (202) 546-4400; www.heritage

.org. Conservative think tank advocating for a smaller federal government role.

National Conference of State Legislatures, 7700 E. First Place, Denver, CO 80230; (303) 364-7700; www.ncsl.org. Provides research and technical assistance for policy makers to exchange ideas on pressing state issues.

National Immigration Law Center, 3435 Wilshire Blvd., Los Angeles, CA 90010; (213) 639-3900; www.nilc.org. Defends the rights and opportunities of low-income immigrants and their families.

Urban Institute, 2100 M St., N.W., Washington, DC 20037; (202) 833-7200; www.urban.org. Research and education think tank working for sound public policy and effective government.

We Are America Alliance, 1050 17th St., N.W., Washington, DC 20036; (202) 463-9222; www.weareamericanalliance.org. Advocacy group for immigrant civic engagement, formed after 2006 pro-immigration rallies.

10

Tea Party Movement

Peter Katel

Republican Scott Brown celebrates in Boston on Jan. 19, 2010, after winning a special election to fill the seat of the late U.S. Sen. Edward M. Kennedy. Tea Party activity typically occurs in Republican territory — "red states" — in the South, West and Midwest. But Tea Party activists also cite Brown's upset election in Massachusetts, considered among the bluest of blue states, as indicative of their broad appeal.

Getty Images/Robert Spencer

From *CQ Researcher*,
March 19, 2010. (Updated May 13, 2011)

It's lock and load time, a pumped up Dana Loesch told several thousand attendees at the Conservative Political Action Conference (CPAC) in Washington last month. "We're in the middle of a war. We're fighting for the hearts, minds and souls of the American people."

Forget politeness, the St. Louis-based radio host and Tea Party activist told the equally energized crowd. "It's all about amplifying your voice." Conservatives, she said, should declare often and loudly, "'I don't like Barack Obama.'"

And as for the president's supporters, said the 31-year-old home-schooling mother, "Make them uncomfortable.... Attack, attack, attack. Never defend."

Many tea partiers may favor a softer approach, but Loesch's take-no-prisoners intensity reflects the dynamic and triumphant spirit emanating from the country's newest political trend, which arose in early 2009 in reaction to economic stimulus legislation, corporate bailouts and the Democrats' health insurance reform effort.

Indeed, as CPAC's enthusiastic embrace of Loesch and other tea partiers makes clear, the Tea Party movement is on the cutting edge of a conservative surge that aims to undercut, or even defeat, the Obama administration and what foes call its big-government, socialist agenda. Tea partiers are also trying to push the national Republican Party to the right, with Tea Party-affiliated candidates this year running in GOP primaries for at least 58 congressional and state offices, including three governorships.

Tea Partiers Running in 25 States

At least 58 candidates — mostly Republican — in 25 states in the upcoming election say their beliefs align with those of the Tea Party movement. Most are running for House seats, but three candidates are in contention for governorships.

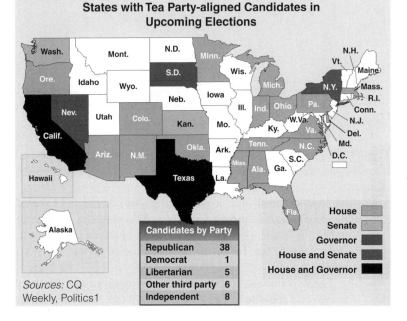

States with Tea Party-aligned Candidates in Upcoming Elections

Candidates by Party

Party	
Republican	38
Democrat	1
Libertarian	5
Other third party	6
Independent	8

House
Senate
Governor
House and Senate
House and Governor

Sources: CQ Weekly, Politics1

A major wing of the movement, Tea Party Patriots, has helped set up a fundraising arm, Liberty Central, in the Washington suburb of Burke, Va. Its president and CEO is Virginia Thomas, wife of Supreme Court Justice Clarence Thomas. She appeared on the same CPAC platform with Loesch and two other movement members. Obama's "hope and change agenda certainly became a leftist agenda pretty fast," she said. "We saw what they were doing, and it was just a big ol' power grab."[1]

The movement proved itself a political force to be reckoned with in the special Senate election in January of Republican Scott Brown for the Massachusetts Senate seat held by the late liberal Democratic lion, Edward M. Kennedy.[2]

"The Tea Party movement had a lot to do with that election," says John Hawkins, publisher of the online *Right Wing News.* "[Brown] had millions and millions of dollars flooding in from the Internet, which showed people getting energized and excited." And some on the

left acknowledge that the Tea Party campaign for Brown could have stirred support among Republican and GOP-leaning independents.

"At a time of heavy recession and joblessness, giving banks a bailout rankles people across the spectrum," says Joseph Lowndes, a University of Oregon political scientist. "A lot of Brown supporters might have been in that camp."

But a vote for Brown doesn't equate to Tea Party membership, he adds, because the movement's sharply defined conservative political perspective doesn't travel well across the left-right divide. "A lot of people who are independents and disenchanted with Obama aren't going to be tea partiers," he says.

The decentralized and loosely defined Tea Party movement takes its name from the Boston Tea Party — the 1773 protest against British taxation. Tea Party Patriots is a national grassroots organization that claims to support more than 1,000 community-based Tea Party groups around the country. The Patriots-organized Tax Day protests last year drew 1.2 million people, says Tea Party activist Jenny Beth Martin of Woodstock, Ga., a founder of the group. She and her husband lost their home and filed for bankruptcy in August 2008 after their business failed. They owed $510,000 to the Internal Revenue Service (IRS). "We've been hit by the financial crisis and the recession," Martin told Fox News, just like other "everyday Americans."[3]

Martin was especially angered by the federal bailouts of ailing banks and financial institutions by the outgoing Bush administration just before the 2008 presidential election and then of the auto companies in 2009 by the incoming Obama administration. After her husband's temp firm failed, "We started cleaning houses and repairing computers to make ends meet," she told Fox News, while big corporations that were struggling got billions in aid from the federal government. "We were saying, these businesses they were bailing out, there's already a [bankruptcy] process in place," she said. "We've gone through it. It sucks and it's not fun, but its part of how the system works."

Grassroots anger at political and business elites has fueled political movements on both the right and left throughout history. A prolific right-leaning blogger, University of Tennessee law professor Glenn Harlan Reynolds, even views the Tea Party as continuing another tradition — the Great Awakening evangelical religious movements that have emerged periodically throughout American history. "It's a symptom of dissatisfaction with politics as usual," he says.

But Republican Indiana Gov. Mitch Daniels is more cautious. "I wouldn't overestimate the number of people involved," he told *The New York Times*, also offering faint praise to tea partiers' "net positive" effects on the party.[4]

Indeed, doctrines supported by some Tea Party followers would give pause to many politicians. Featured speakers at a Nashville Tea Party convention in February included, aside from former Alaska Gov. Sarah Palin, Web news entrepreneur Joseph Farah, who said Obama may not qualify for the presidency because of his possible foreign birth. Another speaker, ex-Republican Rep. Tom Tancredo of Colorado — known for his anti-immigrant stance — urged voter literacy tests, a discriminatory practice rooted in the Jim Crow South. "Because we don't have a civics literacy test to vote," Tancredo said, "people who couldn't even spell 'vote' — or say it in English — put a committed socialist ideologue in the White House named Barack Hussein Obama."[5]

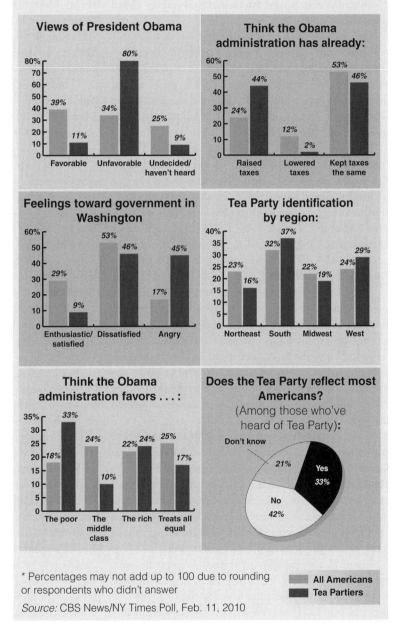

Tea Partiers Have 'Unfavorable' View of Obama

More than three-quarters of Tea Party supporters have unfavorable views of President Obama, compared with a third of all Americans. Forty-four percent of tea partiers think erroneously that the administration has raised taxes, compared with 24 percent of all Americans.

* Percentages may not add up to 100 due to rounding or respondents who didn't answer

Source: CBS News/NY Times Poll, Feb. 11, 2010

For some on the left, the Tancredo and Farah appearances — along with xenophobic and racist signs and slogans that have popped up at other Tea Party events — represent the core identity of the movement. "Tea Partiers have unjustly and unfairly targeted the Latino community to further their political agenda," say the organizers of a new Facebook community called *Cuéntame* ("tell me about it").[6]

Others insist that anti-immigrant xenophobia represents only a fringe. "I was concerned that the anti-immigrant people would try to hijack the Tea Party movement, and they have tried," said Grover Norquist, president of Americans for Tax Reform and a longtime Washington-based conservative who favors liberalized immigration policies. "Not succeeded to date."[7]

In any event, most Tea Party activists stayed away from the $549-per-person Nashville event, organized by the group Tea Party Nation, a social-networking site focusing on social issues that some other Tea Party activists discourage; among Tea Party Nation's "strategic partners" is Farah's *WorldNetDaily*. "It wasn't the kind of grassroots organization that we are, so we declined to participate," said Mark Meckler, a cofounder of Tea Party Patriots (TPP).[8]

The TPP network, which represents the movement's mainstream, steers away from social issues and instead has forged a consensus largely on economic matters: Government spending should be cut, government should be limited and the free-market system should prevail. Specifically, members argue, the federal government shouldn't expand its role in a health-care system that they say already provides adequate care to the poor and the elderly.

"Even if this bill were to have me insured tomorrow, it's still not the right thing to do for America," says Georgia TPP activist Martin. Although she and her husband lost their health coverage when his business failed, they oppose pending health-care legislation on the grounds it would add to the federal budget. "There are a lot of people in this movement who are unemployed. They don't want to burden future generations."

Martin shares a background in Republican politics with many other Tea Party activists — and a critical attitude toward the party. "There's no question the GOP has lost the mantle of fiscal responsibility and small government," writes John M. O'Hara, a former Labor Department

staffer in the George W. Bush administration. But, he adds, "The GOP is the most likely breeding ground for the fiscally responsible constitutionalists the Tea Party movement — and America — craves."[9]

A rally O'Hara helped to organize last year in Washington was part of a series of protests that launched the movement. A cable TV moment provided the mobilizing spark: On Feb. 19, 2009, CNBC business reporter Rick Santelli launched a tirade against a plan by the new Obama administration to help homeowners facing foreclosure.

"How about this, President and new administration?" Santelli yelled from the floor of the Chicago Board of Trade. "Why don't you put up a Web site to have people vote on the Internet as a referendum to see if we really want to subsidize the losers' mortgages."[10]

Santelli went on: "We're thinking of having a Chicago Tea Party in July. All you capitalists that want to show up to Lake Michigan, I'm gonna start organizing." Within four days, Santelli's rant had been viewed 1.7 million times on the CNBC Web site.[11]

O'Hara and others used Twitter and other social-network links to find compatriots and launched their rallies on Feb. 27. Protesters showed up in more than a dozen cities — including Atlanta, Fort Worth, Nashville, New York, St. Louis, San Diego Omaha and Tampa.[12] Later events included a Sept. 12 march on Washington promoted by conservative Fox News commentator Glenn Beck.

But fledgling activist Keli Carender — who blogs as "Liberty Belle" — beat them all to the punch. The 30-year-old Republican convert organized a Feb. 16 rally in her hometown, liberal Seattle, against the Obama administration's economic stimulus bill, which she dubbed "porkulus."[13]

Carender's playful approach — she distributed pulled pork at the event — seems distant from Loesch's militancy at the CPAC convention. So distant, in fact, that the conservative *Washington Examiner* issued a warning that echoed the remarks of some in the Republican establishment. "The approach [Loesch] suggests ... could easily be mistaken for a rallying cry for angry yelling," the paper said. "She must realize that when it comes to making change, it's not about who yells loudest but who actually makes people want to listen. Claiming that the tea parties and conservative activists have declared war on the left only serves to marginalize the right."

As the tea partiers gear up to challenge politics as usual in the 2010 congressional elections later this year, here are some of the questions being raised about the movement:

Does the Tea Party represent only a narrow segment of the population?

Some Tea Party activists are quite candid about what they see as the movement's base. "They've been listening to Rush Limbaugh for years, they've been railing against the mainstream media for years, they've been voting Republican for years," J. P. Freire, a *Washington Examiner* editor and Tea Party activist, said at a Washington panel discussion in February organized by the America's Future Foundation, which trains young conservatives in economics. "I'm talking about mom-and-pop suburban dwellers."

Indeed, some key Tea Party issues do coincide with key Republican positions: The federal budget deficit is out of control; the administration's health-care proposal is unnecessary and fiscally risky; the $787 billion stimulus represented a grave threat to the nation's economic health.

Only three Republican senators voted for the stimulus. And party leaders have been arguing ever since that the stimulus didn't fulfill Obama's promise to jumpstart the economy and create and save jobs. Celebrating Republican gubernatorial victories in New Jersey and Virginia last November, GOP Chairman Michael Steele condemned "an incredibly arrogant government in Washington that has put our country, our freedoms and our economy at risk with unprecedented spending."[14]

Tea partiers insist they don't just blame Obama and the Democrats for excessive spending. "There was a loss of enthusiasm for Republicans" triggered by deficit spending, says blogger and law professor Reynolds, who co-founded Porkbusters, a political initiative that attacked Republicans as well as Democrats for allegedly wasteful spending. "It was one of the things that cost them Congress, and cost them the whole 2008 election."

Tea Party activity typically occurs in Republican territory —"red states" — in the South and Midwest. Like the GOP itself, Tea Party event attendees are overwhelmingly white. But Tea Party activists also cite Brown's upset election in Massachusetts, considered among the bluest of blue states, as indicative of their broad appeal.

"A lot of Democrats voted for Scott Brown," says Reynolds. "And he had massive Tea Party support. That is at least an indicator we're moving beyond the red state-blue state thing."

While labeling the Tea Party a red-state trend "isn't entirely false," he says, the number of "disaffected Democrats" is growing. "I actually think you'll see this spread to an insurgency in the Democratic Party." The theory is that the Tea Party appeals to a bipartisan sense that Congress and the White House are listening only to powerful lobbyists and not looking out for the interests of the average American.

But non-tea partiers view the movement as fitting comfortably within the Republican fold. "Given the pretty fervent conservatism that exists in this group, it is unlikely that there are a significant number of Democrats in it," says John Sides, a political scientist at George Washington University who studies political polarization. "You may be able to find people who say they voted for Obama, but I don't think that is the central tendency of the movement."

In fact, he argues, the concentration of conservatism in suburbs and smaller cities will make it difficult for the Tea Party to build strength in big urban centers. But the movement could play a big role in areas that are up for grabs. "You can imagine that activism by the Tea Party could have a measurable impact on 'blue dog' [conservative, usually Southern] Democrats in close races," he says.

Indeed, a cofounder of the TPP points to the movement's popularity outside of red-state America. "Three of the five coordinators in New York City are Democrats," says Georgia activist Martin. And she says she's ready for the emergence of a New York politician of either party who supports Tea Party principles but who is too socially liberal to win an election in her state.

Martin spent years as a Republican Party volunteer, heading Sen. Saxbe Chambliss' reelection campaign in her county. But she deplored his vote for the TARP (Troubled Asset Relief Program) bill — the emergency "bank bailout" legislation enacted in October 2008, signed into law by George W. Bush a month before Obama was elected. She has renounced completely

Tenets of the Tea Party

The Tea Party Patriots organization says its impetus comes from "excessive government spending and taxation," according to the TPP's Web site. Here are the group's three core values:

"Fiscal Responsibility — Fiscal Responsibility by government honors and respects the freedom of the individual to spend the money that is the fruit of their own labor. . . . Such runaway deficit spending as we now see in Washington, D.C., compels us to take action as the increasing national debt is a grave threat to our national sovereignty and the personal and economic liberty of future generations.

Constitutionally Limited Government: We, the members of the Tea Party Patriots, are inspired by our founding documents and regard the Constitution of the United States to be the supreme law of the land. . . . Like the founders, we support states' rights for those powers not expressly stated in the Constitution. As the government is of the people, by the people and for the people, in all other matters we support the personal liberty of the individual, within the rule of law.

Free Markets: A free market is the economic consequence of personal liberty. The founders believed that personal and economic freedom were indivisible, as do we. Our current government's interference distorts the free market and inhibits the pursuit of individual and economic liberty. Therefore, we support a return to the free-market principles on which this nation was founded and oppose government intervention into the operations of private business."

Source: Tea Party Patriots, www.teapartypatriots.org

---

partisan activity and doesn't exempt the GOP from criticism on big spending. But she acknowledges, "I think the Republican Party is probably the one most Tea Party people more closely align with."

Georgetown University historian Michael Kazin says the movement's espousal of strict market principles determines the Tea Party's political makeup. "It's hard to think of too many people who voted for Barack Obama who really care about the budget deficit."

Kazin, who specializes in populism and other social movements, draws a distinction between the Tea Party and other grassroots upsurges. "Social movements aren't as connected to one of the main parties as this one seems to be. I know that leaders of the Republican Party are trying to appear more moderate, but clearly if you have tens or hundreds of thousands of people whose views

you would like to use, you don't push them out."

Will the Tea Party movement reshape the Republican Party?

It remains to be seen whether the Tea Party can foment national political change. But some political observers think the movement is well-placed to drive the GOP rightward, especially on economic policy issues. Others say it's a fringe faction that ultimately will lose steam.

One outcome is fairly certain: The Tea Party movement would be seriously undercut if it evolved into a third political party — historically the route taken by new movements that want to broaden the national debate. Most Tea Party activists argue against such a move. "If you create a third party you guarantee that it's going to split Republican votes and guarantee socialist Democrat victories," says *Right Wing News* publisher Hawkins. He predicts that the Tea Party instead will effectively take over the GOP.

To be sure, the prevailing view in liberal circles is that the Republican Party has already moved far to the right. Even some senior Republicans are delivering much the same message.

"To those people who are pursuing purity, you'll become a club not a party," Republican Sen. Lindsey Graham of South Carolina told *Politico*, a Washington-based online newspaper, last November. He spoke following the failed attempt by Conservative Party candidate Doug Hoffman to win a congressional seat in upstate New York, replacing the Republican incumbent, who was judged by the party establishment as too liberal. (Democrat Bill Owens won the seat.)

"Those people who are trying to embrace conservatism in a thoughtful way that fits the region and the state and the district are going to do well," Graham said. "Conservatism is an asset. Blind ideology is not."[15]

Some Washington-based conservatives question the possibility that any movement based on political principles can exert deep and lasting influence on the political process, where fulltime participants tend to act as much — or more — from self-interest as from ideology.

A movement that channels itself into a party inevitably suffers the dilution of its ideas, a conservative writer argued during the February panel discussion in Washington organized by the America's Future Foundation. "Politics is a profession, and the temptation, once we're in charge, is to say, 'We're going to fix everything, we're going to solve everything,' not realizing that people involved in these parties are human beings and susceptible to compromise," said Kelly Jane Torrance, literary editor of the Washington-based *American Conservative* magazine.

The absence of a Tea Party institutional presence makes its absorption by professional politicians inevitable, she added. "People seem to need a charismatic leader or organizer or an institution, which is why I think the movement is basically being eaten up by the Republican Party," she said.

But some Tea Party activists argue that promoting their ideas within the GOP is essential if the movement is to avoid being marginalized. "There's got to be communication with the political party establishment," says Karin Hoffman, a veteran Republican activist from Lighthouse Point, Fla. "The Democratic Party has done everything to ridicule the movement," she says, while the GOP platform "matches what the grassroots movement feels."

Hoffman orchestrated a Washington meeting this February between 50 Tea Party-affiliated activists and Republican Chairman Steele. Hoffman says she's on guard against the danger of Tea Party activists becoming nothing more than Republican auxiliaries.

"I've not been happy with how Republicans have behaved," she says, citing the reduced-price system for prescription drugs under Medicare that President Bush pushed through in 2003. "We don't need an increase in government."

Disillusionment with Bush is commonplace among tea partiers, who tend to have been Bush voters in 2000 and 2004. The shift in their support — or, alternatively, their view that he abandoned principles they thought he shared with them — underscores the potential obstacles

to reshaping national parties. "Even with a relatively diffuse organization, they can have influence just because of visibility, and can pull conventions and rallies," says Sides of George Washington University. "But that's not a recipe for transformational change."

Sides cites the history of the Club for Growth, an organization of economic conservatives that rates lawmakers on their votes on taxes, spending and related issues. "No one would say that the Club for Growth has been able to remake the Republican Party," Sides says, "but it has exerted influence in certain races."

Republican consultant and blogger Soren Dayton disputes that view. "If you look at the electoral and policy successes of the conservative movement — look at the Republican Party," Dayton said at the America's Future Foundation event. "Abortion, guns and taxes are settled issues. If you're an activist on these issues, the point is actually changing the minds of Democrats."

The reason for that ideological victory is easy to identify, Soren said. "We're winning these [electoral] fights on the ground because the Republican Party is solid — because it's been taken over in certain significant ways by conservatives."

Does the Tea Party attract conspiracy theorists?

Advocates of ideas and policies from far outside the mainstream are the bane of grassroots movements of any stripe. A classic case is the takeover in the 1960s of the New Left by self-styled revolutionaries, who cited Communist Vietnam and China as economic and political models.

Conservative movements, for their part, have always faced the danger of identification with far-right defenders of segregation and, more recently, with those who question President Obama's legitimacy on the grounds of his supposed foreign birth — a notion that has been laid to rest.

Tensions over ideas tinged with discredited notions about race and conspiracies surfaced publicly at the controversial Tea Party convention in Nashville. Speechmakers included Tancredo, the former Republican House member from Colorado. He advocated voter-literacy tests — a now-illegal procedure that was part of segregation law in the Deep South designed to deny black citizens the right to vote. And *WorldNetDaily*'s Farah insisted that Obama's birthplace remains an unsettled issue. "The president refuses to produce documents proving he meets the Constitution's natural-born citizen requirement," *WorldNetDaily* said in paraphrasing his argument.[16]

The publication reported that "the crowd cheered wildly, whistled and applauded" when Farah made his claim. But observers from both right and left reported a different impression.

Jonathan Raban, writing in the left-leaning *New York Review of Books*, said the favorable response was not universal: "I saw as many glum and unresponsive faces in the crowd as people standing up to cheer."[17] And conservative blogger, columnist and professor Reynolds says, "I did not hear a single person say a good thing about Farah or the 'birther' issue."

In fact, the dispute went public. After his speech, Farah engaged in a heated argument outside the convention hall with Andrew Breitbart, publisher of the conservative *Breitbart.com* news and commentary sites.[18] Breitbart called Farah's focus on Obama's citizenship "a fundamentally controversial issue that forces a unified group of people to have to break into different parts."[19]

The surfacing of the tensions among the tea partiers did lend substance to press reports of fringe constituencies attaching themselves to the movement, whose primary concerns publicly center on economic policy.

Les Phillip, a Tea Party candidate for the Republican nomination for a House seat in Alabama, blames the mainstream media for characterizing the Tea Party constituency as "white, racist old men." To be sure, he says, "You do have some folks on the far right." But, he adds, "Most are in the center."

Himself a black immigrant from Barbados, Phillip calls Farah's insistence on the Obama birth issue a diversion. But he voices sympathy for Tancredo's call for voter-literacy tests, despite their unsavory history. "I know more about the country than many people who were born here," he says. "If you're going to be a voter, you need to understand the history and governing documents and how the government should work."

Nevertheless, Lowndes of the University of Oregon argues that racial fears and xenophobia do play a role in some Tea Party movements, whose agendas may vary widely from place to place. "Certainly one does get the sense that the movement is made up mostly of older folks, 50 and older," he says. "I think these are people

who are most likely to be uncomfortable with cultural differences and certainly with racial differences."

Racial and cultural concerns may outweigh suspicion of the business establishment, which used to predominate among many of today's Tea Party supporters. They also denounce excessive government intrusion in citizens' lives, though typically with little reference to the Patriot Act, the Bush-era law that expanded government's surveillance and monitoring authority over e-mail and other communications. "If these folks are concerned about overweening executive power, then why did the movement not arise during the Bush years?" Lowndes asks.

Hawkins of *Right Wing News* counters that the same kind of inconsistency shadows the liberal activist world. Antiwar marches and protests of all kinds marked the Bush presidency, he observes. Yet, with tens of thousands of U.S. troops fighting hard in Afghanistan and still present in Iraq, "Where's the antiwar movement?" he asks.

Similarly, he argues, the presence of fringe activists who attach themselves to a broader cause is no less a problem on the left than on the right. "There's a very tiny percentage of people who generally are not welcome at tea parties," Hawkins says, adding that he distinguishes members or sympathizers of the militia movement from those who question Obama's presidential eligibility. "I guarantee you that, percentage-wise, there are as many Democrats who think Bush stole the election in 2004 as people who think Barack Obama is not a citizen. I would put those as complete equivalents."

Sides, of George Washington University argues, however, that the Tea Partys' big tent may limit the movement's effectiveness for reasons that go beyond issues of political respectability. The presence of the "birthers" and some militia members, along with people concerned about taxes and spending, likely will add to what he sees as a fundamental weakness. "There is an extraordinarily diffuse organizational structure with a lot of internecine conflict," he says. "That makes coalescing extremely difficult."

BACKGROUND

People's Party

Historians trace the origins of populism to the early years of the new republic. President Andrew Jackson, who served two terms (1829-1837), helped formulate the fear

CHRONOLOGY

1830s-1900s *Movements expressing citizen outrage at government and business elites begin.*

1832 President Andrew Jackson vetoes a bill to expand the national bank, calling it a tool of the "rich and powerful."

1892 People's Party of America (populists) formed in St. Louis by small farmers, evangelical Christians, labor unions and alcohol prohibition advocates.

1896 Populists unite with Democratic Party behind presidential candidate William Jennings Bryan, who is defeated.

1908 People's Party dissolves, unable to develop an urban base to match its rural constituency.

1930s-1950s *Populist politicians begin directing anger toward government, and sometimes ethnic minorities, and away from big business.*

1938 The Rev. Charles E. Coughlin, a Catholic priest with a large radio following, switches from support of President Franklin D. Roosevelt's New Deal to virulent opposition.

1954 After leaping to prominence by accusing the State Department and other agencies of harboring Soviet loyalists, Sen. Joseph R. McCarthy wrecks his career by charging the U.S. Army is also protecting communists.

1955 Liberal academics alarmed by McCarthyism argue that far-right tendencies lurk within all populist-oriented movements.

1960s-1970s *Civil rights and antiwar movements prompt middle-class whites to become Republicans.*

1966 Activists in Oakland, Calif., form Black Panther Party, embodying the worst fears of many middle-class whites about surging left-wing radicalism and "black power."

1968 Violence at Democratic National Convention in Chicago deepens divide between pro- and anti-Vietnam War Democrats and further alienates middle-class whites from protest movements .... Alabama Gov. George C. Wallace wins 13 percent of ballots for his third-party candidacy, built on anti-Washington message.

1969 Referring to Americans turned off by protesters, President Richard M. Nixon calls on "great silent majority" to support his plan to end the war.

1972 Sen. George S. McGovern, D-S.D., the Democratic presidential candidate, wins only one state as incumbent Nixon successfully ties Democrats to privileged, unpatriotic elites who look down on "good, decent people."

1979 Former Gov. Ronald Reagan, R-Calif., wins the presidency, largely by appealing to the "silent majority" constituency identified by Nixon.

1990s-2000s *Populism returns as a third-party movement, and then as a group with strong political party ties.*

1992 Texas billionaire H. Ross Perot launches himself as a third-party presidential candidate, attacking deficit spending and outsourcing of jobs abroad .... Perot wins 19 percent of the vote, drawing votes from both winning candidate Bill Clinton and the defeated George H. W. Bush.

2008 Congressionally approved financial bailout creates discontent among grassroots Republicans and Democrats.

2009 Seattle woman outraged by Obama administration-proposed economic stimulus holds protest against "porkulus." ... CNBC reporter Rick Santelli calls for a "tea party" while denouncing administration's rescue plan for homeowners facing foreclosure .... Dozens of activists network to plan "tea party" demonstrations on Feb. 27 .... Tea Party activists take part in town hall meetings with lawmakers, denouncing administration's health-care proposal .... Fox News commentator Glenn Beck promotes a "9/12" rally in Washington, which draws heavy crowd of Tea Party supporters.

2010 Tea Party activists contribute to surprise election victory of Republican Sen. Scott Brown in Massachusetts .... "Tea Party Nation" convention in Nashville sparks dissension in movement due to high ticket price and presence of anti-immigration and "birther" speakers ....

(Continued)

(Continued)

Tea Party opponents begin organizing Coffee Party alternative.

2010

November — Tea Party protests and marches provide momentum to Republican candidates who win a decisive House majority, though Senate remains majority-Democrat.

2011

Jan. 5 — Congress convenes with more than 50 House members in Tea Party Caucus; only four senators join Senate counterpart.

Jan. 25 — House Tea Party Caucus Chair Michele Bachmann, R-Minn., delivers response to president's State of the Union speech that is separate from official Republican response.

Feb. 22 — Newly elected Sen. Scott Brown, R-Mass., declines to join Tea Party Caucus in Senate.

March 31 — Tea Party Republican Mike Pence of Indiana urges House leaders negotiating with the Senate and White House to maintain demands for major spending cuts even at cost of shutting down government.

April 28 — Arizona Legislature authorizes Tea Party license plates, but some movement members oppose the move as government intrusion.

May 9 — Group of Tea Party leaders attacks House Republican leaders for willingness to accept raising the national debt limit.

---

that a financial elite threatened popular control of national institutions.[20]

Jackson's distrust of "money power" led him to veto a bill to extend the charter of a privately owned national bank that served the federal government as well as private interests. "It is to be regretted that the rich and powerful too often bend the acts of government to their selfish purposes," his veto message said.[21]

Jackson's admonition resounded for generations. But it wasn't until the late 19th century that a national political movement was organized to wrest control of the country from intertwined political and business classes. The People's Party of America, formed in 1892 in St. Louis, united an array of activists that included small farmers from the South and Great Plains who were overwhelmed by debt; the Woman's Christian Temperance Union, which advocated alcohol prohibition; two early union organizations, the Knights of Labor and the American Federation of Labor; and evangelical Christians with socialist politics.

All saw themselves as oppressed by big business and its political allies. The prohibitionists viewed big business as profiting from the vice of alcoholism. But the Populists — as they were dubbed — dodged the issue of race because they counted on Southern supporters of segregation.

Still, the Populist alliance generated enough enthusiasm to drive a presidential campaign in the 1892 election. The Populist candidate, former Union Army officer James B. Weaver, garnered 8.5 percent of the national vote, an impressive showing for a third-party candidate.

Realizing that their party stood no chance of winning the presidency on its own, the Populists forged an electoral alliance in 1896 with the Democratic Party (founded by Jackson). The Democrats' nominee was William Jennings Bryan, who had worked closely with the Populists as a House member from Nebraska.

Known for his spellbinding oratory, Bryan wanted the U.S. currency based on both gold and silver, not just gold. That would lower the value of debt-ridden farmers' obligations by lowering the value of the dollar.

"Having behind us the commercial interests and the laboring interests and all the toiling masses," Bryan said in his electrifying speech to the Democratic Convention that nominated him, "we shall answer their demands for a gold standard by saying to them, you shall not press down upon the brow of labor this crown of thorns. You shall not crucify mankind upon a cross of gold."[22]

However, the Democrat-Populist alliance proved no match for the Republicans. Populists' weaknesses included their strong ties to the Farm Belt and support of strict Protestant moral codes — turn-offs to big-city voters, many of them Catholic immigrants.

Republican William McKinley won the election, which marked the high point of the People's Party's fortunes. By 1908 it had dissolved.

Right Turn

Populist leaders spoke eloquently of corporate oppression, a classic issue of the left. But their handling of race would seem to place them on the political right. While Tom Watson, a Georgia Populist leader, made joint speaking appearances with black populists (who had their own organization), he defended Jim Crow laws, as did party rank and file. (After the party ceased to exist, Watson incited and then defended the lynching of Jewish factory manager Leo Frank of Atlanta, wrongly accused of the rape and murder of a 13-year-old girl.)[23]

In other respects, the Populists' attacks on big business, as well as ties to the early labor movement, marked them as left-liberal. President Franklin D. Roosevelt's New Deal policies of 1933-1940 drew on the Populists' doctrines. They influenced his campaigns to impose regulatory controls — such as creation of the Securities and Exchange Commission — on the "economic royalists" of Wall Street. And his administration's agricultural policies, which sought to stabilize prices by subsidizing farmers for not overproducing, also grew out of the Populists' search for solutions to farmers' financial woes.[24]

Nevertheless, Watson's career had shown that populism can whip up hatred as well as inspire ordinary citizens to demand that government serve their interests, as was exemplified during the Roosevelt era by the career of the Rev. Charles E. Coughlin, a figure of far greater influence than Watson. The Catholic priest from Royal Oak, Mich., went from being a New Deal supporter to a furious critic, whose weekly radio speeches became wildly popular. He then took a sharp right turn into anti-Semitism in 1938, attempting to link Jews to communism — a longtime target of his wrath — and financial manipulation.[25]

Dislike of Jews was commonplace in pre-World War II America, but Coughlin's calls for action against Jews found little support outside the ranks of his hardcore supporters. He raised enough concern in the Catholic hierarchy, however, to lead the archbishop of Detroit to order Coughlin to end his radio broadcasts in 1941. And in 1942, at the U.S. Justice Department's request, the church ordered him to stop publishing his weekly newspaper.

Although the infamous "radio priest" never returned to the public arena, he left his mark. In depicting communism as a menace to ordinary Americans, Coughlin anticipated the early-1950s career of Sen. Joseph R. McCarthy, R-Wis., and his supporters. To be sure, some of McCarthy's followers abhorred anti-Semitism; *National Review* founder William F. Buckley Jr., a leading defender of McCarthy, was credited with purging that prejudice from mainstream conservatism.[26] Ethnic hatred aside, McCarthy owed an intellectual debt to Coughlin with his portrayal of working people preyed upon by communist-inspired elites or outright communist agents.

McCarthy himself saw his career go down in flames in 1954 after a conflict with the U.S. Army in which the senator accused the military of harboring communists. But McCarthyism left a foundation upon which later conservative politicians built, writes Georgetown historian Kazin.

By stirring up distrust of the highly educated graduates of elite schools who predominated in the top reaches of public life — especially the foreign policy establishment — McCarthy and his allies caused serious alarm among liberal academics. McCarthyism "succeeded in frightening many liberals into mistrusting the very kinds of white Americans — Catholic workers, military veterans, discontented families in the middle of the social structure — who had once been foot soldiers of causes such as industrial unionism, Social Security and the GI Bill."[27]

The 'Silent Majority'

The tensions fanned by McCarthy burst into flame in the mid-1960s. Some of the most active and visible leaders of the civil rights movement — such as Stokely Carmichael of the Student Non-Violent Coordinating Committee — adopted the "black power" slogan. The term was elastic — covering everything from affirmative action to armed self-defense — but many whites heard a threat.

Adding to the tension, the Black Panther Party, formed in 1966 in Oakland, Calif., paraded with firearms to illustrate its goal of "self-defense" against police officers

Tea Partiers Take Aim at Health Reform

Movement plans a replay of last summer's town hall meetings.

Joblessness hovers near 10 percent. Yet in a country where most Americans get health insurance through their employers, opposing health insurance reforms proposed by congressional Democrats at the urging of President Barack Obama has been a driving force in the Tea Party movement.

"The Tea Party ... did help destroy health reform," Kelly Jane Torrance, literary editor of the *American Conservative*, claimed at a Washington panel discussion in February. "I think that's an amazing accomplishment."

Torrance's remarks at the America's Future Foundation event may have been premature. Since the event, prospects for passage of the legislation seem to have improved.

With a congressional recess starting on March 29, tea partiers are aiming for a replay of last summer's fractious "town hall" meetings with legislators, when the movement's opposition to health reform — especially its added cost to the deficit — first erupted. "We're gonna hit 'em when we know they're back in [the] district, and we're gonna hit 'em hard," Tom Gaitens, a Tampa Tea Party organizer, told Fox News.

Final passage of the legislation before the recess would short-circuit that plan. But the prospects are uncertain.

In any event, plans to destroy the health-care plan, a longtime centerpiece of the Democratic agenda, might seem counter-intuitive, given that the Tea Party hopes to grow — in a country with up to 45 million uninsured residents.[1]

Among them is Tea Party organizer Jenny Beth Martin of Woodstock, Ga. Martin's family lost health coverage when her husband's business failed more than two years ago. When one of the Martins' children gets sick, "We tell the doctor we don't have insurance, and make arrangements to pay cash," Martin says.

The hardships brought on by the Great Recession hit even deeper for Martin's family. She and her husband lost their home, and for a while the couple was cleaning houses to make ends meet.

Nevertheless, she opposes the Obama plan. "I think that we do need health insurance reform," she says. "I just don't think this bill is a good idea."

Her political response, even in the face of personal hardship, illustrates a major facet of the movement, and of American conservatism in general. "People don't connect the economic crisis to the need for any kind of government intervention," says Joseph Lowndes, a political scientist at George Washington University. "People come to this movement with a pretty strong level of conservatism in place already. So there is that irony: to some extent these movements are facilitated by a poor economy, but their reaction ... does not embrace the government's effort to fix things."

---

and soon embraced the Cuban and North Korean versions of communist doctrines.[28]

The anti-Vietnam War movement also was gathering strength on college campuses, where potential male foot soldiers benefited from draft deferments, unlike working-class high school graduates who weren't going on to college. Antiwar activists also began openly advocating draft-dodging and draft resistance, some even burning their draft cards in protest — stirring outrage among many among the World War II-Korean War generations.

Political and social tensions exploded in 1968. First, the April 4 assassination of civil rights leader the Rev. Dr. Martin Luther King Jr. led to rioting in black communities across the country, notably in Washington, D.C., where the National Guard was called out to quell the violence. Also that spring, tensions over the Vietnam War within the Democratic Party — and within the country as a whole — came to a head during the Democratic Convention in Chicago, marked by large antiwar demonstrations and violent police repression. Although Vice President Hubert H. Humphrey won the nomination, his campaign against Republican Richard M. Nixon was hobbled by the escalation of the war under outgoing President Lyndon B. Johnson.

Nixon's victory enabled him to indulge a deep grudge against the East Coast-based Democratic political elite.

John Hawkins, publisher of the *Right Wing News* Web site, suggests another reason for conservative distrust of the health-reform plan. "I think people fear there is going to be a massive decrease in the quality of care," he said. "The idea that you'll cover more people, but the quality won't drop and it won't cost more — people don't believe that."

And, Hawkins says, conservatives understand another deep-seated element of American political culture. "People don't, with good reason, trust the competence of government."

Martin opposes health reformers' plans to penalize businesses that don't provide health insurance for employees and to raise taxes to help subsidize mandatory coverage for those who couldn't afford it. Although the legislation hasn't been finalized, proposals so far would pay for the expanded insurance coverage by raising taxes on high-end health insurance plans or on wealthy Americans (those earning more than $250,000 a year). Martin also does not like the proposal to delay implementation of benefits until 2014, after some higher taxes take effect (though a prohibition would be immediate on insurance companies refusing clients with pre-existing conditions).[2]

A tea partier protests President Obama's health-care reform plans before his arrival at Arcadia University in Glenside, Pa., on March 8, 2010.

Martin does favor making coverage "portable," not dependent on employment — which would be compatible with the Obama plan, in principle. And she agrees that individuals who can't qualify for insurance could benefit from high-risk insurance pools, which some states have set up. Tea Party organizer John M. O'Hara laid out these and other proposals in a book on the movement.[3]

The book doesn't propose dismantling Medicare, the massive health-care subsidy program for the elderly, and neither does Martin. "It's there now, and we need to deal with it as it is."

And, she adds, "I don't think there is anything wrong with government providing safety nets. I understand that sometimes things happen to people."

— *Peter Katel*

[1] Carl Bialik, "The Unhealthy Accounting of Uninsured Americans," *The Wall Street Journal*, June 24, 2009, http://online.wsj.com/article/SB124579852347944191.html#articleTabs%3Darticle. Some question that U.S. Census Bureau estimate, in part because it includes illegal aliens who wouldn't be covered under a new law.

[2] Alec MacGillis and Amy Goldstein, "Obama offers a new proposal on health care," *The Washington Post*, Feb. 23, 2010, p. A1.

[3] John M. O'Hara, *A New American Tea Party: The Counterrevolution Against Bailouts, Handouts, Reckless Spending, and More Taxes* (2010), pp. 175-201.

In 1969, soon after taking office, he used a term that echoed old-school populist rhetoric, urging the "great silent majority" to support his peace plan.[29] In effect, Nixon was effectively telling ordinary Americans repelled by the civil disorder and protests that they were the backbone of the nation, despite all the noise generated by the demonstrators.

But another high-profile politician tapped even deeper into the vein of outrage that ran through blue-collar America. Gov. George C. Wallace of Alabama had propelled himself into the national spotlight by dint of his fervent resistance to the civil rights movement. As the presidential candidate of the American Independent Party,

he tried to expand his segregationist appeal (he later repudiated Jim Crow) to cast himself as the voice of the common American. He demonstrated his familiarity with his constituency by ticking off its members' occupations: "The bus driver, the truck driver, the beautician, the fireman, the policeman and the steelworker, the plumber and the communications worker and the oil worker and the little businessman." They knew more about the nation's problems, he said, than snobbish politicians, academics and journalists.[30]

As a third-party candidate, Wallace had no chance of winning, but he garnered nearly 10 million votes — 13 percent of ballots — showing that his appeal ran strong.[31]

Sarah Palin Shines at Tea Party Convention

Some see her as a potential party leader.

Tea partiers pride themselves on their lack of formal leadership, but that hasn't stopped speculation about who will emerge to lead the movement. So far, the speculation largely has zeroed in on Sarah Palin. And the former vice-presidential candidate's insistence that she isn't seeking a leadership role hasn't squelched the topic.

In fact, Palin has actually fueled the speculation, possibly inadvertently. After her surprise resignation last year as Alaska's governor and the publication of *Going Rogue*, her best-selling book, she addressed the Tea Party's February convention in Nashville — the only speech she's given this year at an overtly political event. Her political ideas, to the extent she has spelled them out, seem consistent with the tea partiers' call for lower taxes and smaller government.

In the eyes of Tea Party activists who skipped Nashville — in part because they objected to its $500-plus ticket price — Palin made a mistake in going. That view was even more prevalent after the influential online political newspaper *Politico* reported she had received $100,000 for the speech. "This has nothing to do with the grassroots movement — nothing," said Robin Stublen, who helped organize a Tea Party group in Punta Gorda, Fla.[1]

Palin didn't deny that account, but she wrote in *USA Today* that "any compensation for my appearance will go right back to the cause." [2] She didn't specify the precise destination for the money.

Some tea partiers saluted her presence in Nashville and its effects on the movement. "I think the Tea Party is gaining respect when we're able to attract some of the quality representation … a caliber of person such as this," said Bob Porto, an attendee from Little Rock.[3]

Palin's star power certainly generated media attention for the convention, even though a relatively modest 600 people attended, and the convention was controversial within the movement. Her speech, in fact, was carried live on C-SPAN, CNN and Fox News.

Palin made a point of waving off the idea that she wants to take the helm. "I caution against allowing this movement to be defined by any one leader or politician," she said. "The Tea Party movement is not a top-down operation. It's a ground-up call to action that is forcing both parties to change the way they're doing business, and that's beautiful." [4]

For all of her attention-getting capabilities, Palin comes with baggage. A new book by Steve Schmidt, top strategist for the McCain-Palin campaign, described her as dishonest. And another book, by journalists Mark Halperin and John Heilemann reported that she was ignorant of even basic national and international matters. "[S]he still didn't really understand why there was a North Korea and a South Korea," Heilemann said on CNN.[5]

Even a friendlier figure, Stephen F. Hayward of the conservative American Enterprise Institute, warned Palin that she's nowhere near as ready for a national position as Ronald Reagan was. "Palin has as much as admitted that she needs to acquire more depth, especially on foreign policy," he wrote in *The Washington Post*. "One thing above all is required: Do your homework. Reagan did his."[6]

Many of those Wallace votes would have gone to Nixon if the Alabama governor hadn't launched his third-party bid, and Nixon concluded that he didn't want to face that challenge again.[32]

Enduring Appeal

In 1972 Wallace had plans for another presidential run. But the outsider candidate apparently wasn't above making insider deals. In a book on Nixon's presidential campaigns, author Rick Perlstein reports that Nixon made moves to benefit Wallace in exchange for the Alabaman dropping his third-party strategy and running instead in the Democratic presidential primary. As a Democratic candidate, Wallace wouldn't siphon off Republican votes in the general election, as he had in 1968.[33]

In the summer of 1971, Wallace met with Nixon during a flight to Alabama from the president's vacation home in Key Biscayne, Fla. Three months later, a federal grand jury investigating alleged tax fraud by Wallace's brother dissolved without issuing indictments. Shortly

But in Nashville, the crowd loved her, wrote Jonathan Raban in the liberal *New York Review of Books*. Many had been cool not only to the anti-immigrant talk of Tom Tancredo, the former Colorado congressman and 2008 GOP presidential candidate, but also the Obama-birthplace suspicions of Web news entrepreneur Joseph Farah, Raban reported.

But the crowd embraced Palin. "A great wave of adoration met the small black-suited woman .... The entire ballroom was willing Sarah to transport us to a state of delirium with whatever she chose to say."[7]

The speech was something of a letdown, Raban added, because Palin's delivery was better suited to the TV cameras than to the live audience. Still, she got a big sendoff. "The huge standing ovation ('Run, Sarah, Run!') was more for the concept of Palin ... than it was for the lackluster speech," Raban wrote.[8]

Palin hasn't revealed whether she'll run for president in 2012, but she pointedly avoids denying it. "I won't close the door that perhaps could be open for me in the future," she told Fox News.[9]

However, University of Tennessee law professor Glenn Harlan Reynolds, who covered the Nashville convention for the Web-based *Pajamas TV*, warned that Palin's popularity could exact the same price that he argues President Obama has made his political allies pay for hero-worshipping him.

"The biggest risk that the Tea Party movement faces is that it will create its own Obama in the person of Sarah Palin and get a similar result," he says. "She made a point of saying she didn't want to be their leader, and most people agreed. But the tendency of people to run after a charismatic leader is probably genetically hardwired."

— *Peter Katel*

Sarah Palin answered questions from attendees at the National Tea Party Convention in Nashville on Feb. 6, 2010.

Getty Images for NASCAR/Jerry Markland

[1] Quoted in Chris Good, "Is Palin's Tea Party Speech a Mistake?" *The Atlantic*, Feb. 4, 2010, www.theatlantic.com/politics/archive/2010/02/is-palins-tea-party-speech-a-mistake-tea-partiers-have-mixed-opinions/35360/.

[2] Ben Smith and Andy Barr, "Tea partiers shell out big bucks for Sarah Palin," *Politico*, Jan. 12, 2010, www.politico.com/news/stories/0110/31409.html; Sarah Palin, "Why I'm Speaking at Tea Party Convention," *USA Today*, Feb. 3, 2010, http://blogs.usatoday.com/oped/2010/02/column-why-im-speaking-at-tea-party-convention-.html.

[3] *Ibid.*

[4] "Sarah Palin Speaks at Tea Party Convention," CNN, Feb. 6, 2010, http://transcripts.cnn.com/TRANSCRIPTS/1002/06/cnr.09.html.

[5] Jonathan Martin, "Steve Schmidt: Sarah Palin has trouble with truth," *Politico*, Jan. 11, 2010, www.politico.com/news/stories/0110/31335.html.

[6] Steven F. Hayward, "Would Reagan Vote for Sarah Palin?" *The Washington Post*, March 7, 2010, p. B1.

[7] Jonathan Raban, "At the Tea Party," *New York Review of Books*, March 25, 2010, www.nybooks.com/articles/23723.

[8] *Ibid.*

[9] Quoted in "Palin says 2012 presidential bid a possibility," CNN, Feb. 8, 2010, www.cnn.com/2010/POLITICS/02/07/palin.presidential.run.tea.party/index.html.

thereafter, the Justice Department announced — "suddenly and improbably," in Perlstein's words — that Alabama's civil rights enforcement plan was superior to other states' plans.

In January 1972 Wallace announced he would run for the Democratic presidential nomination. In Florida, the first primary, he won first place in a five-man race, with 42 percent of the vote.

In the end, Wallace (who was shot and paralyzed midway through the campaign) won only two primaries outside the Old Confederacy, in Michigan and Maryland. The Democratic nomination went to Sen. George S. McGovern of South Dakota, an anti-Vietnam War candidate.

Unfortunately for McGovern, he came to symbolize a social gap between hard-working, ordinary Americans, and pampered liberals and radicals. In fact, he had earned a Distinguished Flying Cross as a bomber pilot in World War II and hardly fit the stereotype.[34]

But McGovern's supporters did include the liberal wing of the Democratic Party, Hollywood stars among them.

New Coffee Party Drawing Supporters

"People are tired of the anger."

An alternative to the Tea Party is taking shape, as citizens who oppose its message and tactics are forming their own grassroots network — the Coffee Party.

The Tea Party's nascent rival takes a deliberately toned-down approach to political conflict. "We've got to send a message to people in Washington that you have to learn how to work together, you have to learn how to talk about these issues without acting like you're in an ultimate fighting session," founder Annabel Park, who launched the movement from a Coffee Party Facebook page, told *The New York Times* recently.[1]

Tea partiers put themselves on the map with rallies, pointed questions to politicians at town hall meetings and election campaign organizing. How the coffee partiers plan to project themselves into the national debate isn't clear yet. But there's no question that the effort grows out of the liberal, Democratic Party-oriented part of the political spectrum — a counterpart to the veteran Republicans who launched the Tea Party. Park, a documentary filmmaker in the Washington suburb of Silver Spring, Md., had worked on the Obama campaign.

By mid-March, when enthusiasts nationwide held a coordinated series of get-togethers in — of course — coffee shops across the country, the Coffee Party page had collected more than 100,000 fans. "Coffee partiers seem to be more in favor of government involvement — as in envisioning a greater role for government in the future of health care — but denounce the 'corporatocracy' that holds sway in Washington," *The Christian Science Monitor* reported from a Coffee Party meeting in Decatur, Ga.[2]

Whether the Coffee Party grows into a full-fledged movement, there's no denying the initial appeal. The organizer of a Dallas-area gathering in March had expected 15 people at most. She got 40. "This is snowballing," Raini Lane said. "People are tired of the anger, tired of the hate."[3]

— Peter Katel

---

[1] Quoted in Kate Zernike, "Coffee Party, With a Taste for Civic Participation, Is Added to the Menu," *The New York Times*, March 2, 2010, p. A12.

[2] Patrik Jonsson, "'Coffee party' movement: Not far from the 'tea party' message?" *The Christian Science Monitor*, March 13, 2010, www.csmonitor.com/USA/Politics/2010/0313/Coffee-party-movement-Not-far-from-the-tea-party-message.

[3] Quoted in Cassie Clark, "Coffee Party energizes fans," *Dallas Morning News*, March 14, 2010, p. B2.

So the "McGovern Democrats" neatly symbolized one side of the social gap that right-wing populists had identified, and that Nixon had done his best to widen. "It is time that good, decent people stop letting themselves be bulldozed by anybody who presumes to be the self-righteous moral judge of our society," Nixon said in a radio address shortly before Election Day.[35]

His strategy proved spectacularly successful. McGovern won only one state, Massachusetts, and Washington, D.C. But Nixon's even more spectacular political downfall during the Watergate scandal prevented him from taking advantage of his victory. He was forced to resign in 1974.

Though President Ronald Reagan, another Republican, adopted Nixon's "silent majority" paradigm, Reagan's overall optimism effectively sanded off the doctrine's sharp edges. And Reagan didn't have to contend with directing an unpopular war.

During the 1992 reelection campaign of Reagan's successor (and former vice president), President George H. W. Bush, another populist figure emerged, Texas billionaire H. Ross Perot. In his brief but influential third-party campaign for president, Perot declared, "America today is a nation in crisis with a government in gridlock. We are deeply in debt and spending beyond our means."[36]

A pro-choice, law-and-order conservative, Perot paid little attention to social issues. Instead, he emphasized the need to cut government spending and strongly opposed the proposed North American Free Trade Agreement (NAFTA) with Mexico and Canada. Business' "job is to create and protect jobs in America — not Mexico," he said shortly before formally announcing.[37]

And he decried what he saw as the lavish perks of government service. "We have government turned upside down, where the people running it act and live at your expense like royalty, and many of you are working two jobs just to stay even."[38]

Perot's intolerance for criticism and a strong authoritarian streak (he praised Singapore, notorious for its rigid enforcement of laws on personal behavior) limited his appeal. Still, he wound up with 19 percent of the vote, including 29 percent of all votes by independents. "He showed the nation's ruling elites," wrote *The Washington Post*'s John Mintz, "that millions of Americans are deeply disturbed by what they believe is a breakdown in American society."[39]

Political professionals had assumed Perot would draw far more Republican votes away from Bush than Democratic ones from Bill Clinton. But post-election surveys showed that Perot voters — often casting what amounted to protest votes — came from both Republican- and Democratic-oriented voters.

"Those who said they voted for Perot," *The Washington Post* reported, "split almost evenly between Bush and Clinton when asked their second choice."[40]

CURRENT SITUATION

The Election Test

Across the country, Tea Party-affiliated candidates — or those who claim the movement's mantle — are running for a range of Republican nominations, in races that will test both the movement's strength and its potential to influence GOP politics. The races will also set the stage for the 2012 Republican presidential nomination.

So far, at least one potential Republican candidate seems to think the Tea Party will have run its course by then. Former Massachusetts Gov. Mitt Romney is criticizing populism among both Republicans and Democrats. "Populism sometimes takes the form of being anti-immigrant ... and that likewise is destructive to a nation which has built its economy through the innovation and hard work and creativity of people who have come here from foreign shores," Romney told *The Boston Globe*.[41]

Some candidates seeking Tea Party votes do take an anti-immigrant line. In Arizona, former Rep. J.D. Hayworth is challenging veteran Sen. John McCain, the GOP candidate for president in 2008. "In Arizona, you can't ignore the Republican animus against Sen. McCain on immigration," Jason Rose, a spokesman for Hayworth, told *Roll Call*, a Washington political newspaper.[42]

Meanwhile, another Tea Party-backed candidate, Mike Lee, is challenging Republican Sen. Bob Bennett of Utah, whose backers include the state's senior senator, Republican Orrin Hatch. And in Kentucky, Tea Party enthusiast Rand Paul (son of libertarian Rep. Ron Paul, R-Texas) is competing against a Republican officeholder, Secretary of State Trey Grayson, for the GOP nomination to a Senate seat left open by a Republican retirement. Florida's GOP Gov. Charlie Crist, whom tea partiers consider insufficiently conservative, is fighting hard for the Senate nomination against Marco Rubio, a lobbyist and former state legislator who has become a national star among conservative Republicans. "America already has a Democrat Party, it doesn't need two Democrat parties," Rubio told CPAC in February.[43]

And Sen. Jim DeMint, the South Carolina Republican who has become a Senate liaison for the Tea Party, made clear to the CPAC crowd where his sympathies lie, tacitly drawing a parallel between Crist and Sen. Arlen Specter of Pennsylvania. who defected from the GOP last year to save his seat. "I would rather have 30 Marco Rubios in the Senate than 60 Arlen Specters."[44]

In the Deep South, where the Tea Party runs along the same conservative Republican tracks, two Tea Party-friendly candidates for Congress are opposing each other in north Alabama. "A lot of Tea Party activists are split between Les Phillip and Mo Brooks," says Christie Carden, who organized a Tea Party group in Huntsville. So far, at least, she and her fellow members have not endorsed either candidate.

Complicating matters, a third Republican is running as well. Incumbent Parker Griffith was welcomed into the GOP fold after he switched from Democrat to Republican last December. Party-establishment backing for Griffith makes sense, given the GOP's interest in providing a defector with a favorable reception, says blogger and Tennessee law professor Reynolds. But, he adds, "One of the Tea Party complaints is that there is too much *realpolitik*" — or compromising — in the GOP establishment.

Elsewhere, even where Tea Party candidates might have traction, Republican organizations won't necessarily welcome them with open arms. "The Republican Party in Pennsylvania is pretty good at controlling its side of the ballot," says Dan Hirschorn, editor and publisher of the Philadelphia-based political news site *pa2010*. "When ... Tea Party candidates are in a race where there already are

Does the Tea Party movement represent another Great Awakening?

YES Glenn Harlan Reynolds
Professor of Law, University of Tennessee

NO Joseph Lowndes
Professor of Political Science, University of Oregon

Written for *CQ Researcher*, March 2010

In the 18th and 19th centuries, America experienced two Great Awakenings, in which mainstream religious institutions — grown too stodgy, inbred and self-serving for many — faced a sudden flowering of new, broad-based religious fervor. Now we're experiencing a third Great Awakening, but this time it's political, not religious, in nature.

Nonetheless, the problem is the same: The existing institutions no longer serve the needs of broad swaths of the public. The choice between the two parties is increasingly seen as a choice between two gangs of thieves and charlatans. While Americans always joked about corruption and venality in politics, now those jokes don't seem as funny.

The Tea Party movement is one symptom of this phenomenon: Millions of Americans are aligning themselves with a bottom-up insurgency angered by bailouts, growing deficits and the treatment of taxpayers as cash cows. Though often treated as a red-state phenomenon, the Tea Party movement is strong even in deep-blue states like Massachusetts, where Scott Brown was elected to the Senate, or California, where one out of three voters told a recent poll that they identified with the Tea Party.

But the Tea Party movement is a symptom of a much broader phenomenon, exemplified by earlier explosions of support for Howard Dean via Meetup and Barack Obama and Sarah Palin via Facebook. They were triggered by the growing sense that politics has become a cozy game for insiders, and that the interests of most Americans are ignored.

Thus, Americans are becoming harder to ignore. Over the past year they've expressed their dissatisfaction at Tea Party rallies and town hall meetings, and at marches on Washington and state capitals. And they're planning what to do next, using the Internet and talk radio.

Traditional politics is still wedded to 20th-century top-down models, where mailing lists, organizations and message control are key. But in the 21st century, the real energy is at the grassroots, where organization can take place on the fly. When Tea Party activists decided to support Brown, they sent him money through his Web site, and put together an online "Moneybomb" campaign to bypass the Republican Party, which got behind Brown's seemingly quixotic campaign only after the momentum was established by the grassroots.

Coupled with widespread dissatisfaction at things as they are, expect a lot more of this grassroots activism, in both parties, over the coming years.

Written for *CQ Researcher*, March 2010

The Tea Party movement is indeed revivalist, but it revives not the egalitarian impulses of the 1740s or 1830s that fed the zeal of the Revolution and abolition. Rather it rehashes a tradition of racial, antigovernment populism that stretches from George Wallace's American Independent Party through Reagan Democrats to Sarah Palin Republicans.

In this tradition's origins mythology, a virtuous white citizenry became squeezed between liberal elites above and black dependents below as a result of civil rights and Johnson's Great Society. Since then, these Americans have resented taxation and social welfare, linking it to those whom they believe are recipients of special rights and government coddling. Thus, for the tea partiers and their immediate forebears the state is what monopoly capital was for 19th-century populists: a parasitic entity controlling their lives through opaque and malevolent machinations. It is worth noting that a significant percentage of tea partiers appear to be in their 60s or older — placing them in the generation that expressed the most negative reaction to the advances of the civil rights movement.

Why are we seeing this wave of protest now? The Tea Party movement has emerged out of the confluence of two momentous events: an enormous economic crisis and the election of a black president. The dislocations produced by the former have stoked the latent racial nationalism ignited by the latter. Obama represents both aspects of modern populist resentment — blackness and the state, and his perceived coziness with Wall Street taps into outrage felt toward banks right now. Add to this Glenn Beck's continual attacks on Obama and progressivism more generally, and you get a demonology that allows tea partiers to see tyranny wherever they look. (If "demonology" seems too strong a word here, look no further than the grotesque Joker-ized image of Obama over the word "Socialism" that has been omnipresent at Tea Party rallies.)

Will this movement transform the landscape? Third-party movements have impact when they can drive a wedge into the two-party system, creating a crisis that reframes the major political questions of the day. But the stated principles of the various Tea Party groups show them to be entirely consistent with the social conservative wing of the GOP. And there is a great overlap in leadership ties and funding sources as well, making it likely that the movement will find itself reabsorbed by the party with little independent impact.

establishment Republicans, the political landscape the Tea Party candidates face is really formidable."

Democrats view the tension between party professionals and conservative insurgents as a potential advantage. "You've got these very divisive primaries," Rep. Chris Van Hollen, D-Md., chairman of the House Democratic campaign organization, told *CQ Weekly*. "In many instances it's driving the primary way to the right."[45]

In some districts, Van Hollen suggested, primary victories by Tea Party-style Republicans could spell victory for centrist Democrats.

Political Realities

Fresh from his victory in Massachusetts, Sen. Brown is now a certified hero to Republicans, especially the Tea Party movement, which worked its heart out for him. Brown's victory was made all the sweeter by its location in the heart of blue-state America. But his first vote on Capitol Hill has conservatives talking about political realities.

Less than three weeks after he formally took office on Feb. 4, Brown joined four other Republicans in voting for a $15-billion jobs bill pushed by the Obama administration and Democratic Senate leader Harry Reid of Nevada. "I came to Washington to be an independent voice, to put politics aside and to do everything in my power to help create jobs for Massachusetts families," Brown said after the vote. "This Senate jobs bill is not perfect. I wish the tax cuts were deeper and broader, but I voted for it because it contains measures that will help put people back to work."[46]

His words did nothing to stem the tide of rage that poured onto his Facebook page — 4,200 comments in less than 24 hours after his Feb. 22 vote, the vast majority of them furious. As gleefully documented by the liberal *Huffington Post* news site, the comments included "LYING LOW LIFE SCUM HYPOCRITE!" and "YOU FAILED AT THE FIRST CHANCE" and "You sir, are a sellout."

But Michael Graham, a radio talk-show host and *Boston Herald* columnist in the Tea Party fold, mocked the outrage. "This is still Massachusetts," Graham wrote. "Brown will have to win a general election to keep this seat…. This one, relatively insignificant vote sent a powerful message to casual, Democrat-leaning voters that Brown isn't in the GOP bag…. It's brilliant politics."[47]

Chris Van Hollen, D-Md., chairman of the influential House Democratic Congressional Campaign Committee, helps guide House Democrats' fundraising and strategizing. He thinks the Tea Party activists may be driving the Republicans to the right and that primary victories by Tea Party-style Republicans could spell victory for centrist Democrats in November.

Graham is a political veteran, unlike many tea partiers. The movement, in fact, prides itself on its many political neophytes. "These are not people," Tea Party activist Freire, the *Washington Examiner* editor, said at the Washington panel discussion in February, "who are used to getting engaged in the process."

Although the panel discussion preceded Brown's vote by about a week, it delved into the tension between principles and pragmatism that surfaced after Brown's move. Other conservative lawmakers also have disappointed conservative backers, Freire noted. Rep. Paul Ryan, R-Wis., Freire said, "is a pretty reliable guy when it comes to his fiscal conservatism; he still voted for the bailout."

Third-Party Option

Democrats are nourishing the fond if unlikely hope that the Tea Party will turn into a full-fledged political party. "[That] would have a negative effect on Republicans, as would threatening to do that and influencing Republican candidates to move further to the right," says Neil Oxman of Philadelphia, cofounder of The Campaign Group political consulting firm.

For that reason, the third-party idea has not caught fire among tea partiers. "We don't need another party," says Carden, the Huntsville organizer. "We just need to use the vehicles for political change that are already there."

History points to that course as the most promising. Socialists, conservatives, libertarians and other political movements have long used third-party campaigns to build national support or at least publicize their ideas. Winning the White House isn't the goal.

In state races, candidates outside the two major parties have won, though such cases at the moment can be counted on one hand. Sen. Bernard Sanders of Vermont, a socialist who ran as an independent, is serving his first Senate term after 16 years in the House. Another senator, lifelong Connecticut Democrat Joseph I. Lieberman, is technically an independent, but he dropped that affiliation after losing a primary race to an Iraq War opponent.

The outcome of a bitter political fight in upstate New York last November would seem to confirm the two-party strategy as best for Republicans. In a special election to fill a newly vacated "safe" GOP House seat, the choice of a Republican legislator raised the hackles of conservatives nationwide, who viewed her as too liberal on abortion and gay rights. Instead, they backed a Conservative Party candidate — who eventually lost to Democrat Owens. His backers included the onetime Republican candidate Dede Scozzafava, who denounced what she viewed as betrayal by the GOP.[48]

"This election represents a double blow for national Republicans and their hopes of translating this summer's Tea Party energy into victories at the ballot box," Van Hollen, the Democratic Congressional Campaign Committee chairman, said.[49]

In New York state, Conservative Party candidate Hoffman's backers included Sarah Palin and former Rep. Dick Armey of Texas, a Tea Party booster and former House Republican leader who is president of FreedomWorks, a Washington-based activist-training organization whose politics run along Tea Party lines.

The New York debacle was followed by Brown's triumph in Massachusetts. That Brown ran as a Republican seemed to confirm the wisdom of channeling Tea Party activism into GOP campaigns.

Republican strategy guru Karl Rove, the top campaign and White House adviser to former President George W. Bush, is warning Tea Party groups to stay in the Republican fold. "There's a danger from them," he told *USA Today* recently, "particularly if they're used by political operators ... to try and hijack" elections.[50]

Rove could have had Nevada in mind. There, a candidate from the "Tea Party of Nevada" has filed to oppose Senate Majority Leader Reid in the GOP primary.

Leaders of Nevada's Tea Party movement told the conservative *Washington Times* that they don't recognize the names on the Tea Party of Nevada filing documents. They claimed the third party was created on Reid's behalf to siphon Republican votes. But the candidate said by mail, "I am not for Harry Reid. . . .

My candidacy is real." The Reid campaign didn't return a call to the *Times*' reporter.[51] Whatever the sincerity of the Nevada Tea Party, grassroots conservatives elsewhere who are disenchanted with the GOP argue that the best course is to fight within the party. "Use the Republican Party to your advantage," Chicago tea partier Eric Odom wrote on his blog. "Move in and take it over."[52]

OUTLOOK

Short Life?

In the hyperspeed political environment, evaluating the 10-year prospects for a newly emerged movement is an iffy proposition. Still, a consensus is emerging that the Tea Party's ideas will last longer than the movement itself.

"These ideas are endemic in American political culture," says Sides of George Washington University. "Whether we will be able to attach them to a movement or an organization we call the Tea Party is an open question."

Georgia Tea Party activist Martin acknowledges the movement may dissolve over the next decade. "If there isn't a movement 10 years from now, I hope it's faded away because people understand what the country's core values are and don't need to be reminded."

Whatever the state of national consciousness in the near future, the life cycle of social movements in their most influential phase arguably has never been very long, even before the pace of modern life quickened to its present pace. "In their dynamic, growing, inspirational, 'we-can-change-the-world' stage, they last five to seven years," says Kazin of Georgetown University.

The labor union movement's high point ran from 1933 to 1938, Kazin says. And the civil rights movement in its nationwide, unified phase ran from just 1960 to 1965. "And those were movements that were more independent of a political party structure," he adds.

As a movement closely linked to the Republican Party, the Tea Party's future will depend greatly on the course of the 2010 elections, Kazin argues. And which GOP candidates are nominated for president in 2012 will offer an even clearer gauge of the movement's influence.

Hawkins of *Right Wing News* thinks he knows where the Tea Party will be in 10 years. "I tend to doubt it will exist," he says. "It will have been absorbed into the Republican Party."

But the University of Oregon's Lowndes argues that beyond the country's Republican strongholds, the Tea Party won't acquire enough influence to reconfigure the entire party. "It will shape politics in certain places, and shape the Republican Party, but it won't take it over."

For now, however, Lowndes credits the Tea Party with effectively pulling together strands of discontent. "With enormous power concentrated in the executive branch and in corporations, there is a sense of powerlessness at work that can be picked up and interpreted different ways by different folks," he says. "These people have found a language for it that the left has not."

Jonah Goldberg, high-profile editor of *National Review Online*, urged conservatives during the America's Future Foundation panel discussion in February to come to terms with the nature of the political system. "The American people aren't as conservative as we would like them to be, and they never will be," he said, despite what seem to be favorable conditions for the right that largely grow out of the Tea Party's success.

"Things are so much better than they seemed to be a little while ago," he continued. "Will Republicans blow it? They have a great history of that. One of the things that movements do is try to keep politicians honest. That's going to be hard work because politicians are politicians."

Reynolds of the University of Tennessee Law School acknowledges that the Tea Party's promise may go unfulfilled. Conservative hopes ran high after the 1994 Republican takeover of Congress midway through the first Clinton administration, he notes. "But that didn't have long-lasting legs."

On the other hand, Reynolds says, the Reagan legacy has been long-lasting. "And this is probably bigger," he says of the Tea Party.

But there are no guarantees, he cautions. "A lot of people are involved in politics who never were before. In 10 years, some will have gone back to their lives. Of the people who stay in, the odds are that many will become politicians as usual. The question is how much this will happen."

UPDATE

A political activist dressed as a hero of the American Revolution joined with a small group of fellow conservatives in early May to denounce Washington politicians in the name of the Tea Party. Nothing surprising in that — except that the politicians under attack are Republicans.

"Yes, we've been deeply disappointed," said William Temple of Brunswick, Ga., at a Washington news conference. He named House Speaker John Boehner, R-Ohio, as the main source of disenchantment. "Mr. Boehner has been a 'surrenderist' who waves the white flag before the first shots are fired." Temple, wearing a tricorner hat, boots and other 18th-century garb, leaned his musket against a wall when he took to the lectern at the National Press Club in Washington. [53]

The episode was one of many marking the complicated follow-up to Tea Party-driven Republican election successes in 2010. Temple and his half-dozen companions vowed that Boehner, House Budget Committee Chairman Paul Ryan, R-Wis., and other House Republicans would pay a political price if they defied demands of the loose-knit Tea Party movement. At the top of their wish list: massive government spending cuts.

Instead, House leaders have signaled they're willing to go along with raising the "debt ceiling," the limit on how much government can borrow. "This debt limit . . . provides the perfect opportunity to substantially reduce the size and scope of the federal government," said Bob Vander Plaats, vice chair of a Tea Party convention scheduled for Kansas City in October. A loser in last year's Republican gubernatorial primary in Iowa, Vander Plaats remains a top political player in a state whose early primaries are a critical early test for presidential candidates. [54]

Sporting patriotic red, white and blue, a Tea Party supporter attends a Tax Day rally in Chicago on April 18, 2011, calling for massive government spending cuts and tax reform. Tea Party members have been angry at House Republican leaders for signaling they may support raising the nation's debt ceiling.

Testing Time

The Tea Party's ability to sustain the support it gathered last November will be tested as well. Tea Party members and sympathizers played a major part in helping shift control of the House to a 242-193 Republican majority — about 30 of whom had been endorsed by Tea Party groups. That victory, which followed months of demonstrations, marches and frenetic organizing activity by Tea Party members, was limited to the House. The Senate remains in the hands of a Democratic majority though Republicans gained six seats. [55]

Speaker Boehner, who presides over the House GOP majority, seemed to confirm the Tea Party activists' increasingly dire view of him in a speech he gave on the evening following their press conference. As they expected, he signaled willingness to approve a debt-ceiling increase. But in a nod to the Tea Party, he conditioned approval on trillions of dollars of cuts in federal spending. [56]

Whether that would satisfy the activists remains to be seen. Joining with their staunchest congressional allies, they had previously failed in an effort to convince Boehner and other leaders to refuse to reach a temporary budget compromise with the Senate and White House. The move averted a government shutdown. But Rep.

Mike Pence, R-Ind. had urged holding fast. "It's time to pick a fight!" he had told a small rally outside the Capitol. "If liberals in the Senate want to play political games . . ., I say shut it down." [57]

'Unrealistic Expectations'

In another show of Tea Party independence from the Republicans, Rep. Michele Bachmann, R-Minn., chair of the Tea Party Caucus in the House, delivered a response to President Obama's State of the Union address separate from the official Republican response. [58]

Political observers have been arguing that politicians who identify with the Tea Party may have overestimated their power. "The standards they set for themselves in terms of budget cutting and deficit reduction were very high, and the expectations were unrealistic," said Robert Bixby, executive director of the Concord Coalition, a nonpartisan organization directed by members of the political establishment that advocates spending cuts. "Some of the leaders in the House, Boehner and Ryan, do have a bit of a problem in trying to write a tough and realistic budget that can get done, and tamping down some of the unrealistic expectations," Bixby told the *Los Angeles Times.* [59]

And Tea Party strategists may have overestimated the movement's appeal outside its red-state, suburban base. Sen. Scott Brown, R-Mass., who scored a stunning victory last year in a special election for the seat of the late Sen. Edward M. "Ted" Kennedy, a Democratic icon, has taken pains to distance himself from the movement. Along with others more closely identified with the movement, Brown didn't join the Senate Tea Party Caucus. And, asked if he was a Tea Party member, he told *USA Today*, "No, I'm a Republican from Massachusetts." [60]

Pressure to Deliver

For their part, Tea Party-backed lawmakers have expressed frustration at being hemmed in on one side by Democratic opposition in the Senate, and on the other by political commitments to constituents.

"If we don't do a real serious job with spending these next two years, then I think that voters in my district will feel that I didn't deliver," Rep. Joe Walsh, R-Ill., a freshman who was part of the Tea Party wave of House members in last year's election, said in January. [61]

Getty Images/Scott Olson

By early May, Walsh was echoing activists' criticisms of Republican House leaders. In his case, he took issue with their abandonment of a proposal to transform Medicare, the program of government subsidies of health-care costs for the elderly. Under a plan that the House passed in March, senior citizens (starting in 2022) would get vouchers to buy private insurance.[62]

"I would be very disappointed if we didn't follow through," Walsh said, after top Republicans indicated they wouldn't try to push the Medicare plan any further. A fellow Illinois Tea Party Republican, Rep. Bobby Schilling, went further. Giving up on the proposal, he said, would amount to surrendering "to lies and deceit told by the other side."[63]

But the Medicare proposal was turning into a rallying cry for Democrats, as well as for some Medicare beneficiaries who had voted for Republicans in 2010. Republican lawmakers came face-to-face with that reality at town hall meetings they held in their districts during the spring recess. Some of those meetings turned into role-reversed versions of constituent meetings in 2009, at which Tea Party opposition to the administration's health-care legislation seized the headlines and spurred the movement's rapid growth.

Signs of Discord

At this year's meetings, however, crowds turned out to grill and heckle Republicans who had voted for the Medicare plan. A woman in Racine, Wis., attending a meeting held by Rep. Ryan, the author of the plan, held up a sign that read, "We use up the voucher, and then what?" In Orlando, shouts and arguments over Tea Party Republican Rep. Daniel Webster's support for the plan grew so loud that Webster at one point quit talking.[64]

Not all town meetings turned raucous. But the Medicare plan seemed to be turning into a liability. Even after top Republicans backed away from the proposal, Democrats vowed to keep exploiting the issue. "The Republicans are slowly realizing their plan to privatize Medicare is a political disaster," said Sen. Charles E. Schumer, D-N.Y., a spokesman for Senate Democrats. "But until they renounce their vote for it, they are still going to own it."[65]

Yet, as they continue marking a distance between themselves and the Republican establishment, Tea Party members are showing signs of discord within their movement.

In Arizona, some Tea Party members have rallied against the creation of automobile license plates emblazoned with a Revolutionary War slogan they've adopted —"Don't Tread on Me." Tea Party groups can sell the tags to raise money. But, Tea Party member Jim Wise of Surprise, Ariz., isn't buying one. "I realize the people behind this had the best of intentions," he said, "but it goes against what we stand for, which is limited government."[66]

Despite such rifts, there's little doubt that Tea Party movement supporters do agree on the issue of federal spending. The anti-Boehner press conference was only one sign of Tea Party members' determination on that score, expressed as resistance to a debt-ceiling increase. The Tea Party Express, one of the movement's national organizations, was planning a national TV ad campaign on that theme.

"The GOP is on probation," the organization's chair, Amy Kremer, told *The Atlantic*, "because under President Bush they spent a lot of money, and added $3 trillion to the national debt." She added, "You will see that the Tea Party will have no problem whatsoever challenging the very freshmen they put in."[67]

NOTES

1. Kathleen Hennessey, "Justice's wife launches 'tea party' group," *Los Angeles Times*, March 14, 2010, www.latimes.com/news/nation-and-world/la-na-thomas142010mar14,0,3190750,full.story.

2. Mark Leibovich, "Discipline Helped Carve Path to Senate," *The New York Times*, Jan. 21, 2010, www.nytimes.com/2010/01/21/us/politics/21brown.html.

3. Zachary Ross, "Top Tea Partier, Husband, Owed IRS Half a Million Dollars," *Talking Points Memo*, Oct. 8, 2009, http://tpmmuckraker.talkingpointsmemo.com/2009/10/top_tea_partier_husband_owed_irs_half_a_million_do.php.

4. Jeff Zeleny, "Daniels Offers Advice to Republicans," *The New York Times*, The Caucus (blog), March 9, 2010, http://thecaucus.blogs.nytimes.com/2010/03/09/daniels-offers-advice-to-republicans/.

5. "Tom Tancredo's Feb. 4 Tea party speech in Nashville," *Free Republic*, Feb. 5, 2010, http://freerepublic.com/focus/f-news/2445943/posts.

6. Cuéntame, www.facebook.com/cuentame?v=app_11007063052.

7. John Maggs, "Norquist on Tea and Taxes," *National Journal*, Feb. 4, 2010, http://insiderinterviews .nationaljournal.com/2010/02/-nj-were-you-sur prised.php.

8. *Ibid.* Also see Tea Party Nation, teapartynation.com; and Kate Zernike, "Seeking a Big Tent, Tea Party Avoids Divisive Social Issues," *The New York Times*, March 13, 2010, p. A1.

9. John M. O'Hara, *A New American Tea Party: The Counterrevolution Against Bailouts, Handouts, Reckless Spending, and More Taxes* (2010), pp. 256-257.

10. "Rick Santelli Rant Transcript," www.reteaparty .com/2009/02/19/rick-santelli-rant-transcript/.

11. *Ibid.*; Brian Stelter, "CNBC Replays Its Reporter's Tirade," *The New York Times*, Feb.23, 2009, p. B7.

12. Mary Lou Pickel, "Tea Party at the Capitol," *Atlanta Journal-Constitution,* Feb. 28, 2009; Aman Batheja, "Several hundred protest Obama stimulus program in Fort Worth," *Fort Worth Star-Telegram*, Feb. 28, 2009; "Tea Party Time," *New York Post*, Feb. 28, 2009, p. 16; Tim O'Neil, "Riverfront tea party protest blasts Obama's stimulus plan," *St. Louis Post-Dispatch*, Feb. 28, 2009, p. A7; Christian M. Wade, "Tax Protesters Converge on Federal Courthouse," *Tampa Tribune*, Feb. 28, 2009, p. A4; "Protesters bemoan stimulus funds at Tenn. Capitol," The Associated Press, Feb. 28, 2009.

13. Kate Zernike, "Unlikely Activist Who Got to the Tea Party Early," *The New York Times*, Feb. 27, 2010, www.nytimes.com/2010/02/28/us/politics/28keli .html.

14. Quoted in David M. Halbfinger and Ian Urbina, "Republicans Bask in Glow of Victories in N.J. and Va.," *The New York Times*, Nov. 5, 2009; Janet Hook, "Stimulus bill battle is only the beginning," *Los Angeles Times*, Feb. 15, 2009, p. A1.

15. Quoted in Manu Raju, "Lindsey Graham warns GOP against going too far right," *Politico*, Nov. 4, 2009, www.politico.com/news/stories/1109/29131 .html.

16. Chelsea Schilling, " 'Government wants to be your one and only god,' " *WorldNetDaily*, Feb. 6, 2010, www.wnd.com/index.php?pageId=124326.

17. Jonathan Raban, "At the Tea Party," *New York Review of Books*, March 25, 2010, www.nybooks.com/articles/23723.

18. For background, see Peter Katel, "Press Freedom," *CQ Researcher*, Feb. 5, 2010, pp. 97-120.

19. Quoted in David Weigel, "Birther Speaker Takes Heat at Tea Party Convention," *Washington Independent*, Feb. 6, 2010 (includes audio clip of argument), http://washingtonindependent.com/75949/birther-speaker-takes-heat-at-tea-party-convention.

20. Except where otherwise indicated, this subsection is drawn from Michael Kazin, *The Populist Persuasion: An American History* (1998).

21. Quoted in Daniel Feller, "King Andrew and the Bank," *Humanities*, National Endowment for the Humanities, January-February, 2008, www.neh.gov/news/humanities/2008-01/KingAndrewandtheBank.html.

22. "Bryan's 'Cross of Gold' Speech: Mesmerizing the Masses," *History Matters*, undated, http://history-matters.gmu.edu/d/5354/.

23. Steve Oney, "The Leo Frank case isn't dead," *Los Angeles Times*, Oct. 30, 2009, http://articles.latimes.com/2009/oct/30/opinion/oe-oney30. Except where otherwise indicated, this subsection is drawn from Kazin, *op. cit.*

24. William E. Leuchtenburg, *Franklin D. Roosevelt and the New Deal* (1963), pp. 33, 255, 335-336.

25. For background, see Peter Katel, "Hate Groups," *CQ Researcher*, May 8, 2009, pp. 421-448.

26. Douglas Martin, "William F. Buckley Jr., 82, Dies," *The New York Times*, Feb. 28, 2008, p. A1.

27. Kazin, *op. cit.*, p. 193. For background on the G.I. Bill, see "Record of 78th Congress (Second Session)," *Editorial Research Reports*, Dec. 20, 1944, available at *CQ Researcher Plus Archive*; K. Lee, "War Veterans in Civil Life," *Editorial Research Reports*, Vol. II, 1946; and William Triplett, "Treatment of Veterans," *CQ Researcher*, Nov. 19, 2004, pp. 973-996.

28. Todd Gitlin, *The Sixties: Years of Hope, Days of Rage* (1993), pp. 348-351.

29. Quoted in Kazin, *op. cit.*, p. 252.

30. *Ibid.*, pp. 234-235.

31. Richard Pearson, "Former Ala. Gov. George C. Wallace Dies," *The Washington Post*, Sept. 14, 1998, p. A1, www.washingtonpost.com/wp-srv/politics/daily/sept98/wallace.htm.

32. Rick Perlstein, *Nixonland: The Rise of a President and the Fracturing of America* (2008), pp. 631-632.

33. Except where otherwise indicated, this subsection draws from *ibid.*

34. "George McGovern Interview," The National World War II Museum, undated, www.nationalww2museum.org/wwii-community/mcgovern.html.

35. Quoted in Perlstein, *op. cit.*, pp. 732-733.

36. H. Ross Perot, "What Americans Must Demand," *The Washington Post*, March 29, 1992, p. C2.

37. Quoted in John Dillin, "Possible Presidential Bid by Perot Is Seen Posing a Threat to Bush," *The Christian Science Monitor*, March 24, 1992, p. 1.

38. Quoted in *ibid.*

39. John Mintz, "Perot Embodied Dismay of Millions," *The Washington Post*, Nov. 4, 1992, p. A26; Jeffrey Schmalz, "Clinton Carves a Wide Path Deep Into Clinton Country," *The New York Times*, Nov. 4, 1992, p. B1.

40. Thomas B. Edsall and E. J. Dionne, "White, Younger, Lower-Income Voters Turn Against G.O.P.," *The Washington Post*, Nov. 4, 1992, p. A21.

41. Quoted in Sasha Issenberg, "In book, Romney styles himself wonk, not warrior," *Boston Globe*, March, 2, 2010, www.boston.com/news/nation/washington/articles/2010/03/02/mitt_romneys_no_apology_is_not_light_reading?mode=PF.

42. Emily Cadei, "Sands of GOP Discord in Arizona," *Roll Call*, Jan. 28, 2010.

43. Quoted in Liz Sidoti, "Excited GOP: Energy on the right, divisions within," The Associated Press, Feb. 19, 2010. Adam Nagourney and Carl Hulse, "Re-energized, G.O.P. Widens Midterm Effort," *The New York Times*, Jan. 25, 2010, p. A1; Thomas Burr, "GOP's Armey backs Lee, scolds Bennett," *Salt Lake Tribune*, Feb. 18, 2010.

44. Quoted in *ibid.*

45. Quoted in Joseph J. Schatz, "Reading the Leaves," *CQ Weekly*, March 1, 2010, pp. 480-489.

46. Quoted in James Oliphant, "Scott Brown's 'tea party' fans feel burned by jobs vote," *Los Angeles Times*, Feb. 23, 2010, http://articles.latimes.com/2010/feb/23/nation/la-na-scott-brown24-2010feb24.

47. Michael Graham, "Still right cup of tea," *Boston Herald*, Feb. 25, 2010, www.bostonherald.com/news/opinion/op_ed/view.bg?articleid=1235356.

48. Jeremy W. Peters, "Conservative Loses Upstate House Race in Blow to Right," *The New York Times*, Nov. 3, 2009, www.nytimes.com/2009/11/04/nyregion/04district.html?_r=1&scp=9&sq=HoffmanScozzafava&st=cse.

49. Quoted in *ibid.*

50. Judy Keen, "Rove: 'Tea Party' may be risk to GOP," *USA Today*, March 10, 2010, p. A1.

51. Quoted in Valerie Richardson, "New party brings its own 'tea' to election," *The Washington Times*, Feb. 22, 2010, p. A1.

52. Quoted in Kate Zernike, "In Power Push, Movement Sees Base in G.O.P.," *The New York Times*, Jan. 15, 2010, p. A1.

53. For a video of the press conference, see "Federal Debt Ceiling and Debt," C-Span, May 9, 2011, www.c-span.org/Events/Tea-Party-Activists-Take-on-GOP-on-Deficit/10737421394-1/.

54. *Ibid.*; Kerry Howley, "The Road to Iowa is Paved With Pizza," *The New York Times*, March 11, 2011, www.nytimes.com/2011/03/13/magazine/mag-13YouRHere-t.html?scp=1&sq=%22Bob%20vander%20Plaats%22&st=cse; Joshua Green, "The Iowa Caucus Kingmaker," *The Atlantic*, May 2011, www.theatlantic.com/magazine/archive/2011/05/the-iowa-caucus-kingmaker/8446/.

55. Rick Rojas, "Last midterm House, governor races end," *Los Angeles Times*, Dec. 9, 2010, p. A24.

56. Carl Hulse, "Boehner Outlines Demands on Debt Limit Fight," *The New York Times*, May 9, 2011, www.nytimes.com/2011/05/10/us/politics/10boehner.html?_r=1&ref=politics.

57. Quoted in Doyle McManus, "No party for John Boehner," *Los Angeles Times*, April 3, 2011, p. A28.

58. David A. Farenthold, "Republicans decry debt, offer few detailed fixes," *The Washington Post*, Jan. 26, 2011, p. A9.

59. Quoted in Lisa Mascaro, "Cracks show as GOP tackles budget," *Los Angeles Times*, Jan. 25, 2011, p. A1.

60. Quoted in Susan Page, "Sen. Brown keeps 'an open mind,' " *USA Today*, Feb. 21, 2011, p. A4.

61. Quoted in *ibid.*

62. Noam N. Levey, "Rep. Paul Ryan's Medicare privatization plan increases costs, budget office says," *Los Angeles Times*, April 7, 2011, http://articles.latimes.com/2011/apr/07/nation/la-na-gop-budget-20110408.

63. Quoted in Carl Hulse and Jackie Calmes, "G.O.P. Rethinking Bid to Overhaul Medicare Rules," *The New York Times*, May 5, 2011, www.nytimes.com/2011/05/06/us/politics/06fiscal.html?ref=politics.

64. Mike Schneider and Dinesh Ramde, "Congressional Republicans go home to mixed reviews," The Associated Press, April 26, 2011.

65. Quoted in Hulse and Calmes, *op. cit.*

66. Quoted in Marc Lacey, "In Arizona, Tea Party License Plate Draws Opposition From its Honorees," *The New York Times*, May 4, 2011, www.nytimes.com/2011/05/05/us/05plates.html.

67. Eliza Newlin Carney, "Tea Party Puts the Screws to House Republicans Over Debt Ceiling," *The Atlantic.com*, May 9, 2011, www.theatlantic.com/politics/archive/2011/05/tea-party-puts-the-screws-to-house-republicans-over-debt-ceiling/238640/.

BIBLIOGRAPHY

Books

Continetti, Matthew, The Persecution of Sarah Palin: How the Elite Media Tried to Bring Down a Rising Star, Sentinel, 2009.
An editor of the conservative *Weekly Standard* chronicles the rise of Tea Party-friendly Palin from a sympathetic perspective.

Kazin, Michael, The Populist Persuasion: An American History, Cornell University Press, 1998.
A Georgetown University historian traces the forms that an enduring American distrust of elites has taken.

O'Hara, John M., A New American Tea Party: The Counterrevolution Against Bailouts, Handouts, Reckless Spending, and More Taxes, John Wiley & Sons, 2010.
A manifesto in book form by one of the first Tea Party activists tells of the movement's formation and ideas.

Perlstein, Rick, Nixonland: The Rise of a President and the Fracturing of America, Scribner, 2008.
A non-academic historian adds to the Tea Party story with this account of Nixon and his appeal to the "silent majority."

Articles

Barstow, David, "Tea Party Lights Fuse for Rebellion on Right," The New York Times, Feb. 15, 2010, www.nytimes.com/2010/02/16/us/politics/16teaparty.html.
A lengthy, detailed report traces the formation of a Tea Party undercurrent of conspiracists and militia members.

Continetti, Matthew, "Sarah Palin and the Tea Party, Cont.," Weekly Standard, Feb. 8, 2010, www.weeklystandard.com/print/blogs/sarah-palin-and-tea-party-cont.
The author of a sympathetic book on Palin argues she made a powerful case for herself as a 2012 presidential candidate.

Good, Chris, "Some Tea Partiers Question Meeting With Steele," The Atlantic, Politics site, Feb. 16, 2010, www.theatlantic.com/politics/archive/2010/02/some-tea-partiers-question-meeting-with-steele/36027/.
Some Florida tea partiers questioned the movement credentials of a political activist who organized a meeting with Michael Steele, the controversial Republican national chairman.

Hennessey, Kathleen, "Justice's wife launches 'tea party' group," Los Angeles Times, March 14, 2010, www.latimes.com/news/nation-and-world/la-na-thomas14-2010mar14,0,3190750,full.story.

This is the first report of the Tea Party activism of Virginia Thomas, wife of Supreme Court Justice Clarence Thomas.

Markon, Jerry, " 'Wired' conservatives get the message out," The Washington Post, Feb. 1, 2010, p. A1.
Tea Party organizers made extensive use of social networking tools and Republican connections in getting the movement up and running, a political correspondent reports.

Naymik, Mark, "GOP stumbles with Tea Party as movement gains foothold," Cleveland Plain Dealer, Feb. 21, 2010, p. A1.
A leading newspaper in a key political state reports on ambivalent relations between tea partiers and the Republican Party.

Parker, Kathleen, "The GOP's misguided hunt for heretics," The Washington Post, Feb. 24, 2010, www .washingtonpost.com/wp-dyn/content/article/2010/ 02/23/AR2010022303783.html.
A conservative columnist warns of a tendency to zealotry and intolerance among tea partiers.

Rucker, Philip, "GOP woos wary 'tea party' activists," The Washington Post, Jan. 20, 2010, p. A4.
Republican officials are courting Tea Party members, Washington's leading newspaper reports.

Sidoti, Liz, "Primary time: Let the political family feuds begin," The Associated Press, Jan. 30, 2010.
The Tea Party movement's political strength will be tested in some key primary elections, a political correspondent reports.

Tanenhaus, Sam, "The Crescendo of the Rally Cry," The New York Times, Jan. 24, 2010, Week in Review, p. 1.
A *Times* editor who writes on the history of conservatism examines the Tea Party movement in light of past populist surges.

Wilkinson, Howard, "Tea Partiers aim to remake local GOP," Cincinnati Enquirer, Jan. 30, 2010.
Tea partiers in southwest Ohio are making a concerted effort to take over Republican precinct organizations.

Zernike, Kate, "Seeking a Big Tent, Tea Party Avoids Divisive Social Issues," The New York Times, March 13, 2010, p. A1.
Some Tea Party activists deliberately bypass controversial social issues, a correspondent specializing in the Tea Party reports.

Reports

"AEI Political Report," American Enterprise Institute for Public Policy Research, February 2010, www.aei .org/docLib/Political-Report-Feb-2010.pdf.
A compilation of survey results from a variety of sources includes data on public knowledge of the Tea Party.

For More Information

Coffee Party, www.coffeepartyusa.com. A new network of Tea Party opponents.

FreedomWorks, 601 Pennsylvania Ave., N.W., North Building, Washington, DC 20004; (202) 783-3870; www .freedomworks.org. Created by former House Republican Leader Dick Armey, the conservative organization trains local activists.

Politics1, 409 N.E. 17th Ave., Fort Lauderdale, FL 33301; www.politics1.com/index.htm. Comprehensive political site offering a guide to races involving Tea Party candidates.

Right Wing News, rightwingnews.com. Independent Web site covers Tea Party movement, often critically.

Talkingpointsmemo, www.talkingpointsmemo.com. Democratic-oriented news site provides critical but fact-based coverage of Tea Party.

Tea Party Patriots, www.teapartypatriots.org. An extensive network of Tea Party groups around the country offering movement news and views from its Web site.

11

Managing Nuclear Waste

Jennifer Weeks

A blue glow bathes nuclear waste submerged in water for cooling at one of the 100-plus waste storage sites throughout the United States. After submersion for several years, the waste still remains dangerously radioactive for thousands of years and must be isolated to protect the environment. The Obama administration recently sought to block longstanding plans to bury the nation's nuclear waste at a single repository under Yucca Mountain, in Nevada.

From *CQ Researcher*, Jan 28, 2011.

U. S. Department of Energy

At Dominion Power's nuclear power station in Waterford, Conn., 14 massive steel canisters lie entombed in concrete bunkers in a high-security area.

The protection is needed because the so-called "dry casks" hold nuclear waste that emits dangerous levels of heat and radiation. The used — or "spent" — nuclear fuel was first cooled in special pools for several years, but it will remain a health hazard for hundreds of thousands of years.

Storing spent fuel on-site wasn't the original plan for the Waterford plant or dozens of others across the nation. A 1982 law made disposing of spent fuel the federal government's responsibility. Waste was supposed to be sent to an underground complex that the Department of Energy (DOE) was developing under Yucca Mountain in the southern Nevada desert.

Starting in the late 1980s, DOE planned to ship spent fuel from local power plants to the site, which was scheduled to open in 1998. The repository plan called for drilling a 40-mile network of tunnels about 1,000 feet below the surface. Burying spent fuel and other radioactive waste in the mountain's "tuff" (hardened volcanic ash) would isolate it from the environment for up to 1 million years, DOE said.[1]

But technical challenges, funding shortfalls and opposition from Nevada officials, including Senate Majority Leader Harry Reid, put work on Yucca Mountain years behind schedule. The project has been dogged by such intense scientific and political controversy that the Center for Public Integrity, a nonpartisan research group in Washington, calls it an example of "broken government."[2] Many critics believe that design flaws and earthquake activity at the site

Illinois Tops Nation in Spent-Fuel Storage

With nearly 8,000 metric tons, Illinois leads the nation in the storage of used commercial nuclear fuel. Only four other states exceed 3,000 tons. Twelve states store no nuclear fuel.

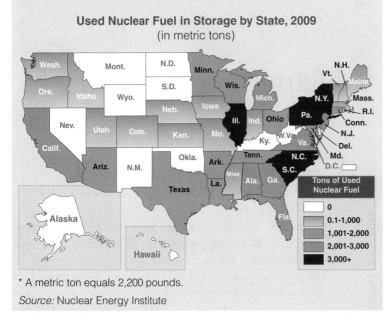

Used Nuclear Fuel in Storage by State, 2009
(in metric tons)

Tons of Used Nuclear Fuel
- 0
- 0.1–1,000
- 1,001–2,000
- 2,001–3,000
- 3,000+

* A metric ton equals 2,200 pounds.

Source: Nuclear Energy Institute

could cause radioactive waste to leak and contaminate groundwater.[3]

President Barack Obama supports expanding nuclear power but says Yucca Mountain is not the right place to store nuclear waste. During the 2008 presidential campaign he argued that "it is time to start exploring new alternatives for safe, long-term solutions based on sound science."[4] Obama has asked Congress to terminate funding for Yucca Mountain and suspended Nuclear Regulatory Commission (NRC) review of a license application for the repository that President George W. Bush submitted in 2008. And last March Obama created a Blue Ribbon Commission, which includes scientists, energy industry executives and former elected officials and regulators, to recommend new waste-storage options.

Nuclear power generates about 20 percent of the nation's electricity, and supporters promote it as a clean energy source that does not generate pollutants or contribute to climate change. But no new reactor has entered operation in the United States since 1996. Orders for new plants fell sharply after the partial meltdown of the

reactor core at the Three Mile Island nuclear plant in Harrisburg, Pa., in 1979. Most of the 104 reactors operating today in the United States were built in the 1970s and '80s, and a few date back to the 1960s.[5] Utilities are planning a handful of new plants today, mainly in Southern states at sites where reactors already operate.[6]

In the near term, experts across the political spectrum say, economics is the biggest obstacle to a nuclear-power renaissance because reactors cost more to build than plants powered by coal, natural gas or wind. But they also agree that the nation needs a consistent policy for handling nuclear waste.[7]

"Sustainability of nuclear power in the U.S. depends on reducing the costs of nuclear plants," says Tom Cochran, a senior scientist at the Natural Resources Defense Council (NRDC), an environmental advocacy group. In Cochran's view, spent nuclear fuel stored at commercial reactors does not pose major public safety risks today. "But if you look hundreds or thousands of years ahead, we have a responsibility to set up institutions for managing it. We're 60 years into the nuclear era, and it's time to get going," he says.

Since the first commercial reactor started up in 1957, nuclear plants have produced about 65,000 metric tons of spent fuel, which is now stored at reactors across the nation. When fuel is unloaded from a reactor, it is extremely hot and highly radioactive. It goes into specially designed cooling pools, where it remains under at least 20 feet of water for a minimum of several years. But there are safety limits on how densely spent fuel can be packed into cooling pools without starting a chain reaction that could cause an accident. As a result, NRC has given 38 nuclear plants permission to build dry cask storage on-site for older, cooler fuel because their spent-fuel pools are full or nearly full.[8]

Spent fuel also is stored at a dozen sites where reactors have shut down. At some of these sites the entire plant has been demolished and removed, leaving only fences and guards protecting fuel canisters.

The federal government is also responsible for disposing of up to 20,000 metric tons of spent fuel and high-level radioactive waste — most of it left over from manufacturing nuclear weapons — at federally owned sites.[9]

Transporting nuclear waste poses special challenges because of the risk of contamination along the route, accidents involving trucks or rail cars carrying waste and the potential threat of attacks by terrorists.

Many critics say that a private or government-owned corporation could solve the nuclear waste problem more effectively than DOE. "Federal agencies aren't well-structured to run programs like this," says Rodney McCullum, director of used-fuel programs for the Nuclear Energy Institute, the industry's policy organization. "Managers change every two to four years; agencies are politically driven and they are subject to annual congressional budget cycles."

Congress is part of the problem, utilities argue, because instead of using mandatory fees that utilities pay into the federal Nuclear Waste Fund to work on radioactive waste disposal, it has spent much of that money on other government activities. Since 1983 nuclear utilities have paid more than $25 billion into the fund — money that they recover in fees charged to their electricity customers — but have not received any waste disposal services in return. Instead, many are paying extra for dry cask storage.

"Money appropriated from ratepayers for a specific purpose should be spent for that purpose," says David Boyd, chair of the Minnesota Public Utilities Commission and head of the National Association of Regulatory Utility Commissioners (NARUC) Subcommittee on Nuclear Issues and Waste Disposal. "We'd like to handle it more like a dedicated trust fund."

Today the waste fund's balance is more than $24 billion. But Boyd says that because Congress has effectively borrowed much of that money, the fund is little more than "a pile of IOUs from previous Congresses."

Obama's Blue Ribbon Commission, which is scheduled to issue a final report next year, is charged with reviewing "all alternatives for the storage, processing and disposal of civilian and defense used nuclear fuel, high-level waste and materials derived from nuclear activities."[10] The commission is not authorized to choose a new repository site but could recommend new guidelines for designing and locating a facility that would be more acceptable to local communities and other stakeholders than Yucca Mountain.

The commission may endorse current U.S. policy, known as the "once-through" cycle, in which nuclear

Spent Fuel Stored in Casks

The need for alternative storage of spent nuclear fuel developed in the late 1970s and early '80s when pools at many nuclear reactors began to fill with stored spent fuel. Dry casks, which typically are steel containers that are welded or bolted shut, keep spent fuel isolated from the environment. Cask storage is considered safe and environmentally sound and is resistant to floods, tornadoes, extreme temperatures and other unusual conditions. The Nuclear Regulatory Commission requires spent fuel to be cooled in pools for at least five years before being transferred to casks.

Dry Storage of Spent Fuel

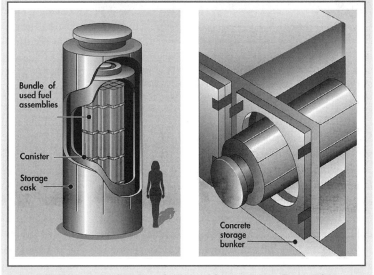

Source: "Fact Sheet on Dry Cask Storage of Spent Nuclear Fuel," U.S. Nuclear Regulatory Commission, December 2008

U.S. Department of Energy

Cleanup workers using breathing tanks and wearing protective suits prepare a cooling basin for demolition at the Hanford nuclear site in Washington state. Radioactive fuel rods that were stored underwater for decades in the plant's basins leaked contaminated water into the surrounding soil.

fuel is irradiated once in the reactor, then permanently stored underground.

Or it could propose new policies, such as reprocessing (chemically treating) spent fuel to recover residual uranium and plutonium that can be reused to generate more electricity. This approach, known as a closed fuel cycle, was the original blueprint for U.S. nuclear power in the 1950s and '60s. But it was abandoned in the 1970s after concern arose that plutonium from commercial reactor fuel could be used in nuclear weapons.

Critics point out that reprocessing is expensive, and that in addition to producing weapon-usable plutonium it also generates new types of high-level radioactive waste, which can be liquids, solids or sludges and are extremely hazardous.[11]

Nuclear engineers say they can develop safer, cleaner reprocessing methods that will not create weapon-usable plutonium. But the United States has worked for years to limit the spread of reprocessing abroad in order to slow the spread of nuclear weapons. Instituting domestic reprocessing would make it harder to justify denying nuclear technology to other countries — even nations such as Iran that are trying to produce their own nuclear arsenals.

As part of either disposal approach, the Blue Ribbon Commission may also recommend building one or more centralized interim storage sites where fuel could be shipped to relieve crowding at operating reactors, free up closed reactor sites for other uses or speed cleanup at military sites. But interim storage can be as hard to place as a permanent repository, because many communities fear that once they accept nuclear waste, they may never be free of it.

As lawmakers, utilities and communities debate options for managing nuclear waste, here are some issues they are considering:

Is transporting radioactive waste dangerous?

Because spent nuclear fuel and high-level waste are extremely radioactive, some observers worry that transporting them poses a health risk for people who handle fuel casks or live along transport routes. Although the United States has more than 40 years of experience with shipping radioactive waste, opening a repository or reprocessing spent fuel would involve moving much larger quantities over thousands of miles.

Utilities routinely ship spent nuclear fuel among storage facilities at different plants. They have made more than 3,000 shipments of commercial spent nuclear fuel by road and rail since the mid-1960s. And DOE has moved many tons of defense nuclear waste as it cleans up nuclear weapons production sites. About a dozen minor accidents have occurred during these shipments, none of which released radioactivity to the environment.[12] A 2006 study by the National Research Council concluded that there were "no fundamental technical barriers to the safe transport of spent nuclear fuel and [high-level waste] in the United States."[13]

But some groups worry that large-scale transport of radioactive waste will increase risks of accidents or low-level exposures. In November 2010 the American Public Health Association (APHA) called spent-fuel transportation "a national public health threat that is largely preventable." The group advocates long-term fuel storage at reactors until a permanent repository is ready.[14]

"The potential hazards and risks are huge, so minimizing transport makes sense. It just takes one accident, and then everyone will be pointing fingers and asking how we got to this point," says Amy Hagopian, a professor of global health at the University of Washington in Seattle who reviewed the statement for APHA.

Spent fuel is transported in massive steel casks that measure four to eight feet in diameter, have walls five to

A Glossary of Nuclear Terminology

Nuclear science has its own language. Here's a guide to key terms used by scientists and nuclear-energy experts.

Dry cask: A large steel canister that can be used to store spent nuclear fuel after it has cooled underwater.

Fast reactor: A reactor that uses fast-moving, high-energy neutrons to sustain a chain reaction. Unlike thermal reactors, fast reactors cannot be cooled with water. Instead they typically use liquid sodium or other liquid metals.

Fission: Splitting an atom of a heavy element to release energy, usually in the form of heat. The main isotopes that can be split by fission using slow neutrons are uranium-233, uranium-235, and plutonium-239. These materials can also be used to power nuclear weapons.

Fission products: Chemical elements formed when atoms of a fuel such as uranium are split into smaller fragments. Roughly 3 to 4 percent of spent fuel is made up of fission products, including iodine, cesium, and strontium. Many of these substances decay within a century (although some are longer-lived), and generate much of the short- and medium-term heat from spent nuclear fuel.

Fuel rod: A long metal tube that contains uranium pellets whose atoms can be split. A commercial nuclear power reactor may hold dozens of fuel assemblies, each of which is a bundle of up to several hundred fuel rods.

High-level radioactive waste: Extremely radioactive nuclear byproducts, including spent fuel rods and liquids and solids from reprocessing.

Isotopes: Different forms of a chemical element, distinguished by the number of neutrons in each atom's nucleus, with distinct nuclear properties. Examples are uranium-235 and uranium-238.

Once-through fuel cycle: A process in which fuel is irradiated once in a nuclear reactor, then permanently disposed of without reusing any of its components.

Plutonium: A heavy metallic element formed when uranium-238 absorbs a neutron in a reactor.

Radioactive waste: Radioactive materials that are at the end of their useful lives or cannot be used productively. Such waste includes spent nuclear fuel, radioactive liquids and solids from reprocessing and equipment, protective clothing or other materials that have been contaminated by radioactivity.

Spent fuel: Nuclear fuel that has been bombarded with neutrons in a reactor until it can no longer sustain a nuclear reaction. The irradiation typically lasts 18 to 24 months.

Thermal (slow) reactor: A nuclear reactor that uses slow-moving neutrons to sustain a chain reaction. U.S. commercial nuclear power reactors are thermal reactors. Often, the neutrons are slowed down by collisions with water, used for this purpose and to cool the reactor core.

Transuranics/actinides: Transuranics are elements heavier than uranium, including plutonium, neptunium and americium. Together with uranium, these elements are also referred to as actinides. About 1 percent of spent reactor fuel consists of plutonium and other actinides, which decay very slowly over thousands of years and produce much of the long-term heat and radioactivity from spent fuel.

Uranium: A radioactive element used to make nuclear reactor fuel. Fresh nuclear fuel contains about 96 percent uranium-238, an isotope that cannot be split using slow neutrons, and 4 percent uranium-235, which can.

— Jennifer Weeks

---

15 inches thick and contain materials that shield the environment from radioactivity. One cask used for shipment by truck holds up to nine bundles of fuel rods and weighs up to 25 tons; a rail shipment cask holds several dozen bundles and can weigh 150 tons. Casks must withstand a range of forces in testing, including a 30-foot drop onto reinforced concrete, a 40-inch drop onto a steel spike, a 30-minute fully engulfing fire and submersion under water for eight hours.[15]

In its 2006 study the National Research Council recommended steps to improve transportation security, including analyzing risks of long-lasting fires that might breach a fuel cask. Researchers were worried about scenarios like a 2001 disaster in which a freight train carrying flammable and toxic chemicals derailed in a tunnel under downtown Baltimore, igniting a fire that burned for five days.[16]

In response the Nuclear Regulatory Commission sought a study that concluded the likelihood of such accidents was extremely low and that rail-shipment casks for spent fuel would not release dangerous levels of radiation even in a similar fire.[17] The agency also negotiated with the railroad industry to revise freight policies so that trains carrying flammable materials would not enter tunnels at the same time as trains carrying spent fuel.[18]

"A significant radiation release would only happen in a very low-probability accident scenario," says the Natural Resources Defense Council's Cochran. "I'd worry more about being in a small car in front of the truck carrying spent fuel than about exposure from an accident."

While the potential for major accidents concerns some industry critics, so too does the possibility of routine radiation exposure. Some cite a 2008 environmental impact study by George W. Bush's administration supporting a proposal for large-scale domestic reprocessing and plutonium recycling starting around 2025.[19] The report estimated that shipping spent fuel and high-level waste cross-country would cause from a handful to hundreds of additional cancer deaths over 50 years from public exposure to low-level radiation, depending on the number of shipments and whether they went by road or rail.[20]

"You can't move spent fuel without irradiating people along the truck routes," argues Gerald Pollet, executive director of Heart of America Northwest (HOANW), a nonprofit group in Washington state. HOANW advocates for cleanup of the Hanford nuclear reservation, a site on the Columbia River covering nearly 600 square miles where workers produced plutonium for nuclear weapons from 1943 through the late 1980s. Hanford remains the most contaminated site in the U.S. nuclear weapons production complex. But Pollet asserts that DOE should find ways to manage Hanford's nuclear waste without increasing risk to the public. "If you move it twice — first to reprocess spent fuel and then to send the leftover high-level waste to a repository — we will see many more cancers," he says.

The National Research Council study also called sabotage of nuclear waste shipments "a major technical and societal concern," especially in the wake of the September 11, 2001, terrorist attacks.[21] Companies transporting nuclear waste are required to use routes approved by the Nuclear Regulatory Commission and monitor shipments in transit. But the federal agency's regulations have changed little since they were enacted in 1980. The agency is proposing new requirements, including joint planning with states along transit routes and use of global positioning systems or radiofrequency identification to track shipments in real time.[22]

The agency's proposed standards are "a vast improvement over the current rule," says Edwin Lyman, a senior scientist with the Union of Concerned Scientists, a nonprofit group that lobbies on environmental issues and oversight of nuclear power. But they would be stronger if they spelled out the size and type of attacking force that security measures must withstand, he argues. "This rule still doesn't provide the same level of security for spent fuel in transit as for spent fuel at reactor pools," Lyman says. "The number of escorts protecting spent fuel shipments is essentially ad hoc and isn't clearly related to a specific and evolving threat."

Should Congress revive the Yucca Mountain repository?

The Obama administration says the Yucca Mountain repository is officially canceled. But many stakeholders contend the administration cannot unilaterally kill the project.

DOE's fiscal 2011 budget request ended support for the department's Office of Civilian Radioactive Waste Management, which oversaw work on the repository. And last March DOE asked the Nuclear Regulatory Commission to withdraw the license application for the repository that President Bush had submitted, and rule out resubmission.

"[T]he Secretary of Energy has decided that a geologic repository at Yucca Mountain is not a workable option for long-term disposition of these materials," DOE's petition stated.[23]

But South Carolina, Washington state and the National Association of Regulatory Utility Commissioners (NARUC) are suing DOE, arguing that only Congress has authority to stop work on the project. Washington and South Carolina both have large quantities of military nuclear waste at DOE sites, some of which was destined for Yucca Mountain. (Idaho, Colorado, Tennessee and New York also have nuclear waste at DOE sites.) NARUC acted on behalf of consumers nationwide who had paid fees into the Nuclear Waste Fund for work on a repository.

"NARUC applauds the president for supporting science-based decisions that aren't trumped by politics, but in this case he's been inconsistent," says Boyd, chair of the group's nuclear waste committee.

South Carolina's newly elected Republican governor, Nikki Haley, put it more bluntly in her gubernatorial campaign. She contended that Obama was terminating Yucca Mountain as a favor to Democratic Majority Leader Reid, who adamantly opposes the repository and narrowly survived a reelection challenge in 2010.

"President Obama and Harry Reid are willing to shut down Yucca and make South Carolina a permanent dumping ground to save Harry Reid's Senate seat," Haley charged. "If the feds want to renege on the promise to keep Yucca open, they must refund the $1.2 billion [in ratepayer fees] our state has spent on the facility. We want our money back."[24]

In June the Nuclear Regulatory Commission's Atomic Safety and Licensing Board ruled that DOE could not unilaterally withdraw the license application. And on December 10, the U.S. Court of Appeals for the District of Columbia Circuit fast-tracked the lawsuit filed by the states and NARUC, requiring briefs to be filed early in 2011. By the fall of 2010, however, DOE had already disbanded the staff of the Office of Civilian Radioactive Waste Management.[25] And NRC chairman Gregory Jaczko had ordered his agency to end work on the Yucca Mountain license application. Jaczko justified this step by observing that DOE's budget proposal sought to terminate work on Yucca Mountain.

Many members of Congress are outraged by these actions. "We are deeply disappointed that DOE has overstepped its bounds and has ignored congressional intent . . . in its actions regarding Yucca Mountain," 91

The Nuclear Fuel Cycle

In a once-through fuel cycle, spent fuel is disposed of after one pass through a reactor (or, if necessary, stored for a period before disposal). In a closed fuel cycle, spent fuel is reprocessed to recover usable plutonium and uranium, which are recycled into fresh fuel. Reprocessing also generates high-level radioactive wastes that require disposal.

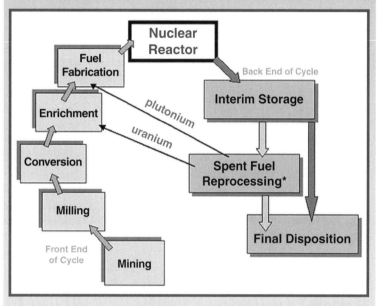

* Spent fuel reprocessing is omitted from the cycle in most countries, including the United States.

Source: Energy Information Administration

House and Senate members (14 Democrats and 77 Republicans) wrote to Energy Secretary Steven Chu in July.[26] And in October, four senior House Republicans called Jaczko's actions "alarming" and "unilateral," charging that NRC and DOE were working together to flout Congress' authority.[27] Because Congress has not yet passed any detailed spending bills for fiscal 2011, many members assert that they have not formally ruled on DOE's request to terminate work on Yucca Mountain.[28]

The nuclear industry supports finishing the license review. "We think it should continue for two reasons," says the Nuclear Energy Institute's McCullum. "First, the law requires it. Second, whether or not the administration or Congress wants to fund Yucca Mountain, we've invested $10 million in the licensing process and addressed a lot of issues. Seeing them resolved in a final determination will be very valuable. Even if NRC doesn't approve Yucca Mountain, the review might help us select an alternative site."

Officials in states where DOE is storing spent fuel and other radioactive waste worry that if Yucca Mountain is canceled, they could be stuck with those materials for decades or centuries. Ending work on Yucca Mountain "significantly sets back cleanup at Hanford and puts our people and our environment at risk," Rob McKenna, attorney general for Washington state, said when his state sued to keep the project going.

Others argue, however, that pushing through what they call a flawed repository would not only be irresponsible but could even backfire on states that want to get rid of radioactive waste. Pollet of Heart of America Northwest points out that less than 10 percent of Hanford's spent fuel and radioactive waste is destined for Yucca Mountain under binding legal cleanup agreements. The remainder will be managed at Hanford well into the future, until a second repository or some other solution is available.[29]

"The state of Nevada has very credibly shown that Yucca Mountain can't meet legal standards for keeping radioactivity out of groundwater," Pollet argues. "If Washington state fights to open Yucca Mountain by relaxing those regulations, Congress is likely to turn around and apply them to Washington for the rest of our radioactive waste. We should be setting standards that protect human health everywhere."

Should the U.S. recycle plutonium from spent fuel?

Reprocessing spent fuel and recycling its plutonium content is one of the most controversial aspects of nuclear power. Inarguably, spent fuel contains unused energy value. According to DOE, about 90 percent of nuclear fuel's energy content is discarded in a once-through fuel cycle. But plutonium can also be used in nuclear weapons, and dissolving fuel rods to extract it generates substantial quantities of high-level waste. For these reasons, environmentalists and many national-security experts have opposed reprocessing spent fuel since the 1970s.

Moreover, when fresh uranium is abundant and affordable, as it is today, reprocessing is considerably more expensive than a once-through fuel cycle. That's because building, operating and safeguarding reprocessing plants is very expensive. During their presidencies, Ronald Reagan and George W. Bush each reversed policies set by their predecessors and encouraged the nuclear industry to reprocess and recycle plutonium. But no utilities were interested in investing their capital to do that.

"If I'm a nuclear executive, I can buy uranium and make it into fuel, or I can take my spent fuel and make it into new fuel. Right now buying uranium is much cheaper. If reprocessing was economic to do, private money would be there to do it," says Charles Forsberg, a research scientist at the Massachusetts Institute of Technology (MIT) and director of a 2010 study on the future of the nuclear fuel cycle.

The MIT study concluded that a once-through cycle was economically preferable for at least the next several decades and would probably dominate the nuclear industry for most of the 21st century. It also recommended research into different nuclear fuel cycles while cautioning that the United States needs to develop new technologies and think broadly about safety, waste management, economics and nonproliferation before making new fuel cycle choices.[30]

"There are a lot of barriers to reprocessing in the U.S.," says Forsberg. "The regulatory structure isn't in place, and nonproliferation experts have a lot of worries about plutonium recycling. We might need to do it in 30 or 40 years, but there's no strong driver."

Energy Secretary Chu has suggested that reprocessing and recycling could become options for breaking down certain components of spent fuel, such as actinides. "We're looking at, instead of the way we do it today, where you're using 10 percent or less of the energy content of fuel, can you actually reduce the amount of waste and the lifetime of the waste," Chu said in a 2009 interview.[31]

Contrary to the Bush administration's proposal to commercialize reprocessing starting in about 2025, Chu speculated that the United States might store spent fuel for a century or more before reprocessing it to recover plutonium and other components. The Obama administration has stretched out federal research on nuclear fuel cycles with a goal of identifying options that could be ready to deploy by 2050. "Nothing has been weeded out. We could take a lot of different pathways, and we need to explore what they look like," says Kathryn McCarthy, deputy associate director at DOE's Idaho National Laboratory.

McCarthy says various reprocessing and recycling methods could address different aspects of the nuclear waste management burden. For example, some approaches could reduce the volume of waste (important if repository space is limited); others could limit how much heat or radioactivity the waste generates at different points in its life cycle by breaking down shorter- or longer-lived components of spent fuel. "We can come up with elegant schemes on paper, but when you look at it from a practical point of view, you need to think about where we can site a repository and what kind of geology it has, and work from there," McCarthy says.

Although environmentalists are strongly concerned about safe and secure management of spent fuel and radioactive waste, they oppose reprocessing as a waste-management strategy. For example, the Natural Resources Defense Council's Cochran points out that recycling to burn up actinides from spent fuel would require constructing dozens of "fast" reactors, which are designed differently from commercial power, or "thermal," reactors operating today. Fast reactors generate fast-moving neutrons that can split actinides to produce energy, but they also are hard to operate and more prone to accidents.

"History has not been kind to fast reactors. They have cost considerably more than thermal reactors, and seem likely to stay that way, and have proven to be much less reliable than thermal reactors," Cochran told the Blue Ribbon Commission last May. "In the view of Admiral Hyman G. Rickover [who led the U.S. Navy's move to nuclear-powered ships in the 1950s and '60], fast reactors were 'expensive to build, complex to operate, susceptible to prolonged shutdown . . . and difficult and time-consuming to repair.' Admiral Rickover got it right," Cochran asserted.[32]

Experts agree on one key point: the United States will need a repository even if it reprocesses nuclear waste, because reprocessing creates high-level waste that cannot be used in a reactor. "Reprocessing doesn't solve the waste problem, because you still have to treat waste that is as difficult to handle as spent fuel," says former NRC commissioner Peter Bradford. "It also adds to the cost of

nuclear power. That harms our ability to deal with climate change, because we could get the same amount of greenhouse gas reduction much sooner from other [energy] sources."

BACKGROUND
Launching a New Industry

The first U.S. radioactive waste was generated in the 1940s at the Hanford military site in eastern Washington. Uranium fuel rods were irradiated in Hanford's nuclear reactors, turning a fraction of their uranium into plutonium. Then chemists dissolved the spent fuel rods in acid and used solvents to separate out the plutonium, which was shipped to other sites for use in nuclear bombs. Over time the process generated millions of gallons of highly radioactive waste, which was stored in massive underground tanks near the Columbia River.

In the early 1950s, as the United States worked to expand its nuclear arsenal, other military sites at Oak Ridge, Tenn., Savannah River, S.C., and Idaho Falls, Idaho, also started reprocessing spent fuel to recover plutonium and uranium for bombs. These sites operated largely in secret, so radioactive waste often was handled expediently — for example, by dumping it into local rivers and streams or burying it.[33]

U.S. leaders wanted to develop a commercial nuclear power industry, so in the mid-1950s Congress authorized private companies to build and run nuclear power plants. Officials assumed that utilities would store spent fuel onsite in cooling ponds for several years, then reprocess it and recycle its plutonium and uranium content into new fuel for "breeder" reactors, which are designed to generate more fissile material than they consume. However, the Atomic Energy Commission (AEC), which was responsible for both promoting and regulating nuclear power, paid much more attention to building up this new industry than to its environmental impacts.

A 1957 report from the National Research Council, commissioned by the AEC, stated that radioactive waste could be safely disposed of underground. The authors, who were prominent scientists, suggested that salt deposits were especially promising because the presence of salt showed that water (which could transport leaking radioactive waste) was not flowing through the zones. Moreover,

CHRONOLOGY

1950s–1960s *U.S. government launches the nuclear power industry.*

1954 Congress passes the Atomic Energy Act, directing the federal government to develop nuclear power for peaceful use. Military sites already have thousands of gallons of high-level radioactive waste left from plutonium production for nuclear weapons.

1966 The first commercial reprocessing plant opens at West Valley, N.Y., generating more liquid high-level waste.

1970s *Federal government bars reprocessing of nuclear waste and commits to underground disposal.*

1970 Atomic Energy Commission (AEC) identifies abandoned salt mine in Lyons, Kan., as a possible waste disposal site.

1974 AEC abandons Kansas site after discovering technical problems. . . . India detonates what it calls a "peaceful" nuclear weapon.

1977 President Jimmy Carter bars reprocessing of spent nuclear fuel to avoid stockpiling plutonium that can be used in weapons.

1980s *U.S. officials commit to underground disposal of nuclear waste at Yucca Mountain in Nevada.*

1982 Nuclear Waste Policy Act directs the Department of Energy (DOE) to locate and build two underground repositories for spent fuel and high-level waste. Utilities are required to pay fees into the Nuclear Waste Fund and to contract with DOE for disposal.

1984 Nuclear Regulatory Commission (NRC) issues its first Waste Confidence Decision, holding that nuclear waste can be stored safely and that a repository will eventually be available.

1985 DOE identifies three possible repository sites in Texas, Washington and Nevada, and seven options for a second site in Eastern states, all of which refuse to accept a facility.

1986 DOE suspends its search for an Eastern nuclear waste site. . . . NRC starts licensing dry cask storage of spent fuel at nuclear plants.

1987 Congress directs DOE to focus research on a repository at a single site at Yucca Mountain in Nevada. The state sues to block the program, losing in federal court in 2004.

1990s *Nuclear industry pushes to expand, but plans for Yucca Mountain fall behind.*

1991 Surface studies begin at Yucca Mountain.

1994 Tunneling at Yucca Mountain begins.

1998 DOE misses its legal deadline for taking ownership of commercial spent fuel and high-level waste. . . . India and Pakistan test nuclear weapons made with materials originally obtained for peaceful purposes.

2000s *Controversy grows over waste disposal.*

2001 President George W. Bush calls for reprocessing spent fuel and using its plutonium content in advanced reactors.

2002 DOE begins work on Yucca Mountain license application.

2005 Energy Policy Act of 2005 provides loan guarantees and energy-production tax credits for new advanced nuclear reactors. . . . DOE revises the projected Yucca Mountain repository opening date from 2012 to 2014.

2008 DOE submits license application for Yucca Mountain to the NRC and projects an opening date of 2020.

2009 President Barack Obama cancels near-term plans for commercial reprocessing of nuclear fuel.

2010 Obama administration calls for halting Yucca Mountain's funding and asks NRC to withdraw its license application, but NRC licensing board refuses. . . . State utility regulators sue to continue work on Yucca Mountain.

they suggested, because salt tended to flow slowly into mined areas and fill them in, it would encase the waste and seal it off. However, the report cautioned, "The research to ascertain feasibility of disposal has for the most part not yet been done."[34]

Over the next five years the AEC studied options for underground radioactive waste disposal. From 1965 through 1968 it conducted tests at an abandoned salt mine in Lyons, Kan., and in 1970 the commission announced a tentative decision to make Lyons the first U.S. nuclear waste repository. But local officials opposed hosting a repository, and technical problems developed at the site, forcing the commission to abandon its plan.[35]

The AEC then tried to develop a surface interim storage facility to give it time to look for a permanent site, but this policy was also unpopular. The effort ended in 1974 when Congress split the commission into separate agencies: the Nuclear Regulatory Commission and the Energy Research and Development Administration (later absorbed into DOE).

Rethinking Reprocessing

U.S. leaders were forced to rethink national fuel cycle policy in 1974, when India carried out what it called a "peaceful" nuclear test, setting off a bomb it had made with plutonium from a civilian reactor. A year later the CIA warned that Taiwan, South Korea, Pakistan, Argentina, Brazil, Libya, South Africa, Iran, Egypt and Spain — all of which had or were considering nuclear power programs — could develop nuclear weapons within a decade.[36]

At the same time, early U.S. reprocessing plants were experiencing problems. A commercial plant that operated at West Valley, N.Y., from 1966 through 1972 shut down after operators decided they could not afford to meet new, stricter environmental standards.[37] General Electric had built a commercial plant in Morris, Ill., but decided in 1972 not to open it because of numerous operating problems.[38] In 1976 President Gerald Ford announced a moratorium on reprocessing unless it could be done without promoting nuclear proliferation. Ford's successor, Jimmy Carter, announced in 1977 that the United States would "defer indefinitely the commercial reprocessing and recycling of plutonium." Carter also barred federal support for a third commercial reprocessing plant under construction in Barnwell, S.C. The plant was never completed.[39]

Carter also canceled funding for the Clinch River Breeder Reactor, a medium-sized commercial plant in Tennessee. Although his successor, Ronald Reagan, sought to revive the breeder (over his budget director's objections), it came to be seen as a symbol of wasteful and unnecessary pork-barrel spending to benefit Tennessee legislators — notably Republican Sen. Howard Baker, the project's strongest advocate.[40] Congress terminated the program in 1983 after its projected cost ballooned from $699 million to $1.6 billion.[41]

"The U.S. nuclear industry made two really bad assumptions: that the costs of power plants would come down and therefore that breeder reactors would become more affordable, and that uranium was scarce and therefore reprocessing would be necessary," says the Natural Resource Defense Council's Cochran. "Everything turned on those theories that we would run out of low-cost uranium and would need to close the fuel cycle" by reprocessing and reusing plutonium. As it became clear that those assumptions were wrong, reprocessing became less necessary. But the need for a final disposal site for waste was, if anything, more urgent.

Meanwhile, spent fuel was piling up at nuclear power stations. Carter announced that he would ask Congress to let the federal government take ownership of spent fuel, although he stressed that it was mainly utilities' responsibility to store it until a repository was ready.

In 1982 Congress passed the Nuclear Waste Policy Act, which set timetables for locating and licensing two underground repositories, one each in the East and West. The law also required DOE to take ownership of spent fuel by Jan. 31, 1998, when the first repository was expected to be ready, and directed the Nuclear Regulatory Commission to help utilities develop dry storage at reactors in the meantime. In addition, the act required utilities to pay a fee of one-tenth of 1 cent per kilowatt-hour of nuclear electricity generation into a federal Nuclear Waste Fund.

Sticking It to Nevada

As the law required, DOE named nine potential repository sites in 1983, including locations in Louisiana, Mississippi, Nevada, Texas, Utah and Washington. Then DOE chose three finalists for the first repository —Yucca Mountain; Deaf Smith County, Texas; and Hanford, Washington — and said it would keep looking for an Eastern site. But all of the communities that DOE considered objected and said the department was moving too

Nuclear Waste Buried for the Ages in New Mexico Desert

"Our mission is to help shrink the footprint of the nuclear weapons complex."

A proposal to build a nuclear waste repository at Yucca Mountain in Nevada has sparked debate for years, but an underground storage site in New Mexico has been operating since 1999 with much less controversy.

The Waste Isolation Pilot Plant (WIPP), located in the remote town of Carlsbad, N.M., was excavated from a 2,000-foot-thick salt bed that dates back to the Permian era, 250 million years ago, when the area was covered by sea water. It was designed specifically to receive transuranic (TRU) waste from nuclear weapons production sites operated by the Department of Energy (DOE).

TRU waste contains slowly decaying manmade radioactive elements such as plutonium and americium, which are not as intensely radioactive as spent fuel from a commercial power reactor. But they emit radiation over millions of years that can be harmful if radioactive particles are inhaled or contaminate groundwater, so the waste must be isolated from the environment.[1]

Typical materials sent to WIPP include rags, tools, soil and protective clothing contaminated with plutonium. Most of these are so-called contact-handled TRU waste, which emits such low radiation that workers can handle the containers they are shipped in without special shielding. A small fraction, known as remote-handled waste, is more heavily contaminated, so workers transport it using equipment that shields them from radiation.[2]

For decades TRU waste at weapons production sites was commonly buried in shallow trenches, sometimes mixed with other waste and packaged in nothing more substantial than cardboard boxes or plastic bags. Starting in 1970 the Atomic Energy Commission, which at that time regulated

U.S. nuclear activities, required the waste to be stored separately in leak-proof drums. When the Cold War ended with the dissolution of the Soviet Union in 1991, states began suing DOE to force it to remove TRU waste from both active and closed weapons sites and clean up contaminated soil and groundwater.

As of early December 2010, WIPP had received 9,207 shipments (72,422 cubic meters) of TRU waste, including 445 shipments (229 cubic meters) of remote-handled waste. (A cubic meter equals 1.3 cubic yards.) The wastes were transported by rail and truck over a total of more than 11 million miles. The Environmental Protection Agency has certified that WIPP will safely contain TRU waste for 10,000 years.[3]

"Our mission is to help shrink the footprint of the nuclear weapons complex," says Casey Gadbury, Carlsbad Field Office Site Operations Director for the Department of Energy, which manages WIPP. "We started with waste at more than 30 sites, and over half of those have been cleaned up, which lets DOE decommission storage buildings, shrink sites and save money." For example, shipping TRU waste to WIPP helped make it possible for DOE to close Rocky Flats, a large facility outside Denver that manufactured plutonium cores for nuclear bombs. Except for a protected landfill at the center of the site, Rocky Flats has been cleaned up and converted to a national wildlife refuge.[4]

In contrast to Yucca Mountain, WIPP is generally accepted by the surrounding community. "Before WIPP, the main industries in this area were potash mines and oil and gas production, which both had cyclical markets and were subject to boom-and-bust cycles," says Gadbury.

fast. In 1986 DOE gave up the search for an Eastern site, further angering Western states.

In 1987 Congress reentered the fray, amending the law to designate Yucca Mountain as the only site DOE could study for a repository, in what became known as the "screw

Nevada bill." Nevada officials were outraged that their state, which had no nuclear power plants and had already been contaminated by above-ground nuclear tests in the 1950s and '60s, was being forced to accept the nation's nuclear waste. (Under the Nuclear Waste Policy Act a host

"When Carlsbad leaders heard that studies were being done that could bring a repository here, they started lobbying officials in Washington, D.C., and asking to be considered. The fact that this area had a lot of scientific and engineering expertise may have helped, since WIPP has provided a new application for those skills."

DOE also has made substantial payments to New Mexico in connection with WIPP, including more than $321 million in highway improvements and $16 million for emergency-response capabilities since 1997.

But New Mexico also negotiated hard with federal agencies, notes Charles Forsberg, an MIT research scientist who studies nuclear waste issues. "The U.S. government had to find a solution for TRU waste so that it could keep the nuclear weapons program going," Forsberg says. "So it grudgingly gave New Mexico some authority to regulate health and environmental impacts at WIPP, plus lots of economic benefits." And, adds Forsburg, Los Alamos National Laboratory — one of three U.S. laboratories that design and maintain nuclear weapons — is located in New Mexico and has a lot of TRU waste. The laboratory gets first priority for shipping those materials to WIPP. [5]

Some observers have suggested that DOE could send commercial spent fuel or high-level waste from weapons plants to WIPP instead of Yucca Mountain. However, that idea raises some difficult issues. WIPP is not big enough to handle the quantity and diversity of waste types that were slated for transport to Yucca Mountain, so a separate repository would have to be built in Carlsbad to receive them. And because salt formations will flow around waste and enclose it over time, spent fuel stored there could not be retrieved if DOE opted to reprocess it in the future. [6]

Moreover, New Mexico officials are not looking for more nuclear waste. "[I]t is crucial that WIPP remain focused on its mission — disposal of the nation's defense-related transuranic waste — and not expand to disposal of other wastes for which it was not contemplated or designed," Ron Curry, then the state's environment secretary, told a

Radioactive military waste has been buried at a Department of Energy site in remote Carlsbad, N.M., for more than a decade.

Blue Ribbon Commission created last year by President Barack Obama to recommend new waste-storage options. [7]

— Jennifer Weeks

[1] U.S. Department of Energy, Waste Isolation Pilot Plant, "Radiation," www.wipp.energy.gov/fctshts/radiation.pdf.

[2] U.S. Department of Energy, "WIPP RH-TRU Waste Study — Summary," www.wipp.energy.gov/library/rhwaste/rhsummry.htm.

[3] Information from U.S. Department of Energy, Carlsbad Field Office, Dec. 7, 2010.

[4] Jennifer Weeks, "From Bombs to Birds," *Defenders Magazine*, Winter 2009, www.defenders.org/newsroom/defenders_magazine/winter_2009/from_bombs_to_birds.php.

[5] See New Mexico Environment Department, "Waste Isolation Pilot Plant (WIPP) Information," www.nmenv.state.nm.us/wipp/.

[6] Christopher M. Timm and Jerry V. Fox, "Should WIPP Replace Yucca Mountain?," paper prepared for the Blue Ribbon Commission appointed by President Barack Obama to recommend new nuclear waste-storage options, November 2010, http://brc.gov/e-mails/November10/Should%20WIPP%20Replace%20Yucca%20Mountain%20-%2011058%20-%20Final%20Draft.pdf.

[7] Ron Curry, Cabinet Secretary, New Mexico Environment Department, summary of statement before the Blue Ribbon Commission, July 7, 2010, http://brc.gov/Disposal_SC/docs/SecretaryCurryBlue%20RibbonSummary.pdf.

state could veto accepting a repository, but Congress could override the veto.) Gov. Richard Bryan called the bill "a legislative atrocity" and predicted that it would be "a nuclear nightmare for the Congress, an avoidable and costly mistake that the taxpayers will have to finance." [42]

Over the next 15 years Nevada tried many tactics to block work on Yucca Mountain, including denying DOE permits to work at the site, passing a state law against storing nuclear waste in the state and denying DOE the water rights it needed to build a rail line to Yucca

AFP/Getty Images/Maxim Kniazkov (both)

Under Yucca Mountain

The unfinished nuclear waste repository under Nevada's Yucca Mountain has been canceled by President Obama. According to government plans for the controversial facility, the entrance (top) would lead to a 40-mile network of tunnels (bottom) about 1,000 feet below the surface. Begun in the 1980s, the repository in Nevada's southern desert was designed to safely store canisters holding thousands of tons of spent nuclear fuel from civilian nuclear power plants and Department of Defense weapons programs for up to 1 million years. Last March Obama created a Blue Ribbon Commission to recommend new waste storage options.

Mountain. The state also questioned whether the repository would actually keep radioactive waste isolated from the environment for millions of years. It presented data about seismic and volcanic activity near Yucca Mountain that it argued showed why the site was unsuitable for a

repository.[43]

At the same time, DOE started to clean up contaminated nuclear weapon production sites that were no longer needed after the end of the Cold War. These sites were now subject to federal and state environmental regulations, and DOE was forced to sign legally binding cleanup agreements with states and the U.S. Environmental Protection Agency that set targets for removing spent fuel and radioactive waste. For example, the agency pledged to remove used fuel from Idaho by 2035 or pay penalties of $60,000 per day. Some of these materials were designated for Yucca Mountain.

Delays and Lawsuits

DOE pressed ahead with work on Yucca Mountain through the 1990s, but design changes, funding shortfalls and quality control problems stretched work well beyond the original 1998 target for accepting spent fuel. By 2000 more than a dozen utilities were using dry casks to store spent fuel at reactors. They also were suing DOE for breach of contract.

At first DOE claimed it was not responsible for damages because its lack of a repository was an "unavoidable delay." After courts rejected that argument, the agency tried to avoid liability by partially refunding utilities for their Nuclear Waste Fund contributions. But courts also struck down that approach.[44]

By 2010 DOE had paid $725 million in legal settlements, and 50 cases were pending against it. DOE estimated that if it started accepting waste from reactors in 2021, its total liability to utilities (funded by taxpayers) would be about $13.1 billion. What's more, it said, that amount would increase by about $500 million in each year beyond 2021 that DOE was not able to accept nuclear waste.[45]

President George W. Bush submitted a license application for Yucca Mountain to the Nuclear Regulatory Commission (NRC) in 2008. The licensing process, which was scheduled to take three years, had two parts: a technical analysis of the repository's design, and hearings at the same time before the NRC's Atomic Safety and Licensing Board to let state and local governments, American Indian tribes and other stakeholders voice their concerns.[46]

But as the commission started work on the license application in the spring of 2009, President Obama submitted his fiscal 2010 budget proposal, which cut

How Other Nations Handle Waste

Few have selected repository sites.

Many nations generate electricity from nuclear power, but only a few have successfully chosen a site for disposing of radioactive waste.

Finland considered six potential repository sites from 1987 through 1998 and chose Olkiluoto, an island off the west coast where two nuclear reactors were operating. Posiva, a private company owned by Finland's utilities, is building a demonstration facility at the site. It expects to apply for a construction license next year and an operating license in 2018.

Sweden studied eight potential sites, then narrowed the competition to two communities in 2002, both of which bid to host the repository. The winner, Osthammar, was selected in 2009 because its dry, crystalline bedrock was considered to be the safest option for isolating nuclear waste. As in Finland, Sweden's utilities formed a private company to manage and dispose of their radioactive waste. The company, SKB, expects to begin site work in 2013 and be operating in 2023.

Other nations are further behind in the repository process:

- Belgium shifted from reprocessing spent fuel to direct disposal in 1994. The country stores spent fuel at reactors and a central interim facility. It is studying sites for underground disposal, with construction expected to start around 2035.

- Canada requires retrievable deep underground disposal. It is researching potential sites, and operation is expected around 2025.
- France reprocesses spent fuel and plans long-term underground disposal of high-level wastes left over from reprocessing. It is studying potential repository sites and expects to apply for a license in 2015 and begin operation in 2025.
- Germany reprocessed spent fuel until 1989, then shifted to direct disposal. It is studying potential repository sites and expects to build a facility by 2035.
- Japan reprocesses spent fuel and is studying potential sites for a high-level-waste repository. It expects to select a site between 2023 and 2027.
- Russia reprocesses spent fuel and stores high-level waste at interim sites. It is studying sites for a final repository.
- The United Kingdom reprocesses spent fuel and is planning for underground disposal, with a repository site to be chosen by community agreement.

— Jennifer Weeks

Source: "Radioactive Waste Management," World Nuclear Association, June 2009, www.world-nuclear.org/info/inf04.html.

---

funding for the project by about one-fourth and called for scaling it back to "costs necessary to answer inquiries from the Nuclear Regulatory Commission, while the Administration devises a new strategy toward nuclear waste disposal."[47] A year later, in early 2010, the Energy Department submitted a budget request that canceled all work on Yucca Mountain.

CURRENT SITUATION

Waste and Licenses

Even with nuclear waste policy in flux, the Nuclear Regulatory Commission is considering proposals for new nuclear plants.

In September the commission affirmed and updated its longstanding finding that nuclear waste can be stored safely for decades at reactors or interim storage sites, and that a repository will eventually be available for disposal. This opinion, known as the Waste Confidence Decision, serves as a generic finding that disposing of spent fuel does not need to be factored into environmental impact studies associated with licensing decisions.

NRC first stated this view in 1984, after a New England advocacy group and a Minnesota state agency challenged its approval of expanded spent-fuel storage at reactors in Vermont and Minnesota.[48] The commission concluded that one or more geologic repositories were likely to be available by 2007-2009 and, if not, that spent fuel could be safely stored at reactors or off-site for at least 30 years after a reactor's 40-year operating license expired. NRC affirmed the rule in 1990, revising its estimate of when a repository would be ready to "the first quarter of the twenty-first century," and endorsed the rule again in 1999 without further change.[49]

NRC revisited the issue again in 2010. This time it ruled that spent fuel could be safely stored at reactors or off-site for at least 60 years after the reactor's license expired. Despite the Obama administration's proposal to cancel Yucca Mountain, the commission also concluded that repository space would be available to dispose of commercial high-level waste and spent reactor fuel. But it gave no specifics, saying only that underground disposal would be ready "when necessary," without a projected date.[50]

The nuclear energy industry applauded NRC's action as a sign that waste management should not be a roadblock to licensing new reactors. "There's a lot of confidence in our ability to store nuclear materials. We've been storing them safely for a long time, and we'll continue to do so," says the Nuclear Energy Institute's McCullum.

Others were negative. "This is more an act of desperation than a finding of science," said Eric Epstein, manager of the Pennsylvania watchdog group Three Mile Island Alert.[51] News accounts pointed out that many operating reactors had already received 20-year extensions on their original 40-year operating licenses; thus, assuming that waste could remain on-site for 60 years after a plant closed, the waste might not be moved for 120 years.[52]

Despite NRC's findings, 10 states have barred new nuclear plant construction until the federal government identifies a means of disposing of high-level waste and spent fuel. California's limit, passed in 1976, was upheld by the U.S. Supreme Court, which ruled in 1983 that states could regulate nuclear power for economic reasons, including the potential cost of storing and disposing of spent fuel.[53] Connecticut, Illinois, Kentucky, Maine, Massachusetts, Oregon, West Virginia and Wisconsin have similar moratoriums in place, and Minnesota has barred any new nuclear plant construction.[54]

Weak Renaissance

For a decade nuclear advocates have predicted that the United States was on the verge of a new growth period

in nuclear power, driven by performance improvements at operating reactors and concerns about global climate change.[55] After Congress approved loan guarantees for a handful of new nuclear plants in the Energy Policy Act of 2005, utilities announced plans to build more than 20 new reactors.[56]

But that expansion has stalled. In late 2007, as the nation entered a sharp economic recession, manufacturing output and demand for electricity slowed. That in turn lowered the price of natural gas, nuclear power's main competitor for generating electricity. The recession also made it harder for utilities to get financing for new reactors, which have high construction costs.

Nuclear advocates expected Congress to set a price on carbon emissions as part of President Obama's energy program, thereby making emission-free nuclear generation more competitive with fossil fuels. But the Democrat-controlled House struggled in 2009 to pass a cap-and-trade bill designed to reduce emissions by allowing utilities to buy and sell emission permits. The House finally succeeded by a mere seven votes. But the Senate — also controlled by Democrats — couldn't pass a bill at all.[57]

Even before Republicans won control of the House in the 2010 midterm elections, observers widely assumed that legal limits on carbon emissions — which opponents argued would cripple the economy — were too unpopular to be enacted into law.[58] President Obama confirmed that view in a press conference following the midterms, although he insisted that "cap and trade was just one way of skinning the cat. . . . It was a means, not an end."[59]

Many Republicans in the new Congress support building more nuclear plants, but the economics of new reactors are still highly unfavorable. Nuclear power is "almost unfinanceable in today's environment," New York Public Service Commissioner Robert Curry said in mid-November. "I don't see how the election changes that for good or ill."[60]

Even a sharp rise in oil prices would do little to boost nuclear power because very few utilities use oil to generate electricity. And new drilling techniques are making it possible to develop abundant natural gas deposits across the United States, from the Northeast to the Rockies.

New reactor projects are moving forward in Georgia and South Carolina — states where regulators allow

Should Congress revive the Yucca Mountain repository?

YES
Rob McKenna
Attorney General, Washington State

Written for *CQ Researcher*, January 2011

NO
Sen. Harry Reid, D-Nev.
Senate Majority Leader

Written for *CQ Researcher*, January 2011

The dispute over whether high-level nuclear waste should be safely stored at Nevada's Yucca Mountain comes down to a political promise between President Barack Obama and Sen. Harry Reid.

Should politics trump science? Should we ignore the law to fulfill a campaign promise between two powerful politicians?

The people of Washington state have worked too hard cleaning up our Hanford Nuclear Reservation — where nearly two-thirds of the nation's defense-related, high-level radioactive waste festers — to let the federal government unilaterally abandon the process for evaluating the nation's only scientifically studied and congressionally approved high-level nuclear waste repository.

The facts are clear. Roughly 53 million gallons — or 2,400 average-sized swimming pools — of untreated nuclear waste are stored at Hanford in 177 large underground tanks. About one-third of these tanks are known or suspected to have leaked, releasing roughly 1 million gallons of waste.

Congress has been seeking suitable storage for more than 30 years, approving the Nuclear Waste Policy Act in 1982 to end political games and provide a detailed process for siting and licensing nuclear waste storage facilities. The Department of Energy (DOE) invested 20 years in scientific research, which consumed millions of hours and more than $4 billion before Energy Secretary Spencer Abraham recommended Yucca Mountain as a repository in 2002.

Congress then designated Yucca Mountain as the nation's sole repository, triggering the licensing phase and putting DOE's application before the Nuclear Regulatory Commission. The licensing process is intended to answer any questions about whether a repository at Yucca Mountain is suitable and safe.

Thanks to recent federal actions, this process has been corrupted. DOE has pulled the plug on the Nuclear Waste Policy Act's process without congressional approval and without providing any evidence Yucca Mountain is technically unsuitable. Instead, listen to the politics at play: "[T]he Secretary's judgment . . . is not that Yucca Mountain is unsafe or that there are flaws . . . but rather that it is not a workable option."

I am in court so Yucca Mountain's fate is decided on its scientific merits, not by political paybacks. The federal government's shenanigans threaten to delay Hanford's entire clean-up mission, creating greater risks to the people and environment of my region.

Sen. Reid has been in prime position to change the law, if that was in the nation's best interests. It's time to put people ahead of politics and follow the law.

The Yucca Mountain repository project is dead, and as long as I am the majority leader of the U.S. Senate it will stay that way.

Yucca Mountain was forced on Nevada nearly 25 years ago as part of what many refer to as the "Screw Nevada" bill. Without a comprehensive study of all potential sites, Congress designated Yucca Mountain the nation's dumping ground for high-level radioactive waste despite having a grossly incomplete understanding of the science and no comprehension of the serious consequences it would pose to Nevadans.

In addition to severe health and safety risks, a nuclear waste dump at Yucca would have a devastating impact on Nevada's tourism industry, dragging down the state's entire economy. It is beyond reckless to ship the most toxic substance known to man across the country to be buried over volcanic fault lines only 90 miles from the world's premier tourist destination. Nevada could not afford these risks in 1987, and we surely cannot afford them today.

The Yucca Mountain project was also the epitome of wasteful government spending until the Obama administration declared an end to the project nearly two years ago. The price tag on Yucca rose to nearly $100 billion, when the proposed site remained riddled with technical, legal and safety problems.

But most important, the dump at Yucca Mountain posed a grave risk to our health and safety as thousands of shipments of nuclear waste would have been carried across America through our neighborhoods, by our schools and right past the Las Vegas strip — the economic engine of southern Nevada.

I am proud that after two decades of fighting, the Yucca Mountain project is history thanks to budget cuts year after year, culminating with President Obama terminating the project and eliminating all funding for it in last year's budget.

I am grateful that Energy Secretary Steven Chu has taken the necessary step of taking Yucca off the table and creating a Blue Ribbon Commission to determine the best path for dealing with nuclear waste based on sound science, 21st-century technologies and the input of all stakeholders. This panel includes the nation's foremost experts on nuclear energy, environmental science and public policy.

Our country has some of the best scientific minds in the world. I am confident they can find a solution to deal with the nation's nuclear waste that ensures the safety and security of all Americans.

utilities to recover the cost of new plants from their customers. But in many Northeastern and Midwestern states, nuclear utilities have to compete against other fuels based on price. "You just can't build reactors in states that use competitive markets to sort out what kind of new generation [plant] gets built," says former NRC commissioner Bradford. "When you rank issues for the nuclear industry, cost is pretty far ahead of waste."

Private Options

Now that President Obama has called for rethinking nuclear waste policy, many stakeholders want to see the task assigned to an entity other than DOE, such as a private contractor working for utilities or a government-owned, single-mission corporation, often nicknamed "Fedcorp."

"DOE is one of the most mistrusted agencies of the federal government, followed by the NRC," says Eugene Rosa, a professor of sociology at Washington State University who has studied public perceptions of risk related to nuclear power and other environmental and technical issues. "The standard model for DOE and pro-nuclear scientists has been to think that if we only educate people about the technical details, they will accept nuclear power. That whole paradigm is bankrupt; it doesn't work that way. People get a lot of technical details wrong, and the pro-nuclear community would like to disenfranchise them because of that. But the public's concerns are still real and need to be taken seriously."

Even if DOE was better at communicating with the public, the scientific studies the department carries out to show that a repository can isolate radioactive waste from the environment are extremely complicated, notes University of California, Berkeley, historian Cathryn Carson. DOE uses sophisticated computer models to predict how the repository will behave far into the future, what paths waste would follow if it escaped and what the consequences would be, over the course of millennia.

"It's so complex that it's extremely hard for the public to understand, and mistrust of DOE makes many people think that the inputs must be cooked," Carson says. "Part of the challenge of making a case for the repository is showing how scientists make projections, and conveying that process to audiences who don't necessarily trust the government or government contractors."

In addition to communicating more effectively with the public, groups such as the National Association of Regulatory Utility Commissioners (NARUC) expect a government-owned corporation to operate more efficiently and manage nuclear waste fees more responsibly than DOE or Congress. "A Fedcorp CEO may be better able to offer states and communities incentives to store nuclear waste than a federal negotiator who has to go back to Congress for money," says NARUC's Boyd. "The corporation could be empowered to set nuclear waste fee levels and collect fees directly, without the federal government getting involved. And it could work more directly with utilities to take advantage of their expertise."

The federal government has set up many corporations to provide public services, including Amtrak for rail passenger service, the Corporation for Public Broadcasting and the Federal Deposit Insurance Corporation for help in stabilizing the banking system. Former Sen. George Voinovich, R-Ohio, and Rep. Fred Upton, R-Mich., introduced legislation in 2010 to create a government corporation for managing nuclear waste; Voinovich retired at the end of 2010, but Upton chairs the House Energy and Commerce Committee and may reintroduce the bill this year.

The design of a Fedcorp is less important than whether it has real authority, says MIT's Forsberg. "There are lots of different corporate structures, but the leaders have to have power to make agreements that everyone can live with. You can't have 535 overseers in Congress," he says. "The system needs to include everyone who has a stake in solving the problem, including utilities and public utility commissions. You have to be in an ownership position to make these deals."

OUTLOOK
No Shortcuts

Most observers agree that the United States does not face an immediate nuclear waste crisis. But given how long it will take to locate, build and license a nuclear waste repository, they also say that it is essential to agree on basic goals and get the process back on track.

After the Blue Ribbon Commission delivers its final report next year, Congress will have to approve and fund new steps, which will likely include either directing the Nuclear Regulatory Commission to continue with licensing Yucca Mountain or laying out rules for a new repository. Assigning nuclear waste policy to an agency outside of DOE would require Congress to charter the new entity and decide how it should be funded. If a search is opened for a new repository site or interim storage sites, politicians and voters in potential host states will no doubt demand extensive input into any decisions.

Each of those steps will require Congress and federal officials to focus on goals many election cycles into the future. "Nuclear waste is so dreaded that we could see a tar-baby syndrome that generates mistrust of whoever has to deal with it," says Washington State University's Rosa. "But something has to be done. We can't go on forever the way we are. Nuclear power is growing internationally, so the world needs to solve this issue."

One key, scholars assert, is to view nuclear waste policy as a social issue, not just a technical problem. "We have tried-and-true methods for ensuring that a process is representative, and we understand the factors that erode public trust and make people afraid of nuclear technology," says Rosa.

Many experts commend Sweden and Finland for thinking hard about nuclear waste storage issues, such as how to offer communities incentives that don't seem like bribes, and how to have real dialogues with citizens about their concerns. Forcing states to accept facilities they don't want — as Congress did when it directed DOE to study only Yucca Mountain for a repository — is expedient but has proved to be self-defeating, observers say.

"Nevada fought Yucca Mountain instead of negotiating with DOE for better benefits because there were perceptions that the federal government was taking shortcuts and that the process was wired," says Boyd at the National Association of Regulatory Utility Commissioners.

MIT's Forsberg points out another lesson that the federal government could learn from other countries: thinking about hazardous waste in broad categories, instead of distinguishing between nuclear waste and other long-lived substances, such as the heavy metals lead, arsenic and cadmium. "U.S. policy says that if something is radioactive, it goes to a geologic repository, which is a

> "Nuclear waste is so dreaded that we could see a tar-baby syndrome that generates mistrust of whoever has to deal with it."
>
> — *Eugene Rosa Professor of Sociology, Washington State University*

good idea. But if it's a heavy metal that remains toxic forever, we dump it and don't worry about it, which is crazy," he contends.

"Europeans have figured out that anything really long-lived and hazardous needs to go to a repository, and the question of whether it's radioactive or a toxic heavy metal is a technical detail for engineers," Forsberg says. "We need a waste management policy based on hazards to people that covers all wastes."

NOTES

1. The U.S. Environmental Protection Agency set standards for the Yucca Mountain repository that sought to limit how much radioactivity people might receive from spent fuel stored there for up to 1 million years. This target was based on an estimate by the National Academy of Sciences that peak exposure risk might occur hundreds of thousands of years after radioactive waste was placed in the repository. See American Nuclear Society, "The EPA Radiation Standard for Spent-Fuel Storage in a Geological Repository," November 2006, www.ans.org/pi/ps/docs/ps81-bi.pdf.

2. Center for Public Integrity, "Nuclear Waste Problem Unsolved," www.publicintegrity.org/investigations/broken_government/articles/entry/956/.

3. For an overview of technical concerns with Yucca Mountain, see Alison Macfarlane and Rodney Ewing, eds., *Uncertainty Underground: Yucca Mountain and the Nation's High-Level Nuclear Waste* (2006).

4. Steve Tetreault, "Waste Site Critics See Opening," *Las Vegas Review-Journal*, Nov. 10, 2008, www.lvrj.com/news/34191604.html.

5. U.S. Energy Information Administration, "U.S. Nuclear Statistics/Reactor Status Table," www.eia.doe.gov/cneaf/nuclear/page/operation/statoperation.html.

6. Many proposed plants are currently on hold while utilities seek loan guarantees and other financial support, but site preparation is under way in Georgia and Tennessee. See U.S. Energy Information Administration, "Status of Potential New Commercial Nuclear Reactors in the United States," July 1, 2010, www.eia.doe.gov/cneaf/nuclear/page/nuc_reactors/com_reactors.pdf; Matthew Wald, "Nuclear 'Renaissance' Is Short on Largess," *The New York Times*, Dec. 7, 2010, http://green.blogs.nytimes.com/2010/12/07/nuclear-renaissance-is-short-on-largess/?scp=2&sq=new%20reactors&st=cse.

7. For background see Jennifer Weeks, "Nuclear Energy," *CQ Researcher*, March 10, 2006, pp. 217-240.

8. U.S. Nuclear Regulatory Commission, "List of Power Reactor Units," updated Sept. 23, 2010, www.nrc.gov/reactors/operating/list-power-reactor-units.html, and "Location of Independent Spent Fuel Storage Installations," www.nrc.gov/waste/spent-fuel-storage/locations.html.

9. "Federal Commitments Regarding Used Fuel and High-Level Wastes," Van Ness Feldman, P.C., paper commissioned for the Blue Ribbon Commission, Aug. 31, 2010, http://brc.gov/library/commissioned_papers/August%202010%20BRC%20Federal%20Committments%20Paper%20REVISED%2011.12.10.pdf.

10. See Commission charter, online at www.brc.gov/pdfFiles/BRC_Charter.pdf.

11. For example, see Idaho Department of Environmental Quality, "Waste at INL: High Level Waste," www.deq.idaho.gov/inl_oversight/waste/high_level.cfm.

12. National Research Council, *Going the Distance? The Safe Transport of Spent Nuclear Fuel and High-Level Radioactive Waste in the United States* (2006), pp. 117-122.

13. *Ibid.*, pp. 2-3.

14. "Policy Statement B-7," summarized at www.apha.org/membergroups/newsletters/sectionnewsletters/occupat/fall10/default.htm#{46E77A7B-722B-4393-94A5-FD04BF5CE736}.

15. U.S. Nuclear Regulatory Commission, *Safety of Spent Fuel Transportation* (2003), pp. 4-5, www.nrc.gov/reading-rm/doc-collections/nuregs/brochures/br0292/br0292.pdf, and "Typical Spent Fuel Transportation Casks," www.nrc.gov/waste/spent-fuel-storage/diagram-typical-trans-cask-system-2.pdf.

16. National Transportation Safety Board, "Railroad Accident Brief," August 2004, www.ntsb.gov/publictn/2004/RAB0408.pdf.

17. U.S. Nuclear Regulatory Commission, "Spent Fuel Transportation Package Response to the Baltimore Tunnel Fire Scenario," NUREG/CR-6886, www.nrc.gov/reading-rm/doc-collections/nuregs/contract/cr6886/r2/cr6886r2.pdf.

18. U.S. Nuclear Regulatory Commission, "Staff actions taken in response to the National Academy of Sciences' study on transportation of high-level waste and spent nuclear fuel in the United States," SECY-07-0995 (June 6, 2007).

19. President Obama changed this plan to focus on basic research, with no reprocessing until mid-century at the earliest.

20. U.S. Department of Energy, Office of Nuclear Energy, "Draft Global Nuclear Energy Partnership Programmatic Environmental Impact Statement — Summary," DOE/EIS-0396 (October 2008), pp. S-52, S-53, www.brc.gov/library/docs/GNEP%20Summary.pdf. Figures cited are for public latent cancer fatalities.

21. National Research Council, *Going the Distance*, *op cit.*, p. 8.

22. "Physical Protection of Irradiated Reactor Fuel in Transit," *Federal Register*, Oct. 13, 2010, pp. 62695-62716.

23. "U.S. Department of Energy's Motion to Withdraw," submitted to the Atomic Safety and Licensing board, U.S. Nuclear Regulatory Commission March 3, 2010, www.energy.gov/news/documents/DOE_Motion_to_Withdraw.pdf.

24. "Haley Slams Reid's Rejection of Yucca Nuclear Waste Site," FoxNews.com, Sept. 19, 2010.

25. Emily Yehle, "Little Hope, Help for DOE's Displaced Yucca Mountain Contract Workers," *The New York*

Times, Aug. 24, 2010, www.nytimes.com/gwire/2010/08/24greenwire-little-hope-help-for-does-displaced-yucca-moun-27266.html.

26. "Bipartisan Coalition to DOE: Halt Actions to Terminate Yucca Mountain," July 6, 2010, https://hastings.house.gov/News/DocumentSingle.aspx?DocumentID=199019.

27. "Members of Congress Urge NRC Chairman to Continue Yucca Mountain Review," *Nuclear Power Industry News*, Oct. 15, 2010.

28. For example, see Jack Spencer, "Yucca Mountain and Nuclear Waste Policy: A New Beginning?" Heritage Foundation, Dec. 16, 2010, www.heritage.org/research/reports/2010/12/yucca-mountain-and-nuclear-waste-policy-a-new-beginning. The 111th Congress passed a short-term continuing resolution late in 2010 funding most government programs through March 4, 2011 at current levels. "2010 Legislative Summary: Appropriations (Overview), *CQ Weekly*, Dec. 27, 2010, p. 2907.

29. For details see Jeff Mapes, "An Activist View: Closing Yucca Good for Hanford," *The Oregonian*, Feb. 26, 2009, http://blog.oregonlive.com/mapesonpolitics/2009/02/an_activist_view_closing_yucca.html.

30. *The Future of the Nuclear Fuel Cycle: Summary Report* (2010), pp. xi-xii.

31. "Q&A: Steven Chu," *TechnologyReview.com*, May 14, 2009.

32. Thomas B. Cochran, statement before the Blue Ribbon Commission on America's Nuclear Future, May 25, 2010, pp. 4-5, http://docs.nrdc.org/nuclear/files/nuc_10062201a.pdf.

33. For background see Mary H. Cooper, "Nuclear Arms Cleanup," *CQ Researcher*, June 24, 1994, and U.S. Department of Energy, *Linking Legacies: Connecting the Cold War Nuclear Weapons Production Processes to Their Environmental Consequences* (1997), www.em.doe.gov/Publications/linklegacy.aspx.

34. National Research Council, *The Disposal of Radioactive Waste On Land* (1957), p. 1, www.biodiversitylibrary.org/ia/disposalofradioa00nati#page/1/mode/1up.

35. James M. Hylko and Robert Peltier, "The U.S. Spent Nuclear Fuel Policy: Road to Nowhere," *Power Magazine*, May 1, 2010.

36. "Managing Nuclear Proliferation: The Politics of Limited Choice," Central Intelligence Agency, December 1975, declassified Aug. 21, 2001, www.gwu.edu/~nsarchiv/NSAEBB/NSAEBB155/prolif-15.pdf.

37. "Record of Decision: Final Environmental Impact Statement for Decommissioning and/or Long-Term Stewardship at the West Valley Demonstration Project," U.S. Department of Energy, April 14, 2010, pp. 3-4, www.westvalleyeis.com/ROD.pdf.

38. Robert Gillette, "Nuclear Fuel Reprocessing: GE's Balky Plant Poses Shortages," *Science*, vol. 185 (Aug. 30, 1974), pp. 770-771.

39. Jan Collins Stucker, "Nuclear White Elephant," *The New Republic*, Jan. 20, 1982.

40. Robert Reinhold, "Controversial Clinch River Reactor Plan Is Poised to Proceed," *The New York Times*, March 10, 1981; Colin Norman, "Clinch River Supporters Pin Hopes on Baker," *Science*, vol. 220 (June 10, 1983), p. 1132.

41. John Abbots, "All the King's Horses and All the King's Men . . ." *Bulletin of the Atomic Scientists*, January/February 1989, pp. 49-50; U.S. General Accounting Office, Department of Energy, "Opportunity to Improve management of Major System Acquisitions," GAO/RCED-97-17 (November 1996), pp. 34, 50.

42. Larry B. Stammer, "Nevada May Get Nuclear Waste Dump," *Los Angeles Times*, Dec. 18, 1987, http://articles.latimes.com/1987-12-18/news/mn-20047_1.

43. For details see the website of the Nevada Agency for Nuclear Projects, www.state.nv.us/nucwaste/.

44. Todd Garvey, "The Yucca Mountain Litigation: Breach of Contract Under the Nuclear Waste Policy Act of 1982," Congressional Research Service, R40996 (Dec. 22, 2009).

45. Kim Cawley, Congressional Budget Office, statement for the record for the Committee on the Budget, U.S. House of Representatives, July 27, 2010.

46. "Licensing Yucca Mountain," U.S. Nuclear Regulatory Commission, April 2009, www.nrc.gov/reading-rm/doc-collections/fact-sheets/fs-yucca-license-review.pdf.

47. Keith Rogers, "Obama Budget Plan Cuts Yucca Mountain Funding," *Las Vegas Review-Journal*, Feb. 26, 2009, www.lvrj.com/news/40348957.html.

48. The rule was prompted by a court decision, *Minnesota v. NRC* (602 F. 2d 412, 1979) consolidating the two cases. In this case, a federal appeals court held that NRC could make generic judgments about whether nuclear waste could be safely handled and disposed of, rather than analyzing the issue every time a utility applied for a new or amended reactor license.

49. For details, see "NRC Waste Confidence Positions," http://brc.gov/library/docs/NRC%20waste%20 confidence%20FRNs%201984-2008.pdf.

50. U.S. Nuclear Regulatory Commission, "Waste Confidence Decision Update," *Federal Register*, Dec. 23, 2010, www.federalregister.gov/articles/2010/12/ 23/2010-31637/waste-confidence-decision-update.

51. Barbara Miller, "NRC Extends Time That Radioactive Waste Can Be Stored at Nuclear Plants," *The Patriot-News* (Penn.), Jan. 10, 2011.

52. For example, see Josh Stilts, "NRC Wants Waste Stored for Century," *Brattleboro Reformer*, Jan. 4, 2011.

53. The case is *Pacific Gas and Electric Company v. State Energy Resources Conservation and Development Commission*, 461 U.S. 190 (1983).

54. Scott Hendrick, "State Restrictions on New Nuclear Power Facility Construction," National Conference of State Legislatures, December 2010, www.ncsl .org/?TabId=21817.

55. Weeks, *op. cit.*

56. "Status of Potential New Commercial Nuclear Reactors in the United States," U.S. Energy Information Administration, July 1, 2010, www.eia .doe.gov/cneaf/nuclear/page/nuc_reactors/reactor-com.html.

57. For background see Marcia Clemmitt, "Energy and Climate," *CQ Researcher*, July 24, 2009, pp. 621-644.

58. For example, see Ezra Klein, "Cap-and-Trade is Dead," *The Washington Post*, July 19, 2010.

59. "Press conference by the President," Nov. 3, 2010, www.whitehouse.gov/the-press-office/2010/11/03/ press-conference-president.

60. Matthew L. Wald, "G.O.P. Gains on Capitol Hill May Not Advance Nuclear Power," *The New York Times*, Nov. 16, 2010, www.nytimes.com/2010/ 11/17/business/energy-environment/17NUCLEAR .html.

BIBLIOGRAPHY

Books

Bernstein, Jeremy, *Plutonium: A History of the World's Most Dangerous Element*, Joseph Henry Press, 2007.
Bernstein, a physicist and former *New Yorker* staff writer, recounts the history of plutonium and shows why the buildup of global plutonium stockpiles is dangerous.

Gerber, Michele Stenehjem, *On the Home Front: The Cold War Legacy of the Hanford Nuclear Site*, 3rd edition, Bison Books, 2007.
A comprehensive history of the Hanford nuclear site, constructed as a secret Manhattan Project facility during World War II, covering its Cold War operations and the ongoing effort to clean it up.

Walker, Samuel J., *The Road to Yucca Mountain: The Development of Radioactive Waste Policy in the United States*, University of California Press, 2009.
The Nuclear Regulatory Commission's historian traces the history of U.S. policy debates over managing spent nuclear fuel and high-level radioactive waste.

Articles

Biello, David, "Spent Nuclear Fuel: A Trash Heap Deadly for 250,000 Years or a Renewable Energy Source?" *Scientific American*, Jan. 28, 2009, www .scientificamerican.com/article.cfm?id=nuclear-waste-lethal-trash-or-renewable-energy-source.
Some experts see spent nuclear fuel as waste, but others call it a valuable energy resource.

Blumenthal, Les, "Nuclear Sites Fear They're the Alternative to Yucca Mountain," *McClatchy Newspapers*, Aug. 30, 2009, www.mcclatchydc.com/2009/ 08/30/74567/nuclear-sites-fear-theyre-the.html.
Washington, South Carolina, Idaho and other states that house former nuclear weapons production sites fear that

they will be permanently stuck with military radioactive waste if Yucca Mountain is not built.

Cochran, Thomas B., *et al.*, **"It's Time to Give Up on Breeder Reactors,"** *Bulletin of the Atomic Scientists*, May/June 2010, pp. 50-56, www.princeton.edu/sgs/ publications/articles/Time-to-give-up-BAS-May_ June-2010.pdf.

Based on experience in six other countries, the authors argue that reactors designed to produce more plutonium than they use are expensive, unreliable, dangerous and unnecessary.

Joyce, Christopher, "For N.M., Nuclear Waste May Be Too Hot to Handle," *National Public Radio*, May 14, 2010, www.npr.org/templates/story/story.php?story Id=126799978.

New Mexicans are divided over whether to expand an existing nuclear waste repository in Carlsbad so that it could store commercial spent fuel.

Rosa, Eugene A., *et al.*, **"Nuclear Waste: Knowledge Waste?"** *Science*, vol. 329, Aug. 13, 2010, pp. 762-763.

To identify a workable U.S. nuclear waste policy, a Blue Ribbon Commission appointed by President Obama should focus on conditions that will make that policy socially and politically acceptable to the public.

Upson, Sandra, "Finland's Nuclear Waste Solution," *IEEE Spectrum*, December 2009, http://spectrum.ieee .org/energy/nuclear/finlands-nuclear-waste-solution/0.

Finland is building one of only two active nuclear waste repositories in the world, with the other next door in Sweden.

Wald, Matthew L., "Giant Holes in the Ground," *Technology Review*, November/December 2010.

A predicted nuclear power renaissance has stalled, but the main reason is high construction costs, not controversy over waste disposal.

Reports and Studies

"The Future of the Nuclear Fuel Cycle," Massachusetts Institute of Technology, 2010, http://web.mit .edu/mitei/docs/spotlights/nuclear-fuel-cycle.pdf.

A panel of scientists and engineers argues that the United States should continue with a once-through fuel cycle for at least several decades, plan to store spent fuel for up to a century at centralized sites and create a new quasi-governmental organization to manage nuclear waste.

Garvey, Todd, "The Yucca Mountain Litigation: Breach of Contract under the Nuclear Waste Policy Act of 1982," Congressional Research Service, Dec . 22, 2009, http://ncseonline.org/NLE/CRSreports/ 10Jan/R40996.pdf.

Utilities have filed more than 70 claims against the Department of Energy for breaching legal agreements to take ownership of civilian spent nuclear fuel. The department's total liability could be up to $50 billion.

"Survey of National Programs for Managing High-Level Radioactive Waste and Spent Nuclear Fuel," U.S. Nuclear Waste Technical Review Board, October 2009, www.nwtrb.gov/reports/nwtrb%20sept%2009 .pdf.

Experts say that deep underground storage is the safest approach for long-term management of nuclear waste, but experience in 13 countries shows that designing and locating a repository raise many technical and political challenges.

For More Information

Heart of America Northwest, 1314 E. 56th St., Suite 100 Seattle, WA 98105; (206) 382-1014; www.hoanw.org. Advocates for cleanup of the Hanford nuclear weapons site in eastern Washington state.

Idaho National Laboratory, 2525 Fremont Ave., Idaho Falls, ID 83415; (866) 495-7440; www.inl.gov. Department of Energy laboratory focusing on nuclear and energy research, science and national defense.

National Association of Regulatory Utility Commissioners, 1101 Vermont Ave., N.W., Suite 200, Washington, DC 20005; (202) 898-2200; www.naruc.org. Represents state public service commissions that regulate energy, water and telecommunications utilities.

Natural Resources Defense Council, 40 West 20th St., New York, NY 10011; (212) 727-2700; www.nrdc.org.

Environmental advocacy group that conducts research and policy work on issues including nuclear energy, waste and weapons.

Nuclear Energy Institute, 1776 I St., N.W., Suite 400, Washington, DC 20006; (202) 739-8000; www.nei.org. Represents the nuclear energy and nuclear technologies industry.

U.S. Department of Energy, Office of Nuclear Energy, 1000 Independence Ave., S.W., Washington, DC 20585; (202) 586-4403; www.ne.doe.gov. Promotes nuclear power through research, development and demonstration projects.

U.S. Nuclear Regulatory Commission, One White Flint North, 11555 Rockville Pike, Rockville, MD 20852; (301) 415-7000; www.nrc.gov. Regulates commercial nuclear power plants, transport of nuclear materials and operation of nuclear waste storage and disposal facilities.

12

Energy Policy

Jennifer Weeks

Stock Photo

Oil rig workers symbolize the environmental and political battles being waged over the nation's energy future. Republicans acknowledge the potential danger of offshore drilling, as reflected in last year's Gulf oil spill, but say a failure to produce more domestic oil, coal and natural gas will cost jobs and leave the U.S. too dependent on foreign oil producers. Democrats say failing to pursue alternative energy sources will hasten climate change and squander opportunities to sell new energy technologies to other countries.

From *CQ Researcher*,
May 20, 2011.

s Americans mark the one-year anniversary of the *Deepwater Horizon* oil disaster, conservationists see a painful irony. At the same time that Americans acknowledge the environmental damage along the Gulf coast, political leaders remain locked in a titanic struggle over the future of national energy policy — a struggle that essentially pits fossil fuels against clean energy.

The Obama administration is pressing for more federal investment in renewable energy, such as solar and wind power, and emerging technology such as "clean" coal plants that could capture and bury their greenhouse gas emissions.[1] Congressional Republicans, on the other hand, advocate increased development of domestic oil and natural gas and other carbon-based energy sources.

The stakes in the debate are huge and far-reaching. Democrats say a failure to pursue alternative energy sources will heighten global damage from climate change, make the nation increasingly beholden to unstable foreign oil producers and hurt the economy, in part because of lost opportunities to sell new environmentally friendly energy technologies to other countries.

Republicans, however, say a failure to produce more domestic oil, coal and natural gas will cost jobs and economic growth. They, too, worry about dependence on foreign oil producers but say renewable and other new technologies, which together supply only about 8 percent of the nation's energy demand, can't begin to substitute for oil and coal in handling the nation's energy needs.

Last week President Barack Obama made several concessions in the face of Republican pressure to expand domestic energy production. Obama announced that annual auctions would begin for oil and gas leases in Alaska's National Petroleum Reserve, and that the

Oil Imports Outpace Domestic Production

The United States imported nearly 10 million barrels of oil per day in 2010 — 71 percent more than was produced domestically. Imports have exceeded domestic production over the past two decades and reached a high in 2006 of more than 12 million barrels daily.

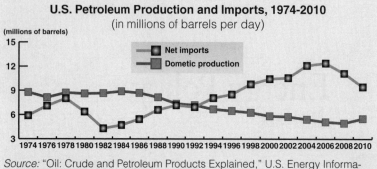

U.S. Petroleum Production and Imports, 1974-2010
(in millions of barrels per day)

Source: "Oil: Crude and Petroleum Products Explained," U.S. Energy Information Administration, October 2010, www.eia.doe.gov/energyexplained/index.cfm?page=oil_home#tab2

Debate over how to meet U.S. energy needs has simmered for several decades, intensifying when supplies grow short and prices rise. Today federal agencies are still cleaning up damage from the Gulf oil disaster, which spilled nearly 5 million barrels of crude into rich fishing grounds, and political turmoil in the oil-rich Middle East has driven gasoline prices above $4 per gallon, lending support to President Obama's argument that the nation needs to wean itself from fossil fuel. To create markets for alternative energy, Obama has set a goal of generating 80 percent of the nation's electricity from cleaner fuels by 2035, including renewable energy, nuclear power, "clean" coal plants and natural gas, which is less polluting than oil and coal but not completely free of environmental effects.

federal government would speed up a review of possible impacts from offshore drilling along the Atlantic coast. He also said that current offshore leaseholders would have additional time to meet new, tighter safety and environmental standards imposed after the BP spill.[2]

The debate is as much about money as it is about energy and the environment. A key issue is whether, as conservatives argue, the federal government should continue to provide oil and gas producers with tax subsidies that total some $4 billion per year.

Many analysts believe it is unlikely that Congress will settle the issue before the 2012 presidential election and that the battle could even outlast a shift in congressional party control or a change in administrations. But others are optimistic that Congress will act this year. "I think $5 a gallon gasoline is the best incentive I know to find a rational energy plan that would create jobs, make us more energy independent, clean up the air," Sen. Lindsey Graham, R-S.C., said in March.[3]

"Energy debates for the past two years have been pretty catastrophic — they've taken an issue that historically has enjoyed pretty strong bipartisan support and created a war dynamic around it," says Jason Grumet, president of the Bipartisan Policy Center, a think tank that proposes policies designed to win support from Republicans and Democrats. "We need to promote more constructive dialogue."

"The United States of America cannot afford to bet our long-term prosperity, our long-term security on a resource that will eventually run out, and even before it runs out will get more and more expensive to extract from the ground," Obama said.[4] Declaring in his State of the Union address in January that "this is our generation's *Sputnik* moment," he said investing in clean energy and other high-tech industries would "strengthen our security, protect our planet, and create countless new jobs for our people."

Yet, conservatives argue that the nation's federal deficit ($1.3 trillion in 2010), 9 percent unemployment rate and relatively young stage of alternative-energy development all lend support to their view that traditional energy sources represent the best way to secure the nation's long-term energy future.

"Wishful thinking about magic bullet alternatives is not going to heat and cool our homes, get us where we need to go, and power the businesses that provide jobs," said Rep. Fred Upton, R-Mich., chair of the House Energy and Commerce Committee. Reflecting the view of many congressional Republicans, Upton said the Obama administration was spending too much money on energy efficiency and renewable energy and not enough on fossil fuel development. "The reality is we still need fossil fuels and will continue to do so for the foreseeable future," he said.[5]

However, clean-energy advocates point out that as well-established industries, fossil fuels have competitive advantages that make it hard for newer technologies to compete, even if those alternatives are environmentally preferable. "It's cheap to finance polluting energy, because big utilities have been building coal and gas plants for a long time, so the market understands them and they can get low-cost capital," says Bracken Hendricks, a senior fellow at the Center for American Progress, a liberal think tank in Washington. "Renewable energy projects often are seen as more risky ventures, so they have higher costs. Also, fossil fuels don't pay for the environmental harms they cause. We underestimate risk and overestimate benefits of fossil fuels, and do the opposite for renewables."

The energy debate doesn't always split neatly along party lines — many legislators in both parties support nuclear energy, for example, despite this spring's nuclear disaster in Japan — but congressional support for Obama's renewable- and clean-energy agenda has come almost exclusively from Democrats. In 2009-2010, Democratic majorities in the House and Senate tried to limit greenhouse gas emissions and require polluters to buy permits for their excess emissions. This system, known as cap-and-trade, was a top priority for environmentalists and was widely expected to push the U.S. toward cleaner energy sources by making it more expensive to generate energy from fossil fuels.

The House passed a cap-and-trade bill in 2009 — albeit by a razor-thin margin — but the Senate did not act. Opponents argued that putting a price on greenhouse gas emissions would make energy more expensive and harm the economy as it struggled to recover from the recession.[6]

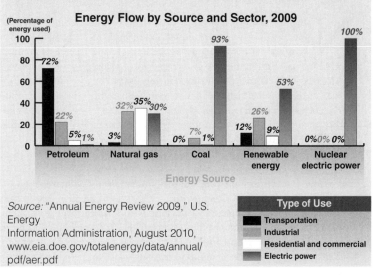

Energy Sources Fit Different Demands

More than 70 percent of petroleum is used in cars, diesel locomotives and other modes of transportation. Twenty-two percent is used for industrial power. By contrast, only 3 percent of natural gas and 12 percent of renewable sources are used for transportation, but natural gas outpaces petroleum as a source of residential and commercial energy. More than 90 percent of coal is used to generate electricity.

Energy Flow by Source and Sector, 2009

(Percentage of energy used)

Type of Use
- Transportation
- Industrial
- Residential and commercial
- Electric power

Source: "Annual Energy Review 2009," U.S. Energy Information Administration, August 2010, www.eia.doe.gov/totalenergy/data/annual/pdf/aer.pdf

Republicans, who gained control of the House and expanded their Senate ranks from 41 seats to 47 in 2010, have other ideas. Most want to focus on established, large-scale energy sources — in particular, oil and gas produced from domestic sources, plus nuclear power, which now supplies 20 percent of the nation's electricity and 9 percent of its total energy. Many advocate cutting government support for energy efficiency and renewable energy, arguing that these sources should compete on their own.

On April 5, House Budget Committee Chairman Paul Ryan, R-Wis., released a long-term budget plan that would slash federal spending for social programs, defense and research and development. The plan would reduce spending on energy from about $8 billion per year, as Obama proposed in his 2012 budget request, to $1 billion per year. Ryan said the plan "rolls back expensive handouts for uncompetitive sources of energy, calling instead for a free and open marketplace for energy development, innovation and exploration."[7]

'Fracking' Dirties Image of Natural Gas Drilling

"Gasland" documentary shows flammable drinking water.

Natural gas is widely hailed as a "clean" fuel because when burned it produces much lower levels of conventional air pollutants and carbon dioxide than oil or coal. And in contrast to nuclear power plants — which generate electricity without producing any carbon dioxide or conventional air pollutants — gas-fired electric plants can be built much more quickly and at lower costs.

But natural gas is stirring controversy because of an increasingly popular method of extracting it from deep inside the earth. Called hydraulic fracturing, or "fracking," the approach involves pumping millions of gallons of water and chemicals under high pressure into rock formations to crack them open and let gas flow upward.

Many landowners complain that fracking is polluting drinking water supplies with chemical additives and flammable methane, the main component of natural gas.[1] Drillers add many types of chemicals to fracking water to help dissolve rock, reduce friction or for other purposes. And when fracking fluids flow to the surface, they can carry dissolved metals and salts from underground.[2]

Fracking has been in use since 1947, but only recently have energy developers combined it with another technique — horizontal drilling — to extract vast quantities of natural gas trapped in underground shale formations. Horizontal drilling allows developers to drill thousands of feet into the earth, then turn the drill sideways to penetrate gas formations trapped tightly between rock layers.

Between 2000 and 2006, production from shale gas formations grew at an average rate of 17 percent annually. Then, as methods improved, production surged, rising at an average yearly rate of 48 percent through 2010.[3] The natural gas industry estimates that fracking and horizontal drilling have increased available domestic supplies from about 60 years' worth to at least 100 years' supply at current levels of production.

Yet fracking has stirred alarm in localities where it is being used. Controversy has been most intense in states located over the Marcellus Shale, an immense formation of gas-rich sedimentary rock that stretches from upstate New York through parts of Pennsylvania, Ohio and West Virginia.

In Pennsylvania alone, more than 2,400 gas wells were drilled in 2006-2010 using either fracking or conventional methods.[4] State officials welcomed the economic activity, but media investigations documented widespread problems, including spills of contaminated wastewater and pollution escaping into drinking water.[5] The documentary film "Gasland" showed homeowners lighting their tap water on fire to demonstrate how much methane it contained.[6]

The natural gas industry, which issued a detailed rebuttal of charges in "Gasland," argues that fracking takes place at levels well below the water table and does not threaten human health or the environment.[7] "No allegations of fracking contaminating drinking water have been proven," says Bruce Vincent, chair of the Independent Petroleum Association of America. He argues that the flammable tap water shown in "Gasland" was caused by naturally occurring methane.

"Fracking has moved into areas that aren't used to gas development, which is raising concern from local communities," Vincent says. "Our industry needs to get out and do a better job of educating and communicating so that people understand how the process works and see the economic benefits."

Nearly all Republicans and some Democrats oppose limiting greenhouse gas emissions. But Obama is using the Environmental Protection Agency to regulate those emissions under the Clean Air Act, citing a 2007 Supreme Court ruling that the EPA has such authority.[8] That move has further polarized Republicans and Democrats and made compromise on an energy policy more elusive.

Yet critics on both sides of the ideological divide argue that more delay in crafting a comprehensive energy policy could make the United States more dependent on

Just this month, however, four Duke University scientists published the first peer-reviewed study linking fracking to contaminated drinking water. The researchers sampled 68 wells near gas-production sites in Pennsylvania and New York and found that water from wells within one kilometer of drilling had much higher levels of dissolved methane than water from wells farther away. The methane's chemical signature was consistent with gas from nearby wells and underground shale formations. The scientists did not find evidence that fracking fluids were contaminating groundwater. [8]

The gas industry argued that the study lacked "key data that would be needed to validate its conclusions," but federal regulators are stepping up oversight of fracking. [9] Currently the process is almost entirely regulated at the state level, but the Environmental Protection Agency is reviewing the drilling method's impacts on drinking water. In April Robert Perciasepe, EPA deputy administrator, accused companies that had injected fracking fluids containing diesel fuel underground without permits of violating the Safe Drinking Water Act, which limits underground injection of fluids. [10] Fracking is exempt from federal regulation under the act except for one additive — diesel fuel, which contains several toxic compounds.

And this month Energy Secretary Steven Chu created another expert panel to review impacts from fracking and recommend ways to make the process cleaner and safer, with initial recommendations due by August. [11]

— Jennifer Weeks

---

[1] Natural gas is a mixture of hydrocarbon gases but is typically 70 to 90 percent methane. See "What is Natural Gas?," www.naturalgas.org.

[2] For background see Jennifer Weeks, "Water Shortages," *CQ Researcher*, June 18, 2010, pp. 529-552.

[3] "Annual Energy Outlook 2011," U.S. Energy Information Administration, April 26, 2011, p. 2, www.eia.doe.gov/forecasts/aeo/pdf/0383%282011%29.pdf.

[4] Bryan Walsh, "Could Shale Gas Power the World?" *Time*, March 31, 2011, www.time.com/time/health/article/0,8599,2062331,00.html.

[5] "Buried Secrets: Gas Drilling's Environmental Threat," *Pro Publica*, Dec. 2, 2010, www.propublica.org/series/buried-secrets-gas-drillings

Tap water containing methane gas is ignited in the documentary film "Gasland."

environmental-threat; Ian Urbina, "Drilling Down," *The New York Times*, Feb. 27-April 8, 2011, http://topics.nytimes.com/top/news/us/series/drilling_down/index.html?scp=2&sq=fracking%20radioactive&st=cse.

[6] Jeremy Egner, "Muckraking Road Movie on Natural Gas Drilling," *The New York Times*, June 21, 2010, http://artsbeat.blogs.nytimes.com/2010/06/21/a-muckraker-targets-onshore-drilling/.

[7] "The Energy You Need, the Facts You Demand," *Energy in Depth*, June 9, 2010, www.energyindepth.org/2010/06/debunking-gasland/.

[8] Stephen G. Osborn, *et al.*, "Methane Contamination of Drinking Water Accompanying Gas-Well Drilling and Hydraulic Fracturing," *Proceedings of the National Academy of Sciences*, Early Edition, published online May 9, 2011, www.pnas.org/content/early/2011/05/02/1100682108.

[9] Bryan Walsh, "Another Fracking Mess for the Shale-Gas Industry," *Time*, May 9, 2011, www.time.com/time/health/article/0,8599,2070533,00.html.

[10] Mike Soraghan, "Fracking for Natural Gas With Diesel Violated Law, EPA Says," *The New York Times*, April 13, 2011, www.nytimes.com/gwire/2011/04/13/13greenwire-fracking-for-natural-gas-with-diesel-violated-81979.html?scp=3&sq=fracking%20diesel&st=cse.

[11] John M. Broder, "Fracture on Fracking," *The New York Times*, May 6, 2011, http://green.blogs.nytimes.com/2011/05/06/fracture-on-fracking/?scp=2&sq=fracking%20diesel&st=cse.

unstable foreign producers and less competitive in the global marketplace.

National energy policy since the 1970s "has stumbled, marked by uncertain goals and shifting priorities, an inability to measure the impact of our choices, and a stark lack of accountability across the government," a Bipartisan Policy Center task force, led by former senators and Cabinet-level officials, declared in April. The group called for clear, achievable energy objectives that gradually shift the U.S. economy away from oil. "Our nation does not want for a lack of ideas," it said. "What we suffer is a lack of discipline and follow-through."[9]

As the Obama administration, Congress and interest groups debate what kind of energy strategy the U.S. should pursue, here are some issues they are considering:

Is a shift away from fossil fuels necessary?

President Obama's energy policy calls for more production from a variety of energy sources, including domestic oil and natural gas and nuclear power.[10] But it also assumes that the nation needs to shift to a clean-energy future that emphasizes energy efficiency, renewable fuels and other advanced low-carbon and carbon-free technologies.

"Instead of subsidizing yesterday's energy sources, we need to invest in tomorrow's," Obama said in his weekly radio address on April 23. In the long term, Obama asserted, "investing in clean, renewable energy" is "the key to helping families at the pump and reducing our dependence on foreign oil."[11] Obama's proposed budget for fiscal 2012 would eliminate $4 billion in yearly tax subsidies for fossil fuel production and spend the money on clean-energy sources instead.[12]

The shift to clean-energy sources is widely supported by scientists, who say the burning of fossil fuels and other human activities are major causes of global climate change. A 2010 review of climate research by the congressionally chartered National Academies of Science put it bluntly: "Climate change is occurring, is caused largely by human activities and poses significant risks for — and in many cases is already affecting — a broad range of human and natural systems."[13]

Many conservatives argue, however, that the core goal of U.S. energy policy should be to deliver abundant, low-cost energy, which is most readily available from fossil fuels. "We want energy to be cheap, and we want a surplus," says Kenneth Green, a scholar at the American Enterprise Institute, a conservative think tank in Washington. "We're a wealthy country, and we can pay more for oil than China or India. Renewables are simply more expensive than fossil fuels, are slower to deploy and are slower to ramp up in times of economic prosperity."

Unlike many congressional Republicans, Green does not deny that climate change is occurring, although he thinks its near-term effects may have been overstated. In his view renewable energy is too small-scale to be a

solution. "The trivial role that low-carbon energy sources could conceivably play in the energy economy would do virtually nothing to influence the climate, except for nuclear power, which is the only non-carbon source of electricity that could be deployed at a large enough scale to displace coal," he asserts. "Even then, there would have to be a global dash to nuclear power, which is unlikely given the disaster in Japan."

The oil and gas industry and its supporters seek to boost domestic production, which they say will be more reliable than relying on imports. In the past several years, improved drilling techniques and other technical advances have enabled energy producers to extract large quantities of natural gas from once inaccessible sources, especially shale formations. That has driven down prices and increased supplies of natural gas, which accounts for 25 percent of the nation's total energy supply.

"Natural gas is an American treasure," says Bruce Vincent, chair of the Independent Petroleum Association of America. "Technical advances have allowed us to unlock an incredible resource that can fuel the country for a long time, and we should take advantage of it."

Those new extraction techniques — specifically, a method called hydraulic fracturing, in which developers pump millions of gallons of fluid underground to crack open rock formations — have triggered protests in areas where opponents say they are polluting drinking water supplies. Nonetheless, many experts say natural gas gradually will replace a significant fraction of older coal-fired power plants over the next 20 to 30 years.[14]

Oil, which accounts for 37 percent of the nation's total energy supply, poses problems as well. It is more carbon intensive than natural gas and produces air pollutants that are ingredients in smog and acid rain. Moreover, since oil is traded on a global market, supply disruptions anywhere in the world can create shortages and price spikes. "'Foreign oil' is a myth," says Grumet of the Bipartisan Policy Center. "Even if the U.S. produced all the oil it needed, our economy would be just as impacted when oil prices rose worldwide as it is now."

Although regulation of greenhouse gas emissions has stalled in Washington, the United States continues to negotiate with other countries over ways to slow long-term climate change. If those talks eventually lead to limits on greenhouse gases, the three main carbon-based fuels — oil, natural gas and coal — will become more expensive and the United States will need alternatives.

"Just because we won't have a carbon policy in the next couple of years doesn't mean that we won't face greenhouse gas limits 10 years out," says Bruce Biewald, president of Synapse Energy Economics, a consulting firm in Cambridge, Mass. "We need to think carefully about the impact of federal energy policies and try to drive investments in a forward-looking direction, instead of locking ourselves into 30- or 40-year-old technologies."

Can clean-energy sources compete?

Although renewable energy provides less than 8 percent of total U.S. energy today, experts say that share could grow substantially over the next several decades. Some renewable fuels are more advanced and affordable than others, but many types are competitive now with conventional energy at good sites — that is, places that are sunny enough to generate significant solar power, breezy enough to generate substantial wind power or rich in some other renewable resource.

"Wind, biomass power, and geothermal energy are used worldwide," says Bobi Garrett, senior vice president at the U.S. Department of Energy's National Renewable Energy Laboratory in Colorado. "Wind is the fastest-growing renewable and can compete economically with conventional sources in many markets." Electricity from solar power costs about four times as much as other sources, but in February the Energy Department announced an initiative called SunShot, which seeks to make solar power competitive by 2020.

"That's a stretch goal and a grand challenge, but it's not unreasonable," says Garrett. "There's been a lot of investment in the underlying science in recent years, and we can draw on it to make new breakthroughs." And, she points out, solar power is already cost-effective in some areas, such as the Southwest, where peak sunlight hours match up with peak electricity demand periods (for example, on hot summer afternoons).

Fossil Fuels Are Big Carbon Emitters

When burned, all fossil fuels produce carbon dioxide, the main greenhouse gas, and sulfur dioxide and nitrogen oxides — pollutants that contribute to acid rain and smog. But emissions from combustion of natural gas are significantly lower than those from coal or oil. Hydropower and nuclear plants do not produce greenhouse gases or conventional air pollutants during energy generation.

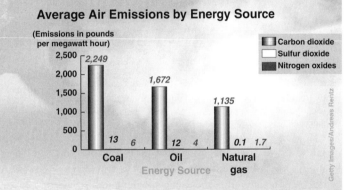

Average Air Emissions by Energy Source

Source: "Air Emissions," Environmental Protection Agency, December 2007, www.epa.gov/cleanenergy/energy-and-you/affect/air-emissions.html

But skeptics argue that solar and wind power and other clean technologies cannot compete without federal support. "Renewables basically rely on subsidies," says the American Enterprise Institute's Green. "Without supports, they just don't get built."

Estimates of the value of government energy measures vary widely. According to one study, from the early 1970s through 2003 solar, wind, biomass and geothermal energy received more than $38 billion in broadly defined federal support.[15] The Environmental Law Institute, a research and education group in Washington that works to strengthen environmental protection, calculates that from fiscal 2002 through 2008, renewable fuels received $29 billion in more narrowly defined federal subsidies — that is, direct spending or tax breaks.[16]

However, the federal government spends much more money on fossil fuels and nuclear power than on renewables. From the early 1970s through 2003, oil received more than $302 billion in federal support, followed by coal ($80 billion) and nuclear power ($63 billion).[17] From 2002 through 2008, the Environmental Law Institute estimates that traditional fossil fuels received more than $70 billion in federal subsidies.[18]

Steam from the cooling towers at the Limerick Generating Station, a nuclear power plant in Pottstown, Pa., rises over a nearby neighborhood.

AFP/Getty Images/Stan Honda

Clean-power advocates argue that these subsidies to large, mature industries make it hard for new, cleaner sources to compete. "Subsidies can help young industries that are growing and developing overcome certain cost barriers," says Hendricks of the Center for American Progress. "They can also be very destructive when they give windfall profits to mature industries. Renewable energy is receiving subsidies to drive its costs down and make it more competitive. Most producers agree that as technology matures, that support should sunset. On a truly level playing field without subsidies, renewables would do quite well."

Oil and gas producers argue, however, that the tax breaks their industry receives are not subsidies at all. "They are cost-recovery mechanisms, similar to what other industries get," says Vincent, at the Independent Petroleum Association of America. "A subsidy is designed to help something become commercially competitive in a market where it otherwise wouldn't be."

Programs such as SunShot seek to help companies in new industries grow from early pilot operations to large-scale commercial operations that can attract funding from major private investors. Advocates say that helping new technologies scale up in this way is smart policy. "Under our last major research grant from the Department of Energy, we commercialized six major innovations within a three-year contract, including high-efficiency panels and high-efficiency photovoltaic cells," says Julie Blunden, executive vice president at SunPower, a San Jose, Calif.,

company that designs and manufactures solar-energy systems. "That's a great return on federal dollars."

In April SunPower and a partner company opened a jointly operated plant in Milpitas, Calif., that will manufacture 75 megawatts of highly efficient solar panels for homes and power plants annually. At the plant opening, Democratic Gov. Jerry Brown signed a bill expanding California's renewable electricity standard, which now requires utilities to generate one-third of their power from renewable sources.[19]

Earlier this year SunPower won a contract to generate and deliver more than 700 megawatts of solar power to Southern California Edison, one of California's largest utilities, for resale to the utility's customers. "We came in at a price that was competitive with a new natural gas plant," Blunden says. "That's something we could never have achieved if we hadn't been able to scale up our manufacturing and if we hadn't had California's renewable electricity standard driving demand."

Based partly on SunPower's recent successes, the popular Motley Fool investment website rated the company as a "Rising Star." Motley Fool's report noted that renewable energy companies still depend heavily on government support and are fairly risky investments. Still, it argued, "the market for alternative energy won't go away. . . . There are myriad reasons why so many people all over the globe are looking for better, cleaner, cheaper alternatives to fossil fuels."[20]

Is the United States in a global clean-energy race?

Investment in clean-energy industries has surged worldwide in the past five years, rising from $51.7 billion in 2004 to $243 billion in 2010.[21] Currently China and Europe are the largest growth centers for clean power. Many observers worry that if the United States does not give clean energy enough support, it will lose the chance to be a global leader and forfeit jobs and investment to other countries. Ultimately, some warn, America might replace its dependence on foreign oil with dependence on imported green-power technologies.

Consulting firm Ernst & Young ranked the United States second after China in its spring 2011 Renewable Energy Country Attractiveness Indices, which rank nations based on how strongly their laws, regulations and investment climates support renewable energy development. Other countries rounding out the top 10 are

Germany, India, the United Kingdom, Italy, France, Spain, Canada and Portugal.

China surpassed the United States in mid-2010, but Ernst & Young noted some positive U.S. developments, including President Obama's proposed goal of generating 80 percent of the nation's electricity from clean sources by 2035.[22]

"We absolutely are in a race," says Hendricks of the Center for American Progress. "Some of the fastest innovation in the energy sector is happening around clean tech in areas like the future of the auto industry, energy storage and materials science. If we lose leadership here, we will lose leadership much more broadly."

U.S. manufacturers have moved production abroad for decades in search of cheap labor, but Hendricks argues that clean-energy companies have other reasons for looking overseas. "China has made a bigger commitment to energy efficiency and renewable energy than the U.S. has," he asserts. "Beijing just issued a five-year plan with very specific targets for adopting different types of energy efficiency in buildings and for building systems like high-speed rail and a smart grid. The U.S. doesn't have a planned economy like China, but our current energy policies are making it hard for clean energy companies to build a clean economy because they're not getting predictable market signals."

Michael El-Hillow, owner of Evergreen Solar, the third-largest U.S. manufacturer of solar panels, cited China's offer of extremely low-interest loans on favorable terms from state-owned banks in his decision to close Evergreen's main factory in Massachusetts early this year and shift production to a plant it owned in Wuhan, China. El-Hillow made the move despite having received more than $58 million in incentives from Massachusetts to locate there.[23]

Massachusetts officials were angry at the company's decision but said the U.S. government was not doing enough to compete with China on clean energy. "The federal government has brought a knife to a gun fight," said Ian Bowles, the state's former secretary of energy and environmental affairs.[24]

Others say, however, that the spread of green-technology industries is good for the United States even if the systems are manufactured elsewhere. "China's investments offer spillover benefits to the rest of the world," UCLA economics professor Matthew Kahn wrote in *The New York Times*. In Kahn's view, China's massive investments

will push clean-energy costs down and make items like solar panels cheaper for everyone who wants them.[25]

Conservatives dismiss the Obama administration's efforts to compare U.S.- China competition in clean energy to the *Sputnik*-era space race. "[I]t is true that China is spending money on energy hand over fist," argued analysts Nicolas Loris and Derek Scissors of the conservative Heritage Foundation think tank. "But China has very little to show for it. Massive regulatory intervention and tens of billions of dollars in annual spending on green energy have produced results that are drastically inferior to those of the United States — both economically and environmentally — and have left China falling behind rather than marching ahead, contrary to the popular myth."[26]

One of the largest U.S. manufacturing companies, General Electric, is betting heavily on solar power. In April GE announced that it would invest $600 million to build the largest solar panel production plant in the nation. The factory, whose location is yet to be chosen, is expected to open in 2013 and employ some 400 workers. Although many solar companies are struggling to compete with inexpensive mass-produced silicon panels from China, GE plans to produce a different type: thin-film panels that convert sunlight to electricity somewhat less efficiently than silicon but are less expensive to make.[27]

"America excels at research and development and at innovation, and U.S. solar companies that are succeeding have developed distinctive technologies," says SunPower's Blunden. "The question is whether they can grow at the pace at which Chinese companies are growing. Growth begets cost reduction, which begets competitiveness. We need policies that will make it possible for companies in the U.S. to make long-term investments in research and development that will drive our costs down and help us be competitive."

BACKGROUND

Cheap and Abundant

Since the Industrial Revolution in the 1800s, fossil fuels have provided most of the energy that drives the U.S. economy. Coal fueled factories, heated homes and powered trains and ships in the 19th century. In the early 1900s a drilling boom in Texas introduced a new, versatile source: oil. And energy companies started developing natural gas

Energy Companies Receive Tax Breaks, Other Federal Aid

Obama seeks to end $4 billion in benefits.

Energy producers receive an abundance of government subsidies and other benefits, from grants and tax breaks to research programs and rules requiring federal agencies to buy certain types of fuel to operate vehicles and heat offices.

Budget analysts typically define subsidies as policies that cost the U.S. Treasury money: direct payments, such as cash grants, and tax breaks, which represent income that the government chooses not to collect.

But many other government policies also benefit specific fuels or technologies. For example, in 2005 Congress required refiners to blend certain amounts of renewable fuel — mainly corn-based ethanol — into gasoline, and lawmakers expanded the policy in 2007 to include bio-based diesel fuel. For 2011 the rule requires use of nearly 14 billion gallons of biofuels. [1]

Because ethanol is more expensive to produce than gasoline, consumers pay the extra cost at the pump. In addition, oil companies receive a tax credit for every gallon of ethanol they blend into gasoline, and domestic ethanol producers are protected by tariffs that block cheaper imports. [2]

President Obama has called for ending eight tax provisions that benefit the oil and natural gas industries at a total cost of about $4 billion annually. Most of the expected revenue ($3.38 billion per year) would come from three programs:

• Tax write-offs in place since 1913 for certain drilling costs, such as labor expenses and drilling fluids. Ending the write-offs would generate $1.9 billion in additional federal tax revenue in 2012, or nearly $12.5 billion from 2012 through 2021.

• Depletion allowances in place since 1926 allow producers to deduct 15 percent from their gross income to compensate for the reduction in supply of a finite resource — oil and natural gas. If the allowance ended, producers would pay $607 million more in taxes in 2012, or an additional $11.2 billion from 2012 through 2021.

• Deductions for domestic manufacturing enacted in 2004 allow oil and natural gas companies to deduct 6 percent of their net income for production in the U.S. The program is intended to lower labor costs and stimulate employment. Ending it would generate $902 million in additional tax revenue in 2012, or about $18.3 billion in the 2012-2021 period. [3]

Other energy sources also receive subsidies. The nonpartisan Environmental Law Institute estimates that renewable fuels received almost $29 billion between 2002 and 2008, including:

• $11.5 billion in tax credits to refiners for blending fuel ethanol into gasoline;

(which was often found along with oil deposits) during World War II, both for energy and as an integral part of making chemicals and fertilizer.

Oil surpassed coal as America's primary fuel in 1950, driven by the postwar economic boom and expansion of the Interstate Highway System. To meet growing demand, developers started drilling for oil in the Gulf of Mexico. But U.S. domestic oil production peaked in 1970. As yields began to decline, the United States cultivated links with oil-producing countries in the Middle East and North Africa and relied increasingly on oil imports.

The natural gas industry grew more slowly because the federal government set price ceilings starting in 1954, based on where gas was produced. This policy sought to protect consumers, but prices were set so low that producers had little incentive to enter the market. As a result, natural gas was not widely sold outside of major producing states such as Texas in the 1950s and '60s.

But the federal government fostered another large-scale energy industry during this time: nuclear power, an outgrowth of the top-secret Manhattan Project to develop an atomic bomb during World War II. Congress allowed private utilities to own nuclear reactors starting in 1954. In 1957 it passed the Price-Anderson Act, which capped private liability for reactor accidents at $560 million. This step sought to allay energy companies' fear that they would have

- $5.4 billion in production tax credits for electricity generation from wind, solar, biomass and other renewable fuels;
- $5 billion in payments to farmers for growing corn used to make ethanol; and
- $294 million in low-cost federal financing for public utilities that distribute electricity from federally owned hydropower dams. [4]

The institute notes that tax credits for renewable energy production were time-limited, while most large tax subsidies for fossil fuels are permanent tax code provisions. [5]

Federal spending for research and development also helps many energy sources by paying for some work on basic science and new technologies. The Department of Energy (DOE) spends about $2 billion each year for applied R&D in energy efficiency, renewable energy, fossil fuels and nuclear power systems. DOE also spends about $4 billion for basic research on fundamental issues, such as energy storage and high-energy physics.

From 1978 through 2008, DOE spent $57.5 billion on energy research and development, not including basic research. At its spending peak, in 1978, when the United States was reacting to severe oil shocks in the Middle East, DOE spent $6 billion on energy R&D. Through the next two decades that figure fell drastically to a low of $505 million in fiscal 1998 before rising gradually to its current level. However, when spending is adjusted for inflation, DOE is spending far less on energy R&D today than it did 30 years ago. [6]

Another major policy that benefits the nuclear industry is the Price-Anderson Act, enacted in 1957, which requires utilities to buy a set amount of primary insurance (currently $375 million) for each nuclear plant and to contribute to a secondary insurance pool for the entire U.S. nuclear industry, which currently stands at about $12.6 billion. If an accident causes damages higher than this amount, however, Congress is responsible for deciding how to pay any higher costs.

The nuclear industry argues that Price-Anderson has not cost taxpayers any money since it was enacted. [7] But critics argue that if nuclear operators had to carry full, private liability insurance, the cost of nuclear power would be much higher. [8] According to the Government Accountability Office, "No credible quantification of the value [of this liability limit] is available."

— *Jennifer Weeks*

[1] U.S. Environmental Protection Agency, "Regulation of Fuels and Fuel Additives: 2011 Renewable Fuel Standards," *Federal Register*, Dec. 9, 2010, p. 76791.

[2] Tom Doggett and Charles Abbott, "Senate Votes to Extend Ethanol Subsidy for 2011," Reuters, Dec. 15, 2010.

[3] Summarized from Robert Pirog, "Oil and Natural Gas Industry Tax Issues in the BY2012 Budget Proposal," Congressional Research Service, March 3, 2011, www.nationalaglawcenter.org/assets/crs/R41669.pdf.

[4] "Estimating U.S. Government Subsidies to Energy Sources: 2002-2008," Environmental Law Institute, September 2009, pp. 21-24,

[5] *Ibid.*, p. 3.

[6] "Advanced Energy Technologies: Budget Trends and Challenges for DOE's Energy R&D Program," U.S. Government Accountability Office, March 5, 2008, www.gao.gov/new.items/d08556t.pdf.

[7] "Price-Anderson Act Provides Effective Public Liability Insurance at No Cost to the Public," Nuclear Energy Institute, June 2010, www.nei.org/resourcesandstats/documentlibrary/safetyandsecurity/factsheet/priceandersonact/.

[8] "Nuclear Power: Still Not Viable Without Subsidies," Union of Concerned Scientists, executive summary, February 2011, p. 9, http://earthtrack.net/files/uploaded_files/nuclear%20subsidies_summary.pdf.

to pay for potentially massive damages if an accident occurred at a commercial nuclear plant. By 1970, 20 reactors were operating, and dozens more were under construction.

Through the 1950s most Americans viewed rapid economic growth and high consumer spending as positive trends. But it gradually became clear that prosperity was fouling air and water and damaging natural resources. In a preface to a 1965 expert study, President Lyndon B. Johnson observed, "Pollution is now one of the most pervasive problems of our society."[28]

The backlash affected some big energy projects. In 1966, when federal officials proposed building hydropower dams on the Colorado River that would have flooded more than 100 miles of the Grand Canyon, thousands of people protested and the project was canceled. Then in 1969 an undersea wellhead off Santa Barbara, Calif., leaked 200,000 gallons of oil, contaminating 35 miles of coastline. The disaster helped to catalyze the first Earth Day rally in 1970 and led to state and federal bans on new offshore drilling along much of the U.S. coastline.

Oil Shocks

The era of cheap oil ended on Oct. 20, 1973, when Arab members of the Organization of Petroleum Exporting Countries (OPEC) cut off oil exports to the United States

CHRONOLOGY

1950s-1960s *U.S. relies on coal and oil, starts to develop nuclear power.*

1953 President Dwight D. Eisenhower proposes "Atoms for Peace" program.

1957 Price-Anderson Act limits nuclear plant owners' liability.

1970s-1980s *Arab oil shocks temporarily boost support for conservation and alternative fuels, but renewable sources struggle to reach commercial scale.*

1970 U.S. oil production peaks at 11.3 million barrels per day and begins gradual decline. . . . Environmentalists hold first Earth Day partly in response to major undersea oil well leak near Santa Barbara, Calif., on April 22, 1969.

1973 Arab members of Organization of Petroleum Exporting Countries (OPEC) embargo oil exports to the U.S., sparking a national energy crisis.

1975 Congress creates the Strategic Petroleum Reserve to reduce the impact of future oil shortages, and adopts Corporate Average Fuel Economy standards.

1977 President Jimmy Carter's energy plan aims to reduce dependence on oil imports through conservation and efficiency standards. . . . Oil from Alaska's North Slope reaches markets.

1977-79 Revolution in Iran halts oil exports, triggering a second global oil shock. . . . Congress begins deregulating natural gas prices. . . . Explosion and partial core meltdown at Pennsylvania's Three Mile Island nuclear power plant undercut public support for nuclear energy.

1986 Major accident at Chernobyl nuclear plant in Ukraine further intensifies safety fears.

1989 *Exxon Valdez* runs aground in Alaska's Prince William Sound, spilling 11 million gallons of oil.

1990s *Environmental concerns dominate energy-policy debates. Natural gas becomes an increasingly popular alternative to oil and coal.*

1990 Congress amends Clean Air Act to limit pollution from electric power plants through a cap-and-trade system.

1992 World Environmental Summit in Rio de Janeiro, Brazil, adopts Framework Convention on Climate Change to cut greenhouse gas emissions voluntarily. . . . Energy Policy Act of 1992 increases U.S. investments in energy efficiency, renewable energy and alternative fuels.

1997 Clinton administration signs Kyoto Protocol, pledging the U.S. to cutting greenhouse gas emissions 7 percent below 1990 levels by 2012; Senate refuses to ratify the treaty.

2000s *National energy policy focuses on production under a Republican administration, then on energy efficiency and low-carbon sources under President Obama.*

2001 President George W. Bush advocates more use of fossil fuels and nuclear power.

2005 Energy Policy Act of 2005 provides loan guarantees and tax credits for new nuclear reactors and extends industry's liability protection.

2007 Supreme Court rules that the Environmental Protection Agency can regulate carbon dioxide as a pollutant under the Clean Air Act.

2009 House passes carbon cap-and-trade legislation, but Senate fails to move a similar bill. . . . Congress approves more than $26 billion in economic stimulus funds for clean-energy development and deployment.

2010 Coal mine explosion in West Virginia kills 29 workers. . . . BP's Macondo well in the Gulf of Mexico suffers a blowout and spills nearly 5 million barrels of oil. . . . Republicans win control of the House and press for major federal spending cuts.

2011 After a massive earthquake and tsunami, three reactors at Japan's Fukushima nuclear power station suffer partial core meltdowns. Used fuel rods at another reactor overheat, releasing radiation into the air. . . . Unrest in North Africa and Middle East drives oil prices well above $100 per barrel.

after it supported Israel in the Yom Kippur War. The embargo, which lasted six months, raised the prices of gasoline, home heating oil and other petroleum-based products and energy-intensive processes, triggering a deep economic recession in the United States from 1973-75.

In response, President Richard M. Nixon imposed gasoline rationing for the first time since World War II. To reduce dependence on oil imports, the Nixon administration started building a pipeline to bring crude oil from Alaska's Prudhoe Bay to the Lower 48 states. In 1975 Congress imposed the first Corporate Average Fuel Economy (CAFE) standards on automakers, requiring them to raise the fuel efficiency of new passenger cars to 27.5 miles per gallon on average by 1987. Congress also created the federally owned Strategic Petroleum Reserve and started deregulating oil prices so that they would rise to market levels.

Shortly after taking office in 1977, President Jimmy Carter delivered a blunt speech about America's energy options. "The oil and natural gas we rely on for 75 percent of our energy are running out," Carter warned. "Each American uses the energy equivalent of 60 barrels of oil per person each year. Ours is the most wasteful nation on earth." Just as coal had replaced wood in the 19th century as the world's primary fuel, and oil and gas had later supplanted coal, Carter argued that it was time to shift again — this time to "strict conservation" and reliance on coal (which the United States still had in abundance) and to renewable sources like wind and solar power.[29]

Carter's words spurred Congress to create a Cabinet-level Department of Energy and approve new energy-efficiency standards and tax incentives for investments in renewable energy sources, such as solar, wind and geothermal power. To encourage more domestic energy production and let prices rise to market levels, Carter also deregulated natural gas prices.

Some of these steps worked. For example, the share of U.S. electricity generation produced from oil dropped from 20 percent to 3 percent as utilities switched to

Subsidies Favor Fossil Fuels

Federal energy subsidies totaled $101.5 billion from 2002 to 2008, according to the Environmental Law Institute. Nearly 70 percent of the total — more than $70 billion — went to traditional fossil-fuel producers, such as oil and natural gas companies.

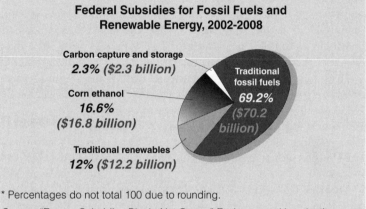

Federal Subsidies for Fossil Fuels and Renewable Energy, 2002-2008

Carbon capture and storage
2.3% ($2.3 billion)

Corn ethanol
16.6% ($16.8 billion)

Traditional fossil fuels
69.2% ($70.2 billion)

Traditional renewables
12% ($12.2 billion)

* Percentages do not total 100 due to rounding.

Source: "Energy Subsidies Black, Not Green," Environmental Law Institute, September 2009, www.eli.org/pdf/Energy_Subsidies_Black_Not_Green.pdf

natural gas and coal.[30] Others were less successful. Notably, developers received tax credits for wind- and solar-power projects based on how much money they invested, not on actual electricity generated, so some facilities were built haphazardly and performed poorly.[31] In another setback, Pennsylvania's Three Mile Island nuclear plant suffered a hydrogen explosion and partial meltdown in 1979. The accident undercut public support for nuclear power, which was already reeling from massive cost overruns and construction delays.[32]

The Iranian Revolution in the winter of 1978-79 brought a militant, fundamentalist Islamic regime to power in Tehran, shutting off Iranian oil exports and triggering a new wave of worldwide panic-buying and price spikes. The outbreak of the Iran-Iraq War in 1980 severely damaged both countries' oil industries, worsening the shortage.

In the 1980s, President Ronald Reagan asserted that markets, not government, were key to meeting energy needs and reviving the economy. Reagan speeded up deregulation of oil and natural gas prices and slashed subsidies for renewable energy. Symbolically, he also had solar panels that had been installed during Carter's term removed from the White House roof. In spite of this philosophical shift, U.S. oil consumption fell in the early 1980s in response to high world prices. But as other oil-producing countries entered the market and made up for Iran and Iraq's lost output, prices fell, and energy use rose again.

Greener Energy

In the late 1980s scientists began to speak publicly about a new concern: global warming, driven mainly by human activities that were raising the concentrations of greenhouse gases (GHGs) in the atmosphere. By far, the largest human-driven contribution to climate change was carbon dioxide emissions from fossil-fuel combustion.

"It is time to stop waffling so much and say that the evidence is pretty strong that the greenhouse effect is here," NASA scientist James Hansen told a Senate committee in a widely publicized June 1988 hearing. Hansen and other panelists called for sharp cuts in fossil-fuel use to avoid impacts such as severe droughts and melting of polar ice caps.[33]

President George H. W. Bush (1989-93), who had worked in the oil industry in Texas as a young man, maintained Reagan's focus on increasing energy supplies. Bush supported opening the Arctic National Wildlife Refuge (ANWR) to oil and gas exploration, but this policy lost support after the tanker *Exxon Valdez* ran aground in Alaska's Prince William Sound in March 1989, spilling 11 million gallons of oil and contaminating more than 1,000 miles of shoreline.

In 1990 Congress amended the Clean Air Act to address smog- and ozone-forming emissions produced by electric power plants that burned fossil fuels. President Bush supported a market-based approach that capped emissions of sulfur dioxide (SO_2), one of the most serious pollutants, and allowed sources to buy and sell emission allowances. Over the next decade, this system reduced SO_2 emissions by nearly 30 percent from 1990 levels. The cost for the program had been projected at $4.6 billion, but actual reductions cost only about $1 billion, partly because polluters were allowed to choose the most cost-effective way to meet their emission targets.[34]

Bush supported other voluntary efforts to conserve energy and reduce pollution — moves that he said also would lower greenhouse-gas emissions. But he argued that too much uncertainty existed about the scale and timing of climate change to take more aggressive action.[35]

Bush's successor, President Bill Clinton (1993-2001), opposed opening ANWR to oil and gas exploration, and he used his executive authority to protect public lands in other regions from energy development. Clinton also proposed higher funding for energy efficiency and renewable fuels and supported action to reduce GHG emissions.

In 1997 the Clinton administration signed the Kyoto Protocol, which committed the United States to reducing greenhouse gas emissions to 7 percent below 1990 levels by 2012. But Republican majorities in Congress opposed budget increases for low-carbon energy research, and the entire Senate passed a resolution opposing the Protocol, so Clinton never submitted it for ratification.

Seesawing Policies

President George W. Bush (2001-2009), who had followed his father's early career path into the oil business, switched the focus back to increasing energy supplies and argued that the case for global warming had not been proven. Bush's energy policy called for boosting supplies of oil, gas and coal, plus expansion of nuclear power. His administration moved to reduce barriers to energy production on public lands, lobbied vigorously for energy development in ANWR and called for building a new generation of nuclear power reactors.

Bush cut spending on energy efficiency and renewable sources, except for hydrogen power for vehicles and electricity production — a long-term goal that its sponsors did not expect to produce results before 2020.[36] Congressional Democrats and environmental advocates harshly criticized the Bush energy plan for emphasizing production over conservation and downplaying the environmental impact of energy development.

During the 2008 presidential campaign, high gasoline prices brought energy issues to the forefront. Sen. John McCain, R-Ariz., the Republican nominee, and his running mate, Alaska Gov. Sarah Palin, called for more domestic oil production, leading chants of "Drill, baby, drill!" at campaign rallies. Illinois Sen. Barack Obama, the Democratic nominee, proposed strategies to move away from oil, including government investments to develop and commercialize cleaner energy sources and higher fuel-economy standards for automobiles.[37]

As president-elect, Obama promised action on these issues, even though oil prices had fallen sharply from their summer peak of $147 per barrel. The United States could not afford complacency just because oil was cheap for the moment, Obama argued.

"We go from shock to trance," Obama said a week after the election. "You know, oil prices go up, gas prices at the pump go up, everybody goes into a flurry of activity. And then the prices go back down, and suddenly we act like it's not important, and we start, you know, filling up our SUVs again. And, as a consequence, we never make any progress. It's part of the addiction, all right. That has to be broken. Now is the time to break it."[38]

CURRENT SITUATION

Budget Focus

After several years of polarized debate over energy and climate change, some observers are cautiously hopeful that Congress will take constructive steps to ease U.S. dependence on oil and shape a more proactive national energy policy. Negotiations over federal spending could provide a framework.

"I think there will be energy legislation before the 2012 elections, especially if gasoline prices keep rising," says Grumet of the Bipartisan Policy Center. "It won't be comprehensive, but there are opportunities. For example, our national political dialogue will be driven by debt issues for the next few years. There's growing concern that our tax system is not encouraging economic growth. We might see energy pricing or a carbon tax emerge in a debate over tax reform."

Budget concerns could also reshape energy subsidies. "Saying 'I don't like yours, you don't like mine' isn't a constructive approach," Grumet contends. "We should take it as given that when Congress decided to devote taxpayer money to a specific energy source, it had a legitimate purpose. But many of the policies we have now were passed years ago. Why don't we go back and try to identify what their purpose was, and whether we're achieving those ends efficiently? If we're not, we can save money by reforming subsidies that aren't working."

So far, however, both parties have engaged in angry debates over oil and gas subsidies. Democrats have seized on the issue as a way to show concern over gasoline prices and federal spending. They cite former Shell Oil CEO

Oil Shocks and Spills

Iranian protestors display a poster of religious leader Ayatollah Khomeini during a demonstration in Tehran against the shah in January 1979 (top). The Iranian Revolution in the winter of 1978-79 brought a militant fundamentalist Islamic regime to power, shutting off Iranian oil exports and triggering a new wave of worldwide panic buying and price spikes. Tugboats tow the oil tanker Exxon Valdez after it went aground in Alaska's Prince William Sound in March 1989, spilling 11 million gallons of crude oil and contaminating more than 1,000 miles of shoreline (bottom).

John Hofmeister, who asserted publicly in February that with oil prices high, tax subsidies were "not an issue" in large energy companies' production decisions — in other words, that companies did not need subsidies to persuade them to drill more wells.[39]

"We go from shock to trance. . . . You know, oil prices go up, gas prices at the pump go up, everybody goes into a flurry of activity. And then the prices go back down, and suddenly we act like it's not important, and we start, you know, filling up our SUVs again."

— *Barack Obama President, United States of America*

"While families across the country are being squeezed, your industry is doing better than ever. And yet the U.S. government continues to dole out $4 billion a year in tax breaks to your companies. These subsidies are not sustainable, and we intend to end them," five Senate Democrats wrote to the CEOs of Exxon Mobil, Chevron, ConocoPhillips, Shell, and BP in May.[40]

But oil companies have resisted these critiques, which Exxon Mobil CEO Rex Tillerson called "misinformed and discriminatory" at a May 12 hearing of the Senate Finance Committee.[41]

Republicans argue that "raising taxes" on oil companies (their wording for eliminating the provisions at issue) will reduce domestic production and drive up gasoline prices. But some key figures have wavered. In April, when House Speaker John Boehner, R-Ohio, was asked about the issue during a television interview, he answered, "We certainly ought to take a look at it. . . . We're in a time when — when the federal government is short on revenues. We need to control spending, but we need to have revenues to keep the government moving. And they ought to be paying their fair share."[42]

Boehner quickly backtracked, but in May House Budget Committee chair Ryan said of his long-term budget plan, "We go after fossil fuel subsidies, we go after renewable subsidies. We propose to go after all that stuff."[43]

And the public is receptive to cutting energy subsidies. In a February NBC News/*Wall Street Journal* poll, 74 percent of respondents thought that eliminating tax credits for the oil and natural gas industries was an acceptable way to reduce the federal deficit, and 57 percent supported "significantly cutting" subsidies to build new nuclear power plants.[44]

On May 17, the Senate voted 52-48 to reject a Democratic resolution to cut five tax breaks for oil companies, but Democrats vowed to pursue the issue as part of negotiations over reducing the federal deficit.[45]

What is 'Clean' Electricity?

As of April 2011, 29 states plus the District of Columbia and Puerto Rico had adopted legally binding renewable portfolio standards (RPSs), which require utilities to generate specific percentages of their electricity from renewable fuels by certain dates. Another seven states have nonbinding renewable electricity targets.[46] These measures have created growing market demand for renewable energy since the early 1990s.

The U.S. does not have a national RPS, although Congress has debated proposals for the past decade. The American Clean Energy and Security Act of 2009 (the House-passed cap-and-trade bill) would have established a national RPS requirement of 20 percent by 2020. In the Senate, Energy Committee Chairman Jeff Bingaman, D-N.M., has proposed a 15 percent RPS several times, most recently in late 2010.

Regions like the Pacific Northwest, where most electricity comes from hydropower, are more receptive to a national RPS than areas like the Midwest that rely heavily on fossil fuels. President Obama's proposal for an 80 percent clean-electricity standard (CES) by 2035 defines the target much more broadly. It includes natural gas plants with newer, more efficient designs; nuclear power; and coal-burning plants that would capture and store their carbon emissions. The Obama administration estimates that about 40 percent of U.S. electricity comes from clean sources today and that that share can be doubled by 2035.

Adding those sources could expand support, since most regions have some of those resources. Importantly, however, carbon capture and storage for power plants has not been commercialized in the United States yet, although the Energy Department is funding research and 25 demonstration projects at industrial sites.[47]

Designing a national CES will be extremely complex, since the rules will have major impacts on utilities' finances (especially for small companies) and on market demand for various fuels. A major concern is whether natural gas would dominate a clean-energy portfolio, since it produces

Should the government end tax breaks for oil and gas production?

YES

Steve Kretzmann
Executive Director, Oil Change International, Washington, D.C.

Written for *CQ Researcher*, May 2011

Let's start with what we agree on. America needs energy for transport, light and heat. America needs to reduce its spending. The questions are, how we are going to get energy in the future, and how we are going to use our limited government funds?

Roughly 10 percent of global oil production is here at home, despite the fact that the U.S. has only 2 percent of global reserves. But as President Bush noted in 2005, "with $55 [per barrel] oil we don't need incentives to the oil and gas companies to explore." Oil is more than twice that price today, and the justification for phasing out subsidies is at least twice as strong.

President Obama has proposed eliminating $4 billion annually in oil subsidies. While these are not all the subsidies that this mature and very profitable industry enjoys, they are some of the most obvious. Responsible policymakers are of course concerned about what impact removing these subsidies (an act the industry deceptively calls imposing new taxes) will have on domestic production, jobs and consumers at the pump. The short answer to those three questions is little to none.

Our reliance on foreign oil has been a fact since the 1970s, and no amount of additional drilling or subsidies is going to change that. The only way to end our reliance on foreign oil is to end our dependence on all oil.

According to the Treasury Department, removing these domestic subsidies will reduce U.S. oil production less than one half of 1 percent and increase exploration and production costs less than 2 percent. Considering the price that the domestic industry receives for crude has more than doubled over the past several years, the industry should be able to afford that — without laying anyone off or jacking up the price at the pump.

The global oil market, not the domestic industry, determines gas prices. The Treasury Department estimates that subsidy removal would cause a loss of less than one-tenth of 1 percent in global oil supply and thus would have no impact on global or U.S. prices.

Many think that money saved from subsidies removed should simply be used to offset the deficit toward the goal of a balanced budget. Others think that at least some of these funds should help level the playing field for clean energy. But that's a different discussion, for another day — hopefully soon.

NO

Lee Fuller
Vice President of Government Relations, Independent Petroleum Association of America, Washington, D.C.

Written for *CQ Researcher*, May 2011

Policymakers in Washington are, once again, talking about raising taxes on U.S. producers of oil and natural gas — tax increases that have been proposed for the last three years and have been soundly rejected.

Contrary to popular belief, these tax proposals do not target "Big Oil," but instead go after 18,000 American independent oil and natural gas producers, who on average employ only 12 workers. American production activities are dominated by these independent producers, who drill 95 percent of the nation's natural gas and oil wells, accounting for 67 percent of total U.S. natural gas and oil production. America's independents are dedicated to finding and producing America's energy resources, creating jobs, generating revenues and supplying reliable and affordable energy all across the United States.

In fact, a recent IHS Global Insight study showed that independent oil and natural gas producers operating onshore in the United States accounted for nearly 4 million American jobs in 2010, a number that represents more than 3 percent of the total U.S. workforce. Very few industries have the potential to create as many better-than-average-paying jobs as quickly and effectively as we do.

The study also projects that onshore independents will return more than $930 billion to state, local and federal governments in the form of taxes, rents and royalties over the next 10 years — all driven by a forecast that predicts an ever-expanding role for U.S. independents in developing more onshore wells and delivering greater volumes of reliable and affordable oil and natural gas to American consumers.

However, these positive forecasts cannot be realized if the government raises taxes on these producers, which will consequently reduce capital investments. Historically, independent producers have reinvested as much as 150 percent of their American cash flow back into new American production. Drilling costs are a key component of capital-expenditure budgets for independent producers.

Without the ability to expense these ordinary and necessary business costs, an independent would have to reduce its drilling budget by 20 to 35 percent almost immediately.

Increasing taxes on independent producers will reduce capital investment in the industry. It also will result in fewer jobs, reduce revenue to federal and state treasuries, hurt American retirees whose mutual funds, pension plans and IRAs are invested in oil and gas companies and harm American energy security.

A coal scraper works at the American Electric Power Co. plant in New Haven, W. Va. In 2009 the facility became the first coal-fired power plant in the nation to capture a portion of its carbon dioxide emissions and inject them underground. The U.S. has the world's largest coal reserves and 1,500 coal-fired electricity generating plants.

fewer carbon emissions than fossil fuels and generates electricity more cheaply than nuclear power or many renewables.

The Obama administration has proposed to award "half credits" for electricity from combined cycle natural gas plants, which are highly efficient. But some experts worry that natural gas could crowd out other, less-mature sources that are even cleaner.

"We could meet an 80 percent clean-electricity goal almost entirely by substituting natural gas generation for power from old coal plants," says the Center for American Progress's Hendricks. Instead, Hendricks recommends developing a renewable electricity standard that will create a predictable path for developing energy efficiency and renewable electricity sources. "You can do this by dividing a clean-electricity standard into tiers and allocating specific shares of generation to renewable electricity and energy efficiency," he says. "Without doing that, a clean-electricity standard won't do enough."

On March 21, Sens. Bingaman and Lisa Murkowski, R-Alaska, the top Republican on the Senate Energy Committee, released a white paper on how to design a CES. The paper illustrated a common criticism of Obama's CES proposal: that it was too vague. "Is the goal to reduce greenhouse gas emissions, lower electricity costs, spur utilization of particular assets, diversify supply, or some combination thereof?" Bingaman and Murkowski asked, inviting comments from industry and advocates.

"It's a pretty good rule of thumb that if you can't lay out the goals of your policy clearly, you're unlikely to design it well," wrote journalist David Roberts in the online environmental magazine *Grist*. In contrast to Bingaman's 2010 recent RPS proposal, Roberts called the CES idea "shapeless" and argued that it would "undercut existing congressional efforts while doing little to build new coalitions."[48]

GHG Regulations

Clean-energy advocates have another tool available: regulating greenhouse gas emissions (GHGs) as pollutants under the Clean Air Act. This approach would have a similar impact to cap-and-trade legislation: It would limit how much carbon dioxide and other GHGs polluters could release, which would make low-carbon and carbon-free energy sources more attractive.

Carbon dioxide and other GHGs have not traditionally been regulated this way because they were not thought to have direct harmful impacts on health or the environment. But as scientists painted an increasingly detailed picture of impacts from extreme climate change (including droughts, floods and heat waves), and Congress failed to pass laws limiting GHG emissions, activists started addressing the issue through the courts.

In a case brought by Massachusetts and 11 other states, the U.S. Supreme Court ruled in 2007 that the Environmental Protection Agency had authority to regulate carbon dioxide and other greenhouse gases.[49] As the Clean Air Act requires, the court directed EPA to conduct a study of whether GHGs in the atmosphere endangered public health and welfare. In late 2009 the agency released a formal finding, based on technical studies, that carbon dioxide and other GHGs in the atmosphere "threaten the public health and welfare of current and future generations."[50]

Although President Obama supported congressional action on climate change as the best way to address the issue, EPA Administrator Lisa Jackson announced in December 2010 that the agency would issue rules to limit GHGs, since it was clear that there would not be enough votes in the new Congress to address the problem through legislation.[51] But opponents — including most congressional Republicans and some Democrats — say that doing so would have the same impacts that they had predicted earlier from a cap-and-trade bill: driving energy prices up and hurting the economy.

"Studies estimated that a cap-and-trade national energy tax would produce job losses in the millions. Yet EPA is unilaterally acting to impose the very same types of policies that Congress rejected [in 2009-2010]," House Energy and Commerce Committee chair Upton asserted in a March 1 hearing.[52]

Some legal experts disagree with that view. "EPA regulation is not cap-and-trade by another name. It's far less efficient, and if we had done a comprehensive cap-and-trade approach, we would be dealing with these major pollution sources more effectively," says Scott Schang, vice president of the Environmental Law Institute.

On April 7 the House voted 255-172 to block EPA from regulating GHGs under the Clean Air Act.[53] No Republicans voted against the bill, and 19 Democrats, mostly from Midwestern and Southern states, supported it. The White House issued a statement saying Obama would veto the bill if it reached his desk, but the Democrat-controlled Senate was not expected to take it up.

Next, opponents may try to deny EPA funds in the final 2012 budget to regulate GHGs. But Schang says that approach would not end the debate. "Defunding EPA doesn't repeal requirements under the Clean Air Act, so companies would still have to comply with the law. States implement the Clean Air Act and issue permits, and Congress can't regulate the states, so defunding EPA could really complicate the issue," he says.

Moreover, Schang notes, an extended fight over this issue will leave the power industry in limbo. "Utilities hate uncertainty, and they don't know what to do here. They have to make multibillion-dollar decisions about power plant investments. That's not fair to them," he says.

OUTLOOK

How Green?

Industry leaders and advocates generally agree that growing America's energy supply and reducing reliance on imported oil are high priorities. But there's less consensus over how large a role green sources should play, and how quickly the U.S. needs to develop cleaner fuels.

"We need an 'all of the above' strategy. World energy needs are growing, and it will be challenging to keep

supplies growing at the same pace," says the Independent Petroleum Association of America's Vincent. "Energy policy should encourage the development of oil and gas resources, because they will be the main sources for decades. Eventually, we'll develop technology that will let us power society in other ways, like advanced nuclear power and renewables. We can't rule anything out, but we need to be practical about how much of the equation they can provide."

Environmentalists want more aggressive efforts to shift away from dirty sources. "We need to reduce emissions from existing fossil fuels. That means making sure that natural gas is produced and transported to minimize leakage, so we get its full low-carbon benefits. It also means closing old, dirty coal plants and replacing them with cleaner resources," says Jim Marston, energy program director with the Environmental Defense Fund, a national environmental advocacy group.

"We also need to put more money into next-generation fuels, and set modest requirements [in a national clean- or renewable energy standard] that will create economies of scale for solar, geothermal and wind power," Marston continues. "You can believe in the market and understand that there are market failures that prevent these new resources from getting into the market and going to scale."

Energy choices will be shaped by the ongoing national debate over how to reduce U.S. budget deficits and stimulate economic growth. "Many Democrats and Republicans agree that we need to invest in advanced technology," says the Bipartisan Policy Center's Grumet. But with total spending shrinking, federal support for energy research and development will have to show significant returns to win support.

"We're going to have to find the right balance of investments in our most critical needs, with an eye toward those that protect our nation and that create jobs — but at a much lower funding level," Rep. Steve Womack, R-Ark., said at a House Appropriations subcommittee hearing on Energy Department programs in March.[54]

Unexpected events around the world may roil the U.S. energy debate even more. For example, many observers speculate that the post-earthquake meltdowns at Japan's Fukushima nuclear reactor will undercut nascent support in the United States for new investments in nuclear power. But the National Renewable

Energy Laboratory's Garrett draws a broader lesson from Fukushima.

"The accident in Japan suggests that government should have an ongoing role in all energy technologies," she says. "As you move forward in time, you face new challenges, and government can accelerate transitions from the status quo to new ways of doing things. Government can speed transitions that need to happen."

NOTES

1. No commercial-scale clean-coal plant is currently operating in the United States. For background, see Jennifer Weeks, "Coal's Comeback," *CQ Researcher*, Oct. 5, 2007, pp. 817-840, and David Hosansky, "Wind Power," *CQ Researcher*, April 1, 2011, pp. 289-312.

2. John M. Broder, "Obama Shifts to Speed Oil and Gas Drilling in U.S.," *The New York Times*, May 14, 2011, p. A1.

3. Jean Chemnick, "Climate: Rising Oil Prices Demand Bipartisan Cooperation On Energy, Graham Says," *E&E News*, March 8, 2011.

4. "Remarks by the President on America's Energy Security," Georgetown University, March 30, 2011, www.whitehouse.gov/the-press-office/2011/03/30/remarks-president-americas-energy-security.

5. Statement prepared for delivery, http://republicans.energycommerce.house.gov/Media/file/Hearings/Energy/031611/Upton2.pdf.

6. For background see Marcia Clemmitt, "Energy and Climate," *CQ Researcher*, July 24, 2009, pp. 621-644.

7. John Collins Rudolf, "Clean Energy Is a Target of Ryan Budget Plan," *The New York Times*, April 6, 2011, http://green.blogs.nytimes.com/2011/04/06/clean-energy-is-a-target-of-ryan-budget-plan/; Paul Ryan, "The GOP Path to Prosperity," *The Wall Street Journal*, April 6, 2011, http://online.wsj.com/article/SB10001424052748703806304576242612172357504.html.

8. The case is *Massachusetts v. Environmental Protection Agency*, 549 U.S. 497 (2007).

9. "An Open Letter to the American People and America's Leaders: A New Era for U.S. Energy Security," April 12, 2011, www.bipartisanpolicy.org/library/energy-project/open-letter.

10. "Blueprint for a Secure Energy Future," March 30, 2011, pp. 4-8, www.whitehouse.gov/sites/default/files/blueprint_secure_energy_future.pdf.

11. Weekly radio address, April 23, 2011, www.whitehouse.gov/the-press-office/2011/04/23/weekly-address-instead-subsidizing-yesterdays-energy-sources-we-need-inv.

12. "Blueprint for a Secure Energy Future," *op. cit.*, p. 39.

13. National Research Council, *Advancing the Science of Climate Change* (National Academies Press, 2010), p. 3, www.nap.edu/catalog.php?record_id=12782.

14. Massachusetts Institute of Technology, *The Future of Natural Gas* (2010), http://web.mit.edu/mitei/research/studies/report-natural-gas.pdf; Dave Roberts, "Chart of the Day: The U.S. Energy Mix in 2035," *Grist*, April 22, 2011, www.grist.org/climate-energy/2011-04-22-chart-of-the-day-the-u.s.-energy-mix-in-2035.

15. Roger H. Bezdek and Robert M. Wending, "A Half Century of U.S. Federal Government Energy Incentives: Value: Distribution, and Policy Implications," *International Journal of Global Energy Issues*, vol. 27, no. 1 (2007), p. 43. This figure includes spending for geothermal energy ($5.7 billion), which the article counts separately from other renewable fuels ($32.6 billion).

16. "Estimating U.S. Government Subsidies to Energy Sources: 2002-2008," Environmental Law Institute, September 2009, www.eli.org/Program_Areas/innovation_governance_energy.cfm.

17. Bezdek and Wending, *op. cit.*, p. 43.

18. Environmental Law Institute, *op. cit.*, p. 3.

19. Ian Bauer, "Governor Dedicates Solar Plant," *San Jose Mercury-News*, April 13, 2011.

20. Alyce Lomax, "Rising Star Buy: SunPower," *Fool.com*, Jan. 11, 2011, www.fool.com/investing/general/2011/01/11/rising-star-buy-sunpower.aspx.

21. "Clean Energy Investment Storms to New Record in 2010," Bloomberg New Energy Finance, Jan. 11, 2011, http://bnef.com/Download/pressreleases/134/pdffile/.

22. Ernst & Young, *Renewable Energy Country Attractiveness Indices*, Issues 26 (August 2010) and 28 (February 2011), www.ey.com/Publication/vwLUAssets/Renewable_energy_country_attractiveness_indices_-_Issue_28/$FILE/EY_RECAI_issue_28.pdf.

23. Todd Wallack, "Plant Will Shut After $58m in State Aid," *The Boston Globe*, Jan. 12, 2011, http://articles.boston.com/2011-01-12/business/29338294_1_evergreen-solar-plant-state-funds.

24. Keith Bradsher, "Solar Panel Maker Moves Work to China," *The New York Times*, Jan. 14, 2011, www.nytimes.com/2011/01/15/business/energy-environment/15solar.html.

25. Matthew E. Kahn, "How We Gain From China's Advances," *The New York Times*, Jan. 18, 2011, www.nytimes.com/roomfordebate/2011/01/18/can-the-us-compete-with-china-on-green-tech/how-we-gain-from-chinas-advances.

26. Nicolas Loris and Derek Scissors, "China's 'Sputnik Moment,' " Heritage Foundation, Jan. 21, 2011, http://origin.heritage.org/Research/Commentary/2011/01/Chinas-Sputnik-Moment.

27. "GE Invests $600m to Build Largest US Solar Plant," Reuters, April 8, 2011.

28. Restoring the Quality of Our Environment: Report of the Environmental Pollution Panel, President's Science Advisory Committee, White House, November 1965, p. iii, http://dge.stanford.edu/labs/caldeiralab/Caldeira%20downloads/PSAC,%201965,%20Restoring%20the%20Quality%20of%20Our%20Environment.pdf.

29. Televised address by President Jimmy Carter, April 18, 1977, online at www.pbs.org/wgbh/americanexperience/features/primary-resources/carter-energy/.

30. Stephen Hoff, "Was Jimmy Carter Right?" *Cleveland Plain Dealer*, Oct. 1, 2005, www.energybulletin.net/node/9657.

31. Joshua Green, "The Elusive Green Economy," *The Atlantic*, July/August 2009, www.theatlantic.com/magazine/archive/2009/07/the-elusive-green-economy/7554/.

32 Michael Grunwald, "Three Mile Island at 30: Nuclear Power's Pitfalls," *Time*, March 27, 2009, www.time.com/time/nation/article/0,8599,1888119,00.html.

33. Philip Shabecoff, "Global Warming Has Begun, Expert Tells Senate," *The New York Times*, June 24, 1988, www.nytimes.com/1988/06/24/us/global-warming-has-begun-expert-tells-senate.html.

34. National Research Council, *Air Quality Management in the United States* (2001), pp. 199-202.

35. Larry Parker and John Blodgett, "U.S. Global Climate Change Policy: Evolving Views on Cost, Competitiveness, and Comprehensiveness," Congressional Research Service, Jan. 29, 2009, pp. 5-7, http://assets.opencrs.com/rpts/RL30024_20090129.pdf.

36. For background, see Mary H. Cooper, "Alternative Energy," *CQ Researcher*, Feb. 25, 2005, pp. 173-196.

37. Council On Foreign Relations, "Barack Obama," www.cfr.org/experts/world/barack-obama/b11603#6.

38. Andrew Revkin, "Obama on the 'Shock to Trance' Energy Pattern," *The New York Times*, Nov. 17, 2008, http://dotearth.blogs.nytimes.com/2008/11/17/obama-on-shock-to-trance-energy-pattern/.

39. Amy Harder, "Ex-Shell CEO Says Big Oil Can Live Without Subsidies," *National Journal.com*, Feb. 11, 2011, www.nationaljournal.com/daily/ex-shell-ceo-says-big-oil-can-live-without-subsidies-20110211.

40. "Democrats Urge Oil CEOs to Admit They No Longer Need Taxpayer-Funded handouts, Use Money to Cut Deficit Instead," online at http://menendez.senate.gov/newsroom/press/release/?id=649ae0ba-6219-4fa6-9173-e1cc83a135a0.

41. John M. Broder, "Oil Executives, Defending Tax Breaks, Say They'd Cede Them if Everyone Did," *The New York Times*, May 12, 2011, www.nytimes.com/2011/05/13/business/13oil.html?_r=1&hp.

42. Jonathan Allen and Darren Goode, "Boehner Gaffe Creates Dem Opening," *Politico.com*, April 26, 2011.

43. Evan Lehmann, "Ryan, the Republicans' Budget Hawk, Opposes Tax Breaks for Clean Energy and Oil," *The New York Times*, May 9, 2011, www.nytimes.com/cwire/2011/05/09/09climatewire-ryan-the-republicans-budget-hawk-opposes-tax-73991.html?scp=1&sq=ryan%20tax%20breaks%20clean%20energy%20oil%20&st=cse.

44. Study # 11091, Hart/McInturff, February 2011, pp. 15-16, http://online.wsj.com/public/resources/documents/wsj-nbcpoll03022011.pdf.

45. Carl Hulse, "Senate Refuses to End Tax Breaks for Big Oil," *The New York Times*, May 18, 2011, p. A1.

46 Database of State Incentives for Renewables & Efficiency, "Summary Maps — RPS Policies," www.dsireusa.org/summarymaps/index.cfm?ee=1&RE=1.

47. U.S. Department of Energy, Office of Fossil Energy, "Carbon Sequestration," http://fossil.energy.gov/sequestration/.

48. David Roberts, "Bingaman Tries to Make Policy Out of Obama's Hopey-Changey Clean Energy Standard," *Grist*, March 23, 2011, www.grist.org/energy-policy/2011-03-23-bingaman-tries-to-make-policy-out-of-obama-clean-energy-standard.

49. *Massachusetts v. Environmental Protection Agency*, 549 U.S. 497 (2007), www.supremecourt.gov/opinions/06pdf/05-1120.pdf.

50. U.S. Environmental Protection Agency, "Endangerment and Cause or Contribute Findings for Greenhouse Gases Under Section 202(a) of the Clean Air Act," Dec. 7, 2009, www.epa.gov/climatechange/endangerment.html.

51. Matthew L. Wald, "E.P.A. Says It Will Press on With Greenhouse Gas Regulation," *The New York Times*, Dec. 23, 2010, www.nytimes.com/2010/12/24/science/earth/24epa.html.

52. Hearing of the Energy and Power Subcommittee, March 1, 2011, http://energycommerce.house.gov/hearings/hearingdetail.aspx?NewsID=8270.

53. H.R. 910, the Energy Tax Prevention Act of 2011.

54. House Committee on Appropriations, Subcommittee on Energy and Water Development, hearing March 31, 2011, http://appropriations.house.gov/_files/033111EnergyandWaterARPAELoanGuaranteeWomack.pdf.

BIBLIOGRAPHY

Books

Buchar, David, *The Rough Guide to the Energy Crisis*, Rough Guides, 2010.
A senior research fellow at the Oxford Institute for Energy Studies surveys current energy choices and options for shifting to cleaner sources.

Hofmeister, John, *Why We Hate the Oil Companies: Straight Talk from an Energy Insider*, Palgrave Macmillan, 2010.
A former president of Shell Oil argues that U.S. energy debates are polarized and that a Federal Energy Resources Board is needed to plan and manage the nation's energy system.

Madrigal, Alexis, *Powering the Dream: The History and Promise of Green Technology*, Da Capo Press, 2011.
A journalist shows that American innovators have refined many green energy concepts for decades, including wind and geo-thermal power and electric cars, but inconsistent policies have often kept them from expanding to a large scale.

National Research Council, *Hidden Costs of Energy: Unpriced Consequences of Energy Production and Use*, National Academies Press, 2010.
The study, conducted in response to a congressional request, concludes that energy production and use cause billions of dollars in damages yearly that are not reflected in energy prices.

Articles

Clayton, Mark, "Is EPA Greenhouse-Gas Plan a Job Killer? History Might Offer Clues," *The Christian Science Monitor*, March 2, 2011, www.csmonitor.com/USA/Politics/2011/0302/Is-EPA-greenhouse-gas-plan-a-job-killer-History-might-offer-clues.
Carbon-intensive industries say regulating greenhouse gases as pollutants would wreck the U.S. economy, but many economists say the impact would be insignificant or positive.

De Gorter, Harry, and Jerry Taylor, "Ethanol: Let Protectionism Expire," *National Review* (online), Dec. 8, 2010, www.cato.org/pub_display.php?pub_id=12623.
Two libertarian scholars argue against continuing federal tax credits and trade protections for ethanol.

Goldberg, Jonah, "Obama's Sputnik Analogy Doesn't Fly," *USA Today*, Jan. 31, 2011, www.usatoday.com/news/opinion/forum/2011-02-01-column01_ST_N.htm.
A conservative argues that the United States should not spend billions of dollars to emulate China's energy policy.

Harder, Amy, "Can Obama Budget a Clean Energy Future?" *National Journal*, **Feb. 14, 2011, http://energy.nationaljournal.com/2011/02/can-obama-budget-a-clean-energ.php.**
Policy experts and energy company leaders debate whether President Obama's proposed investments will help create a green economy.

Klare, Michael T., "The Relentless Pursuit of Extreme Energy," *The Nation*, **May 18, 2010, www.thenation.com/article/relentless-pursuit-extreme-energy.**
A professor of peace and world security studies at Hampshire College argues that more major accidents like the 2010 BP oil spill can be expected.

"Room for Debate: Can the U.S. Compete with China on Green Tech?" *The New York Times*, **Jan. 19, 2011, www.nytimes.com/roomfordebate/2011/01/18/can-the-us-compete-woth-china-on-green-tech.**
Lawyers, economists and other policy experts give their perspectives on American companies' efforts to win global market shares in clean-energy industries.

Rotman, David, "Praying for an Energy Miracle," *Technology Review*, **March/April 2011, www.technologyreview.com/energy/32383/.**
Many companies are developing new clean-energy sources, but deploying new technologies into the market is harder than inventing them and requires government support.

Reports and Studies

"Estimating U.S. Government Subsidies to Energy Sources: 2002-2008," Environmental Law Institute, 2009, www.elistore.org/reports_detail.asp?ID=11358.
The United States provided $72 billion in subsidies for fossil fuels and $29 billion for renewable-energy sources.

Hendricks, Bracken, and Lisbeth Kaufman, "Cutting the Cost of Clean Energy 1.0," Center for American Progress, November 2010, www.americanprogress.org/issues/ 2010/11/cleanenergycosts.html.
A liberal think tank lays out a strategy for clean-energy investments led by the private sector but spurred by government policies, including regulatory reforms.

MIT Energy Initiative, "The Future of Natural Gas: Interim Report," Massachusetts Institute of Technology, 2010, web.mit.edu/mitei/research/studies/report-natural-gas.pdf.
An interdisciplinary study finds that abundant natural gas could serve as a "bridge" fuel to a low-carbon future, especially as a substitute for coal to generate electricity, but that it should not be allowed to crowd out cleaner fuels.

For More Information

Petroleum Institute, 1220 L St., N.W., Washington, DC 20005; (202) 682-2000; www.api.org. National association for the oil and natural gas industry.

Center for American Progress, 1333 H St., N.W., 10th Floor, Washington, DC, 20005; (202) 682-1611; www.americanprogress.org. Liberal think tank that advocates in fields including energy and the environment.

Environmental Defense Fund, 257 Park Ave. South, New York, NY 10010; (800) 684-3322; www.edf.org. National advocacy group known for promoting market-based solutions to environmental challenges.

Institute for 21st Century Energy, 1615 H St., N.W., Washington, DC 20062; (202) 463-5558; www.energyxxi.org. Research initiative affiliated with the U.S. Chamber of Commerce that advocates strategies to ensure affordable, reliable and diverse energy supplies, improve environmental stewardship, promote economic growth and strengthen national security.

Lawrence Berkeley National Laboratory, 1 Cyclotron Road, Berkeley, CA 94720; (510) 486-4000; www.lbl.gov. Laboratory of the U.S. Department of Energy, managed by the University of California, that conducts unclassified research on subjects including energy efficiency and advanced energy technologies.

MIT Energy Initiative, Massachusetts Institute of Technology, 77 Massachusetts Ave., E19-307, Cambridge, MA 02139-4307; (617) 258-8891; http://web.mit.edu/mitei/. University-wide initiative at MIT designed to help transform the global energy system through research, classroom teaching and campus energy-use reductions.

Synapse Energy Economics, 22 Pearl St., Cambridge, MA 02139; (617) 661-3248; www.synapse-energy.com. Research and consulting firm specializing in energy, economic and environmental issues that works to inform sound regulatory and policy decisions.

U.S. Department of Energy, 1000 Independence Ave., S.W., Washington, DC 20585; (202) 586-5000; www.energy.gov. Manages research, development and policy initiatives to meet U.S. energy needs. Key offices for energy supply include Energy Efficiency and Renewable Energy, Fossil Energy and Nuclear Energy.

13

Climate Change

Reed Karaim

Erosion is washing away beachfront land in the Maldives. The island nation in the Indian Ocean faces possible submersion as early as 2100, according to some climate change predictions. President Mohamed Nasheed said the voluntary emission cuts goal reached in Copenhagen last December was a good step, but at that rate "my country would not survive."

From *CQ Researcher*, February 2010. (Updated May 16, 2011)

It was the global gathering many hoped would save the world. For two weeks in December, delegates from 194 nations came together in Copenhagen, Denmark, to hammer out an international agreement to limit global warming. Failure to do so, most scientists have concluded, threatens hundreds of millions of people and uncounted species of plants and animals.

Diplomatic preparations had been under way for years but intensified in the months leading up to the conference. Shortly before the sessions began, Yvo de Boer, executive secretary of the United Nations Framework Convention on Climate Change — the governing body for negotiations — promised they would "launch action, action and more action," and proclaimed, "I am more confident than ever before that [Copenhagen] will be the turning point in the fight to prevent climate disaster."[1]

But delegates found themselves bitterly divided. Developing nations demanded more financial aid for coping with climate change. Emerging economic powers like China balked at being asked to do more to limit their emissions of the greenhouse gases (GHGs) — created by burning carbon-based fuels — blamed for warming up the planet. The United States submitted proposed emissions cuts that many countries felt fell far short of its responsibility as the world's dominant economy. As negotiations stalled, frustration boiled over inside the hall and on the streets outside, where tens of thousands of activists had gathered to call world leaders to action. A historic opportunity — a chance to reach a global commitment to battle climate change — seemed to be slipping away.

Then, on Dec. 18 — the final night of the conference — leaders from China, India, Brazil, South Africa and the United States emerged

Major Flooding, Drought Predicted at Century's End

Significant increases in runoff — from rain or melting snow and ice — are projected with a high degree of confidence for vast areas of the Earth, mainly in northern regions. Up to 20 percent of the world's population lives in areas where river flood potential is likely to increase by the 2080s. Rainfall and runoff are expected to be very low in Europe, the Middle East, northern and southern Africa and the western United States.

Projected Changes in Annual Runoff (Water Availability), 2090-2099
(by percentage, relative to 1980-1999)

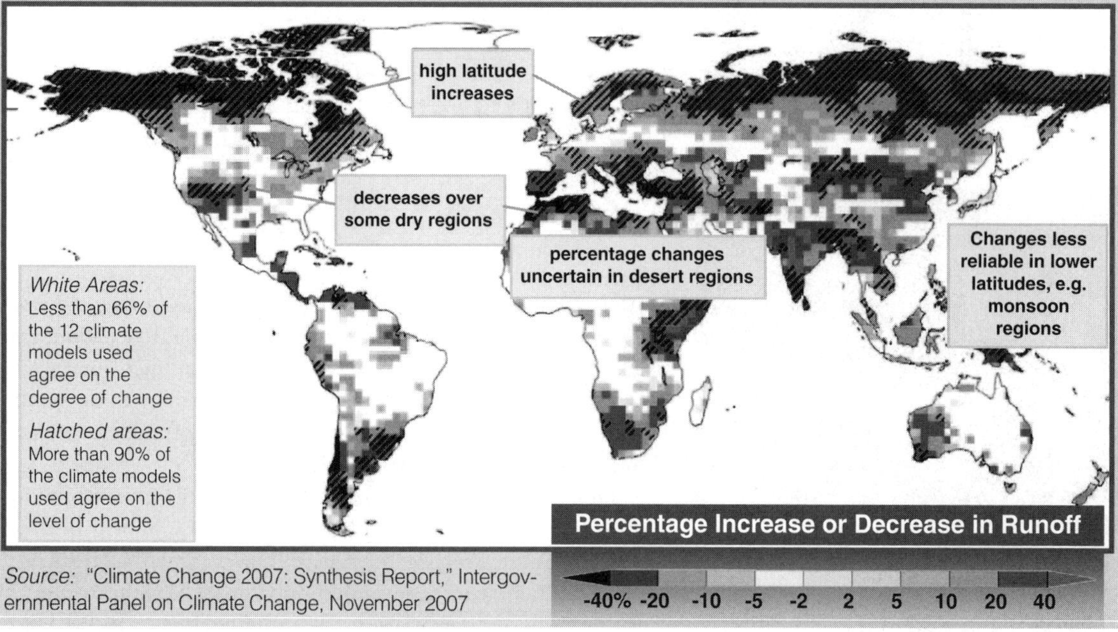

Source: "Climate Change 2007: Synthesis Report," Intergovernmental Panel on Climate Change, November 2007

from a private negotiating session with a three-page, nonbinding accord that rescued the meeting from being judged an abject failure.

But the accord left as much confusion as clarity in its wake. It was a deal, yes, but one that fell far short of the hopes of those attending the conference, and one largely lacking in specifics. The accord vowed to limit global warming to 2 degrees Celsius (3.6 Fahrenheit) above pre-Industrial Revolution levels, provide $30 billion in short-term aid to help developing countries cope with the effects of climate change — with more promised longer-term — and included significant reporting and transparency standards for participants, including emerging economic powers such as China and India.

The accord did not, however:

- Include earlier language calling for halving global greenhouse gas emissions by 2050;
- Set a peak year by which greenhouse gases should begin to decline;
- Include country-specific targets for emission reductions (signatories began filling in the numbers by the end of January);
- Include a timetable for reaching a legally binding international treaty, or
- Specify where future financial help for the developing world to cope with climate change will come from.[2]

Called back into session in the early morning hours, delegates from much of the developing world reacted with dismay to a deal they felt left their countries vulnerable to catastrophic global warming.

"[This] is asking Africa to sign a suicide pact — an incineration pact — in order to maintain the economic dependence [on a high-carbon economy] of a few countries," said Lumumba Di-Aping, the Sudanese chair of the G77 group of 130 poor countries.[3]

British Prime Minister Gordon Brown, however, hailed the deal as a "vital first step" toward "a green and low-carbon future for the world."[4] A total of 55 countries, including the major developed nations, eventually signed onto the deal.

But at the Copenhagen conference, delegates agreed only to "take note" of the accord, without formally adopting it.

Since then, debate has raged over whether the accord represents a step backward or a realistic new beginning. "You had the U.S., China and India closing ranks and saying it's too hard right now to have a binding agreement," says Malini Mehra, an Indian political scientist with 20 years of involvement in the climate change debate. "It's really worse than where we started off."

Others are more upbeat. Michael Eckhart, president of the American Council on Renewable Energy, points out that the convention had revealed how unworkable the larger effort — with 194 participants — had become. "The accord actually sets things in motion in a direction that is realistic," he says. "To have these major nations signed up is fantastic."

Copenhagen clearly demonstrated how extremely difficult and complex global climate negotiations can be. Getting most of the world's nations to

Carbon Emissions Rising; Most Come from China

Global emissions of carbon dioxide (CO_2) — the most common greenhouse gas (GHG) blamed for raising the planet's temperature — have grown steadily for more than 150 years. Since 1950, however, the increases have accelerated and are projected to rise 44 percent between 2010 and 2030 (top graph). While China emits more CO_2 than any other country, Australians produce the most carbon emissions per person (bottom left). Most manmade GHG comes from energy production and transportation (pie chart).

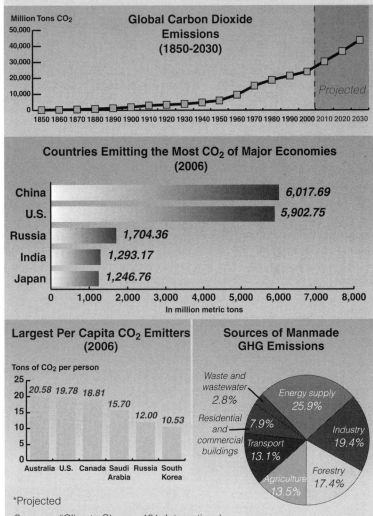

*Projected

Sources: "Climate Change 101: International Action," Pew Center on Global Climate Change, undated; "Climate Change 2007: Synthesis Report," Intergovernmental Panel on Climate Change, November 2007; Union of Concerned Scientists

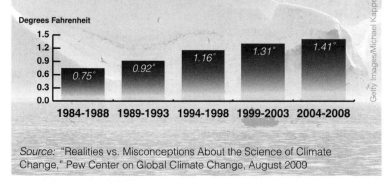

Warming Trends Continue to Accelerate

During the last 25 years the Earth's average temperature steadily increased — and at increasingly higher increments — compared to the average temperature from1880-1910. From 2004-2008, the increase was about 1.4 degrees F., or nearly double the increase from 1984 to 1988.

Average Temperature Increases in Five-year Periods, Relative to the Average Temperature in 1880-1910

Degrees Fahrenheit

1984-1988: 0.75°
1989-1993: 0.92°
1994-1998: 1.16°
1999-2003: 1.31°
2004-2008: 1.41°

Source: "Realities vs. Misconceptions About the Science of Climate Change," Pew Center on Global Climate Change, August 2009

agree on anything is no easy task, but climate change straddles the biggest geopolitical fault lines of our age: the vast economic disparity between the developed and developing worlds, questions of national sovereignty versus global responsibility and differences in political process between democratic and nondemocratic societies.

Climate change also involves a classic example of displaced hardship — some of the worst effects of global warming are likely to be felt thousands of miles from those nations that are most responsible for the higher temperatures and rising seas, making it easier for responsible parties to delay action. Finally, tackling the problem is likely to take hundreds of billions of dollars.

None of this is comforting to those already suffering from climate change, such as Moses Mopel Kisosion, a Maasai herdsman who journeyed from Kenya to tell anyone who would listen how increasingly severe droughts are destroying his country's traditional way of life. But it does explain why reactions to the Copenhagen Accord — which even President Barack Obama acknowledged is simply a "beginning" — have varied so widely.[5]

For some U.S. environmental groups, the significance of the accord was in the commitment Obama secured from emerging economies to provide greater transparency and accountability, addressing one of the U.S. Senate's

objections to earlier climate change proposals. The Senate never ratified the previous international climate agreement, known as the Kyoto Protocol.

Carl Pope, executive director of the Sierra Club, called the accord "historic — if incomplete," but said, "Now that the rest of the world — including countries like China and India — has made it clear that it is willing to take action, the Senate must pass domestic legislation as soon as possible."[6]

But to nongovernmental organizations focused on global poverty and economic justice, the accord represented an abdication of responsibility by the United States and other developed countries. Tim Jones, chief climate officer for the United Kingdom-based anti-poverty group World Development Movement, called the accord "a shameful and monumental failure that has condemned millions of people around the world to untold suffering."[7]

Easily lost in the heated rhetoric, however, is another part of the Copenhagen story: The conference illustrated how a consensus now unites most of the globe about the threat climate change poses. And although skeptics continue to speak out the scientific community has overwhelmingly concluded that average global temperatures are rising and that manmade emissions — particularly carbon dioxide from burning coal, oil and other fossil fuels — are largely to blame. According to a comprehensive assessment released in June 2009 by the U.S. Global Change Research Program, "Observations show that warming of the climate is unequivocal."[8] The conclusion echoes earlier findings by the U.N.'s Intergovernmental Panel on Climate Change (IPCC).[9]

The costs of climate change, both economic and in human lives, already appear significant. Disasters tied to climate change kill around 300,000 people a year and cause roughly $125 billion in economic losses, according to the Global Humanitarian Forum, a Geneva-based think tank led by former U.N. Secretary General Kofi Annan.[10] Evidence widely cited during the conference strengthens the conclusion the world is heating up. The World Meteorological Organization (WMO) reported that the last decade appeared to be the warmest on record, continuing a trend. The years 2000 through 2009 were "warmer than the 1990s, which were warmer than the 1980s, and so on," said Michel Jarraud, the secretary general of the WMO, as Copenhagen got under way.[11] Other reports noted that sea levels appeared likely to rise higher than previously estimated by 2100, with one estimating seas could rise more than six feet by then. The Antarctic ice shelves and the Greenland ice sheet are also melting faster than the U.N. scientific body previously found.[12]

Copenhagen also provided evidence of a growing international political consensus about climate change. About 120 heads of state attended the final days of the conference, hoping to sign their names to an agreement, an indication of the seriousness with which the global community now views the issue.

"It was remarkable the degree to which Copenhagen galvanized the public," says David Waskow, Oxfam America's climate change policy adviser, who attended the conference. "That's true with the literally millions who came out to show their support for strong action on climate change around the world. It's true with the number of heads of state who showed up, and even in terms of the number of developing countries making substantial offers to tackle their emissions."

As observers try to determine where the world is headed on climate change and how the Copenhagen Accord helps or hinders that effort, here are some of the questions they are considering:

Is the Copenhagen Accord a meaningful step forward in the fight against global warming?

No one claims that a three-page accord that leaves out hard emission-reduction targets or a firm timetable is the final answer to global climate change. But does it bring the world closer to adequately addressing the problem?

Accord supporters range from the dutiful to the enthusiastic. But the unifying thread is a feeling that the accord is better than no deal at all, which is where the conference seemed to be headed until the 11th-hour negotiations.

"If the standard is — were we going to get a blueprint to save the world? The fact is, we were never going to

Reuters/Christian Charisius

Protesters outside the U.N. Climate Change Conference in Copenhagen on Dec. 10, 2009, call for rich countries to take responsibility for their disproportionate share in global warming. Greenhouse gas emissions by industrial countries are causing climate changes in poor countries thousands of miles away. The nonbinding Copenhagen Accord calls for $10 billion a year for the next three years to help them deal with climate change.

meet it. None of the documents circulating were a feasible basis for agreement among the major players," says Michael A. Levi, director of the Program on Energy Security and Climate Change for the U.S. Council on Foreign Relations. "What we ended up with is something that can be useful if we use it the right way. It has pieces that empower all sorts of other efforts, like increased transparency, some measure of monitoring and reporting. It sets a political benchmark for financing. It can be a meaningful step forward."

Levi also notes that countries signing the accord agreed to fill in their targets for emissions cuts (as the major signatories and other nations did at the end of January), addressing one of the main criticisms of the deal.

But the Indian political scientist Mehra says even if countries abide by their commitments to cut emissions, the accord will not meet its target of holding global warming to 2 degrees Celsius (3.6-degrees Fahrenheit), which U.N. scientists consider the maximum increase that could avoid the worst effects of climate change, including a catastrophic rise in sea levels and severe damage to world food production.

She cites an IPCC conclusion that says in order to meet the 2-degree goal industrialized countries must reduce their emissions to 25-40 percent of 1990 levels by 2020 and by 50 percent by 2050. "What we actually got in the various announcements from the developed nations are far below that, coming in at around 18 percent," Mehra says.

Indeed, research by Climate Interactive — a joint effort by academic, nonprofit and business entities to assess climate policy options — found that the countries' commitments would allow temperatures to rise about 3.9 degrees Celsius (7 degrees Fahrenheit) by 2100 — nearly twice the stated goal.[13] "If you're looking at an average of 3 to 4 degrees, you're going to have much higher rises in significant parts of the world. That's why so many of the African negotiators were so alarmed by this," says Mehra. "It's worse than where we started because it effectively sets in stone the lowest possible expectations."

But other analysts point out that President Obama and other leaders who backed the accord have acknowledged more must be done.[14] They add that focusing on the initial emissions goals ignores the areas where the deal breaks important ground. "A much bigger part of the story, I think, is the actual money the developed world is putting on the table, funds for mitigation and adaptation," says Mike Hulme, a professor at the University of East Anglia in Great Britain who has been studying the intersection between climate and culture. "This is as much part of the game as nominal reduction targets."

The accord calls for $10 billion a year to help poorer, more vulnerable countries cope with climate change over the next three years, rising to $100 billion a year by 2020. The money will come from "a wide variety of sources, public and private, bilateral and multilateral, including alternative sources of finance," according to the agreement.[15]

Equally important, say analysts, is the fact that the agreement sets new standards of participation and accountability for developing economies in the global warming fight. "The developing countries, particularly China, made a step forward and agreed not only to undertake some actions to reduce emissions, but to monitor and report those. I think that's significant," says Stephen Eule, a U.S. Chamber of Commerce climate expert and former George W. Bush administration climate official.

However, to many of the accord's critics, the accord mostly represents a failure of political leadership. "It was hugely disappointing. Watching world leaders lower expectations for three months coming into this, and then actually having them undershoot those expectations was unbelievable," says Jason Blackstock, a research scholar at the International Institute for Applied Systems Analysis in Austria, who studies the intersection of science and international affairs. He places some of the blame at the feet of President Obama: "This is clearly not one of his top issues, and that's disappointing."

But Thomas Homer-Dixon, who holds an international governance chair at the Balsillie School of International Affairs in Waterloo, Canada, and studies climate policy, believes critics are underestimating the importance of leaders from around the globe sitting down face-to-face to tackle the problem. "Symbolically, that photograph of the leaders of those countries sitting around the table with their sleeves rolled up was enormous," he says. "All of a sudden we're having a direct conversation among the actors that matter, both in the developed and developing world."

He also credits the conference for tackling difficult questions such as how much money developed countries need to transfer to the developing world to fight climate change and how much countries have to open themselves up to international inspection. "There's been sort of an agreement not to talk about the hard stuff," he says, "and now, at Copenhagen, it was finally front and center."

But to those who believe that the time for talk is running out, the dialogue meant nothing without concrete results. "This [deal], as they themselves say, will not avert catastrophic climate change," said Kumi Naidoo, Greenpeace International's executive director. "That's the only thing on which we agree with them. Everything else is a fudge; everything else is a fraud, and it must be called as such."[16]

Is the U.N.'s climate change negotiating framework outdated?

Although delegations from most of the world's nations came to Copenhagen, the final deal was hammered out by the leaders of only five countries. Those nations — the United States, China, India, Brazil and South Africa — provide a snapshot of the changing nature of geopolitical power.

Although they had been involved in larger group discussions of about 30 nations, the traditional European powers and Japan were not involved in the final deal. The five key players represented the world's largest economy (the United States), the largest emitter of greenhouse gases and second-biggest economy (China) and significant emerging economies in South America (Brazil), Africa (South Africa) and India, with the world's second-largest population.

The five-nation gathering could be seen as an effort to fashion a thin cross-section of the global community. But the U.N.-sponsored Copenhagen conference was supposed to embody the entire world community. To some observers, the fact that the accord was fashioned outside the official sessions appeared to be an attempt to undermine the U.N. effort.

Anne Petermann, co-director of the Global Justice Ecology Project, an international grassroots organization, notes the Bush administration also worked outside the U.N., setting up a smaller meeting of major economies to discuss climate change. "It wasn't particularly surprising the U.S. negotiated an accord that was completely outside the process," she says. "This wasn't the first time that the U.S. had come in with a strategy of undermining the U.N. Framework Convention."

To other analysts, however, the ability of the small group of leaders to come together where the larger conference had failed shows that the U.N. effort no longer fits the crisis. "The Framework Convention is actually now an obstacle to doing sensible things on climate change," says East Anglia's Hulme. "Climate change is such a multifaceted problem that we need to find sub-groups, multiple frameworks and initiatives to address it."

To others, the U.N. effort remains both the best chance for the world to reach a binding climate change agreement and essential to proceeding. "Because you've really got to have a global solution to this problem, it's essential that all the interested parties, including the most vulnerable countries, be around the table," says Oxfam's Waskow. "There's no question the U.N. Framework Convention, which has been working on this for many years, is the right place for that."

But Homer-Dixon, of the Balsillie School of International Affairs, believes the U.N. Framework process "has too many parties." He expects that on the negotiating side "we're going to migrate to something like the G-20 [economic forum], which includes all the major emitters. It would make sense to have the G-20 responsible."

However, Kassie Siegel, the climate law expert for the Center for Biological Diversity, a U.S. environmental group, thinks critics underestimate the U.N. effort. "Both the U.N. Framework Convention and the Intergovernmental Panel on Climate Change have been building capacity since 1992," she says. "There's not any other institution that came close to their experience on this issue. The U.N. Framework process is the best and fastest way forward."

Supporters also note that the United States and other signatories to the Copenhagen Accord have called for efforts to continue toward reaching a binding agreement at the next U.N. climate gathering in Mexico City at the end of this year. "I don't think the U.N. negotiations are irrelevant because the U.S. is still engaged in the Framework Convention," says Nicola Bullard, a climate change analyst and activist with Focus on the Global South, a nongovernmental group in Bangkok, Thailand.

But Eckhart believes the results in Copenhagen mean that key countries will now focus most of their efforts outside the U.N. framework. "I doubt Mexico City is still relevant," he says. "What can they get done in Mexico City that they couldn't get done in Copenhagen?"

The relationship between the Copenhagen Accord and the U.N. Framework Convention is somewhat ambiguous. Jacob Werksman, a lawyer specializing in international environmental and economics law at the World Resources Institute, concludes the conference's decision to only "take note" of the accord means that some provisions, including the call for setting up a Copenhagen Green Climate Fund to manage billions of dollars in aid through the U.N. mechanism, cannot occur without a conference decision to accept the accord.

U.N. Secretary General Ban Ki-moon has called on all U.N. countries to back the accord.[17] But some analysts believe the U.N. Framework Convention can't legally adopt it until the Mexico City conference, which would push the Climate Fund and possibly other accord provisions down the road another year — a delay climate change activists say the world can't afford.

Would a carbon tax reduce emissions more effectively?

Obscured by the immediate furor over Copenhagen is a longer-term debate over whether the developed world

Residents grin and bear flooding in Jakarta, Indonesia, in December 2007. Similar scenes would be played out in coastal cities and communities around the world if climate change causes glaciers and polar ice caps to melt, which many researchers predict. Analysts say the worst effects of climate change are expected to be felt in Asia.

is taking the right tack in its approach to reducing emissions.

The most popular approach so far has been the so-called cap-and-trade programs.[18] Progressively lower caps on overall emissions allow power companies and other entities to trade their emission quotas, creating a market-based approach to cutting greenhouse gases. Several European nations have embraced "cap-and-trade," and the climate change legislation that passed the U.S. House last June takes such an approach. But the system has been criticized for its complexity and susceptibility to manipulation and abuse.

Some analysts believe a carbon tax — a levy on carbon-emitting fuels, coupled with a system to rebate most of the tax back to consumers, is a more straightforward and effective way to control emissions. Robert Shapiro, former undersecretary of commerce during the Clinton administration and chair of the U.S. Climate Task Force, advocates such a program and works to educate the public on the need for action on climate change.

Shapiro's plan would use 90 percent of the carbon tax revenue to cut payroll taxes paid by workers and businesses, with the remaining 10 percent going to fund research and development of clean energy technology. The tax would provide a price incentive for discouraging the use of carbon emitting fuels and encouraging the use of green energy, while the tax cut would keep the approach from unduly burdening lower-income Americans. "A carbon tax would both directly reduce greenhouse gas emissions and provide powerful incentives for technological progress in this area," Shapiro wrote. "It offers the best way forward in both the national and global debate over climate change."[19]

However, carbon tax opponents argue it would be no more effective than cap-and-trade and would lead to a huge expansion of government. Analysts at the Heritage Foundation, a conservative U.S. think tank, wrote that a carbon tax "would cause significant economic damage and would do very little to reduce global temperatures." Even coupling it with a payroll tax cut, they continue, "would do little to offset the high energy prices that fall particularly hard on low-income households." The real agenda of a carbon tax, they charge, is "about raising massive amounts of revenue to fund a huge expansion in government."[20]

Several Scandinavian countries have adopted carbon taxes, with mixed results. Norway has seen its per capita CO_2 emissions rise significantly. But Denmark's 2005 emissions were 15 percent below what they were in 1990, and the economy still remained strong.[21]

But to Bullard, at Focus on the Global South, a carbon tax is the approach most likely to spur changes in personal behavior. "Reducing consumption is really important, reducing our own dependence on fossil fuels," she says. "I think it's very important to have a redistributive element so that working people and elderly people don't end up with a huge heating bill. But it's really a simpler and more effective route than a complicated solution like cap-and-trade."

However, Bill McKibben — an American environmentalist and the founder of 350.org, an international campaign dedicated to scaling back GHG emissions — says a carbon tax faces an almost insurmountable political hurdle in the United States. "Even I can't convince myself that America is going to sit very long with something called a carbon tax," he says.

McKibben thinks "cap and rebate" legislation recently introduced by Sens. Maria Cantwell, D-Wash., and Susan Collins, R-Maine, would be more palatable to voters. It would cap total emissions — a limit that would be tightened over time — with the government auctioning off available carbon credits. The money raised would be rebated to consumers to offset any higher energy bills.[22]

Congressional efforts, however, have focused on cap-and-trade. But as wariness grows in the U.S. Senate toward the ramifications of cap-and-trade, Shapiro believes a carbon tax could prove a more appealing option. "A real public discussion and debate about a carbon tax tied to offsetting cuts in payroll or other taxes," he said, "could be the best news for the climate in a very long time."[23]

BACKGROUND

Road to Copenhagen

The road to Copenhagen was a long one. In one sense, it began with the Industrial Revolution in the 18th and 19th century, which brought with it the increased burning of coal and the beginning of large-scale carbon dioxide emissions in Europe and America. It also started with scientific speculation in the 1930s that manmade emissions could be changing the planet's climate.

Those first studies were widely discounted, a reflection of the difficulty humanity has had coming to grips with the idea it could be changing the global climate. But by the mid-1980s, thanks in large part to the work of David Keeling at the Mauna Loa Observatory in Hawaii, the world had a nearly three-decade record of rising carbon dioxide levels in the atmosphere.[24] Scientists were also reporting an overall warming trend in the atmosphere over the last 100 years, which they considered evidence of a "greenhouse effect" tied to CO_2 and other manmade emissions.

Humankind began a slow, often painful struggle to understand and deal with a global challenge. From the beginning, there were doubters, some well-intentioned, some with a vested interest in making sure that the world continued to burn fossil fuels. Even as the scientific consensus on climate change has grown stronger, and many nations have committed themselves to tackling global warming, the issue continues to provoke and perplex.

Climate and Culture

In her book *Field Notes from a Catastrophe, Man, Nature and Climate Change*, American writer Elizabeth Kolbert visits, among other spots, Greenland's ice fields, a native village in Alaska and the countryside in northern England, surveying how global warming is changing the Earth. In the opening section, she admits her choices

about where to go to find the impact of climate change were multitudinous.

"Such is the impact of global warming that I could have gone to hundreds if not thousands of other places," Kolbert writes, "From Siberia to the Austrian Alps to the Great Barrier Reef to the South African *fynbos* (shrub lands)."[25]

Despite mounting evidence, however, climate change remains more a concept than a reality for huge parts of the globe, where the visible impacts are still slight or nonexistent. Research scholar Blackstock, whose work focuses on the intersection between science and international affairs, points out that for many people this makes the issue as much a matter of belief as of fact.

"It really strikes to fundamental questions on how we see the human-nature interface," he says. "It has cultural undertones, religious undertones, political undertones." Blackstock thinks many climate scientists have missed this multifaceted dimension to the public dialogue. "Pretending this is just a scientific debate won't work," he says. "That's important, but we can't have that alone."

The heart of the matter, he suggests, is how willing we are to take responsibility for changes in the climate and how we balance that with other values. This helps to explain the varying reactions in the United States, which has been reluctant to embrace limits on carbon emissions, and Europe, which has been more willing to impose measures. "You're seeing the cultural difference between Europe and America," Blackstock says, "the American values of individualism and personal success versus the communal and collective good, which Europe has more of a sense of being important."

Other analysts see attitudes about climate deeply woven into human culture. The University of East Anglia's Hulme, author of *Why We Disagree About Climate Change*, notes that climate and weather have been critical to humanity for most of its history. The seasons, rains and hot or cold temperatures have been so essential to life — to the ability to obtain food and build stable communities — that they have been attributed to deities and formed the basis for religious ceremonies. Even in the modern age, Hulme says, "People have an instinctive sense that weather and climate are natural phenomena, that they work at such scales and complexity that humans could not possibly influence them."

He points out that weather was once the realm of prophets, "and part of our population is still resistant to the idea that science is able to predict what the weather

Climate Change Could Force Millions to Relocate

"Climate Refugees" from Africa to the Arctic could be affected.

Maasi herdsman Moses Mopel Kisosion had never been outside Kenya before. He'd never ridden on a plane. But he flew across parts of two continents to deliver a message to anyone who would listen at the Copenhagen climate conference in December.

Climate change, he believes, is destroying the ability of his people, the Kajiado Maasi, to make a living. "I am a pastoralist, looking after cattles, walking from one place to another looking for grass and pastures," Kisosion said. "And now, for four years, we have a lack of rain, so our animals have died because there's no water and no grass. . . . We are wondering how our life will be because we depend on them."[1]

The Maasi are hardly alone in worrying if they will be able to continue living where they are. From small South Pacific island nations to the Arctic, hundreds of millions of people might have to relocate to survive as a result of climate change. If global warming predictions prove accurate, some researchers believe the world could soon find itself dealing with a tidal wave of "climate refugees."

A study by the U.N. Office for the Coordination of Humanitarian Affairs and the Internal Displacement Monitoring Centre found that "climate-related disasters — that is, those resulting from hazards that are already being or are likely to be modified by the effects of climate change — were responsible for displacing approximately 20 million people in 2008."[2]

Norman Myers, a British environmentalist, sees the situation worsening as the effects of climate change grow. In a 2005 study, he concluded that up to 200 million people could become climate refugees.[3] But he recently revised his estimate significantly. "We looked at the best prognosis for the spread of desertification and sea level rise, including the associated tsunamis and hurricanes, and we meshed those figures with the number of people impoverished or inhabiting coastal zones," says Myers. "We believe we could see half a billion climate refugees in the second half of the century."

The human displacement is likely to take place over several decades, experts say, and determining who is a climate refugee and who is simply a political or economic refugee could be difficult. International organizations have just begun the discussion about their status and what kind of assistance they might require.

The European Commission is funding a two-year research project, "Environmental Change and Forced Migration Scenarios," based on case studies in 24 vulnerable countries.[4] An African Union Summit in Kampala, Uganda, also met last October to consider how it would address the growing number of displaced Africans.[5]

Wahu Kaara, a Kenyan political activist, says the need for action is pressing. Kenya has recorded four major droughts in the last decade, significantly higher than the average over the previous century. "Very many people are dislocated and have to move to where they can salvage their lives," she says. "We have seen people die as they walk from one place to another. It's not a hardship; it's a catastrophe. They not only have lost their animals, they have lost their lives, and the framework of their lives for those who survive."

While Africa already may be suffering population movement due to climate change, the worst consequences are will be. This deep cultural history makes climate change a categorically different phenomenon than other scientifically observed data."

Climate is also often confused with weather. England, for example, has a temperate, damp climate, but can have dry, hot years. The human inclination is to believe what's before our eyes, so every cold winter becomes a reason to discount global warming.

Sander van der Leeuw, director of the School of Human Evolution and Social Change at Arizona State University in Tempe, Ariz., notes that facing climate change also means contemplating the costs of consumerism. "Those of us in the developed world have the most invested in this particular lifestyle," he says. "If that lifestyle has to change, we'll be facing the most wrenching dislocations."

likely to be felt in Asia, analysts say. Rising sea levels threaten low-lying coastal areas, which constitute only 2 percent of the land surface of the Earth but shelter 10 percent of its population. About 75 percent of the people living in those areas are in Asia.[6]

The Maldives, a nation of low-lying islands in the Indian Ocean that could be submerged if predictions prove accurate, has taken the lead in trying to organize smaller island nations in the global warming debate. President Mohamed Nasheed initially supported the Copenhagen Accord and its 2-degree Celsius target for limiting global warming as a beginning. But before the deal was struck, he declared, "At 2 degrees, my country would not survive."[7]

Rising sea levels threaten every continent, including the Americas. Until recently, Kivalina Island, an eight-mile long barrier island in northern Alaska, had survived the punishing storms that blew in from the ocean because of ice that formed and piled up on the island.[8]

Inupiat hunters from the island's small village began noticing changes in the ice years ago, says the island's tribal administrator, Colleen Swan, but the change has accelerated in recent years. "In early September and October, the ice used to start forming, but now it doesn't form anymore until January and it's not building up," she says. "When that happened, we lost our barrier from fall sea storms, and our island just started falling apart. We started losing a lot of land beginning in 2004."

The U.S. Army Corps of Engineers is building a seawall to protect what's left of Kivalina, but Swan says it is expected to buy only 10 or 15 years. "People in the United States are still debating whether climate change is happening. The U.N. is focusing on the long-term problem of emissions," Swan says, "but we're in the 11th hour here. The bottom line is we need someplace to go."

— *Reed Karaim*

A house tumbles into the Chukchi Sea in Shishmaref, Alaska. Like other victims of climate change, residents may have to abandon the tiny community due to unprecedented erosion caused by intense storms.

[1] Moses Mopel Kisosion spoke in a video blog from Kilmaforum09, the "people's forum" on climate change held in Copenhagen during the official conference. It is available online at http://en.cop15.dk/blogs/view+blog?blogid=2929.

[2] "Monitoring disaster displacement in the context of climate change," the U.N. Office for the Coordination of Humanitarian Affairs and The Internal Displacement Monitoring Centre, September 2009, p. 12.

[3] Norman Myers, "Environmental Refugees, an Emergent Security Issue," presented at the 13th Economic Forum, Prague, May 2005.

[4] "GLOBAL: Nowhere to run from nature," IRIN, Nov. 9, 2009, www.irinnews.org/report.aspx?ReportId=78387.

[5] "AFRICA: Climate change could worsen displacement — UN," IRIN, Nov. 9, 2009, www.irinnews.org/report.aspx?ReportId=86716.

[6] Anthony Oliver-Smith, "Sea Level Rise and the Vulnerability of Coastal Peoples," U.N. University Institute for Environment and Human Security, 2009, p. 5, www.ehs.unu.edu/file.php?id=652.

[7] "Address by His Excellency Mohamed Nasheed, President of the Republic of Maldives, at the Climate Vulnerable Forum," Nov. 9, 2009, www.actforclimatejustice.org/2009/11/address-by-his-excellency-mohamed-nasheed-president-of-the-republic-of-maldives-at-the-climate-vulnerable-forum/.

[8] See John Schwartz, "Courts As Battlefields in Climate Fights," *The New York Times*, Jan. 26, 2010.

Van der Leeuw, who worked for the European Union on climate change issues in the 1990s, is actually optimistic about the progress the world has made on climate change in the face of these challenges. "It's a very long process," he says, "but I'm encouraged by my students. It's wonderful to see how engaged they are, how open to thinking differently on these issues. I know we have very little time, but history is full of moments where we've reacted in the nick of time."

However, there are still those who doubt the basic science of climate change.

The Doubters

To enter the world of the climate change skeptics is to enter a mirror reflection of the scientific consensus on the issue. Everything is backwards: The Earth isn't warming; it may be cooling. If it is warming, it's part of the

CHRONOLOGY

1900-1950s *Early research indicates the Earth is warming.*

1938 British engineer Guy Stewart Callendar concludes that higher global temperatures and rising carbon dioxide levels are probably related.

1938 Soviet researchers confirm that the planet is warming.

1957 U.S. oceanographer Roger Revelle and Austrian physicist Hans Suess find that the oceans cannot absorb carbon dioxide as easily as thought, indicating that manmade emissions could create a "greenhouse effect," trapping heat in the atmosphere.

1958 U.S. scientist David Keeling begins monitoring atmospheric carbon dioxide levels, creating a groundbreaking record of their increase.

1960s *Climate science raises the possibility of global disaster.*

1966 U.S. geologist Cesare Emiliani says ice ages were created by tiny shifts in Earth's orbit, backing earlier theories that climate reacts to small changes.

1967 Leading nations launch 15-year program to study the world's weather.

1968 Studies show Antarctica's huge ice sheets could melt, raising sea levels.

1970s-1980s *Research into climate change intensifies, and calls for action mount.*

1975 A National Aeronautics and Space Administration (NASA) researcher warns that fluorocarbons in aerosol sprays could help create a greenhouse effect.

1979 The National Academy of Sciences finds that burning fossil fuels could raise global temperatures 6 degrees Fahrenheit in 50 years.

1981 U.S. scientists report a warming trend since 1880, evidence of a greenhouse effect.

1985 Scientists from 29 nations urge governments to plan for warmer globe.

1988 NASA scientist James Hansen says global warming has begun; he's 99 percent sure it's manmade.

1988 Thirty-five nations form a global panel to evaluate climate change and develop a response.

1990s *As the world responds to global warming, industry groups fight back.*

1990 The carbon industry-supported Global Climate Coalition forms to argue that climate change science is too uncertain to take action.

1995 The year is the hottest since the mid-19th century, when records began being kept.

1997 More than 150 nations agree on the Kyoto Protocol, a landmark accord to reduce greenhouse gases. The U.S. signs but never ratifies it.

2000s *The political battle over climate change action escalates worldwide.*

2000 Organization of Petroleum Exporting Countries (OPEC) demands compensation if global warming remedies reduce oil consumption.

2006 National Academy of Sciences reports the Earth's temperature is the highest in 12,000 years, since the last Ice Age.

2007 A U.N. report concludes that global warming is "unequivocal" and human actions are primarily responsible.

2009 The 194 nations attending the Copenhagen Climate Change Conference cannot agree on a broad treaty to battle global warming. After two weeks of contentious discussion, five nations create a nonbinding climate change accord, which 55 nations eventually sign, but which falls far short of delegates' hopes.

2010 The U.N effort to get a global, legally binding climate change treaty is scheduled to continue in November-December in Mexico City.

2009 December — The U.N. climate change conference in Copenhagen fails to reach a comprehensive legally binding accord to limit global warming.

2010 February — Yvo de Boer, the Dutch diplomat who led the U.N. Framework Convention on Climate Change effort for four years, resigns less than two months after Copenhagen, furthering the sense of a process in disarray.

November — A Republican majority, largely skeptical about climate change, sweeps into the U.S. House of Representatives, reducing the chance of comprehensive legislation to deal with greenhouse gas emissions anytime soon.

December — U.N. conference in Cancún, Mexico, agrees to take modest steps in the battle against climate change; supporters hail the agreement as a sign the U.N. process is still alive.

December — Environmental Protection Agency (EPA) says it will act to curb greenhouse gas emissions at power plants and oil refineries, possibly as early as 2011.

2011 January — National Climate Data Center announces that 2010 tied with 2005 as the hottest and wettest year on record, based on average annual precipitation.

February — Another investigation — the sixth — concurs that no scientific misconduct was revealed by researchers in connection with "climategate," the controversy that erupted in 2009 when more than 1,000 climatologists' emails were made public. Skeptics had claimed the emails cast doubt on the legitimacy of climate change findings.

April — U.S. House of Representatives blocks the EPA from regulating greenhouse gases, but a similar measure fails in the Senate.

December — Representatives from the 194 nations participating in the U.N. process are scheduled to meet in Durban, South Africa, to continue efforts to forge a meaningful international agreement to reduce manmade greenhouse gases and limit global warming.

planet's natural, long-term climate cycles. Manmade carbon dioxide isn't the heart of the problem; it's a relatively insignificant greenhouse gas. But even if carbon dioxide is increasing, it's beneficial for the planet.

And that scientific consensus? It doesn't exist. "What I see are a relatively small number, perhaps a few hundred at most, of extremely well-funded, well-connected evangelistic scientists doing most of the lobbying on this issue," says Bob Carter, a geologist who is one of Australia's more outspoken climate change skeptics.

Many scientists who take funds from grant agencies to investigate global warming, he says, "don't speak out with their true views because if they did so, they would lose their funding and be intimidated."

It's impossible to know if people are keeping views to themselves, of course. But professional science has a method of inquiry — the scientific method — and a system of peer review intended to lead to knowledge that, as much as possible, is untainted by prejudice, false comparison or cherry-picked data. The process isn't always perfect, but it provides our best look at the physical world around us.

In December 2004, Naomi Oreske, a science historian at the University of California, San Diego, published an analysis in *Science* in which she reviewed 928 peer-reviewed climate studies published between 1993 and 2003. She did not find one that disagreed with the general consensus on climate change.[26]

The U.S. National Academy of Sciences, the Royal Society of London, the Royal Society of Canada, the American Meteorological Society, the American Association for the Advancement of Science and 2,500 scientists participating in the IPCC also have concluded the evidence that humans are changing the climate is compelling. "Politicians, economists, journalists and others may have the impression of confusion, disagreement or discord among climate scientists, but that impression is incorrect," Oreske wrote, after reviewing the literature.[27]

The debate over climate change science heated up last fall, when, shortly before the Copenhagen conference, hackers broke into the University of East Anglia's computer network and made public hundreds of e-mails from scientists at the school's climate research center — some prominent in IPCC research circles. Climate

Climate Scientists Thinking Outside the Box

"Geoengineering" proposes futuristic solutions that sound like science fiction.

Imagine: A massive squadron of aircraft spewing sulfur particles into the sky. An armada of oceangoing ships spraying sea mist into the air. A swarm of robotic mirrors a million miles out in space reflecting some of the sun's harmful rays away from the Earth. Thousands of giant, air-filtering towers girdling the globe.

The prospect of devastating global warming has led some scientists and policy analysts to consider the kind of planet-altering responses to climate change that were once the province of science fiction. The underlying concept, known as "geoengineering," holds that manmade changes in the climate can be offset by futuristic technological modifications.

That idea raises its own concerns, both about the possibility of unintended consequences and of technological dependence. But from an engineering perspective, analysts say the sulfur particle and sea vapor options — which would reflect sunlight away from the Earth, potentially cooling the planet — appear feasible and not even that expensive.

"Basically, any really rich guy on the planet could buy an ice age," says David Keith, a geoengineering expert at the University of Calgary, estimating that sulfur injection could cost as little as $1 billion or so a year. "Certainly, it's well within the capability of most nations."

"Technologically, it would be relatively easy to produce small particles in the atmosphere at the required rates," says Ken Caldiera, a climate scientist at the Carnegie Institution for Science's Department of Global Ecology in Stanford, Calif. "Every climate-model simulation performed so far indicates geoengineering would be able to diminish most climate change for most people most of the time."

To spread sulfur, planes, balloons or even missiles could be used.[1] For sea vapor, which would be effective at a lower altitude, special ships could vaporize seawater and shoot it skyward through a rotor system.[2]

A global program of launching reflective aerosols higher into the atmosphere would cost around $5 billion annually — still small change compared to the economic costs of significant global warming, says Caldiera. Other geoengineering options are considerably more expensive. The cost of launching the massive (60,000 miles by 4,500 miles) cloud of mirrors into space to block sunlight would cost about $5 trillion.[3] Building air-scrubbing towers would also be expensive and would require improved technology.[4]

change skeptics were quick to point to the "Climategate" e-mails as evidence researchers had been squelching contrary opinions and massaging data to bolster their claims.

Reviews by *Time*, *The New York Times* and the Pew Center on Climate Change, however, found the e-mails did not provide evidence to alter the scientific consensus on climate change. "Although a small percentage of the e-mails are impolite and some express animosity toward opponents, when placed into proper context they do not appear to reveal fraud or other scientific misconduct," the Pew Center concluded.[28]

Some skeptics are scientists, but none are climate researchers. Perhaps the most respected scientific skeptic is Freeman Dyson, a legendary 86-year-old physicist and mathematician. Dyson does not dispute that atmospheric carbon-dioxide levels are rapidly rising and humans are to blame. He disagrees with those who project severe consequences. He believes rising CO_2 levels could have some benefits, and if not, humanity could bioengineer trees that consume larger amounts of carbon dioxide or find some other technological solution. He is sanguine about the ability of the Earth to adapt to change and is suspicious of the validity of computer models.

"The climate-studies people who work with models always tend to overestimate their models," Dyson has said. "They come to believe models are real and forget they are only models."[29]

Unlike Dyson, many climate change skeptics are connected to groups backed by the oil, gas and coal industries, which have worked since at least 1990 to discredit global warming theories. A 2007 study by the Union of Concerned Scientists found that between 1998 and 2005 ExxonMobil had funneled about $16 million to 43 groups that sought to manufacture uncertainty about global warming with the public.[30]

But cost is not what worries those studying geoengineering. "Everyone who's thinking about this has two concerns," says Thomas Homer-Dixon, a political scientist at Canada's Balsillie School of International Affairs in Waterloo, Ontario. "One is unintended consequences — because we don't understand climate systems perfectly — something bad could happen like damage to the ozone layer. The second is the moral-hazard problem: If we start to do this, are a lot of people going to think it means we can continue the carbon party?"

Keith thinks the consequences could be managed. "One of the advantages of using aerosols in the atmosphere is that you can modulate them," he says. "If you find it's not working, you can stop and turn the effect off." But he shares a concern with Caldiera and Homer-Dixon that geoengineering could be used as an excuse to avoid reducing carbon-dioxide emissions.

Geoengineering also raises geopolitical concerns, in part because it could be undertaken unilaterally. Unlike lowering greenhouse gas emissions, it doesn't require a global agreement, yet its effects would be felt around the planet — and not evenly.

That could aggravate international tensions: Any sustained bad weather in one nation could easily raise suspicion that it was the victim of climate modifications launched by another country. "If China, say, were to experience a deep drought after the deployment of a climate-intervention system," says Caldiera, "and people were starving as a result, this could cause them to lash out politically or even militarily at the country or countries that were engaged in the deployment."

Such scenarios, along with the fear of undercutting global negotiations to reduce emissions, make serious international consideration of geoengineering unlikely in the near term, says Homer-Dixon. But if the direst predictions about global warming prove accurate that could change. "You could see a political clamor worldwide to do something," he says.

Some scientists believe stepped-up geoengineering studies need to start soon. "We need a serious research program, and it needs to be international and transparent," says Keith. "It needs to start small. I don't think it needs to be a crash program, but I think there's an enormous value in doing the work. We've had enough hot air speculation. We need to do the work. If we find out it works pretty well, then we'll have a tool to help manage environmental risk."

— *Reed Karaim*

[1] Robert Kunzig, "A Sunshade for Planet Earth," *Scientific American*, November 2008.

[2] *Ibid.*

[3] *Ibid.*

[4] Seth Borenstein, "Wild ideas to combat global warming being seriously entertained," *The Seattle Times*, March 16, 2007, http://seattletimes.nwsource.com/html/nationworld/2003620631_warmtech16.html.

The tactics appear to be patterned after those used by the tobacco industry to discredit evidence of the hazards of smoking. According to the study, ExxonMobil and others have used ostensibly independent front groups for "information laundering," as they sought to sow doubts about the conclusions of mainstream climate science.

Several prominent climate change skeptics — including physicist S. Fred Singer and astrophysicists Willie Soon and Sallie Baliunas — have had their work published by these organizations, some of which seem to have no other purpose than to proliferate the information. "By publishing and re-publishing the non-peer-reviewed works of a small group of scientific spokespeople, ExxonMobil-funded organizations have propped up and amplified work that has been discredited by reputable climate scientists," the study concludes.[31]

Is the world cooling? Is global warming a natural phenomenon? Is more CO_2 really good for the planet?

Science and media watchdog groups have published detailed rebuttals to the claims of climate change skeptics.[32] To cite one example, assertions that the Earth is actually cooling often use 1998 as the base line — a year during the El Niño weather system, which typically produces warmer weather. The Associated Press gave temperature numbers to four statisticians without telling them what the numbers represented. The scientists found no true declines over the last 10 years. They also found a "distinct, decades-long" warming trend.[33]

James Hoggan, a Canadian public relations executive who founded DeSmogblog to take on the skeptics, feels climate scientists have done a poor job of responding to the skeptics, too often getting bogged down in the minutiae of detail. "We need to start asking these so-called skeptics a number of basic questions," says Hoggan, the author of *Climate Cover-Up: The Crusade to Deny Global Warming*. "The first one is, 'Are you actually a climate scientist?' The

Hunger and Thirst

A young Turkana girl in drought-plagued northern Kenya digs for water in a dry river bed in November 2009 (top). Momina Mahammed's 8-month-old son Ali suffers from severe malnutrition in an Ethiopian refugee camp in December 2008 (bottom). Food and water shortages caused by climate changes are already affecting many countries in Africa. A sudanese delegate to the Copenhagen Climate Change Conference called the nonbinding accord reached at the convention "an incineration pact" for poor countries.

second one is, 'Have you published peer-reviewed papers on whatever claims you're making?' And a third one is, 'Are you taking money directly or indirectly from industry?' "

Untangling the Threads

Since nations first began to seriously wrestle with climate change, most of the effort has gone into fashioning a legally binding international treaty to cut greenhouse gas emissions while helping poorer nations cope with the effects of global warming.

The approach has a powerful logic. Climate change is a worldwide problem and requires concerted action around the planet. Assisting those most likely to be affected — populations in Africa and Asia who are among the poorest on the globe — is also a burden that is most equitably shared.

But the all-in-one-basket approach also comes with big problems. The first is the complexity of the negotiations themselves, which involve everything from intellectual-property rights to hundreds of billions of dollars in international finance to forest management. Global nations have been meeting on these issues for nearly two decades without a breakthrough deal.

Some observers believe the best chance for moving forward is untangling the threads of the problem. "We don't have to try to set the world to rights in one multilateral agreement," says East Anglia's Hulme. "It's not something we've ever achieved in human history, and I doubt we can. It seems more likely it's acting as an unrealistic, utopian distraction."

Analysts cite the 1987 Montreal Protocol, which phased out the use of chlorofluorocarbons that were damaging the ozone layer, as an example of a successful smaller-scale deal.

So far, the effort to control global warming has focused on limiting carbon-dioxide emissions from power plants and factories. But CO_2 accounts for only half of manmade greenhouse gas emissions.[34] The rest comes from a variety of sources, where they are often easier or cheaper to cut.

Black carbon, mainly produced by diesel engines and stoves that burn wood or cow dung, produces from one-eighth to a quarter of global warming.[35] Promoting cleaner engines and helping rural villagers move to cleaner-burning stoves would cut global warming gases, yet hardly requires the wrenching shift of moving from coal-fired electricity. Hydrofluorocarbons (HFCs) are more than a thousand times more potent as greenhouse gases than CO_2, but are used in comparably minuscule amounts and should be easier to limit.

"Why are we putting all the greenhouse gases into one agreement? CO_2 is very different from black soot, or methane or HFCs," Hulme says. "Tropical forests, why do they have to be tied to the climate agenda? They sequester carbon, yes, but they're also valuable resources in other regards."

Those who support negotiating a sweeping climate change accord believe that untangling these threads could weaken the whole cloth, robbing initiative from critical parts of the deal, such as assistance to developing countries. But Hulme believes the poorer parts of the world could benefit.

"We can tend to the adaptation needs of the developing world without having them hitched to the much greater complexity of moving the economy in the developed world away from fossil fuels," he says.

Other analysts, however, are unconvinced that climate change would be easier to deal with if its constituent issues were broken out. "There are entrenched interests on each thread," says Blackstock, at Austria's International Institute in Applied Systems Analysis. "That's the real problem at the end of the day."

CURRENT SITUATION

Next Steps

The whole world may be warming, but as has been said, all politics is local — even climate change politics. "It's still the legislatures of the nation states that will really determine the pace at which climate policies are driven through," notes the University of East Anglia's Hulme. "In the end, that's where these deals have to make sense."

Nations around the globe are determining their next steps in the wake of Copenhagen. Most greenhouse gases, however, come from a relative handful of countries. The United States and China, together, account for slightly more than 40 percent of the world's manmade CO_2 emissions.[36] If India and the European Union are added, the total tops 60 percent.[37] The post-Copenhagen climate change status is different for each of these major players.

More Countries Agree to Emissions Cuts

The nonbinding climate agreement reached in Copenhagen, Denmark, on Dec. 18 was originally joined by 28 countries, which were to send the United Nations by the end of January their individual goals for reducing carbon emissions by 2020. But other nations also were invited to sign on by submitting their own plans to cut emissions. On Feb. 1, the U.N. reported that a total of 55 nations had submitted targets for cutting greenhouse gases. Analysts say while these countries produce 78 percent of manmade carbon emissions, more cuts are needed. The U.N. will try to use the accord as a starting point for a binding treaty at the next international climate conference in Mexico City, Nov. 29-Dec. 10.

Key provisions in the Copenhagen Accord:

- Cut global greenhouse gas emissions so global temperatures won't rise more than 2 degrees Celsius above the pre-Industrial Revolution level.
- Cooperate in achieving a peak in emissions as soon as possible.
- Provide adequate, predictable and sustainable funds and technology to developing countries to help them adapt to climate change.
- Prioritize reducing deforestation and forest degradation, which eliminate carbon-consuming trees.
- Provide $30 billion in new and additional resources from 2010 to 2012 to help developing countries mitigate climate change and protect forests; and provide $100 billion a year by 2020.
- Assess implementation of the accord by 2015.

Sources: "Copenhagen Accord," U.N. Framework Convention on Climate Change, Dec. 18, 2009; "UNFCCC Receives list of government climate pledges," press release, United Nations Framework Convention on Climate Change, Feb. 1, 2010, http://unfccc.int/files/press/news_room/press_releases_and_advisories/application/pdf/pr_accord_100201.pdf

---

China — China presents perhaps the most complex case of any of the countries central to climate change. It was classified as a developing country in the Kyoto Protocol, so it was not required to reduce carbon emissions.[38] But as the country's economy continued to skyrocket, China became the world's largest carbon dioxide emitter in 2006, passing the United States.[39]

But with roughly 700 million poorer rural citizens, promoting economic growth remains the Chinese government's essential priority. Nevertheless, shortly before Copenhagen, China announced it would vow to cut CO_2 emissions by 40 to 45 percent *per unit of gross domestic product* below 2005 levels by 2020. The complicated formula meant that emissions would still rise, but at a slower rate. China subsequently committed to

Is the Copenhagen Accord a meaningful step forward in halting climate change?

YES
Ban Ki-moon
Secretary-General, United Nations

NO
Nnimmo Bassey
Chair, Friends of the Earth International

From opening remarks at press conference, U.N. Climate Change Conference, Copenhagen, Dec. 19, 2009

Written for *CQ Global Researcher,* February 2010

The Copenhagen Accord may not be everything that everyone hoped for. But this decision of the Conference of Parties is a new beginning, an essential beginning.

At the summit I convened in September, I laid out four benchmarks for success for this conference. We have achieved results on each.

- All countries have agreed to work toward a common, long-term goal to limit global temperature rise to below 2 degrees Celsius.
- Many governments have made important commitments to reduce or limit emissions.
- Countries have achieved significant progress on preserving forests.
- Countries have agreed to provide comprehensive support to the most vulnerable to cope with climate change.

The deal is backed by money and the means to deliver it. Up to $30 billion has been pledged for adaptation and mitigation. Countries have backed the goal of mobilizing $100 billion a year by 2020 for developing countries. We have convergence on transparency and an equitable global governance structure that addresses the needs of developing countries. The countries that stayed on the periphery of the Kyoto process are now at the heart of global climate action.

We have the foundation for the first truly global agreement that will limit and reduce greenhouse gas emission, support adaptation for the most vulnerable and launch a new era of green growth.

Going forward, we have three tasks. First, we need to turn this agreement into a legally binding treaty. I will work with world leaders over the coming months to make this happen. Second, we must launch the Copenhagen Green Climate Fund. The U.N. system will work to ensure that it can immediately start to deliver immediate results to people in need and jump-start clean energy growth in developing countries. Third, we need to pursue the road of higher ambition. We must turn our back on the path of least resistance.

Current mitigation commitments fail to meet the scientific bottom line.

We still face serious consequences. So, while I am satisfied that we have a deal here in Copenhagen, I am aware that it is just the beginning. It will take more than this to definitively tackle climate change.

But it is a step in the right direction.

The Copenhagen Accord is not a step forward in the battle to halt climate change. Few people expected the Copenhagen climate talks to yield a strong outcome. But the talks ended with a major failure that was worse than predicted: a "Copenhagen Accord" in which individual countries make no new serious commitments whatsoever.

The accord sets a too-weak goal of limiting warming to 2 degrees Celsius, but provides no means of achieving this goal. Likewise, it suggests an insufficient sum for addressing international solutions but contains no path to produce the funding. Individual countries are required to do nothing.

The accord fails the poor and the vulnerable communities most impacted by climate change. This non-agreement (it was merely "noted," not adopted, by the conference) is weak, non-binding and allows false solutions such as carbon offsetting. It will prove completely ineffective. Providing some coins for developing countries to mitigate climate change and adapt to it does not help if the sources of the problem remain unchecked.

The peoples' demands for climate justice should be the starting point when addressing the climate crisis. Instead, in Copenhagen, voices of the people were shut out and peaceful protests met brutal suppression. Inside the Bella Center, where the conference took place, many of the poor countries were shut out of back-room negotiations. The accord is the result of this anti-democratic process.

The basic demands of the climate justice movement remain unmet. The U.N. climate process must resume, and it must accomplish these goals:

- Industrialized countries must commit to at least 40 percent cuts in emissions by 2020 by using clean energy, sustainable transport and farming and cutting energy demand.
- Emission cuts must be real. They cannot be "achieved" by carbon offsetting, such as buying carbon credits from developing countries or by buying up forests in developing countries so they won't be cut down.
- Rich countries must make concrete commitments to provide money for developing countries to grow in a clean way and to cope with the floods, droughts and famines caused by climate change. Funding must be adequate, not the minuscule amounts proposed in the accord.

Wealthy nations are most responsible for climate change. They have an obligation to lead the way in solving the problem. They have not done so with the Copenhagen Accord.

this reduction when confirming its Copenhagen pledge at the end of January.

U.N. climate policy chief de Boer hailed the move as a critical step. But the United States — especially skeptical members of the U.S. Congress — had hoped to see more movement from China and wanted verification standards.

Some participants say China's recalcitrance is why Copenhagen fell short. The British seemed particularly incensed. Ed Miliband, Great Britain's climate secretary, blamed the Chinese leadership for the failure to get agreement on a 50-percent reduction in global emissions by 2050 or on 80-percent reductions by developed countries. "Both were vetoed by China," he wrote, "despite the support of a coalition of developed and the vast majority of developing countries."[40]

But the Global Justice Ecology Project's Petermann places the blame elsewhere. "Why should China get involved in reducing emissions if the U.S. is unwilling to really reduce its emissions?" she asks.

Jiang Lin, director of the China Sustainable Energy Program, a nongovernmental agency with offices in Beijing and San Francisco, thinks China's leaders take the threat of climate change seriously. "There's probably a greater consensus on this issue in China than the United States," says Jiang. "The Chinese leadership are trained engineers. They understand the data."

Jiang points out that China already is seeing the effects predicted by climate change models, including the weakening of the monsoon in the nation's agricultural northwest and the melting of the Himalayan glaciers. "The Yellow River is drying up," he adds. "This is very symbolic for the Chinese. They consider this the mother river, and now almost half the year it is dry."

The Copenhagen Accord is not legally binding, but Jiang believes the Chinese will honors its provisions. "When they announce they're committed to something, that's almost as significant as U.S. law," he says, "because if they don't meet that commitment, losing facing is huge for them."

While attention has focused on international negotiations, China is targeting improved energy efficiency and renewable power. In 2005, China's National People's Congress set a goal of generating 20 gigawatts of power through wind energy by 2020. The goal seemed highly ambitious, but China expected to meet it by the end of 2009 and is now aiming for 150 gigawatts by 2020. The

target for solar energy has been increased more than 10-fold over the same period.[41]

Coal still generates 80 percent of China's power, and the country continues to build coal-fired plants, but Chinese leaders clearly have their eyes on the green jobs that President Obama has promoted as key to America's future.[42] "Among the top 10 solar companies in the world, China already has three," says Jiang, "and China is now the largest wind market in the world. They see this as an industry in which China has a chance to be one of the leaders."

The United States — To much of the world, the refusal of the United States so far to embrace carbon emission limits is unconscionable. U.S. emissions are about twice Europe's levels per capita, and more than four times China's.

"The United States is the country that needs to lead on this issue," says Oxfam's Waskow. "It created a lot of problems that the U.S. wasn't able to come to Copenhagen with congressional legislation in hand."

In the Copenhagen Accord, President Obama committed the United States to reduce its carbon dioxide emissions to 17 percent below 2005 levels by 2020. That equates to about 4 percent below 1990 levels, far less stringent than the European and Japanese pledges of 20 percent and 25 percent below 1990 levels, respectively. However, Congress has not passed global warming legislation. Last year, the House of Representatives passed a bill that would establish a cap-and-trade system, which would limit greenhouse gases but let emitters trade emission allowances among themselves. The legislation faces stiff opposition in the Senate, however.

In 1997, after the Kyoto Protocol was adopted, the Senate voted 95-0 against signing any international accord unless it mandated GHG emission reductions by developing countries as well. Securing such commitments in Copenhagen — especially from China, along with improved verification — was considered critical to improving the chances a climate change bill would make it through the Senate.

Some analysts also blamed the lack of U.S. legislation for what was considered a relatively weak American proposal at Copenhagen. "Obama wasn't going to offer more than the U.S. Senate was willing to offer," says the International Institute for Applied System's Blackstock. "He could have done more and said, 'I cannot legally commit to this, but I'll go home and fight for it.' He didn't."

But Obama's negotiating effort in Copenhagen impressed some observers. "He could have stood back and worried about looking presidential," says the American Council on Renewable Energy's Eckhart. "He didn't. He rolled up his sleeves and got in there and tried to do good for the world."

Early reviews of the Copenhagen Accord were favorable among at least two key Republican senators, Lisa Murkowski of Alaska and Richard Lugar of Indiana. "Whenever you have developing countries, and certainly China and India stepping forward and indicating that they have a willingness to be a participant ... I think that that is progress," said Murkowski.[43]

Still, analysts remain skeptical whether it will make a real difference on Capitol Hill. "I don't see Congress doing anything, even in line with the position in the Copenhagen Accord unless Obama makes it his 2010 priority," says 350.org's McKibben. "There's no question it's going to be hard because it's going to require real change."

The administration is planning to regulate some greenhouse gases through the Environmental Protection Agency (EPA). The Center for Biological Diversity has petitioned the EPA to make further use of regulation to reduce greenhouse emissions. "The president has the tools he needs. He has the Clean Air Act," says the center's Siegel. "All he has to do is use it."

However, some Senate Republicans are already calling for a resolution to undo the EPA's limited actions, and polls show a rising number of Americans skeptical about global warming, particularly Republicans.[44] Given the highly polarized nature of American politics, any significant move on climate change is likely to prove a bruising battle. President Obama has made promoting green energy jobs a priority, but with health care and joblessness still leading the administration's agenda, further action on climate change seems unlikely in the next year. Chances for major legislative action shrunk even further with the election of Republican Scott Brown, a climate change skeptic, to the Senate from Massachusetts. Brown's win ended the democrats' 60-vote, filibuster-proof majority.[45]

India — Although India's economy has grown almost as rapidly as China's in recent years, it remains a much poorer country. Moreover, its low coastline and dependence on seasonal monsoons for water also make it sensitive to the dangers of global warming. Jairam Ramesh, India's environment minister, said, "The most vulnerable country in the world to climate change is India."[46]

India's leaders announced recently they will pursue cleaner coal technology, higher emissions standards for automobiles and more energy-efficient building codes. Prior to Copenhagen, India also announced it would cut CO_2 emissions per unit of GDP from 2005 levels, but rejected legally binding targets.

After the negotiations on the accord, Ramesh told the *Hindustan Times* that India had "upheld the interest of developing nations."[47] But some analysts said India had largely followed China's lead, a position that could cost India some prestige with other developing nations, whose cause it had championed in the past.

"The worst thing India did was to align itself uncritically to China's yoke," says Indian political scientist Mehra, "because China acted purely in its own self interest."

The European Union — European leaders are calling for other countries to join them in backing the Copenhagen Accord, but they've hardly tried to hide their disappointment it wasn't more substantial. The European Union had staked out one of the stronger positions on emissions reductions beforehand, promising to cut emissions by 20 percent from 1990 levels to 2020, or 30 percent if other countries took similarly bold action. They also wanted rich nations to make 80 to 95 percent cuts in GHG emissions by 2050.[48]

Some national leaders also had expended political capital on global warming before the conference. French President Nicolas Sarkozy had announced a proposal to create a French "carbon tax" on businesses and households for use of oil, gas and coal. The proposal was blocked by the French Constitutional Council, but Sarkozy's party plans to reintroduce it this year.[49]

In the United Kingdom, Prime Minister Brown's government passed legislation committing to an 80 percent cut in U.K. greenhouse gas emissions by 2050.[50] Brown also pressed publicly for $100 billion a year in aid to the developing world to cope with climate change.

The European efforts were designed to lead by example. But analysts say the approach yielded little fruit in Copenhagen. "The European perspective that they could lead by example was the wrong strategy. This was a negotiation. Countries do not check their national interests at the door when they enter the U.N.," says the Chamber of Commerce's Eule, who worked on climate change in the Bush administration.

Although Europe's leaders finally backed the accord and formally pledged 20 percent emission reductions, they had only limited influence on the deal's final shape. "Europe finds itself now outside the driver's seat for how this is going to go forward," says Hulme at the University of East Anglia. "I think in Brussels [home of the E.U. headquarters], there must be a lot of conversations going on about where Europe goes from here." He believes Europe's stricter emissions regulations could now face a backlash.

Framework Conference chief de Boer, who is a citizen of the Netherlands, captured the resignation that seemed to envelope many European diplomats during his post-Copenhagen comments to the press. Before the climate conference kicked off, de Boer had predicted that Copenhagen would "launch action, action and more action" on climate change.

But in his December 19 press conference, when asked what he hoped could be accomplished in the year ahead, he responded, "Basically, the list I put under the Christmas tree two years ago, I can put under the Christmas tree again this year."

OUTLOOK

Too Late?

The world's long-term climate forecast can be summed up in a word: warmer. Even if the nations of the world were to miraculously agree tomorrow to reduce global greenhouse gas emissions, global warming could continue for some time because of the "lag" in how the climate system responds to GHG emission reductions.

In the last decade, researchers have poured a tremendous amount of effort into trying to foresee where climate change could take us. But the projections come with an element of uncertainty. Still, taken together, the most startling forecasts amount to an apocalyptic compendium of disaster. Climate change could:

- Lead to droughts, floods, heat waves and violent storms that displace tens of millions of people, particularly in Asia and sub-Saharan Africa;
- Create a high risk of violent conflict in 46 countries, now home to 2.7 billion people, as the effects of climate change exacerbate existing economic, social and political problems;[51]

AFP/Getty Images STR

Getty Images/Robert Nickelsberg

Causes of Climate Change

Rapidly industrializing China has surpassed the United States as the world's largest emitter of carbon dioxide—one of the greenhouse gases (GHG) responsible for rising world temperatures. Although most GHGs are invisible, air pollution like this in Wuhan, China, on Dec.3, 2009 (above) often includes trapped greenhouse gases. The destruction of tropical rainforests decreases the number of trees available to absorb carbon dioxide. Palm oil trees once grew on this 250-acre plot being cleared for farming in Aceh, Indonesia (below).

- Cause the extinction of about a quarter of all land-based plant and animal species — more than a million — by 2050;[52]
- Effectively submerge some island nations by 2100,[53] and create widespread dislocation and damage to coastal areas, threatening more than $28 trillion worth of assets by 2050; and[54]
- Cause acidification of the oceans that renders them largely inhospitable to coral reefs by 2050, destroying a fragile underwater ecosystem important to the world's fisheries.[55]

If temperatures climb by an average of 3.5 to 4 degrees Celsius (6.3 to 7.2 Fahrenheit) by the end of the century, as some projections predict, it would mean "total devastation for man in parts of the world," says the Global Justice Ecology Project's Petermann. "You're talking about massive glaciers melting, the polar ice caps disappearing. It would make life on this planet completely unrecognizable."

But some analysts, while endorsing the potential dangers of climate change, still back away from the view that it's a catastrophe that trumps all others. "The prospective tipping points for the worst consequences are just that, prospective tipping points, and they're resting on the credibility of scientific models," says East Anglia University's Hulme. "We should take them seriously. But they're not the Nazis marching across Belgium. We need to weigh our response within the whole range of needs facing the human race."

The critical question likely to determine the shape of the planet's future for the rest of this century and beyond is when humans will stop pouring greenhouse gases into the atmosphere. If done soon enough, most scientists say, climate change will be serious but manageable on an international level, although billions of dollars will be needed to mitigate the effects in the most vulnerable parts of the globe.

But if emissions continue to rise, climate change could be far more catastrophic. "It is critically important that we bring about a commitment to reduce emissions effectively by 2020," said IPCC Chairman Rajendra Pachauri, shortly before Copenhagen.[56]

To accomplish Copenhagen's goal of holding warming to 2 degrees Celsius, Pachauri said emissions must peak by 2015. The agreement, however, sets no peaking year, and the emission-reduction pledges by individual nations fall short of that goal, according to recent analysis by Climate Interactive, a collaborative research effort sponsored by the Sustainability Institute in Hartland, Vt.[57]

World leaders acknowledge they need to do more, and some observers remain hopeful the upcoming climate conference in Mexico City could provide a breakthrough that will avert the worst, especially if pressure to act continues to grow at the grassroots level. "Right now there is a massive gulf between where the public is and where the political process is," says India's Mehra. "But I think

[in 2010] you will see government positions mature. And I think you will see more politicians who have the conviction to act."

Canadian political scientist Homer-Dixon considers bold action unlikely, however, unless the world's major emitting nations, including the United States and China, start suffering clearly visible, serious climate-change consequences.

"In the absence of those really big shocks, I'm afraid we're probably achieving about as much as possible," he says. "Because of the lag in the system, if you wait until the evidence is clear, it's too late."

UPDATE

The long-term forecast for planet Earth remains the same: warmer climate, with increased severe weather events likely. But the outlook for government action on the problem of global climate change is cloudier and has cooled on a couple of fronts.

On the international level, the U.N.-led effort to forge a comprehensive accord to battle climate change has focused on incremental steps, after falling short of its most ambitious goals at a discordant Copenhagen conference in 2009. Leaders of the U.N. Framework Convention on Climate Change — the governing body for international treaty negotiations — sought to temper expectations during the most recent climate change conference, held last year in Cancún, Mexico.

In the United States, the chances of comprehensive climate change legislation being enacted have been put in a deep freeze by a new, Republican-led House of Representatives that includes key members openly dismissive of the idea of climate change being affected by human activity.

Meanwhile, 2010 tied with 2005 as the warmest year on record, according to the National Climactic Data Center, marking the 34th year in a row that the global temperature was above average.[58]

The scientific consensus that climate change is occurring and that human activity is most likely responsible remains firm. "A few years ago, we were seeing a lot of new research, papers coming out that indicated, wow, everything is happening faster than we thought. That trend has solidified," says Jay Gulledge, senior scientist and director for science and impacts at the Pew Center on Global Climate Change.

Extreme Weather More Likely

Although no earth-shattering new findings have come to light, climate researchers continue to advance their understanding of what's happening in the atmosphere and the likely consequences for life on Earth.

"There's some recent work that's provided computer-modeling support for the conjecture that climate change is making extreme weather events more likely," Gulledge says.

A study in the *Journal of Great Lakes Research*, for example, looked at the likelihood of more extreme heat waves such as the unprecedented event that killed nearly 800 people in Chicago in July 1995. Such extreme weather could become more commonplace, researchers have concluded, depending on the rise in greenhouse gas emissions, the carbon dioxide and other gases that heat up the Earth's atmosphere. "Before the end of the century, 1995-like heat waves could occur every other year on average under lower emissions and as frequently as three times per year under higher" emissions, researchers concluded. Thousands could die as a result, they said. [59]

Other research indicates that global warming is helping to spread malaria into Africa's highland areas, where it has been almost unknown. Experts believe the death toll from the disease, which already kills about 1 million people a year, could rise dramatically because upland inhabitants have developed less resistance to the disease. [60]

New research also shows that climate change is affecting a wide variety of plants and animals. In fact, changes in the planet's temperatures may be ushering in a wave of mass extinctions like those that have occurred only rarely in the planet's history, according to a new study. Scientists caution that a complex interplay of factors is at work. But other research has bolstered the conclusion that global warming is challenging lots of different species, and many scientists believe it is playing a significant role in extinction rates. [61]

All in all, much of the recent research supports the idea that the risks to Earth from climate change aren't "far away in the future," says Gulledge, "but are already here in some cases."

AFP/Getty Images/Olivier Morina

Yvo de Boer, a Dutch diplomat who led the U.N. Framework Convention on Climate Change, speaks at a press briefing during a conference in Copenhagen on Dec. 19, 2009. De Boer resigned less than two months later, furthering a sense that U.N. efforts to deal with climate issues were in disarray.

International Negotiations

The last two U.N. climate change conferences provide a study in contrasts and an example of hard lessons learned.

In 2009 the Copenhagen conference kicked off with high hopes that world leaders would sign a landmark agreement setting firm targets for reducing manmade greenhouse gases and a timetable for reaching a legally binding treaty to cut those emissions.

Instead, the negotiations nearly collapsed in acrimony, exposing fault lines between the developed and developing worlds and between China and leading Western nations. As thousands of activists from around the world filled the streets of Copenhagen to urge the delegates to act, negotiators inside the meeting hall haggled in increasing frustration.

In the end, the so-called Copenhagen Accord was negotiated at the 11th hour by a small group of world leaders, including President Barack Obama and Chinese Premier Wen Jiabao. It kept the international dialogue alive and included a pledge to provide billions in aid to help developing countries cope with climate change, along with new reporting and transparency standards for participating countries.

But it failed to include a timetable for reaching a legally binding treaty and in most other ways fell short of expectations. Many nations reacted with dismay. Africa was being asked "to sign a suicide pact," declared Sudanese delegate Lumumba Di-Aping, referring to the dire consequences of higher temperatures on his desert nation and other African countries. A bitterly divided conference agreed only to "take note" of the accord, not adopt it.

A year later, the U.N. conference in Cancún was notable for the relative modesty of its goals and the low-key manner in which leading nations approached the session, inviting none of the large expectations that attended Copenhagen. Instead, negotiators focused on smaller steps, including strengthening nations' non-binding pledges to reduce greenhouse gas emissions, creating a mechanism to spread clean-energy technology and formally establishing the new Green Climate Fund to help poor countries deal with climate change. It also clarified reporting and verification requirements important to U.S. negotiators.[62]

Participants declared they were back on track. "This is not the end, but it is a new beginning," said Christiana Figueres, executive secretary of the U.N. Framework Convention on Climate Change. "Governments have given a clear signal that they are headed towards a low-emissions future together."[63]

But skeptics noted that negotiators from the 194 participating countries reached agreement only by once again avoiding the hard questions. "They kicked the can down the road," says Patrick J. Michaels, a senior fellow in environmental studies at the Cato Institute, a libertarian think tank in Washington. "What we're seeing, pretty much globally, is a retreat from expansive global-warming policies and global agreements."

Michaels attributes this to a shift in world public opinion against the idea that climate change requires immediate action. "The more realistic people on this planet are saying we have to see what climate change is going to take place," he says.

But Elliot Diringer, vice president for international strategies at the Pew center, believes Cancún helped re-establish the relevance of the U.N. negotiations. "Essentially what happened in Cancún," he says, "was importing the Copenhagen Accord into the U.N. process and taking some initial steps to implement its essential elements."

Diringer acknowledges that negotiators in Cancún sidestepped difficult issues, specifically binding commitments to limit emissions. "And I'm glad they did because for a long time the process seemed stuck in a binding or nothing mode," he says. "Ultimately, we'd like to see this resolve in the direction of binding commitments, but that's going to take time, and concrete, incremental steps can help us get there."

Outside the U.N. process, some nations are making progress on an individual basis or within smaller groups. For example, the Arctic Council, an organization of eight nations with northern territories that ring the Arctic Circle, recently agreed to reduce emissions of black carbon — essentially soot — a significant contributor to Arctic global warming.[64]

The U.N. effort will reconvene in Durban, South Africa, later this year to continue working toward a more substantial agreement. Pressure will be ratcheted up in 2012, when the initial commitment period of the Kyoto Protocol expires. Under the protocol, 37 industrialized nations (but not the United States) promised to cut greenhouse gases, but some have indicated they will not renew their Kyoto commitments.[65]

"The question for Durban is whether this new sense of realism carries over," Diringer says, "or do we fall back into this binding-or-nothing syndrome?"

U.S. Impasse

The prospect, already slight, that Congress would pass comprehensive climate change legislation this session died in January when the Republicans swept back into control of the U.S. House of Representatives.

Skepticism about global warming runs high among congressional Republicans, and they have pressed the administration on a couple of fronts. The budget deal hammered out between Republicans and Democrats in April eliminated funding for the National Oceanic and Atmospheric Administration's Climate Service and the position of assistant to the president for energy and climate change. It significantly reduced U.S. commitments to international climate change efforts. [66]

House Republicans also have voted to block Environmental Protection Agency (EPA) plans to regulate and limit greenhouse gases as pollutants under the Clean Air Act. But President Obama threatened to veto the bill, and the Senate failed to pass similar legislation.[67]

Given the mood in Washington, the likelihood of the bipartisan effort that would be necessary to move a bill limiting manmade greenhouse gases forward seems remote. "We don't expect to see any major legislation in this Congress," says Diringer.

But further Republican efforts to curb the EPA's regulatory effort also seem unlikely to succeed. "That's not going to happen unless there's a president and a Senate of a different persuasion," says Michaels.

In other words, the current impasse is almost certain to continue, at least until the 2012 elections.

NOTES

1. Yvo de Boer, the United Nation's Framework Convention on Climate Change video message before the opening of the Cop15 conference, Dec. 1, 2009, www.youtube.com/climateconference#p/u/11/xUTXsdkinq0.

2. The complete text of the accord is at http://unfccc.int/resource/docs/2009/cop15/eng/l07.pdf.

3. John Vidal and Jonathan Watts, "Copenhagen closes with weak deal that poor threaten to reject," *The Guardian*, Dec. 19, 2009, www.guardian.co.uk/environment/2009/dec/19/copenhagen-closes-weak-deal.

4. *Ibid.*

5. "Remarks by the President," The White House Office of the Press Secretary, Dec. 18, 2009, www.whitehouse.gov/the-press-office/remarks-president-during-press-availability-copenhagen.

6. http://action.sierraclub.org/site/MessageViewer?em_id=150181.0.

7. See Jones' complete comments at http://wdm.gn.apc.org/copenhagen-'deal'-'shameful-and-monumental-failure'.

8. Jerry Melillo, Karl Thomas and Thomas Peterson, editors-in-chief, "Global Climate Change Impacts in the United States," U.S. Global Change Research Program, executive summary, June 16, 2009, www.education-research-services.org/files/USGCRP_Impacts_US_executive-summary.pdf.

9. Intergovernmental Panel on Climate Change staff, "Climate Change 2007: Synthesis Report," The U.N. Intergovernmental Panel on Climate Change, Nov. 17 2007, www.ipcc.ch/pdf/assessment-report/ar4/syr/ar4_syr_spm.pdf.

10. "Climate Change responsible for 300,000 deaths a year," Global Humanitarian Forum, http://ghfgeneva.org/NewsViewer/tabid/383/vw/1/ItemID/6/Default.aspx.

11. Andrew C. Revkin and James Kanter, "No Slowdown of Global Warming, Agency Says," *The New York Times*, Dec. 8, 2009, www.nytimes.com/2009/12/09/science/earth/09climate.html.

12. "Key Scientific Developments Since the IPCC Fourth Assessment Report," in Key Scientific Developments Since the IPCC Fourth Assessment Report, Pew Center on Global Climate Change, June 2009.

13. "Final Copenhagen Accord Press Release," The Sustainability Institute, Dec. 19, 2009, http://climateinteractive.org/scoreboard/copenhagen-cop15-analysis-and-press-releases.

14. "Remarks by the President," *op. cit.*

15. "Copenhagen Accord," draft proposal, United Nations Framework Convention on Climate Change, Dec. 18, 2009, p. 3. http://unfccc.int/resource/docs/2009/cop15/eng/l07.pdf.

16. Kumi Naidoo, speaking at Copenhagen in a video blog posted by Greenpeace Australia, www.facebook.com/video/video.php?v=210068211237.

17. Ban Ki-moon, remarks to the General U.N. Assembly, Dec. 21, 2009, www.un.org/News/Press/docs/2009/sgsm12684.doc.htm.

18. Jennifer Weeks, "Carbon Trading, Will it Reduce Global Warming," *CQ Global Researcher*, November 2008.

19. Robert Shapiro, "Addressing the Risks of Climate Change: The Environmental Effectiveness and Economic Efficiency of Emissions Caps and Tradable Permits, Compared to Carbon Taxes," February 2007, p. 26, http://67.23.32.13/system/files/carbon-tax-cap.pdf.

20. Nicolas Loris and Ben Lieberman, "Capping Carbon Emissions Is Bad, No Matter How You Slice the Revenue," Heritage Foundation, May 14, 2009, www.heritage.org/Research/EnergyandEnvironment/wm2443.cfm.

21. Monica Prasad, "On Carbon, Tax and Don't Spend," *The New York Times*, March 25, 2008, www.nytimes.com/2008/03/25/opinion/25prasad.html.

22. "Cantwell, Collins Introduce 'Cap and Rebate' Bill," Clean Skies, Energy and Environment Network, Dec. 11, 2009, www.cleanskies.com/articles/cantwell-collins-introduce-cap-and-rebate-bill.

23. Robert J. Shapiro, "Carbon Tax More Likely," *National Journal* expert blog, Energy and the Environment, Jan. 4, 2010, http://energy.national-journal.com/2010/01/whats-next-in-the-senate.php-1403156.

24. A concise history of Keeling and his work is at "The Keeling Curve Turns 50," Scripps Institution of Oceanography, http://sio.ucsd.edu/special/Keeling_50th_Anniversary/.

25. Elizabeth Kolbert, *Field Notes from a Catastrophe: Man, Nature, and Climate Change* (2006), p. 2.

26. Naomi Oreskes, "Beyond the Ivory Tower: The Scientific Consensus on Climate Change," *Science*, Dec. 3, 2004, www.sciencemag.org/cgi/content/full/306/5702/1686.

27. *Ibid.*

28. "Analysis of the Emails from the University of East Anglia's Climatic Research Unit," Pew Center on Global Climate Change, December 2009, www.pewclimate.org/science/university-east-anglia-cru-hacked-emails-analysis.

29. Quoted by Nicholas Dawidoff, "The Civil Heretic," *The New York Times Magazine*, March 23, 2009, p. 2, www.nytimes.com/2009/03/29/magazine/29Dyson-t.html?pagewanted=1&_r=1.

30. "Smoke, Mirrors & Hot Air: How ExxonMobil Uses Big Tobacco's Tactics to Manufacture Uncertainty on Climate Science," Union of Concerned Scientists, January 2007, p. 1, www.ucsusa.org/assets/documents/global_warming/exxon_report.pdf.

31. *Ibid.*

32. Many are summarized in a policy brief by the non-profit Pew Center on Global Climate Change, "Realities vs. Misconceptions about the Science of Climate Change," August 2009, www.pewclimate.org/science-impacts/realities-vs-misconceptions.

33. Seth Borenstein, "AP IMPACT: Statisticians Reject Global Cooling," The Associated Press, Oct. 26, 2009, http://abcnews.go.com/Technology/wireStory?id=8917909.

34. Unpacking the problem," *The Economist*, Dec. 5-11, 2009, p. 21, www.economist.com/specialreports/displaystory.cfm?story_id=14994848.

35. *Ibid.*

36. It is important to note that if CO_2 emissions are calculated on a per capita basis, China still ranks far below most developed nations. The highest emitter on a per capita basis is Australia, according to the U.S. Energy Information Agency, with the United States second. See www.ucsusa.org/global_warming/science_and_impacts/science/each-countrys-share-of-co2.html.

37. A chart of the top 20 CO_2 emitting countries is at www.ucsusa.org/global_warming/science_and_impacts/science/graph-showing-each-countrys.html.

38. "China ratifies global warming treaty," CNN.com, Sept. 4, 2002, http://archives.cnn.com/2002/WORLD/africa/09/03/kyoto.china.glb/index.html.

39. "China overtakes U.S. in greenhouse gas emissions," *The New York Times*, June 20, 2007, www.nytimes.com/2007/06/20/business/worldbusiness/20iht-emit.1.6227564.html.

40. Ed Miliband, "The Road from Copenhagen," *The Guardian*, Dec. 20, 2009, www.guardian.co.uk/commentisfree/2009/dec/20/copenhagen-climate-change-accord.

41. "A Long Game," *The Economist*, Dec. 5-11, 2009, p. 18.

42. *Ibid.* Keith Bradsher, "China Leading Global Race to Make Clean Energy," *The New York Times*, Jan. 31, 2010, p. A1.

43. Darren Samuelsohn, "Obama Negotiates 'Copenhagen Accord' With Senate Climate Fight in Mind," *The New York Times*, Dec. 21, 2009, www.nytimes.com/cwire/2009/12/21/21climatewire-obama-negotiates-copenhagen-accord-with-senat-6121.html.

44. Juliet Elperin, "Fewer Americans Believe in Global Warming, Poll Shows," *The Washington Post*, Nov.

25, 2009, www.washingtonpost.com/wp-dyn/content/article/2009/11/24/AR2009112402989.html.

45. Suzanne Goldenberg, "Fate of US climate change bill in doubt after Scott Brown's Senate win," *The Guardian*, Jan. 20, 2010, www.guardian.co.uk/environment/2010/jan/20/scott-brown-climate-change-bill.

46. "India promises to slow carbon emissions rise," BBC News, Dec. 3, 2009, http://news.bbc.co.uk/2/hi/8393538.stm.

47. Rie Jerichow, "World Leaders Welcome the Copenhagen Accord," Denmark.dk, Dec. 21, 2009, www.denmark.dk/en/menu/Climate-Energy/COP15-Copenhagen-2009/Selected-COP15-news/World-leaders-welcome-the-Copenhagen-Accord.htm.

48. "Where countries stand on Copenhagen," BBC News, undated, http://news.bbc.co.uk/2/hi/science/nature/8345343.stm.

49. James Kantor, "Council in France Blocks Carbon Tax as Weak on Polluters," *The New York Times*, Dec. 31, 2009, www.nytimes.com/2009/12/31/business/energy-environment/31carbon.html.

50. Andrew Neather, "Climate Change could still be Gordon Brown's great legacy," *The London Evening Standard*, Dec. 15, 2009, www.thisislondon.co.uk/standard/article-23783937-climate-change-could-still-be-gordon-browns-great-legacy.do.

51. Dan Smith and Janini Vivekananda, "A Climate of Conflict, the links between climate change, peace and war," *International Alert*, November 2007, www.international-alert.org/pdf/A_Climate_Of_Conflict.pdf.

52. Alex Kirby, "Climate Risk to a Million Species," BBC Online, Jan. 7, 2004, http://news.bbc.co.uk/2/hi/science/nature/3375447.stm.

53. Adam Hadhazy, "The Maldives, threatened by drowning due to climate change, set to go carbon-neutral," *Scientific American*, March 16, 2009, www.scientificamerican.com/blog/post.cfm?id=maldives-drowning-carbon-neutral-by-2009-03-16.

54. Peter Wilkinson, "Sea level rise could cost port cities $28 trillion," CNN, Nov. 23, 2009, www.cnn.com/2009/TECH/science/11/23/climate.report.wwf.allianz/index.html.

55. "Key Scientific Developments Since the IPCC Fourth Assessment Report," *op. cit.*

56. Richard Ingham, "Carbon emissions must peak by 2015: U.N. climate scientist," Agence France-Presse, Oct. 15, 2009, www.google.com/hostednews/afp/article/ALeqM5izYrubhpeFvOKCRrZmWSYWCkPoRg.

57. "Final Copenhagen Accord Press Release," *op. cit.*

58. Doyle Rice, "2010 tied for Earth's warmest year on record," *USA Today*, Jan. 13, 2011, www.usatoday.com/tech/science/environment/2011-01-12-2010-warmest-year-climate-change_N.htm.

59. Katherine Hayhoe, *et al.*, "Climate change, heat waves, and mortality projections for Chicago," *Journal of Great Lakes Research 36* (2010), pp. 65-73, www.as.miami.edu/geography/research/climatology/JGR_manuscript.pdf.

60. Paul Epstein and Dan Ferber, "Malaria on the Rise as East African Climate Heats Up," *Scientific American*, April 1, 2011, www.scientificamerican.com/article.cfm?id=east-africa-malaria-rises-under-climate-change.

61. Carl Zimmer, "Multitude of Species Face Climate Threat," *The New York Times*, April 4, 2011, www.nytimes.com/2011/04/05/science/earth/05climate.html.

62. Elliot Diringer, *et al.*, "Summary: Cancún Climate Change Conference," The Pew Center on Global Climate Change, December 2010, www.pewclimate.org/international/cancun-climate-conference-cop16-summary.

63. "UN Climate Change Conference in Cancún delivers balanced package of decisions, restores faith in multilateral process," press release, United Nations Framework Convention on Climate Change, Dec. 11, 2010, http://unfccc.int/files/press/news_room/press_releases_and_advisories/application/pdf/pr_20101211cop16_closing.pdf.

64. See Joby Warrick, "In Greenland, many like it warmer," *The Washington Post*, May 13, 2011, p. A6.

65. Suzanne Goldenberg, "Cancún climate change conference: Russia will not renew Kyoto protocol,"

Guardian.co.uk, Dec. 10, 2010, www.guardian.co
.uk/environment/2010/dec/10/cancun-climate-
change-conference-kyoto.

66. "Climate Action in Congress," Pew Center on
Global Climate Change, www.pewclimate.org/
federal/congress.

67. John Broder, "House Votes to Bar E.P.A. From
Regulating Industrial Emissions," *The New York
Times*, April 7, 2011, www.nytimes.com/2011/
04/08/us/politics/08emit.html.

BIBLIOGRAPHY

Books

**Hoggan, James, *Climate Cover-Up: The Crusade to
Deny Global Warming*, Greystone Books, 2009.**
A Canadian public relations executive who founded the
anti-climate-skeptic Web site DeSmogblog takes on
what he considers the oil and gas industry's organized
campaign to spread disinformation and confuse the public about the science of climate change.

**Hulme, Mike, *Why We Disagree About Climate
Change: Understanding Controversy, Inaction and
Opportunity*, Cambridge University Press, 2009.**
A professor of climate change at East Anglia University
in Great Britain looks at the cultural, political and scientific forces that come into play when we consider climate
and what that interaction means for dealing with climate
change today.

**Kolbert, Elizabeth, *Field Notes from a Catastrophe:
Man, Nature and Climate Change*, Bloomsbury, 2006.**
A *New Yorker* writer summarizes the scientific evidence on
behalf of climate change and looks at the consequences for
some of the world's most vulnerable locations.

**Michaels, Patrick J., and Robert C. Balling, *Climate
of Extremes: Global Warming Science They Don't
Want You to Know*, The Cato Institute, 2009.**
Writing for a libertarian U.S. think tank, the authors
argue that while global warming is real, its effects have
been overstated and do not represent a crisis.

Articles

**"Stopping Climate Change, A 14-Page Special
Report," *The Economist*, Dec. 5, 2009.**

The authors provide a comprehensive review of the state
of global climate change efforts, including environmental, economic and political conditions.

**Broder, John and Andrew Revkin, "A Grudging
Accord in Climate Talks," *The New York Times*, Dec.
19, 2009.**
The Times assesses the Copenhagen Accord and reports
on the final hours of the climate change convention.

**Kunzig, Robert, "A Sunshade for Planet Earth,"
Scientific American, November 2008.**
An award-winning scientific journalist examines the
various geoengineering options that might reduce global
warming, their costs and possible consequences.

**Schwartz, John, "Courts as Battlefields in Climate
Fights," *The New York Times*, Jan. 26, 2009.**
A reporter looks at environmental groups' and other
plaintiffs' efforts to hold corporations that produce
greenhouse gases legally liable for the effects of climate
change on vulnerable areas, including Kivalina Island off
the coast of Alaska.

**Walsh, Bryan, "Lessons from the Copenhagen
Climate Talks," *Time*, Dec. 21, 2009.**
Time's environmental columnist provides predictions
about the future of the climate change battle, based on
the final Copenhagen Accord.

**Walsh, Bryan, "The Stolen Emails: Has 'Climategate'
been Overblown," *Time Magazine online*, Dec. 7, 2007.**
The stolen East Anglia University e-mails, the author
concludes, "while unseemly, do little to change the overwhelming scientific consensus on the reality of manmade climate change."

Reports and Studies

**"Climate Change 101: Understanding and Res-
ponding to Global Climate Change," Pew Center on
Global Climate Change, January 2009.**
This series of reports aims to provide an introduction to
climate change science and politics for the layman.

**"World Development Report 2010: World Development
and Climate Change," World Bank, November 2009,
http://econ.worldbank.org/WBSITE/EXTERNAL/
EXTDEC/EXTRESEARCH/EXTWDRS/EXTWDR20
10/0,,contentMDK:21969137~menuPK:5287816~page**

PK:64167689~piPK:64167673~theSitePK:5287741,00.html.

This exhaustive, 300-page study examines the consequences of climate change for the developing world and the need for developed nations to provide financial assistance to avert disaster.

Bernstein, Lenny, *et al.*, "Climate Change 2007: Synthesis Report," The Intergovernmental Panel of Climate Change, 2007, www.ipcc.ch/pdf/assessment-report/ar4/syr/ar4_syr_spm.pdf.

The international body tasked with assessing the risk of climate change caused by human activity gathered scientific research from around the world in this widely quoted report to conclude, "warming of the climate system is unequivocal."

Thomas, Karl, Jerry Melillo and Thomas Peterson, eds., "Global Climate Change Impacts in the United States," United States Global Change Research Program, June 2009, www.globalchange.gov/publications/reports/scientific-assessments/us-impacts.

U.S. government researchers across a wide range of federal agencies study how climate change is already affecting the United States.

For More Information

Cato Institute, 1000 Massachusetts Avenue, N.W., Washington, DC 20001; (202) 842-0200; www.cato.org/global-warming. A conservative U.S. think tank that maintains an extensive database of articles and papers challenging the scientific and political consensus on climate change.

Climate Justice Now; www.climate-justice-now.org. A network of organizations and movements from around the world committed to involving people in the fight against climate change and for social and economic justice at the grassroots level.

Climate Research Unit, University of East Anglia, Norwich, NR4 7TJ, United Kingdom; +44-1603-592722; www.cru.uea.ac.uk. Recently in the news when its e-mail accounts were hacked; dedicated to the study of natural and manmade climate change.

Greenpeace International, Ottho Heldringstraat 5, 1066 AZ Amsterdam, The Netherlands; +31 (0) 20 7182000; www.greenpeace.org/international. Has made climate change one of its global priorities; has offices around the world.

Intergovernmental Panel on Climate Change, c/o World Meteorological Organization, 7bis Avenue de la Paix, C.P. 2300 CH- 1211, Geneva 2, Switzerland; +41-22-730-8208; www.ipcc.ch. U.N. body made up of 2,500 global scientists; publishes periodic reports on various facets of climate change, including a synthesis report summarizing latest findings around the globe.

Pew Center on Global Climate Change, 2101 Wilson Blvd., Suite 550, Arlington, VA, 22201; (703) 516-4146; www.pewclimate.org. Nonprofit, nonpartisan organization established in 1998 to promote research, provide education and encourage innovative solutions to climate change.

United Nations Framework Convention on Climate Change, Haus Carstanjen, Martin-Luther-King-Strasse 853175 Bonn, Germany; +49-228-815-1000; http://unfccc.int/2860.php. An international treaty that governs climate change negotiations.

Voices From Abroad:

JOHN ASHE

Chair, Kyoto Protocol Talks

A reason for hope

"Given where we started and the expectations for this conference, anything less than a legally binding and agreed outcome falls far short of the mark. On the other hand . . . perhaps the bar was set too high and the fact that there's now a deal . . . perhaps gives us something to hang our hat on."

BBC, December 2009

Peter Broelman, Australia

JOHN SAUVEN

Executive Director Greenpeace UK

Copenhagen = Crime Scene

"Copenhagen is a crime scene tonight, with the guilty men and women fleeing to the airport. It seems there are too few politicians in this world capable of looking beyond the horizon of their own narrow self-interest, let alone caring much for the millions of people facing the threat of climate change."

The Guardian (England), December 2009

JOSÉ MANUEL BARROSO

President European Commission

All countries have a role

"Developed countries must explicitly recognise that we will all have to play a significant part in helping to finance mitigation action by developing countries. . . . The counterpart is that developing countries, at least the economically advanced amongst them, have to be much clearer on what they are ready to do to mitigate carbon emissions as part of an international agreement."

Business Day (South Africa), September 2009

MOHAMED NASHEED

President, Maldives

A critical number

"Anything above 1.5 degrees [Celsius], the Maldives and many small islands and low-lying islands would vanish. It is for this reason that we tried very hard during the course of the last two days to have 1.5 degrees in the document. I am so sorry that this was blatantly obstructed by big-emitting countries."

BBC, December 2009

NELSON MUFFUH

Senior Climate Change Advocacy Advisor Christian Aid England

Climate change kills 300,000 a year

"Already 300,000 people die each year because of the impact of climate change, most in the developing world. The lack of ambition shown by rich countries in Copenhagen means that number will grow."

The Observer (England), December 2009

NICOLAS SARKOZY
President, France

A vital contract
"The text we have is not perfect. . . . If we had no deal, that would mean that two countries as important as India and China would be freed from any type of contract . . . [and] the United States, which is not in Kyoto, would be free of any type of contract. That's why a contract is absolutely vital."

BBC, December 2009

STANISLAS KAMANZI
Environment and Lands Minister, Rwanda

Progress regardless of Copenhagen
"Our policy is that every industrialized investment in the country should come up with an environment friendly technology. So, with or without Copenhagen, we are safe with policies in place."

New Times (Rwanda), December 2009

KYERETWIE OPOKU
Member, Forest Watch Ghana

Relationships are key
"I accept the technological challenges and all that, but the real challenges are restructuring relationships. If we don't resolve these, forget about going to Copenhagen and getting a deal."

Public Agenda (Ghana), October 2009

VICTOR FODEKE
Chief Climate Officer, Nigeria

Kyoto: the only hope
"The Kyoto Protocol is the only hope of the developing countries; it is the only legally binding instrument requiring developed countries to cut their emission, killing it is dashing the hope of developing countries."

Daily Trust (Nigeria), December 2009

14

Afghanistan Dilemma

Thomas J. Billitteri and Alex Kingsbury

An Afghan security officer guards two tons of burning heroin, opium and hashish near Kabul, Afghanistan's capital, on March 18, 2009. Nearly eight years after U.S.-led forces first entered Afghanistan, many challenges still confront the U.S., Afghan and coalition forces seeking to stabilize the country: fanatical Taliban and al Qaeda fighters, rampant police corruption, shortages of Afghan troops and a multibillion-dollar opium economy that supports the insurgents.

From *CQ Researcher*,
August 7, 2009. (Updated May 23, 2011)

O n the outskirts of Now Zad, a Taliban stronghold in southern Afghanistan's violent Helmand Province, the past, present and future of the war in Afghanistan came together this summer.

The past: After the U.S.-led invasion of Afghanistan in 2001, Now Zad and its surrounding poppy fields and stout compounds were largely tranquil, thanks in part to the clinics and wells that Western money helped to build in the area. But three years ago, when the war in Iraq intensified and the Bush administration shifted attention from Afghanistan to Iraq, insurgents moved in, driving out most of Now Zad's 35,000 residents and foreign aid workers.

The present: This summer U.S. Marines engaged in withering firefights with Taliban militants dug in on the northern fringes of the town and in nearby fields and orchards.

The future: The situation in Now Zad and the surrounding war-torn region of southern Afghanistan is a microcosm of what confronts the Obama administration as it tries to smash the Taliban, defang al Qaeda and stabilize governance in Afghanistan. "In many ways," wrote an Associated Press reporter following the fighting, Now Zad "symbolizes what went wrong in Afghanistan and the enormous challenges facing the United States." [1]

Nearly eight years after U.S.-led forces first entered Afghanistan to pursue al Qaeda and its Taliban allies in the wake of the Sept. 11, 2001, terrorist attacks, the country remains in chaos, and President Barack Obama faces what many consider his biggest foreign-policy challenge: bringing stability and security to Afghanistan and denying Islamist militants a permanent foothold there and in neighboring nuclear-armed Pakistan.

An Unstable Nation in a Volatile Neighborhood

Almost as large as Texas, Afghanistan faces Texas-size problems, including desperate poverty, an economy dominated by illicit drugs and an unstable central government beset by Taliban militants. Afghanistan's instability is compounded by longstanding tensions between neighboring Pakistan and India, both armed with nuclear weapons. Many Western experts also say Pakistan has failed, despite promises, to rein in Taliban and other Islamist extremists.

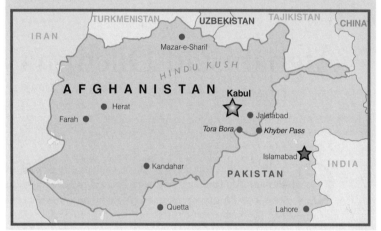

The challenge is heightened by the war's growing casualty figures. July was the deadliest month in Afghanistan for U.S. soldiers since the 2001 invasion began, with 43 killed. [2] Twenty-two British troops also died last month, including eight in a 24-hour period. In nearly eight years of war in Afghanistan, 767 U.S. troops have died there, along with 520 coalition forces, according to the Web site iCasualties.org. Thousands of Afghan civilians also have died.

The Afghanistan-Pakistan conflict —"Af-Pak" in diplomatic parlance — poses a witch's brew of challenges: fanatical Taliban and al Qaeda fighters, rampant corruption within Afghanistan's homegrown police force and other institutions, not enough Afghan National Army forces to help with the fighting and a multibillion-dollar opium economy that supplies revenue to the insurgents.

But those problems pale in comparison with what foreign-policy experts call the ultimate nightmare: Pakistan's nuclear weapons falling into the hands of jihadists and terrorists, a scenario that has become more credible this summer as suicide bombers and Taliban fighters have stepped up attacks in Pakistani cities and rural areas,

using Pakistan's lawless western border region as a sanctuary. [3]

"The fact that Pakistan has nuclear weapons and the question of the security of those weapons presses very hard on the minds of American defense planners and on the mind of the president," says Bruce Riedel, who led a 60-day strategic policy review of Afghanistan and Pakistan for the Obama administration. "If you didn't have that angle," adds Riedel, who has since returned to his post as a Brookings Institution senior fellow, "I think this would all be notched down one level of concern."

Pakistan is important to the Afghan conflict for reasons that go beyond its nuclear arsenal. Pakistan has been a breeding ground for much of the radical ideology that has taken root in Afghanistan. A failure of governance in Afghanistan would leave a void that Islamist militants on either side of the border could wind up filling, further destabilizing the entire region.

In March Obama announced what he called a "comprehensive, new strategy" for Afghanistan and Pakistan that rests on a "clear and focused goal" for the region: "to disrupt, dismantle and defeat al Qaeda in Pakistan and Afghanistan, and to prevent their return to either country in the future." [4]

Key to the strategy is winning over the local Afghan population by protecting it from insurgent violence and improving governance, security and economic development. [5]

The effort includes new troop deployments — a total of 21,000 additional U.S. soldiers to fight the insurgency in Afghanistan and train Afghan security forces, plus other strategic resources. By year's end, U.S. troop levels are expected to reach about 68,000. NATO countries and other allies currently are supplying another 32,000 or so, though many are engaged in development and relief work but not offensive combat operations. [6]

An immediate goal is to heighten security in Afghanistan in the run-up to a high-profile presidential election on

Aug. 20. None of Afghan President Hamid Karzai's main challengers are expected to beat him flat out, *The Washington Post* noted, but some observers said other candidates could "do well enough as a group to force a second round of polling, partly because of recent blunders by Karzai and partly because many Afghans are looking for alternative leadership at a time of sustained insurgent violence, economic stagnation and political drift." [7]

Observers say Obama's approach to the Af-Pak conflict represents a middle path between counterterrorism and counterinsurgency — protecting civilians, relying on them for information on the enemy and providing aid to build up a country's social and physical infrastructure and democratic institutions. [8]

Among the most notable features of the new approach is a vow among military officials — beginning with Gen. Stanley A. McChrystal, the newly appointed commander of U.S. and NATO forces in Afghanistan — to avoid civilian casualties. McChrystal pledged to follow a "holistic" approach in which protecting civilians takes precedence over killing militants. [9]

"I expect stiff fighting ahead," McChrystal told the Senate Armed Services Committee at his confirmation hearing. But "the measure of effectiveness will not be the number of enemy killed," he added, "it will be the number of Afghans shielded from violence." [10]

The United Nations said that 1,013 civilians died in the first six months of 2009, up from 818 during the same period last year. The U.N. said 310 deaths were attributed to pro-government forces, with about two-thirds caused by U.S. air strikes. [11]

As part of his strategy, Obama called for a "dramatic" increase in the number of agricultural specialists, educators, engineers and lawyers dispatched to "help the Afghan government serve its people and develop an economy that isn't dominated by illicit drugs." He also

supports economic-development aid to Pakistan, including legislation to provide $1.5 billion annually over the next five years. But Obama's approach on Pakistan also reflects long-held Western concerns that the Pakistani government has been at best negligent — and perhaps downright obstructionist — in bringing Taliban and other Islamist extremists to heel. Pakistan, whose situation is complicated by long-standing tensions with nearby India, will get no free pass in exchange for the aid, Obama vowed. "We will not, and cannot, provide a blank check," he said, because Pakistan had shown "years of mixed results" in rooting out terrorism. [12]

As Obama goes after the insurgency, his Af-Pak policy is under the microscope here at home.

Some have demanded that the administration describe its plans for ending military operations in Afghanistan.

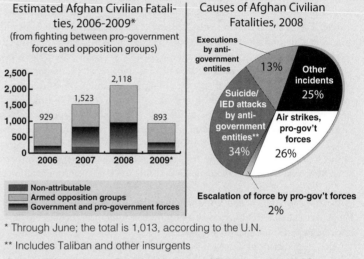

Gates Warns About Civilian Deaths

The number of civilians killed in Afghanistan more than doubled from 2006 to 2008, but based on the toll for the first six months of 2009, the rate may be somewhat lower in 2009 (graph at left). In 2008 nearly half of the civilian deaths were caused by executions or suicide and IED (improvised explosive device) attacks by the Taliban and other anti-government groups (graph at right). Concern over civilian deaths prompted Defense Secretary Robert Gates to call such casualties "one of our greatest strategic vulnerabilities."

Estimated Afghan Civilian Fatalities, 2006-2009*
(from fighting between pro-government forces and opposition groups)

Causes of Afghan Civilian Fatalities, 2008

* Through June; the total is 1,013, according to the U.N.

** Includes Taliban and other insurgents

Source: "Afghan Index: Tracking Variables of Reconstruction and Security in Post-9/11 Afghanistan," Brookings Institution, July 15, 2009

Opium Trade Funds Taliban, Official Corruption

"It's clear that drug money is paying for the Taliban's operational costs."

In the crowded Afghan capital of Kabul, opulent marble homes sit behind guard houses and razor wire. "Most are owned by Afghan officials or people connected to them, men who make a few hundred dollars a month as government employees but are driven around in small convoys of armored SUVs that cost tens of thousands of dollars," reporter Tom Lasseter noted recently. "[M]any of the houses were built with profits harvested from opium poppy fields in the southern provinces of Helmand and Kandahar." [1]

The so-called "poppy palaces" are outward signs of a cancer eating Afghanistan to its core: illicit drugs and narcoterrorism, aided by official corruption.

According to the United Nations Office on Drugs and Crime, Afghanistan grows more than 90 percent of the world's opium, which is used to produce heroin and morphine. [2] Total opium production for 2008 was estimated at 7,700 metric tons, more than double the 2002 level. [3]

In her new book, *Seeds of Terror: How Heroin Is Bankrolling the Taliban and Al Qaeda*, journalist Gretchen Peters says militant groups are raising hundreds of millions of dollars a year from the opium trade.

"It's clear that drug money is paying for the Taliban's operational costs within Afghanistan," she told *Time* magazine. "That means that every time a U.S. soldier is killed in an IED attack or a shootout with militants, drug money helped pay for that bomb or paid the militants who placed it. . . . The Taliban have now thrown off their old masters and are a full-fledged criminal force on both sides of the [Afghan-Pakistan] border." [4]

The biggest challenge to curbing the drug trade, Peters said, is corruption. "As much money as the insurgents are earning off the drug trade, corrupt officials in Afghanistan and Pakistan are earning even more," she said. "It's going to be very complex for the U.S. and for the international community, for NATO, to find reliable and trustworthy partners to work with. I don't think that it is widely understood how high up the corruption goes within the Pakistani government, particularly within their military and intelligence forces."

In recent weeks, the Obama administration has shifted U.S. drug policy in Afghanistan from trying to eradicate poppy fields to seizing drugs and related supplies and helping farmers grow alternative crops. [5]

"The Western policies against the opium crop, the poppy crop, have been a failure," Richard C. Holbrooke, the administration's special representative for Afghanistan and Pakistan, said. "They did not result in any damage to the Taliban, but they put farmers out of work and they alienated people and drove people into the arms of the Taliban." [6]

The Bush administration had advocated intense efforts to eradicate poppy fields, but some experts have said the approach is counterproductive.

"The United States should de-emphasize opium eradication efforts," Air Force Lt. Col. John A. Glaze wrote in a 2007 report for the U.S. Army War College. It recommended a multi-pronged strategy including higher troop levels, more economic aid for Afghanistan, pursuit of drug lords and corrupt officials and development of alternative

A measure proposed by Rep. Jim McGovern, D-Mass., requiring a report from the Obama administration by the end of the year on its exit strategy, drew significant support from Democrats but was defeated in the House this summer amid heavy Republican opposition.

And some critics question the validity of Obama's rationale for the fighting in Afghanistan, particularly the assumption that if the Taliban were victorious they would invite al Qaeda to return to Afghanistan and use it as a base for its global jihad. John Mueller, a political science professor at Ohio State University and author of *Overblown: How Politicians and the Terrorism Industry Inflate National Security Threats, and Why We Believe*

Them, contends that al Qaeda does not need Afghanistan as a base. The 2001 terrorist attacks were orchestrated mostly from Hamburg, Germany, he points out.

What's more, he argues, "distinct tensions" exist between al Qaeda and the Taliban. Even if the Taliban were to prevail in Afghanistan, he says, "they would not particularly want al Qaeda back." Nor, he says, is it clear that al Qaeda would again view Afghanistan as a safe haven. [13]

But administration officials disagree. The Taliban are "the frontrunners for al Qaeda," said Richard Holbrooke, Obama's special envoy to Pakistan and Afghanistan. "If they succeed in Afghanistan, without any shadow of a

livelihoods for Afghans, plus exploration of the possibility of participating in the market for legal opiates used for morphine and other medicines.

"U.S.-backed eradication efforts have been ineffective and have resulted in turning Afghans against U.S. and NATO forces . . . ," Glaze wrote. "While the process of eradication lends itself well to the use of flashy metrics such as 'acres eradicated,' eradication without provision for long-term alternative livelihoods is devastating Afghan's poor farmers without addressing root causes."[7]

Brookings Institution scholar Vanda Felbab-Brown, an expert on Afghanistan's opium-poppy economy, says rural development, not poppy eradication, is the best way to attack the drug economy. "Any massive eradication right now . . . , we would lose Afghanistan," she says. "In the absence of resources available to farmers, any eradication would just prompt massive destabilization and invite the Taliban in."

Felbab-Brown says the development of new crops is key, but that such crops must be "high-labor-intensive, high-value crops" that offer more than subsistence income.

"People don't have to become rich, but they cannot continue existing in excruciating poverty. Many people will be willing and motivated to switch to a legal crop," she says, but "it needs to offer some chance of advancement."

Vegetable, fruit and horticultural crops are better options, Felbab-Brown says. Wheat, on the other hand, "has no traction" because the prices are low, people in vast parts of the country don't have enough land to make the crop pay, and wheat is much less labor-intensive than poppy growing, affording fewer opportunities for employment, she says.

For rural development to offer an alternative to illicit poppy production, it must include not only access to land,

legal microcredit and other features, but security for Afghan farmers, Felbab-Brown stresses.

"The lack of security in many ways is the key structural driver of illicit crop cultivation, because the risks of cultivating legal crops in insecure settings are just tremendous," she says.

Rural development, for example, "needs to involve roads, and not just their physical presence but also security on the roads," Felbab-Brown says. Roads are now insecure due to both the insurgents and the Afghan National Police.

"In much of the south, travel on the road is three times as expensive as travel in the north because of the number of bribes that one needs to pay at check stops. For many people, simply to take crops from Laskar Gah to Kandahar, by the time they pay the bribes that they need to pay, they will have lost all profit."

---

[1] Tom Lasseter, "Western Military Looked Other Way as the Afghan Drug Trade Boomed," *Charlotte Observer*, May 10, 2009, p. 13A.

[2] "World Drug Report 2009 Highlights Links Between Drugs and Crime," United Nations Office on Drugs and Crime, June 2009, www.unodc.org/unodc/en/press/releases/2009/june/world-drug-report-2009-highlights-links-between-drugs-and-crime.html.

[3] "World Drug Report 2009," United Nations Office on Drugs and Crime, www.unodc.org/documents/wdr/WDR_2009/WDR2009_eng_web.pdf.

[4] Bobby Ghosh, "Q&A: Fighting the New Narcoterrorism Syndicates," *Time*, July 17, 2009, www.time.com/time/nation/article/0,8599,1910935,00.html.

[5] Rachel Donadio, "New Course for Antidrug Efforts in Afghanistan," *The New York Times*, June 28, 2009, www.nytimes.com/2009/06/28/world/asia/28holbrooke.html?scp=1&sq=holbrooke+drug%20policy+afghanistan+rome&st=cse.

[6] Quoted in *ibid*.

[7] John A. Glaze, "Opium and Afghanistan: Reassessing U.S. Counternarcotics Strategy," U.S. Army War College, www.strategicstudiesinstitute.army.mil/Pubs/Display.Cfm?pubID=804.

---

doubt al Qaeda would move back into Afghanistan, set up a larger presence, recruit more people and pursue its objectives against the United States even more aggressively."[14]

As the war in Afghanistan continues, here are some of the questions people are asking:

Is the Obama administration pursuing the right course in Afghanistan?

Early in July, thousands of U.S. Marines began a massive assault in Afghanistan's Helmand River valley, the biggest American offensive of the Obama presidency and a key test of his new strategy in the region.

The operation included 4,000 troops from the 2nd Marine Expeditionary Brigade, who poured into the area in helicopters and armored vehicles. The Marines have run into stiff opposition, but the ultimate goal remains intact: protect local Afghans from insurgent violence and strengthen Afghanistan's legal, judicial and security institutions.

"Our focus must be on getting this [Afghan] government back up on its feet," Brig. Gen. Lawrence D. Nicholson, commander of the brigade, told his officers.[15]

But the mission is fraught with huge risks and challenges, and skepticism about it runs deep, even among some of Obama's fellow Democrats.

Social Conditions Worsened in Many Areas

Living conditions deteriorated between 2007 and 2008 in areas such as education, water quality and availability of electricity, according to surveys of Afghan citizens.

Condition of Infrastructure in Localities, 2007 and 2008

	Very/Quite Good (%)		Quite/Very Bad (%)	
	2007	2008	2007	2008
Availability of clean drinking water	63%	62%	36%	38%
Availability of water for irrigation	59	47	40	49
Availability of jobs	30	21	69	78
Supply of electricity	31	25	68	74
Security situation	66	No data	33	No data
Availability of medical care	56	49	44	50
Availability of education for children	72	70	28	29
Freedom of movement	72	No data	28	No data

Source: "Afghan Index: Tracking Variables of Reconstruction and Security in Post-9/11 Afghanistan," Brookings Institution, July 15, 2009

In May, House Appropriations Chairman David Obey, D-Wis., suggested that if the White House doesn't demonstrate progress by next year, funding for the war could slow. Asked if he could see Congress halting funding completely, Obey said, "If it becomes a fool's errand, I would hope so," according to *The Hill* newspaper. The success or failure of the Afghan policy is not in the hands of the president or Congress, Obey said, but "in the hands of the practicing politicians in Pakistan and Afghanistan. And I'm dubious about those hands." [16]

Much of the American public is similarly dubious. A June *New York Times*-CBS News poll found that 55 percent of respondents believed the war in Afghanistan was going somewhat or very badly for the United States, an increase of two points since April. Only 2 percent said the war was going "very well." [17]

Critics question the prospect of success in a country long divided by ethnic rivalries, a resistance to central governance and rampant graft that ranges from demands for petty bribes to drug corruption in high levels of government. [18]

"To pacify the place in the absence of reconciliation of the main tribes,* you'd need a very large national army" — one that would have to be financially subsidized by outside powers, says Stephen Walt, a professor of international affairs at Harvard University's Kennedy School of Government. Such an army "would have to be drawn from all these groups and imbued with central loyalty to the state. And there's never been a strong central state. Politics [in Afghanistan is defined by] factional alignments." And, he adds, the challenge is "compounded by levels of corruption and lack of institutions."

"We're sort of trying to impart a Western model of how the Afghan state should be created — with a central government, ministries, defense and so on. That's not the way Afghanistan has been run for centuries. The idea that we know how to do that, especially in the short term," Walt says, is "far-fetched."

Malou Innocent, a foreign-policy analyst at the conservative Cato Institute think tank, says America faces the prospect of an "ambiguous victory" because it is caught amid long-simmering tensions between Pakistan and India, a dynamic, she argues, that the Obama administration has failed to adequately take into account.

Pakistan has long feared an alliance between Afghanistan and India. To hedge its bets, Pakistan aids the insurgency in Afghanistan by providing shelter to the Taliban and other militants, Innocent says. At the same time, she says, Pakistan has accused India of funneling weapons through Afghanistan to separatists in Pakistan's unstable Balochistan province. [19] The ongoing India-Pakistan dispute over Kashmir also remains a cause of friction in the region.

"The regional dynamics are too intractable," Innocent says. "The countries in the region have an incentive to foment and maintain Afghanistan's instability. So we should be looking to get out of Afghanistan within a reasonable time frame — say at least in the next five years."

Innocent sees a U.S. role in training Afghanistan's own security forces and says covert operations against specific insurgent targets could make sense. But the Taliban threat centered along the Afghanistan-Pakistan

---

* The main ethnic groups are the Pashtun (42%), Tajik (27%), Hazara (9%), Uzbek (9%), Aimak (4%), Turkmen (3%) and Baloch (2%).

border cannot be definitively eradicated, she argues. "We can contain the militancy" and weaken it, she says, "but we can't believe we can have a victory with a capital V."

But Peter Bergen, a counterterrorism analyst and senior fellow at the New America Foundation, is more sanguine about the war's prospects in Afghanistan. In a *Washington Monthly* article, he challenged those who say Afghanistan is an unconquerable and ungovernable "graveyard of empires" where foreign armies have come to ignominious ends.

One telling fact, in Bergen's view, is that "the Afghan people themselves, the center of gravity in a counterinsurgency, are rooting for us to win." He cited BBC/ABC polling data indicating that 58 percent of Afghans named the Taliban — viewed favorably by only 7 percent of Afghans — as the biggest threat to their country, while only 8 percent named the United States.

"[T]he growing skepticism about Obama's chances for success in Afghanistan is largely based on deep misreadings of both the country's history and the views of its people, which are often compounded by facile comparisons to the United States' misadventures of past decades in Southeast Asia and the Middle East," wrote Bergen. "Afghanistan will not be Obama's Vietnam, nor will it be his Iraq. Rather, the renewed and better-resourced American effort in Afghanistan will, in time, produce a relatively stable and prosperous Central Asian state."[20]

Stephen Biddle, a senior fellow at the Council on Foreign Relations, a think tank in New York City, said victory in Afghanistan is possible but only if steps are taken to strengthen Afghanistan's governance. "I do think it's possible to succeed," Biddle said in late July after spending a month as part of a group helping McChrystal formulate a strategic assessment report on the war, due this month. But, he added, "there are two very different requirements for success.

"One is providing security, [and] the other is providing enough of an improvement in Afghan governance to

Afghanistan Ranks Low in Developing World

Afghanistan ranked as the second-weakest state in the developing world, after Somalia, in 2008, according to the Brookings Institution* (left). It consistently ranks near the bottom among countries rated for corruption by Transparency International (right).

Afghanistan's Rank

Index of State Weakness in Developing World, 2008			Corruption Perceptions Index		
Rank	Country	Overall Score	Year	Rank	No. of Countries Surveyed
1	Somalia	0.52	2008	176	180
2	Afghanistan	1.65	2007	172	180
3	Dem. Rep. Congo	1.67	2006	No data	163
4	Iraq	3.11	2005	117	159
5	Burundi	3.21			

* Brookings surveyed 141 nations, allocating a score of 0-10 points for each of four categories: economic, political, security and social welfare. Benin had the median score, 6.36; the Slovak Republic was the least weak, with a score of 9.41.

Source: "Afghan Index: Tracking Variables of Reconstruction and Security in Post-9/11 Afghanistan," Brookings Institution, July 15, 2009

enable the country to function without us. We can keep the patient on life support by providing security assistance indefinitely, but if you don't get an improvement in governance, you'll never be able to take the patient off the ventilator. Of those two challenges, providing security we know how to do. It's expensive, it's hard, it takes a long time, but if we invest the resources there's a substantial probability that we can provide security through our assistance. Governance improvement is a more uncertain undertaking. There are a lot of things we can do that we have not yet done to improve governance, but ultimately the more uncertain of the two requirements is the governance part."[21]

Another member of McChrystal's strategic assessment group, Anthony Cordesman, a scholar with the Center for Strategic and International Studies, also believes the war is winnable, but that the United States and its allies must "act quickly and decisively" in a number of ways, including "giving the Afghan government the necessary legitimacy and capacity" at national, regional and local levels, reducing official corruption and "creating a level of actual governance that can ensure security and stability."[22]

CHRONOLOGY

1838-1930s *Afghanistan gains independence, but ethnic and religious conflicts persist.*

1838-42; 1878 Afghan forces defeat Britain in two wars, but Britain retains control of Afghanistan's foreign affairs under 1879 treaty.

1893 British draw Afghan-Pakistan border, split Pashtun ethnic group.

1919 Afghanistan gains independence after Third Anglo-Afghan War.

1934 Diplomatic relations between United States and Afghanistan established.

1950s-1980s *Political chaos wracks Afghanistan during Cold War.*

1950s-1960s Soviets and Americans funnel aid to Afghanistan.

1953 Gen. Mohammed Daoud becomes prime minister, seeks aid from Soviets, institutes reforms.

1964 New constitution establishes constitutional monarchy.

1973 Daoud overthrows king, is killed in Marxist coup in 1978.

1979-1989 Civil war rages between communist-backed government and U.S.-backed Mujahedeen. Soviets withdraw in 1989, 10 years after they invaded.

1990-2001 *Taliban emerges amid postwar chaos; al Qaeda forges ties with Afghan militants.*

1992 Burhanuddin Rabbani, an ethnic Tajik, rises to power, declares Afghanistan an Islamic state.

1994 Taliban emerges; the militant Islamist group is mainly Pashtun.

1996 Taliban gains control of Kabul.

1996 Taliban leader Mullah Omar invites al Qaeda leader Osama bin Laden to live with him in Kandahar.

1997 Osama bin Laden declares war on U.S. in interview with CNN.

2001 U.S. and coalition forces invade Afghanistan on Oct. 7 after Sept. 11 terrorist attacks; Taliban retreats.

2002-Present *U.S.-led invasion of Iraq shifts focus off Afghanistan; Taliban resurges.*

2002 Hamid Karzai elected head of Afghan Transitional Authority; International Security Assistance Force deployed in Kabul; international donors pledge $4.5 billion for reconstruction.

2003 U.S.-led invasion of Iraq begins, leading to charges Bush administration shifted focus and resources away from Afghanistan; commission drafts new Afghan constitution.

2004 Draft constitution approved; Karzai elected president; Pakistani nuclear scientist A. Q. Khan admits international nuclear-weapons trading; President Pervez Musharraf pardons him.

2005 Afghanistan holds its first parliamentary elections in some three decades.

2006 NATO takes over Afghan security; donors pledge $10.5 billion more.

2007 Musharraf and Karzai agree to coordinate efforts to fight Taliban, al Qaeda; allied troops kill Taliban leader Mullah Dadullah.

2008 More than 50 die in suicide bombing of Indian Embassy in Kabul in July. . . . More than 160 die in November terror attacks in Mumbai, India; India accuses Pakistani militants of carrying out the attacks; in July 2009 a young Pakistani admits to taking part in the attacks as a soldier for Lashkar-e-Taiba, a Pakistan-based Islamic group.

2009 Obama announces new strategy "to disrupt, dismantle and defeat al Qaeda in Pakistan and Afghanistan"; Gen. Stanley McChrystal replaces Gen. David McKiernan as top U.S. commander in Afghanistan; Marines attack Taliban in southern Helmand Province; July is bloodiest month for U.S. and foreign troops in Afghanistan, with 43 Americans killed. . . . Concern grows over security surrounding Aug. 20 presidential election.

2009

July — U.S. and NATO forces launch major offensive against the Taliban in Afghanistan's southern Helmand province; more than 4,000 Marines take part, along with a smaller contingent of Afghan forces.

August — Numerous Taliban attacks mark presidential and provincial elections, which are largely seen as fraudulent by outside observers.

November — Hamid Karzai is sworn in as Afghan president, despite concerns about election fraud.

December — After months of consideration, President Obama opts to send 30,000 additional troops to Afghanistan; at the same time, he announces that U.S. forces will begin a partial withdrawal in 2011. . . . In one of the deadliest days for the CIA in decades, a CIA base in Khost, Afghanistan, is attacked by a double agent turned suicide bomber, killing seven CIA officers.

2010

July — WikiLeaks begins publishing thousands of formerly classified documents detailing the Pakistani security service's backing of the Taliban. . . . Gen. David Petraeus takes command of U.S. forces in Afghanistan after Gen. Stanley McChrystal resigns over comments published in Rolling Stone.

August — Dutch troops end Afghan mission.

2011

May 1 — Al-Qaida leader Osama bin Laden is killed in a U.S. raid; he apparently had been hiding in the same house in Abbottabad, Pakistan, for more than five years, according to U.S. intelligence officials. The raid also netted dozens of computer drives and other materials that the CIA hopes will reveal terrorist planning strategies and show who helped bin Laden remain hidden over the past decade.

Are troop levels in Afghanistan adequate?

When the Marine assault in Helmand Province got under way this summer, only about 400 effective Afghan fighters had joined the American force of nearly 4,000, according to *The New York Times*, citing information from Gen. Nicholson. [23]

Commanders expressed concern that not enough homegrown forces were available to fight the insurgency and build ties with the local population. Gen. Nicholson said, "I'm not going to sugarcoat it. The fact of the matter is, we don't have enough Afghan forces. And I'd like more." [24] Capt. Brian Huysman, a Marine company commander, said the lack of Afghan forces "is absolutely our Achilles' heel." [25]

"We've seen a shift over the past few years to put a lot more resources, including money and attention, toward building Afghan national security forces, army and police forces," Seth Jones, a political scientist at the RAND Corporation, told the "NewsHour" on PBS. "I think the problem that we're running into on the ground in Afghanistan, though: There are not enough Afghan national security forces and coalition forces to do what

Gen. McChrystal and others want, and that is to protect the local population." [26]

Worries about the size of the Afghan force have been accompanied by concerns over whether U.S. forces are adequate to overcome the Taliban threat and secure local areas long enough to ensure security and build governance capabilities.

According to a report this summer by veteran *Washington Post* reporter Bob Woodward, National Security Adviser James L. Jones told U.S. commanders in Afghanistan the Obama administration wants to keep troop levels steady for now. Gen. Nicholson, though, told Jones that he was "a little light," suggesting he could use more troops, and that "we don't have enough force to go everywhere," Woodward reported. [27]

"The question of the force level for Afghanistan . . . is not settled and will probably be hotly debated over the next year," Woodward wrote. "One senior military officer said privately that the United States would have to deploy a force of more than 100,000 to execute the counterinsurgency strategy of holding areas and towns after clearing out the Taliban insurgents. That is at least 32,000 more than the 68,000 currently authorized." [28]

The Many Faces of the Taliban

Adherents include violent warlords and Islamist extremists.

When President Barack Obama announced his administration's new Afghanistan strategy in March, he declared that if the Afghan government were to fall to the Taliban, the country would "again be a base for terrorists who want to kill as many of our people as they possibly can."[1]

But defining "the Taliban" is tricky. Far from a monolithic organization, the Taliban is a many-headed hydra, and a shadowy one at that. It is a mélange of insurgents and militants, ranging from high-profile Islamist extremists and violent warlords to local villagers fighting for cash or glory. Western military strategists hope to kill or capture the most fanatical elements of the Taliban while persuading others to abandon their arms and work within Afghanistan's political system.

"You have a whole spectrum of bad guys that sort of get lumped into this catch-all term of Taliban . . . because they're launching bullets at us," a senior Defense official told *The Boston Globe*. "There are many of the groups that can probably be peeled off."

The Defense official quoted by *The Globe* was among "hundreds of intelligence operatives and analysts" in the United States and abroad involved in a broad study of tribes tied to the Taliban, the newspaper said. The aim is to figure out whether diplomatic or economic efforts can persuade some to break away, according to the paper. The examination "is expected to culminate later this year in a detailed, highly classified analysis of the different factions of the Taliban and other groups," *The Globe* said.[2]

Many experts break down the Taliban into four main groups:

• **The Early Taliban** — Insurgents emerged under Mullah Omar and other leaders during the civil war that wracked Afghanistan in the mid-1990s, following the end of the Soviet occupation of the country. Early members were a mix of fighters who battled the Soviets in the 1980s and Pashtuns who attended religious schools in Pakistan, where they were aided by the Pakistani Inter-Services Intelligence agency.[3]

• **The Pakistani Taliban** emerged under a separate organizational structure in 2002, when Pakistani forces entered the country's tribal region in the northwest to pursue Islamist militants.[4]

"At the time of the U.S.-led military campaign in Afghanistan in late 2001, allies and sympathizers of the Taliban in Pakistan were not identified as 'Taliban' themselves," wrote Hassan Abbas, a research fellow at Harvard's Belfer Center for Science and International Affairs. "That reality is now a distant memory. Today, Pakistan's indigenous Taliban are an effective fighting force and are engaging the Pakistani military on one side and NATO forces on the other."[5]

• **Hizb-e-Islami** — Formed by the brutal warlord Gulbuddin Hekmatyar, the group is "a prominent ally under the Taliban umbrella," says *Christian Science Monitor* journalist Anand Gopal.[6]

Hizb-e-Islami ("Islamic Party") was allied with the United States and Pakistan during the decade-long Soviet war, Gopal wrote, but after the 2001 U.S. invasion of Afghanistan a segment led by Hekmatyar joined the insurgency. *The New York Times* has described Hekmatyar as having "a record of extreme brutality."[7]

Hizb-e-Islami fighters have for years "had a reputation for being more educated and worldly than their Taliban

Adm. Mike Mullen, chairman of the Joint Chiefs of Staff, said on CBS News' "Face the Nation" on July 5 that in southern Afghanistan, where the toughest fighting is expected, "we have enough forces now not just to clear an area but to hold it so we can build after. And that's really the strategy." He noted that Gen. McChrystal was due to produce his 60-day assessment of the war this summer, adding "we're all committed to getting this right and resourcing it properly."[29]

But senior military officials told *The Washington Post* later that week that McChrystal had concluded Afghan security forces must be greatly expanded if the war is to be won. According to officials, the *Post* said, "such an expansion would require spending billions

counterparts, who are often illiterate farmers," Gopal wrote last year. In the 1970s, Hekmatyar studied engineering at Kabul University, "where he made a name for himself by hurling acid in the faces of unveiled women."[8]

Today the group has a "strong presence in the provinces near Kabul and in Pashtun pockets in the country's north and northeast," Gopal wrote. In 2008 Hizb-e-Islami participated in an assassination attempt on President Hamid Karzai and was behind a 2008 ambush that killed 10 NATO soldiers, according to Gopal.

"Its guerrillas fight under the Taliban banner, although independently and with a separate command structure," Gopal wrote. "Like the Taliban, its leaders see their task as restoring Afghan sovereignty as well as establishing an Islamic state in Afghanistan."

- **The Haqqani network** — Some of the most notorious terrorist actions in recent months have been linked to the network, including the kidnapping of a *New York Times* reporter and the abduction of a U.S. soldier. Haqqani is "not traditional Taliban, they're more strongly associated with al Qaeda," said Haroun Mir, director of Afghanistan's Center for Research and Policy Studies in Kabul.[9]

Thought to control major parts of eastern Afghanistan, the network in recent years "has emerged . . . as a powerful antagonist to U.S. efforts to stabilize that country and root out insurgent havens in the lawless tribal areas of Pakistan," according to *The Washington Post.*[10]

The network is controlled by Jalaluddin Haqqani and his son, Sirajuddin, the *Post* said. Analysts call the son a "terrorist mastermind," according to *The Christian Science Monitor.*[11]

New York Times reporter David Rohde, who was abducted in Logar Province in Afghanistan and taken across the Pakistani border to North Waziristan, was held by the Haqqani network until he escaped in June after seven months in captivity.[12]

The network also is suspected of the suicide bombing of the Indian Embassy in Kabul in July 2008 that left more than 50 dead, *The Post* said.[13]

According to Gopal, "The Haqqanis command the lion's share of foreign fighters operating in [Afghanistan] and tend to be even more extreme than their Taliban counterparts. Unlike most of the Taliban and Hizb-e-Islami, elements of the Haqqani network cooperate closely with al Qaeda."[14]

---

[1] "Remarks by the President on a New Strategy for Afghanistan and Pakistan," The White House, March 27, 2009, www.whitehouse.gov.

[2] Bryan Bender, "U.S. probes divisions within Taliban," *The Boston Globe,* May 24, 2009, p. 1.

[3] See Eben Kaplan and Greg Bruno, "The Taliban in Afghanistan," Council on Foreign Relations, July 2, 2008, www.cfr.org/publication/10551/taliban_in_afghanistan.html.

[4] *Ibid.*

[5] Hassan Abbas, "A Profile of Tehrik-i-Taliban Pakistan," *CTC Sentinel,* Vol. 1, Issue 2, pp. 1-4, www.ctc.usma.edu/sentinel/CTCSentinel-Vol1Iss2.pdf.

[6] Anand Gopal, "Briefing: Who Are the Taliban?" *The Christian Science Monitor,* April 16, 2009, http://anandgopal.com/briefing-who-are-the-taliban/.

[7] Dexter Filkins, "Taliban said to be in talks with intermediaries about peace; U.S. withdrawal is called a focus," *The New York Times,* May 21, 2009, p. 4.

[8] Anand Gopal, "Who Are the Taliban?" *The Nation,* Dec. 22, 2008, www.thenation.com/doc/20081222/gopal.

[9] Quoted in Issam Ahmed, "Captured U.S. soldier in Taliban video: Held by Haqqani network?" *The Christian Science Monitor,* Global News blog, July 19, 2009, http://features.csmonitor.com/globalnews/2009/07/19/captured-us-soldier-in-taliban-video-held-by-haqqani-network/.

[10] Keith B. Richburg, "Reporters Escape Taliban Captors," *The Washington Post,* June 21, 2009, p. A1.

[11] Ahmed, *op. cit.*

[12] *Ibid.*

[13] Richburg, *op. cit.*

[14] Gopal, *The Nation, op. cit.*

---

more than the $7.5 billion the administration has budgeted annually to build up the Afghan army and police over the next several years, and the likely deployment of thousands more U.S. troops as trainers and advisers."[30]

As combat has intensified this spring and summer and more troops entered the war zone, commanders focused on one of the most pernicious threats to the U.S.-led counterinsurgency strategy: the potential for civilian casualties, which can undermine efforts to build trust and cooperation with the local population. Concern over civilian deaths rose sharply in May, when a high-profile U.S. air strike in western Farah province killed at least 26 civilians, according to American investigators.[31]

This spring commanders instituted strict new combat rules aimed at minimizing civilian deaths, and Defense Secretary Robert M. Gates has called such casualties "one of our greatest strategic vulnerabilities." [32]

While some fear that the deployment of more troops to Afghanistan could heighten civilian casualties, others say the opposite is true.

"In fact, the presence of more boots on the ground is likely to *reduce* civilian casualties, because historically it has been the over-reliance on American air strikes — as a result of too few ground forces — which has been the key cause of civilian deaths," wrote Bergen of the New America Foundation. [33]

Should the United States negotiate with the Taliban?

In early March, shortly before announcing his new strategy for Afghanistan and Pakistan, *The New York Times* reported that Obama, in an interview aboard Air Force One, "opened the door to a reconciliation process in which the American military would reach out to moderate elements of the Taliban." [34]

In broaching the idea of negotiating with the Taliban, the president cited successes in Iraq in separating moderate insurgents from the more extreme factions of al Qaeda. Still, he was cautious about reconciliation prospects in Afghanistan.

"The situation in Afghanistan is, if anything, more complex" than the one in Iraq, he said. "You have a less governed region, a history of fierce independence among tribes. Those tribes are multiple and sometimes operate at cross-purposes, and so figuring all that out is going to be much more of a challenge." [35]

Nevertheless, the notion of seeking some sort of reconciliation with elements of the Afghan Taliban has received fresh attention recently.

Opponents of the idea argue that it could project an image of weakness and embolden the insurgency and that Taliban leaders cannot be trusted to uphold any deals they may make.

But proponents argue the Taliban is not a unified bloc, but rather an amalgam that includes those who joined the insurgency out of frustration at the lack of security in their villages or because they were forcibly drafted, among other reasons.

"If you look at a security map of Afghanistan between, say, 2003 and today, you have this creep of the insurgency sort of moving up from the south and east into other parts of the country," J. Alexander Thier, senior rule of law adviser with the United States Institute of Peace. That trend, he says, suggests many local communities and commanders that may have once supported the Afghan government have turned neutral or are actively supporting the Taliban. "There's real room in there to deal with their grievances and concerns about security and justice and the rule of law so as to change that tide."

Thier says he's not talking about seeking a "grand bargain" with the Taliban leadership now ensconced in Pakistan. "If what you're envisioning is [Afghan President] Karzai and [Taliban leader] Mullah Omar sitting on the deck of an aircraft carrier signing an armistice, I don't think that's feasible or realistic," he says. What is feasible are "micro level" negotiations.

"There is an enormous opportunity to work on what I would call mid- and low-level insurgents who, for a variety of reasons, were likely not engaged in the insurgency just a few years ago and were either pro-government or at least neutral. And I think they can and should be brought back to that position."

In an article this summer in *Foreign Affairs*, Fotini Christia, an assistant professor of political science at MIT, and Michael Semple, former deputy to the European Union special representative to Afghanistan, wrote that while "sending more troops is necessary to tip the balance of power against the insurgents, the move will have a lasting impact only if it is accompanied by a political 'surge,' a committed effort to persuade large groups of Taliban fighters to put down their arms and give up the fight." [36]

For reconciliation to work, say Fotini and Semple, Afghans first must feel secure. "The situation on the ground will need to be stabilized, and the Taliban must be reminded that they have no prospect of winning their current military campaign," they wrote. "If the Afghan government offers reconciliation as its carrot, it must also present force as its stick — hence the importance of sending more U.S. troops to Afghanistan, but also, in the long term, the importance of building up Afghanistan's own security forces. Reconciliation needs to be viewed as part of a larger military-political strategy to defeat the insurgency."

Some favor waiting to begin negotiation efforts, while others say they should occur simultaneously with the military campaign. Riedel of Brookings says he sees reason to believe that "a fair number" of Taliban foot soldiers and local commanders are not deeply dedicated to the core extremist cause as espoused by leaders such as Omar. Many rank and file Taliban may be "in this for one reason or another" — perhaps because "their tribe is aligned with the Taliban for local reasons, they're getting paid by the Taliban to do this better than they could be paid by anyone else, or simply because if you're a 17-year-old Pashtun male in Kandahar, fighting is kind of how you get your right of passage," Riedel says.

If the momentum changes on the battlefield "and it's a lot more dangerous to support the Taliban," Riedel continues, "my sense . . . is that these people will either defect or simply go home — they just won't fight."

Still, he says, it's not yet time to begin negotiations. First must come intelligence networks and greater political savvy in each district and province to capitalize on any Taliban inclinations to bend, he argues. "That is primarily an Afghan job, because they're the only people who are going to know the ins and outs of this. That's one of the things the new [U.S.] command arrangement needs to focus on the most. I don't think we're there. This requires really intense local information."

Yet, while the hour for negotiating may not be ripe, "the time is now to do the homework to do that," Riedel says, in order to develop "fine-grained knowledge of what's going on."

But Rajan Menon, a professor of international relations at Lehigh University, says "not coupling" the military campaign against the Taliban "with an olive branch is probably not effective."

Because huge challenges face the military operation — from the threat of civilian casualties to the weakness of the country's central government — the prospect of a long and costly war looms, he says. To avoid that, Menon says, the military effort should be occurring simultaneously with one aimed at encouraging "pragmatic" elements of the Taliban to buy into a process in which they "have to sell [their] ideas in the political marketplace."

The Taliban pragmatists, he says, would be offered a choice: either a long, open-ended war with heavy insurgent casualties or the opportunity to enter the political process as a group seeking victory through the ballot box.

"The question is, can you fracture the [insurgency] movement by laying down terms that are pretty stringent

and test their will," Menon says. Nobody knows if the arms-and-olive branch approach would work, he says, but "you lose nothing by trying."

BACKGROUND

'Graveyard of Empires'

Afghanistan has long been known as the "crossroads of Central Asia," an apt name given the long list of outsiders who have ventured across its borders. It also is known as the "graveyard of empires," reflecting the difficulty faced by would-be conquerors of its remote terrain and disparate peoples.

The list is long. It includes the Persian king Darius I in the 6th century B.C. and the Macedonian conqueror Alexander the Great in 328 B.C., followed by the Scythians, White Huns, Turks, Arabs (who brought Islam in the 7th century A.D.), and the Mongol warrior Genghis Khan in 1219 A.D. [37]

Afghanistan's more recent history is a story of struggle against foreign domination, internal wrangling between reformists and traditionalists, coups, assassinations and war.

Modern Afghanistan began to take shape in the late 19th century, after a bitter fight for influence in Central Asia between the burgeoning British Empire and czarist Russia in what is known as "the Great Game." The contest led to Anglo-Afghan wars in 1839 and 1878. In the first, Afghan warriors forced the British into a deadly retreat from Kabul. The Afghans also had the upper hand over the British in the second war, which resulted in a treaty guaranteeing internal autonomy to Afghanistan while the British had control of its foreign affairs.

In 1880 Amir Abdur Rahman rose to the throne, reigning until 1901. Known as the "Iron Amir," he sought to institute reforms and weaken Pashtun resistance to centralized power but used methods, later emulated by the Taliban, to bring Uzbeks, Hazaras and Tajiks under Kabul's authority. [38] During his reign, Britain drew the so-called Durand Line separating Afghanistan from what was then India and later became Pakistan.

Rahman's son succeeded him but was assassinated in 1919. Under his successor, Amanullah — Rahman's grandson — Afghanistan gained full independence as a result of the Third Anglo War. Amanullah brought reforms that included ties with other countries and coeducational

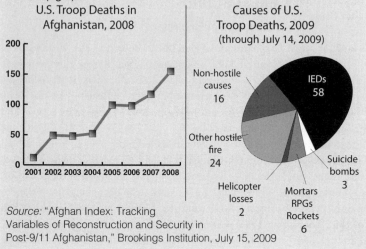

U.S. Troop Deaths Rose Steadily

U.S. troop fatalities have risen steadily since the United States entered Afghanistan in 2001 (graph at left). So far this year, IEDs (improvised explosive devices) caused slightly more than half the deaths (right).

U.S. Troop Deaths in Afghanistan, 2008

Causes of U.S. Troop Deaths, 2009 (through July 14, 2009)

Non-hostile causes 16

IEDs 58

Other hostile fire 24

Suicide bombs 3

Helicopter losses 2

Mortars RPGs Rockets 6

Source: "Afghan Index: Tracking Variables of Reconstruction and Security in Post-9/11 Afghanistan," Brookings Institution, July 15, 2009

schools. But the moves alienated traditionalists, and Amanullah was forced to abdicate in 1929. His successor and cousin, Nadir Shah, was assassinated in 1933.

His death led to the 40-year reign of Crown Prince Mohammad Zahir Shah, Nadir Shah's son, who assumed power at 19.

Chaos and War

Under Zahir, Afghanistan sought to liberalize its political system. But the effort collapsed in the 1970s, and the country became a battleground between communist-backed leftists and a U.S.-backed Islamist resistance movement.

Afghanistan had tilted toward the Soviets in the Cold War era of the 1950s, partly because of U.S. ties to Pakistan, a country created by the partition of India in 1947. Afghan leaders wanted independence or at least autonomy for the Pashtun-dominated areas beyond the Durand Line.

Border tensions led Kabul to seek help from the Soviets, who responded with development loans and other aid in 1950. The United States sought to counter the Soviet Union's influence, and in the 1960s both countries were helping to build up Afghanistan's infrastructure.

Between 1956 and 1978, according to Pakistani journalist Ahmed Rashid, Afghanistan received some $533 million in economic aid from the United States and $2.5 billion in both economic and military aid from the Soviets.[39]

In the 1960s Zahir introduced a constitutional monarchy and pressed for political freedoms that included new rights for women in voting, schooling and employment. "These changes, in a deeply traditional Islamic society, were not popular with everyone," the *Times* noted in a 2007 obituary of Zahir. "But his years were characterized by a rare long period of peace. This tranquility is recalled now with immense nostalgia. On the other hand, peace was not accompanied by prosperity, and the king was faulted for not developing the economy."[40]

Zahir's "experiment in democracy" did not lead to many lasting reforms, but "it permitted the growth of unofficial extremist parties on both the left and the right," including the communist People's Democratic Party of Afghanistan that was ideologically aligned with the Soviets, the U.S. State Department noted. The party split into rival groups in 1967 in a rift that "reflected ethnic, class and ideological divisions within Afghan society."[41]

In 1973 Zahir was ousted while in Europe for medical treatment. His cousin, former Prime Minister Sardar Mohammad Daoud Khan, whom Zahir had forced out in the 1960s, seized power in a bloodless coup. Daoud tried to institute reforms, but political unrest persisted. He aligned closely with the Soviets, but his efforts to build his own political party and forge some links with the United States alienated communist radicals. In 1978, the People's Democratic Party overthrew Daoud, killing him and most of his family.

Soviet Invasion

More upheaval followed. The new leader, Nur Mohammad Taraki, imposed Marxist reforms that angered Islamic traditionalists and ethnic leaders, sparking revolts. Taraki was ousted and killed, and his successor, Hafizullah Amin, who resisted Soviet pressure to moderate his policies, was himself executed in 1979 by the Soviets.

Shortly before Amin's killing, the Soviets mounted a massive invasion of Afghanistan, starting a decade-long war that would permanently alter Afghanistan's profile in world affairs. In Amin's place, the Soviets installed Babrak Karmal. With Soviet military aid, he tried to impose authority throughout Afghanistan but ran into stiff opposition, especially in rural regions. An Islamist resistance movement called the Mujahedeen began receiving weapons and training from the United States and other countries in 1984, and soon the Soviet invasion was on the ropes.

In 1986 Karmal was replaced by Muhammad Najibullah, former head of the Afghan secret police, but the war continued to sour for the Soviets, who also were dealing with powerful political opposition at home. In 1988 Moscow signed agreements, along with the United States, Pakistan and Afghanistan, calling for an end to foreign intervention in Afghanistan. The Soviets withdrew early the following year, and in 1991 the USSR collapsed.

The Soviet invasion affirmed the idea of Afghanistan as a "graveyard" for invaders. Between 1979 and the Soviet withdrawal in 1989, some 14,500 Soviets died. [42] For the Afghan people, however, the war was a bloodbath that all but destroyed the economy and educational system and uprooted much of the population. The U.S. State Department estimates a million died. [43] Some estimates are higher.

Yet the end of the Soviet invasion brought no peace, but rather more chaos. After the Soviets departed, President George H. W. Bush withdrew support from Afghanistan, setting the stage for the conflict engulfing Afghanistan today. "Having won the Cold War," journalist Rashid wrote, "Washington had no further interest in Afghanistan or the region. This left a critical power vacuum for which the United States would pay an enormously high price a decade later." [44]

When the Soviet Union collapsed and the United States disengaged from Afghanistan, they left a country "that had become a cockpit for regional competition, a shattered state with no functioning security forces or civilian political process, a highly mobilized and armed population increasingly dependent on international organizations and cash for livelihood (including through the

Afghan President Hamid Karzai may face a runoff after the presidential election on Aug. 20, partly because many Afghans are looking for alternative leadership in the face of sustained insurgent violence, economic stagnation and political drift.

drug trade), and a multiplicity of armed groups linked transnationally to both state and non-state patrons," wrote Barnett Rubin, director of studies at the Center on International Cooperation at New York University, where he directs a program on Afghan reconstruction. [45]

The Mujahedeen were not a party to the accord leading to Soviet withdrawal, and through the early 1990s they continued fighting the Najibullah regime. In 1992 his government fell, and Burhanuddin Rabbani, an ethnic Tajik, became president. He declared Afghanistan an "Islamic state" but failed to ensure order.

By 1994 Afghanistan "was fast disintegrating," Rashid wrote. "Warlord fiefdoms ruled vast swathes of countryside. President Rabbani . . . governed only Kabul and the northeast of the country, while the west, centered on Herat, was under the control of warlord Ismael Khan. Six provinces in the north were ruled by the Uzbek general Rashid Dostum, and central Afghanistan was in the hands of the Hazaras. In the Pashtun south and east there was even greater fragmentation. . . . Warlords seized people's homes and farms for no reason, raped their daughters, abused and robbed the population and taxed travelers at will. Instead of refugees returning to Afghanistan, more began to leave the south for Pakistan." [46]

In 1994 a militant Islamist group — known as the Taliban and made up mainly of Pashtuns — sprang up in the south to oppose Rabbani. Their rise stemmed directly from the chaos wracking Afghanistan, Rashid wrote. "Frustrated young men who had fought against the Soviets and then returned to madrassas in Pakistan to resume their religious studies or to their villages in Afghanistan gathered around their elders demanding action." [47]

The Taliban took over Kabul in 1996, and by the early 2000s Rabbani's anti-Taliban Northern Alliance was limited to a slice of northern territory. "The Taliban instituted a repressive version of sharia law that outlawed music, banned women from working or going to school and prohibited freedom of the press," wrote Jones, the RAND political scientist. "While it was a detestable regime that committed gross human rights violations, the Taliban succeeded in establishing law and order throughout most of the country." [48]

At the same time, the Taliban was forging links to al Qaeda. In 1996 Taliban leader Mullah Omar invited Osama bin Laden to stay with him in Kandahar, and even though "the CIA already considered bin Laden a threat . . ., he was left alone to ingratiate himself with Omar by providing money, fighters and ideological advice to the Taliban," Rashid wrote. "Bin Laden gathered the Arabs left behind in Afghanistan and Pakistan from the war against the Soviets, enlisted more militants from Arab countries, and established a new global terrorist infrastructure." [49]

The al Qaeda threat reached full force with the Sept. 11, 2001, attacks on the United States. In October President George W. Bush responded with a military assault called Operation Enduring Freedom. The Taliban promptly collapsed, and its leadership, along with that of al Qaeda, fled, in the view of many analysts, to Pakistan.

Yet still more trouble was to follow.

A Weakening Government

"The collapse of the Taliban government . . . created a condition of emerging anarchy," Jones wrote. In late 2001 a United Nations-sponsored conference in Bonn, Germany, laid down a process to rebuild Afghanistan's political system. With the Bonn agreement, "on paper, Afghanistan looked like it had a central government," Jones wrote. But "in practice . . ., Afghanistan had a fragile government that became weaker over time." [50]

The new government couldn't provide essential services, especially in rural areas, and a 2005 World Bank study found that "the urban elite" were the main beneficiaries of help, Jones wrote. [51] Meanwhile, the Afghan government had various problems, including the inability to provide security outside of Kabul, in large measure due to "the inability of the U.S. government to build competent Afghan security forces, especially the police." [52]

American force levels were low, too, with "the number of U.S. troops per capita in Afghanistan . . . significantly less than in almost every state-building effort since World War II," Jones wrote. [53] Moreover, the United States gave "significant assistance to local warlords, further undermining governance and weakening the ability of the Afghan state to establish law and order." [54]

The Taliban rebounded, aided by what critics have called a lack of focus by the Bush administration after its decision to invade Iraq in 2003. In Afghanistan, reconstruction and security issues were left unattended, critics say, leaving an opening for the Taliban — along with criminals, warlords, drug traffickers and others — to assert brutal control. Afghan opium production soared, al Qaeda sanctuaries in the border region of Pakistan festered and once again the region threatened to unleash a new wave of global terrorism.

The threat came not only from Afghanistan, but Pakistan, too.

In an article last year on the emboldened Taliban and al Qaeda forces in the Pakistani border region, celebrated *New York Times* war correspondent Dexter Filkins noted that Islamist militants continued to be backed by Pakistani military and intelligence services. Then, in 1994, came Pakistan's "most fateful move," he wrote. Concerned about the mayhem that swept through Afghanistan after the Soviet withdrawal, Pakistani Prime Minister Benazir Bhutto and her administration intervened on behalf of the Taliban, Filkins wrote.

"We created the Taliban," Bhutto's interior minister, Nasrullah Babar, told Filkins. "Mrs. Bhutto had a vision: that through a peaceful Afghanistan, Pakistan could extend its influence into the resource-rich territories of Central Asia." Her dream didn't materialize — the Taliban's conquest of Afghanistan fell short, and Bhutto was assassinated in late 2007. But as Filkins noted, the Taliban training camps, sometimes supported by Pakistani intelligence officials, "were beacons to Islamic militants from around the world." [55]

Concerns persist about Pakistan's intentions and security capabilities. In recent weeks, as militants threatened Islamabad and other Pakistani cities, Pakistan has gone after insurgents in the Swat Valley and elsewhere. But Pakistani officials also have criticized U.S. attacks on insurgent strongholds using unmanned drone planes.

The big question, as posed by Filkins and others, is whether Pakistan is willing — or able — to control the radical forces within its border region. "This was not supposed to be a major worry," Filkins wrote, noting that after the Sept. 11 attacks Pakistani President Pervez Musharraf backed the United States, helped find al Qaeda suspects, attacked militants in Pakistan's remote tribal areas and vowed to fight terrorism — all in return for $10 billion in U.S. aid since 2001.

But Pakistani military and civilian leaders have survived by playing a "double game," Filkins wrote, promising the United States they were cracking down on militants, and sometimes doing so, while also allowing, and even helping, the same militants.

One reason for the "double game" is Pakistan's long-standing tension with India, especially over the disputed border region of Kashmir. "You can't address Pakistan without dealing with India," says Riedel, the Brookings scholar.

Some experts say Pakistan views its support of the Taliban as a hedge against an India-friendly government coming to power in Afghanistan.

"The Pakistanis have convinced themselves that India's objective is a friendly Afghanistan that can pose a second front against Pakistan," says Riedel. "They see the Afghan Taliban, in particular, as a very useful asset. It keeps Afghanistan from becoming an Indian client state, and their conviction is that . . . it's only a matter of time" until the United States leaves Afghanistan. The Pakistanis believe that "if they wait it out, their client will be the dominant power at least in southern and eastern Afghanistan."

The Cato Institute's Innocent says the Obama administration has made a "profound strategic miscalculation" by not recognizing how much Pakistani leaders fear a non-Pashtun, India-leaning government assuming power in Kabul.

India has used its influence in Afghanistan, she says, to funnel weapons to a separatist movement in southwest Pakistan's sprawling Baluchistan region — a movement

that some say could pose an existential threat to Pakistan. That, in turn, has given Pakistan an incentive to keep Afghanistan from growing closer to India.

Says Innocent, "This rivalry between [Pakistan and India] is the biggest impediment to stabilizing Afghanistan."

CURRENT SITUATION

Measurable Metrics

In the weeks leading up to this summer's Helmand River operation, Defense Secretary Gates expressed optimism about the war in Afghanistan, but acknowledged that the American public's patience with its progress could be limited.

"I think what the people in the United States want to see is the momentum shifting to see that the strategies that we're following are working," he said on CBS' "60 Minutes." "And that's why I've said in nine months to a year, we need to evaluate how we're doing." [56]

Part of that evaluation will be done through "metrics," statistical measurements on everything from civilian casualties to the strength of the Afghan National Army. The approach is part of the Obama strategy.

"Going forward, we will not blindly stay the course," Obama said, but rather "we will set clear metrics to measure progress and hold ourselves accountable. We'll consistently assess our efforts to train Afghan security forces and our progress in combating insurgents. We will measure the growth of Afghanistan's economy and its illicit narcotics production. And we will review whether we are using the right tools and tactics to make progress towards accomplishing our goals." [57]

One measure attracting rising attention in recent weeks is that of troop levels. Michael E. O'Hanlon, a senior fellow at Brookings, wrote this summer in the *Washington Examiner* that "for all its virtues," the Obama administration's Afghan strategy "may still lowball requirements for the Afghanistan mission to succeed."

"The administration's decisions in March to increase U.S. troop numbers to 68,000 (making for about 100,000 foreign troops in all), and Afghan army and police to about 215,000 will leave combined coalition forces at only half the levels in Iraq during the surge," O'Hanlon wrote, "and Afghanistan is slightly larger and more populous."

Should the president announce an Afghanistan exit strategy?

YES
Malou Innocent
Foreign Policy Analyst
Cato Institute

Written for *CQ Researcher*, July 2009

No strategic, political or economic gains could outweigh the costs of America maintaining an indefinite military presence in Afghanistan. Washington can continue to disrupt terrorist havens by monitoring the region with unmanned aerial vehicles, retaining advisers for training Afghan forces and using covert operatives against specific targets.

Many policy makers and prominent opinion leaders are pushing for a large-scale, long-term military presence in Afghanistan. But none of their rationales for such a heavy presence withstands close scrutiny.

Al Qaeda poses a manageable security problem, not an existential threat to America. Washington's response, with an open-ended mission in Afghanistan, is both unnecessary and unsustainable.

Policy makers also tend to conflate al Qaeda with indigenous Pashtun-dominated militias, such as the Taliban. America's security, however, will not necessarily be at risk even if an oppressive regime takes over a contiguous fraction of Afghan territory.

Additionally, the argument that America has a moral obligation to prevent the reemergence of reprehensible groups like the Taliban seems instead a justification for the perpetuation of American empire. After all, America never made a substantive policy shift toward or against the Taliban's misogynistic, oppressive and militant Islamic regime when it controlled Afghanistan in the 1990s. Thus, the present moral outrage against the group can be interpreted as opportunistic.

Some policy makers claim the war is worth waging because terrorists flourish in failed states. But that cannot account for terrorists who thrive in states with the sovereignty to reject external interference. That is one reason why militants find sanctuary in Pakistan. In fact, attempts to stabilize Afghanistan destabilize Pakistan. Amassing troops in Afghanistan feeds the perception of a foreign occupation, spawning more terrorist recruits for Pakistani militias and thus placing undue stress on an already-weakened, nuclear-armed nation.

It's also important to recognize that Afghanistan's land-locked position in Central Asia will forever render it vulnerable to meddling from surrounding states. This factor will make sealing the country's borders from terrorists impossible.

Finally, Americans should not fear appearing "weak" after withdrawal. The United States accounts for almost half of the world's military spending, wields one of the planet's largest nuclear arsenals and can project its power around the globe. Remaining in Afghanistan is more likely to weaken the United States militarily and economically than would withdrawal.

NO
Ilan Berman
Vice President for Policy
American Foreign Policy Council

Written for *CQ Researcher*, July 2009

It has been called the "graveyard of empires," a place that for thousands of years has stymied invading armies. Today, Afghanistan remains one of the West's most vexing international security conundrums — and a pressing foreign policy challenge for the Obama administration.

Indeed, for almost as long as Obama has been in office, critics have counseled the new U.S. president to set a date certain for an American exit from Afghanistan. To his credit, Mr. Obama has done no such thing. To the contrary, through the "Af-Pak" strategy unveiled in March, the White House has effectively doubled down on the American investment in Afghanistan's security. It has done so for two principal reasons.

The first has to do with Afghanistan's importance to the overall struggle against radical Islam. In the years before Sept. 11, Afghanistan became an incubator of international terrorism. And the sinister synergy created there between al Qaeda and the ruling Taliban movement was directly responsible for the most devastating terrorist attack in American history. Preventing a repeat occurrence remains an overriding priority, which is why Washington has committed to propping up the fragile government of Afghan President Hamid Karzai with the troops and training necessary to hold its ground.

The second is an understanding that Afghanistan is essentially a derivative problem. Much of the instability that exists there today is a function of radicalism nurtured next door, in Pakistan. The Taliban, after all, was an invention of Pakistan's Inter-Services Intelligence back in the mid-1990s, and Islamabad's intelligence czars (as well as their military counterparts) remain heavily invested in its future. Today, the Taliban poses perhaps a greater threat to Pakistan's own stability than to that of Afghanistan. But a retraction of U.S. and allied forces from the latter is sure to create a political vacuum that Islamic radicals will be all too eager to exploit.

These realities have defined the Obama administration's approach. Unlike previous foreign powers that have gotten involved in Afghanistan, the United States today is interested simply in what the military calls "area denial." The goal is not to conquer and claim, but to deny the Taliban the necessary breathing room to regroup and re-entrench.

Setting a firm date for an American withdrawal would fundamentally undermine that objective. It would also serve to provide regional radicals with far greater certainty that the U.S. investment in Afghanistan's stability is both limited and reversible.

O'Hanlon cautioned against closing the door on adding more troops and pointed to "troubling signs that the Obama administration may be digging in against any future troop requirements." While "we may or may not have enough forces in Afghanistan" to accomplish the mission's full range of goals, he concluded, "let's not close off the conversation until we learn a little bit more." [58]

NATO's Cold Shoulder

Among the thorniest of the troop-level issues is the role of NATO forces in Afghanistan. As of June, countries participating in the NATO-led International Security Assistance Forces (ISAF), a mission mandated by the U.N. under the 2001 Bonn agreement, have committed about 32,000 troops to Afghanistan, not counting those from the United States, according to the Brookings Institution. The top three were the United Kingdom, which had committed 8,300 troops, Germany (3,380) and Canada (2,830). Several countries, including the U.K. and Germany, were expected to send a small number of additional troops to provide security for the Aug. 20 election.

The Obama administration has been largely unsuccessful in prodding European nations to send more troops to Afghanistan. In April, in what the online edition of the *Times* of London billed as a "charm offensive" by Obama on his "debut international tour," leaders on the European continent "turned their backs" on the president, with British Prime Minister Gordon Brown "the only one to offer substantial help." Brown offered to send several hundred extra troops to provide election security, the *Times* noted, "but even that fell short of the thousands of combat troops that the U.S. was hoping to [gain] from the prime minister." [59]

Nonetheless, Obama has mustered some recent support for his Afghan policy. In late July Spain's prime minister, José Luís Rodriguez Zapatero, said his country was willing to increase its force on long-term deployment to Afghanistan, *The New York Times* reported. [60]

Early this month, NATO approved a reorganized command structure for Afghanistan, agreeing to set up a New Intermediate Joint Headquarters in Kabul under U.S. Lt. General David M. Rodriquez, who will manage the war on a day-to-day basis and report to McChrystal. NATO made the move at the first meeting of its governing body, the North Atlantic Council, under new NATO Secretary General Anders Fogh Rasmussen, former Danish prime minister. [61] Rasmussen, in his first comments as secretary general, called on the United Nations and European Union to help defeat the Taliban. "NATO will do its part, but it cannot do it alone," he said. "This needs to be an international effort, both military and civilian." [62]

The effectiveness of having more NATO troops in Afghanistan has been a matter of debate. At a forum in June, Brookings scholar Jeremy Shapiro, recently back from a visit to southern Afghanistan, suggested U.S. commanders have had little faith in the NATO command structure.

"Each of the main countries there is really running its own provincial war," Shapiro said. "The overall problem is that there really is no unity of command in Afghanistan so we're unable . . . to prioritize and to shift resources to deal with the most important problems. . . . It's related to the fact that for every NATO force in Afghanistan including the Americans, there are two chains of command, one up through the NATO commander who is an American, and one to the national capital, and in case of conflict, the national capital command always takes priority.

"The result is that each of the lead countries in the south, the Canadians in Kandahar, the British in Helmand, the Dutch in Uruzgan, are focused on their own priorities, on improving specific indicators in their piece of the war in their own province or district without a great deal of attention to the impact of that measure on the overall fight."

In impoverished Uruzgan Province, for example, the Dutch are doing "impressive things" with development efforts, but Uruzgan "is to a large degree serving as a sanctuary for insurgents to rest and refit and plan and to engage in the struggle in Kandahar and Helmand" province, Shapiro said.

The Canadians and British "would argue . . . that the priority for Afghanistan is not Uruzgan, it is Kandahar and Helmand and [if] the development of Uruzgan comes at the cost of strengthening the insurgency in other provinces, it's perhaps not the best use of resources."

Shapiro said he believes that as the number of U.S. troops has increased, especially in southern Afghanistan, "the focus for the U.S. military command is on . . . assigning roles to coalition partners that don't require intense coordination. . . . What that presages is an Americanization of the war, including in the south." By next year, Shapiro said, NATO will remain in command, "but I would be very dubious that we'll be truly fighting a NATO war at that point." [63]

Americanizing the War

Such predictions of an Americanized war are at odds with the administration's perception of the Afghan mission. Obama told *Sky News*, a British news outlet, that British contributions to the war effort are "critical" and that "this is not an American mission. The mission in Afghanistan is one that the Europeans have as much if not more of a stake in what we do. . . . The likelihood of a terrorist attack in London is at least as high, if not higher, than it is in the United States." [64]

Any further Americanization of the war will doubtlessly fuel scrutiny of the Afghan strategy in Congress and bolster demands for the Obama administration to set forth an exit strategy.

This summer, the U.S. House of Representatives strongly rejected an amendment calling on the defense secretary to submit a report no later than Dec. 31 outlining an exit strategy for U.S. forces in Afghanistan.

"Every military mission has a beginning, a middle, a time of transition and an end," said Rep. McGovern, the Massachusetts Democrat who sponsored the measure. "But I have yet to see that vision articulated in any document, speech or briefing. We're not asking for an immediate withdrawal. We're sure not talking about cutting or running or retreating, just a plan. If there is no military solution for Afghanistan, then please just tell us how we will know when our military contribution to the political solution has ended." [65]

But "focusing on an exit versus a strategy is irresponsible and fails to recognize that our efforts in Afghanistan are vital to preventing future terrorist attacks on the American people and our allies," argued Rep. Howard McKeon, R-Calif. [66]

The amendment's defeat did nothing to allay scrutiny of the war. Sen. John F. Kerry, D-Mass., chairman of the Senate Foreign Relations Committee, told *Global-Post*, an online international-news site, that he planned to hold oversight hearings on U.S. involvement in Afghanistan. [67]

"End of summer, early fall," Kerry said, "we are going to take a hard look at Afghanistan."

OUTLOOK

More Violence

Military strategists say the Afghan war is likely to get more violent in coming months as U.S. and NATO forces battle the insurgency.

One immediate concern is whether the Taliban will make good on threats to disrupt this month's presidential election. While additional troops are being deployed to guard against attacks, officials have said ensuring the security of all 28,000 polling places is impossible. [68]

Meanwhile, tensions are likely to remain between those calling for a strict timetable for de-escalating the war and those arguing in favor of staying the course.

"I certainly do not think it would be a wise idea to impose a timeline on ourselves," says Riedel of Brookings, although he points to "political realities" that include the idea "that some measure of improvement in the security situation on the ground needs to be apparent over the course of the next 18 to 24 months."

Riedel expresses confidence that will occur. Once all scheduled troop deployments are in place, he says, "it's reasonable to expect that you can see some impact from [those deployments] in 18 to 24 months. Not victory, not the surrender of [Taliban leader] Mullah Omar, but some measurable decline in the pace of Taliban activity, some increase in the number of districts and provinces which are regarded as safe enough for [non-governmental organizations] to work in."

Beyond demands for on-the-ground progress in Afghanistan, the Obama administration faces other pressures as it struggles to get a grip on the Afghanistan and Pakistan region. One is helping U.S. allies maintain support for the war. In Britain, Prime Minister Brown has faced an uproar over growing British casualties that critics say stem from an underfunded defense budget that led to inadequate troop levels and equipment. [69] At home, as the financial crisis, health-care reform and other issues put pressure on the federal budget, Obama is likely to face opposition in Congress over additional war funding.

And Obama also is under pressure to address incendiary issues left over from the Bush administration. In July, a *New York Times* report detailed how the Bush administration repeatedly sought to discourage an investigation of charges that forces under U.S.-backed warlord Gen. Abdul Rashid Dostum massacred hundreds or even thousands of Taliban prisoners of war during the 2001 invasion of Afghanistan. [70]

In an editorial, the *Times* said Obama has directed aides to study the issue and that the administration is pressing Afghan President Karzai not to return Dostum to power. But, it added, Obama "needs to order a full investigation into the massacre." [71]

In the long run, one of the biggest challenges facing the Obama administration is its effort to instill sound governance in a country saturated with graft.

Afghanistan's corruption "reveals the magnitude of the task," says Walt, the Harvard international affairs professor. "Fixing corrupt public institutions is really hard once a pattern of behavior has been established, where money is flowing in non-regular ways. It's very difficult for outsiders to re-engineer those social and political practices, even if we were committed to staying five or 10 years."

Walt says he hopes he's wrong — "that the injection of the right kind of American power will create space for some kind of political reconciliation." But he's not optimistic. "I believe several years from now, [Afghanistan] will look like a sinkhole."

UPDATE

The dramatic Navy Seal commando raid that killed al-Qaida leader Osama bin Laden on May 1 undoubtedly will affect U.S. anti-terrorism efforts, including the war in Afghanistan. How much remains to be seen.

But even before members of elite Seal Team 6 swooped into Abbottabad, Pakistan, the Obama administration planned to shrink the number of U.S. and NATO soldiers in Afghanistan. Reportedly the reduction would amount to about 5,000 troops out of more than 100,000 currently deployed, not to mention an even larger force of private security contractors. [72] The conflict is now in its 10th year, and analysts predict that 2011 will be its most violent. Many see the conflict as one in which neither side can defeat the other. Nic Lee, director of the Afghanistan NGO Safety Office, a group that advises nongovernmental organizations about security

Defense Secretary Robert Gates and Afghan President Hamid Karzai arrive at a joint press conference in Kabul on March 7, 2011. Karzai's weak, U.S.-backed government is widely viewed as corrupt and dysfunctional, and many Afghans see it as illegitimate.

in Afghanistan, describes it as a "perpetually escalating stalemate." [73]

Moreover, in the decade since the terrorist attacks of Sept. 11, 2001, critics of the conflict, including Richard Haass, president of the Council on Foreign Relations, and former Republican National Committee Chairman Michael Steele say it has gone from a war of necessity to one of choice. [74]

Many argue that Afghanistan is no longer a significant global terrorist threat, a view underscored in May, when bin Laden — the *raison d'etre* behind the conflict — was discovered living in Pakistan, a scant hour's drive from the capital, Islamabad. It appears that he had sheltered there for many years, even as U.S. forces blasted away with bombs and missiles at suspected terrorists and other militants believed to be living in the remote tribal regions between Afghanistan and Pakistan.

U.S intelligence officials — with the aid of materials captured in the bin Laden raid — are now racing to rewrite the history of al-Qaida, in light of bin Laden's decade on the lam. The results will clearly have major implications for the larger conflict between the West and the radical Islamist terrorist organization and others.

It had long been thought that bin Laden was living in a cave, in limited contact with the outside world and not coordinating terrorist attacks worldwide. Those assumptions are now being reconsidered after his lair was discovered just yards from the top Pakistani military academy, and his walled compound yielded a vast trove of al-Qaida information stored on computer hard drives and thumb drives, including plans to attack the United States on the 10th anniversary of 9/11.

Meanwhile, the scheduled drawdown of U.S. forces in Afghanistan, slated to begin in July, will be an important indicator of Washington's long-term plans for the war. The size and nature of the drawdown have yet to be announced.

Even the authorization of military force against perpetrators of the 9/11 attacks and those who harbored them, passed three days after the attacks, is up for consideration. The authorization legally underpins the war effort in Afghanistan and detention of terror suspects at Guantánamo Bay, Cuba. But with the death of bin Laden and capture of others responsible for the 9/11 attacks, experts say the war resolution will need congressional updating. That process will allow lawmakers to craft a long-term framework for any continued military and counterterrorism actions. [75]

Changes on the Ground

There are only a few dozen al-Qaida operatives, at most, in Afghanistan, according to the CIA. [76] But numbers are only one measure of al-Qaida's strength: There were only 200 sworn members of the group when key operatives met in the German city of Hamburg to plan the 2001 attacks on the World Trade Center and Pentagon.

Most troubling for Washington is the weak, U.S.-backed government of President Hamid Karzai in Kabul. It is widely viewed as corrupt and dysfunctional, and many Afghans see it as illegitimate. [77] "The Vietnam War showed us that we shouldn't prop up corrupt governments, and that's what we've got in Afghanistan," said former Democratic National Committee Chairman. Howard Dean. [78]

Dean, who rallied Democratic support as an anti-war presidential candidate in 2004, initially had supported the Obama administration's surge last year of 30,000 additional troops in Afghanistan, but no longer. Republicans, too, are questioning the continued importance of the war. Rep. Jason Chaffetz, a freshman Republican from Utah, bucked his party and twice voted in the House to force the Obama administration to detail a withdrawal plan. "I believe that it is time to bring our troops home," Chaffetz proclaimed on his website. [79]

Sen. Richard Lugar, R-Ind., the senior Republican on the influential Foreign Relations Committee, is even blunter in his criticism of the war effort. "Nearly a decade later, with al-Qaida largely displaced from the country but franchised in other locations, Afghanistan does not carry a strategic value that justifies 100,000 American troops and a $100 billion a year cost, especially given current fiscal restraints in the United States," Lugar said in May. [80]

Just days after the raid on bin Laden's compound, a bipartisan group of House members wrote a letter to Obama urging that the Afghan mission be recalibrated. "We believe it is no longer the best way to defend America against terror attacks, and we urge you to withdraw all troops from Afghanistan that are not crucial to the immediate national security objective of combating al-Qaida," the lawmakers said. [81]

But other members of Congress have said it would be reasonable to stay the course well into 2014. "A precipitous withdrawal from Afghanistan would be a mistake, and I, for one, would take that option off the table," Democratic Sen. John Kerry, chairman of the Foreign Relations Committee, said in mid-May. [82]

End Game

Many Americans outside Washington are calling for a new direction in Afghanistan. In a *Washington Post/ABC News* poll conducted in March, 64 percent of respondents said the war was no longer worth the cost, though there was nearly an even split on the question of how well things were going. [83]

"For a decade, this country has expended an inordinate amount of its resources, not to mention the more than 1,500 soldiers killed, to fight a war in Afghanistan that never promised to yield comparable strategic results," argued an editorial in the *Philadelphia Inquirer* days after the Navy Seals' raid. "With bin Laden's death, this nation has an opportunity to take emotionalism and politics out of the equation and make some rational decisions about U.S. strategic interests in South Asia, and how best to achieve them." [84]

For the U.S. military, which bears the brunt of the burden in the Afghan War, 10 years of combat in the region have taken an emotional toll as well. The latest survey of military morale found it to be the lowest in five years, even as the intensity of the fighting has spiked to levels comparable to combat in Iraq in 2006-07. Many soldiers have served three or more deployments, and half of the respondents said they had killed enemy fighters, a crucial psychological event for a combat veteran. [85] And the costs are not limited to members of the military and their families: The $110 billion price for the war consumes $1 of every $7 the nation spends on defense. [86]

One of NATO's primary goals in Afghanistan has been to bolster the Afghan national army, seen as crucial for lasting stability and a prerequisite for U.S. troop withdrawal. The Afghan army is on track to meet its growth target of 171,000 troops by October 2011. It's currently short of that goal by about 10,000 soldiers. But desertion rates are high, and there is a severe shortage of officers. What's more, 86 percent of enlisted men are illiterate, and drug abuse is rampant. [87]

Combat Continues

Since the surge in U.S. forces into Afghanistan last year, the strategy has involved both repositioning soldiers to better protect population centers and drastically boosting aerial bombardment, often using the CIA's unmanned aerial drones to target enemy fighters. The two-pronged approach was developed by Gen. David Petraeus, the commander of U.S. Forces in Afghanistan, who is expected to take over as CIA chief in September. [88]

The drone campaign has been crucial in "taking the fight to the enemy," as military officials like to say. Bill Roggio, a military analyst and editor of *The Long War Journal* who has studied the secretive campaign, has kept a running tally of drone strikes, which rose to 117 in 2010, compared with 35 in 2008. There have been 22 reported strikes during the first four months of 2011. In May, on the eve of the summer battle season, NATO announced that the Taliban and other insurgents in Kabul had been "weakened" by both the increase in the number of troops on the ground and an uptick in airstrikes.

But because the drone campaign is classified, no full public accounting has been provided of the targets and success rates for the strikes, including how many civilians have been killed and the number and nature of militants' deaths. Roggio argues that international fighters and terrorist leaders are targeted, but Gilles Dorronsoro, a visiting scholar at the Carnegie Endowment for International Peace, says the drone campaign is problematic. "Now, we're seeing drone airstrikes against low-level foot soldiers and more civilian casualties," he says. "Is it working to use drones to break the back of the Taliban? No."

Airstrikes in the tribal regions alone have not forced the Taliban to the negotiating table, nor have they broken their will to fight on. Moreover, the high number of civilian casualities has made the U.S. war against terrorist groups wildly unpopular in Pakistan. But the death of Osama bin Laden might be the break that many people have been hoping for. Afghanistan's ambassador to Washington said that the demise of the world's most wanted terrorist "created the hope for leadership of the Taliban to join the reconciliation and reintegration process." [89]

In addition, Pakistani security officials announced a new operation to sweep through Quetta, long thought to be the home of the Taliban's government in exile, to make sure that one-eyed Taliban chief Mullah Mohammed Omar and Ayman al-Zawahiri, formerly bin Laden's second in command, aren't also hiding in Pakistan.

NOTES

1. Chris Brummitt, "Afghan firefight shows challenge for U.S. troops," The Associated Press, June 21, 2009, http://news.yahoo.com/s/ap/20090621/ap_on_re_as/as_afghan_taking_on_the_taliban.

2. Laura King, "6 U.S. troops killed in Afghanistan," *Los Angeles Times*, Aug. 3, 2009, www.latimes.com/news/nationworld/world/la-fg-afghan-deaths3-2009aug03,0,3594308.story.

3. For background, see Robert Kiener, "Crisis in Pakistan," *CQ Global Researcher*, December 2008, pp. 321-348, and Roland Flamini, "Afghanistan on the Brink," *CQ Global Researcher*, June 2007, pp. 125-150.

4. "Remarks by the President on a New Strategy for Afghanistan and Pakistan," White House, March 27, 2009, www.whitehouse.gov.

5. See www.boston.com/news/nation/washington/articles/2009/07/23/obama_victory_not_right_word_for_afghanistan/.

6. For background, see Roland Flamini, "Future of NATO," *CQ Global Researcher*, January 2009, pp. 1-26.

7. Pamela Constable, "For Karzai, Stumbles On Road To Election," *The Washington Post*, July 13, 2009, www.washingtonpost.com/wp-dyn/content/article/2009/07/12/AR2009071202426.html.

8. See, for example, Fred Kaplan, "Counterinsur gen-terrorism," *Slate*, March 27, 2009, www.slate.com/id/2214726/.

9. Ann Scott Tyson, "New Approach to Afghanistan Likely," *The Washington Post*, June 3, 2009, www.washingtonpost.com/wp-dyn/content/article/2009/06/02/AR2009060203828.html.

10. *Ibid.*

11. Sharon Otterman, "Civilian death toll rises in Afghanistan," *The New York Times*, Aug. 1, 2009, www.nytimes.com/2009/08/01/world/asia/01afghan.html?scp=1&sq=civilian%20death%20toll%20rises&st=cse.

12. White House, *op. cit.*

13. See also John Mueller, "How Dangerous Are the Taliban?" *foreignaffairs.com*, April 15, 2009, www.foreignaffairs.com/articles/64932/john-mueller/how-dangerous-are-the-taliban.

14. Matthew Kaminski, "Holbrooke of South Asia," *The Wall Street Journal*, April 11, 2009.

15. Quoted in Rajiv Chandrasekaran, "Marines Deploy on Major Mission," *The Washington Post*, July 2, 2009, www.washingtonpost.com/wp-dyn/content/article/2009/07/01/AR2009070103202.html.

16. Jared Allen and Roxana Tiron, "Obey warns Afghanistan funding may slow unless significant progress made," *The Hill*, May 4, 2009, http://thehill.com/leading-the-news/obey-warns-afghanistan-funding-may-slow-unless-significant-progress-made-2009-05-04.html.

17. *The New York Times*/CBS News Poll, June 12-16, 2009, http://graphics8.nytimes.com/packages/images/nytint/docs/latest-new-york-times-cbs-news-poll/original.pdf.

18. See Dexter Filkins, "Afghan corruption: Everything for Sale," *The New York Times*, Jan. 2, 2009, www.nytimes.com/2009/01/02/world/asia/02iht-corrupt.1.19050534html?scp=2&sq=everything%20for%20sale&st=cse.

19. See Malou Innocent, "Obama's Mumbai problem," *The Guardian*, Jan. 27, 2009, www.guardian.co.uk/commentisfree/cifamerica/2009/jan/27/obama-india-pakistan-relations.

20. Peter Bergen, "Winning the Good War," *Washington Monthly*, July/August 2009, www.washington-monthly.com/features/2009/0907.bergen.html#Byline.

21. Greg Bruno, "U.S. Needs a Stronger Commitment to Improving Afghan Governance," Council on Foreign Relations, July 30, 2009, www.cfr.org/publication/19936/us_needs_a_stronger_commitment_to_improving_afghan_governance.html?breadcrumb=%2Fpublication%2Fpublication_list%3Ftype%3Dinterview.

22. Anthony H. Cordesman, "The Afghanistan Campaign: Can We Win?" Center for Strategic and International Studies, July 22, 2009. Cordesman expands on his ideas in a paper available at http://csis.org/files/publication/090722_CanWeAchieveMission.pdf.

23. Richard A. Oppel Jr., "Allied Officers Concerned by Lack of Afghan Forces," *The New York Times*, July 8, 2009, www.nytimes.com/2009/07/08/world/asia/08afghan.html?ref=world.

24. Quoted in Associated Press, "Marines: More Afghan Soldiers Needed in Helmand," CBS News, July 8, 2009, www.cbsnews.com/stories/2009/07/08/ap/politics/main5145174.shtml.

25. Quoted in Oppel, *op. cit.*

26. Transcript, "Death Toll Mounts as Coalition Forces Confront Taliban," "The NewsHour with Jim Lehrer," PBS, July 15, 2009, www.pbs.org/newshour/bb/military/july-dec09/afghancas_07-15.html.

27. Bob Woodward, "Key in Afghanistan: Economy, Not Military," *The Washington Post*, July 1, 2009, www.washingtonpost.com/wp-dyn/content/article/2009/06/30/AR2009063002811.html.

28. *Ibid.*

29. "Face the Nation," CBS News, July 5, 2009.

30. Greg Jaffe and Karen De Young, "U.S. General Sees Afghan Army, Police Insufficient," *The Washington Post*, July 11, 2009, www.washingtonpost.com/wp-dyn/content/article/2009/07/10/AR2009071002975 .html.

31. Greg Jaffe, "U.S. Troops Erred in Airstrikes on Civilians," *The Washington Post*, June 20, 2009, www.washingtonpost.com/wp-dyn/content/article/2009/06/19/AR2009061903359.html.

32. Quoted in Robert Burns, "Analysis: reducing Afghan civilian deaths key goal," The Associated Press, June 13, 2009, www.google.com/hostednews/ap/article/eqM5hyNJNBigtMGe2M12B2s3w6OCoAbQD98Q2VP80.

33. Bergen, *op. cit.*

34. Helene Cooper and Sheryl Gay Stolberg, "Obama Ponders Outreach to Elements of Taliban," *The New York Times*, March 8, 2009, www.nytimes.com/2009/ 03/08/us/politics/08obama.html?scp=1&sq=obama %20ponders%20outreach%20to%20elements%20of%20taliban&st=cse.

35. Quoted in *ibid.*

36. Fotini Christia and Michael Semple, "Flipping the Taliban: How to Win in Afghanistan," *Foreign Affairs*, July/August 2009, p. 34, www.foreignaffairs .com/articles/65151/fotini-christia-and-michael-semple/flipping-the-taliban. Co-author Semple, who has significant background in holding dialogues with the Taliban, was expelled from Afghanistan in 2007 by the Karzai government amid accusations he and another diplomat held unauthorized talks with the Taliban.

37. See, "Background Note: Afghanistan," U.S. Department of State, November 2008, www.state.gov/r/pa/ei/bgn/5380.htm; also, *Grolier Encyclopedia of Knowledge*, Vol. 1, 1991. See also Kenneth Jost, "Rebuilding Afghanistan," *CQ Researcher*, Dec. 21, 2001, pp. 1041-1064.

38. Ahmed Rashid, *Descent into Chaos* (2008), p. 8.

39. *Ibid.*

40. Barry Bearak, "Mohammad Zahir Shah, Last Afghan King, Dies at 92," *The New York Times*, July 24, 2007, www.nytimes.com/2007/07/24/world/asia/24 shah.html.

41. U.S. State Department, *op. cit.*

42. *Ibid.*

43. *Ibid.*

44. Rashid, *op. cit.*, p. 11.

45. Barnett R. Rubin, "The Transformation of the Afghan State," in J. Alexander Thier, ed., *The Future of Afghanistan* (2009), p. 15.

46. Rashid, *op. cit.*, pp. 12-13.

47. *Ibid.*, p. 13.

48. Seth G. Jones, "The Rise of Afghanistan's Insurgency," *International Security*, Vol. 32, No. 4, spring 2008, p. 19.

49. Rashid, *op. cit.*, p. 15.

50. Jones, *op. cit.*, p. 20.

51. *Ibid.* The reference to "the urban elite" comes from "Afghanistan: State Building, Sustaining Growth, and Reducing Poverty," World Bank Report No. 29551-AF, 2005, p. xxvi.

52. *Ibid.*, pp. 20, 22.

53. *Ibid.*, p. 24.

54. *Ibid.*, p. 25.

55. Dexter Filkins, "Right at the Edge," *The New York Times*, Sept. 7, 2008, www.nytimes.com/2008/09/07/magazine/07pakistan-t.html.

56. "Bob Gates, America's Secretary of War," "60 Minutes," May 17, 2009, www.cbsnews.com/stories/ 2009/05/14/60minutes/main5014588.shtml.

57. White House, *op. cit.*

58. Michael O'Hanlon, "We Might still Need More Troops In Afghanistan," *Washington Examiner*, July 7, 2009, www.washingtonexaminer.com/politics/50044002 .html.

59. Michael Evans and David Charter, "Barack Obama fails to win NATO troops he wants for Afghanistan," *Timesonline*, April 4, 2009, www.timesonline.co.uk/tol/news/world/us_and_americas/article6032342 .ece.

60. Victoria Burnett and Rachel Donadio, "Spain Is Open to Bolstering Forces in Afghanistan," *The New York Times*, July 30, 2009, www.nytimes.com/2009/ 07/30/world/europe/30zapatero.html?ref=world.

61. Steven Erlanger, "NATO Reorganizes Afghan Command Structure," *The New York Times*, Aug. 4, 2009, www.nytimes.com/2009/08/05/world/05nato .html.

62. Thomas Harding, "New NATO head calls for 'international effort' in Afghanistan," *Telegraph*, Aug. 3, 2009, www.telegraph.co.uk/news/worldnews/asia/ afghanistan/5967377/New-Nato-head-calls-for-international-effort-in-Afghanistan.html.

63. "Afghanistan and Pakistan: A Status Report," Brookings Institution, June 8, 2009, www.brook ings.edu/~/media/Files/events/2009/0608_afghani stan_pakistan/20090608_afghanistan_pakistan .pdf.

64. "Taliban pushed back, long way to go: Obama," Reuters, July 12, 2009, www.reuters.com/article/ topNews/idUSTRE56A2Q420090712?feedType=R SS&feedName=topNews&rpc=22&sp=true.

65. Quoted in Dan Robinson, "U.S. Lawmakers Reject Amendment Calling for an Exit Strategy from Afghanistan," VOA News, June 26, 2009, www .voanews.com/english/2009-06-26-voa1.cfm.

66. Quoted in *ibid*.

67. John Aloysius Farrell, "Kerry: 'We are going to take a hard look at Afghanistan,' " *GlobalPost*, updated July 10, 2009, www.globalpost.com.

68. Pamela Constable, "Karzai's Challengers Face Daunting Odds," *The Washington Post*, July 6, 2009, p. 7A.

69. John F. Burns, "Criticism of Afghan War Is on the Rise in Britain," *The New York Times*, July 12, 2009, www .nytimes.com/2009/07/12/world/europe/12britain .html?scp=1&sq=criticism%20of%20afghan%20 war%20is%20on%20the%20rise&st=cse.

70. James Risen, "U.S. Inaction Seen After Taliban P.O.W.'s Died," *The New York Times*, July 11, 2009, www.nytimes.com/2009/07/11/world/asia/11afghan .html?scp=1&sq=U.S.%20Inaction% 20Seen%20 After%20Taliban&st=cse.

71. "The Truth About Dasht-i-Leili," *The New York Times*, July 14, 2009, www.nytimes.com/2009/ 07/14/opinion/14tue2html?scp=5&sq=U.S.% 20Inaction%20Seen%20After%20Taliban&st=cse.

72. Julian Barnes and Adam Entous, "Military Draws Up Afghan Exit Plan," *The Wall Street Journal*, May 10, 2011.

73. "Glimmers of hope; it's been a long slog, but Afghanistan may at last be able to contemplate more stable government," *The Economist*, May 12, 2011.

74. Statement of Richard Haass before the Senate Committee on Foreign Relations, May 3, 2011, http://i.cfr.org/content/publications/attachments/ Testimony.Haass.SFRC.5.3.2011.pdf.

75. Josh Gerstein, "GOP seeks to redefine the war on terror," *Politico*, May 10, 2011.

76. Felicia Sonmez, "Panetta: Maybe 50 to 100 al Qaeda left in Afghanistan," *The Washington Post*, June 27, 2010.

77. Larry Goodson and Thomas H. Johnson, "Parallels With Past: How Soviets Lost In Afghanistan, How US Is Losing — Analysis," *Eurasia Review*, April 26, 2011.

78. McKay Coppins, "Howard Dean to Obama: Get Out of Afghanistan!" *The Daily Beast*, May 18, 2011, www.thedailybeast.com/blogs-and-sto ries/2011-04-18/howard-dean-to-president-obama-get-our-troops-out-of-afghanistan/?cid=hp:beastori ginalsC1.

79. http://chaffetz.house.gov/legislation/strong-national-defense.shtml.

80. "Indiana Senator calling for troop withdrawal from Afghanistan," FOX News, May 3, 2011, www. fox59.com/news/wxin-richard-lugar-indiana-senator-calling-for-troop-withdrawal-from-afghanistan-20110503,0,3670876.story.

81. Letter to President Obama, http://welch.house.gov/ index.php?option=com_content&view=article &id=1466:welch-and-chaffetz-lead-bipartisan-house-group-urging-obama-to-pull-out-of-afghani-stan-and-recalibrate-anti-terrorismstrategy&ca tid=39:2011-press-releases&Itemid=32.

82. "Key US senators warn against hasty Afghan pull-out," Agence France-Press, May 10, 2011.

83. "Washington Post-ABC News Poll," March 13, 2011, www.washingtonpost.com/wp-srv/politics/polls/post-poll_03142011.html.

84. "Rethink Afghanistan," *Philadelphia Inquirer*, May 9, 2011, www.philly.com/philly/opinion/121482579.html.

85. Gregg Zoroya, "Strain on forces in the field at a five-year high," *USA Today*, May 8, 2011.

86. "Prepared Statement of Richard Haass," *op. cit.*

87. C. J. Radin, "Afghan National Army Update May 2011," *The Long War Journal*, May 9, 2011, www.longwarjournal.org/archives/2011/05/afghan_national_army_4.php.

88. Yochi Dreazen, "National Security Reshuffle has Implications for Afghan War," *National Journal*, April 27, 2011.

89. Ashish Kumar Sen, "Without bin Laden, Taliban may talk peace," *The Washington Times*, May 8, 2011.

BIBLIOGRAPHY

Books

Coll, Steve, *Ghost Wars*, Penguin Press, 2004.
The former *Washington Post* managing editor, now president of the New America Foundation think tank, traces the CIA's involvement in Afghanistan since the Soviet invasion in the 1970s.

Kilcullen, David, *The Accidental Guerrilla*, Oxford University Press, 2009.
A former Australian Army officer and counterterrorism adviser argues that strategists have tended to conflate small insurgencies and broader terror movements.

Peters, Gretchen, *Seeds of Terror*, Thomas Dunne Books, 2009.
A journalist examines the role of Afghanistan's illegal narcotics industry in fueling the activities of the Taliban and al Qaeda.

Rashid, Ahmed, *Descent into Chaos*, Viking, 2008.
A Pakistani journalist argues that "the U.S.-led war on terrorism has left in its wake a far more unstable world than existed on" Sept. 11, 2001.

Wright, Lawrence, *The Looming Tower*, Knopf, 2006.
In a Pulitzer Prize-winning volume that remains a must-read for students of the wars in Afghanistan and Iraq, a

New Yorker staff writer charts the spread of Islamic fundamentalism and emergence of al Qaeda that gave rise to the Sept. 11 attacks.

Articles

Bergen, Peter, "Winning the Good War," *Washington Monthly*, July/August 2009, www.washingtonmonthly.com/features/2009/0907.bergen.html.
A senior fellow at the New America Foundation argues that skepticism about the Obama administration's chances of victory in Afghanistan are based on a misreading of that nation's history and people.

Christia, Fotini, and Michael Semple, "Flipping the Taliban," *Foreign Affairs*, July/August 2009.
A political scientist (Christia) and a specialist on Afghanistan and Pakistan who has talked with the Taliban argue that while more troops are necessary, "the move will have a lasting impact only if it is accompanied by a political 'surge' " aimed at persuading large groups of Taliban fighters to lay down arms.

Hogan, Michael, "Milt Bearden: Afghanistan Is 'Obama's War,' " *Vanityfair.com*, Feb. 5, 2009, www.vanityfair.com/online/politics/2009/02/milt-bearden-afghanistan-is-obamas-war.html.
Bearden, the former CIA field officer in Afghanistan when U.S. covert action helped expel the Soviet Union, says in this Q&A that "the only thing that is absolutely certain about this war is that it's going to be Obama's war, just as Iraq will be Bush's war."

Jones, Seth G., "The Rise of Afghanistan's Insurgency," *International Security*, Vol. 32, No. 4, spring 2008, http://belfercenter.ksg.harvard.edu/files/IS3204_pp007-040_Jones.pdf.
A RAND Corporation political scientist analyzes the reasons a violent insurgency began to develop in Afghanistan earlier this decade.

Mueller, John, "How Dangerous Are the Taliban?" *Foreignaffairs.com*, April 15, 2009, www.foreignaffairs.com/articles/64932/john-mueller/how-dangerous-are-the-taliban.
An Ohio State University political science professor questions whether the Taliban and al Qaeda are a big

enough menace to the United States to make a long war in Afghanistan worth the cost.

Riedel, Bruce, "Comparing the U.S. and Soviet Experiences in Afghanistan," *CTC Sentinel*, Combating Terrorism Center, May 2009, www.brookings.edu/~/media/Files/rc/articles/2009/05_afghanistan_riedel/05_afghanistan_riedel.pdf.
A Brookings Institution scholar and former senior adviser to President Barack Obama examines the "fundamental differences" between the Soviet and U.S. experiences in the region.

Rosenberg, Matthew, and Zahid Hussain, "Pakistan Taps Tribes' Anger with Taliban," *The Wall Street Journal*, June 6-7, 2009, p. A14.
Pakistani anger at the Taliban in tribal regions bordering Afghanistan is growing, and Pakistan's military leaders hope to capitalize on that anger as they mount a grueling campaign against insurgents in North and South Waziristan.

Reports and Studies

Campbell, Jason, Michael O'Hanlon and Jeremy Shapiro, "Assessing Counterinsurgency and Stabilization Missions," Brookings Institution, Policy Paper No. 14, May 2009, www.brookings.edu/~/media/Files/rc/papers/2009/05_counterinsurgency_ohanlon/05_counterinsurgency_ohanlon.pdf.
Brookings scholars examine the status of change in Afghanistan and Iraq and explain why "2009 is expected by many to be a pivotal year in Afghanistan."

Tellis, Ashley J., "Reconciling With the Taliban?" Carnegie Endowment for International Peace, 2009, www.carnegieendowment.org/files/reconciling_with_taliban.pdf.
Efforts at reconciliation today would undermine American credibility and jeopardize the success of the U.S.-led mission in Afghanistan, argues a senior associate at the endowment.

For More Information

American Foreign Policy Council, 509 C St., N.E., Washington, DC 20002; (202) 543-1006; www.afpc.org. Provides analysis on foreign-policy issues.

Brookings Institution, 1775 Massachusetts Ave., N.W., Washington, DC 20036; (202) 797-6000; www.brookings.edu. Liberal-oriented think tank that provides research, data and other resources on security and political conditions in Afghanistan and Pakistan and global counterterrorism.

Cato Institute, 1000 Massachusetts Ave., N.W., Washington, DC 20001; (202) 842-0200; www.cato.org. Libertarian-oriented think tank that provides analysis on U.S. policy toward Afghanistan and Pakistan.

RAND Corp., 1776 Main St., Santa Monica, CA 90401; (310) 393-0411; www.rand.org. Research organization that studies domestic and international policy issues.

United Nations Office on Drugs and Crime, U.N. Headquarters, DC1 Building, Room 613, One United Nations Plaza, New York, NY 10017; (212) 963-5698; www.unodc.org. Helps member states fight illicit drugs, crime and terrorism; compiles data on opium poppy production.

United States Institute of Peace, 1200 17th St., N.W., Washington, DC 20036; (202) 457-1700; www.usip.org. Provides analysis, training and other resources to prevent and end conflicts.

15

Government Secrecy

Alex Kingsbury

Pvt. Bradley Manning, the 23-year-old Army intelligence analyst suspected of providing WikiLeaks with thousands of classified documents, reportedly is being held in solitary confinement at the Quantico Marine Corps Base in Virginia. WikiLeaks' disclosure of classified diplomatic, military and intelligence documents has intensified the battle of words between open-government advocates and those who say too much transparency threatens national security.

From *CQ Researcher*,
Feb 11, 2011.

L ast summer, the biggest security breach ever to hit the U.S. government exploded on the international scene, but the leaker wasn't a renegade CIA operative or a National Security Agency mole.

It was a tousled 39-year-old former computer hacker from Australia named Julian Assange, founder of the controversial whistle-blowing website WikiLeaks. Aided by a shadowy band of associates in several countries, Assange has posted hundreds of thousands of classified U.S. military and State Department documents. His source may have been Bradley Manning, a U.S. Army private with access to one of the government's classified databases.

A small portion of the trove of hundreds of thousands of documents obtained by Assange, including sensitive diplomatic cables and combat field reports from Iraq and Afghanistan, has appeared in newspapers around the world, including *The New York Times*, and new leaks continue to emerge online.[1]

Last December, however, lawmakers condemned Assange and pressured the online shopping behemoth Amazon.com to stop hosting the controversial site on its powerful servers.

"WikiLeaks' illegal, outrageous and reckless acts have compromised our national security and put lives at risk around the world," declared Sen. Joseph Lieberman, I-Conn., chairman of the Senate Homeland Security and Governmental Affairs Committee. "No responsible company — whether American or foreign — should assist WikiLeaks in its efforts to disseminate these stolen materials."[2]

But not everyone agrees that groups like WikiLeaks are illegal or ought to be stifled.

Government Secrecy Efforts Increased

Government efforts to classify information* more than doubled in 2009 over 2008 and were nearly 10 times greater than in 1996 (line graph). The number of classification decisions increased largely because classifying agencies used new guidelines to provide more accurate data. However, the number of "original" decisions dropped from more than 500,000 in 1989 to fewer than 200,000 in 2009 (inset). The drop reflected a declining number of people and agencies with classification authority and a change in the way the number of classification decisions was tabulated by federal agencies.

Combined Original and Derivative Classification Activity, FY 1996-FY 2009

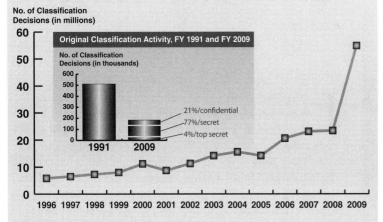

* Government information is classified in one of two ways: The initial determination that certain information must be protected — in other words a new secret created — is known as "original" classification; "derivative" classification involves the reuse of already classified information in a new form. There are three basic levels of classification: Top Secret, Secret, and Confidential.

Note: In 2009 67 percent of the information protected was designated for declassification in 10 years or less, the highest percentage to date.

Source: "Report to the President, 2009," Information Security Oversight Office, March 31, 2010

The conflicting views over WikiLeaks point to a much broader ideological rift between advocates of greater government transparency — conducting government business in full view of the public — and those who fear that loosening the secrecy reins could put the nation at risk.

President Barack Obama has satisfied neither side in the debate. On his first full day in office, Obama signed an executive order aimed at reducing government secrecy and increasing the flow of information across federal agencies. He also created the National Declassification Center to speed and coordinate the release of government information that no longer needed to be kept from public view. Both actions were designed to fulfill campaign pledges.

But critics say Obama has fallen short in fulfilling all the promises he made on the stump. For example, they note, the White House has invoked the "state secrets" privilege to thwart lawsuits challenging the jailing of people who leak sensitive information to the press.* Candidate Obama decried such legal maneuvers when his predecessor, George W. Bush, was in office.

"The administration's record on transparency is mixed," says Hina Shamsi, director of the National Security Project at the liberal American Civil Liberties Union. "The longer he is in office, the less importance secrecy reform appears to have. [Obama] should recommit to the ideals about openness and transparency that he invoked when he first took office."

Obama is hardly the first president to struggle with the secrecy issue. But the rise of the Internet as a tool to

"What is really going on here is a war over control of the Internet, and whether or not the Internet can actually serve its ultimate purpose — which is to allow citizens to band together and democratize the checks on the world's most powerful factions," *Salon.com*'s Glenn Greenwald, a lawyer and prominent civil liberties blogger, proclaimed soon after the Amazon affair unfolded.[3]

Indeed, a Norwegian lawmaker this month nominated WikiLeaks for a Nobel Prize, saying the site and its work promote world peace by disclosing government documents.[4]

* The state secrets privilege is a controversial rule of evidence whereby the government tells a court that its proceedings might disclose secret information and thereby endanger national security. Courts rarely deny or challenge a state secrets claim.

disseminate sensitive information, coupled with international tensions wrought by the Sept. 11, 2001, terror attacks and the wars in Iraq and Afghanistan, have brought the issue to a boil.

And nothing has raised the temperature of the debate as much as the WikiLeaks controversy. To fully understand it, one must first know about a little-known Defense Department computer network that sounds like it was conjured up by a Hollywood sci-fi screenwriter. Known as SIPRNet — Secret Internet Protocol Router Network — the system allows the U.S. military, the State Department and other agencies around the globe to share classified information. Although the information is supposed to be protected from prying eyes, nearly 500,000 people have access to it — from senior military and law-enforcement officials to low-level military analysts and government contractors.[5]

That accessibility apparently contributed to the WikiLeaks affair. Pvt. Manning, a 23-year-old intelligence analyst with SIPRNet access, is suspected of downloading the classified military communiqués and diplomatic cables from the Defense Department computer system while he was deployed in Iraq.[6] According to friends, Manning was despondent after being demoted for fighting with a fellow soldier and felt that his military career was headed nowhere.[7] He was arrested on suspicion of unauthorized disclosure of classified information and reportedly is being held under harsh conditions at the Marine Corps Base in Quantico, Va.

Last summer Assange gave the documents to selected media outlets, including *The Times*. Recently, the paper's executive editor, Bill Keller, described a prickly relationship with Assange. "Julian Assange has been heard to boast that he served as a kind of puppet master, recruiting several news organizations, forcing them to work in concert and choreographing their work. This is characteristic braggadocio," Keller wrote in a long article last month detailing the paper's WikiLeaks dealings.[8]

In the end, several international newspapers besides *The Times* — Britain's *The Guardian*, France's *Le Monde* and Madrid's *El Pais* — plus the German newsmagazine *Der Spiegel* — published some of the documents, along with articles explaining the significance of the material. Some names and other information in the WikiLeaks files were redacted, or blacked out.[9]

The documents did not expose the government's most sensitive secrets, many of which are kept off SIPRNet because of its wide accessibility.[10] Still, the disclosures were explosive. They marked the first time in history that such a large collection of candid communiqués among diplomats and military officials was exposed to public view. What's more, publication spurred concern that human-rights workers, government informants and collaborators mentioned in the dispatches could be identified and put at personal risk.

Defense Secretary Robert Gates condemned the leaks but suggested that fears of their effects on American foreign policy have been exaggerated.

Yet politicians in both parties have expressed deep outrage over what they view as WikiLeaks' compromise of national security. Democrats objected even though they previously supported leaks exposing controversial national security practices such as warrantless wiretapping during the Bush administration. Republicans are upset even though they earlier praised the publication of stolen e-mails suggesting that some climatologists tried to hide evidence that undermined their global warming research.

Lieberman, an Independent who has sided with Republicans on many foreign-policy issues, said, "The recent dissemination by WikiLeaks . . . is just the latest example of how our national security interests, the interests of our allies, and the safety of government employees and countless other individuals are jeopardized by the illegal release of classified and sensitive information." Lieberman's statement came as he introduced legislation making it a federal crime to publish the name of a U.S. intelligence source.[11]

The WikiLeaks disclosures have already had a far-reaching impact on government operations. The State Department suspended its use of SIPRNet, forcing the military and diplomatic corps to share less information with each other than in the past. The government also has warned human-rights activists, foreign officials and others who have been identified in leaked diplomatic cables that they could be in jeopardy; some have been moved to more secure sites.[12] In addition, foreign leaders reportedly have become more reluctant to candidly discuss issues with U.S. diplomats.[13]

Efforts to discourage information-sharing are viewed as troubling in light of a government panel's conclusion that the failure of federal agencies to share intelligence information aided the 9/11 terrorists.[14]

Half of Pages Reviewed Were Declassified

Federal agencies declassified more than 28 million pages of government data in 2009, or about 55 percent of the 52 million pages it reviewed. The number of pages declassified dropped 8 percent from the previous year. The percentage of pages declassified has remained constant at 55 percent of total pages reviewed since 2004.

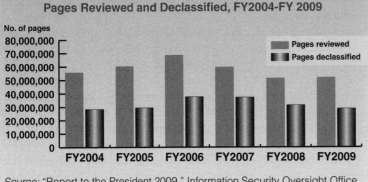

Pages Reviewed and Declassified, FY2004-FY 2009

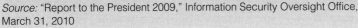

Source: "Report to the President 2009," Information Security Oversight Office, March 31, 2010

Meanwhile, Congress and some government agencies have told employees not to download classified material from the WikiLeaks site.

The leaks may also affect broader transparency efforts far into the future, including fulfilling Freedom of Information Act (FOIA) requests made by government watchdog groups and the news media, some analysts say.

Media representatives have been wary in their dealings with Assange.[15] Keller wrote that *The Times* was "confident that reporting on the secret documents could be done within the law." But, he said, the paper's editors "felt an enormous moral and ethical obligation to use the material responsibly. . . . From the beginning, we agreed that in our articles and in any documents we published from the secret archive, we would excise material that could put lives at risk."[16]

Reporters Without Borders, an international organization that promotes press freedom, was more equivocal. In a scathing letter to Assange, general secretary Jean-François Julliard charged, "The precedent you have set leaves all those people throughout the world who risk their freedom and sometimes their lives for the sake of online information even more exposed to reprisals."[17] Yet Reporters Without Borders also has lashed out at attempts to stifle WikiLeaks. "It is up to the courts, not

politicians, to decide whether or not a website should be closed," it declared in December.[18]

WikiLeaks' staunchest defenders have cast it as a modern-day whistle-blowers' clearinghouse, saying that its disclosures show evidence of government malfeasance on the scale of the top-secret Pentagon Papers, which were leaked to *The Times* and *The Washington Post* in 1971 and revealed official misgivings and deception about the Vietnam War.[19]

But critics have another view of WikiLeaks. "I think a lot of their talk about fighting injustice is pretty woolly and a little hard to take seriously," said Steven Aftergood, editor of *Secrecy News*, a Web publication of the Federation of American Scientists. * "[T]here are lots of potential consequences of just this latest release that may turn out to be really positive and constructive, including a change of course in the war, perhaps, and there are potential consequences that are disastrous, including the potential loss of life and future difficulties in assembling new intelligence networks, because sources will lack confidence that the U.S. can keep the secrets it commits to keeping."[20]

As the government tries to manage vast amounts of sensitive information in the age of WikiLeaks, here are some questions being asked:

Has WikiLeaks threatened national security?

To be sure, the WikiLeaks documents embarrassed the U.S. government. They document the deaths of civilians in war zones, the close relations that the United States has with some despotic regimes and countless other details, both explosive and mundane, that were never meant for public consumption.

---

* Aftergood directs the federation's Project on Government Secrecy, which promotes the reform of official secrecy practices. In 1997 his Freedom of Information Act lawsuit against the CIA led to the declassification and publication of a prior year's intelligence budget, for the first time in 50 years.

In some instances, the documents also show that the U.S. government has lied. A case in point: For years the Pentagon insisted publicly that it was not keeping a tally of Iraqi civilians and soldiers killed during the war and that counts provided by private aid groups and journalists were wildly inflated. In reality, the Pentagon did keep count, and its numbers were, if anything, slightly higher than the most widely cited press tallies.[21]

But does embarrassment and scandal rise to the level of a national security threat?

Defense Secretary Gates denounced the release of thousands of once secret battlefield reports from troops in Iraq and Afghanistan, but sounded a word of caution. "I've heard the impact of these releases on our foreign policy described as a meltdown, as a game-changer and so on. I think those descriptions are fairly significantly overwrought," Gates said.

"The fact is, governments deal with the United States because it's in their interest, not because they like us, not because they trust us and not because they believe we can keep secrets. Many governments — some governments — deal with us because they fear us, some because they respect us, most because they need us. We are still essentially, as has been said before, the indispensable nation."[22]

Concerns over the disclosures have centered on two issues. First, that those who had provided information to, or cooperated with, the U.S. government — on the battlefield in Afghanistan, for instance — would face immediate reprisal. Second, that the release sowed mistrust that would make governments and individuals unwilling to cooperate candidly with the government in the future, for fear they would later be identified in leaked documents.

The first concern has been the more immediate and serious. In the wake of the first release of Afghan documents last July, Admiral Mike Mullen, chairman of the Joint Chiefs of Staff, put it bluntly: "Mr. Assange can say whatever he likes about the greater good he thinks he and his source are doing, but the truth is they might already have on their hands the blood of some young soldier or that of an Afghan family."[23]

Highlighting what it sees as the seriousness of the issue, the State Department released a letter to WikiLeaks from its legal adviser, Harold Koh, warning that the site was jeopardizing "the lives of countless innocent individuals — from journalists to human-rights activists and

bloggers to soldiers to individuals providing information to further peace and security."

John Bellinger III, a State Department legal adviser in the Bush administration from 2005-2009, says WikiLeaks undoubtedly caused damage, especially regarding the willingness of people to cooperate with the U.S. government in the future. "What if WikiLeaks had published the internal source list for Human Rights Watch, which relies on confidential sources to write its reports?" he asks. "Not many people would agree that transparency in that case was a good idea. Foreign Service officers routinely meet with dissidents, human-rights workers [and] environmental activists, and they do good work that may be compromised."

But months after the leaks were published, nearly 100 government intelligence analysts reported to Congress that the disclosures had done little actual damage to U.S. national interests. "We were told [by intelligence analysts that the impact of WikiLeaks revelations] was embarrassing but not damaging," a government official familiar with the report told the Reuters news agency.[24] The State Department did note, however, that it helped relocate a small number of people who had been compromised through the release of the documents.[25]

Some intelligence experts say the release of sensitive information may actually have had benefits. The documents showed frequent duplicity on the part of foreign governments. The Yemeni president, for instance, allowed U.S. forces to operate in his country and lied about it to the country's parliament.[26] On the other hand, the State Department comes across as rather honest, experts say. As Blake Hounshell, managing editor of *Foreign Policy* magazine noted, WikiLeaks actually showed that "the U.S. is remarkably consistent in what it says publicly and privately."[27]

But others contend that analysis misses the point. "Undermining the confidentiality of diplomatic communication harms our national security all by itself," says Stephen Sestanovich, a former U.S. diplomat and current fellow at the Council on Foreign Relations. "Yes, the leaks may show that American diplomats are good, honest, capable people, but that isn't reason enough to think that the affair helps us."

Others have mixed views. Professor Peter Feaver, who heads the Triangle Institute for Security Studies at Duke University, says the WikiLeaks disclosures have imposed "costs on friends and allies in other countries who trusted us, making diplomacy and cooperation harder, feeding noxious conspiracy theories and contributing to an image of a weak administration incapable of protecting items it has claimed must be kept secret to protect our national security." Then again, he says, "for fair-minded and careful observers, many of the files disprove certain critiques of the United States and so, in this limited sense, there are some silver linings."

Should the government prosecute Julian Assange?

Attorney General Eric Holder announced in December that the Justice Department was considering prosecuting Assange. Meanwhile, a *Washington Post*/ABC News poll found that some 60 percent of Americans want the WikiLeaks founder arrested and charged with something.[28] (Assange faces unrelated sex-crime accusations in Sweden.) But legal experts say it will be difficult to prosecute Assange for the disclosure of the classified government documents, primarily because it is unclear whether he broke any U.S. laws when he received and posted them online.

The government doesn't normally have the right to stop publication of stolen classified material, the Supreme Court ruled in the Pentagon Papers case.[29] In another important case, *Barnicki v. Vopper*, the court said the press has the right to publish truthful information that is leaked, even if the leaker gained the information illegally.[30] In fact, the government has never successfully prosecuted a media organization for a leak. Nor is there a law criminalizing the simple disclosure of classified information. In 2000, President Bill Clinton vetoed a bill that would have explicitly criminalized all leaking.[31]

The most likely approach to prosecuting Assange would be under the Espionage Act, which prohibits the "willful" disclosure of "information relating to the national defense." Courts have interpreted that to mean that the defendant must know the information will hurt national security and that disclosure violates the law. But what constitutes harm to national security can be a highly contentious issue.

"Here, Assange can make the department's case especially difficult," contends Baruch Weiss, a lawyer who has defended clients against charges of violating the Espionage Act. "Well before publishing the cables, he wrote a letter to the U.S. government, delivered to our ambassador in London, inviting suggestions for redactions."[32] The

government declined that offer and demanded that the documents be returned.

Adding to the confusion is the fact that the Espionage Act refers to "national security," not "national defense." Experts say it is unclear how the two concepts may differ. Indeed, lawyers reviewing the WikiLeaks situation have noted that the first witness called in Assange's defense could theoretically be Defense Secretary Gates, who said the leaks were likely to cause the nation minimal long-term damage.

But the limitations of existing law shouldn't dissuade the government from pursuing prosecution, others argue. "The Obama administration should, within the limits of the law, of course, seek to indict and prosecute those who have stolen classified documents, particularly when they have done so with the express purpose of hurting the United States, as Assange has done," says Duke University's Feaver.

If anything, prosecution should be considered for its deterrent value, Kenneth Wainstein, former assistant attorney general for national security, told a congressional committee in December. "If Assange and WikiLeaks pay no penalty for their recent audacious releases, that sense of security will become one of invulnerability, they will redouble their efforts to match or exceed their recent exploits, and copycat operations will start to appear throughout the Internet," he said.[33] Wainstein thinks the government stands a "fighting chance" of successfully prosecuting the case.

But the problem with prosecuting Assange under the Espionage Act, media and civil liberties groups say, is that such a judicial remedy could just as easily be turned against traditional news outlets that publish stories based on the leaks of classified information.[34] The ACLU's Shamsi says any effort to prosecute Assange would be catastrophic for the news media. "From what we know in the public record, there's no difference between what Julian Assange has done that is any different than what's done by *The New York Times*. Criminalizing the publication of classified information is not the step that the government should take. It would have a chilling effect on the First Amendment."

But that chilling effect would be a good thing, argues historian Gabriel Schoenfeld, author of *Necessary Secrets: National Security, the Media, and the Rule of Law*. "In publishing leaked materials, journalists indefatigably demand openness in government and claim to defend the people's 'right to know,' " he told a congressional panel in December. "But along with the public's 'right to know,' constantly invoked by the press, there is also something rarely spoken about, let alone defended: namely the public's right not to know."[35]

Is too much government information classified?

Over the past 50 years, a half-dozen commissions have examined classification, and all came to essentially the same conclusion: Too much information is kept from the public, and the practice runs contrary to the national interest. One advocacy group estimated that in 2009 the government spent at least $196 maintaining secrets already on the books for every dollar it spent declassifying documents.[36]

Obama talked frequently on the campaign trail about a culture of transparency. And on his first day in office he relaxed Bush administration restrictions on photographing the return of service members killed in combat, posted more government documents online and ordered his agencies to be more transparent with the public. But advocates of open government argue that isn't enough.

"Too much government information is being classified," says Lucy Dalglish, who heads the Reporters Committee for Freedom of the Press.

Yet, even trying to understand how much information is classified, and why, is difficult. For instance, in 2005 the federal government had 50 different designations for secret information. Many of those categories, such as "sensitive but unclassified," were improvised — meaning that there was neither clear legal precedent for their creation nor clear avenues for declassification.[37] Congress has taken steps in recent years to standardize those designations and reduce the number of people authorized to classify information.

The Reducing Over-Classification Act, signed into law by Obama in October 2010, directs the Department

Freedom of Information Requests Dropped

The number of public requests for government records under the Freedom of Information Act (FOIA) dropped 8 percent from 2008 to 2009. Meanwhile, the cost of processing FOIA requests rose to nearly $400 million in the past decade.

Freedom of Information Act Requests and Costs, 1999-2009*

Year	FOIA requests received	Total cost of FOIA
1999	1,908,083	$286,546,488
2000	2,174,570	$253,049,516
2001	2,188,799	$287,792,041
2002	2,429,980	$300,105,324
2003	3,266,394	$323,050,337
2004	4,080,737	$336,763,628
2005	19,950,547	$334,853,222
2006	21,412,736	$304,280,766
2007	21,758,628	$352,935,673
2008	605,471	$338,677,544
2009	557,825	$382,244,225

* Year-to-year figures are not comparable because some agencies included Privacy Act numbers in their annual totals.

Source: "Secrecy Report Card 2010," OpentheGovernment.org

of Homeland Security and the intelligence community to standardize classification and declassification procedures and improve information sharing across the government. The importance of sharing information has been an important motivator for reform. After the 9/11 attacks, numerous reviews cited a failure to share information among different agencies — often for fear of disclosure — as a critical failing of the government in the run-up to the disaster.

Yet the government does need to do some things in private, experts say. Bellinger, the former State Department legal adviser, says that while the government may overclassify some information, the problem is perhaps exaggerated by transparency advocates. "There's probably no one who has served in government who hasn't seen something that was classified that probably shouldn't have been," he says. "But I think that it's more of a peripheral problem."

So, how much secrecy is too much? Rodney McDaniel, National Security Council secretary in the

WikiLeaks Sheds Light on U.S. Diplomatic Actions

Thousands of cables posted by the controversial website WikiLeaks have put the U.S. State Department and its allies under the spotlight. Notable disclosures include payment to other nations in exchange for accepting Guantánamo detainees, suspected corruption in the Afghan government and potential Korean unification.

• **Yemen takes responsibility for attacks.** The Yemeni government covered up American drone attacks against al-Qaida in the country by saying the attacks were its own. "We'll continue saying the bombs are ours, not yours," President Ali Abdullah Saleh told Gen. David Petraeus in January 2010.

• **China hacks Google.** The Chinese government initiated a cyberattack on Google's computer network in January 2010, according to what a contact told the U.S. Embassy in Beijing. Attacks were also targeted against the computers and e-mail accounts of adversaries such as the Dalai Lama.

• **Saudi King pushes for U.S. strike against Iran.** King Abdullah of Saudi Arabia has repeatedly pleaded for the United States to attack Iran. "Cut off the head of the snake," he said in 2008, referring to a military strike against Iran's nuclear program.

• **U.S. pays others to take in Guantánamo detainees.** U.S. authorities, in an effort to resettle Guantánamo detainees, offered the island nation of Kiribati millions of dollars to accept Chinese Muslim prisoners. Slovenian officials were offered a meeting with President Obama in exchange for accepting a former prisoner.

• **Korean unification discussed.** American and South Korean officials have presented plans to unite North and South Korea after a collapse of the North. They floated the idea of persuading China to accept unification in exchange for economic incentives.

• **Corruption suspected in Afghan government.** During a visit by Afghan Vice President Ahmed Zia Massoud to the United Arab Emirates in 2009, officials from the U.S. Drug Enforcement Administration discovered that he was carrying $52 million in cash, which they ultimately allowed him to keep without revealing its source.

Sources: "The 9 Most Shocking WikiLeaks Secrets," The Daily Beast, Nov. 28, 2010, www.thedailybeast.com/blogs-and-stories/2010-11-28/wikileaks-documents-chinas-google-hack-un-spying-more-secrets/full/; Scott Shane and Andrew W. Lehren, "Leaked Cables Offer Raw Look at U.S. Diplomacy," The New York Times, Nov. 28, 2010, www.nytimes.com/2010/11/29/world/29cables.html?pagewanted=all; The Telegraph, www.telegraph.co.uk.

Reagan administration, estimated 20 years ago that only 10 percent of what the government classified was for the "legitimate protection of secrets," implying that the government should reveal 90 percent of its protected data.[38]

Former New Jersey Gov. Thomas Kean, co-chair of the 9/11 Commission, said after reviewing thousands of documents related to the terror attacks that "maybe 60 to 70 percent of the materials that I went over that are classified shouldn't have been."[39]

Meanwhile, over the past 15 years, the Interagency Security Classification Appeals Panel, where denied FOIA requests are appealed, has overruled agency secrecy claims in whole or in part in about two-thirds of its cases.[40]

Tom Blanton, head of the National Security Archive, a nonprofit research organization that collects and publishes declassified government documents, says his group has found dozens of examples of identical documents that are both classified and unclassified at the same time, "sometimes with different versions from different agencies or different reviewers, all because the secrecy is so subjective and overdone."

And while there are many examples of information redacted in one document and released in another, what may get lost in the debate is the corrosive effect the sometimes arbitrary secrecy decisions have on the public debate. Jack Goldsmith, who headed the Office of Legal Counsel in the Bush administration, said, "A root cause of the perception of illegitimacy inside the government that led to leaking (and then to occasional irresponsible reporting) is, ironically, excessive government secrecy."[41]

BACKGROUND

Growth of Secrecy

The country's oldest official secret is a recipe for invisible ink that predates World War I. The information remains classified, not because the recipe is still in use (though it may be), but because it is evidence of the intelligence community's "sources and methods," which are exempt from declassification laws.[42]

In 1916, as the United States edged closer to entering the war, German saboteurs destroyed a munitions dump in New Jersey with an explosive blast so powerful that it was heard as far away as Maryland, and shrapnel hit the Statue of Liberty. The next year, the country joined the war, and Congress passed the Espionage Act, which made disclosure of information related to the national defense a crime.

Soon after, Congress passed laws that criminalized "treasonable utterances," while President Woodrow Wilson pushed to expand the scope of the Espionage Act to include "profane, scurrilous, or abusive language about the form of government . . . the Constitution . . . or the flag of the United States, or the uniform of the Army and Navy."[43]

Former President Theodore Roosevelt aptly captured the zeitgeist when he said that "the men who oppose the war; who fail to support the government in every measure which really tends to the efficient prosecution of the war; and above all who in any shape or way champion the cause and the actions of Germany, show themselves to be the Huns within our own gates and the allies of men whom our sons and brothers are crossing the ocean to fight."[44]

The emergence of the United States as a global military power during and after World War II led to what critics say is a system that keeps too much government information secret.

By the early years of the Cold War, overclassification was already identified as a problem in need of remedy. The 1956 Coolidge Committee, led by Assistant Defense Secretary Charles Coolidge, identified widespread overclassification and traced it to a chaotic and largely unaccountable classification system.[45] Subsequently, the Wright and Moss commissions, in 1957 and 1958, respectively, came to nearly identical conclusions.[46]

Even as the Defense Department and other agencies kept more and more information secret, there was competing pressure for citizens, businesses, and others to make more government business transparent. The growth in government regulation, in particular, created a need to publish more information and increased demand for that information from businesses, journalists and others.

The 1935 Federal Register Act mandated the daily publication of agency regulations, executive orders, and presidential orders. A decade later, the Administrative Procedure Act of 1946 directed federal agencies to allow the public to participate in the rule-making process.[47]

In 1966, a reluctant Lyndon B. Johnson signed the Freedom of Information Act (FOIA), which allowed public access to government records. (He did so, however, in a ceremony closed to the public, and he attached a statement that limited the law's reach.) As first written, the law set no minimum times for agencies to respond to requests, no penalties for noncompliance and no minimum fees that agencies could charge. Amendments to the law addressed some of those issues, such as requiring a 20-day response time and capping fees — and in some cases waiving them altogether.

Though FOIA receives much attention in discussions about government transparency, critics note that it only provides the public with a way to try to access government records — and only some of those records. It doesn't address the issue of overclassification, nor does it change the procedures government officials use to make documents secret in the first place.[48]

During the 1960s, conflicts arose with the FBI and the CIA over secret practices and classified documents. Investigations detailing the CIA's overthrow of foreign governments and a host of other controversial actions led to calls for stricter congressional oversight and greater transparency.

The FBI, meanwhile, was forced to answer questions about infiltrating and subverting the civil rights and anti-war movements. Later investigations by the 1975 Church

Committee, chaired by Sen. Frank Church, D-Idaho, found that the CIA had, among other things, spied on Americans, assassinated some foreign leaders and overthrown others, and administered the drug LSD ("acid") to unwitting human test subjects, all in secret.

At the same time, the classification of other government information was growing. In 1970, the Defense Science Board's Task Force on Secrecy concluded that the amount of scientific and technical information that was being classified "could profitably be decreased perhaps as much as 90 percent by limiting the amount of information classified and the duration of its classification."[49]

The board recommended limiting the classification of most technical and scientific information to five years, but the recommendation was ignored. It also noted the costs of keeping secrets, both in terms of dollars and also the harm to an informed public and the suppression of innovation. In addition, the board said that "secrecy has limited effectiveness. . . . Classification may sometimes be more effective in withholding information from our friends than from potential enemies."[50]

In 1971, open-government advocates won their most significant victory when the Supreme Court denied an effort by the Nixon administration to halt publication of the Pentagon Papers, a classified study of U.S. involvement in Vietnam. Daniel Ellsberg, a defense analyst turned anti-war activist, leaked the study to *The Times* and *The Washington Post*, which began to publish the study before the Justice Department contended the government had the right to block publication.

In a 6-3 ruling against the Nixon administration, the Supreme Court held that the government had failed to meet the high constitutional burden required to justify press censorship. Justice Potter Stewart, who voted with the majority, wrote that "the only effective restraint upon executive policy and power in the areas of national defense and international affairs may lie in an enlightened citizenry — in an informed and critical public opinion which alone can here protect the values of democratic government."[51]

History proved that the Pentagon Papers didn't damage national security. In 1989, Erwin Griswold, who as Nixon's solicitor general argued the government's position but was barred from seeing the documents at issue, called the case an instance of "massive overclassification." He said he saw

no "trace of a threat to the national security" in what was eventually published in the press.[52]

Secrecy Blowback

The Pentagon Papers case, coupled with growing consumer-rights and open-government movements in the 1970s, spurred even greater public calls for transparency. In 1974, Congress overhauled FOIA and overturned a veto by President Gerald Ford aimed at nullifying the changes. The amendments provided for judicial review of contested declassification decisions and narrowed exemptions enjoyed by law enforcement agencies. They also mandated a 10-day response time for FOIA requests.

Presidents in the past few decades have pushed the margins of FOIA in various directions. In the late 1970s and early '80s the Carter administration generally expanded government transparency and liberalized classification policy. For instance, the administration specified that those with classification authority must use the lowest necessary level of classification as their default position.

In the 1980s, the Reagan administration tightened government control of information, directing officials to use the highest level of classification as their default and broadening exemptions that agencies could claim to deny FOIA requests.[53] In 1984, Congress passed the Central Intelligence Agency Information Act, putting most CIA records essentially off-limits to FOIA requests. Nevertheless, overclassification was still seen as a problem. In 1985, a Pentagon review, the Stilwell Commission, concluded once again that "too much information appears to be classified and at much higher levels than is warranted."[54] The panel's recommendations, including the simplification of the classification system, were ignored.

Some Reagan-era restrictions to FOIA were rolled back during Clinton's presidency. In 1995, he signed an executive order allowing the public to request access to classified documents that are at least 25 years old, provided that their disclosure doesn't demonstrably damage national security. The order also established the Interagency Security Classification Appeals Panel to hear appeals to denied disclosure requests.

A year later, another Clinton order required agencies responding to FOIA requests to make their records available electronically. It also lengthened the maximum

CHRONOLOGY

1960s–1970s *Open-government and consumer-rights groups push for more public access to information.*

1966 President Lyndon B. Johnson signs Freedom of Information Act (FOIA).

1971 Supreme Court refuses Nixon administration's plea to stop publication of Pentagon Papers.

1974 Congress strengthens FOIA by setting deadlines for agencies to release information and providing for judicial review. . . . Privacy Act allows individuals to see information the government has compiled about them.

1978 Presidential Records Act mandates release of presidential papers 12 years after an administration ends.

1980s *Reagan administration resists transparency.*

1982 President Ronald Reagan eliminates requirement that government documents eventually be declassified.

1986 Congress broadens FOIA exemption for law enforcement materials.

1990s *Clinton administration allows greater access to government information.*

1995 President Bill Clinton orders a 25-year limit on secrecy classification unless the information would harm national security.

1996 Electronic Freedom of Information Act requires agencies to make requested records available in electronic format whenever possible.

1997 Commission on Protecting and Reducing Government Secrecy headed by Sen. Daniel Patrick Moynihan, D-N.Y., criticizes excessive secrecy and calls for various reforms; proposed legislation fails.

2000s–Present *President George W. Bush expands scope of government secrecy.*

2000 President Bill Clinton vetoes bill criminalizing leaking of classified information.

2001 January: Energy task force headed by Vice President Dick Cheney meets secretly. . . . September: After 9/11 terrorist attacks, government secrecy expands exponentially. . . . USA Patriot Act further limits the release of information related to national security and terrorism investigations. . . . November: Bush signs executive order allowing White House or former presidents to veto the release of presidential papers.

2005 American Civil Liberties Union wins court ruling for release of additional photos of detainee abuse at Abu Ghraib prison in Baghdad.

2007 WikiLeaks is launched with mandate to "expose oppressive regimes."

2009 Jan. 21: On his first full day in office, President Obama signs executive order directing agencies to make more information public; establishes National Declassification Center at the National Archives; and orders study of classification system reforms. . . . May: Obama administration reneges on an earlier promise and withholds publication of additional Abu Ghraib photos, calling their release a danger to combat troops. . . . September: In a victory for open-government advocates, the director of national intelligence for the first time reveals the current U.S. intelligence budget. . . . By the end of fiscal 2009, the number of "original classification decisions" (new secrets) has decreased 10 percent from the previous year. . . . November: WikiLeaks publishes e-mails suggesting British climate scientists had fudged research data; a later investigation disproves those claims.

2010 July: In coordination with several media partners, including *The Guardian* (London) and *The New York Times*, WikiLeaks publishes thousands of classified military reports from Iraq and Afghanistan, as well as State Department cables dating back decades. . . . Oct. 7: Obama signs Reducing Over-Classification Act mandating evaluations by agency inspector generals' offices and other oversight bodies. . . . Nov. 30: Amazon. com stops hosting WikiLeaks. . . . Dec. 1: Interpol places Assange on its most-wanted list in connection with sexual misconduct accusations in Sweden. . . . Dec. 10: Former WikiLeaks employees announce plans to launch a rival site, OpenLeaks. . . . Dec. 16: Assange is released on bail in London as he prepares to fight extradition to Sweden.

Secrets of the Man Behind WikiLeaks

By age 16, Julian Assange had become the master hacker known as "Mendax."

Long before Julian Assange launched WikiLeaks and became a crusader — both celebrated and vilified — against government secrecy worldwide, he was no ordinary hacker.

Calling himself "Mendax," he prided himself on his uncanny ability to hack into secure computer networks — including those belonging to the Department of Defense and the national nuclear laboratory in Los Alamos, N.M. That was back in 1987, before most households had personal computers, when Assange was 16 years old.[1]

Since then, Assange has turned networked computers worldwide into a giant farm, of sorts, from which he harvests the secrets that have made him and his website notorious. For his efforts, Assange has won a medal from Amnesty International for publishing material about extrajudicial killings in Kenya.[2] Politicians in the United States, meanwhile, have called for Assange — an Australian citizen — to be tried for treason; others have called for his assassination.[3]

Though Assange has never claimed to be a journalist, many see him as a 21st-century, wired-world version of one, albeit with some ethical caveats. Daniel Ellsberg, the one-time defense analyst who leaked the Pentagon Papers during the Vietnam War, called Assange a hero in December,

shortly before chaining himself to a fence at the White House in protest of the wars in Iraq and Afghanistan. Ellsberg sees "fundamental similarities" between the Pentagon Papers and the WikiLeaks document dumps related to the Iraq and Afghanistan wars.[4] Indeed, some credit Assange with "one of the greatest journalistic scoops of the last 30 years."[5]

Assange launched WikiLeaks in 2006 specifically to end government secrecy through the leaking and publication of information. "The more secretive or unjust an organization is, the more leaks induce fear and paranoia in its leadership," Assange wrote. He said that, faced with sufficient threats to its ability to keep secrets, sclerotic organizations are forced to either adapt and improve or face collapse. Keeping secrets inside an organization, he added, results in a "secrecy tax" as a result of inefficiency.[6]

Since WikiLeaks went online three years ago, it has published military manuals on detainee treatment at Guantánamo Bay, Cuba; the so-called "climate-gate" e-mails from scientists at the University of East Anglia; the contents of Sarah Palin's personal e-mail account; and thousands of stolen and formerly classified military and diplomatic reports from the U.S. government. In the past few

---

response time from 10 to 20 days, as the shorter deadlines had proved largely unworkable. By 1997, Clinton had authorized 20 federal officials to classify materials as "top secret," a cadre that a few years later expanded to include more than 1,300 "original classifiers." Today, some 4,407 people have that authority, not to mention the 140,000 plus people who have the authority to stamp less important materials "secret."[55]

But even as FOIA was allowing the public greater access to government documents, the classification system continued to raise concerns. In 1994, a commission reported to the secretary of Defense that "[d]espite the best of intentions, the classification system, largely unchanged since the Eisenhower administration, has grown out of control."[56]

Three years after that, the Commission on Protecting and Reducing Government Secrecy, headed by Sen. Daniel

Patrick Moynihan, D-N.Y., concluded that "[t]he classification system, for example, is used too often to deny the public an understanding of the policymaking process, rather than for the necessary protection of intelligence activities and other highly sensitive matters." Accompanying that condemnation of the status quo was a series of modest recommendations on how to fix the system. Congress ignored them. A bill enacting the changes expired without coming to a vote.

From the outset of his presidency, George W. Bush ramped up government secrecy. The Bush administration was so diligent in its effort to remove government information from public view that it classified information on the vulnerabilities of drinking-water supplies, data on airline safety and the exposure of communities to dangerous chemicals. The administration even limited the disclosure of car tire safety data submitted to the government by

months, Assange has claimed to have other, equally explosive troves of documents, including Swiss banking records,[7] the contents of a U.S. bank executive's hard drive[8] and documentation of corruption in Russia.[9]

But Assange's personal behavior has been as controversial as his projects. Bill Keller, executive editor of *The New York Times*, which published redacted versions of military documents and State Department cables provided by WikiLeaks, called him "elusive, manipulative and volatile." Last year, when a disgruntled WikiLeaks employee provided journalists with copies of some unpublished WikiLeaks material, Assange threatened to sue, claiming that he had a financial interest in keeping his stolen secrets secret.[10]

And last year, Assange turned himself in to authorities in England in connection with sex-crime allegations against him in Sweden at the same time that WikiLeaks began releasing the stolen State Department cables. In what many commentators called a delicious irony, the police report on the incident in question was leaked to a British newspaper, which one of Assange's close supporters called "a selective smear through the disclosure of material."[11]

A full hearing on Sweden's request for Assange's extradition began Feb. 7.

— Alex Kingsbury

[1] Raffi Khatchadourian, "No Secrets: Julian Assange's mission for total transparency," *The New Yorker*, June 7, 2010, www.wired.com/threatlevel/2010/06/assange-newyorker/.

[2] "Amnesty announces Media Awards," Amnesty International, June 2, 2009, www.amnesty.org.uk/news_details.asp?NewsID=18227.

[3] Alex Newman, "WikiLeak's Assange Accuses Some Critics of Terror, Calls for Prosecution," *New American*, Jan. 4, 2010, www.thenewamerican.com/index.php/world-mainmenu-26/north-america-mainmenu-36/5752-wikileaks-assange-accuses-some-critics-of-terror-calls-for-prosecution.

[4] Cameron Joseph, "Ellsberg Calls Assange a Hero," *The National Journal*, Dec. 16, 2010, http://nationaljournal.com/nationalsecurity/from-the-pentagon-papers-to-wikileaks-daniel-ellsberg-calls-julian-assange-a-hero-20101216.

[5] Sarah Ellison, "The Man Who Spilled the Secrets," *Vanity Fair*, February 2011, www.vanityfair.com/politics/features/2011/02/the-guardian-201102.

[6] Julian Assange, "Selected Correspondence," http://web.archive.org/web/20071020051936/http://iq.org/.

[7] Ed Vulliamy, "Swiss whistleblower Rudolf Elmer plans to hand over offshore banking secrets of the rich and famous to WikiLeaks," *The Guardian*, Jan. 16, 2011, www.guardian.co.uk/media/2011/jan/16/swiss-whistleblower-rudolf-elmer-banks.

[8] Sarah Halzack, "Bank of American braces for WikiLeaks," *The Washington Post*, Jan. 3, 2011, http://voices.washingtonpost.com/political-economy/2011/01/bank_of_america_prepares_for_p.html.

[9] Fred Weir, "WikiLeaks ready to drop a bombshell on Russia. But will Russians get to read about it?" *The Christian Science Monitor*, Oct. 26, 2010, www.csmonitor.com/World/Europe/2010/1026/WikiLeaks-ready-to-drop-a-bombshell-on-Russia.-But-will-Russians-get-to-read-about-it.

[10] Sarah Ellison, "The Man Who Spilled the Secrets," *Vanity Fair*, February 2011, www.vanityfair.com/politics/features/2011/02/the-guardian-201102.

[11] David Leppard, "Lawyers cry foul over leak of Julian Assange sex-case papers," *The Australian*, Dec. 20, 2010, www.theaustralian.com.au/news/world/lawyers-cry-foul-over-leak-of-julian-assange-sex-case-papers/story-e6frg6so-1225973548657.

tire manufacturers in the wake of hundreds of tire-related crashes and deaths. Bush also reversed the Clinton order to classify information at the lowest possible level.

In the wake of the 9/11 attacks, government secrecy expanded greatly. Despite the fact that the 9/11 Commission later concluded that secrecy within the government was a contributing factor in the failure to disrupt al-Qaida's plans to attack the United States, the government went on a classification binge.

In 2002, Bush issued an order making it easier to reclassify information that previously had been declassified. Some reclassifications occurred as early as 1999 but greatly accelerated after the 2001 attacks. More than 55,000 documents were taken off the public shelves of the National Archives and marked classified. The details of what was re-classified and why were also classified. The effort even reclassified some documents that had been widely published in the State Department's own publicly available series, "The Foreign Relations of the United States."[57]

The War on Transparency

In the early 1950s, the widows of three crewmen killed in a military plane crash filed a wrongful death suit against the government. They wanted officials to release the crash report, but the government argued that it couldn't do so without compromising national security because the plane carried secret radio gear.[58] It was the first invocation of what came to be known as the "state secrets" privilege. At the time, fearing future abuse, the court admonished the government that the privilege was "not to be lightly invoked."

From 1953 through 1976, the government asserted the privilege just six times, but from 1977 through 2000, it invoked it 59 times — a nearly tenfold increase.

Many Recent Leakers Ended Up Behind Bars

Obama administration takes hard line against unauthorized disclosures.

The Obama administration has jailed more leakers during its first two years than any other administration in modern times.

In August 2010, a month after WikiLeaks began releasing classified U.S. military documents about the Afghan war, Samuel Shamai Leibowitz, a former Hebrew linguist for the FBI, took up temporary residence at the low-security federal prison in Petersburg, Va. He is the first person incarcerated during the Obama administration for leaking classified material. [1]

Leibowitz was sentenced to 20 months after pleading guilty to providing information to a blogger, who was not identified in open court. In a strange twist, the sentencing judge confessed to being "in the dark as to the kind of documents" that had been leaked. "I don't know what was divulged, other than some documents, and I don't know how it's compromised things," District Court Judge Alexander Williams Jr. said. Leibowitz and the prosecutors, however, had stipulated that the disclosed information related to "the communications intelligence activities of the United States." [2]

Leibowitz's importance pales in comparison to that of U.S. Army Pvt. Bradley Manning, who is believed to have given hundreds of thousands of documents to WikiLeaks. He's currently being held at the Quantico Marine Corps Base in Virginia. Manning's supporters have objected to his treatment; he reportedly is being held in solitary confinement for 23 hours per day, without a pillow, sheets or personal possessions. [3] Amnesty International sent a letter to the Pentagon decrying the treatment of Manning, who has yet to be convicted of a crime. [4]

So far, government officials apparently have been unable to link Manning to WikiLeaks, perhaps because of the website's highly complex and largely untraceable method of publishing information. Donations of information to WikiLeaks are frequently made through an anonymous, encrypted e-mail system that doesn't record the identity of the leaker. Consequently, WikiLeaks founder Julian Assange and others at the controversial site have long said they are unsure if Manning is the source of the material. Nonetheless, in July the website promised to foot half the cost of Manning's legal defense. Manning's lawyers have set that figure at $100,000. In January, WikiLeaks donated $15,100 to Manning's legal defense fund and now contends it has fulfilled its obligations to the 23-year-old intelligence analyst. [5]

Other leakers also are behind bars. In April, a grand jury indicted Thomas Drake, a former senior official at the super-secret National Security Agency (NSA), on charges that he provided classified information to a reporter — likely from the *Baltimore Sun* — between 2006 and 2007. [6] Reports in that newspaper around the same time detailed wasteful and mismanaged electronic intelligence collection programs at the NSA that cost billions of dollars. In yet another case, a trial is pending for Jeffrey Sterling, a former senior CIA officer accused of leaking information on Iran to a reporter.

With the exception of Manning, these cases were little noticed outside the intelligence community. They were unusual because they resulted in jail time. Media reports based on classified information are common — in major newspapers, television and, increasingly, on blogs and in so-called niche publications. Cases often have been referred to prosecutors, experts say, but only rarely do they actually lead to charges, trials or imprisonment. Indeed, between 2005 and 2010, the federal government made 183 complaints about leaks to the FBI. Only 26 cases actually were opened by the bureau, and only 14 leakers were ever identified. [7]

In U.S. history, one of the most prominent cases involving leaked classified material was that of defense

Bush asserted the "state secrets" privilege at an even faster clip. From 2001 through 2008, the White House asserted it 48 times. [59] The government used the privilege not only to block parts of documents from public view but also to dismiss requests for information in their entirety. The two most prominent cases in which the administration used the privilege were in challenges to the National Security Agency's warrantless eavesdropping program and the CIA's use of "extraordinary renditions," in which suspected terrorists in U.S. custody were sent to nations where they were allegedly tortured by intelligence services.

The Bush administration also won court victories allowing it to keep secret the records of Vice President

analyst Daniel Ellsberg, who leaked a secret study of U.S. involvement in the Vietnam War to *The New York Times* in 1971. The White House attempted to prevent *The Times* from publishing the documents in a groundbreaking legal case that went to the Supreme Court, which ruled in favor of the newspaper.[8] The incident became known as the Pentagon Papers case. Ellsberg was prosecuted, though the charges were later dropped because of government misconduct.

There have been other, less prominent cases in recent decades, including that of Samuel Morison, a naval intelligence analyst convicted of providing three satellite photographs to a British trade journal in 1985,[9] and Lawrence Franklin, a defense official who pleaded guilty to providing classified information to a pro-Israeli lobbying group in 2005.[10]

Some question why the government has made such a concerted effort to punish leakers, but government attorneys hinted at a cause in a recent court filing during the Sterling case. Leaking, the government contended in the brief, is "more pernicious than the typical espionage case where a spy sells classified information for money. Unlike the typical espionage case where a single foreign country or intelligence agency may be the beneficiary of the unauthorized disclosure of classified information, this defendant elected to disclose the classified information publicly through the mass media. Thus, every foreign adversary stood to benefit from the defendant's unauthorized disclosure of classified information, thus posing an even greater threat to society."[11]

— *Alex Kingsbury*

Thomas Drake, a former senior official at the super-secret National Security Agency (NSA), was indicted on charges that he gave classified information to a newspaper reporter.

[1] Josh Gerstein, "Obama sends first leaker to prison," *Politico*, Aug. 4, 2010.

[2] Maria Glod, "Former FBI employee sentenced for leaking classified papers," *The Washington Post*, May 25, 2010.

[3] Raphael Satter, "Amnesty urges UK to intervene in Manning case," The Associated Press, Feb. 1, 2011.

[4] Amnesty International letter to Robert Gates, Jan. 11, 2011, www.amnesty.org/en/library/asset/AMR51/006/2011/en/df463159-5ba2-416a-8b98-d52df0dc817a/amr510062011en.pdf.

[5] Joshua Norman, "WikiLeaks finally gives funds to Bradley Manning," CBS News, Jan. 13, 2011.

[6] Scott Shane, "Former N.S.A. official is charged in leak case," *The New York Times*, April 15, 2010.

[7] Pete Yost, "FBI uncovered 14 suspected leakers in five years," The Associated Press, June 22, 2010.

[8] *New York Times Co. v. United States*, 403 U.S. 713 (1971).

[9] "Ex-analyst for Navy convicted of spying," The Associated Press, Oct. 18, 1985.

[10] Mark Sherman, "More charges in leak of Pentagon material," The Associated Press, Aug. 5, 2005.

[11] Motion for Pretrial detention; case 1:10-cr-00485-LMB Document 9; Jan. 11, 2011, www.politico.com/static/PPM176_110114_detention.html.

Dick Cheney's energy task force. The task force aided in the formulation of national energy policy, but critics charged it was unduly influenced by industry groups.

The Bush White House also beat back legal challenges to immigration policies it initiated after the 9/11 attacks. Following the attacks, hundreds of Muslim foreigners in the United States were detained for suspected immigration violations, and in some cases deported after closed hearings.

Congress allowed the government to keep more information secret when it passed the USA Patriot Act in October 2001. The law gave the FBI broad authority to investigate terrorism cases and issue "national security letters," allowing certain government agencies to request

Secretary of Defense Robert Gates has denounced WikiLeaks' release of battlefield reports from the Iraq and Afghan wars while sounding a word of caution. "I've heard the impact of these releases on our foreign policy described as a meltdown, as a game-changer, and so on," he said. "I think those descriptions are fairly significantly overwrought."

records and data pertaining to individuals without probable cause or judicial oversight. The letters also imposed a gag order on those named, preventing recipients from disclosing that the letters were even issued. While initially limited, the use of the letters skyrocketed. From 2003 through 2006 the FBI issued more than 192,500 letters — an average of almost 50,000 a year.[60]

The Bush administration increased the number of government officials with "classification authority" to include the secretary of Health and Human Services, Agriculture secretary and head of the Environmental Protection Agency. Traditionally, that authority had been limited to officials in the national security and intelligence communities. The change put vast amounts of previously unclassified information in these departments out of the public view.

When it came to historical records, the Bush administration was equally resistant to disclosure. In November 2001, Bush allowed the White House and living former presidents to block the release of presidential papers indefinitely. Bush issued his order shortly before the scheduled release of the papers of President Ronald Reagan, for whom his father, George H.W. Bush, served

as vice president. Historians were outraged, and President Bill Clinton called the order unnecessary. A legal challenge to the Bush order was rejected in 2004.[61]

Throughout his term as Bush's attorney general, John Ashcroft staunchly defended the administration's approach to government secrecy. Testifying before a Senate panel, he said, to "those who scare peace-loving people with phantoms of lost liberty, my message is this: Your tactics only aid terrorists — for they erode our national unity and diminish our resolve. They give ammunition to America's enemies, and pause to America's friends. They encourage people of good will to remain silent in the face of evil."[62]

In October 2001, Ashcroft directed federal agencies in a memo: "When you carefully consider FOIA requests and decide to withhold records, in whole or in part, you can be assured that the Department of Justice will defend your decisions unless they lack sound legal basis or present an unwarranted risk of adverse impact on the ability of other agencies to protect other important records."

CURRENT SITUATION

Opening Up

As WikiLeaks continues to publish new documents from the trove of State Department cables, releasing a few every week, Assange is focusing his attention on another matter: accusations that he sexually assaulted two women last year in Sweden.

Assange has been confined to a mansion owned by one of his supporters outside London, as he awaits possible extradition in the case. He is required to check in daily with the police and wear an electronic tag to monitor his location. He also has launched a fundraising campaign for his legal defense fund.

Still, despite the conditions of his bail, Assange has managed to do dozens of interviews with journalists and sign a $1.5 million book deal for his memoirs.[63]

Assange says WikiLeaks has more secrets to disclose, including the contents of a hard drive from a senior official at a major U.S. bank (Assange wouldn't say which one), along with records from some Swiss bank accounts.[64] At the same time, the group has released only about 1 percent of the estimated State Department trove.

Meanwhile, even as the Obama administration's Justice Department tries to build a case against Assange,

Should the Espionage Act of 1917 be updated?

YES — Abbe Lowell
Chief, White-Collar Criminal Defense Group, McDermott Will & Emery

Testimony before House Judiciary Committee, Dec. 16, 2010

What is primarily missing in the act right now is clarity. The statute has been attacked often as vague and overbroad. Because of its breadth and language, it can be applied in a manner that infringes on proper First Amendment activity: discussions of foreign policy between government officials and private parties or proper newsgathering to expose government wrongdoing.

If the Espionage Act were used to bring charges against WikiLeaks or its founder, Julian Assange, this too would be unprecedented because it would be applying the law to a (a) nongovernment official, (b) who had no confidentiality agreement, (c) who did not steal the information, (d) who did not sell or pay for the information involved, (e) who was quite out front and not secretive about what he was doing, (f) who gave the U.S. notice and asked if the government wanted to make redactions to protect any information, and (g) in a context that can be argued to be newsgathering and dissemination protected by the First Amendment.

If the act applies to this disclosure, then why does it not apply as well to the articles written by *The New York Times* and other traditional media with the same disclosures? On its face, the Espionage Act does not distinguish between these two disclosures and would apply equally to both and to any even further dissemination of the same information.

Of course, the First Amendment would not and should not provide blanket immunity, for example, to a newspaper that tips off enemy forces by publishing a story that describes, in advance, a planned assault by the U.S. military on an al-Qaida or Taliban stronghold. While such a news report might arguably provide some benefit to public understanding of our government, the imminent and likely risk of harm to American troops would far outweigh any such benefit, and there would be no First Amendment protection for such a publication.

The act's breadth and vagueness can, intentionally or not, result in a powerful chill on the kinds of open government, freedom of the press and transparency in proper foreign policy formulation that make this country stronger. It does not serve proper national security or law enforcement interests to have this possibility of improper application of the act to conduct that was not targeted in 1917 and has even less reason to be targeted today. Accordingly, Congress should revise the act. It is almost 100 years old and was passed at a time and in an era that has little resemblance to the type of threats the county faces now or for the way information is disseminated today.

NO — Gabriel Schoenfeld
Senior Fellow, Hudson Institute

Testimony before House Judiciary Committee, Dec. 16, 2010

On the one hand, we're a wide-open society. On the other hand, we have too much secrecy. On the one hand, we have authorized, innocuous leaks of government secrets. On the other hand, we have unauthorized, highly dangerous leaks. And this is a very unsatisfactory state of affairs, and we have begun to pay a high price for it. There are five things we need to do:

First, we need to devote more attention and resources to declassification and to combating overclassification. Fewer secrets and a more rational secrecy policy will help us to preserve truly necessary secrets. Second, we need to make sure that legitimate whistle-blowers have viable avenues other than the media to which they can turn.

Third, we need to reestablish deterrents and prosecute those in government who violate their confidentiality agreements and pass secrets to the press or to an outfit like WikiLeaks. The Obama administration has been doing this with unprecedented energy. The last 24 months have witnessed four prosecutions of leakers, more than all previous presidencies combined.

Fourth, we need at the very least to bring down the weight of public opprobrium on those in the media who disseminate vital secrets.

And, finally, we sometimes need to take legal action. We have never had a prosecution of a media outlet in our history, although we came close during World War II, when *The Chicago Tribune* revealed that we had broken Japanese naval codes. While I believe that the First Amendment would not protect a news outlet that endangered the nation as *The Chicago Tribune* did in 1942, reasons of prudence suggest that such a prosecution should be a last resort, used against the media outlet only in the face of reckless disregard for the public's safety.

WikiLeaks — whether it is or is not a news organization — has certainly exhibited such reckless disregard. Thanks in part to the march of technology, it has been able to launch what might be called LMDs, leaks of mass disclosure. Leaks so massive in volume and so indiscriminate in what they convey that it becomes very difficult to assess the overall harm, precisely because there are so many different ways in which that harm is occurring.

The purpose of these leaks is to cripple our government, which Mr. Assange believes is a, quote, "authoritarian conspiracy," close quote. But the United States is not such a conspiracy; it is a democracy. And as a democracy it has every right to create its own laws concerning secrecy, and to see to it that those laws are respected. And, as a democracy, it has every right to protect itself against those who would do it harm.

RuLeaks.net — a copycat site calling itself the "Russian WikiLeaks" — recently published photographs of a palace constructed near the Black Sea, reportedly for Prime Minister Vladimir Putin at a cost of $1 billion.

it is still publicly committed to reducing secrecy within the government.

William J. Bosanko, director of the Information Security Oversight Office, who is wrapping up work on his office's annual report on government secrecy, says the Obama administration may be pushing for change but that change promises to be a lengthy process. "Obama's executive order [signed on his first full day in office] drives us towards the standardization of secrecy policy across agencies and does promote greater openness, but it will take years to change the classification and secrecy system even a little bit," he says.

Even after WikiLeaks began publishing its classified documents, the Obama administration signed an executive order that standardizes and limits the use of "Controlled Unclassified Information," one of the numerous secrecy classifications that has emerged in recent years. In October, the administration also published the total intelligence budget for 2010 (it was $80.1 billion) — the first time a current intelligence budget was officially released by an administration. While it might not seem like a large concession, open government advocates have sought the declassification of the intelligence budget for years.

Obama's new openness is a departure from the secrecy of the past administration, which famously blurred satellite imagery of the vice presidential residence on Massachusetts Avenue on public websites such as GoogleMaps.[65] Indeed, when Obama took office, one of his first acts was

to create the National Declassification Center. In 2010, the center reviewed some 83 million pages of classified historical records, but only 12 million of those pages have been declassified and released to the open shelves at the National Archives.[66]

In Obama's first year in office, his administration also released once-classified Justice Department memos detailing coercive interrogation techniques — including waterboarding — that were authorized by the Bush administration in terrorism cases and that many international law experts said constituted torture. But Obama reneged on an earlier promise to release a complete archive of photographs depicting the abuse of detained Iraqis by U.S. soldiers at the Abu Ghraib prison. "[T]he most direct consequence of releasing them, I believe, would be to further inflame anti-American opinion and to put our troops in greater danger," Obama said.[67]

Report Card

The annual "Government Secrecy Report Card," compiled by a coalition of open-government advocates, has given the Obama administration qualified praise for its transparency record.

"The elections of 2008 were viewed by many as a referendum on the secrecy and unaccountability of the Bush administration, and the country elected a president who has promised the most open, transparent, and accountable federal Executive Branch in history," it said. "The record to date is mixed, but some indicators are trending in the right direction."

Among the issues that the report card raised: Fewer pages were declassified governmentwide during the reporting period, and the backlog of declassification requests continues to grow. On the other side of the ledger, the number of "original classification" decisions decreased by 10 percent, there was a 40 percent decrease in the backlog of FOIA requests, and the head of the U.S. intelligence community for the first time revealed the total size of the current intelligence budget, a key statistic that has long been considered a vital national secret.[68]

A few months ago, an investigation by The Associated Press found that political appointees at the Department of Homeland Security may have delayed release of some 500 FOIA requests to examine what was being sought, and by whom. A memo from the department's chief

FOIA officer asked for weekly updates on requesting activities.[69] Once the practice had been publicized, however, the department quickly stopped it, though Congress and the department's inspector general say they are investigating the incident. The House of Representatives may hold hearings on the matter in coming months.[70]

Government secrecy issues aside, the WikiLeaks episode is hitting the open government movement like an atomic bomb. Indeed, WikiLeaks itself has spawned a rival, OpenLeaks, created by former WikiLeaks staffer Daniel Domscheit-Berg with the aim of avoiding the aura of celebrity that has surrounded Assange and his outfit.

In January, a copycat site billing itself as a "Russian WikiLeaks" published numerous photos of a palace reportedly constructed for Russian Prime Minister Vladimir Putin near the Black Sea. RuLeaks.net apparently acquired the photos from workers at the site of the gargantuan estate.[71]

Another prominent anti-secrecy website, cryptome.org, frequently publishes national security-related documents after they have inadvertently been placed online by the government, such as a Transportation Safety Administration security manual detailing how airport screeners operate.

It's long been said in certain corners of Washington that all officials in the CIA or State Department need to do is speak their minds during a meeting for it to be printed on the front pages the next day. In the wake of the WikiLeaks scandal, the cynicism doesn't seem so far-fetched. One of the most candid U.S. diplomats, Gene Cretz, whose cables on Libya were published by the site, has already been recalled to Washington.[72] The veteran diplomat famously wrote that Libyan leader Moammar Gadhafi relied on a "voluptuous" Ukrainian nurse. The cable's release may have been embarrassing, but now the government could have to worry about less candor from its diplomats.

OUTLOOK

'Tsunami of Information'

Sitting in his paper-filled office a few blocks north of the White House, Aftergood, the *Secrecy News* editor, says he worries about the long-term impact that WikiLeaks may have on the government's ability to reform itself.

"Will things be better on the secrecy front in 20 years? I can't say, but I do know that the WikiLeaks disclosures have probably made it less likely that the government will become more transparent."

Bellinger, the former State Department legal adviser, concurs. "We'll see the pendulum swing back the other way, towards greater government control in the wake of the WikiLeaks," he says. "I think a lot of senior people in government are asking at a practical level why the system allowed someone so junior [Manning] to access so much information, and they'll try to limit that type of 'need-to-know' access in the future."

While some foresee the flow of government information slowing, declassification nonetheless is continuing at a rapid clip. "We're declassifying maybe 30 million pages per year, which is three times what was being released in 1995," says Bosanko of the Information Security Oversight Office. "There's a tsunami of information that is being released and it is growing. What I also see happening already, which will continue in the future, is that the wave of newly released information has outstripped both the government's and the public's ability to assimilate it."

As more information — whether officially released or purloined — becomes available, WikiLeaks or groups similar to it may represent an emerging third category of stakeholders in the secrecy debate, alongside citizens and government. "It is likely that there will be other sites besides WikiLeaks that try to disclose classified information in the future, which is why the Congress should update the laws on the books so that they won't be forced to do so when tensions over the issue are high," says the ACLU's Shamsi.

Meanwhile, regardless of what happens to Assange in the courtroom, all eyes will be on a single computer file posted on the WikiLeaks site designated "insurance.aes256."[73]

Some 100,000 people around the world have downloaded the file, believed to be encrypted with a 256-character password. The file is large enough to contain countless documents or other materials, but little is known about its contents, though speculation has been rampant on the Internet. Several people familiar with the WikiLeaks case suspect that it is designed to be unlocked in the event that Assange faces prison

— or perhaps meets an even worse fate at the hand of enemies who oppose his work.

The file's encryption is reputedly so powerful that not even the government's supercomputers could crack it without a key.

Bruce Schneier, a cryptographer and one of the country's top computer security experts, writes that the mystery file, like any secret, could be important or not. "It's either 1.4 gig of embarrassing secret documents, or 1.4 gig of random data bluffing. There's no way to know."[74]

NOTES

1. Bill Keller, "The Boy Who Kicked the Hornet's Nest," *The New York Times Magazine*, Jan. 30, 2011, p. 32; see also, Ellen Nakashima, "Amazon.com stops hosting WikiLeaks on its servers," *The Washington Post*, Dec. 1, 2010.

2. Anahad O'Connor, "Amazon Removes WikiLeaks From Servers," *The New York Times*, Dec. 2, 2010, www.nytimes.com/2010/12/02/world/02amazon.html?_r=1&scp=9&sq=lieberman+wikileaks+amaz&st=cse.

3. Amy Goodman, "Democracy Now!," Dec. 7, 2010, http://mwcnews.net/focus/analysis/7119-glenn-greenwald-on-assange-arrest.html.

4. Selah Hennessy, "WikiLeaks receives 2011 Nobel Peace Prize nomination," Voice of America, Feb. 3, 2011.

5. Sharon Weinberger, "What is SIPRNet?" *Popular Mechanics*, Dec. 1, 2010.

6. Nancy Youssef, "Probe: Army was warned not to deploy WikiLeaks suspect," *The Miami Herald*, Jan. 27, 2011, www.miamiherald.com/2011/01/27/2037978/probe-army-was-warned-not-to-deploy.html.

7. Ellen Nakashima, "Messages from alleged leaker Bradley Manning portray him as despondent soldier," *The Washington Post*, June 10, 2010, www.washingtonpost.com/wp-dyn/content/article/2010/06/09/AR2010060906170.html.

8. Keller, *op. cit.*

9. Mike Barber, "A WikiLeaks Timeline," *The National Post*, Nov. 28, 2010.

10. The Central Intelligence Agency is so sensitive about potential breaches of SIPRNet that it doesn't generally use it to distribute information. See Bruce Berkowitz, "Failing to keep up with the information revolution: the DI and IT," *Studies in Intelligence*, Vol. 47, No. 1, 2003. After the WikiLeaks scandal broke open, some CIA officials felt vindicated in their reluctance to share information on the system. See Alex Kingsbury, "CIA seen as the winner in WikiLeaks scandal," *U.S. News & World Report*, Dec. 15, 2010.

11. Kevin Poulsen, "Lieberman Introduced Anti-WikiLeaks Legislation," *Wired*, Dec. 2, 2010, www.wired.com/threatlevel/2010/12/shield.

12. Mark Landler and Scott Shane, "U.S. Sends Warning to People Named in Cable Leaks," *The New York Times*, Jan. 6, 2011, www.nytimes.com/2011/01/07/world/07wiki.html.

13. Mark Hosenball, "Officials privately say WikiLeaks damage limited," Reuters, Jan. 18, 2011.

14. "National Commission on Terrorist Attacks Upon the United States," p. 19, www.9-11commission.gov/report/911Report_Exec.pdf.

15. Nancy Youssef, "In WikiLeaks fight, journalists take a pass," McClatchy Newspapers, Jan. 9, 2010.

16. Bill Keller, "Dealing With Assange and the WikiLeaks Secrets," *The New York Times*, Jan. 26, 2010.

17. http://en.rsf.org/united-states-open-letter-to-wikileaks-founder-12-08-2010,38130.html.

18. "Wikileaks hounded?," Reporters Without Borders, Dec. 4, 2010, http://en.rsf.org/wikileaks-hounded-04-12-2010,38958.html.

19. "Pentagon Papers," *Encyclopedia Britannica*, www.britannica.com/EBchecked/topic/450326/Pentagon-Papers.

20. "From One Transparency Advocate to Another," "On The Media," NPR (transcript), July 30, 2010, www.onthemedia.org/transcripts/2010/07/30/02.

21. "Iraq death toll higher: WikiLeaks," CBC News, Oct. 23, 2010, www.cbc.ca/world/story/2010/10/23/wikileaks-iraqi-death-toll.html.

22. Robert Gates, Pentagon briefing, Nov. 30, 2010.

23. Mike Mullen, Pentagon briefing, July 29, 2010, www.jcs.mil/speech.aspx?id=1432.

24. Quoted in Hosenball, *op. cit.*

25. *Ibid.*

26. Nick Allen, "WikiLeaks: Yemen covered up US drone strikes," *The Telegraph*, Nov. 28, 2010.

27. Daniel Drezner, "The Utopianism of Julian Assange," *Foreign Policy*, Nov. 29, 2010.

28. Meredith Chaiken, "Poll: Americans say WikiLeaks harmed public interest; most want Assange arrested," *The Washington Post*, Dec. 14, 2010.

29. *New York Times Co. v. United States*, 403 U.S. 713 (1971). For an account of the case, see Paul Finkelman and Melvin I. Urofsky, Landmark Decisions of the United States Supreme Court (2d ed.), 2008, pp. 413-414.

30. *Bartnicki v. Vopper*, 532 U.S. 514 (2001), www.law.cornell.edu/supct/html/99-1687.ZS.html.

31. Deb Riechmann, "Clinton vetoes leakers bill," ABC News, Nov. 4, 2000.

32. Baruch Weiss, "Why prosecuting WikiLeaks' Julian Assange won't be easy," *The Washington Post*, Dec. 5, 2010.

33. Testimony of Kenneth Wainstein, House Judiciary Committee, "Concerning the espionage act and the legal and constitutional issues raised by WikiLeaks," Dec. 16, 2010.

34. American University law professor Stephen Vladeck notes further that "the potentially sweeping nature of the Espionage Act may inadvertently interfere with federal whistleblower laws."

35. House Judiciary Committee, *op. cit.*

36. "Secrecy Report Card 2010," *OpenTheGovernment.org*, p. 4.

37. "Secrecy Report Card 2005," *OpenTheGovernment.org*.

38. Daniel Patrick Moynihan, "Secrecy: Report of the Commission on Protecting and Reducing Government Secrecy," 1997, p. 36.

39. Thomas Kean, "Frontline," www.pbs.org/wgbh/pages/frontline/enemywithin/interviews/kean.html.

40. Tom Blanton, congressional testimony, Dec. 16, 2010, www.gwu.edu/~nsarchiv/news/20101216/Blanton101216.pdf.

41. Jack Goldsmith, "Secrecy and Safety," *The New Republic*, Aug. 13, 2008.

42. Bill Miller, "The very visible battle over invisible ink," *The Washington Post*, June 13, 2001.

43. Daniel Patrick Moynihan, *Secrecy: the American Experience* (1998), p. 106.

44. John Podesta and Judd Legum, "A secret history of secrecy: the closing of the American government," *Salon.com*, March 22, 2004.

45. Steven Aftergood, "Reducing Government secrecy: finding what works," *Yale Law & Policy Review*, Vol. 27, No. 2, 2009, p. 404.

46. "Appendix G: Major Reviews of the U.S. Secrecy System," www.gpo.gov/congress/commissions/secrecy/pdf/18form1.pdf.

47. Kenneth Jost, "Government Secrecy," *CQ Researcher*, Dec. 2, 2005, p. 1014.

48. Aftergood, *op. cit.*, p. 406.

49 "Report of the Defense Science Board Taskforce on Secrecy," July 1, 1970, p. 1, www.fas.org/sgp/othergov/dsbrep.pdf.

50. *Ibid.*, p. 3.

51. *New York Times Co. v. United States*, 403 U.S. 713 (1971).

52. John Correll, "The Pentagon Papers," *Air Force Magazine*, Vol. 90, No. 2, 2007.

53. Jost, *op. cit.*, p. 1016.

54. www.gpo.gov/congress/commissions/secrecy/pdf/18form1.pdf.

55. "Report to the President for FY 2009," Information Security Oversight Office, p. 2, www.archives.gov/isoo/reports/2009-annual-report.pdf.

56. "Redefining Security. A Report by the Joint Security Commission," Feb. 24, 1994, p. 6.

57. Scott Shane, "U.S. reclassifies many documents in secret review," *The New York Times*, Feb. 21, 2006.

58. When the crash report was finally declassified in 2004, historians found that it contained no details that would have compromised national security, leading many to conclude that the government invoked the privilege simply to shield itself from liability.

59. "Secrecy Report Card, 2010," *op. cit.*, p. 10.

60. Ellen Nakashima, "Plaintiff who challenged FBI's national security letters reveals concerns," *The Washington Post*, Aug. 10, 2010.

61. Jost, *op. cit.*, p. 1019.

62. Testimony before Senate Judiciary Committee, Dec. 6, 2001.

63. Jill Lawless, "Julian Assange extradition hearing begins Monday as WikiLeaks founder faces legal battle," The Associated Press, Feb. 2, 2011.

64. Theunis Bates, "WikiLeaks handed data on secret Swiss bank accounts," *AOL News*, Jan. 17, 2011.

65. Sharon Weinberger, "Why is Google Earth hiding Dick Cheney's House?" *Wired*, July 23, 2008.

66. "Bi-annual Report on Operations of the National Declassification Center," Jan. 1, 2010-Dec. 31, 2010, www.fas.org/sgp/othergov/ndc-123110.pdf.

67. Statement of the President, May 13, 2009, www .whitehouse.gov/the_press_office/Statement-by-the-President-on-the-Situation-in-Sri-Lanka-and-Detainee-Photographs/.

68. "Secrecy Report Card, 2010," *op. cit.*, p. 4.

69. Mary Ellen Callahan, "Memorandum for all DHS FOIA officers," July 7, 2009, http://papersplease.org/wp/wp-content/uploads/2010/10/foia-blocking-policy.pdf.

70. Alan Fram, "House panel wants Homeland Security documents," The Associated Press, Jan. 16, 2010.

71. "Putin Palace Pics: it's good to the PM," Radio Free Europe — Radio Liberty, Jan. 21, 2011.

72. Warren Strobel, "WikiLeaks: 'Voluptuous' nurse cable costs diplomat his job," McClatchy Newspapers, Jan. 4, 2011.

73. For more on the file, see www.wired.com/threatlevel/2010/07/wikileaks-insurance-file/.

74. Bruce Schneier, "Schneier on Security," www.schneier .com/blog/archives/2010/08/wikileaks_insur.html.

BIBLIOGRAPHY

Books

Goldman, Jan, and Susan Maret, *Government Secrecy: Classic and Contemporary Readings*, **Libraries Unlimited, 2008.**
This collection of 45 readings on government secrecy in the United States dates back to a piece by Thomas Jefferson from 1787. The readings detail and critique the history, philosophy, theory, practice and justification for secrecy. They also explain how the CIA, NSA and other intelligence agencies operate and how they affect the government's overall approach to secrecy.

Moynihan, Daniel, *Secrecy: The American Experience*, **Yale University Press, 1998.**
The late senator from New York served for eight years on the Senate Select Committee on Intelligence and came to abhor the "culture of secrecy" that he felt impeded enlightened public discourse and the proper functioning of government. His book traces the growth of the modern secrecy system from the early 20th century to the post-Cold War years.

Schneier, Bruce, *Secrets and Lies: Digital Security in a Networked World*, **John Wiley & Sons, 2000.**
A cryptographer, mathematician and security expert says that in the digital age even the most elegant security systems can be breached and exploited because of human weakness by users. People break the rules, he concludes, no matter how well-designed those rules may be. Schneier traces the history of computer security in witty prose that has made him one of the more engaging and popular voices on a rather dense topic.

Schoenfeld, Gabriel, *Necessary Secrets: National Security, the Media, and the Rule of Law*, **W.W. Norton, 2010.**
Conservative thinker Schoenfeld has said *The New York Times* and others could be prosecuted under the country's espionage laws for exposing secret intelligence operations. He expands that argument here within the context of a broader discussion of the history of American government secrecy. He argues that secrecy is important and that the government should be more forthright in its prosecution of those who undermine it.

Articles

Aftergood, Steven, "Reducing Government secrecy: finding what works," *Yale Law & Policy Review*, **Vol. 27, No. 2, 2009.**
A leading security expert traces a history of government secrecy, charting the effectiveness of various policy approaches to reducing it.

Anderson, Joseph, "Hidden from the Public by Order of the Court: The Case Against Government-Enforced

Secrecy," *South Carolina Law Review*, **Vol. 55, No. 4, 2004, pp. 711-760.**
The author examines the use of secrecy inside the courtroom and how it affects the public's right to know about the proceedings of a trial, including its procedural history and details of settlements. Anderson contends that keeping court proceedings secret undermines public confidence in the legal system.

Feldman, Noah, "The Way We Live Now: In Defense of Secrecy," *The New York Times*, **Feb. 10, 2009.**
There are "many circumstances in which secrets are critical," argues Feldman, a fellow at the Council on Foreign Relations. He traces how secrecy can impact not just the national security realm but also transparency in the financial markets and other areas.

Schmitt, Christopher, and Edward Pound, "Keeping Secrets," *U.S. News & World Report*, **Dec. 22, 2003, p. 18.**
Investigative reporters trace the Bush administration's penchant for secrecy. They conclude that from day one, the administration "quietly but efficiently dropped a shroud of secrecy across many critical operations of the federal government — cloaking its own affairs from scrutiny and removing from the public domain important information on health, safety and environmental matters."

Stone, Geoffrey, "Government Secrecy vs. Freedom of the Press," *Harvard Law and Policy Review*, **No. 185, 2007.**
The author explores whether the measures taken and suggested by the executive branch to prevent and punish disclosure of classified materials are consistent with the First Amendment.

Sunstein, Cass, "Government Control of Information," *California Law Review*, **Vol. 74, No. 3, Symposium: New Perspectives in the Law of Defamation, May 1986, pp. 889-921.**
The noted legal scholar critically examines the government's history and incentives to manage information — secret and otherwise.

Reports and Studies

"Report of the Commission on Protecting and Reducing Government Secrecy," Commission on Protecting and Reducing Government Secrecy, 1997.
The late Sen. Moynihan chaired this landmark, 12-member panel, which aimed to reduce secrecy within the federal government as a means of increasing its transparency and efficiency. The commission's work caused a stir when it was released, but the commission was unable to mobilize the political will to enact legislation in line with its recommendations.

"Secrecy Report Card 2010," *OpenTheGovernment .org*, **September 2010.**
This yearly update is issued by a coalition of more than 70 groups advocating for open government and a reduction in the number and nature of classified materials. It concludes that secrecy as reflected by several indicators has declined during the first years of the Obama administration and that backlogs in the declassification system are easing as well. Yet in other areas, the system "continues to fall further behind."

For More Information

American Civil Liberties Union, 125 Broad St., 18th Floor, New York, NY 10004-2400; (212) 549-2500; 122 Maryland Ave., N.E., Washington, DC 20002; (202) 544-1681; www .aclu.org. Frequently uses the Freedom of Information Act in litigation against the government for infringements on civil liberties, particularly in cases involving national security and technology.

Brechner Center for Freedom of Information, P.O. Box 118400, 3208 Weimer Hall, University of Florida, Gainesville, FL 32611-840; (352) 392-2273; http://brechner.org. Focuses on media law and the Freedom of Information Act.

Federation of American Scientists, Project on Government Secrecy, 1725 DeSales St., N.W., Washington, DC 20036; (202) 546-3300, fas@fas.org; www.fas.org. Publishes the Secrecy News blog and newsletter focusing on declassification and secrecy issues.

Freedom of Information Advocates Network, www.foiadvocates.net/. An international information-sharing network of organizations and individuals who promote the right of access to information.

Freedominfo.org, www.freedominfo.org. An online portal describing best practices, lessons learned and future strategies for freedom of information advocates worldwide.

Information Security Oversight Office, National Archives and Records Administration, 700 Pennsylvania Ave., N.W., Room 500, Washington, DC 20408; (202) 219-5250; www. archives.gov/isoo/. Compiles and publishes statistical reports on government classification and secrecy.

James Madison Project, 1380 Monroe St., N.W., Unit 269, Washington, DC 20010; (202) 498-0011, www.james-madisonproject.org. Advocates for less government secrecy and more education on intelligence and national security issues.

National Security Archive, The George Washington University, Gelman Library, Suite 701, 2130 H St., N.W., Washington, DC 20037; (202) 994-7000; www.gwu .edu/~nsarchive. A private research center that files FOIA requests and publishes the results, often with scholarly commentary.

OpenTheGovernment.org, 1742 Connecticut Ave., N.W., Washington, DC 20009; (202) 234-8494; www.openthe-government.org. A coalition of journalism, consumer watchdog and related organizations that promotes open and accountable government.

Reporters Committee for Freedom of the Press, 1101 Wilson Blvd. Suite 1100, Arlington, VA 22209; (703) 807-2100; www.rcfp.org. Works with journalists and media companies on issues involving journalism and the government. Its website offers help for reporters and citizens seeking access to government documents and records.

16

Health-Care Reform

Marcia Clemmitt

House Speaker Nancy Pelosi, D-Calif., greets 11-year-old Brian McCann during a news conference on health care in September 2009, months before she helped engineer passage of the landmark health reform law. The sweeping new law enables people with preexisting medical conditions, like Brian, to get affordable insurance.

AP Photo/Matt Slocum

From *CQ Researcher*,
June 11, 2010. (Updated May 16, 2011)

Enactment of the most far-reaching health-care law in at least four decades pumped emotions to a fever pitch among opponents and supporters alike.

"Today, after almost a century of trying; today, after over a year of debate; today, after all the votes have been tallied — health insurance reform becomes law in the United States of America. Today," President Barack Obama proclaimed at the March 23 White House signing ceremony.[1]

With equal passion, Republicans unanimously rejected the landmark Patient Protection and Affordable Health Care Act, refusing to award it even a single vote.

The law "is an historic betrayal of the clear will of the American people," scolded Republican National Committee Chairman Michael Steele. Referring to the new requirement that all Americans carry health-insurance coverage, he said the law represented "an historic loss of liberty."[2]

The landmark law will extend coverage to about 32 million of the nation's 45 million uninsured people by:

- Expanding Medicaid;
- Providing subsidies to help low- and middle-income families buy insurance;
- Creating regulated insurance markets where people without employer-sponsored insurance can buy subsidized coverage; and
- Using Medicare's economic clout to cut health care costs.

Health Reforms Opposed in Majority of States

State lawmakers in at least 39 states have introduced legislation to limit, alter or oppose aspects of the health-reform plan. The measures largely seek to make or keep health insurance optional and allow people to purchase any type of coverage they choose. Such legislation passed and is in effect in three states — Idaho, Utah and Virginia — and legislation passed in Oklahoma and Georgia is ready for approval by the governors. The bills did not pass in 21 states.

State Legislation Opposing Certain Health Reforms, 2009-2010

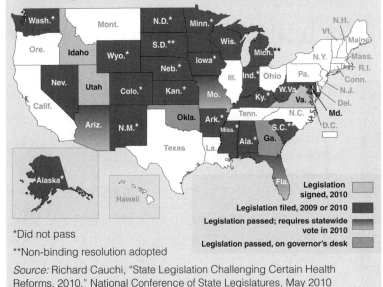

*Did not pass

**Non-binding resolution adopted

Legislation signed, 2010
Legislation filed, 2009 or 2010
Legislation passed; requires statewide vote in 2010
Legislation passed, on governor's desk

Source: Richard Cauchi, "State Legislation Challenging Certain Health Reforms, 2010," National Conference of State Legislatures, May 2010

sections contain provisions designed to essentially reengineer health care to favor efficient, effective treatments and preventive medicine over expensive but relatively ineffective services, she says. This is "urgent for a variety of reasons," including the fact that the high cost of health care is the main reason people are uninsured, says Feder.

The law launches a variety of "institutions and experiments" that policymakers hope can eventually slow the huge annual increases in health-care costs, says Michael E. Chernew, a professor of health policy at Harvard Medical School. Some are simple payment cuts to health-care players like private "Medicare Advantage" plans that most health-care economists agree have long been overpaid, he says.

But the law also will launch numerous demonstration projects aimed at developing ways to pay doctors, hospitals and other providers for delivering good health outcomes efficiently rather than continuing the current system, which mostly pays for services whether they are successful and necessary or not, Chernew explains.

"We can't be sure the [cost-cutting] things in the law will work, and critics can argue that they are not pursued aggressively enough or quickly enough," says Chernew. "Nevertheless, we have to do them, and from a pure cost-curve standpoint, [the law's framers] did whatever they could possibly do, what is politically possible."

The law also has some "pro-competitive" elements to encourage private insurers to emphasize cost and quality control as well, Chernew says. The "insurance exchanges" that will be set up in states to help people without employer coverage buy insurance "are very pro-competition" since they get insurers to compete against each other for individuals' business, Chernew says.

"It's very easy for those not in power to argue that those in power haven't done enough," Chernew says, but

While supporters tout the law's multifaceted approach to access and cost problems, conservatives argue the federal government has no right to require individuals to purchase insurance or states to participate in coverage-expansion programs. At least 20 state attorneys general and several private groups are suing to stop the law.

The law has two main facets — expanding health coverage and developing cost-control measures, says Judith Feder, a professor of public policy at Georgetown University and former staff director of the 1990 U.S. Bipartisan Commission on Comprehensive Health Care, which called for universal health coverage.

For the first time in history, the law "establishes access to affordable health care as a national responsibility," with "the great bulk of the dollars coming from taxpayers" to fund the coverage expansion, says Feder. The cost-cutting

those in power "can only do what is politically possible" in a system where health-care providers and insurers hold enormous influence.

Ultimately, Chernew acknowledges, "the law could turn out to be a disaster" because, when the results are in from cost-cutting experiments, "the solution [to rising costs] may require tough choices" to impose cost-trimming measures that doctors and patients won't like.

If that happens "and we end up not having the political will" to impose the changes, the federal budget deficit will soar because, under the law, the nation has committed itself to "a new entitlement program" — subsidizing health coverage for most low- and middle-income Americans, Chernew says.

The law takes some good steps but also leaves a few important things undone, says Mark McClellan, a former chief of Medicare and Medicaid under President George W. Bush and now director of the Engelberg Center for Health Care Reform at the centrist Brookings Institution think tank. For example, McClellan says the law's tax on high-cost employer-provided health insurance with rich benefit packages is a good way to raise money for coverage, but the tax should kick in sooner.

"It got pushed back to 2018," after complaints about unfairness, he says. But he argues that it is fair to end the tax-favored status of the most benefit-rich coverage, in favor of spending those dollars to help lower-income people gain coverage. Currently, "we pay about $250 billion a year for those employer subsidies, and most of that goes to higher-income people," he says.

One set of conservative-backed cost-trimming provisions that didn't make it into the law are so-called "consumer-side" incentives for people to take steps on their own to reduce health spending, McClellan says. For example, private insurers are implementing "wellness

Wealthy to Pay Higher Medicare Tax

Before passage of the health-care plan, middle-income families paid a higher Medicare tax than wealthy families. Under the plan, middle-income families will continue to pay a 2.9 percent tax but the tax on couples making $10 million annually would nearly triple.

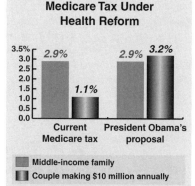

Medicare Tax Under Health Reform

Middle-income family
Couple making $10 million annually

Source: Chuck Marr, "Changes in Medicare Tax on High-Income People Represent Sound Additions to Health Reform," Center on Budget and Policy Priorities, March 2010

plans" to give consumers financial incentives to take common-sense steps like stopping smoking or losing weight, which should save health-system dollars down the line, he says.

Limits on lawsuits against health-care providers also should have been included, says McClellan. Such reforms can trim 2-3 percent annually from medical spending, and while that amount may seem minimal, "it could add to the other reforms" and increase the law's cumulative cost-cutting effect, he says.

The new law also has its critics among proponents of guaranteed, universal access to health care.

"The law does not solve the problem," says Steffie Woolhandler, an associate professor of medicine at Harvard and longtime advocate of national, single-payer health care.

"If the bill works as planned, there will still be 23 million uninsured people in 2019, of whom about a quarter will be illegal immigrants," she says. Furthermore, many who get insurance under the bill will end up underinsured, she added, partly because about 16 million of the newly insured will be enrolled in Medicaid, which most doctors don't accept because of its lower payments. "They can go to the emergency room (ER), but they'll have trouble getting primary care for conditions like high blood pressure" and the like, where early treatment could keep ER-type health emergencies from happening, she says.

Many who buy insurance in the law's new exchanges also "will get woefully inadequate coverage," since the insurance available there "will cover only 60 percent" of medical costs, says Woolhandler.

"Because the law was sold largely on the basis of cost containment, the critics are able to fire at it by saying, 'It won't save as much money as you say,' " says Arthur L.

Health Reforms That Begin This Year

A few programs expand coverage for the neediest.

Most Americans won't see many effects of the health-care reform law this year. However, the law does launch a few programs that start expanding coverage for some of the neediest people and some who are easier to cover.[1]

High-risk pool — Many people with preexisting medical conditions can't get affordable insurance under current laws. To help close that gap, this year a temporary "high-risk pool" will begin offering price-capped coverage to people with pre-existing illnesses. In 2014 the new law will require insurers to take all comers.

Young adult coverage — Young adults are one of the largest uninsured groups. Beginning this year, for the first time, young adults up to age 26 can get coverage under their parents' health insurance.

Benefit limits — In the past, patients with serious illnesses were likely to lose their insurance coverage when they ran into a lifetime limit on the dollar value of their coverage. Beginning this year, the law bans lifetime dollar limits on coverage and also bans insurers from canceling a patient's

insurance policy for any reason except fraud by the patient. Also beginning this year, children may not be refused health insurance because of preexisting medical conditions.

Medicaid expansion — For the first time, states may offer Medicaid coverage to all poor people, not just to mothers and their young children or the disabled.

Business tax credit — Small businesses whose workers' annual wage is under $50,000 get tax credits if they provide health insurance.

Regulating insurance premiums — Insurers must report the proportion of premium dollars they spend on actual medical services, and the federal government will establish a process for judging whether annual premium increases are justified.

— Marcia Clemmitt

[1] See "Focus on Health Reform: Summary of New Health Reform Law," The Henry J. Kaiser Family Foundation, March 26, 2010, and "Timeline for Health Care Reform Implementation: System and Delivery Reform Provisions," The Commonwealth Fund, April 1, 2010.

Caplan, a professor of bioethics at the University of Pennsylvania. "If, instead, you had had the discussion of whether there is a right to health care, critics would have to explicitly make their arguments for why health care is not a right," bringing out into the open the real issue, which the country must face sooner or later, he says.

"Only critics looking for some way to derail reform give a hoot about details" like individual mandates or tax provisions, Caplan said. "No nation on Earth has ever reformed its health care system by asking the public to wallow around in the details of health reform." Instead, nations including Canada, Britain, Singapore, Taiwan, Germany and Australia "secured agreement that health care is a right and then, and only then, moved on to figure out how to guarantee that right to all citizens," he said.[3]

As health reform is implemented amid protests in Washington and the states, here are some of the questions being debated:

Is the new health-care reform law a good idea?

The new law's supporters say it puts in place most of the mechanisms for coverage expansion and cost control that are politically possible in the complex, private-sector-dominated American health system, but many conservative critics have called for the law's partial rollback or repeal. They argue that increased government involvement in health care can only damage the job market, interfere with individual freedom and worsen cost problems. Critics on the left, meanwhile, say there was little point in enacting provisions that will only temporarily lower the number of uninsured Americans without creating a permanent solution.

The bill's so-called "individual mandate," requiring everyone to purchase insurance, is unconstitutional, said Sen. Orrin Hatch, R-Utah.

The purpose of insurance is to spread costs across the population — with people paying in even in years

Health Reforms That Begin in 2011 and Beyond

Changes spread costs, reduce spending increases.

The health-reform law contains hundreds of provisions designed to expand insurance coverage, spread the tax burden of paying for the new coverage fairly and eventually tame steep annual increases in spending while improving care. Most of the provisions will be phased in over the next eight years.[1]

2011

Long-term care — People may enroll in an insurance plan to fund future long-term care needs, including services that can help them stay in their own homes.

Drug company fees — Annual fees paid by large pharmaceutical manufacturers will help pay for expanding health coverage.

Hospital-acquired illnesses — Medicare won't pay hospitals to care for infections caused by a patient's hospital stay.

OTC drugs — To raise money, the law bans paying for over-the-counter drugs from tax-favored accounts like flexible spending accounts unless a doctor has prescribed the drugs.

2012

Paying health-care providers — To hold down rising medical costs and improve care, Medicare will begin paying doctors and hospitals less when patients develop preventable illnesses and study other potential incentives to get medical providers to work together to deliver care more efficiently.

2013

Standardize insurance operations — To save money and set the stage for the new health-insurance exchanges that launch in 2014, health-insurance eligibility, enrollment and claims procedures will be standardized nationwide.

Higher Medicare taxes — To raise money to expand insurance coverage, individuals with adjusted gross incomes over $200,000 ($250,000 for couples who file jointly) will pay higher Medicare taxes.

2014

Individual mandate — U.S. citizens and legal residents must carry health coverage or pay a tax penalty.

Employer contributions — To help pay for coverage expansion, employers with more than 50 workers must either offer health coverage or pay a per-worker fee.

Insurance exchanges — State-based regulated markets will help individuals and small businesses buy health coverage that is tax-subsidized on a sliding scale for people earning up to 400 percent of the federal poverty level. The federal government will establish a minimum benefit package for health coverage.

Medicaid expansion — The federal government will pay to expand Medicaid to all non-elderly Americans earning up to 133 percent of the federal poverty level.

Insurance rules — Insurance companies will no longer be able to refuse new coverage or coverage renewal to anyone, regardless of preexisting conditions or other factors. To keep insurance affordable for all, older and sicker people can't be charged more than three times what the average person in the community pays for coverage. Annual dollar limits on benefits are banned.

Insurer fees — Insurance companies will pay fees based on their size.

2018

Benefit tax — To raise funds, tax breaks will end for health plans with annual premiums exceeding $10,000 for an individual (or $27,500 for a family). Such so-called Cadillac plans benefit only richer Americans and are believed to be inefficient.

— Marcia Clemmitt

---

[1] See "Focus on Health Reform: Summary of New Health Reform Law," The Henry J. Kaiser Family Foundation, March 26, 2010, and "Timeline for Health Care Reform Implementation: System and Delivery Reform Provisions," The Commonwealth Fund, April 1, 2010.

when they don't use much health care. Those payments serve as a buffer against times when they are sick and use services — and if people wait until they become ill to sign up for insurance, insurers are unable to spread costs in this way.

For this reason, an individual mandate has been part of some Republican coverage-expansion proposals over the years, as well as the 1993 proposal by President Bill Clinton.

Hatch raised no objection to the individual mandates in the Clinton plan, "but . . . 17 years later . . . I looked at it and, constitutionally, I came to the conclusion . . . that this would be the first time in history that the federal government requires you to buy something you don't want," he said. "If we allow the federal government to tell us what we can or can't buy, then our liberties are gone."[4]

"Forcing employers to offer health insurance . . . will cost America jobs and revenue, and inhibit small businesses from growing," according to the small-business lobbying group National Federation of Independent Businesses. "It's a bad idea any time but is particularly destructive in the current economic environment."[5]

By requiring employers to pay a penalty if they don't offer workers substantial health-insurance coverage, the law "creates an incentive for employers to avoid hiring workers from low-income families, hurting those who need jobs the most," said Kathryn Nix, a research assistant at the conservative Heritage Foundation. (Low-income workers are the least likely to receive employer-based health insurance because its cost is more than most employers are willing to shoulder as an added cost of employing a worker.)[6]

Tax increases to pay for expanding coverage will damage the economy, Nix continued. For example, the law raises some taxes on investment income, a move that "will discourage investment in the U.S. economy . . . reducing the potential for economic growth."

"Families with incomes greater than $250,000 will pay a higher Medicare payroll tax — up to 2.35 percent, plus a new 3.8 percent tax on interest and dividend income. With this stroke, Democrats have managed to punish both work and the savings of American families," wrote Sally C. Pipes, chief executive officer of the free-market-oriented Pacific Research Institute in San Francisco.[7]

Increasing government involvement in health care will likely drive some doctors out of Medicare and perhaps out of practice altogether, said Robert E. Moffit, director of health policy studies at Heritage. Having public and private insurers pay for health care rather than allowing individuals to pay directly out of their own pockets for it "already [compromises] the independence and integrity of the medical profession," and the new law "will reinforce the worst of these features," because "physicians will be subject to more government regulation and oversight," said Moffit.[8]

Some critics on the left also see more harm than good in the reforms.

The law "hurts many more people than it helps," wrote blogger Jane Hamsher of the liberal website Firedoglake. "A middle-class family of four making $66,370 will be forced to pay $5,243 per year for insurance," an amount that will leave many without enough discretionary income to cover other bills, she said.[9]

But reform supporters counter that expanding coverage is worth the law's cost and that its provisions are not unconstitutional.

"There is a long line of [Supreme Court] cases holding that Congress has broad power to enact laws that substantially affect prices, marketplaces and commercial transactions," including cases decided by the current conservative-dominated court, wrote Ian Millhiser, a policy analyst at the liberal Center for American Progress. "A law requiring all Americans to hold health insurance does all of these things," so its constitutionality is not in question, he said. The 2005 case *Gonzales v. Raich*, for example, "establishes that Congress can regulate even tiny insurance providers who serve only a handful of local residents because such local activity substantially affects a multistate market," said Millhiser.[10]

"The Supreme Court decades ago held that the business of insurance fell within Congress' regulatory authority under the Commerce Clause," wrote Simon Lazarus, public policy counsel to the National Senior Citizens Law Center.[11]

The court noted that "perhaps no modern commercial enterprise directly affects so many persons in all walks of life as does the insurance business," said Lazarus. Consequently, the 1944 finding "could hardly be more consonant with Congress' identical case for expanding federal regulation of health insurance in 2009," including the "individual mandate" to buy coverage, since "many independent experts, studies and analyses concur" that without such a requirement "overall health reform will be unsustainable," he said.[12]

The law is "an enormously positive step to expand access and put in tools" to begin driving down costs, says Jacob Hacker, a Yale University professor of political science who was the chief architect of a proposal — eventually dumped from the legislation — to include a public, government-run health insurance plan to compete against private insurers. "I was a very strong advocate of the bill even after the public-plan option was off the table," he says.

Half of Unemployed Workers Are Uninsured

Out of nearly 6 million unemployed workers with incomes below 200 percent of the poverty level, more than 50 percent are uninsured. The new law will allow unemployed people and others without job-sponsored coverage to buy tax-subsidized insurance.

Health coverage status of non-elderly unemployed workers with incomes below 200% of poverty level, December 2008

Private or military coverage 1,214,324 20.8%

Uninsured 3,149,847 54.0%

Public coverage 1,467,874 25.2%

Source: Claire McAndrew, "Unemployed and Uninsured in America," Families USA, February 2009

Supporters argue that by making it easier for people to get non-job-based health coverage and beginning to trim costs, the law will actual improve businesses' ability to create jobs. Inability to find affordable health coverage under current law "is one of the major reasons why small businesses close their doors and corporations ship jobs overseas," said Obama.[13]

By establishing a system in which fewer people experience breaks in insurance coverage, the law will improve health and trim some costs, according to Mathematica Policy Research, a consulting firm in Princeton, N.J. Studies show that "adults with continuous insurance coverage are healthier and at lower risk for premature death than those who are uninsured or whose coverage is intermittent," the firm reported in April.[14]

"Continuous coverage also can reduce administrative costs," Mathematica said. For example, "guaranteed eligibility for Medicaid and the Children's Health Insurance Program for six or 12 months can lower states' administrative costs by reducing the frequent movement (called 'churning')" of people in and out of the programs," drastically cutting paperwork and staff time.[15]

Will people with insurance lose out under the new law?

Critics say the new law will change things for the worse for people who have either public or private insurance

today. Reform supporters argue, however, that while the law will change how many people get coverage and care, it will ultimately provide better options for everyone.

Many provisions that raise revenue to pay for coverage expansion will leave insured Americans worse off, said John Berlau, director of the Center for Investors and Entrepreneurs at the free-market think tank Competitive Enterprise Institute. For example, a provision to raise tax money to fund the law's coverage expansion will ban using pre-tax dollars from a flexible-spending account or health-savings account to buy over-the-counter drugs unless a doctor has prescribed them, creating "an effective tax increase of up to 40 percent on these items," said Berlau.[16]

About 7 million Medicare enrollees will lose the more generous benefits they now receive from "Medicare Advantage" private health insurers that serve the Medicare program, said Grace-Marie Turner, president of the Galen Institute, a free-market think tank in Alexandria, Va. Payments to those insurers will be cut under the law, based on recommendations by many economists that Medicare has long overpaid the plans. But the resulting pullout of the plans from Medicare will be a significant hardship for the Medicare enrollees who've come to rely on the richer benefits Medicare Advantage plans provide, compared to traditional Medicare, Turner said.[17]

Before the law was enacted, the United States already faced a shortage of primary-care doctors and, with an estimated 32 million newly insured people by 2019 under the law, primary-care physicians will be stretched even thinner, according to *Kaiser Health News*.[18]

If Congress actually implements Medicare payment cuts named in the law, "15 percent of hospitals and other care facilities that rely on Medicare reimbursements would become unprofitable, meaning that they might drop Medicare patients," limiting "the availability of care for millions of seniors," the *Columbus* [Ohio] *Dispatch* editorialized.[19]

But health-reform supporters say that, contrary to critics' warnings, the law, on balance, will make it easier for virtually everyone to maintain continuous access to health insurance and care.

Rather than losing money, hospitals actually "come out winners" under the law, so access won't become a greater problem, said Maggie Mahar, a fellow at the liberal Century Foundation.[20]

Hospitals got in on early negotiations for the law and negotiated some payment rate cuts that they found acceptable, said Urban Institute senior fellow Robert Berenson. Now "hospitals are off-limits until 2020" from pay cuts proposed by the new board established by the law to make sure that Medicare hits its spending targets, Berenson said.[21]

Moreover, hospital payment cuts "will be offset by the fact that hospitals will be seeing an influx of paying patients" as more people gain insurance, Mahar said.[22]

And Medicare cuts will actually benefit enrollees, some analysts argue. Cutting payments for ineffective care such as hospital readmissions, for example, will not only make Medicare more economically sustainable over the long haul but help eliminate hospital stays that amount to unnecessary "hardship for the patient," said a report published by the liberal-leaning Commonwealth Fund in Manhattan.[23]

The law will help insured people avoid unwarranted insurance-premium rate increases by requiring annual review of premium increases in a public process that will, for the first time, require public input, not just explanations of their charges by the insurance company, according to the liberal consumer group Families USA. Before the law went into effect, many states had "no process for obtaining consumer input in the rate-review process," so state officials heard "only the insurers' side of the story"

and often were unaware that the proposed rates were unaffordable.[24]

Changes brought about by the law "do not pose a risk to the public," says Georgetown University's Feder. "What insured people are currently at risk of is higher costs" that will force them out of their coverage, either because they lose a job, become self-employed or an employer stops offering it, she says. Under the new law, "if there's an employment change, now for the first time they'll have a real option," she says.

In another boon for patients, "beginning this year, if you become seriously ill, insurers won't be able to drop your coverage on the grounds that you forgot some detail of your medical history when you applied for insurance," as they could in the past, said Mahar. From now on, insurers "will be able to rescind your policy only if they can prove fraud, or that you intentionally set out to deceive them. This won't be easy."[25]

Will health care reform make care more affordable?

Supporters of the new law say its tax-funded subsidies will help low-income people afford health coverage and that health-provider payment initiatives will slow out-of-control health spending. But skeptics say that the law's affordability provisions are all unproven.

Using incentives and accountability, the new law tries to nudge doctors, hospitals and other health-care providers toward eliminating unnecessary illness and treatment, said David Kendall, a senior fellow at Third Way, a center-left advocacy group in Washington. For example, "the current system . . . lets doctors who cause infections through improper hand-washing send [insurers] more bills to treat" infections that patients may get as a result, Kendall explained. The new law institutes cost-saving provisions such as requiring hospitals to "effectively put a warranty on their care by limiting the payments they get from Medicare if a patient is readmitted" too soon or in circumstances that suggest his or her earlier care was ineffective or harmful.[26]

If such an outcomes-based payment system — often referred to as a "bundled" payment system — can be developed "that providers can live with, we'll be in a much better place" than we are today when it comes to holding down costs, says Harvard Medical School's Chernew. Whether the law is making inroads should begin to become evident in about five years, he says.

Other proposed provider-payment measures "include just about everything we know" about cost control, making it a best effort at implementing cost savings on the provider side, says McClellan, the former Medicare and Medicaid chief under George W. Bush.

The "history of previous legislation is auspicious," because earlier laws that cut health-care provider payments have almost always had a bigger cost-cutting effect than analysts first predicted, said Peter Orszag, director of the White House Office of Management and Budget.[27]

In academic analyses of health-system reorganization plans that stamp out inefficient care — as the law aims to do — "the estimates of possible efficiency savings range up to 30 percent or more of medical spending," said Harvard University professor of economics David M. Cutler. Because previous analyses have underestimated the cost-saving effects of such measures, there's a good chance that "costs will fall more rapidly than expected," Cutler said.[28]

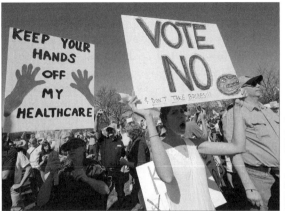

Supporters of the Tea Party movement demonstrate against the health care bill at the Capitol on March 20, 2010, just before a cliffhanger vote on the sweeping legislation the next day. Critics say the plan will cost too much and give the government too much control over Americans' health decisions.

Nevertheless, even some analysts who see significant good in the law have doubts about its ability to make health care affordable.

"I suspect that the legislation is going to be more successful at coverage goals than at cost-containment goals," says Katherine Baicker, a professor of health economics at the Harvard School of Public Health. "You can throw money" at patients and providers and increase individuals' access to health care, "but we simply don't yet know how" to slow health-care cost growth, even though scholars do have ideas about what may work, she says.

Also unknown is "whether Congress will have the political will" to enforce cost-cutting measures that the law's demonstration projects find to be effective, says Baicker. Health-care providers always fight such changes because they affect income, and that means "all these things could easily be left to wither on the vine," she says. "While the demos may be promising, there is no built-in mechanism in the law to give them teeth."

For example, the law sets up a program for testing the "comparative effectiveness" of health treatments — with the goal of spending health-care dollars only for what works best, notes a report by Medicare's actuary. Requiring Medicare to base payments on comparative-effectiveness findings would reap "substantial savings," says the actuary's office. However, the law does not

authorize establishment of a federal board "with authority over payment and coverage policies" to force Medicare and other programs to stop paying for less effective treatments, said the actuary. Instead, the legislation only requires dissemination of the research as a recommendation for payment changes. Because of lawmakers' reluctance to impose tough changes, therefore, a program that could save a lot of money will result only in "small savings," and even those will "take many years to develop," the report predicts.[29]

"If there were an FDA [Food and Drug Administration] of cost containment, none of these measures would be considered safe and effective," quipped Mark Pauly, a professor of health-care systems, business and public policy at the University of Pennsylvania's Wharton School. Nevertheless, a few provisions, such as reducing rates of hospital readmission by letting nurses counsel patients about staying healthy and requiring hospitals to take stringent steps to ward off hospital-acquired infections, likely will save money, Pauly conceded.[30]

But some conservative critics say the law's cost-cutting initiatives simply cannot work.

"You cannot control costs unless someone does the controlling. And there is nothing in the legislation that would free either patients or doctors to do that job," said John Goodman, president of the National Center for

AFP/Getty Images/Nicholas Kamm

Policy Analysis, a free-market think tank in Dallas. Goodman is among conservatives who argue that the entire system of third-party insurance — not just public programs like Medicare — shields patients too much from the high cost of health care. Therefore, he argues that since the new law preserves an insurance system, it cannot succeed at cost control. Goodman argues that health costs will only be controlled when patients must fully confront the cost of the care they seek, so that they will bargain hard to force their medical providers "to use their intelligence, creativity and innovative ability to seek efficiencies the way people do in other markets."[31]

Furthermore, several provisions in the law "are sure to increase health-insurance premiums in the short term," says the Galen Institute's Turner. A ban on health insurers placing a lifetime or annual limit on the benefits an individual receives will raise premiums for all policyholders, she said.[32]

Meanwhile, liberal opponents say the law lacks the most powerful known means of holding down costs. For example, allowing Americans to buy prescription drugs from Canada "could have saved American consumers roughly $100 billion," but that didn't make it into the bill because drug manufacturers strenuously object to the practice, wrote liberal blogger Jon Walker. Creating a centralized federal government authority to negotiate payments with health-care providers would also lower payment rates, and requiring insurance-benefit packages to be standardized would reduce administrative costs and allow for better comparison shopping. But neither of those common-sense measures is in the new law either, Walker said.[33]

BACKGROUND

Exceptional America

Virtually all other industrialized countries have concluded that health care is a right that nations owe their people and have created taxpayer-funded public or combination public-private systems to provide it. By contrast, the U.S. Congress has never seriously debated establishing a universal right to care.[34]

"We had a little of this conversation after the Civil War," resulting in a basic guarantee of health care as a right for veterans, says University of Pennsylvania ethicist

Caplan. Other nations have gone much farther, however. For example, after World War II, Britain explicitly discussed whether health care should be guaranteed as a right and decided that "it was part of what the nation owed to a people who had lived through the blitz" — Nazi Germany's sustained seven-month bombing of Britain during the early years of World War II, he says.

"Canada had the conversation and concluded that" a guaranteed right to health care "is part of what would bind [the geographically vast country] together as a nation," says Caplan.

"We're the only county that finds it quite this difficult to discuss" whether health care should be a right, in part because of historical struggles to harmonize a racially and ethnically diverse society, Caplan says. It's easier for a smaller, homogeneous nation to discuss using taxpayer dollars to offer health care to all, he says.

As a result, health insurance in America developed as a purely private enterprise in the first half of the 20th century. At first, there was limited concern about paying for coverage. Gradually, however, as care grew more expensive, employers began offering hospitalization insurance as a benefit for workers.

By the 1940s, large unionized companies dominated the American economy, and many used health-insurance benefits as a bargaining chip in labor negotiations. Employer-sponsored health plans successfully spread out health-care costs among large pools of workers and, by doing so, allowed each individual to pay relatively low and consistent premiums, even in years when they had accidents or illnesses. Furthermore, since the sickest people are unlikely to be employed, private insurance companies prospered in an insurance market almost entirely made up of employer-sponsored coverage.

Hybrid Solutions

Beginning as early as the 1940s, however, some lawmakers grew troubled by the realization that vulnerable populations — such as the elderly and the disabled — did not have workplace-based coverage. Many of these people couldn't afford individual policies, which in most states insurers could price according to the individual's own health risk.

Members of Congress made unsuccessful attempts to launch discussion of health coverage for all in 1943, 1945, 1947, 1949 and 1957, and Presidents Franklin D. Roosevelt,

CHRONOLOGY

1880s-1930s *As the cost and effectiveness of health care increase, industrialized countries mull universal access, and Americans worry about affording health care.*

1883 Germany creates first universal health-care system.

1929 School system in Dallas, Texas, launches first prepaid hospital insurance plan for employees.

1932 Committee on the Cost of Medical Care details Americans' growing difficulties in paying for care.

1935 Attempts fail to include health coverage in the Social Security Act.

1940s-1980s *Employer-sponsored insurance becomes the dominant form of U.S. health coverage. Congress enacts Medicare and Medicaid to fill coverage gaps for the elderly, the disabled and poor mothers with children.*

1943 Wagner-Murray-Dingell bill for compulsory national health insurance is introduced in Congress. . . . National War Labor Board declares employer contributions to insurance are income-tax free, opening the way for companies to use health insurance packages to attract workers.

1946 United Kingdom launches fully nationalized universal coverage system — National Health Service.

1960 U.S. health spending totals $28 billion, or 5.2 percent of gross domestic product (GDP).

1965 President Lyndon B. Johnson signs Medicare and Medicaid into law.

1971 President Richard M. Nixon places wage and price controls on medical services.

1980 Health spending tops $255 billion, or 9.1 percent of GDP.

1990s-2009 *Rising health costs force some Americans to drop coverage, prompting Congress to enact a public insurance program for children in working families.*

1993 President Bill Clinton and first lady Hillary Clinton propose sweeping health-system reforms. Insurance industry launches opposition campaign.

1994 Senate abandons the Clinton health plan without debate.

1997 President Clinton signs State Children's Health Insurance Program (SCHIP) to provide coverage for children in working families.

2000 Health spending totals $1.4 trillion, or 13.8 percent of GDP.

2002 Congress enacts Health Care Tax Credit for those who lose their jobs to foreign competition.

2006 Massachusetts enacts mandatory, universal health-coverage program.

2009 Massachusetts officials consider implementing "payment bundling" — paying doctors and hospitals a flat fee upfront to cover patients — to control cost growth in their universal-coverage plan. . . . Congress votes to expand SCHIP program. . . . President Obama and congressional Democrats slowly push coverage-expansion plans through Congress in the face of heated opposition; bill passes Senate on Dec. 24.

2010s *Implementation begins of the most wide-ranging health-reform legislation in U.S. history.*

2010 Health reform clears Congress on March 21; President Obama signs legislation intended to cover about 32 million uninsured people and re-engineer the health-care payment system to trim costs; the law's main provisions take effect in 2014. . . . The 2009 federal SCHIP expansion falters as state budgets suffer from recession. . . . Connecticut becomes first state to sign up for the 2010 reform law's option to immediately extend Medicaid coverage to poor adults outside the traditional

(Continued)

(Continued)

Medicaid categories of disabled people and mothers and their young children. . . . At least 20 state attorneys general sue the federal government to stop the health-care law.

2014 Main provisions of the 2010 health law are slated to begin, including a requirement for all Americans to buy health insurance.

2010

March — President Obama signs the Patient Protection and Affordable Care Act and its companion legislation, the Health Care and Education Reconciliation Act of 2010. . . . First lawsuits challenging the law's constitutionality are filed, including one brought by the state of Virginia. . . . Virginia is first state to enact a law barring the government from requiring individuals to buy health insurance.

April — Thirteen states file a court challenge to the health-care reform law. . . . States may expand Medicaid to cover childless adults with incomes up to 133 percent of poverty level.

July — Federal government opens "high-risk" health plan where people with preexisting health conditions can get more affordable coverage.

September — Young adults up to age 26 become eligible for coverage by their parents' health plans.

2011

January — Some Medicare enrollees get rebates for their prescription-drug spending. . . . Very small businesses become eligible for tax credits for providing health insurance to workers. . . . Newly elected House Republican majority votes to repeal health-reform law; Senate does not take up the bill.

May — House Republicans vote to defund several health-reform provisions; Senate does not take up the bills, and President Obama says he would veto them.

May-June — Federal appeals courts take up four legal challenges to the Affordable Care Act; in initial rulings, judges strike down two of the challenges and uphold two others; Supreme Court declines to expedite hearing on challenges to the law.

Harry S. Truman, Richard D. Nixon and Clinton all proposed guaranteed universal coverage.

Ultimately, however, Congress backed off even debating such proposals because of strong opposition from big employers, insurers and health-care providers — who feared that increased government involvement in health care would mean less autonomy in practice and lower pay. Even organized labor opposed the discussions, largely because it liked bargaining for good health-care benefits.

But the growing size of the population without coverage eventually forced Congress to act. To supplement the private health-insurance system, which left many people behind, Congress launched two large public insurance programs in 1965, effectively creating a right — or "entitlement" — to health care for two specific groups of Americans. The Medicare program covers the elderly, while Medicaid covers poor mothers with young children and some poor and seriously disabled people.

Congress expanded public coverage one more time to reach another population that was increasingly priced out of employer-sponsored coverage. The State Children's Health Insurance Program (SCHIP), launched in 1997, covers children in low- and middle-income working families.

History, then, leaves the United States with a hybrid system — about half public and half private. While the arrangement matches the policy preferences of many Americans, who tend to be political centrists, it poses a complex challenge for lawmakers faced with high rates of uninsurance and fast-rising costs.

When Nixon and Democratic Presidents Jimmy Carter, in the 1970s, and Clinton, in the 1990s, proposed health-care overhauls intended to help provide affordable care for all Americans, all three plans were complicated by their attempts to leave both public and private coverage intact. Further, because of their hybrid nature, all invited harsh criticism both from conservative Republicans, who

States Will Be Ground Zero for Many Changes

"A lot is resting on the shoulders of the states."

Public-policy experts agree that the states will play a crucial role in implementing the new health-care reforms, but they aren't all sure the states are up to the task.

"A lot is resting on the shoulders of the states" for the success of health-care reform, says Stan Dorn, a senior research associate at the Washington-based Urban Institute, a centrist think tank.

"This federalism aspect of the law is one of the biggest worries" in some respects "because reliance on states leads to enormous variation" in a program, which likely will leave some residents of the country with low benefits and little protection under the new law, says Georgetown University professor of public policy Judith Feder. Some analysts tout states as "laboratories of democracy," where innovative ideas are often pioneered and tested, but Feder argues that studies show that most states rarely innovate. "Federalism is overrated," she says.

Yale University professor of political science Jacob Hacker says ultimate success will heavily depend on the states and federal government working together. "To me, one of the biggest challenges of implementation is that the law creates dual authority in many areas," he says. "Hopefully, good partnerships will develop." Specifically, Hacker explains, the federal government will be funding subsidies for people without employer-based coverage to buy insurance in new markets, called exchanges, but the states are charged with setting up and running the exchanges.

Most of the money to fund actual new insurance coverage under Medicaid and in the new exchanges will come from the federal government, which should prove a boon to states in some respects, since it's state and local authorities who often see the consequences as uninsured people develop severe medical problems. States will end up bearing a large share of administrative expenses for the programs, however.

"The states that do the least now" to provide Medicaid coverage "will get the most money from the expansion" of Medicaid to a new group of eligible people — everyone with incomes under 133 percent of the federal poverty level, says Judith Solomon, a senior fellow at the left-leaning Center on Budget and Policy Priorities.

States generally will benefit from the Medicaid expansion because currently "very, very large numbers of the low-income people" who will become eligible for the mostly federally funded Medicaid expansion "are currently in some state-funded programs," such as mental-health programs, Solomon says.

State officials who are fretting about the cost of the new programs tend to "assume that 100 percent" of eligible people will participate, "but we've never seen any such number" in previous programs, so it's unlikely to happen this time either, says Solomon.

"That's not to say that there won't be some expenses" for states, Solomon says. Just as in the current Medicaid program, states will pick up half the administrative costs for the new, much larger Medicaid population — beginning in 2014 — while the federal government will pay for the other 50 percent of the administration.

"I'm worried about the administration side, where there's only a 50 percent federal match," says Dorn. "No state person will want to brag about hiring more state employees" since all state governments are constrained by legal requirements to balance their budgets annually, he says.

Nevertheless, when it comes to getting high numbers of eligible people enrolled, intensive outreach is crucial, plus having as many as possible automatically enrolled based on information government agencies already possess, rather than requiring them to fill out application forms, Dorn says. That makes administrative "resources the greatest implementation question."

Unless they opt out of the responsibility, states also are supposed to set up and manage the health-insurance exchanges that in 2014 are slated to begin selling coverage to people without employer-sponsored health insurance.

"But if I were a state legislator or governor, the last thing I would want to do would be to run an exchange," says Dorn. "The federal money [to administer the exchanges] runs from 2014 to Jan. 1, 2015," and after that "each exchange must raise its own money by charging fees" to insurers or health-care providers, Dorn explains. All of these players "will want services the exchanges provide but won't want to pay." That will give states a difficult balancing act: raising money while also tightly regulating the health-care market, Dorn says.

If many states are leery, "the feds might end up doing it all, which might not be a bad outcome," he says, although it's not what the law anticipates.

— *Marcia Clemmitt*

Reforms Face Many Hurdles

"The war to make health-care reform an enduring success has just begun."

As the health-reform law is implemented, the number of things that can go wrong is as big as the health-care system is complicated. Besides the fact that not only states but also doctors and hospitals may balk at the new provisions, future Congresses must ante up continued funding to administer the law, never a certain outcome.

The law's coverage-expansion portions "are so state-based that the states can stymie a lot," says Judith Solomon, a senior fellow at the left-leaning Center on Budget and Policy Priorities. "There can be a great deal of stalling" on getting some initiatives like a large Medicaid expansion up and running. The law also will largely rely on increased state regulation of health insurers, which could lead to large variations" around the country in how tightly insurers are held to consumer-friendly standards.

Furthermore, "Medicaid rolls in some states will expand by 50 percent or more" beginning in 2014, and "it is unclear whether these states will be able to find enough providers who are willing to accept the anticipated payment rates," wrote Henry J. Aaron, a senior fellow at the centrist Brookings Institution think tank, and Robert D. Reischauer, president of the centrist Urban Institute. Will states "raise provider payment rates, curtail Medicaid benefits (as states are legally authorized to do), or simply let patients fail to find doctors who are willing to provide them with care?" they ask.[1]

One of the balancing acts that face lawmakers seeking to expand coverage in the employer-based U.S. system is keeping enough employer money in the game to avoid overwhelming taxpayers with new costs. Accordingly, the law was developed in hopes of limiting incentives for employers to drop workers' coverage.

But already "there are some troubling signs that employers will back off coverage because of the existence of the exchanges," where workers can buy insurance — using tax-funded subsidies — if their employers don't offer it, says Yale University professor of political science Jacob Hacker. If that happens on a large scale, "for society as a whole it might be a better thing and more fair, because having employers as the basis for coverage distorts labor markets" because the fear of losing health insurance often traps people in jobs or careers they don't want, Hacker says. "Nevertheless, it's not a direction that most people want to go in."

Federal agencies must transform the law's rather general language into specific rules, and some observers say that might produce rules that are unworkable. Moreover, there's evidence that the agencies are already falling behind in the process.

"They're not going to meet their deadlines, so they should push the whole thing back," says Joseph Antos, a scholar at the free-market American Enterprise Institute think tank and a former assistant director of the

oppose taxpayer-financed, government-regulated health care, and from liberal Democrats, who often argue that private health-insurance markets simply don't work and ought to be replaced by all-public coverage.

The Clinton Plan

In 1993 and 1994, when Bill and Hillary Clinton, now Secretary of State, proposed their health-care overhaul plan, Congress came as close as it ever has to debating a full-fledged health overhaul. The times seemed to favor action. When the Clintons' Health Security Act was proposed, up to two-thirds of Americans told pollsters they favored tax-financed national health insurance.

The Clinton proposal attempted to thread the needle of the hybrid U.S. system by maintaining large public-coverage programs while creating new, tightly regulated private-insurance markets where people could buy coverage that was tax subsidized for low-income people. In an attempt to hold onto the private business dollars that had long financed health care in the United States for workers, the plan would have required all employers to contribute to the cost.

But the proposal's complexity helped make the plan an easy target for political opponents and businesses and health-care insurers and providers who feared its complicated rules and high costs. Less than a year after the proposal was announced, Congress informed the White House that it had no plans to move the plan forward.

Congressional Budget Office. "It's going to take more than the three years" the law has set aside to get the massive coverage-expansion program up and running.

Already there's evidence that agencies like the Centers for Medicare and Medicaid Services (CMS) are overwhelmed, Antos says. Neither CMS nor the Department of Health and Human Services (HHS) "is an insurance company" or has much experience in insurance, a serious lack since a massive insurance expansion is a central portion of the law, and Congress has relied on the agencies to flesh out virtually all the details, Antos says. HHS Secretary Kathleen Sebelius is a former Kansas insurance commissioner, "but she admitted that she doesn't have any particular influence in health-care reform."

Drafters of the law made little use of the expertise of the insurance industry and insurance analysts and regulators, "so there will be mistakes" in implementation, charges Antos. "It was done without consultation with the many, many experts, and HHS looks as if it's not going to ask experts now."

But Hacker says it's "too soon to be that critical of the implementation." The critical judgments will be made in the next year or so, when it will be possible to begin judging whether implementation will be smooth, he says. And while rules for how much premium revenue must fund health care "are inevitably going to be contentious, I don't believe it'll preclude insurers from participating," says Hacker. "The fact is that insurers were supportive of these things because they want the revenue" that will accompany expanded, subsidized coverage.

Nevertheless, "there's such a long time before the law goes fully into effect that critics can paint it any way they want," making it very easy for opponents to turn the public against the law, says Hacker. "The best thing advocates could do for themselves is not to trumpet their achievements but to make clear that the law is a first step."

In another setback to implementation, Senate Republicans are blocking the nomination of physician Donald Berwick, a professor of health policy and management at the Harvard School of Public Health, to head CMS. Conservatives say that Berwick's work with Britain's National Health Service is a sign he would use government to destroy American physicians' independence. Supporters argue that, to advance the health-reform law's cost-cutting initiatives, CMS must have a leader dedicated to emphasizing effectiveness and efficiency in U.S. medical practice.[2]

"The war to make health-care reform an enduring success has just begun" and "will require administrative determination and imagination and as much political resolve as was needed to pass the legislation," Aaron and Reischauer warn.[3]

— *Marcia Clemmitt*

[1] Henry J. Aaron and Robert D. Reischauer, "The War Isn't Over," *The New England Journal of Medicine online*, March 24, 2010, www.nejm.org.

[2] For background, see Linda Bergthold, "Who Is Don Berwick and Why Do the Republicans Want to Kill His Nomination," *Huffington Post blog*, June 1, 2010, www.huffingtonpost.com/linda-bergthold/who-is-don-berwick-and-wh_b_596859.html.

[3] Aaron and Reischauer, *op. cit.*

"The failure of the Clinton health plan . . . vividly demonstrates . . . that most Americans — even the underinsured and the soon-to-be-uninsured, the potentially uninsurable and the one-illness-from-bankruptcy — can be scared into fearing that changing America's inadequate public-private patchwork means higher costs and lower quality," Yale's Hacker wrote. "This is the legacy of an insurance structure that lulls many into believing they are secure when they are not, that hides vast costs in quiet deductions from workers' pay, [and] that leaves government paying the tab for the most vulnerable and the least well," he said. "It is the very failings of our insurance system that make dealing with those failings so devilishly hard."[35]

But many conservatives continue to argue that too-strict government regulation of health care along with insurance and public programs like Medicare are the culprits that have hopelessly damaged the health-care market and made effective overhaul difficult.

"The problems in American health care have not been caused by a failure in the health care market, but mainly by distortions imposed on the market," such as "federal tax subsidies and programs that have created a third-party payment system," said Rep. Paul Ryan, R-Wis. The key to a successful overhaul is to convert to an all-private system, by means such as creating "a standard Medicare [cash] payment to be used for the purchase of private health coverage," he said.[36]

Massachusetts Plan

Over the years, many states have attempted to enact systemwide reforms on their own, frustrated by the federal government's reluctance even to discuss universal health care. The pioneers of sweeping reform included Tennessee, Oregon, Washington, Vermont and Minnesota.

Those states generally attempted to expand public coverage for the poorest residents and provide some form of tax-funded subsidies to help other low- to middle-income and sick people purchase coverage in more tightly regulated private insurance markets. But while the programs have increased coverage, at least temporarily, all have eventually foundered as costs continued rising while taxpayer willingness to fund coverage for sick or lower-income people waned.

Massachusetts first began expanding coverage to all its citizens in 1988 and enacted its latest plan in 2006. The law shifted Medicaid funding to provide more subsidies to individuals to get insurance; placed requirements to buy or help pay for coverage on both employers and individuals; and set up a statewide regulated insurance market — known as an insurance "Connector" — which state officials hoped would force insurers to compete for enrollees based on quality and price of benefits.[37]

Reactions to Massachusetts' latest initiative are mixed.

Costs are the big challenge, and it's not yet clear how state attempts to change the medical culture to favor efficiency over excess services and high price tags are working, says Chernew, of Harvard Medical School. "Some say that the culture in the state is changing, but others say we're on the verge of collapse."

People using the Connector to buy insurance "have had lots of different choices of health plans, and there's been good consumer service and information," says the Urban Institute's Dorn.

Furthermore, "they've been good at negotiating for low premiums" with insurers, he says. For example, Massachusetts has several extremely expensive hospital systems, which have had enormous clout in winning high payment from insurers over the years because patients want access to them, Dorn explains. But the Connector set up price competition by establishing a low-cost coverage option that didn't include the big-name systems, and consumers concerned with price, such as young people earning lower wages, have signed up for it, he says.

The state also has rewarded health insurers who keep premiums low by enrolling the most "default" enrollees — people who don't seek out the health coverage on their own — with the insurer who quotes the lowest premium. Default enrollees are often the healthiest, cheapest-to-cover people, thus helping that insurer hold down costs by having an extra helping of healthy people in their pool, Dorn says.

Advocates of single-payer systems, however, say Massachusetts' attempt at health-care expansion is doomed, just like earlier attempts. "Unfortunately, competition in health insurance involves a race to the bottom," said Harvard Medical School's Woolhandler. "Insurers compete by not paying for care: by denying payment and shifting costs onto patients or other payers."[38]

CURRENT SITUATION

Democrats in Power

With Democrats holding not only the White House but also substantial majorities in both the House and the Senate for the first time in three decades, advocates of health-care reform hoped that the 111th Congress — whose term runs from 2009 through 2010 — would finally be the one to debate a health-care overhaul for the entire population.

In his first address to a joint session of Congress, on Feb. 24, 2009, newly inaugurated President Barack Obama declared that "we must . . . address the crushing cost of health care" and thus "can no longer afford to put health-care reform on hold." High-cost health care "now causes a bankruptcy in America every thirty seconds. . . . In the last eight years, [health-insurance] premiums have grown four times faster than wages. And in each of these years, 1 million more Americans have lost their health insurance."[39]

Furthermore, he said, "already, we have done more to advance the cause of health-care reform in the last 30 days than we have in the last decade." For example, "when it was days old, this Congress passed a law to provide and protect health insurance for 11 million American children whose parents work full time" by using a cigarette tax to expand funding for the public-sector SCHIP program that covers children in working families, he said.[40]

Does Health Reform Create Winners and Losers?

More affordable coverage for sicker people will boost costs for healthier people.

Critics charge that the health-care reform plan makes some Americans winners and others losers. Some liberal critics charge that, by relying on private insurance for much of the tax-subsidized coverage expansion, Congress will essentially just direct more taxpayer dollars into the already bloated coffers of the insurance industry.

Other analysts aren't so sure, however.

Many of the people who will enroll in tax-subsidized coverage will not have had consistent insurance coverage for several years, and as a result often have developed significant health needs that will drive their spending up, said Maggie Mahar, a fellow at the liberal, New York City-based Century Foundation.[1]

According to recent analyses, around 11 percent of uninsured people are in "fair" or "poor" health, compared to only 5 percent of privately insured people who report poor health. Unlike in the past, "under the new reform law, insurance companies will not be able to charge these new customers more than they charge others in their community," said Mahar. This means that insurers are unlikely to reap a big windfall from the tax-funded subsidies, she argued.[2]

The same legislative provision that Mahar cites as making coverage more affordable for sicker people will cause health premiums to rise for younger, healthier people, however — an example of the way the law creates some winners and losers in the attempt to get more people covered, noted Trudy Lieberman, a longtime health-care journalist who is a contributing editor to the *Columbia Journalism Review.*[3]

"This is not national health insurance we're talking about, where everyone, no matter how old or young, is treated equally," Lieberman wrote. "We are talking about a private insurance market where companies have to make money to stay in business" and where one key way of making money in the past has been for companies to simply avoid insuring the sickest people so that healthier people can pay lower premiums.

Under the new law, however, insurance companies will be "required to take sick people who will file large claims" and also will be banned from charging them the extremely high premiums that they are liable for in the individual insurance market today, she said. Instead, older or sicker

people will be on the hook for premiums that are "no more than three times what [insurers] charge a younger person," and as a result premiums for younger, healthier people will rise by an estimated 15 to 17 percent. Insurers "have to make up the revenue shortfall somehow, and they'll do it by increasing the premiums for younger people. It's a balancing act Congress has permitted," she wrote. However, for young adults earning $43,000 per year or less, some of the premium increase will be offset by a federal tax credit.

In another financial balancing act, lawmakers had to determine whether to offer larger taxpayer-funded subsidies to a smaller population of people — with lower incomes — or spread out the subsidies to a larger population. More subsidies might make the law more politically popular but also would require making subsidies for the lowest-income people smaller than they might have been otherwise. Some analysts fear that lawmakers came down on the wrong side of that question.

"One big worry that I have is affordability," says Stan Dorn, a senior research associate at the Urban Institute think tank. In the 2006 coverage expansion launched in Massachusetts, the state provided "much bigger subsidies" and "much more extensive coverage" to people with incomes up to 300 percent of the federal poverty level — the group most in danger of being priced out of coverage, says Dorn. (In 2009, for example, a family of four earning about $66,000 had an income 300 percent of the poverty level.)

But the federal law took a different tack, offering smaller subsidies for every income group — including the lowest — in order to provide some level of subsidy for people with incomes up to 400 percent of the poverty level, he says. "It would have been better to concentrate more on the people up to 300 percent of the poverty level rather than spread the subsidies so far."

— *Marcia Clemmitt*

---

[1] Maggie Mahar, "Myths & Facts About HealthCare Reform: Who Wins & Who Loses?" *Healthbeat* blog, April 6, 2010, www.healthbeat-blog.com.

[2] *Ibid.*

[3] Trudy Lieberman, "The White House vs. the Associated Press," *Columbia Journalism Review online*, April 7, 2010, www.cjr.org.

Will the health-care reform law harm the federal budget?

 Grace-Marie Turner
President, Galen Institute

 Paul N. Van de Water
Senior Fellow, Center on Budget and Policy Priorities

Written for *CQ Researcher*, May 2010

Written for *CQ Researcher*, May 2010

President Obama's health overhaul law will have a devastating impact on the federal budget, both because of what it does and what it fails to do.

It does increase federal health spending, creates expensive open-ended entitlements and uses budget gimmicks to hide the true costs of the massive expansion of federal spending.

And it fails to lower health costs, bend the cost curve down or provide real solutions to the trillions of dollars in red ink facing existing entitlement programs, especially Medicare and Medicaid.

Nonetheless, to win passage of the health law, supporters insisted the law would be fiscally responsible and would reduce the deficit. Not a chance.

The Congressional Budget Office (CBO) recently said the law will cost $115 billion more than originally estimated, pushing the total cost above $1 trillion. But this underestimates the true costs by hundreds of billions — if not trillions of dollars — due to the law's deception and budget gimmicks.

Part of the true cost was concealed by delaying expensive subsidies until 2014 while starting many of the tax hikes and Medicare cuts much earlier. Further, the law is purportedly paid for with $569 billion in tax increases and $528 billion in cuts to Medicare. But these Medicare cuts are highly suspect given Congress' history of pushing them off to keep doctor payments level — and keep physicians in the Medicare program. Keeping payments just at current rates will cost $276 billion over 10 years, according to the CBO.

When these and other costs are included, the more accurate price tag for ObamaCare is $2.5 trillion over a decade.

Rather than helping contain escalating health spending, as promised, ObamaCare pushes it higher. Medicare's chief actuary, Rick Foster, says federal health spending will rise by $311 billion by 2019 thanks to the law.

And this estimate doesn't include tens of millions more people who could lose their health insurance at work. The law threatens employers with big fines and subjects them to unpredictable health insurance cost increases; many are considering dropping coverage. If they do, millions more workers would be dumped onto health exchanges where they'll be subsidized by taxpayers. If this happens, federal spending will explode.

Gimmicks, new entitlements and unrealistic assumptions are just some of the many ingredients in ObamaCare that will have a crippling impact on the federal budget. We simply can't afford this law.

The Congressional Budget Office (CBO) estimates that the new health reform law will reduce deficits by $143 billion over the first decade (2010-2019) and by about one-half of 1 percent of gross domestic product, or about $1.3 trillion, over the second decade (2020-2029).

The law will extend coverage to over 30 million uninsured Americans and provide important consumer protections to tens of millions of insured Americans whose coverage may have critical gaps. It will more than pay for these improvements by making specific reductions in Medicare, Medicaid and other programs and by increasing tax revenues (such as by raising the Medicare tax on high-income people).

Despite CBO's finding that the law will reduce deficits, some people have argued that it will actually increase deficits, claiming that CBO's cost estimate includes savings that won't occur, omits costs that should be included, or both. Those claims don't withstand scrutiny (see "Health Reform Will Reduce the Deficit," www.cbpp.org/files/3-25-10health.pdf).

For example, some claim that the law's Medicare savings are unrealistic because Congress never lets Medicare reductions take effect. History shows this is untrue. Over the past 20 years Congress has enacted four pieces of legislation that include significant Medicare savings; virtually all of the savings in three of them (the 1990, 1993 and 2005 budget reconciliation bills) took effect, as did nearly four-fifths of the savings in the fourth piece of legislation (the Balanced Budget Act of 1997).

Some contend that the health-reform law should include the cost of permanently fixing Medicare's sustainable growth rate (SGR) formula for setting physician payments. The poorly designed formula turned out to require much larger cuts in physician payments than Congress intended when it enacted SGR, so Congress has regularly acted in recent years to prevent the full SGR cuts from taking effect. But the SGR cost is in no way a result of health reform — the government will incur this cost regardless of health reform, not because of it.

Because rising health-care costs represent the single largest cause of the federal government's long-term budget problems, fundamental health reform is key to their solution. Experts agree that slowing the growth of health-care costs will require an ongoing process of testing, experimentation and rapid implementation of what is found to work. The health-reform law begins that process. It starts to transform a system that delivers ever more services into one that provides effective, high-value health care.

"I suffer no illusions that this will be an easy process," said Obama. "But I . . . know that nearly a century after Teddy Roosevelt first called for reform, the cost of our health care has weighed down our economy and the conscience of our nation long enough. . . . Health-care reform cannot wait, it must not wait, and it will not wait another year."[41]

In the House, the legislation waited nearly 10 months, passing on a 220-215 vote on Saturday evening, Nov. 7, 2009, with one Republican voting in favor and 39 Democrats opposed.[42]

In the Senate, however, where the minority party wields much more power, debate dragged on into spring 2010, with the measure all but given up for dead on several occasions. Republican senators repeatedly threatened to filibuster — hold the floor without allowing the health-care legislation to come to a vote — forcing Senate leaders to muster 60-vote majorities five times to move the bill forward.

On Dec. 24, 2009, by a 60-39 margin, Senate Democrats finally passed their version of the legislation with no Republican votes. The Senate and House bills varied considerably, however, and, in such a case, both houses of Congress must — one way or another — pass identical bills before they can become law.

Thus, the cliffhanger continued for an additional three months as Democrats struggled to piece together a reform package that could win all the needed conservative Democratic votes in the Senate while retaining liberal support in the House. In addition, by 2010, Democrats' previous 60-vote, filibuster-stymieing Senate majority was reduced to 59 votes, as Sen. Scott Brown, R-Mass., was seated as the elected replacement of the late Sen. Edward M. Kennedy, D-Mass. — longtime ardent champion of health-care reform — who died of brain cancer on Aug. 26, 2009.

Ultimately, using several parliamentary maneuvers, Senate Majority Leader Harry Reid, D-Nev., and Speaker of the House Nancy Pelosi, D-Calif., engineered passage of a bill acceptable to Democrats in both houses. On March 21, the House passed the Senate's version of the bill. Then, under a process called "reconciliation," first the Senate and then the House passed a package of changes to the Senate legislation to make it acceptable to the generally more liberal House Democratic majority.

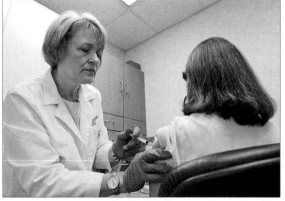

Nurse practitioner Kathryn Quinn administers a flu shot at a clinic in a CVS store in Wyckoff, N.J. Proponents of the health-reform law say using nurse practitioners for more tasks often performed by physicians will help keep health-care costs down.

Reconciliation bills — which are permitted to include only provisions that relate to the federal budget — may not be filibustered and thus require only a 51-vote majority in the Senate to pass.[43]

"Part of Obama's frustration" over health care "is that he thought that in the end some Republicans would approve" the legislation, "which is not as radical as the overhaul that Nixon proposed" in the early 1970s, says Bryan D. Jones, a professor of congressional studies at the University of Texas, in Austin.

The new law is "a much more conservative policy than was considered in the past," says the Urban Institute's Dorn. For example, in the Clinton plan, "we were going to leave behind our employer-based coverage, and there would have been a uniform benefit standard" for all health insurance. The Clinton proposal also included "explicit regulation of insurance premiums" to prevent them from rising too high and largely dictated what insurance benefit packages could contain, says Dorn. "This bill doesn't have any of that."

In fact, many Democrats liken the bill to the 2006 Massachusetts plan, passed by a Democrat-dominated legislature and signed into law by then-Gov. Mitt Romney, a Republican.

"A lot of commentators have said . . . this is sort of similar to the bill that Mitt Romney . . . passed in Massachusetts," said Obama.[44]

Many conservatives, including Romney, heatedly deny that the Massachusetts plan has much in common with the 2010 federal law, however.

"We don't like . . . the intrusion of the federal government on the rights of states" in the federal law, which requires states to participate in health-coverage expansions, nor the taxes the law will raise to pay for coverage, said Romney.[45]

Implementing the Law

Perhaps the biggest difference the law will make for most people is that, beginning in 2014, it will provide a new, regulated insurance marketplace. People who cannot get employer-sponsored coverage can shop for health insurance at the so-called state exchanges. The law also will provide many people with subsidies to help pay for that coverage.[46]

Also in 2014, people with incomes up to 133 percent of the federal poverty level can get Medicaid coverage, paid for mostly by the federal government. Currently, only certain groups of people, mainly poor mothers and their young children and some severely disabled poor people, are eligible for Medicaid.

Health insurers will face a very different set of rules and expectations in the new system, says Georgetown University's Feder. Today U.S. health insurers compete for profits largely based on "risk selection" — trying to be the insurer whose benefit packages attract the healthiest people, because money that doesn't go to medical care can go to profits. While the law "doesn't stamp out risk selection, it sure as hell treads on it," she continues, mainly because, ultimately, it will require insurers to take all comers and will also require that a certain minimum percentage of premiums go towards medical care, she explains.

Many of the law's provisions aimed at cost containment involve "putting new [health-care-delivery and payment] arrangements in place and getting providers into them," says Feder. Under the new arrangements, providers like doctors and hospitals "would retain earnings if they're efficient and deliver high-quality care rather than delivering a high volume of care," as occurs under current systems, she says.

"It's going to take a lot of money and new resources for Medicare to implement and implement quickly" the law's many new programs, says former Medicare and Medicaid chief McClellan. "It normally takes seven to 10 years" for a good idea to actually become part of the Medicare program. "But we don't have that kind of time."

Furthermore, there's the fear that, as in the past when Medicare has proven that certain techniques for saving money worked, Congress may block nationwide rollout of the methods, because of providers who worry they'll lose money, McClellan says.

"The risk is not that the bill is repealed but that pieces of it" won't be supported by future Congresses, says Robert Blendon, a professor of health policy at the Harvard School of Public Health. For example, a Republican Congress that opposes taxes may cut funding for federal subsidies that are required to help people afford insurance, he says.

Meanwhile, congressional Democrats are mulling additional changes they say may be needed to improve the health-care system for patients, such as tightening government oversight of health-insurance premium price increases.[47]

Fighting the Law

Conservatives continue to argue that the law involves government too much in health care.

"The new law requires all Americans to purchase health insurance or pay a penalty . . . an unprecedented extension of congressional power," wrote the Heritage Foundation's Nix. Furthermore, she said, "the health-care overhaul . . . diminishes the federalist system upon which the U.S. was founded, which grants certain powers to the states in order to limit those of the federal government." The law requires that states expand their Medicaid programs, whether or not they want to, and also includes new federal regulations on health insurers, which have been largely state regulated, Nix said.[48]

One of the most prominent initiatives to halt the law is a lawsuit now backed by 20 states and the National Federation of Independent Business.

"After all the political deals were made, small businesses were left with a law that does little to address costs and instead is filled with new mandates, taxes and paperwork requirements that increase the cost of doing business," said Karen Harned, head of the federation's legal office.[49]

The Obama administration has already filed a brief in federal district court in Detroit in one of the earliest lawsuits against the law. The suit was filed by the Thomas More Law Center, a conservative legal group in Ann Arbor, which argues that the law's individual mandate to buy health insurance violates constitutionally protected freedoms.

The administration argues that decisions to opt out of health insurance are more than personal choices but have consequences for the entire country — thus making them suitable targets of federal lawmaking. The administration's brief argues that when uninsured people get sick, people who have been paying insurance, as well as taxpayers, pick up the bill for their care. Thus, "individual decisions to forgo insurance coverage, in the aggregate, substantially affect interstate commerce by shifting costs to health-care providers and the public," making them a fair target for federal legislation under the Commerce Clause.[50]

Ironically, former Gov. Romney — who signed Massachusetts' health-reform law — is among opponents who've called most loudly for stopping the new federal law. Rather than seeking judicial repeal, however, Romney this spring urged voters to support Republican candidates to win back a congressional majority in November. Then "we can clamp down on this bill . . . by not funding it," he said.[51]

OUTLOOK
Dealing with Rationing

Supporters argue that as people learn more about the new law, most will back it. However, expanding taxpayers' responsibility to help provide health coverage for most Americans will ultimately require wrestling with the toughest question: As costs rise, how should taxpayer-supported health benefits be limited — or rationed?

"As people come to understand the basic approach" of the new law, "they'll like most of it," says the Urban Institute's Dorn. Many already support "providing more help for people who can't afford insurance, requiring employers to help and setting up new rules that help people buy" insurance in a more transparent, regulated marketplace, he says.

"Once the law is implemented, people won't have to worry that, 'Oh, if I get laid off, I'll lose coverage for my asthmatic daughter' " because they will be able to buy subsidized coverage elsewhere, he says.

But single-payer advocate Woolhandler of Harvard says the new law will only temporarily slow momentum for much larger reform "because we didn't really solve anything. The cost curve was absolutely not fixed" by the legislation, "so a lot of middle-class people" will eventually find their coverage threatened again. "Very quickly people are going to see that nothing is solved."

With a program in place to ensure basic health coverage to most Americans, the next debate will be about "rationing" care, says Baicker of the Harvard School of Public Health. As the number of available health services — and their price tags — increases, "public programs, at least, almost certainly won't be able to pay for anything that has any benefit at all," but, eventually, "will need to have a higher threshold" — paying only for things that have a certain level of benefit — to avoid having health costs squeeze out all other government spending, she says.

Merely broaching the conversation — let alone reaching conclusions about what care to fund — will be extremely difficult, Baicker says.

Currently, our system rations care by pricing some people out of care altogether, except for emergencies treated in the emergency room, says University of Pennsylvania ethicist Caplan.

Because lawmakers "avoided any discussion of rationing" in the recent debate, the public is running around with the delusion that we don't ration now," Caplan says. "But the discussion we need to have should start now, because the public will need many years to accept" the notion of health spending limits, he says.

UPDATE

Almost as soon as President Obama signed the Patient Protection and Affordable Care Act into law on March 23, 2010, federal officials and many state governments frantically began implementation efforts for the complex health-care-reform legislation. At the same time, however, Republicans in Congress, conservative groups and

Getty Images/Brendan Hoffman

Former House Speaker Newt Gingrich, R-Ga., speaking on Capitol Hill on March 31, 2011, wants to repeal the health-care reform law, which he calls Obamacare. National and state Republican leaders argue that expanding coverage to 30 million uninsured Americans would cost too much and lead to unwelcome government interference in the health-care system.

officials in more than half the states began exploring legal and legislative means to stop the law.

Scheduled to go into effect over the next eight years, the law is intended to reshape the health-insurance market and expand coverage to millions of uninsured Americans while holding down medical costs. The federal government's implementation of the early-stage changes appears to be basically on track. All 26 legislative provisions scheduled to take effect in 2010 have been implemented, along with 18 of 21 provisions scheduled for 2011 rollout. [52] Provisions that have already gone into effect include: [53]

- Grants to improve the process by which states review and approve proposed rate hikes by health-insurance companies;
- Rebates of $250 to Medicare enrollees who paid for some of their own prescriptions because of a so-called "doughnut hole" in Medicare prescription-drug coverage enacted in 2003;
- Tax credits to very small businesses with low-paid workforces for providing health insurance to their employees;
- Requirements that health insurers spend at least 85 percent of premium revenue on health-care-related items and provide rebates to consumers if they spend less;

- Approval for young adults up to age 26 to remain covered by their parents' health plans.

The law's effectiveness in expanding coverage to some 30 million additional Americans has yet to be fully tested, but early results include both promising and worrisome data.

For example, the creation of "high-risk" pools to help people with preexisting medical conditions find affordable coverage got off to a much slower start than lawmakers had hoped. Only about 12,500 people were enrolled nationwide by Feb. 1, 2011, the most recent date for which enrollment has been reported.

Hundreds of thousands of people around the country remain unable to afford coverage because insurers charge high premiums for people with preexisting conditions such as cancer, high blood pressure and high cholesterol. Nevertheless, federal officials have "an aggressive strategy to encourage enrollment of eligible individuals, meeting with local doctors, hospitals, consumer groups and chapters of advocacy groups like the American Cancer Society and American Diabetes Association," Steven B. Larsen, deputy administrator of the federal Center for Medicare and Medicaid Services, told a House subcommittee in April. As a result, he said, officials expect to see enrollment grow significantly between now and 2014, when insurers will no longer be allowed to refuse coverage or charge extremely disparate rates to people with preexisting conditions. [54]

Other parts of the law are off to a faster start. For example, at least 600,000 young adults under 26 are estimated to have insurance coverage now under the law's dependent-coverage provision, which debuted in September 2010. [55]

Legislative and Legal Opposition

Even before the Affordable Care Act became law, national and state Republican leaders vociferously opposed it, arguing that the coverage expansion would cost too much and lead to unwelcome government interference in the U.S. health-care system. State and federal GOP lawmakers have proposed legislation to repeal or defund the law, and several legal challenges to the legislation have been mounted.

In Congress' first major legislative action of 2011, a newly elected House Republican majority — joined by three Democrats — voted 245 to 189 to repeal the entire law. [56] The vote was mainly a symbolic gesture, however, because Democrats maintain control of the Senate and would not vote for repeal, and President Obama would veto repeal legislation should it reach his desk.

By spring, congressional Republicans widely acknowledged that attempts to repeal the entire program were "dead," as House Ways and Means Committee Chairman Dave Camp, R-Mich., put it. However, most Republicans still strongly oppose the law, especially the legal requirement for individuals to carry health insurance, which is set to take effect in 2014. "I do think we may have a vote to repeal that provision some time in this Congress," said Camp. [57]

Meanwhile, a series of 2011 spending bills and budget proposals by congressional Republicans aims to stop the law by blocking funds for federal agencies' implementation efforts.

In April, for example, four House Democrats joined Republicans to approve legislation defunding the law's so-called "prevention and public health fund," which would award grants to states and localities for preventive-health services. [58] In May, House Republicans voted to defund a federal grant program intended to help states set up "insurance exchanges" — regulated markets — in which individuals and small businesses could find information about and purchase insurance under the law. [59] Also in May, the House GOP voted to block a funding provision in the law for building school-based health centers. [60]

Action by the States

Much of the law's implementation, including funding, is left up to the states, some of which are actively executing the law's requirements while others are approving legislation to block the measure.

In Illinois, for example, Gov. Pat Quinn, a Democrat, declared this spring that a health-reform panel he'd appointed struck "the unifying theme" that the Affordable Care Act "must be implemented quickly, efficiently and fairly" to expand health coverage to more than a million currently uninsured state residents by 2014 and that state agencies would "work together to deliver" on the law's promise. [61]

In March 2010, however, Virginia lawmakers became the first in the nation to approve legislation declaring it illegal for the government to require individuals to buy health insurance. Republican Gov. Robert F. McDonnell signed the bill the next day. Later in 2010, Idaho, Utah, Georgia, Louisiana and Arizona legislators passed laws designed to block state implementation of the federal reform law by various means, and other states, including Indiana, Missouri, Montana, North Dakota, Tennessee and Wyoming, enacted similarly intentioned statutes in 2011. [62]

Legal Challenges

Meanwhile, conservative groups and state attorneys general have filed about 20 lawsuits challenging the health-care reform law, beginning soon after its enactment in spring 2010. The suits raise various arguments against the law's constitutionality, but virtually all focus on its requirement that individuals buy health insurance.

Supporters of the law say the Constitution permits Congress to regulate business that crosses state lines — a point that many of the measure's opponents challenge. In addition, supporters argue that the mandate requiring insurance coverage for all Americans is needed because, without it, too many people would purchase coverage only when they were ill. That, the law's supporters say, would subvert the purpose of insurance, which is to spread the costs of those who are ill at any given time across the whole, mostly healthy, population. [63]

Twenty-six states are now party to a lawsuit filed against the law in Florida on March 23, 2010. On Jan. 23, 2011, U.S. District Judge Roger Vinson sided with those states, ruling the entire law is unconstitutional based on the individual requirement to buy insurance. In December 2010, U.S. District Judge Henry Hudson also ruled against the mandate, in a lawsuit filed on March 23, 2010, by Virginia's attorney general, Kenneth Cuccinelli, a Republican. Unlike Vinson, Hudson struck down the individual mandate but left the rest of the law intact. In two other cases, filed in Detroit and Lynchburg, Va., however, judges have upheld the individual mandate and the health-care reform law as constitutional. [64]

The rulings in all four cases have been appealed. In April, Cuccinelli asked the U.S. Supreme Court to fast-track the appeals and place the health-care reform challenges onto its docket before the four appeals courts rule on the cases. The high court denied the request to expedite the matter, however. [65]

NOTES

1. Quoted in Scott Wilson, "With a Signature, Obama Seals His Health-care Victory," *The Washington Post*, March 24, 2010, p. A1.

2. Steven Thomma and David Lightman, "Obama Signs Health-care Bill, but GOP Protests Continue," McClatchy Newspapers/*Miami Herald*, March 23, 2010, www.miamiherald.com/2010/03/23/1543254/obama-signs-health-care-legislation.html.

3. Arthur L. Caplan, "Right to Reform," *The Journal of Clinical Investigation*, October 2009, p. 2862, www.jci.org.

4. Quoted in Michael Sweeney, "Hatch Attacks Individual Mandate He Previously Supported," *TPM LiveWire*, *Talking Points Memo* blog, March 26, 2010, http://tpmlivewire.talkingpointsmemo.com.

5. Quoted in "Health Care Reform: Not Ready to Be Discharged Yet," *Knowledge at Wharton* newsletter, March 31, 2010, http://knowledge.wharton.upenn.edu/article.cfm?articleid=2457.

6. Kathryn Nix, "Top 10 Disasters of Obamacare," Web Memo, The Heritage Foundation, March 30, 2010, www.heritage.org.

7. Sally C. Pipes, "Obamacare Wins: Now the Pain Begins," *New York Post*, March 22, 2010, www.nypost.com.

8. Robert E. Moffit, *Obamacare: Impact on Doctors*, WebMemo No. 2895, The Heritage Foundation, May 11, 2010, www.heritage.org.

9. Jane Hamsher, "Fact Sheet: The Truth About the Health Care Bill," *Firedoglake* blog, March 19, 2010, http://fdlaction.firedoglake.com.

10. Ian Millhiser, "If at First You Don't Succeed, Hope for Activist Judges," Center for American Progress website, March 23, 2010, www.americanprogress.org; for background, see *Gonzales v. Raich*, 545 U.S. 1 (2005), www.law.cornell.edu/supct/html/03-1454.ZS.html.

11. Simon Lazarus, "Mandatory Health Insurance: Is It Constitutional?" Issue Brief, American Constitution Society, December 2009, www.acslaw.org/node/15654; for background, see *United States v. Southeastern Underwriters Association*, 322 U.S. 533 (1944), http://supreme.justia.com/us/322/533/.

12. *Ibid.*

13. "President Barack Obama State of the Union Address, Feb. 24, 2009," About.com: US Politics website, http://uspolitics.about.com/od/speeches/l/bl_feb2009_obama_SOTU.htm.

14. Jill Bernstein, Deborah Chollet and Stephanie Peterson, "How Does Insurance Coverage Improve Health Outcomes?" Issue Brief, Mathematica Policy Research, April 2010, www.mathematica-mpr.com.

15. *Ibid.*

16. John Berlau, "Health Care: Fix Middle-Class 'Medicine Cabinet Tax' in Reconciliation," Competitive Enterprise Institute, March 23, 2010, www.cei.org.

17. Grace-Marie Turner, "Foster's Report Validates Fears," *National Journal Expert Blogs*, May 3, 2010, http://healthcare.nationaljournal.com.

18. Quoted in "True or False? Top Seven Health Care Fears," msnbc.com/*Kaiser Health News*, April 2, 2010, www.msnbc.com.

19. "Flaws of Health-care Overhaul Grow More Apparent Every Day," *Columbus* [Ohio] *Dispatch*, April 29, 2010.

20. Maggie Mahar, "Myths & Facts About HealthCare Reform: The Impact on Hospitals, and Patients Who Need Hospital Care — Part 3," *Healthbeat* blog, April 21, 2010, www.healthbeatblog.com.

21. Quoted in *ibid.*

22. Mahar, *op. cit.*

23. Stuart Guterman, Karen Davis, and Kristof Stremikis, "How Health Reform Legislation Will Affect Medicare Beneficiaries," The Commonwealth Fund, March 2010, www.cmwf.org.

24. "Rate Review: Holding Health Plans Accountable for Your Premium Dollars," Families USA Issue Brief, April 2010, www.familiesusa.org.

25. Maggie Mahar, "Myths & Facts About HealthCare Reform: Who Wins and Who Loses?" *Healthbeat* blog, April 6, 2010, www.healthbeatblog.com.

26. David B. Kendall, "A Foundation for Cost Control," *National Journal* blogs, March 22, 2010, http://healthcare.nationaljournal.com.

27. "In Search of a Fiscal Cure," *Newsweek*, May 10, 2010, p. 12.

28. David M. Cutler, "Time to Prove the Skeptics Wrong on Health Reform," Center for American Progress, April 23 ,2010, www.americanprogress.org.

29. Richard S. Foster, "Estimated Financial Effects of the 'Patient Protection and Affordable Care Act' as Amended," Office of the Actuary, Centers for Medicare and Medicaid Services, April 22, 2010.

30. Quoted in "Health Care Reform: Not Ready to Be Discharged Yet," *op. cit.*

31. John Goodman, "The Most Important Feature of ObamaCare Is Something No One Is Talking About," John Goodman's blog, March 29, 2010, www.john-goodman-blog.com.

32. Testimony before Senate Committee on Health, Education, Labor and Pensions, April 20, 2010.

33. Jon Walker, "Former Obama Aide David Cutler Ignores Proven Cost Control ideas to Inflate Grade on President's Health Care Plan," *Firedoglake* blog, March 10, 2010, http://fdlaction.firedoglake .com.

34. For background, see the following *CQ Researcher* reports by Marcia Clemmitt, "Rising Health Costs," April 7, 2006, pp. 289-312; "Universal Coverage," March 30, 2007, pp. 265-288; and "Health Care Reform," Aug. 28, 2009, pp. 693-716.

35. Jacob S. Hacker, "Yes We Can? The New Push for American Health Security," *Politics & Society*, March 2009, p. 14.

36. Paul Ryan, "A Roadmap for America's Future: Description of the Legislation," House Budget Committee Republican website, www.roadmap .republicans.budget.house.gov.

37. For background, see John E. McDonough, Brian Rosman, Fawn Phelps and Melissa Shannon, "The Third Wave of Massachusetts Health Care Access Reform," *Health Affairs online*, Sept. 14, 2006, http://content.healthaffairs.org/cgi/content/ full/25/6/w420.

38. Testimony before House Energy and Commerce Subcommittee on Health, June 24, 2009, www .pnhp.org/news/2009/june/testimony_of_steffie .php.

39. "President Barack Obama State of the Union Address, Feb. 24, 2009," About.com: US Politics website, http://uspolitics.about.com/od/speeches/l/ bl_feb2009_obama_SOTU.htm.

40. For background see Ceci Connolly, "Senate Passes Health Insurance Bill for Children," *The Washington Post*, Jan. 30, 2009, p. A1, www.washingtonpost .com/wp-dyn/content/article/2009/01/29/AR2009 012900325.html.

41. "President Barack Obama State of the Union Address, Feb. 24, 2009," *op. cit.*

42. For background see "House Passes Health Care Reform Bill," CNN.com, Nov. 8, 2009, www.cnn .com/2009/POLITICS/11/07/health.care.

43. For background see Timothy Noah, "Health Reform: An Online Guide," *Slate*, April 12, 2010, www.slate .com.

44. Quoted in Eric Kleefeld, "Romney Spokesman: 'Romney Plan' Is Not Like Obama's Health Care Reform, Despite What Obama Says," *Talking Points Memo* blog, March 31, 2010, http://tpmdc.talking-pointsmemo.com.

45. Quoted in Andrew Romano, "Mitt Romney on RomneyCare," *Newsweek online*, April 19, 2010, www.newsweek.com.

46. For background see "Side-by-Side Comparisons of Major Health Care Reform Proposals," Focus on Health Reform website, Kaiser Family Foundation, April 8, 2010, www.kff.org/healthreform/sidebyside .cfm.

47. For background see "Senate Democrats Seek Legislation to Regulate Insurer Rate Hikes," *Kaiser Health News* website, April 21, 2010, www.kaiser-healthnews.org/daily-reports/2010/april/21/insur ers.aspx?referrer=search.

48. Nix, *op. cit.*

49. Quoted in Tom Brown, "States Joined in Suit Against Healthcare Reform," Reuters, May 14, 2010, www.reuters.com.

50. Quoted in Ricardo Alonso-Zaldivar, "U.S. Files First Defense of Health Care Law in Court," The Associated Press, May 12, 2010, http://news.yahoo .com/s/ap/20100512/ap_on_bi_ge/us_health_care_ challenge.

51. Quoted in Jonathan Chait, "Could Republicans Repeal Health Care Reform?" *The New Republic online*, March 19, 2010, www.tnr.com.

52. "Implementation Timeline," Health Reform Source, Henry J. Kaiser Family Foundation website, http://healthreform.kff.org/Timeline.aspx.

53. *Ibid.*

54. Testimony before House Energy and Commerce Subcommittee on Oversight and Investigations, April 1, 2011, http://republicans.energycommerce.house.gov/Media/file/Hearings/Oversight/040111/Larsen.pdf.

55. Phil Galewitz, "At Least 600,000 Young Adults Join Parents' Health Plans Under New Law," Kaiser Health News website, May 3, 2011, www.kaiser-healthnews.org/Stories/2011/May/01/young-adult-health-insurance-coverage.aspx.

56. Amy Goldstein and N. S. Aizenman, "House Votes to Repeal Health-Care Law," *The Washington Post*, Jan. 20, 2011, www.washingtonpost.com/wp-dyn/content/article/2011/01/19/AR2011011903344.html.

57. Sam Stein, "Health Care Repeal Is 'Dead,' Says Top Republican, Sights Turn to Repealing Individual Mandate," *Huffington Post*, May 5, 2011, www.huffingtonpost.com/2011/05/05/health-care-repeal-dead-republican_n_858015.html.

58. Felicia Sonmez, "House Passes Repeal of Health Care Law Provision; Obama Issues Veto Threat," *The Washington Post blogs*, April 13, 2011, www.washingtonpost.com/blogs/2chambers/post/house-passes-repeal-of-health-care-law-provision-obama-issues-veto-threat/2011/04/13/AF52PSYD_blog.html.

59. Catherine Dodge, "House Votes to Bar U.S. Funding for Insurance Exchanges," Bloomberg, May 4, 2011, www.bloomberg.com/news/2011-05-04/house-votes-to-bar-u-s-funding-for-insurance-exchanges-1-.html.

60. Jessica Zigmond, "House Approves Bill to Defund School-based Health Centers," *Modern Healthcare*, May 4, 2011, www.modernhealthcare.com/article/20110504/NEWS/305049963.

61. "Illinois Health Care Reform Implementation Panel Releases Initial Recommendations," press release, Illinois Government News Network, March 2, 2011, www.illinois.gov/PressReleases/ShowPressRelease.cfm?SubjectID=1&RecNum=9252.

62. Stephen Groves, "Gov. McDonnell Keeps Up Fight to Strike Down Health Insurance Mandate," *Virginia Statehouse News*, July 27, 2010; "State Legislation and Actions Challenging Certain Health Reforms," 2011, National Conference of State Legislatures website, May 6, 2011, www.ncsl.org/?tabid=18906.

63. For background, see Melissa Maleske, "Health Reform Lawsuits Likely Headed to Supreme Court," *Inside Counsel*, Feb. 1, 2011, www.insidecounsel.com/Issues/2011/February-2011/Pages/Health-Care-Reform-Lawsuits-Likely-Headed-to-Supreme-Court.aspx?page=1.

64. Robert Lowes, "Federal Judge Strikes Down Entire Healthcare Reform Law," *Medscape News Today*, Jan. 31, 2011, www.medscape.com/viewarticle/736539.

65. Warren Richey, "Supreme Court Says No to Expedited Hearing on Health-Care Reform Law," *The Christian Science Monitor*, April 25, 2011, www.csmonitor.com/USA/Justice/2011/0425/Supreme-Court-says-no-to-expedited-hearing-on-health-care-reform-law.

BIBLIOGRAPHY
Books

Grater, David, *The Cure: How Capitalism Can Save American Health Care*, Encounter Books, 2008.
A psychiatrist who has practiced in the United States and Canada makes the conservative case for reforming the health care system by ending government regulation and third-party payment through insurance and instead having consumers pay directly for care.

Hacker, Jacob S., ed., *Health at Risk: America's Ailing System — and How to Heal It*, Columbia University Press, 2008.
A Yale University professor of political science who was chief architect of the proposal — eventually abandoned

by Congress — to include a public, government-run insurance plan to compete with private insurers, assembles essays by health-policy scholars on topics including the state of health-care quality.

Reid, T. R., *The Healing of America: A Global Quest for Better, Cheaper, and Fairer Health Care*, Penguin Press, 2009.

A former foreign affairs correspondent for *The Washington Post* reports his impressions of a round-the-world tour to explore health care systems.

Articles

Cohn, Jonathan, "How They Did It," *The New Republic*, June 10, 2010, www.tnr.com, p. 14.

In the early days of his administration, President Obama switched from opposition to support of an individual mandate to buy insurance.

Meyer, Harris, "Group Health's Move to the Medical Home: For Doctors, It's Often a Hard Journey," *Health Affairs*, May 2010, p. 844.

At a private health plan that's trying to reengineer medical practice to favor primary and preventive care, as the new health-reform law seeks to do nationally, many physicians balk at the change.

Milligan, Susan, "GOP Targets Nominee to Run Health Agency," *The Boston Globe*, May 13, 2010, www.boston.com, p. 1.

In a move that could hamper implementation of the health-reform law, congressional Republicans have been blocking President Obama's nomination of Donald Berwick, a Massachusetts pediatrician, to head the Centers for Medicare and Medicaid Services, on the grounds that Berwick believes that cost controls and pay-for-performance are required.

Ostrom, Carol M., "Health-care Law Will Alter High-Risk Pool, but Just How Hasn't Been Worked Out," *Seattle Times*, April 18, 2010, p. A1.

Under the new health-care reform law, states and the federal government starting this summer will set up temporary programs to help people with serious illnesses obtain affordable coverage. In 2014, private insurers will be required to enroll people regardless of health status.

Currently, 35 states already have such programs, and enrollees in those programs worry that Congress' legislative language may lock them out of the federal plan even though they might get more affordable coverage there.

Reichard, John, "After the Win, No Time to Lose," *CQ Weekly*, April 5, 2010, p. 814.

Federal health agencies face unprecedented challenges in developing rules for the huge, multifaceted health-reform law and making its multiple, complex programs work.

Reports and Studies

Butler, Stuart M., "Evolving Beyond Traditional Employer-Sponsored Health Insurance," The Hamilton Project, Brookings Institution, May 2007, www.brookings.edu/papers/2007/05healthcare_butler .aspx.

A health-policy scholar from the conservative Heritage Foundation, a Washington think tank, explains the legal, regulatory and business changes he believes would be required to create a stable health-insurance system based on conservative principles, as the current employer-based system crumbles.

Cauchy, Richard, "State Legislation Challenging Certain Health Reforms, 2010," National Conference of State Legislatures, May 2010, www.ncsl.org.

States and the federal government share a complex set of responsibilities for regulating health insurance and health care in the United States, which has often set some states at odds with the federal government. As federal health-reform legislation slowly moved through Congress over the past year, at least 39 state legislatures have proposed bills to limit, change or oppose certain federal actions on health care.

Lazarus, Simon, "Mandatory Health Insurance: Is It Constitutional?" American Constitution Society, December 2009, www.acslaw.org/node/15654.

A lawyer for the National Senior Citizens Law Center argues that contested provisions in the recently passed health-reform law, including the individual requirement to buy health insurance, are constitutional, based on longtime legal precedent.

For More Information

Alliance for Health Reform, 1444 I St., N.W., Suite 910, Washington, DC 20005-6573; (202) 789-2300; www.all-health.org. Nonpartisan group providing information on all facets of health coverage and access, including transcripts and videos of Capitol Hill briefings from experts with a wide spectrum of views on reform.

The Commonwealth Fund, One East 75th St., NY, NY 10021; (212) 606-3800; www.commonwealthfund.org. Private foundation that supports research on and advocates for universal access to affordable, high-quality health care.

The Heritage Foundation, 214 Massachusetts Ave., N.E., Washington, DC 20002-4999; (202) 546-4400; www.heritage.org. Public-policy think tank provides analysis of health reform and health care from a conservative viewpoint.

John Goodman's Health Policy Blog, National Center for Policy Analysis, 12770 Coit Rd., Suite 800, Dallas, TX 75251-1339; (972) 386-6272; www.john-goodman-blog.com. Conservative analyst who advocates for free-market policies provides daily commentary on health care and health reform.

Kaiser Health News, www.kaiserhealthnews.org. Foundation-funded, editorially independent nonprofit news group provides information on current events affecting health care.

National Conferences of State Legislatures, 444 North Capitol St., N.W., Suite 515, Washington, DC 20001; (202) 624-5400; www.ncsl.org. Nongovernmental group that tracks proposed state legislation related to health-care reform.

National Journal Expert Blogs: Health Care, http://healthcare.nationaljournal.com. Reporters from the political magazine and a wide variety of health-care experts and analysts provide commentary.

The White House Blog: Health Care, www.whitehouse.gov/blog/issues/Health-Care. Obama administration officials comment on implementation of the new law.